D1432440

6 SAINT☆YOUNG MEN

C O N T E N T S

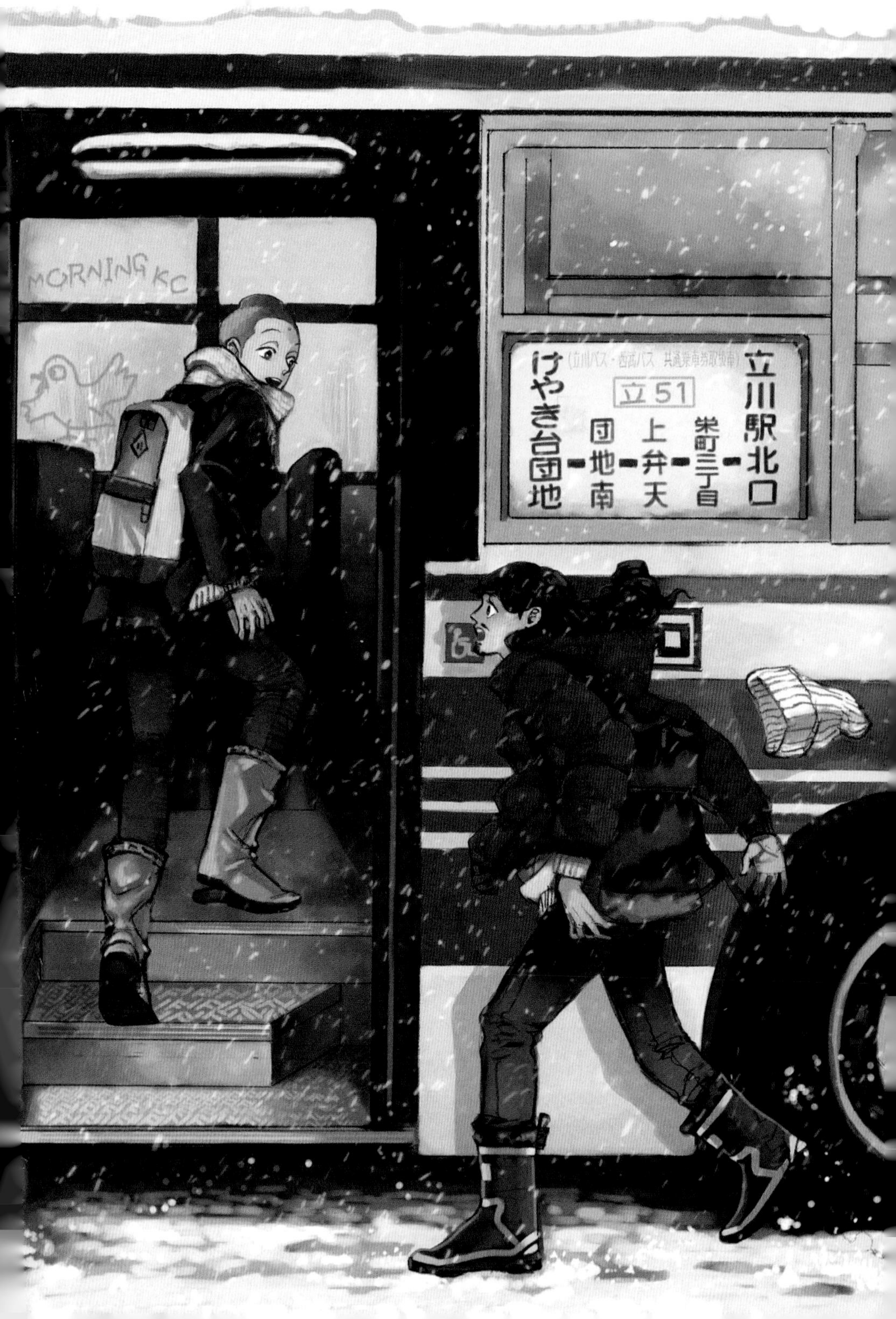
（立川バス・西武バス　共通乗車券取扱車）
立51
立川駅北口
栄町三丁目
上弁天
団地南
けやき台団地
MORNING KC

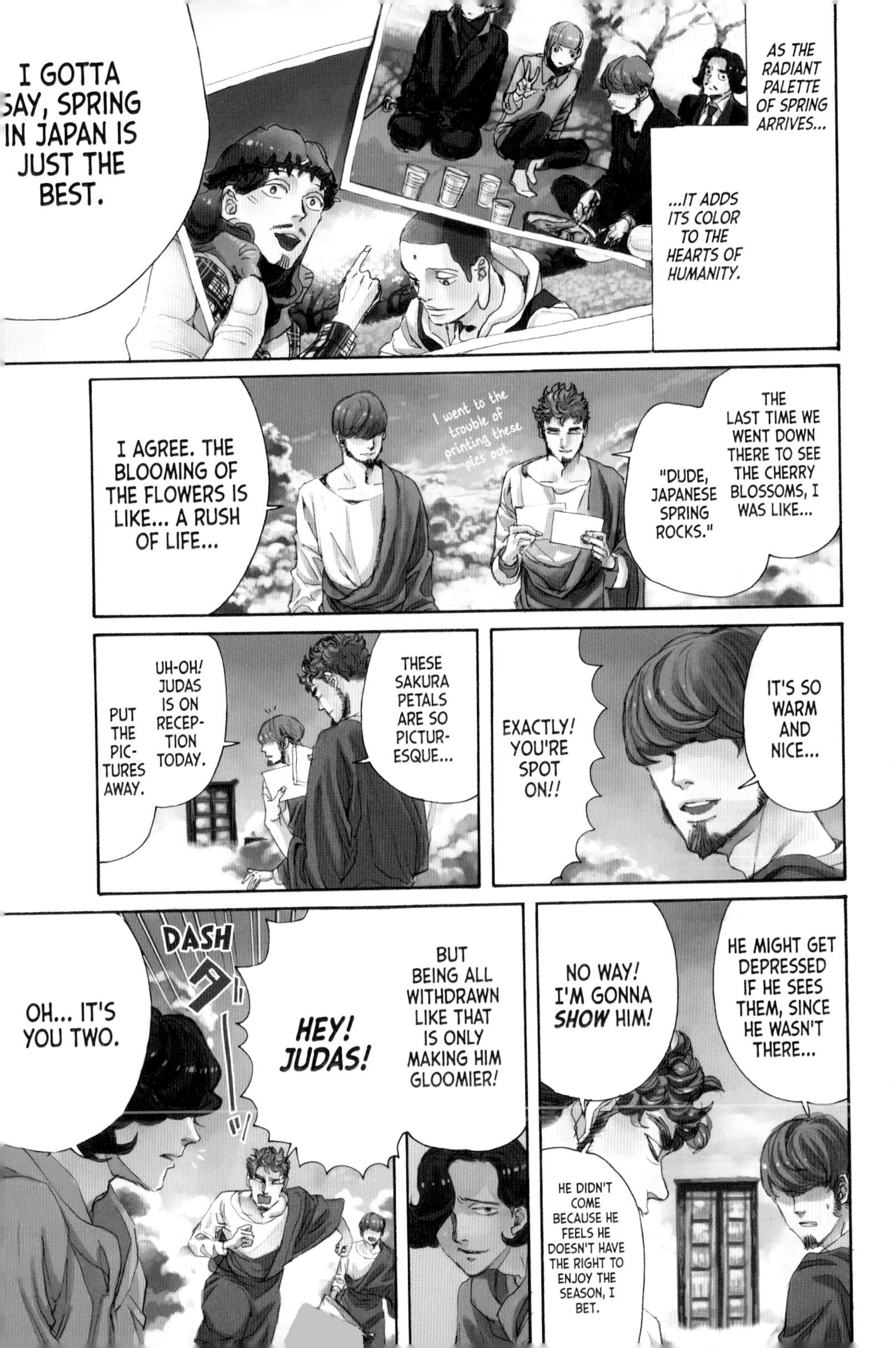
AS THE RADIANT PALETTE OF SPRING ARRIVES...
...IT ADDS ITS COLOR TO THE HEARTS OF HUMANITY.
I GOTTA SAY, SPRING IN JAPAN IS JUST THE BEST.
THE LAST TIME WE WENT DOWN THERE TO SEE THE CHERRY BLOSSOMS, I WAS LIKE...
"DUDE, JAPANESE SPRING ROCKS."
I went to the trouble of printing these pics out.
I AGREE. THE BLOOMING OF THE FLOWERS IS LIKE... A RUSH OF LIFE...
IT'S SO WARM AND NICE...
EXACTLY! YOU'RE SPOT ON!!
THESE SAKURA PETALS ARE SO PICTURESQUE...
UH-OH! JUDAS IS ON RECEPTION TODAY.
PUT THE PICTURES AWAY.
HE MIGHT GET DEPRESSED IF HE SEES THEM, SINCE HE WASN'T THERE...
NO WAY! I'M GONNA *SHOW* HIM!
HE DIDN'T COME BECAUSE HE FEELS HE DOESN'T HAVE THE RIGHT TO ENJOY THE SEASON, I BET.
BUT BEING ALL WITHDRAWN LIKE THAT IS ONLY MAKING HIM GLOOMIER!
HEY! JUDAS!
DASH
OH... IT'S YOU TWO.

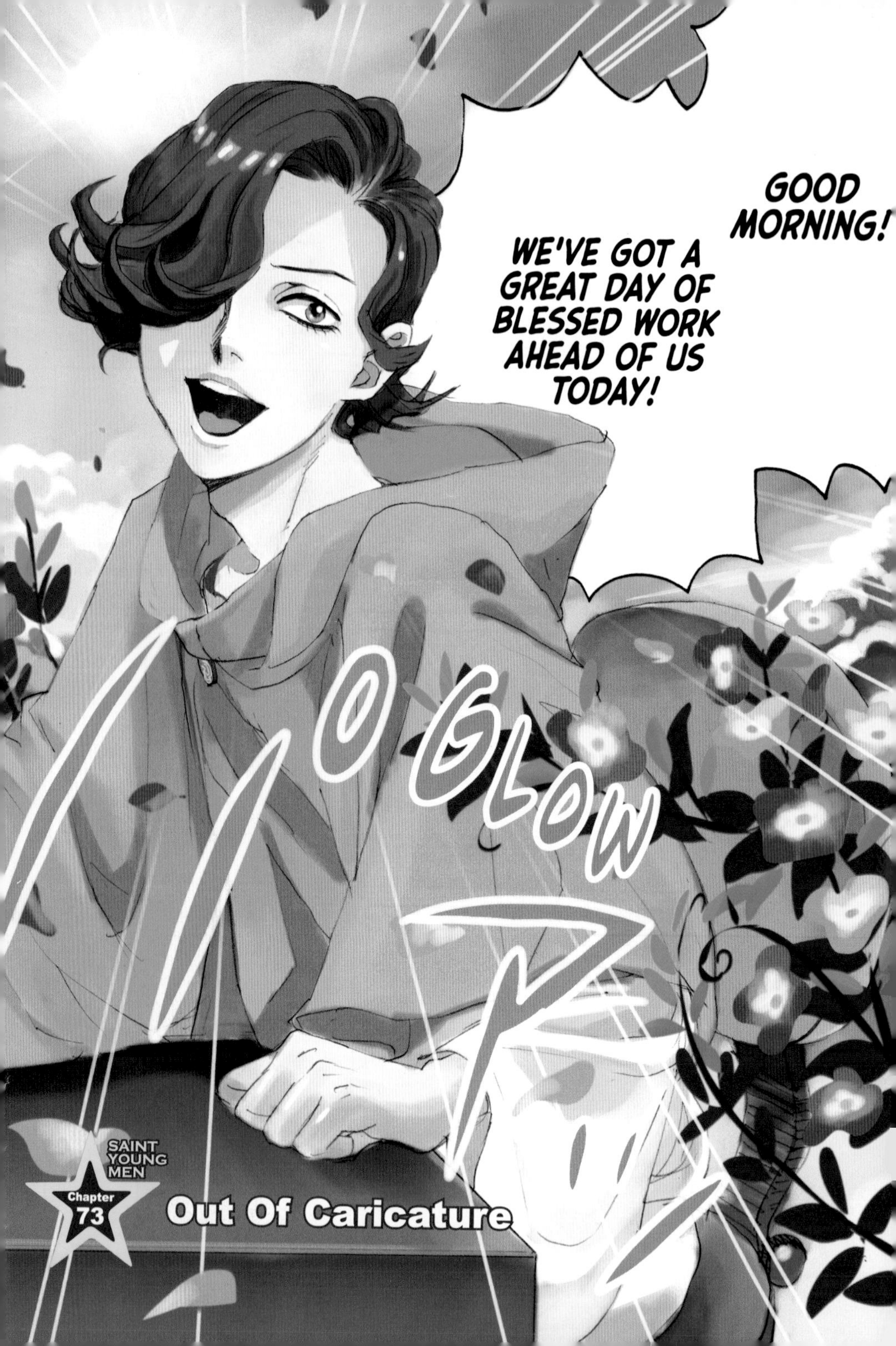
GOOD MORNING!
WE'VE GOT A GREAT DAY OF BLESSED WORK AHEAD OF US TODAY!
GLOW
SAINT YOUNG MEN
Chapter 73
Out Of Caricature

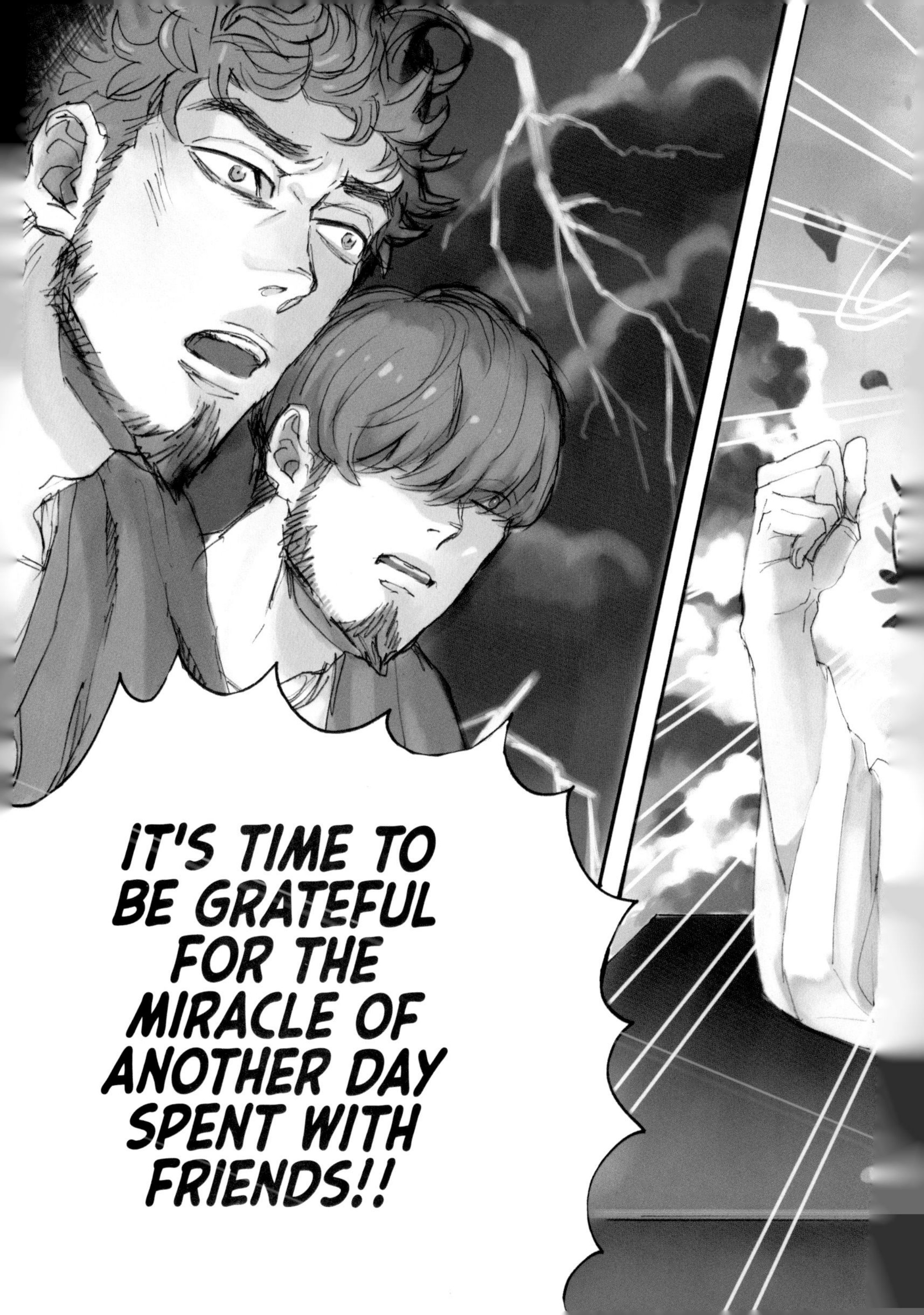
IT'S TIME TO BE GRATEFUL FOR THE MIRACLE OF ANOTHER DAY SPENT WITH FRIENDS!!

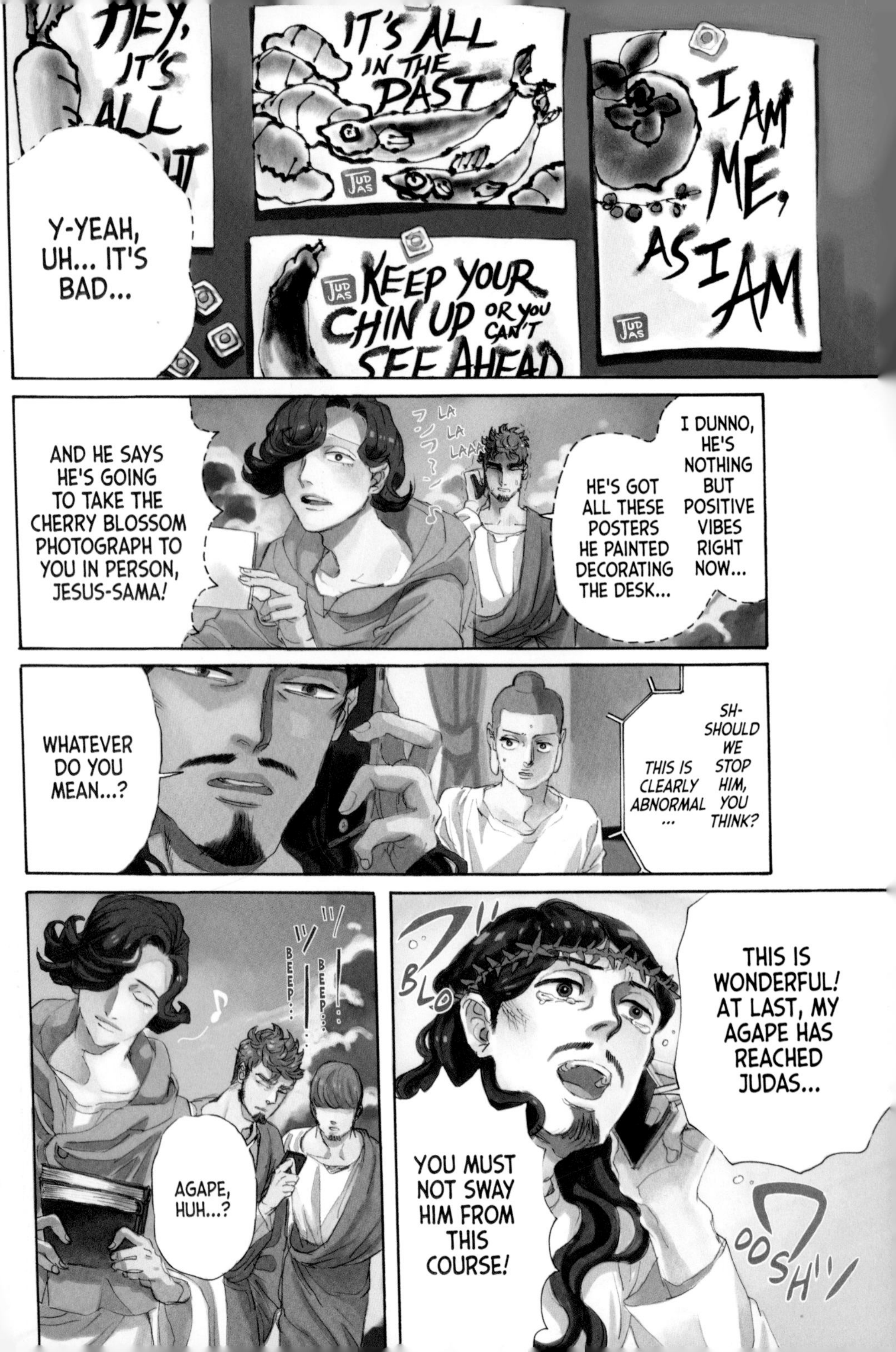

I AM ME, AS I AM
IT'S ALL IN THE PAST
KEEP YOUR CHIN UP OR YOU CAN'T SEE AHEAD
HEY, IT'S ALL
Y-YEAH, UH... IT'S BAD...
I DUNNO, HE'S NOTHING BUT POSITIVE VIBES RIGHT NOW...
HE'S GOT ALL THESE POSTERS HE PAINTED DECORATING THE DESK...
LA LA LAAA
AND HE SAYS HE'S GOING TO TAKE THE CHERRY BLOSSOM PHOTOGRAPH TO YOU IN PERSON, JESUS-SAMA!
SH-SHOULD WE STOP HIM, YOU THINK?
THIS IS CLEARLY ABNORMAL...
WHATEVER DO YOU MEAN...?
THIS IS WONDERFUL! AT LAST, MY AGAPE HAS REACHED JUDAS...
BLO
OOSH
YOU MUST NOT SWAY HIM FROM THIS COURSE!
BEEP...
BEEP...
AGAPE, HUH...?

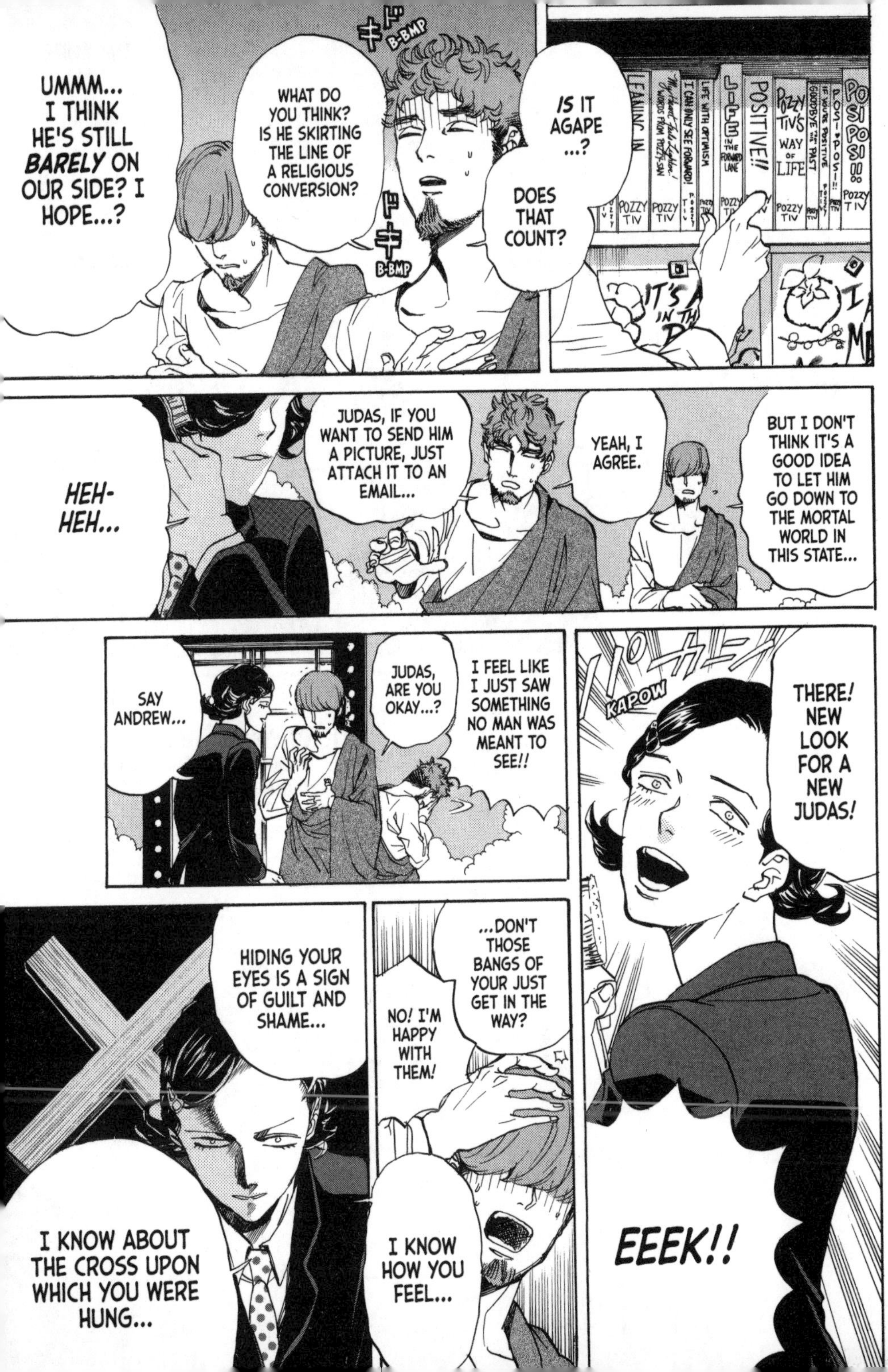
LEANING IN
I CAN ONLY SEE FORWARD!
LIFE WITH OPTIMISM
LIFE IN THE FORWARD LANE
POSITIVE!!
POZZY TIV'S WAY OF LIFE
GOODBYE TO THE PAST
IF YOU'RE POSITIVE
POSI-POSI-!!
POSI POSI!!
POZZY TIV
IS IT AGAPE ...?
DOES THAT COUNT?
B-BMP
WHAT DO YOU THINK? IS HE SKIRTING THE LINE OF A RELIGIOUS CONVERSION?
B-BMP
UMMM... I THINK HE'S STILL BARELY ON OUR SIDE? I HOPE...?
BUT I DON'T THINK IT'S A GOOD IDEA TO LET HIM GO DOWN TO THE MORTAL WORLD IN THIS STATE...
YEAH, I AGREE.
JUDAS, IF YOU WANT TO SEND HIM A PICTURE, JUST ATTACH IT TO AN EMAIL...
HEH-HEH...
KAPOW
THERE! NEW LOOK FOR A NEW JUDAS!
EEEK!!
I FEEL LIKE I JUST SAW SOMETHING NO MAN WAS MEANT TO SEE!!
JUDAS, ARE YOU OKAY...?
SAY ANDREW...
...DON'T THOSE BANGS OF YOUR JUST GET IN THE WAY?
NO! I'M HAPPY WITH THEM!
I KNOW HOW YOU FEEL...
HIDING YOUR EYES IS A SIGN OF GUILT AND SHAME...
I KNOW ABOUT THE CROSS UPON WHICH YOU WERE HUNG...

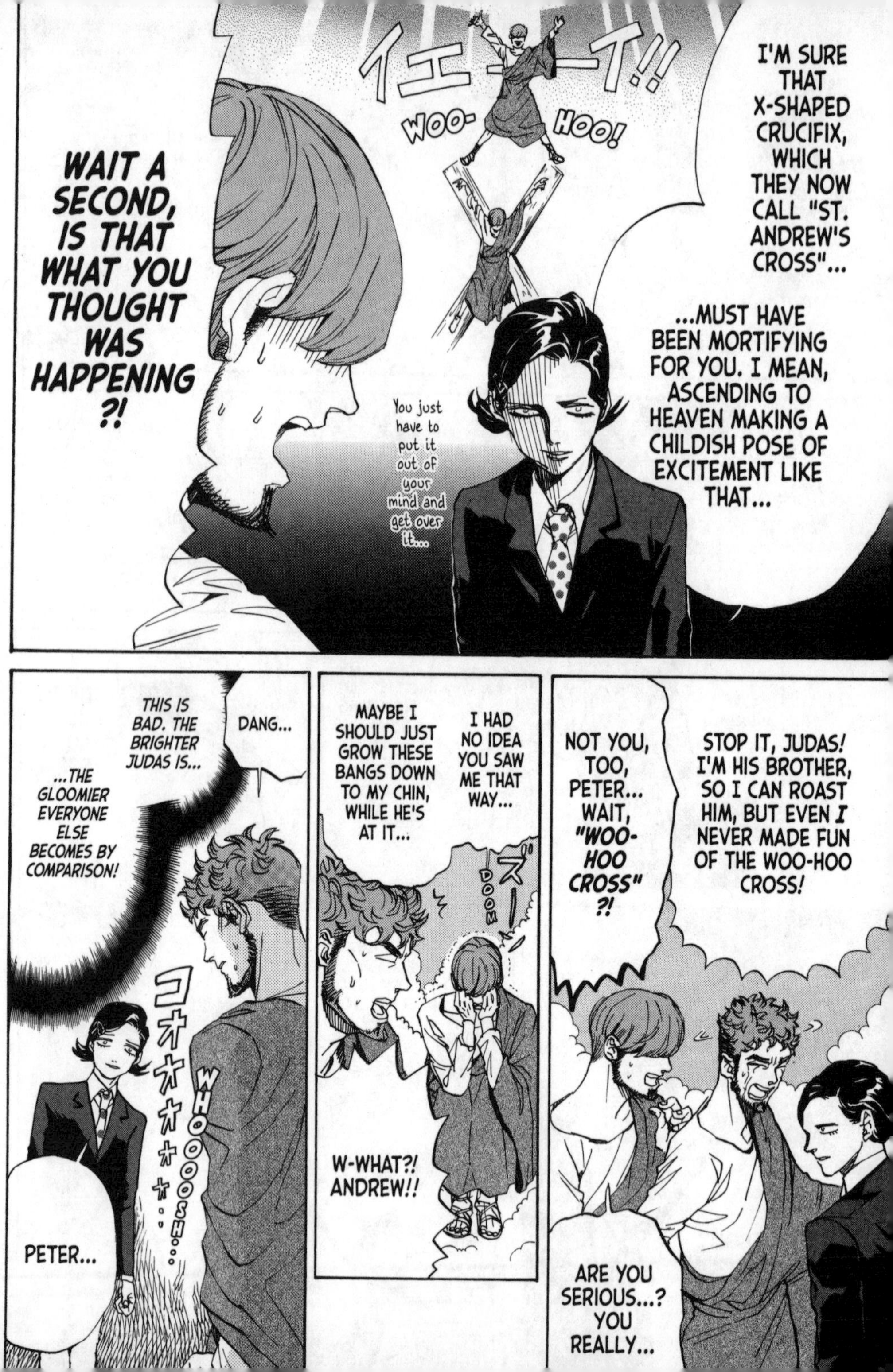
I'M SURE THAT X-SHAPED CRUCIFIX, WHICH THEY NOW CALL "ST. ANDREW'S CROSS"...
...MUST HAVE BEEN MORTIFYING FOR YOU. I MEAN, ASCENDING TO HEAVEN MAKING A CHILDISH POSE OF EXCITEMENT LIKE THAT...
イエーイ!!
WOO-HOO!
You just have to put it out of your mind and get over it...
WAIT A SECOND, IS THAT WHAT YOU THOUGHT WAS HAPPENING?!
STOP IT, JUDAS! I'M HIS BROTHER, SO I CAN ROAST HIM, BUT EVEN I NEVER MADE FUN OF THE WOO-HOO CROSS!
NOT YOU, TOO, PETER... WAIT, "WOO-HOO CROSS"?!
ARE YOU SERIOUS...? YOU REALLY...
I HAD NO IDEA YOU SAW ME THAT WAY...
MAYBE I SHOULD JUST GROW THESE BANGS DOWN TO MY CHIN, WHILE HE'S AT IT...
ズーン
DOOM
W-WHAT?! ANDREW!!
DANG...
THIS IS BAD. THE BRIGHTER JUDAS IS...
...THE GLOOMIER EVERYONE ELSE BECOMES BY COMPARISON!
コォオオォォ...
WHOOOOOSH...
PETER...

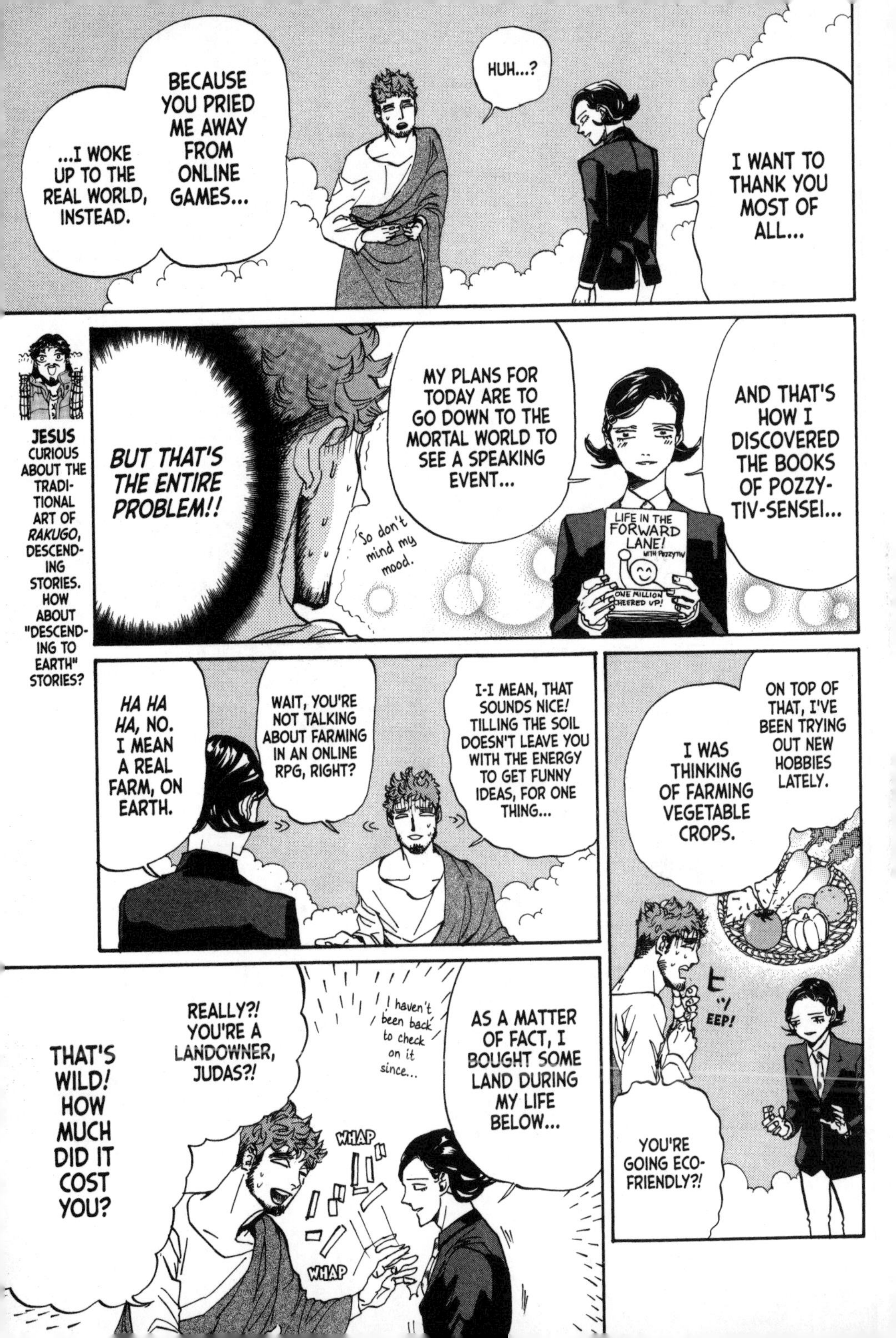
I WANT TO THANK YOU MOST OF ALL...
HUH...?
BECAUSE YOU PRIED ME AWAY FROM ONLINE GAMES...
...I WOKE UP TO THE REAL WORLD, INSTEAD.
AND THAT'S HOW I DISCOVERED THE BOOKS OF POZZY-TIV-SENSEI...
LIFE IN THE FORWARD LANE! WITH POZZYTIV
ONE MILLION CHEERED UP!
MY PLANS FOR TODAY ARE TO GO DOWN TO THE MORTAL WORLD TO SEE A SPEAKING EVENT...
So don't mind my mood.
BUT THAT'S THE ENTIRE PROBLEM!!
JESUS CURIOUS ABOUT THE TRADITIONAL ART OF RAKUGO, DESCENDING STORIES. HOW ABOUT "DESCENDING TO EARTH" STORIES?
ON TOP OF THAT, I'VE BEEN TRYING OUT NEW HOBBIES LATELY.
I WAS THINKING OF FARMING VEGETABLE CROPS.
EEP!
YOU'RE GOING ECO-FRIENDLY?!
I-I MEAN, THAT SOUNDS NICE! TILLING THE SOIL DOESN'T LEAVE YOU WITH THE ENERGY TO GET FUNNY IDEAS, FOR ONE THING...
WAIT, YOU'RE NOT TALKING ABOUT FARMING IN AN ONLINE RPG, RIGHT?
HA HA HA, NO. I MEAN A REAL FARM, ON EARTH.
AS A MATTER OF FACT, I BOUGHT SOME LAND DURING MY LIFE BELOW...
I haven't been back to check on it since...
REALLY?! YOU'RE A LANDOWNER, JUDAS?!
THAT'S WILD! HOW MUCH DID IT COST YOU?
WHAP
WHAP

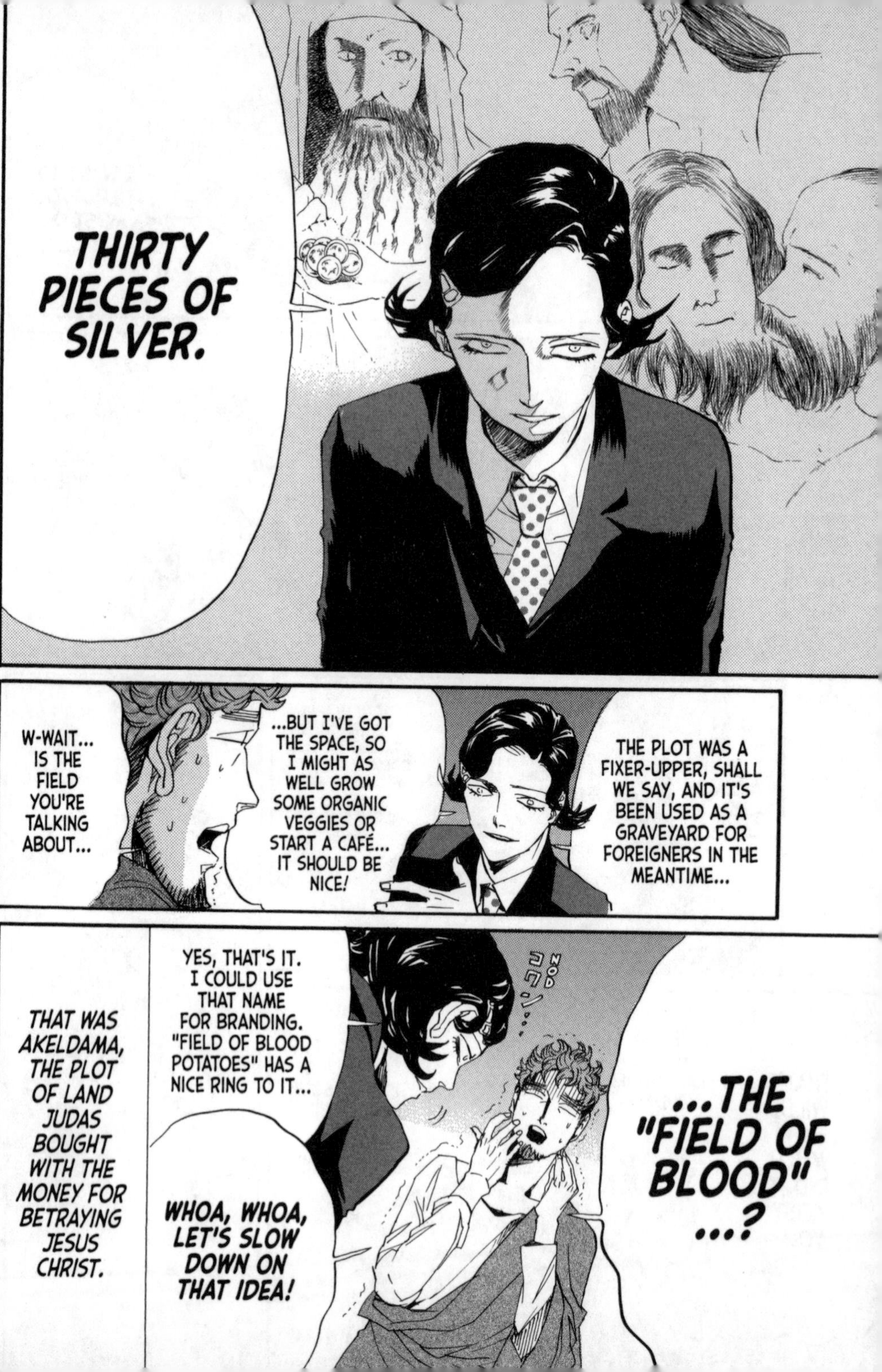
THIRTY PIECES OF SILVER.
THE PLOT WAS A FIXER-UPPER, SHALL WE SAY, AND IT'S BEEN USED AS A GRAVEYARD FOR FOREIGNERS IN THE MEANTIME...
...BUT I'VE GOT THE SPACE, SO I MIGHT AS WELL GROW SOME ORGANIC VEGGIES OR START A CAFÉ... IT SHOULD BE NICE!
W-WAIT... IS THE FIELD YOU'RE TALKING ABOUT...
...THE "FIELD OF BLOOD" ...?
コクン NOD
YES, THAT'S IT. I COULD USE THAT NAME FOR BRANDING. "FIELD OF BLOOD POTATOES" HAS A NICE RING TO IT...
WHOA, WHOA, LET'S SLOW DOWN ON THAT IDEA!
THAT WAS AKELDAMA, THE PLOT OF LAND JUDAS BOUGHT WITH THE MONEY FOR BETRAYING JESUS CHRIST.

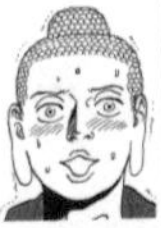

BUDDHA
CURIOUS ABOUT THE FORM OF TRADITIONAL JAPANESE ART. YOU'VE SEEN ART OF MT. FUJI... WHAT ABOUT MT. BUDHI?

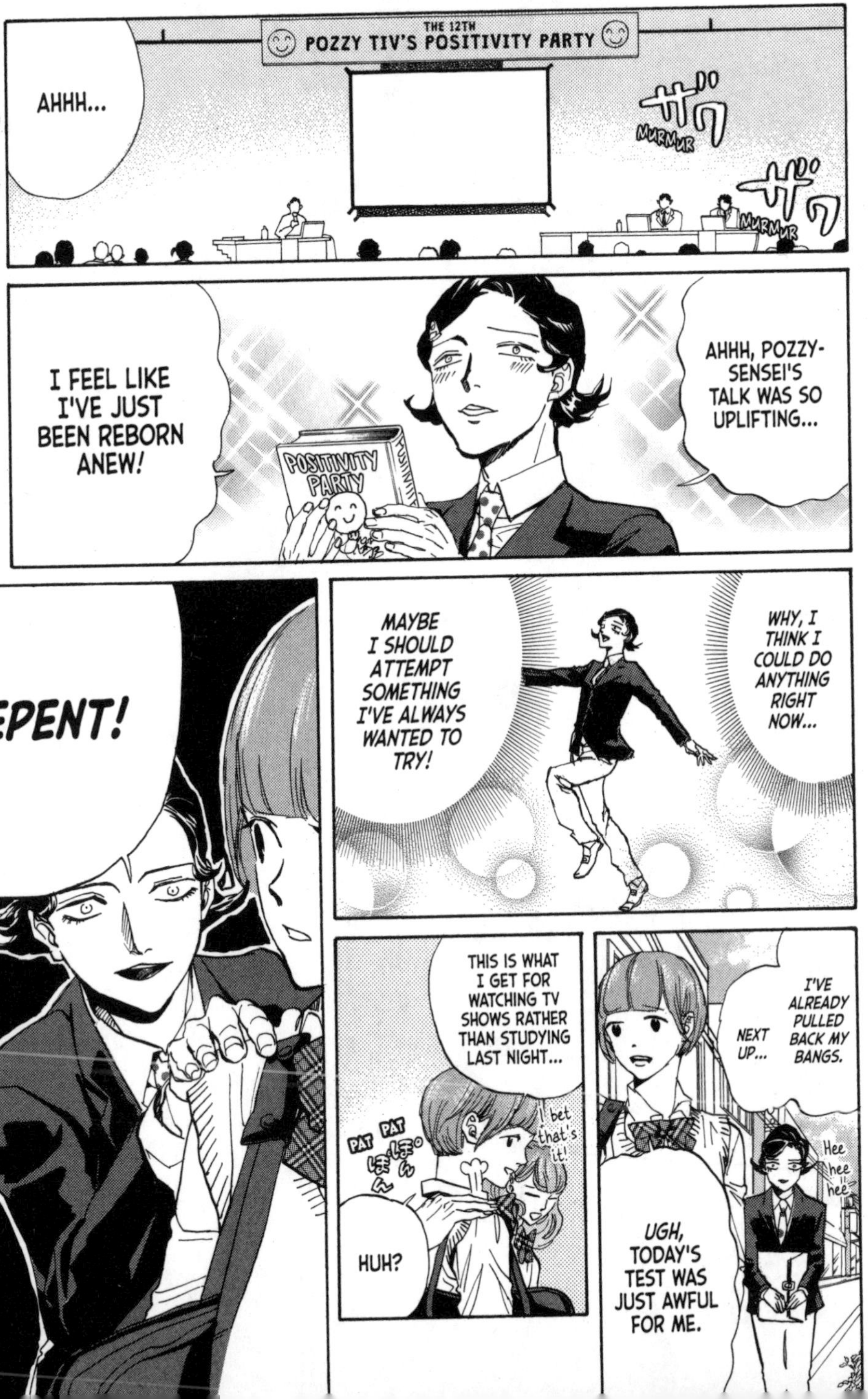
THE 12TH
POZZY TIV'S POSITIVITY PARTY
ザワ
MURMUR
ザワ
MURMUR
AHHH...
AHHH, POZZY-SENSEI'S TALK WAS SO UPLIFTING...
I FEEL LIKE I'VE JUST BEEN REBORN ANEW!
POSITIVITY PARTY
WHY, I THINK I COULD DO ANYTHING RIGHT NOW...
MAYBE I SHOULD ATTEMPT SOMETHING I'VE ALWAYS WANTED TO TRY!
I'VE ALREADY PULLED BACK MY BANGS.
NEXT UP...
Hee hee hee
UGH, TODAY'S TEST WAS JUST AWFUL FOR ME.
THIS IS WHAT I GET FOR WATCHING TV SHOWS RATHER THAN STUDYING LAST NIGHT...
I bet that's it!
PAT PAT
ぽんぽん
HUH?
REPENT!

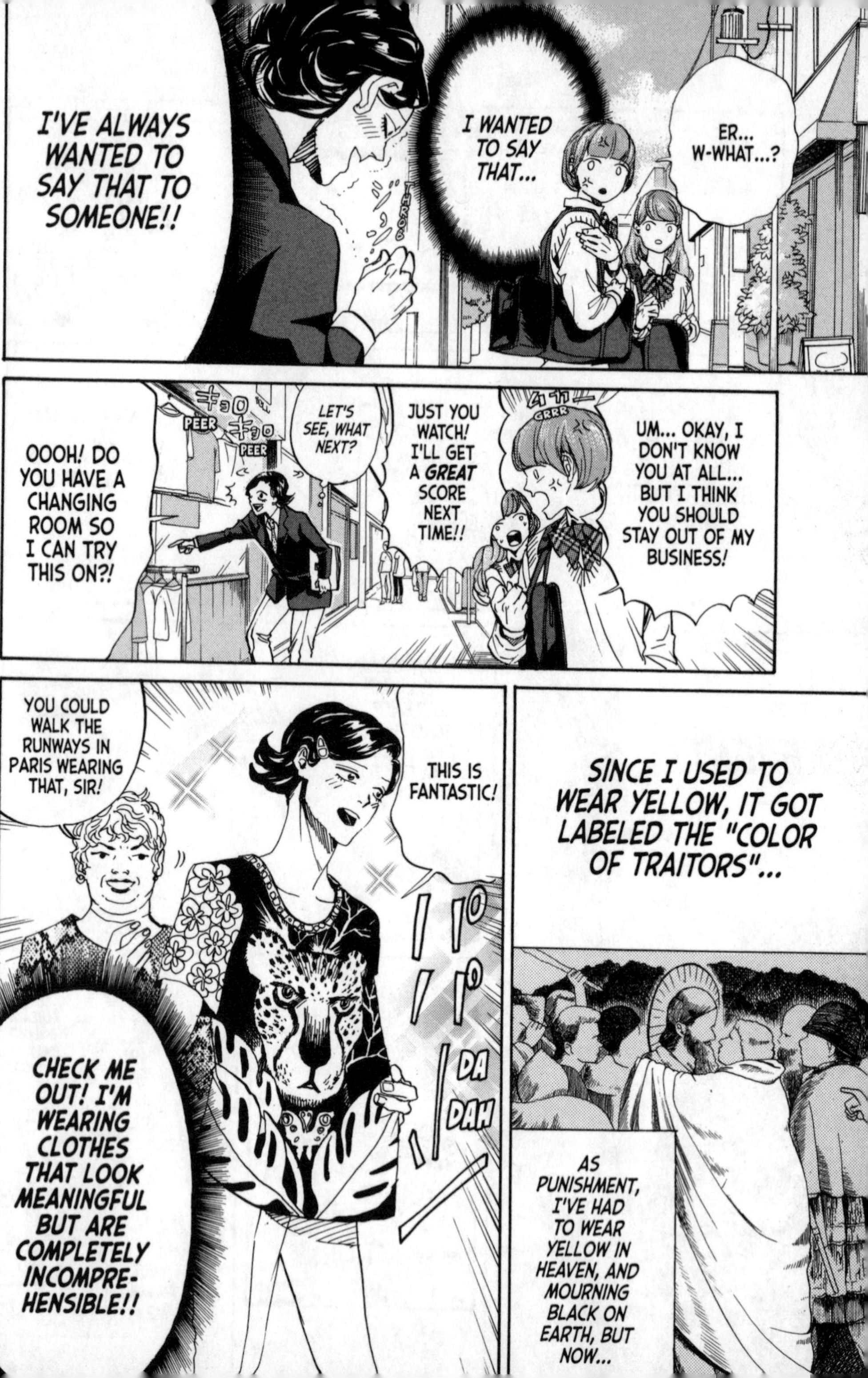
ER... W-WHAT...?
I WANTED TO SAY THAT...
THROB
I'VE ALWAYS WANTED TO SAY THAT TO SOMEONE!!
UM... OKAY, I DON'T KNOW YOU AT ALL... BUT I THINK YOU SHOULD STAY OUT OF MY BUSINESS!
GRRR
JUST YOU WATCH! I'LL GET A GREAT SCORE NEXT TIME!!
LET'S SEE, WHAT NEXT?
PEER
PEER
OOOH! DO YOU HAVE A CHANGING ROOM SO I CAN TRY THIS ON?!
SINCE I USED TO WEAR YELLOW, IT GOT LABELED THE "COLOR OF TRAITORS"...
AS PUNISHMENT, I'VE HAD TO WEAR YELLOW IN HEAVEN, AND MOURNING BLACK ON EARTH, BUT NOW...
THIS IS FANTASTIC!
YOU COULD WALK THE RUNWAYS IN PARIS WEARING THAT, SIR!
DA DAH
CHECK ME OUT! I'M WEARING CLOTHES THAT LOOK MEANINGFUL BUT ARE COMPLETELY INCOMPRE-HENSIBLE!!

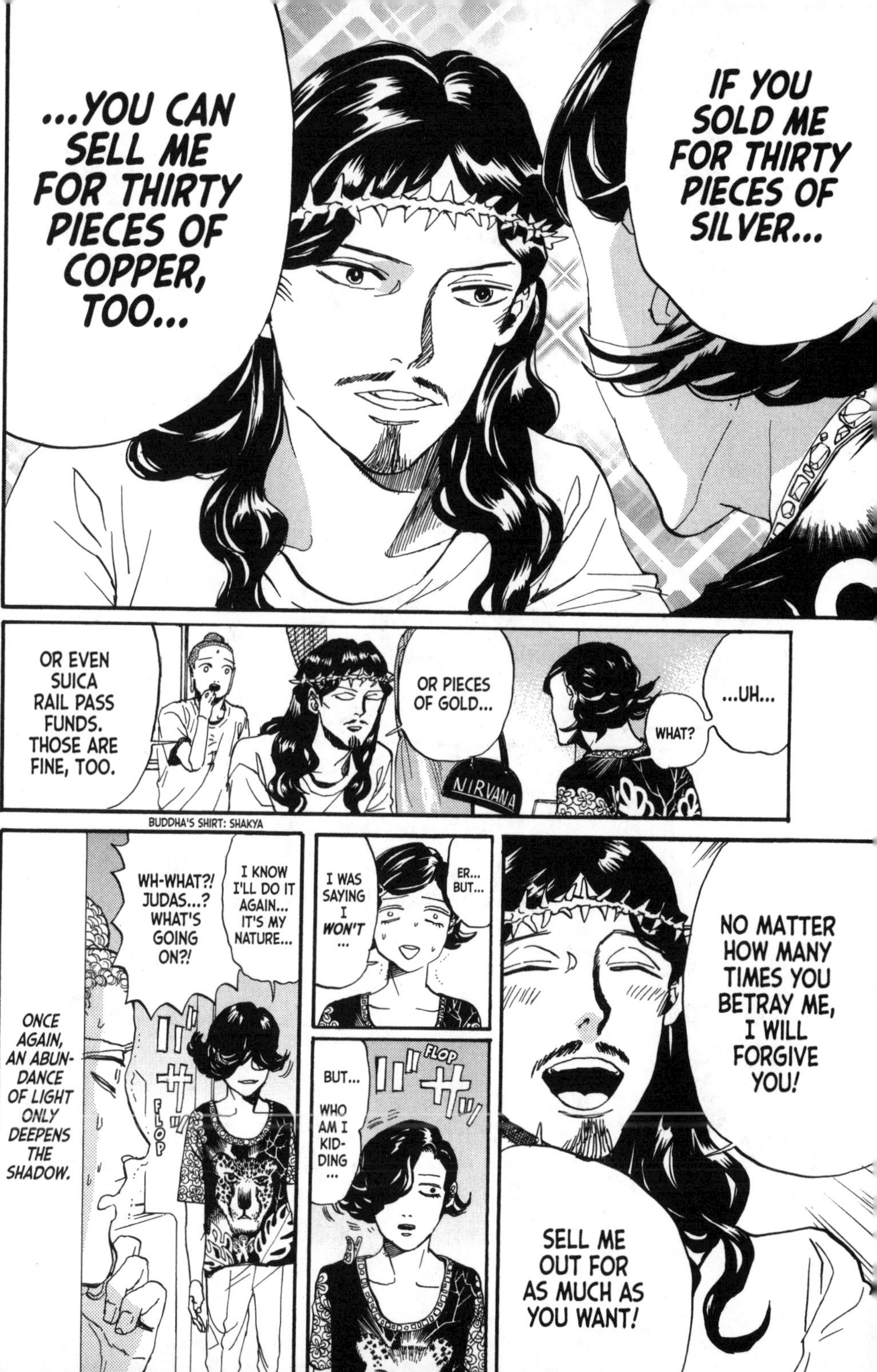
IF YOU SOLD ME FOR THIRTY PIECES OF SILVER...
...YOU CAN SELL ME FOR THIRTY PIECES OF COPPER, TOO...
...UH...
WHAT?
OR PIECES OF GOLD...
NIRVANA
OR EVEN SUICA RAIL PASS FUNDS. THOSE ARE FINE, TOO.
BUDDHA'S SHIRT: SHAKYA
NO MATTER HOW MANY TIMES YOU BETRAY ME, I WILL FORGIVE YOU!
SELL ME OUT FOR AS MUCH AS YOU WANT!
ER... BUT...
I WAS SAYING I *WON'T* ...
FLOP
BUT...
WHO AM I KID-DING ...
I KNOW I'LL DO IT AGAIN... IT'S MY NATURE...
WH-WHAT?! JUDAS...? WHAT'S GOING ON?!
FLOP
ONCE AGAIN, AN ABUN-DANCE OF LIGHT ONLY DEEPENS THE SHADOW.

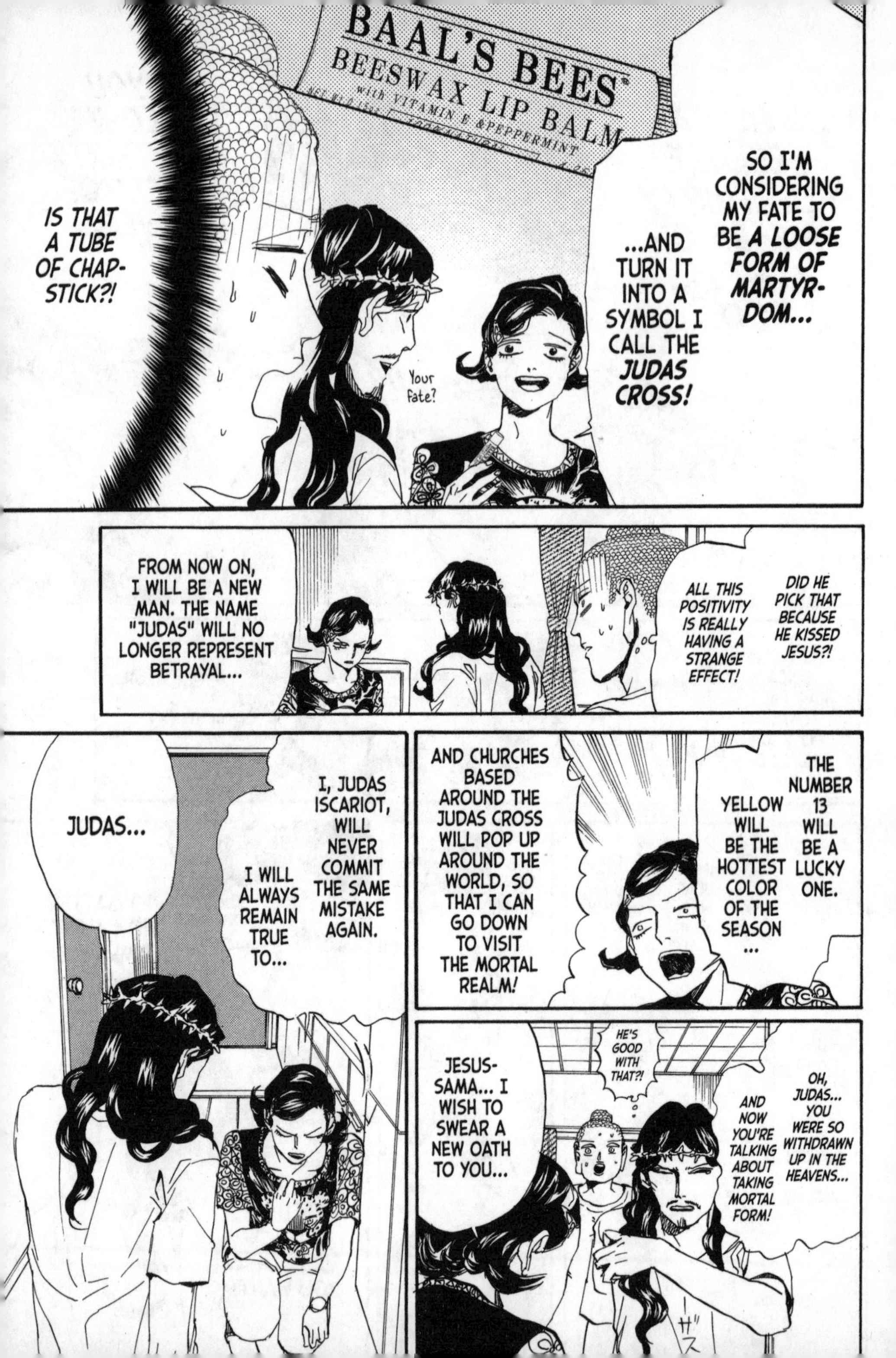
BAAL'S BEES
BEESWAX LIP BALM
with VITAMIN E &PEPPERMINT
SO I'M CONSIDERING MY FATE TO BE A LOOSE FORM OF MARTYRDOM...
...AND TURN IT INTO A SYMBOL I CALL THE JUDAS CROSS!
Your fate?
IS THAT A TUBE OF CHAP-STICK?!
DID HE PICK THAT BECAUSE HE KISSED JESUS?!
ALL THIS POSITIVITY IS REALLY HAVING A STRANGE EFFECT!
FROM NOW ON, I WILL BE A NEW MAN. THE NAME "JUDAS" WILL NO LONGER REPRESENT BETRAYAL...
THE NUMBER 13 WILL BE A LUCKY ONE.
YELLOW WILL BE THE HOTTEST COLOR OF THE SEASON ...
AND CHURCHES BASED AROUND THE JUDAS CROSS WILL POP UP AROUND THE WORLD, SO THAT I CAN GO DOWN TO VISIT THE MORTAL REALM!
OH, JUDAS... YOU WERE SO WITHDRAWN UP IN THE HEAVENS...
AND NOW YOU'RE TALKING ABOUT TAKING MORTAL FORM!
HE'S GOOD WITH THAT?!
JESUS-SAMA... I WISH TO SWEAR A NEW OATH TO YOU...
I, JUDAS ISCARIOT, WILL NEVER COMMIT THE SAME MISTAKE AGAIN.
I WILL ALWAYS REMAIN TRUE TO...
JUDAS...

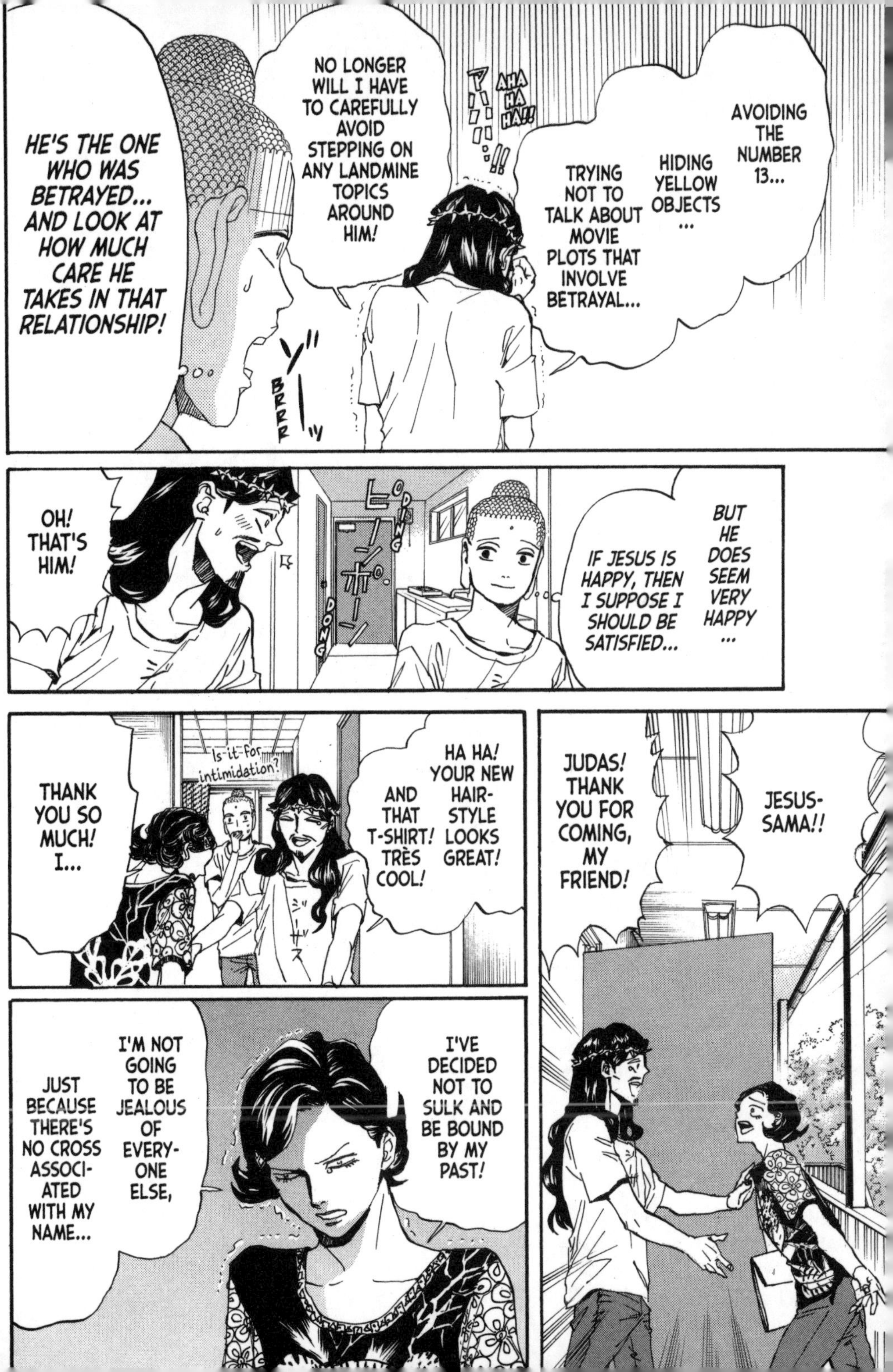
AVOIDING THE NUMBER 13...
HIDING YELLOW OBJECTS...
TRYING NOT TO TALK ABOUT MOVIE PLOTS THAT INVOLVE BETRAYAL...
AHA HA HA!!
NO LONGER WILL I HAVE TO CAREFULLY AVOID STEPPING ON ANY LANDMINE TOPICS AROUND HIM!
HE'S THE ONE WHO WAS BETRAYED... AND LOOK AT HOW MUCH CARE HE TAKES IN THAT RELATIONSHIP!
BRRR
BUT HE DOES SEEM VERY HAPPY...
IF JESUS IS HAPPY, THEN I SUPPOSE I SHOULD BE SATISFIED...
DING
DONG
OH! THAT'S HIM!
JESUS-SAMA!!
JUDAS! THANK YOU FOR COMING, MY FRIEND!
HA HA! YOUR NEW HAIR-STYLE LOOKS GREAT!
AND THAT T-SHIRT! TRÈS COOL!
Is it for intimidation?
THANK YOU SO MUCH! I...
I'VE DECIDED NOT TO SULK AND BE BOUND BY MY PAST!
I'M NOT GOING TO BE JEALOUS OF EVERY-ONE ELSE,
JUST BECAUSE THERE'S NO CROSS ASSOCI-ATED WITH MY NAME...

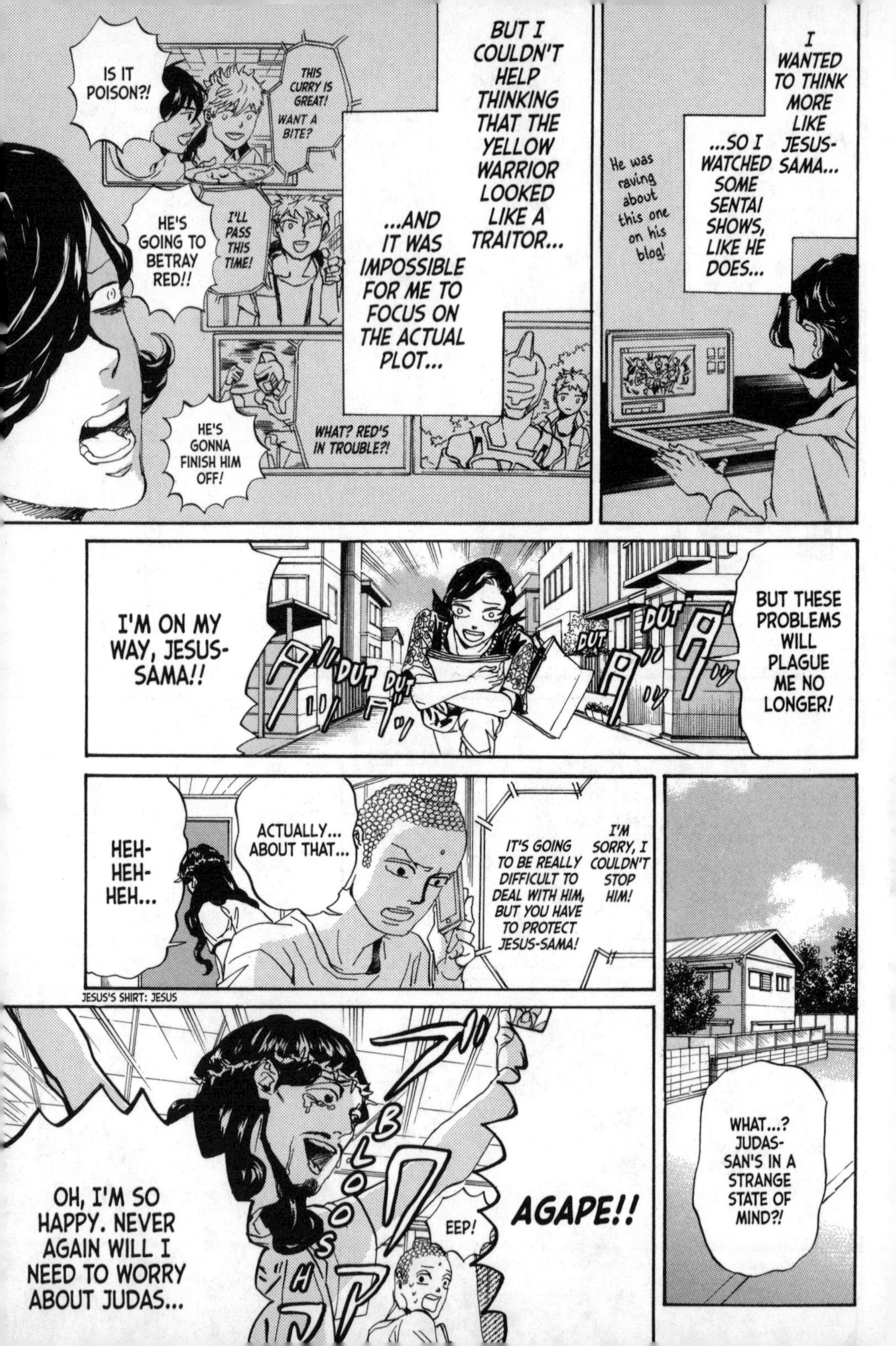
I WANTED TO THINK MORE LIKE JESUS-SAMA...
...SO I WATCHED SOME SENTAI SHOWS, LIKE HE DOES...
He was raving about this one on his blog!
BUT I COULDN'T HELP THINKING THAT THE YELLOW WARRIOR LOOKED LIKE A TRAITOR...
...AND IT WAS IMPOSSIBLE FOR ME TO FOCUS ON THE ACTUAL PLOT...
WHAT? RED'S IN TROUBLE?!
THIS CURRY IS GREAT! WANT A BITE?
IS IT POISON?!
I'LL PASS THIS TIME!
HE'S GOING TO BETRAY RED!!
HE'S GONNA FINISH HIM OFF!
BUT THESE PROBLEMS WILL PLAGUE ME NO LONGER!
DUT DUT
DUT DUT
I'M ON MY WAY, JESUS-SAMA!!
WHAT...? JUDAS-SAN'S IN A STRANGE STATE OF MIND?!
I'M SORRY, I COULDN'T STOP HIM!
IT'S GOING TO BE REALLY DIFFICULT TO DEAL WITH HIM, BUT YOU HAVE TO PROTECT JESUS-SAMA!
ACTUALLY... ABOUT THAT...
HEH-HEH-HEH...
JESUS'S SHIRT: JESUS
AGAPE!!
BLOOSH
EEP!
OH, I'M SO HAPPY. NEVER AGAIN WILL I NEED TO WORRY ABOUT JUDAS...

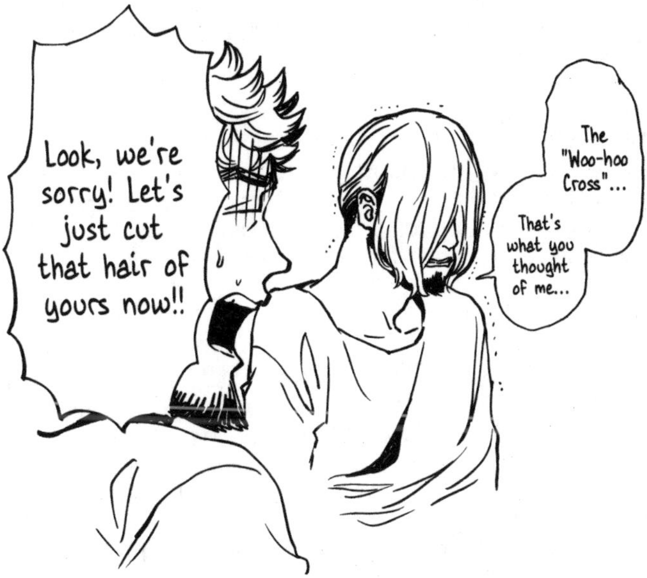
The "Woo-hoo Cross"...
That's what you thought of me...
Look, we're sorry! Let's just cut that hair of yours now!!

CHAPTER 73 TRANSLATION NOTES

St. Andrew's Cross, page 6

St. Andrew is said to have been crucified on an X-shaped cross, rather than the straight crucifix associated with Jesus. Iconography typically depicts him as being trussed to the cross, rather than nailed to it. The geometric X-shape is called a "saltire" or "St. Andrew's Cross," and can be seen in several pieces of heraldry and flags, most prominently the flag of Scotland, where St. Andrew is a major patron saint.

Rakugo, page 7

A Japanese form of storytelling. Rakugo is performed by a single person, acting out a story that is typically comical but sometimes dramatic, playing multiple distinct characters using only voices and mannerisms. Despite being "old-fashioned," rakugo maintains a strong popularity in Japan and can even be seen in manga/anime such as Descending Stories: *Showa Genroku Rakugo Shinju.*

Akeldama, page 8

Depending on the book in the Bible, Judas either bought Akeldama with the thirty pieces of silver for betraying Jesus, or returned the money to the temple, where the authorities used it to buy a burial ground for foreigners. Akeldama's location is known for producing excellent clay, which is the origin of the term "potter's field" in reference to a graveyard of unidentified bodies or paupers.

Yellow, page 10

The color yellow became associated with Judas in the Middle Ages through religious iconography. This developed into other negative associations for yellow, including non-Christians, heretics, and the emotions of jealousy and avarice.

Suica, page 14

An electronic prepaid card-based fund system for train lines in Japan (plus buses in the Tokyo area). The smart cards work on contactless readers at fare gates, and because they are essentially just electronic cash cards, they can also be used regularly at convenience stores and other businesses on general purchases.

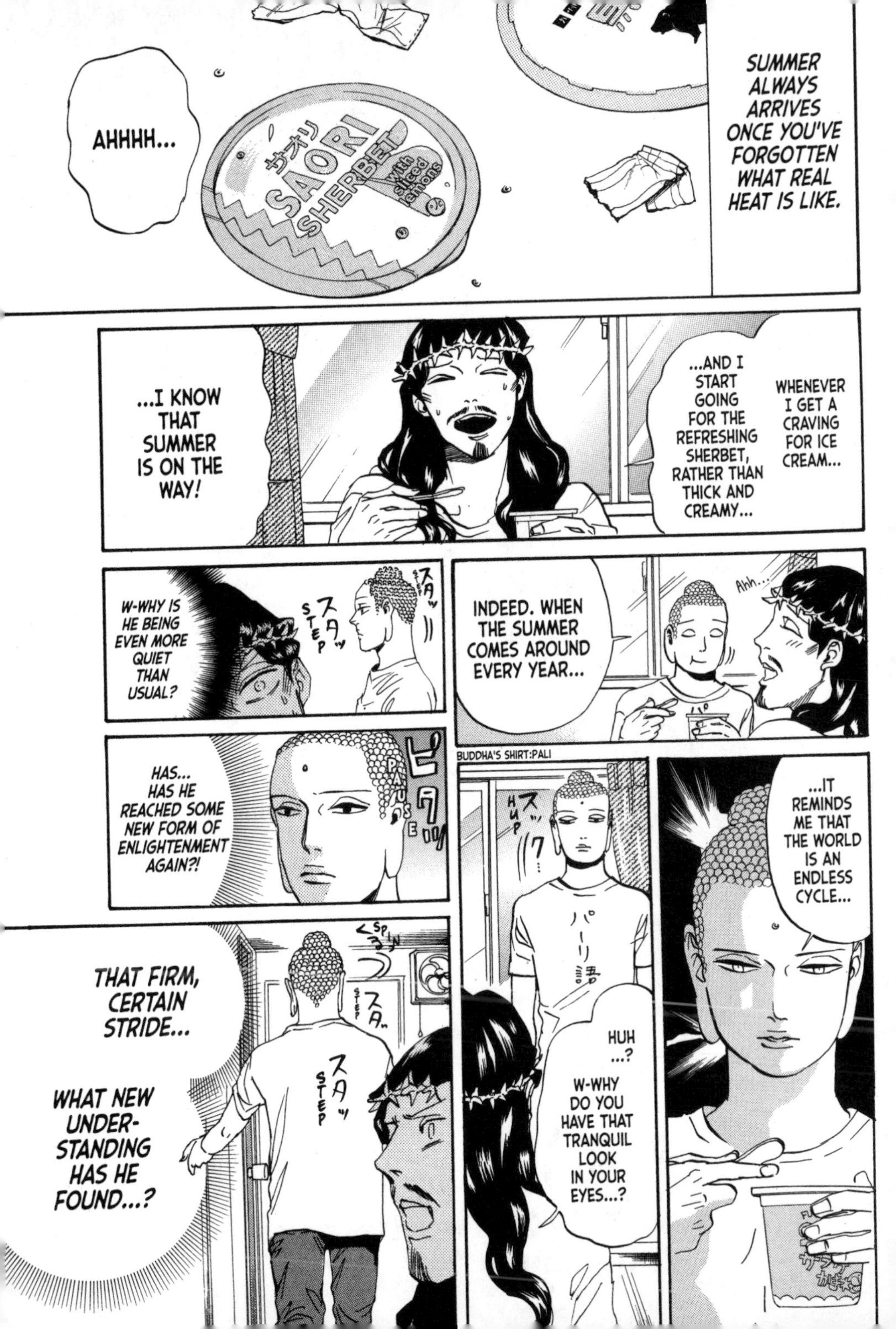
SUMMER ALWAYS ARRIVES ONCE YOU'VE FORGOTTEN WHAT REAL HEAT IS LIKE.
サオリ SAORI SHERBET with sliced lemons
AHHHH...
WHENEVER I GET A CRAVING FOR ICE CREAM...
...AND I START GOING FOR THE REFRESHING SHERBET, RATHER THAN THICK AND CREAMY...
...I KNOW THAT SUMMER IS ON THE WAY!
Ahh...
INDEED. WHEN THE SUMMER COMES AROUND EVERY YEAR...
パ
スタッ STEP
スタッ STEP
W-WHY IS HE BEING EVEN MORE QUIET THAN USUAL?
...IT REMINDS ME THAT THE WORLD IS AN ENDLESS CYCLE...
BUDDHA'S SHIRT:PALI
スック HUP
パーリ語
HUH...?
W-WHY DO YOU HAVE THAT TRANQUIL LOOK IN YOUR EYES...?
ピタ PAUSE
HAS... HAS HE REACHED SOME NEW FORM OF ENLIGHTENMENT AGAIN?!
くるっ SPIN
スタッ STEP
スタッ STEP
THAT FIRM, CERTAIN STRIDE...
WHAT NEW UNDER-STANDING HAS HE FOUND...?

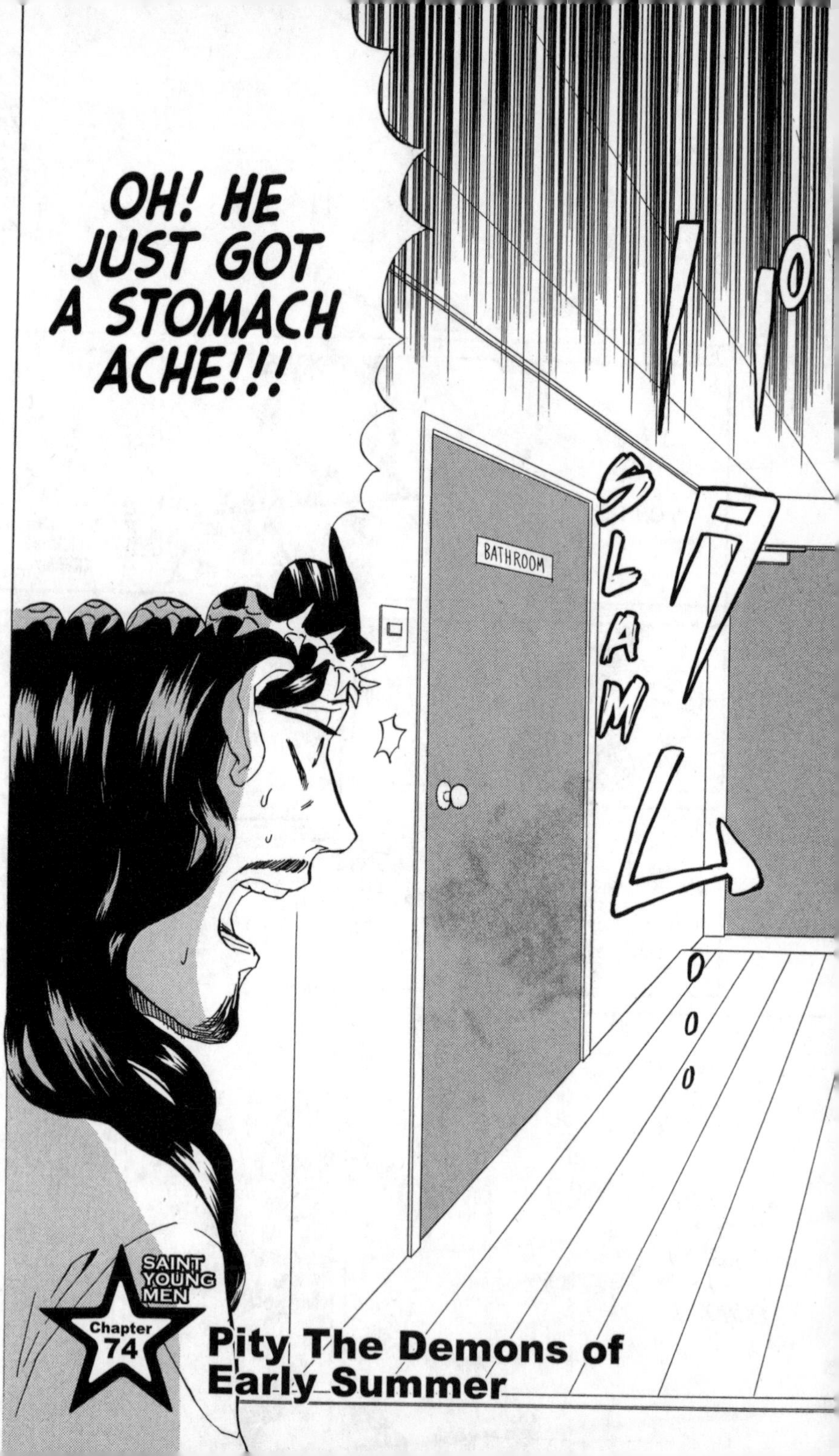
SLAM
OH! HE JUST GOT A STOMACH ACHE!!!
BATHROOM
SAINT YOUNG MEN
Chapter 74

HE NEEDED TO USE THE REST-ROOM.

Pity The Demons of Early Summer

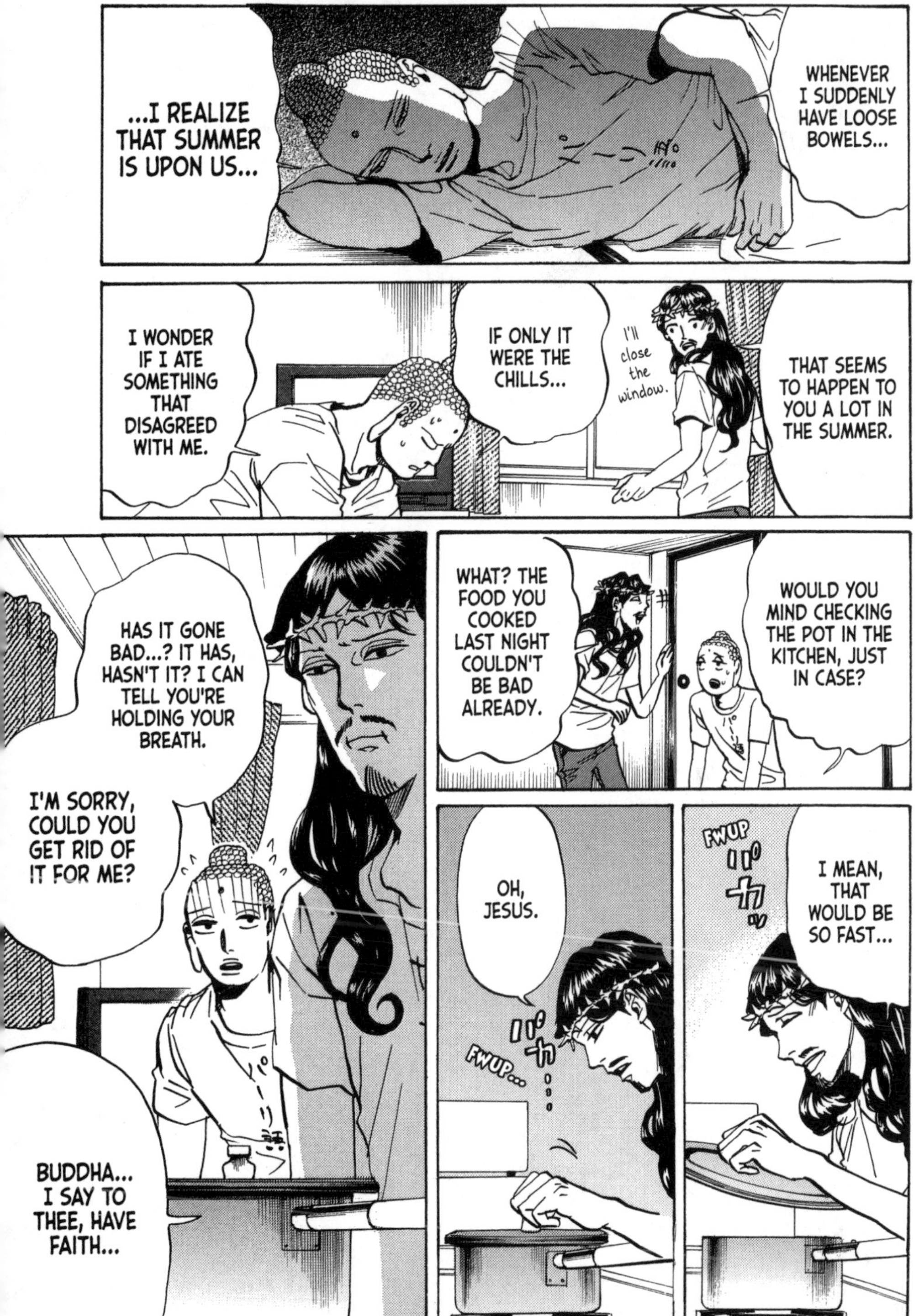
WHENEVER I SUDDENLY HAVE LOOSE BOWELS...
...I REALIZE THAT SUMMER IS UPON US...
THAT SEEMS TO HAPPEN TO YOU A LOT IN THE SUMMER.
I'll close the window.
IF ONLY IT WERE THE CHILLS...
I WONDER IF I ATE SOMETHING THAT DISAGREED WITH ME.
WOULD YOU MIND CHECKING THE POT IN THE KITCHEN, JUST IN CASE?
WHAT? THE FOOD YOU COOKED LAST NIGHT COULDN'T BE BAD ALREADY.
FWUP
I MEAN, THAT WOULD BE SO FAST...
OH, JESUS.
FWUP...
HAS IT GONE BAD...? IT HAS, HASN'T IT? I CAN TELL YOU'RE HOLDING YOUR BREATH.
I'M SORRY, COULD YOU GET RID OF IT FOR ME?
BUDDHA... I SAY TO THEE, HAVE FAITH...

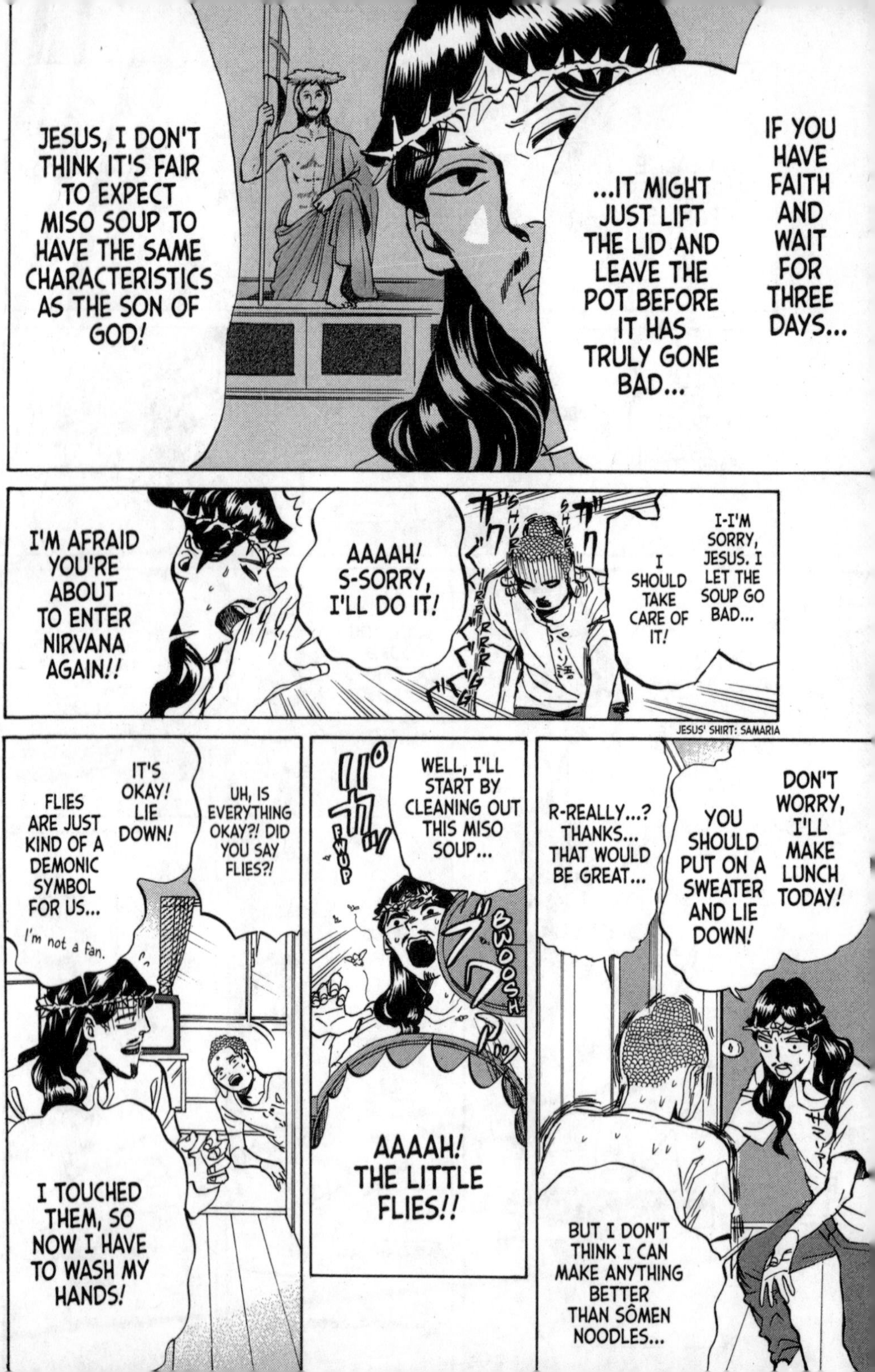
IF YOU HAVE FAITH AND WAIT FOR THREE DAYS...
...IT MIGHT JUST LIFT THE LID AND LEAVE THE POT BEFORE IT HAS TRULY GONE BAD...
JESUS, I DON'T THINK IT'S FAIR TO EXPECT MISO SOUP TO HAVE THE SAME CHARACTERISTICS AS THE SON OF GOD!
I-I'M SORRY, JESUS. I LET THE SOUP GO BAD...
I SHOULD TAKE CARE OF IT!
AAAAH! S-SORRY, I'LL DO IT!
I'M AFRAID YOU'RE ABOUT TO ENTER NIRVANA AGAIN!!
JESUS' SHIRT: SAMARIA
DON'T WORRY, I'LL MAKE LUNCH TODAY!
YOU SHOULD PUT ON A SWEATER AND LIE DOWN!
R-REALLY...? THANKS... THAT WOULD BE GREAT...
BUT I DON'T THINK I CAN MAKE ANYTHING BETTER THAN SÔMEN NOODLES...
WELL, I'LL START BY CLEANING OUT THIS MISO SOUP...
FWUP
BWOOSH
AAAAH! THE LITTLE FLIES!!
UH, IS EVERYTHING OKAY?! DID YOU SAY FLIES?!
IT'S OKAY! LIE DOWN!
FLIES ARE JUST KIND OF A DEMONIC SYMBOL FOR US...
I'm not a fan.
I TOUCHED THEM, SO NOW I HAVE TO WASH MY HANDS!

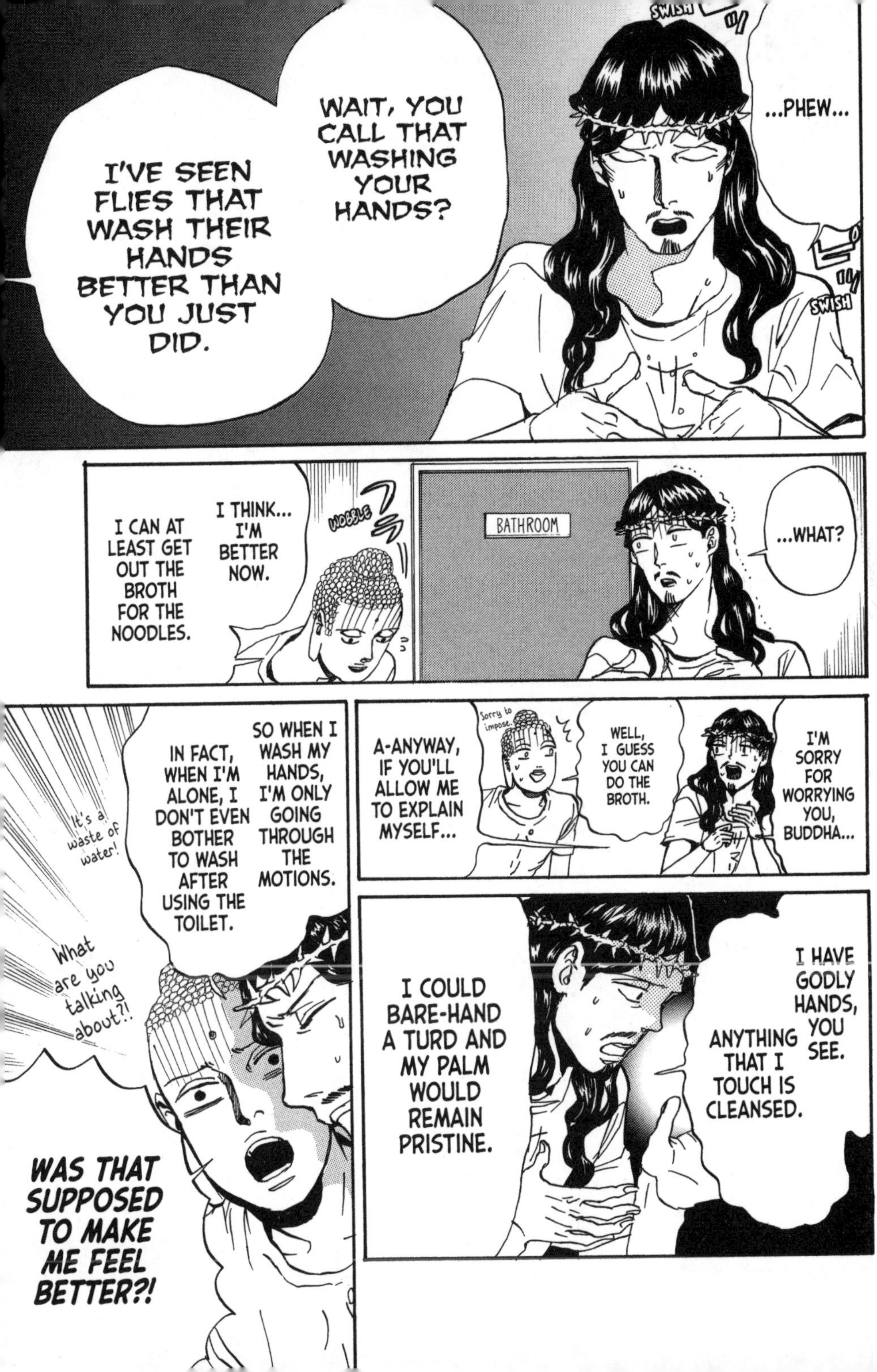
SWISH
...PHEW...
SWISH
WAIT, YOU CALL THAT WASHING YOUR HANDS?
I'VE SEEN FLIES THAT WASH THEIR HANDS BETTER THAN YOU JUST DID.
...WHAT?
BATHROOM
WOBBLE
I THINK... I'M BETTER NOW.
I CAN AT LEAST GET OUT THE BROTH FOR THE NOODLES.
I'M SORRY FOR WORRYING YOU, BUDDHA...
WELL, I GUESS YOU CAN DO THE BROTH.
Sorry to impose.
A-ANYWAY, IF YOU'LL ALLOW ME TO EXPLAIN MYSELF...
I HAVE GODLY HANDS, YOU SEE.
ANYTHING THAT I TOUCH IS CLEANSED.
I COULD BARE-HAND A TURD AND MY PALM WOULD REMAIN PRISTINE.
SO WHEN I WASH MY HANDS, I'M ONLY GOING THROUGH THE MOTIONS.
IN FACT, WHEN I'M ALONE, I DON'T EVEN BOTHER TO WASH AFTER USING THE TOILET.
It's a waste of water!
What are you talking about?!
WAS THAT SUPPOSED TO MAKE ME FEEL BETTER?!

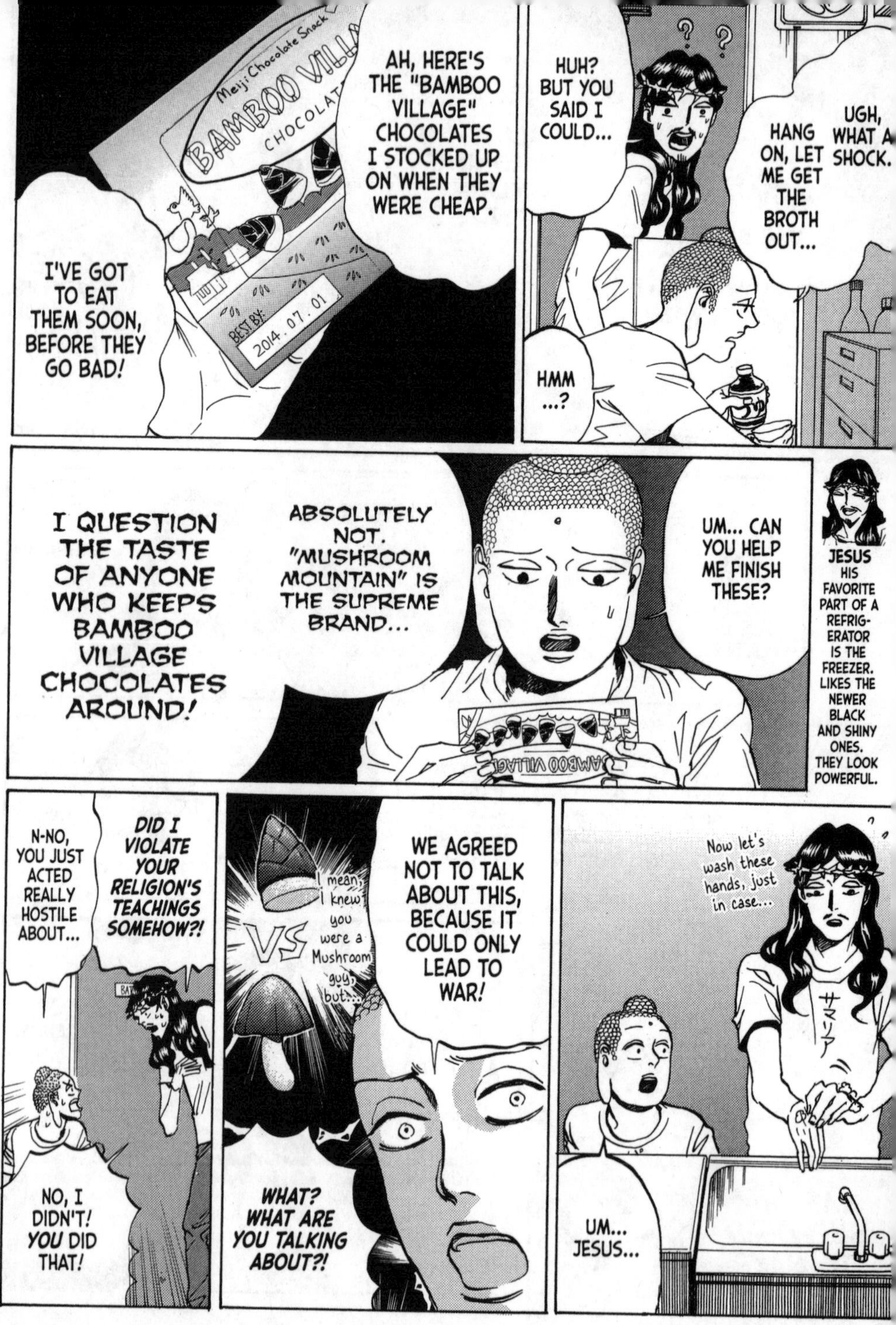
UGH, WHAT A SHOCK.
HANG ON, LET ME GET THE BROTH OUT...
HUH? BUT YOU SAID I COULD...
HMM ...?
AH, HERE'S THE "BAMBOO VILLAGE" CHOCOLATES I STOCKED UP ON WHEN THEY WERE CHEAP.
Meiji Chocolate Snack
BEST BY: 2014.07.01
I'VE GOT TO EAT THEM SOON, BEFORE THEY GO BAD!
JESUS
HIS FAVORITE PART OF A REFRIGERATOR IS THE FREEZER. LIKES THE NEWER BLACK AND SHINY ONES. THEY LOOK POWERFUL.
UM... CAN YOU HELP ME FINISH THESE?
ABSOLUTELY NOT. "MUSHROOM MOUNTAIN" IS THE SUPREME BRAND...
I QUESTION THE TASTE OF ANYONE WHO KEEPS BAMBOO VILLAGE CHOCOLATES AROUND!
Now let's wash these hands, just in case...
UM... JESUS...
WE AGREED NOT TO TALK ABOUT THIS, BECAUSE IT COULD ONLY LEAD TO WAR!
I mean, I knew you were a Mushroom guy, but...
VS
WHAT? WHAT ARE YOU TALKING ABOUT?!
DID I VIOLATE YOUR RELIGION'S TEACHINGS SOMEHOW?!
N-NO, YOU JUST ACTED REALLY HOSTILE ABOUT...
NO, I DIDN'T! YOU DID THAT!

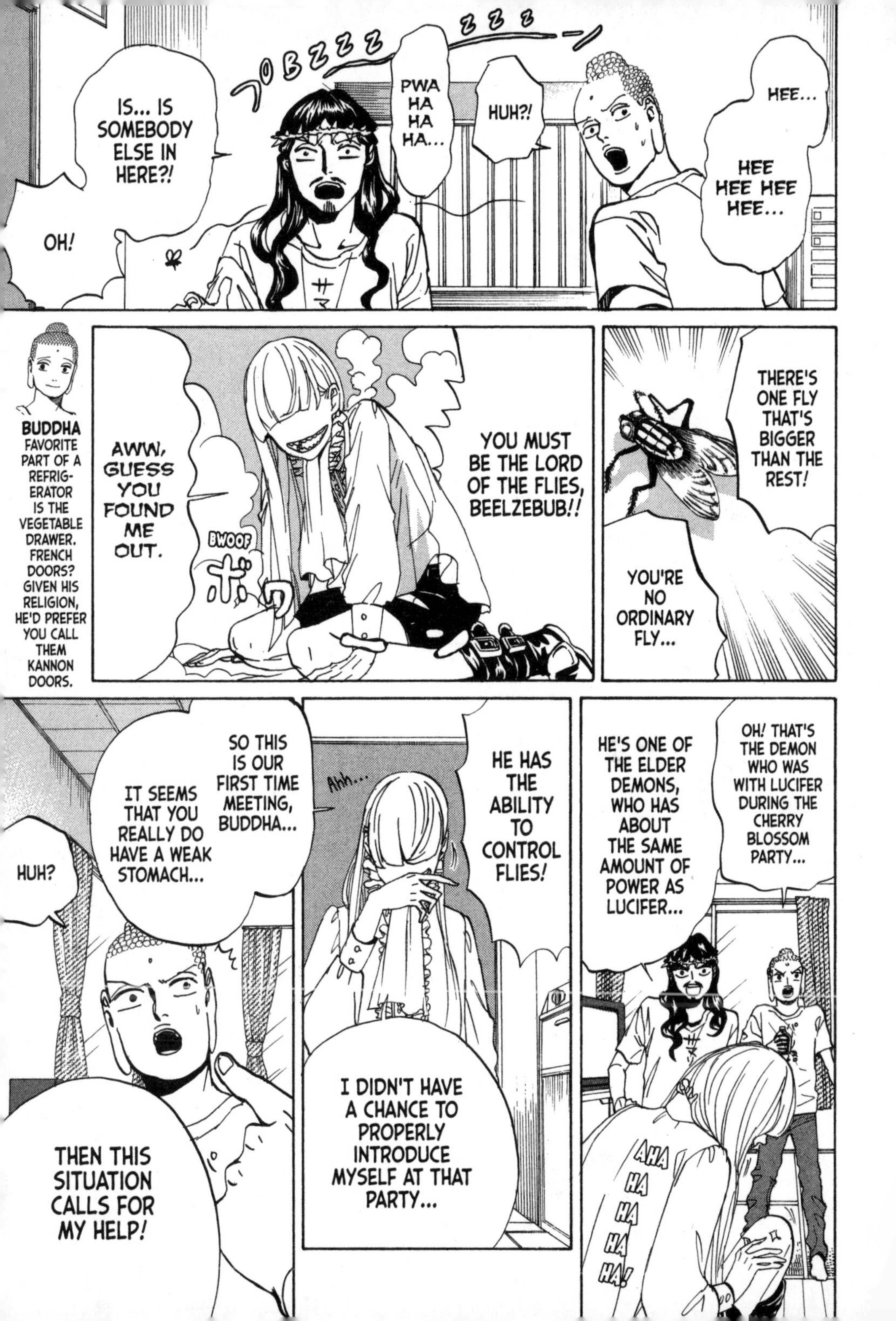
HEE...
HEE HEE HEE HEE...
HUH?!
PWA HA HA HA...
プBZZZZ ZZZ—!
IS... IS SOMEBODY ELSE IN HERE?!
OH!
THERE'S ONE FLY THAT'S BIGGER THAN THE REST!
YOU'RE NO ORDINARY FLY...
YOU MUST BE THE LORD OF THE FLIES, BEELZEBUB!!
AWW, GUESS YOU FOUND ME OUT.
BWOOF
ボワ
BUDDHA
FAVORITE PART OF A REFRIG-ERATOR IS THE VEGETABLE DRAWER. FRENCH DOORS? GIVEN HIS RELIGION, HE'D PREFER YOU CALL THEM KANNON DOORS.
OH! THAT'S THE DEMON WHO WAS WITH LUCIFER DURING THE CHERRY BLOSSOM PARTY...
HE'S ONE OF THE ELDER DEMONS, WHO HAS ABOUT THE SAME AMOUNT OF POWER AS LUCIFER...
AHA HA HA HA HA HA!
HE HAS THE ABILITY TO CONTROL FLIES!
Ahh...
I DIDN'T HAVE A CHANCE TO PROPERLY INTRODUCE MYSELF AT THAT PARTY...
SO THIS IS OUR FIRST TIME MEETING, BUDDHA...
IT SEEMS THAT YOU REALLY DO HAVE A WEAK STOMACH...
HUH?
THEN THIS SITUATION CALLS FOR MY HELP!

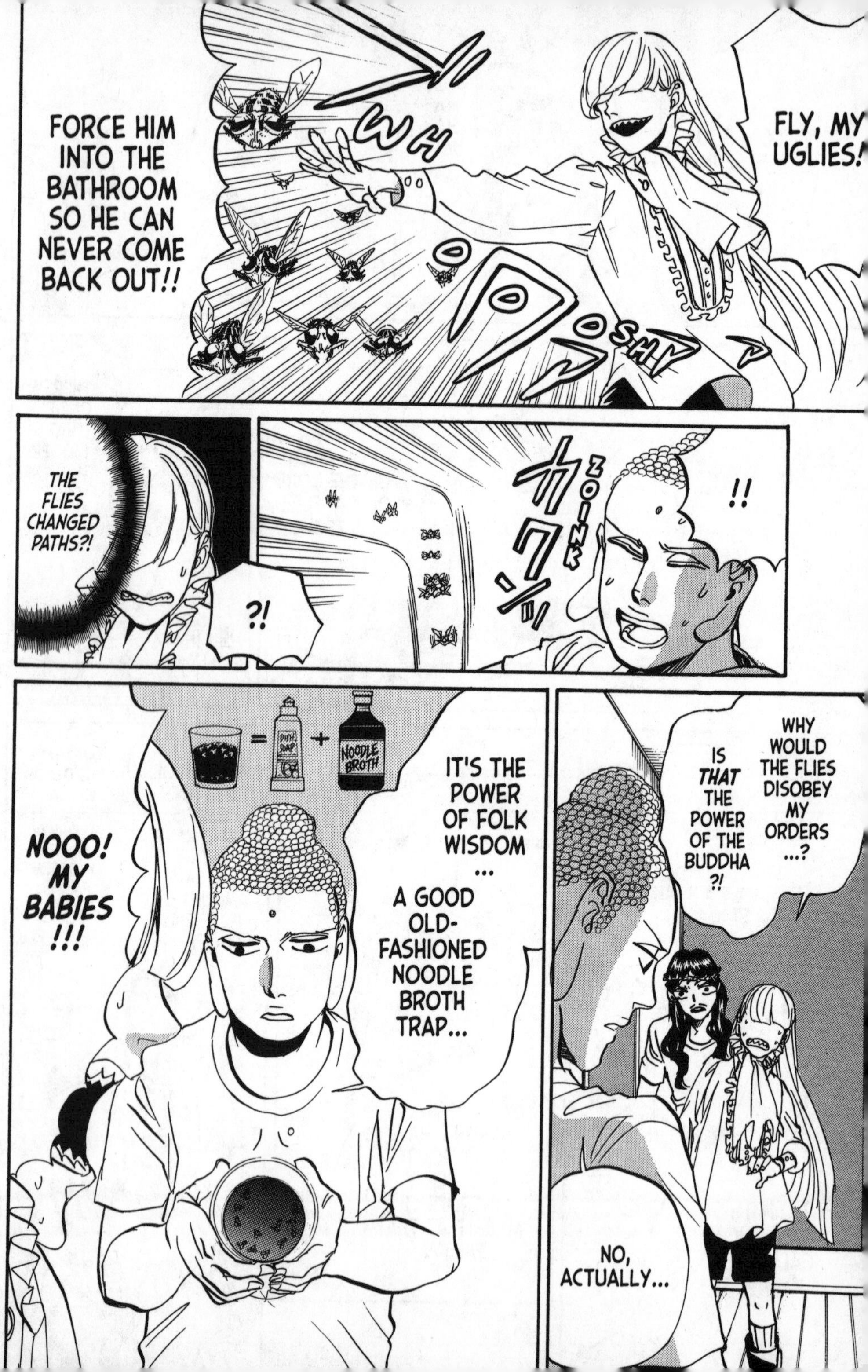
FLY, MY UGLIES!
FORCE HIM INTO THE BATHROOM SO HE CAN NEVER COME BACK OUT!!
!!
ZOINK
THE FLIES CHANGED PATHS?!
?!
WHY WOULD THE FLIES DISOBEY MY ORDERS ...?
IS THAT THE POWER OF THE BUDDHA ?!
NO, ACTUALLY...
IT'S THE POWER OF FOLK WISDOM ...
A GOOD OLD-FASHIONED NOODLE BROTH TRAP...
NOODLE BROTH
NOOO! MY BABIES !!!

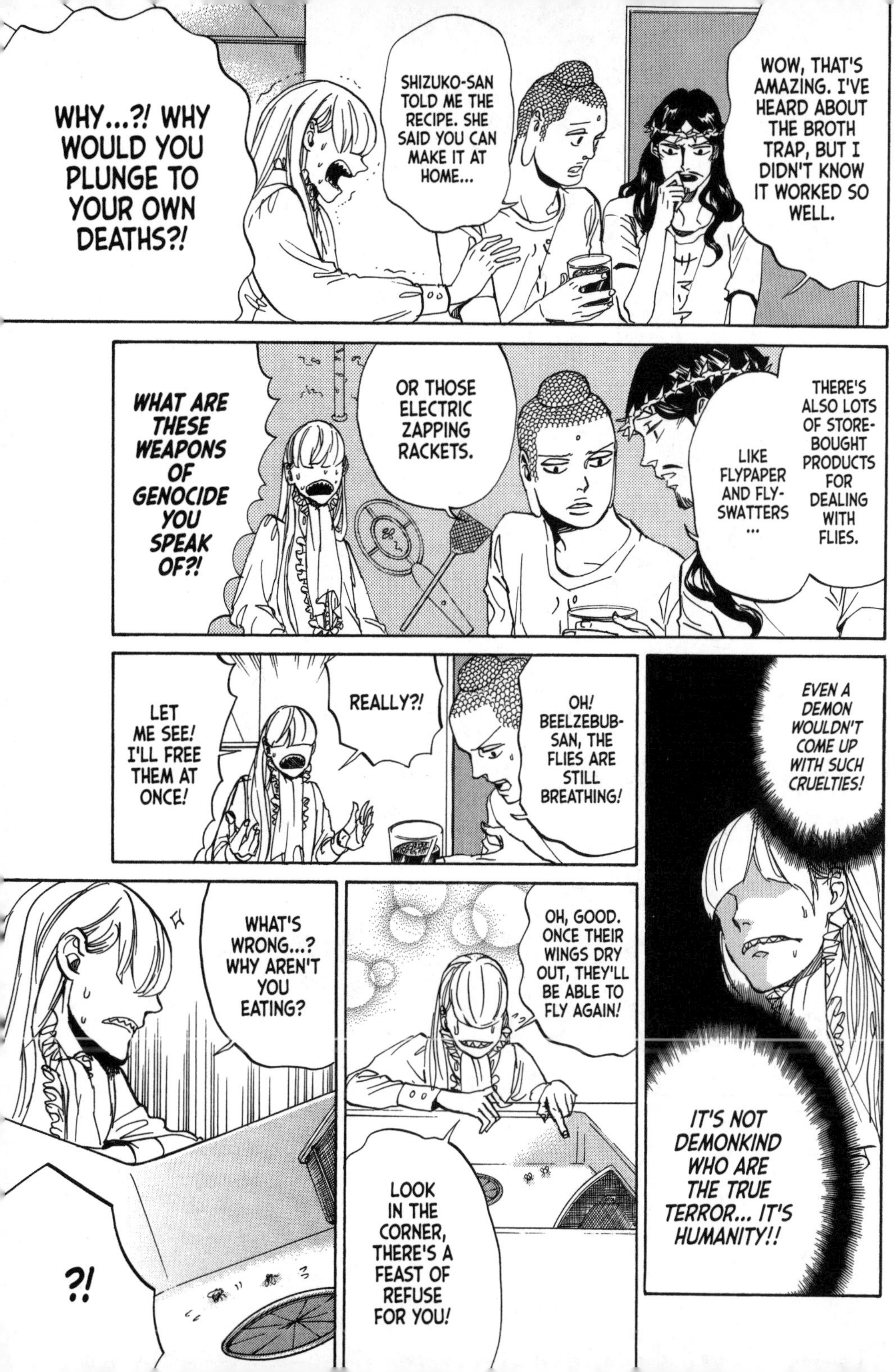
WOW, THAT'S AMAZING. I'VE HEARD ABOUT THE BROTH TRAP, BUT I DIDN'T KNOW IT WORKED SO WELL.
SHIZUKO-SAN TOLD ME THE RECIPE. SHE SAID YOU CAN MAKE IT AT HOME...
WHY...?! WHY WOULD YOU PLUNGE TO YOUR OWN DEATHS?!
THERE'S ALSO LOTS OF STORE-BOUGHT PRODUCTS FOR DEALING WITH FLIES.
LIKE FLYPAPER AND FLY-SWATTERS...
OR THOSE ELECTRIC ZAPPING RACKETS.
WHAT ARE THESE WEAPONS OF GENOCIDE YOU SPEAK OF?!
EVEN A DEMON WOULDN'T COME UP WITH SUCH CRUELTIES!
IT'S NOT DEMONKIND WHO ARE THE TRUE TERROR... IT'S HUMANITY!!
OH! BEELZEBUB-SAN, THE FLIES ARE STILL BREATHING!
REALLY?!
LET ME SEE! I'LL FREE THEM AT ONCE!
OH, GOOD. ONCE THEIR WINGS DRY OUT, THEY'LL BE ABLE TO FLY AGAIN!
LOOK IN THE CORNER, THERE'S A FEAST OF REFUSE FOR YOU!
WHAT'S WRONG...? WHY AREN'T YOU EATING?
?!

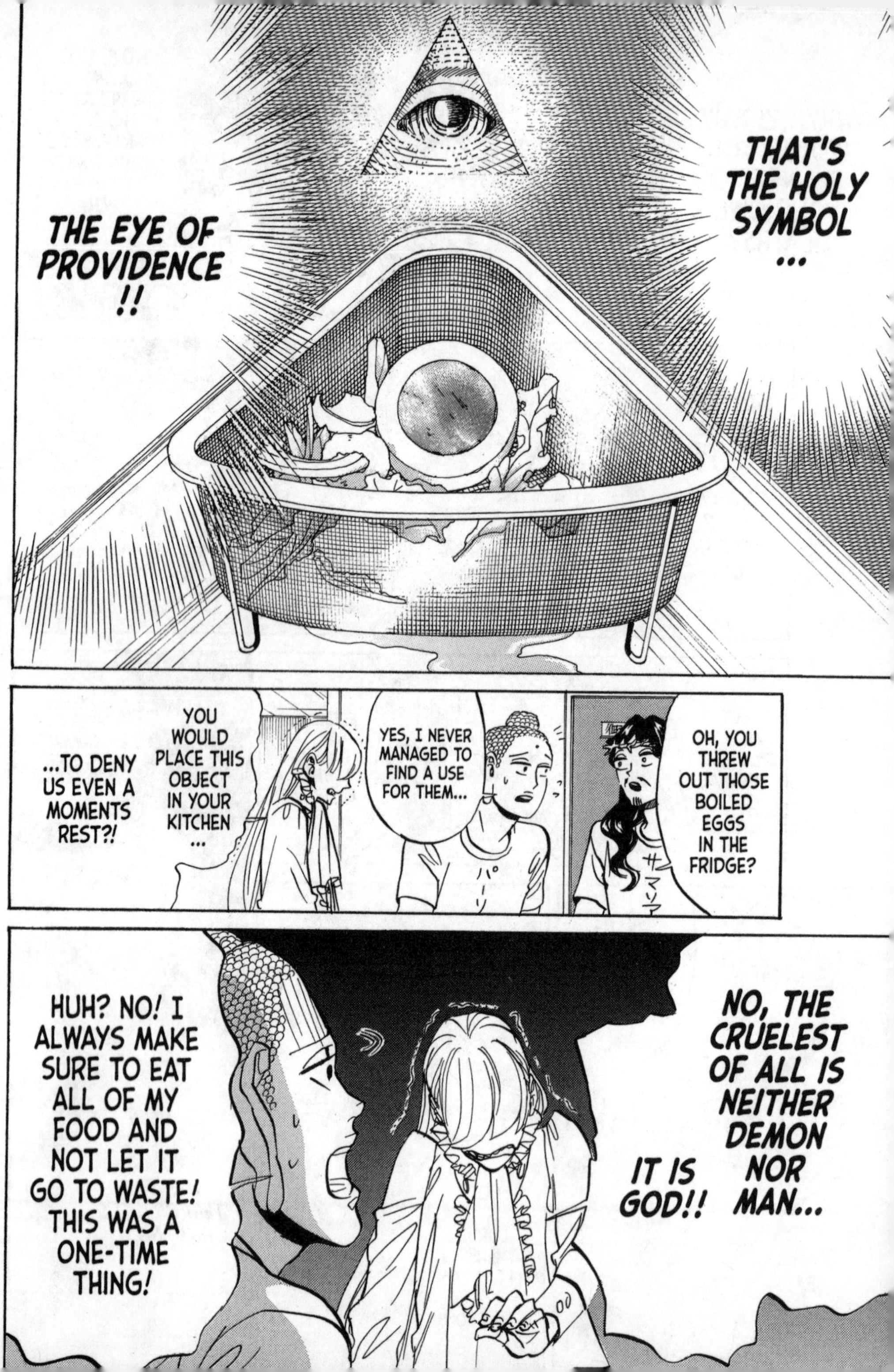
THAT'S THE HOLY SYMBOL ...
THE EYE OF PROVIDENCE !!
OH, YOU THREW OUT THOSE BOILED EGGS IN THE FRIDGE?
YES, I NEVER MANAGED TO FIND A USE FOR THEM...
YOU WOULD PLACE THIS OBJECT IN YOUR KITCHEN ...
...TO DENY US EVEN A MOMENTS REST?!
NO, THE CRUELEST OF ALL IS NEITHER DEMON NOR MAN...
IT IS GOD!!
HUH? NO! I ALWAYS MAKE SURE TO EAT ALL OF MY FOOD AND NOT LET IT GO TO WASTE! THIS WAS A ONE-TIME THING!

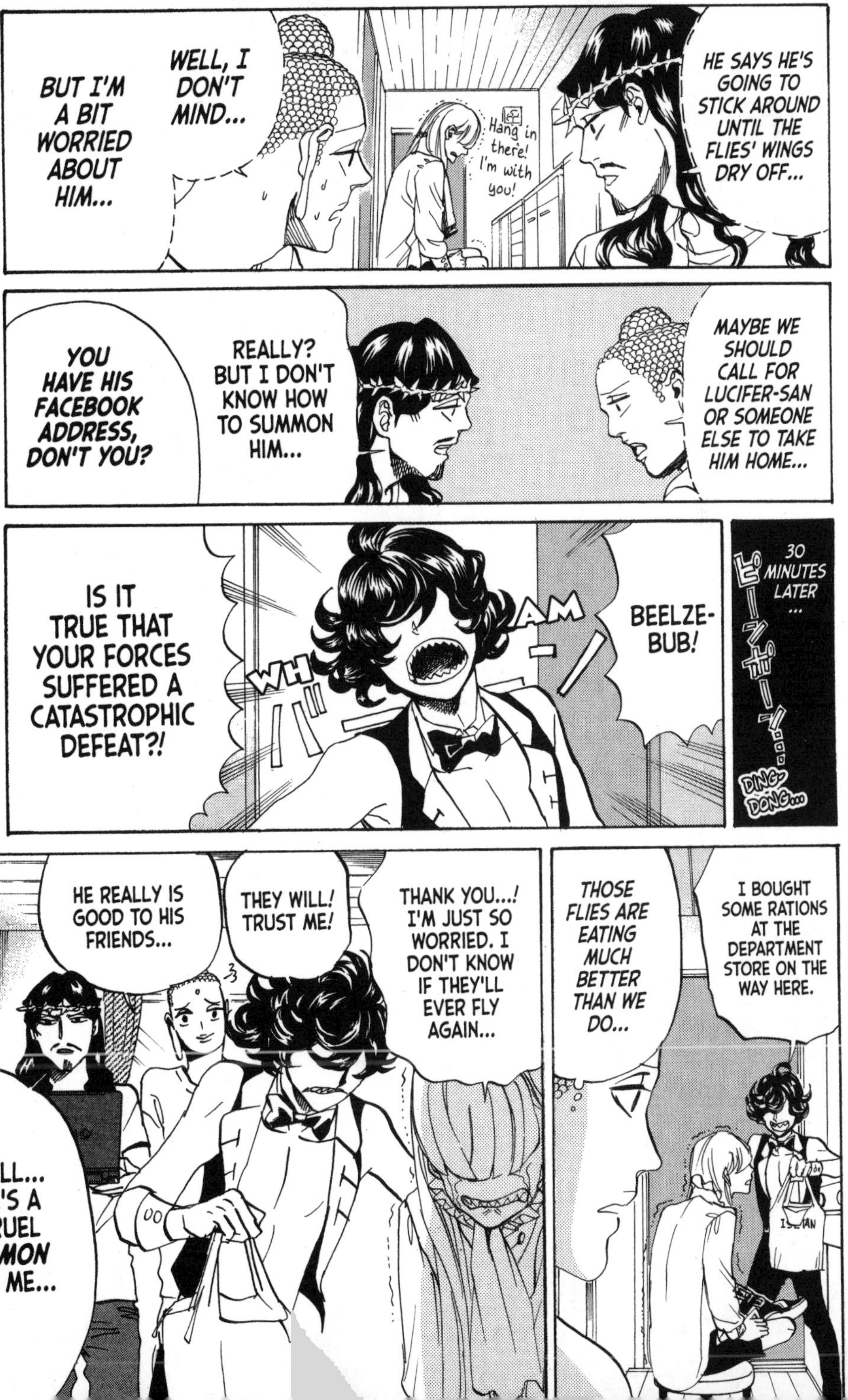
HE SAYS HE'S GOING TO STICK AROUND UNTIL THE FLIES' WINGS DRY OFF...
Hang in there! I'm with you!
WELL, I DON'T MIND...
BUT I'M A BIT WORRIED ABOUT HIM...
MAYBE WE SHOULD CALL FOR LUCIFER-SAN OR SOMEONE ELSE TO TAKE HIM HOME...
REALLY? BUT I DON'T KNOW HOW TO SUMMON HIM...
YOU HAVE HIS FACEBOOK ADDRESS, DON'T YOU?
30 MINUTES LATER...
DING-DONG...
BEELZEBUB!
WH AM
IS IT TRUE THAT YOUR FORCES SUFFERED A CATASTROPHIC DEFEAT?!
I BOUGHT SOME RATIONS AT THE DEPARTMENT STORE ON THE WAY HERE.
THOSE FLIES ARE EATING MUCH BETTER THAN WE DO...
THANK YOU...! I'M JUST SO WORRIED. I DON'T KNOW IF THEY'LL EVER FLY AGAIN...
THEY WILL! TRUST ME!
HE REALLY IS GOOD TO HIS FRIENDS...
WELL... HE'S A CRUEL DEMON TO ME...

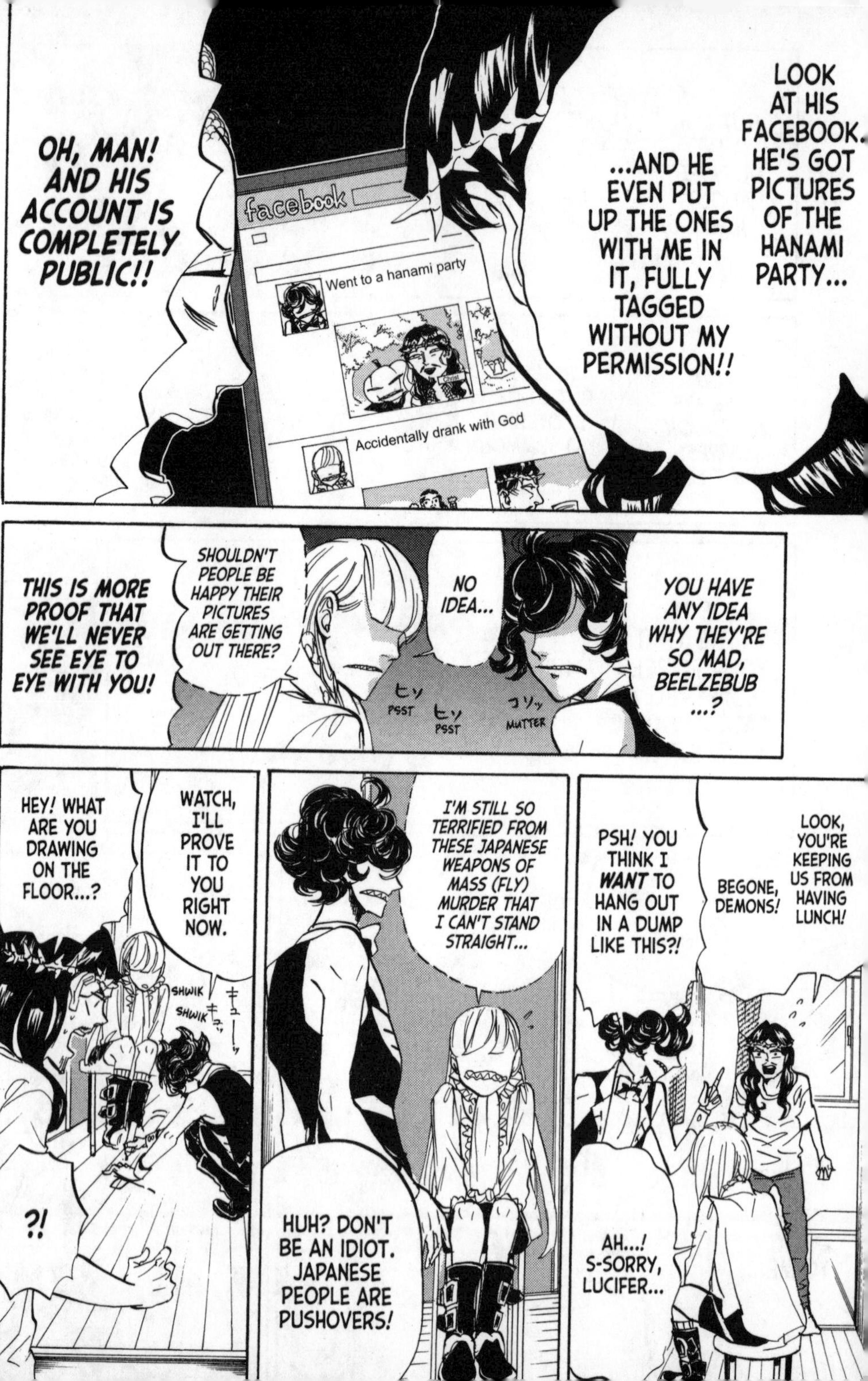
LOOK AT HIS FACEBOOK. HE'S GOT PICTURES OF THE HANAMI PARTY...
...AND HE EVEN PUT UP THE ONES WITH ME IN IT, FULLY TAGGED WITHOUT MY PERMISSION!!
OH, MAN! AND HIS ACCOUNT IS COMPLETELY PUBLIC!!
facebook
Went to a hanami party
Accidentally drank with God
YOU HAVE ANY IDEA WHY THEY'RE SO MAD, BEELZEBUB...?
NO IDEA...
SHOULDN'T PEOPLE BE HAPPY THEIR PICTURES ARE GETTING OUT THERE?
THIS IS MORE PROOF THAT WE'LL NEVER SEE EYE TO EYE WITH YOU!
ヒソ PSST
ヒソ PSST
コソッ MUTTER
LOOK, YOU'RE KEEPING US FROM HAVING LUNCH!
BEGONE, DEMONS!
PSH! YOU THINK I *WANT* TO HANG OUT IN A DUMP LIKE THIS?!
AH...! S-SORRY, LUCIFER...
I'M STILL SO TERRIFIED FROM THESE JAPANESE WEAPONS OF MASS (FLY) MURDER THAT I CAN'T STAND STRAIGHT...
HUH? DON'T BE AN IDIOT. JAPANESE PEOPLE ARE PUSHOVERS!
WATCH, I'LL PROVE IT TO YOU RIGHT NOW.
HEY! WHAT ARE YOU DRAWING ON THE FLOOR...?
SHWIK
SHWIK
?!

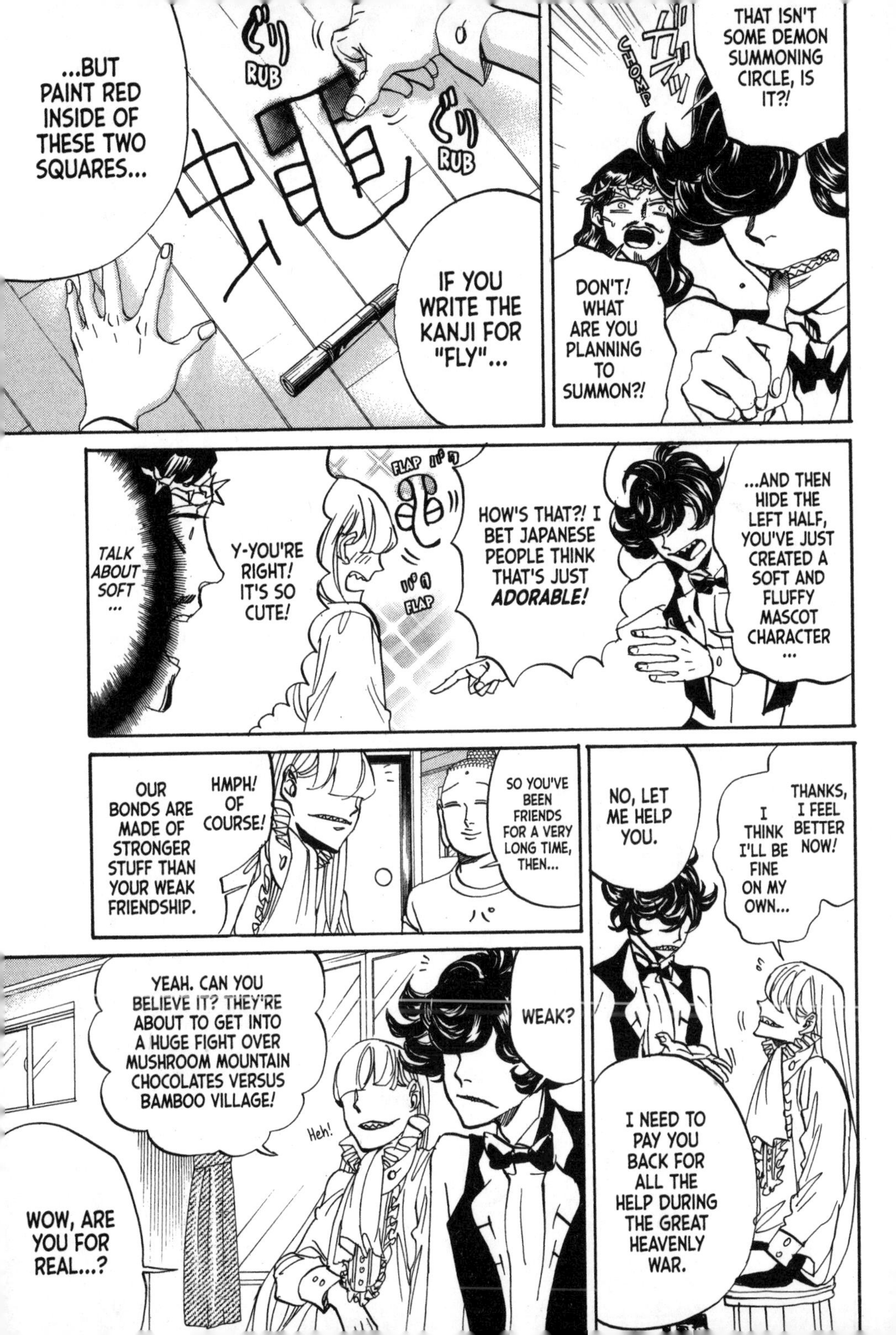
THAT ISN'T SOME DEMON SUMMONING CIRCLE, IS IT?!
CHOMP
DON'T! WHAT ARE YOU PLANNING TO SUMMON?!
RUB
RUB
IF YOU WRITE THE KANJI FOR "FLY"...
...BUT PAINT RED INSIDE OF THESE TWO SQUARES...
...AND THEN HIDE THE LEFT HALF, YOU'VE JUST CREATED A SOFT AND FLUFFY MASCOT CHARACTER...
HOW'S THAT?! I BET JAPANESE PEOPLE THINK THAT'S JUST ADORABLE!
FLAP
FLAP
Y-YOU'RE RIGHT! IT'S SO CUTE!
TALK ABOUT SOFT...
THANKS, I FEEL BETTER NOW!
I THINK I'LL BE FINE ON MY OWN...
NO, LET ME HELP YOU.
I NEED TO PAY YOU BACK FOR ALL THE HELP DURING THE GREAT HEAVENLY WAR.
SO YOU'VE BEEN FRIENDS FOR A VERY LONG TIME, THEN...
HMPH! OF COURSE!
OUR BONDS ARE MADE OF STRONGER STUFF THAN YOUR WEAK FRIENDSHIP.
WEAK?
YEAH. CAN YOU BELIEVE IT? THEY'RE ABOUT TO GET INTO A HUGE FIGHT OVER MUSHROOM MOUNTAIN CHOCOLATES VERSUS BAMBOO VILLAGE!
Heh!
WOW, ARE YOU FOR REAL...?

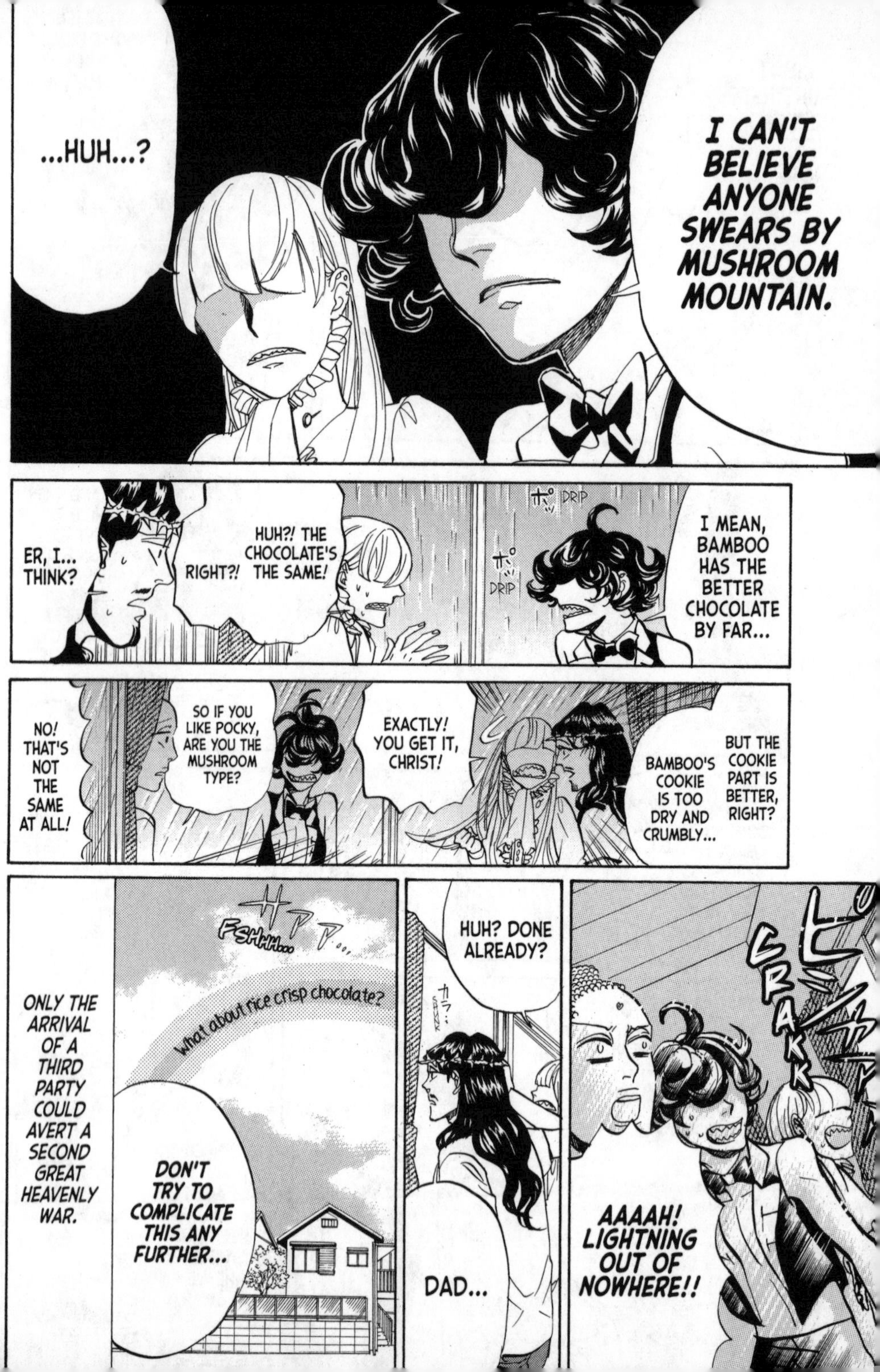
I CAN'T BELIEVE ANYONE SWEARS BY MUSHROOM MOUNTAIN.
...HUH...?
DRIP
DRIP
I MEAN, BAMBOO HAS THE BETTER CHOCOLATE BY FAR...
HUH?! THE CHOCOLATE'S THE SAME!
RIGHT?!
ER, I... THINK?
BUT THE COOKIE PART IS BETTER, RIGHT?
BAMBOO'S COOKIE IS TOO DRY AND CRUMBLY...
EXACTLY! YOU GET IT, CHRIST!
SO IF YOU LIKE POCKY, ARE YOU THE MUSHROOM TYPE?
NO! THAT'S NOT THE SAME AT ALL!
CRAKK
AAAAH! LIGHTNING OUT OF NOWHERE!!
HUH? DONE ALREADY?
SHUNK
DAD...
FSHHH...
What about rice crisp chocolate?
ONLY THE ARRIVAL OF A THIRD PARTY COULD AVERT A SECOND GREAT HEAVENLY WAR.
DON'T TRY TO COMPLICATE THIS ANY FURTHER...

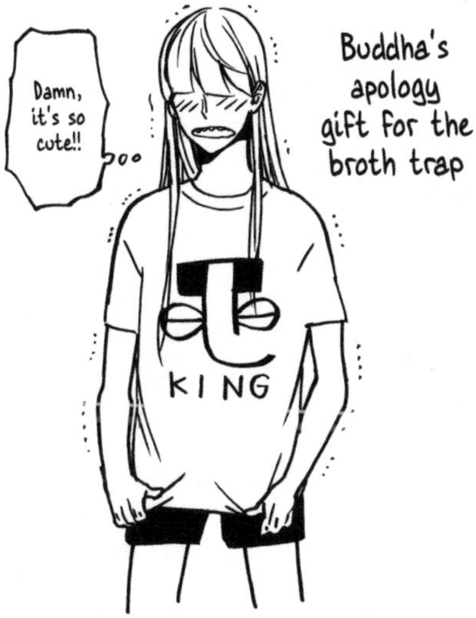
Damn, it's so cute!!
KING
Buddha's apology gift for the broth trap

CHAPTER 74 TRANSLATION NOTES

Pali, page 17
A historical language from the Indian subcontinent. Pali is a liturgical language in Buddhism, similar to Ecclesiastical Latin used in the Catholic Church. Pali is the language of many important Buddhist texts in the Theravada tradition, which is practiced among Southeast Asian cultures.

Three days, page 20
Referring to the three day period between Jesus's crucifixion and his disappearance from the tomb.

Samaria, page 20
An area of Israel. People from Samaria are known as Samaritans, most famous for the biblical tale of the Good Samaritan, who helped a traveler on the road in need despite the enmity between Samaritans and Jews.

Sômen, page 20
A kind of thin wheat noodle popular in the summer, when they are served cold with a small cup of dipping sauce.

Kannon doors, page 23
In Japanese, double doors (or "French doors") are typically called Kannon doors, after the Kannon bodhisatva. This is because such doors were most common in Japan on compartments and altars for Kannon statues.

Eye of Providence, page 26
A symbol consisting of an eye inside a triangle. In Christian symbolism, this represents the omnipresent eye of God within the Trinity of Father, Son, and Holy Ghost. It's been used in many settings, such as on American paper currency and in various conspiracy theories.

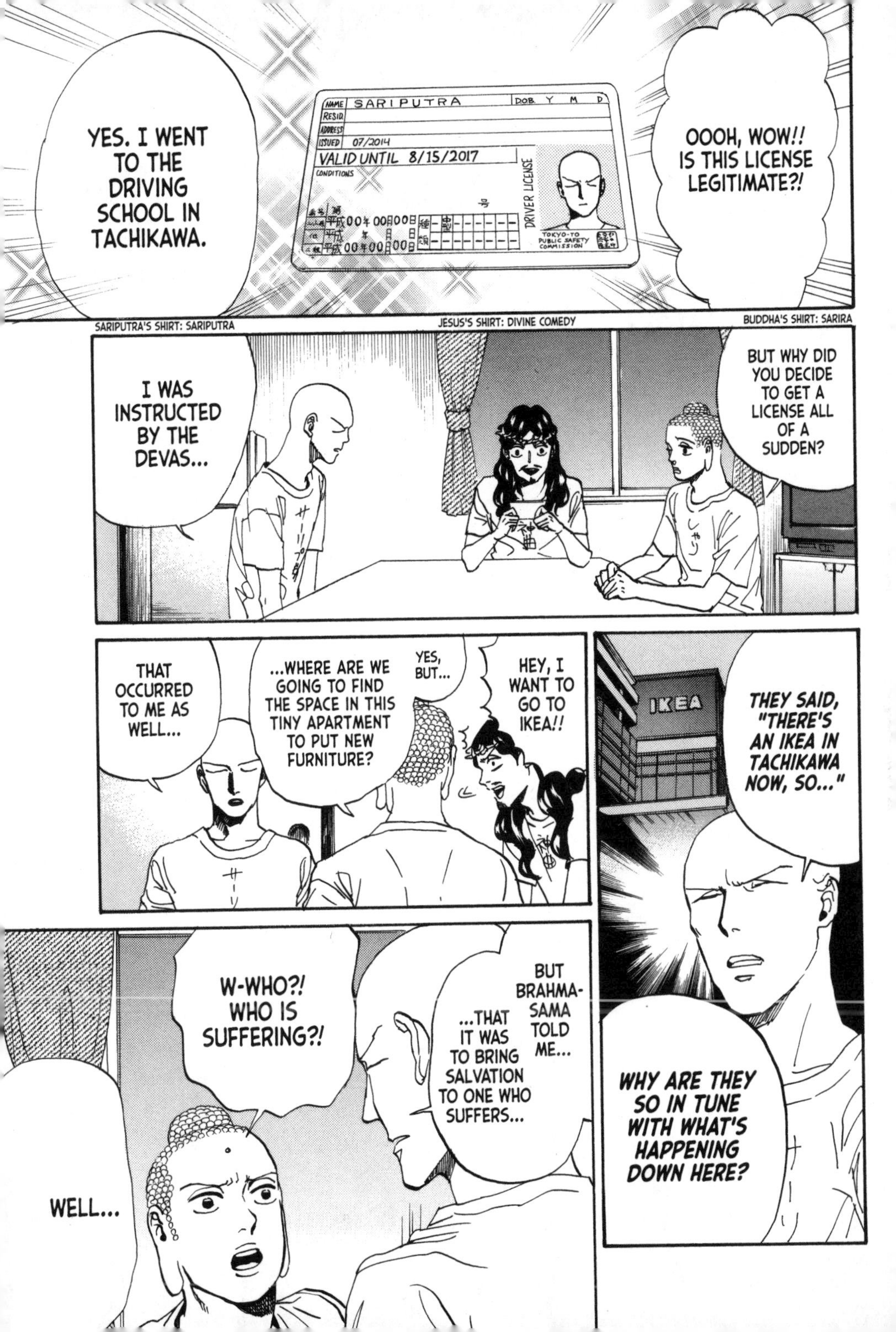
OOOH, WOW!! IS THIS LICENSE LEGITIMATE?!
NAME SARIPUTRA
DOB. Y M D
RESID.
ADDRESS
ISSUED 07/2014
VALID UNTIL 8/15/2017
CONDITIONS
DRIVER LICENSE
TOKYO-TO PUBLIC SAFETY COMMISSION
YES. I WENT TO THE DRIVING SCHOOL IN TACHIKAWA.
BUDDHA'S SHIRT: SARIRA
JESUS'S SHIRT: DIVINE COMEDY
SARIPUTRA'S SHIRT: SARIPUTRA
BUT WHY DID YOU DECIDE TO GET A LICENSE ALL OF A SUDDEN?
I WAS INSTRUCTED BY THE DEVAS...
IKEA
THEY SAID, "THERE'S AN IKEA IN TACHIKAWA NOW, SO..."
WHY ARE THEY SO IN TUNE WITH WHAT'S HAPPENING DOWN HERE?
HEY, I WANT TO GO TO IKEA!!
YES, BUT...
...WHERE ARE WE GOING TO FIND THE SPACE IN THIS TINY APARTMENT TO PUT NEW FURNITURE?
THAT OCCURRED TO ME AS WELL...
BUT BRAHMA-SAMA TOLD ME...
...THAT IT WAS TO BRING SALVATION TO ONE WHO SUFFERS...
W-WHO?! WHO IS SUFFERING?!
WELL...

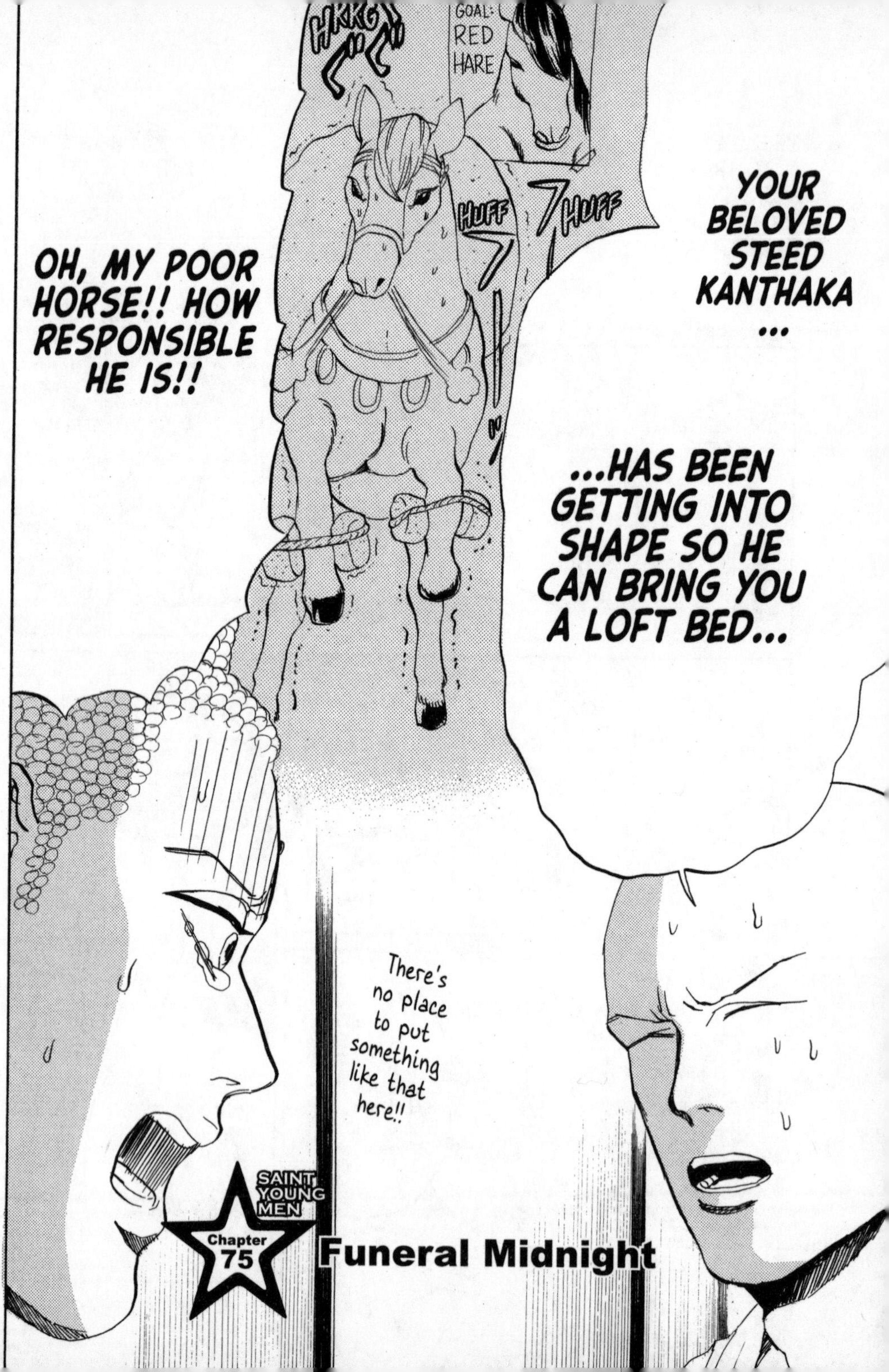
GOAL: RED HARE
HKKG
YOUR BELOVED STEED KANTHAKA ...
HUFF HUFF
OH, MY POOR HORSE!! HOW RESPONSIBLE HE IS!!
...HAS BEEN GETTING INTO SHAPE SO HE CAN BRING YOU A LOFT BED...
There's no place to put something like that here!!
SAINT YOUNG MEN
Chapter 75
Funeral Midnight

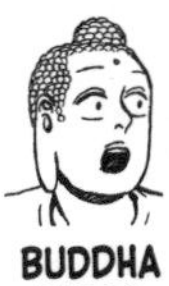

BUDDHA
WHY DO YOU HAVE TO STEP ON THE GAS AND BRAKE PEDALS? IF YOU COULD DRIVE WITH REINS, I WOULD HAVE MY LICENSE TOMORROW.

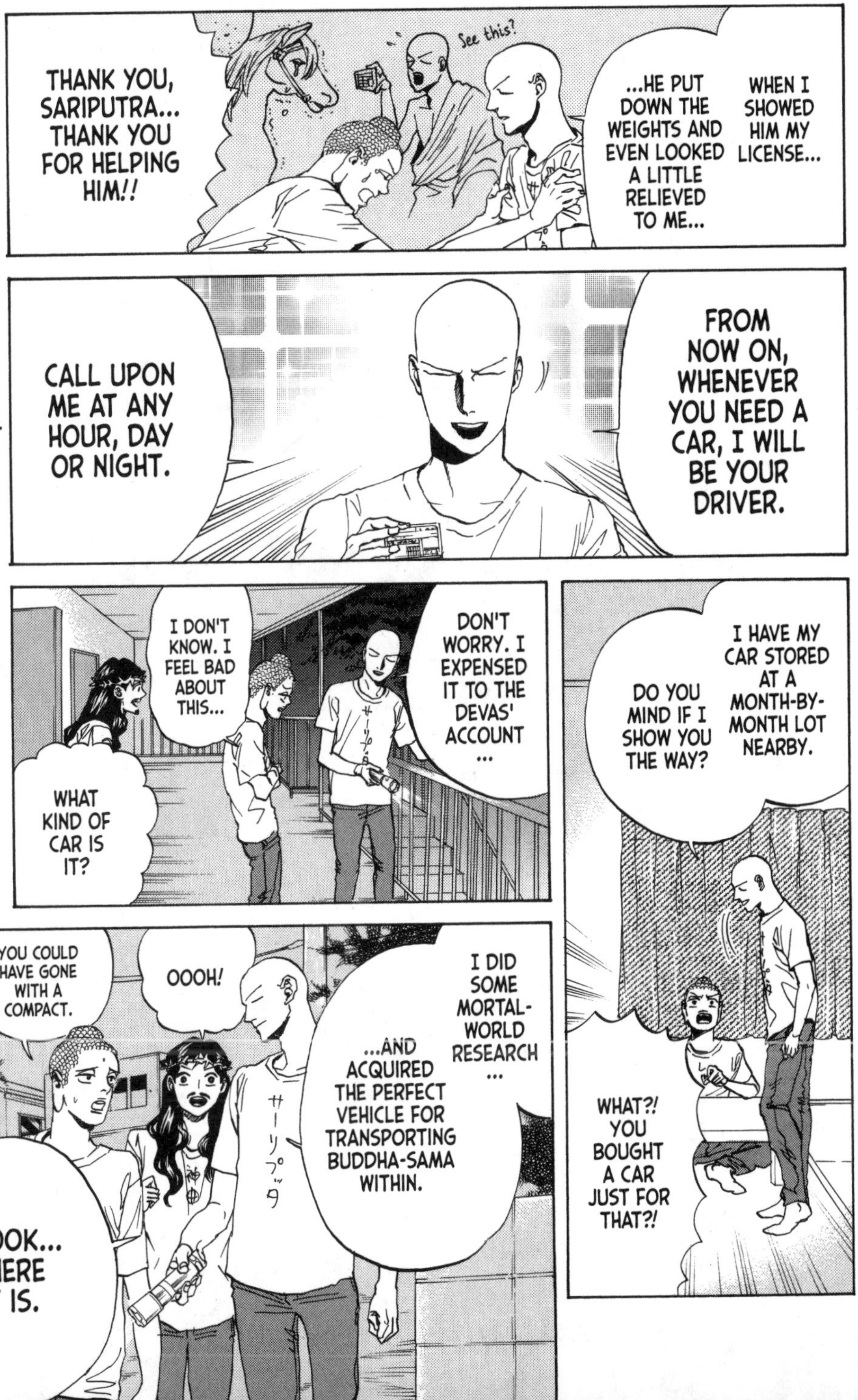
WHEN I SHOWED HIM MY LICENSE...
...HE PUT DOWN THE WEIGHTS AND EVEN LOOKED A LITTLE RELIEVED TO ME...
See this?
THANK YOU, SARIPUTRA... THANK YOU FOR HELPING HIM!!
FROM NOW ON, WHENEVER YOU NEED A CAR, I WILL BE YOUR DRIVER.
CALL UPON ME AT ANY HOUR, DAY OR NIGHT.
I HAVE MY CAR STORED AT A MONTH-BY-MONTH LOT NEARBY.
DO YOU MIND IF I SHOW YOU THE WAY?
WHAT?! YOU BOUGHT A CAR JUST FOR THAT?!
DON'T WORRY. I EXPENSED IT TO THE DEVAS' ACCOUNT...
I DON'T KNOW. I FEEL BAD ABOUT THIS...
WHAT KIND OF CAR IS IT?
I DID SOME MORTAL-WORLD RESEARCH...
...AND ACQUIRED THE PERFECT VEHICLE FOR TRANSPORTING BUDDHA-SAMA WITHIN.
サーリプッタ
OOOH!
YOU COULD HAVE GONE WITH A COMPACT.
LOOK... THERE IT IS.

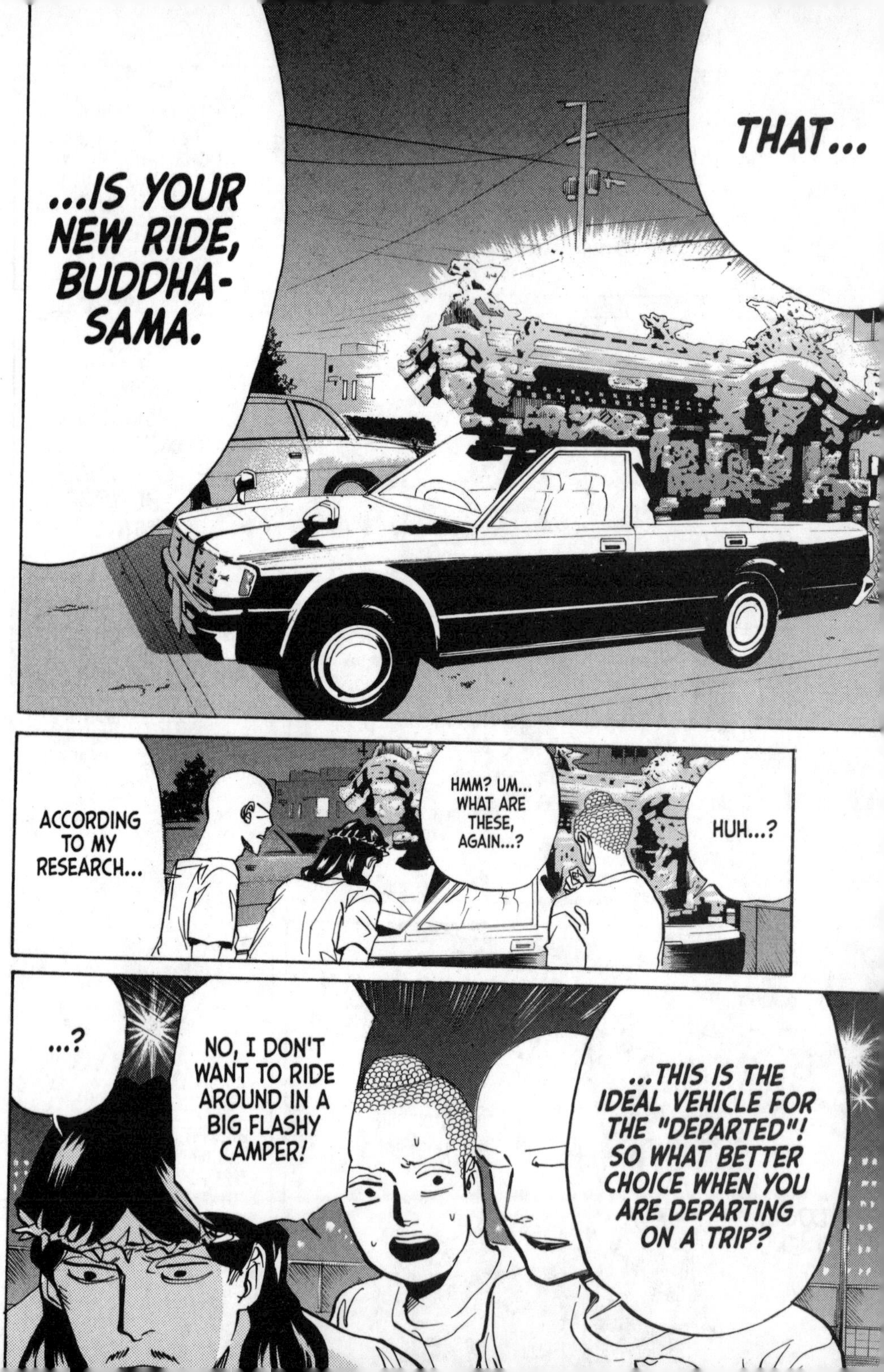
THAT...
...IS YOUR NEW RIDE, BUDDHA-SAMA.
HUH...?
HMM? UM... WHAT ARE THESE, AGAIN...?
ACCORDING TO MY RESEARCH...
...THIS IS THE IDEAL VEHICLE FOR THE "DEPARTED"! SO WHAT BETTER CHOICE WHEN YOU ARE DEPARTING ON A TRIP?
NO, I DON'T WANT TO RIDE AROUND IN A BIG FLASHY CAMPER!
...?

JESUS
WHO DECIDED THE STEERING WHEEL SHOULD BE ROUND? IF YOU CONTROLLED THE CAR WITH A D-PAD AND BUTTONS, I COULD BE AN F1 RACER.

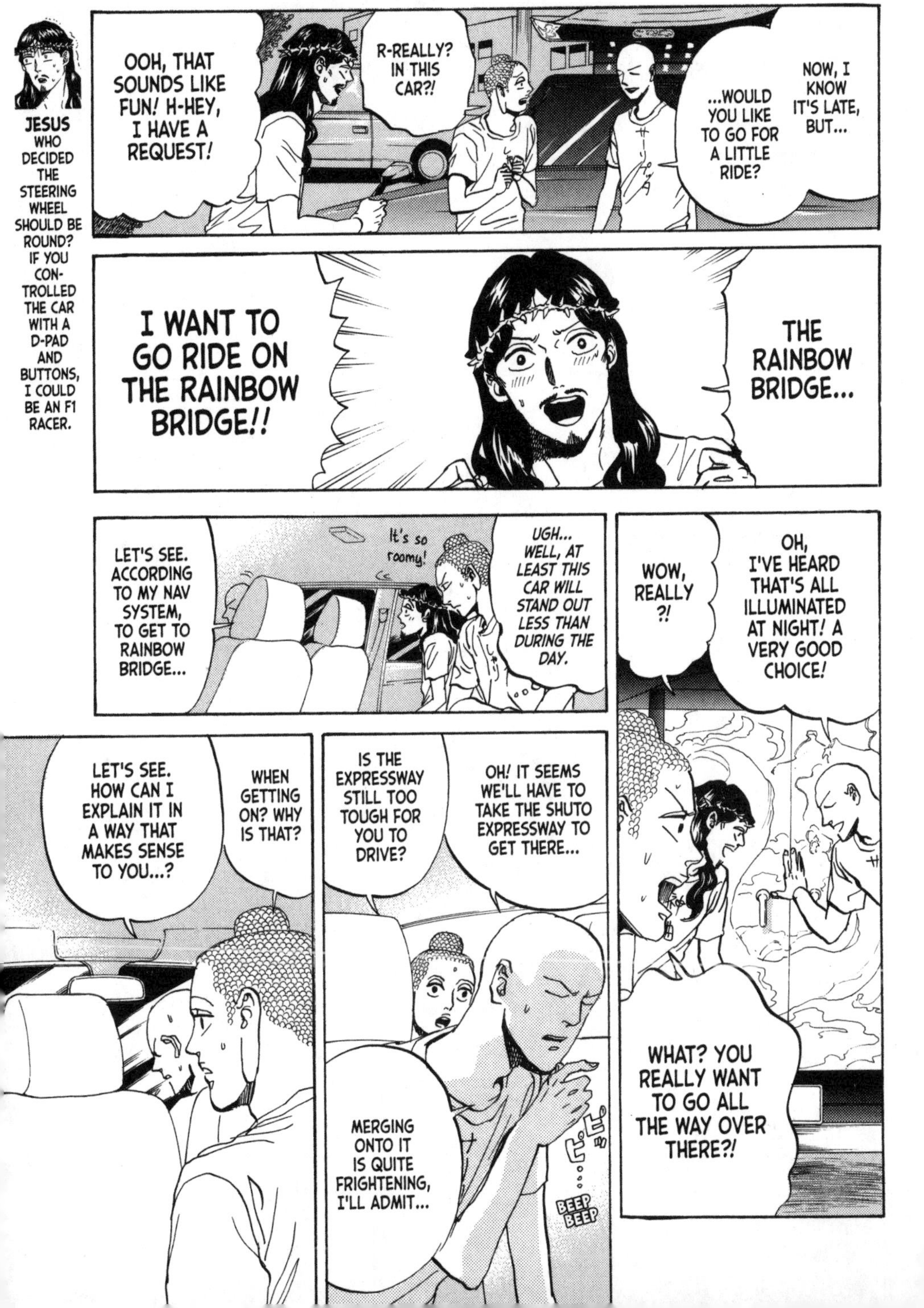
NOW, I KNOW IT'S LATE, BUT...
...WOULD YOU LIKE TO GO FOR A LITTLE RIDE?
R-REALLY? IN THIS CAR?!
OOH, THAT SOUNDS LIKE FUN! H-HEY, I HAVE A REQUEST!
THE RAINBOW BRIDGE...
I WANT TO GO RIDE ON THE RAINBOW BRIDGE!!
OH, I'VE HEARD THAT'S ALL ILLUMINATED AT NIGHT! A VERY GOOD CHOICE!
WOW, REALLY?!
WHAT? YOU REALLY WANT TO GO ALL THE WAY OVER THERE?!
UGH... WELL, AT LEAST THIS CAR WILL STAND OUT LESS THAN DURING THE DAY.
It's so roomy!
LET'S SEE. ACCORDING TO MY NAV SYSTEM, TO GET TO RAINBOW BRIDGE...
OH! IT SEEMS WE'LL HAVE TO TAKE THE SHUTO EXPRESSWAY TO GET THERE...
IS THE EXPRESSWAY STILL TOO TOUGH FOR YOU TO DRIVE?
MERGING ONTO IT IS QUITE FRIGHTENING, I'LL ADMIT...
BEEP BEEP
WHEN GETTING ON? WHY IS THAT?
LET'S SEE. HOW CAN I EXPLAIN IT IN A WAY THAT MAKES SENSE TO YOU...?

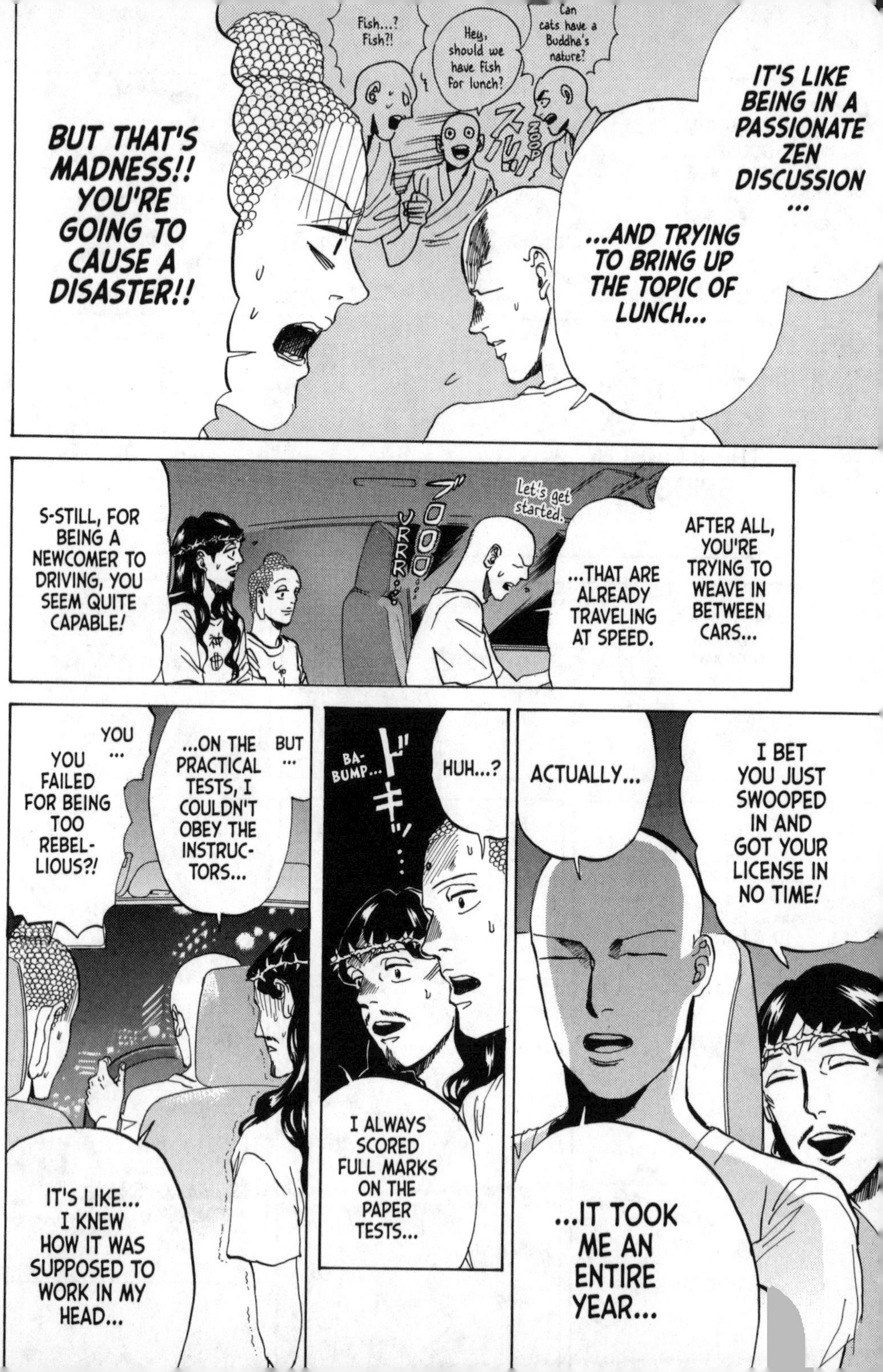
IT'S LIKE BEING IN A PASSIONATE ZEN DISCUSSION ...
...AND TRYING TO BRING UP THE TOPIC OF LUNCH...
Can cats have a Buddha's nature?
Hey, should we have fish for lunch?
ZOOP
Fish...? Fish?!
BUT THAT'S MADNESS!! YOU'RE GOING TO CAUSE A DISASTER!!
AFTER ALL, YOU'RE TRYING TO WEAVE IN BETWEEN CARS...
...THAT ARE ALREADY TRAVELING AT SPEED.
Let's get started...
VRRR
S-STILL, FOR BEING A NEWCOMER TO DRIVING, YOU SEEM QUITE CAPABLE!
I BET YOU JUST SWOOPED IN AND GOT YOUR LICENSE IN NO TIME!
ACTUALLY...
...IT TOOK ME AN ENTIRE YEAR...
HUH...?
BA-BUMP...
I ALWAYS SCORED FULL MARKS ON THE PAPER TESTS...
BUT ...
...ON THE PRACTICAL TESTS, I COULDN'T OBEY THE INSTRUCTORS...
YOU ...
YOU FAILED FOR BEING TOO REBELLIOUS?!
IT'S LIKE... I KNEW HOW IT WAS SUPPOSED TO WORK IN MY HEAD...

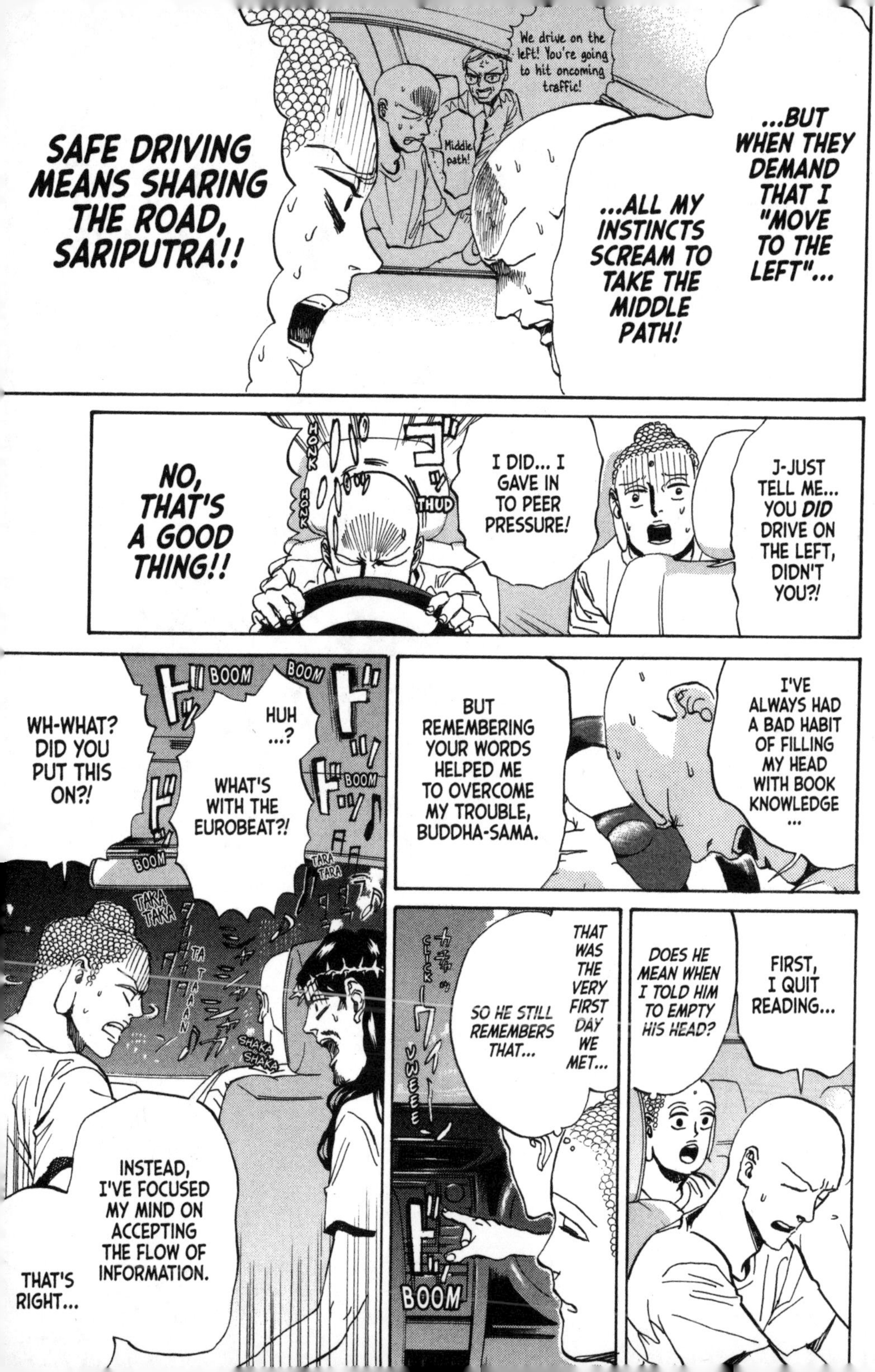
...BUT WHEN THEY DEMAND THAT I "MOVE TO THE LEFT"...
...ALL MY INSTINCTS SCREAM TO TAKE THE MIDDLE PATH!
We drive on the left! You're going to hit oncoming traffic!
Middle path!
SAFE DRIVING MEANS SHARING THE ROAD, SARIPUTRA!!
J-JUST TELL ME... YOU *DID* DRIVE ON THE LEFT, DIDN'T YOU?!
I DID... I GAVE IN TO PEER PRESSURE!
THUD
HONK HONK
NO, THAT'S A GOOD THING!!
I'VE ALWAYS HAD A BAD HABIT OF FILLING MY HEAD WITH BOOK KNOWLEDGE ...
BUT REMEMBERING YOUR WORDS HELPED ME TO OVERCOME MY TROUBLE, BUDDHA-SAMA.
FIRST, I QUIT READING...
DOES HE MEAN WHEN I TOLD HIM TO EMPTY HIS HEAD?
THAT WAS THE VERY FIRST DAY WE MET...
SO HE STILL REMEMBERS THAT...
CLICK
VWEEE
BOOM
BOOM
BOOM
HUH ...?
WH-WHAT? DID YOU PUT THIS ON?!
BOOM
WHAT'S WITH THE EUROBEAT?!
BOOM
TARA TARA
TAKA TAKA
TA TA TAAAAN
SHAKA SHAKA
INSTEAD, I'VE FOCUSED MY MIND ON ACCEPTING THE FLOW OF INFORMATION.
THAT'S RIGHT...

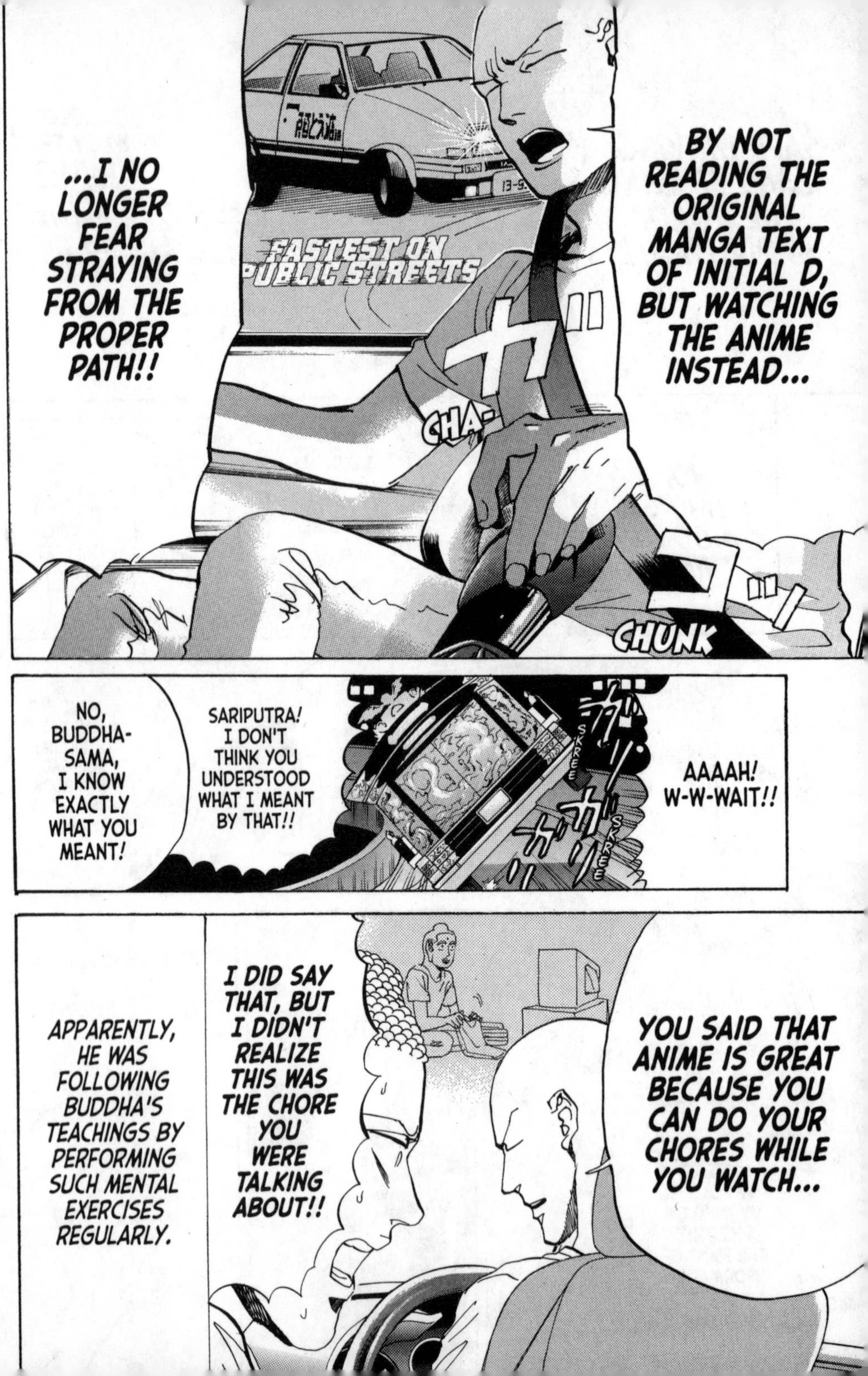
BY NOT READING THE ORIGINAL MANGA TEXT OF INITIAL D, BUT WATCHING THE ANIME INSTEAD...
...I NO LONGER FEAR STRAYING FROM THE PROPER PATH!!
FASTEST ON PUBLIC STREETS
CHA-
CHUNK
AAAAH! W-W-WAIT!!
SKREE
SKREE
SARIPUTRA! I DON'T THINK YOU UNDERSTOOD WHAT I MEANT BY THAT!!
NO, BUDDHA-SAMA, I KNOW EXACTLY WHAT YOU MEANT!
YOU SAID THAT ANIME IS GREAT BECAUSE YOU CAN DO YOUR CHORES WHILE YOU WATCH...
I DID SAY THAT, BUT I DIDN'T REALIZE THIS WAS THE CHORE YOU WERE TALKING ABOUT!!
APPARENTLY, HE WAS FOLLOWING BUDDHA'S TEACHINGS BY PERFORMING SUCH MENTAL EXERCISES REGULARLY.

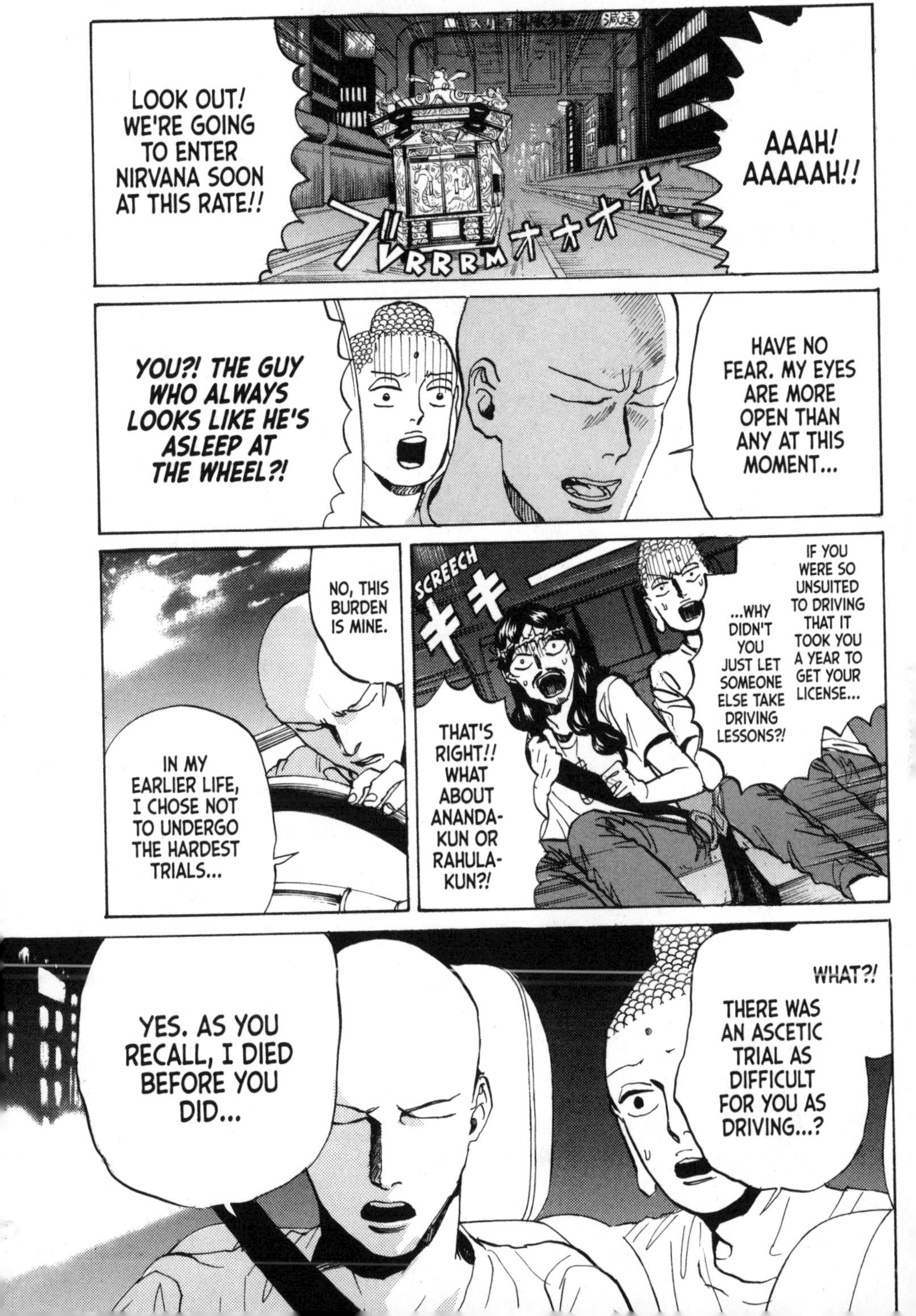
AAAH! AAAAAH!!
LOOK OUT! WE'RE GOING TO ENTER NIRVANA SOON AT THIS RATE!!
VRRRM
HAVE NO FEAR. MY EYES ARE MORE OPEN THAN ANY AT THIS MOMENT...
YOU?! THE GUY WHO ALWAYS LOOKS LIKE HE'S ASLEEP AT THE WHEEL?!
IF YOU WERE SO UNSUITED TO DRIVING THAT IT TOOK YOU A YEAR TO GET YOUR LICENSE...
...WHY DIDN'T YOU JUST LET SOMEONE ELSE TAKE DRIVING LESSONS?!
SCREECH
THAT'S RIGHT!! WHAT ABOUT ANANDA-KUN OR RAHULA-KUN?!
NO, THIS BURDEN IS MINE.
IN MY EARLIER LIFE, I CHOSE NOT TO UNDERGO THE HARDEST TRIALS...
WHAT?!
THERE WAS AN ASCETIC TRIAL AS DIFFICULT FOR YOU AS DRIVING...?
YES. AS YOU RECALL, I DIED BEFORE YOU DID...

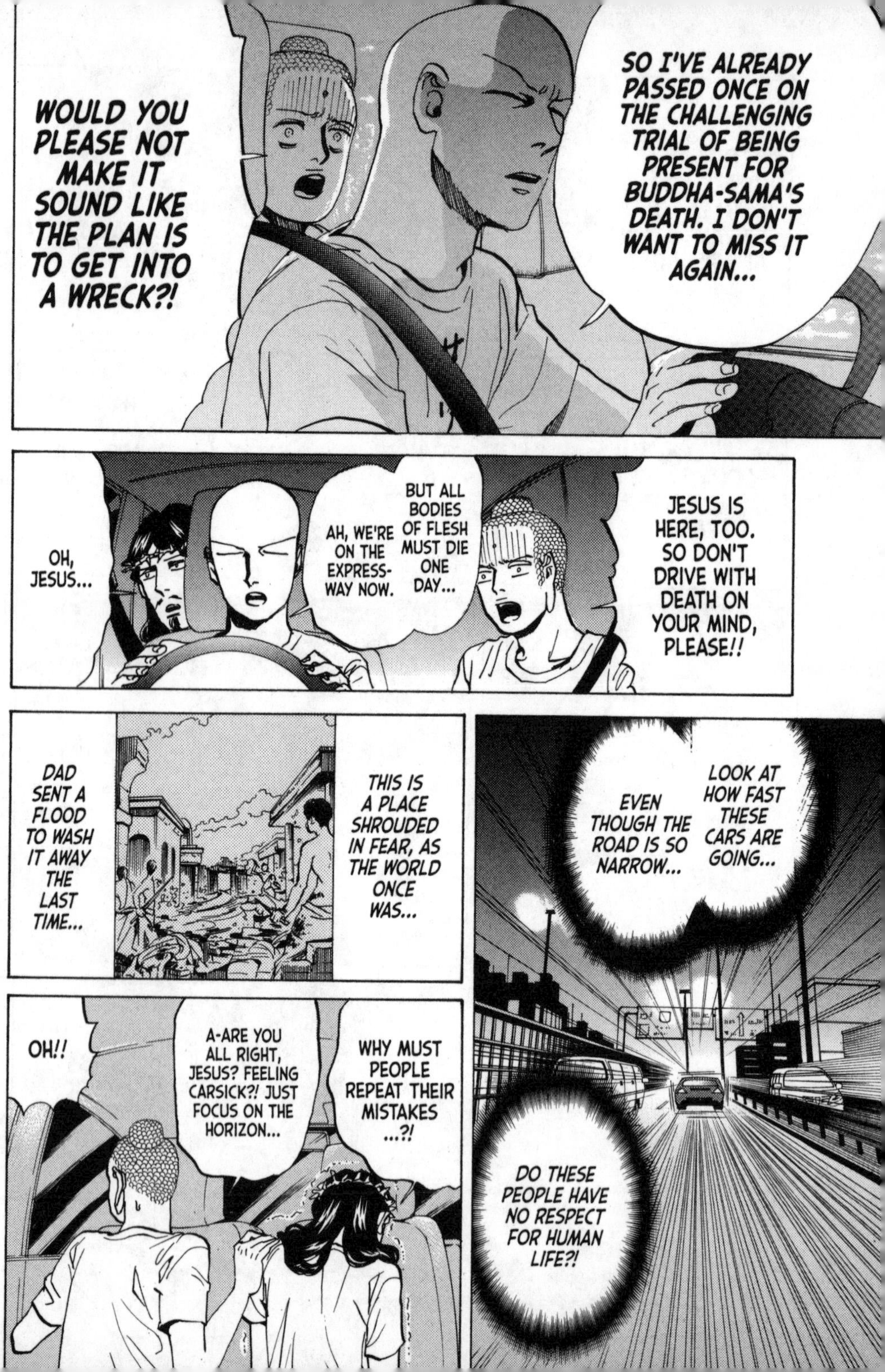
SO I'VE ALREADY PASSED ONCE ON THE CHALLENGING TRIAL OF BEING PRESENT FOR BUDDHA-SAMA'S DEATH. I DON'T WANT TO MISS IT AGAIN...
WOULD YOU PLEASE NOT MAKE IT SOUND LIKE THE PLAN IS TO GET INTO A WRECK?!
JESUS IS HERE, TOO. SO DON'T DRIVE WITH DEATH ON YOUR MIND, PLEASE!!
BUT ALL BODIES OF FLESH MUST DIE ONE DAY...
AH, WE'RE ON THE EXPRESS-WAY NOW.
OH, JESUS...
LOOK AT HOW FAST THESE CARS ARE GOING...
EVEN THOUGH THE ROAD IS SO NARROW...
DO THESE PEOPLE HAVE NO RESPECT FOR HUMAN LIFE?!
THIS IS A PLACE SHROUDED IN FEAR, AS THE WORLD ONCE WAS...
DAD SENT A FLOOD TO WASH IT AWAY THE LAST TIME...
WHY MUST PEOPLE REPEAT THEIR MISTAKES ...?!
A-ARE YOU ALL RIGHT, JESUS? FEELING CARSICK?! JUST FOCUS ON THE HORIZON...
OH!!

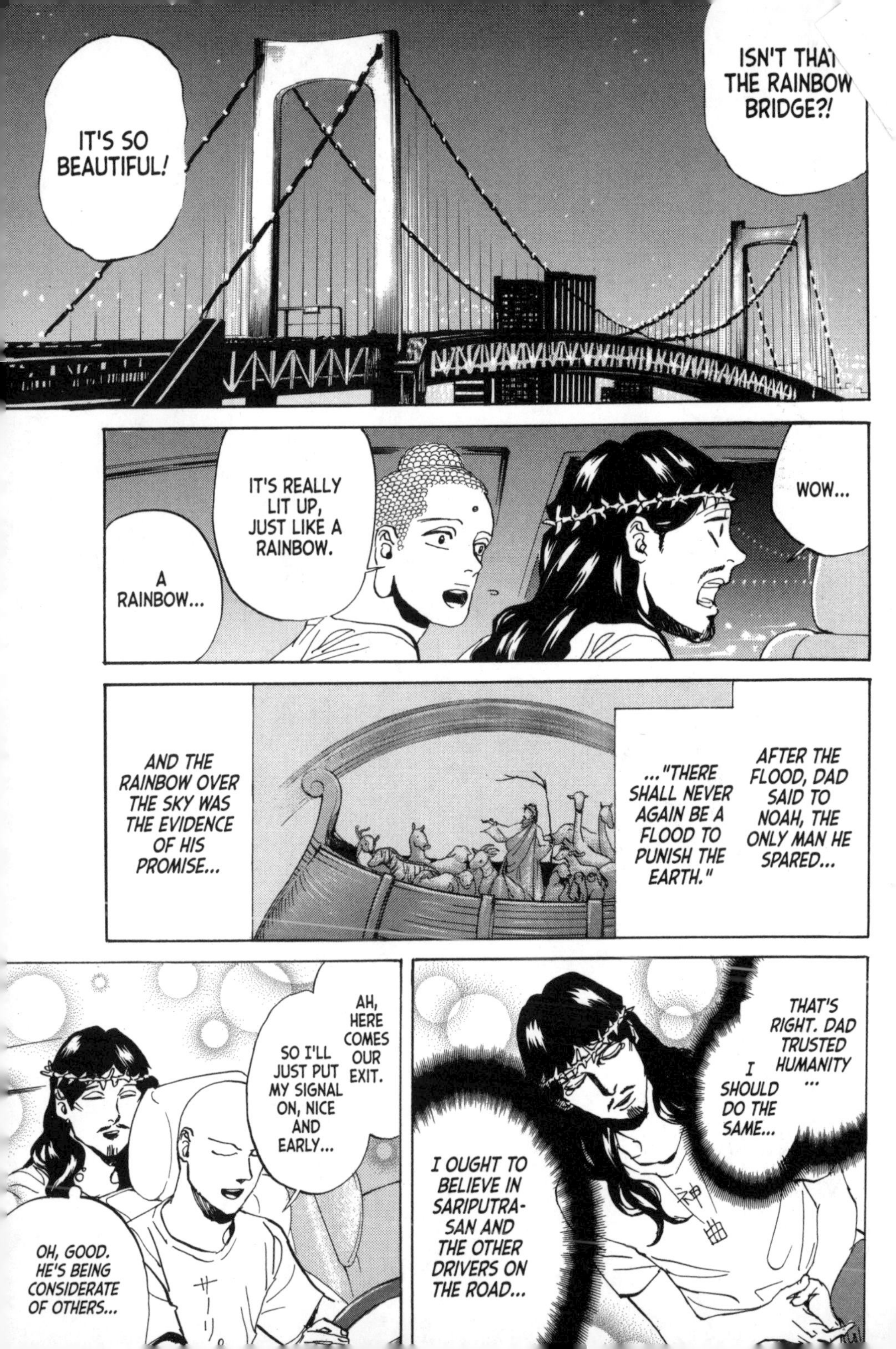
ISN'T THAT THE RAINBOW BRIDGE?!
IT'S SO BEAUTIFUL!
WOW...
IT'S REALLY LIT UP, JUST LIKE A RAINBOW.
A RAINBOW...
AFTER THE FLOOD, DAD SAID TO NOAH, THE ONLY MAN HE SPARED...
..."THERE SHALL NEVER AGAIN BE A FLOOD TO PUNISH THE EARTH."
AND THE RAINBOW OVER THE SKY WAS THE EVIDENCE OF HIS PROMISE...
THAT'S RIGHT. DAD TRUSTED HUMANITY...
I SHOULD DO THE SAME...
I OUGHT TO BELIEVE IN SARIPUTRA-SAN AND THE OTHER DRIVERS ON THE ROAD...
AH, HERE COMES OUR EXIT.
SO I'LL JUST PUT MY SIGNAL ON, NICE AND EARLY...
OH, GOOD. HE'S BEING CONSIDERATE OF OTHERS...

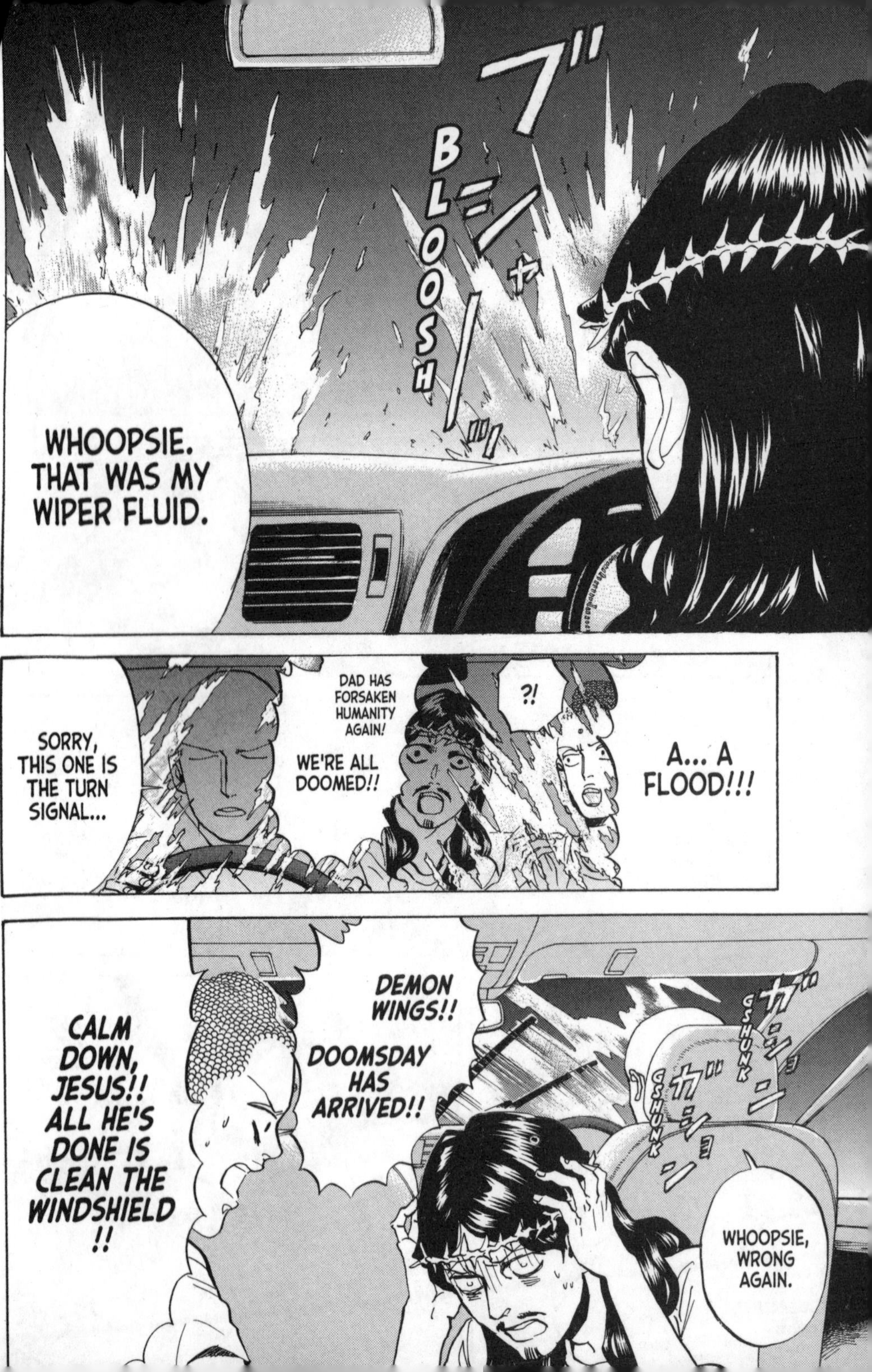
BLOOSH
WHOOPSIE. THAT WAS MY WIPER FLUID.
A... A FLOOD!!!
?!
DAD HAS FORSAKEN HUMANITY AGAIN!
WE'RE ALL DOOMED!!
SORRY, THIS ONE IS THE TURN SIGNAL...
GSHUNK
GSHUNK
WHOOPSIE, WRONG AGAIN.
DEMON WINGS!!
DOOMSDAY HAS ARRIVED!!
CALM DOWN, JESUS!! ALL HE'S DONE IS CLEAN THE WINDSHIELD!!

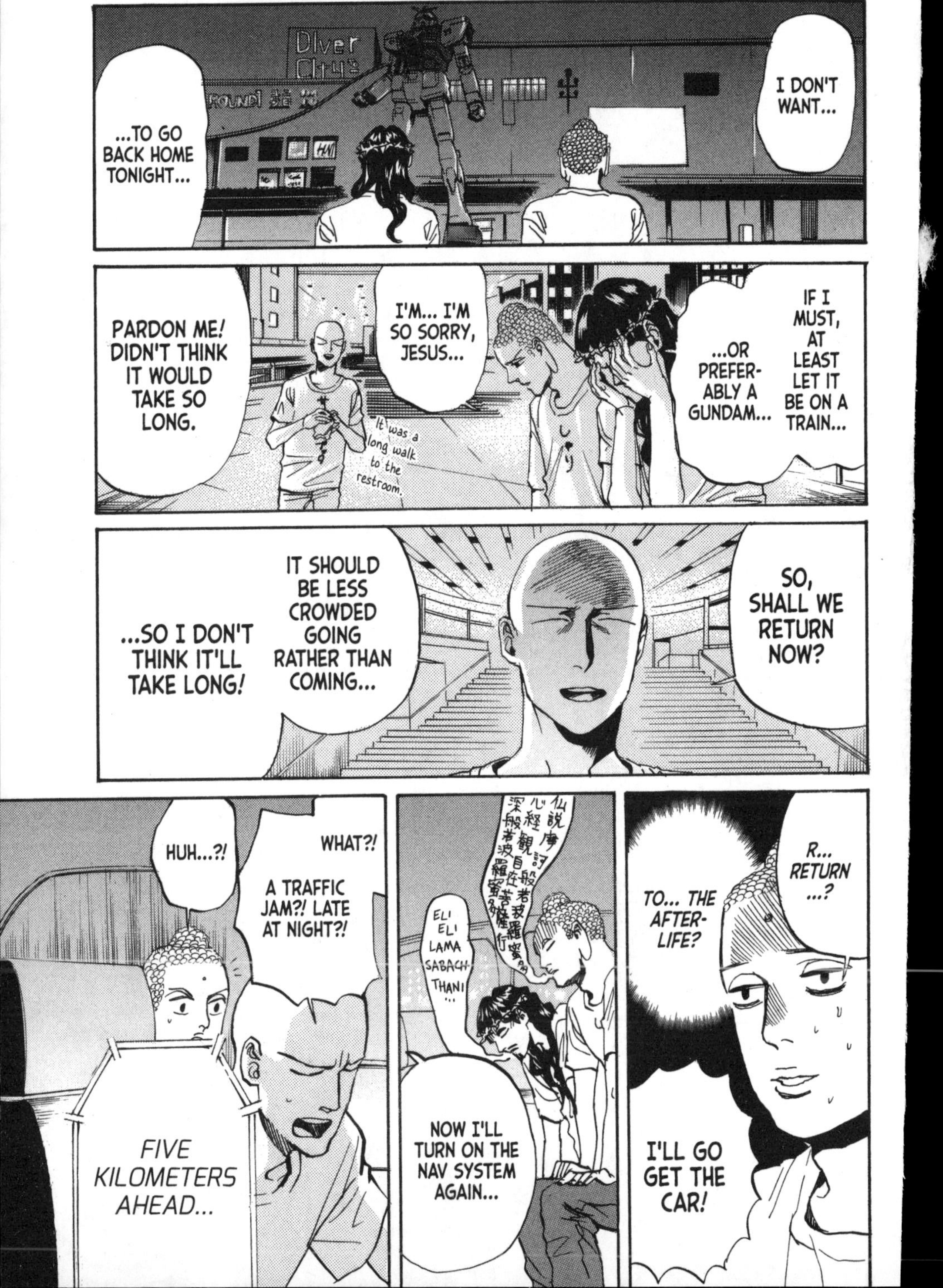
I DON'T WANT...
...TO GO BACK HOME TONIGHT...
IF I MUST, AT LEAST LET IT BE ON A TRAIN...
...OR PREFER-ABLY A GUNDAM...
I'M... I'M SO SORRY, JESUS...
PARDON ME! DIDN'T THINK IT WOULD TAKE SO LONG.
It was a long walk to the restroom.
SO, SHALL WE RETURN NOW?
IT SHOULD BE LESS CROWDED GOING RATHER THAN COMING...
...SO I DON'T THINK IT'LL TAKE LONG!
R... RETURN ...?
TO... THE AFTER-LIFE?
I'LL GO GET THE CAR!
仏説摩訶般若波羅蜜多心経観自在菩薩行深般若波羅蜜多
ELI ELI LAMA SABACHTHANI...
NOW I'LL TURN ON THE NAV SYSTEM AGAIN...
WHAT?!
HUH...?!
A TRAFFIC JAM?! LATE AT NIGHT?!
FIVE KILOMETERS AHEAD...

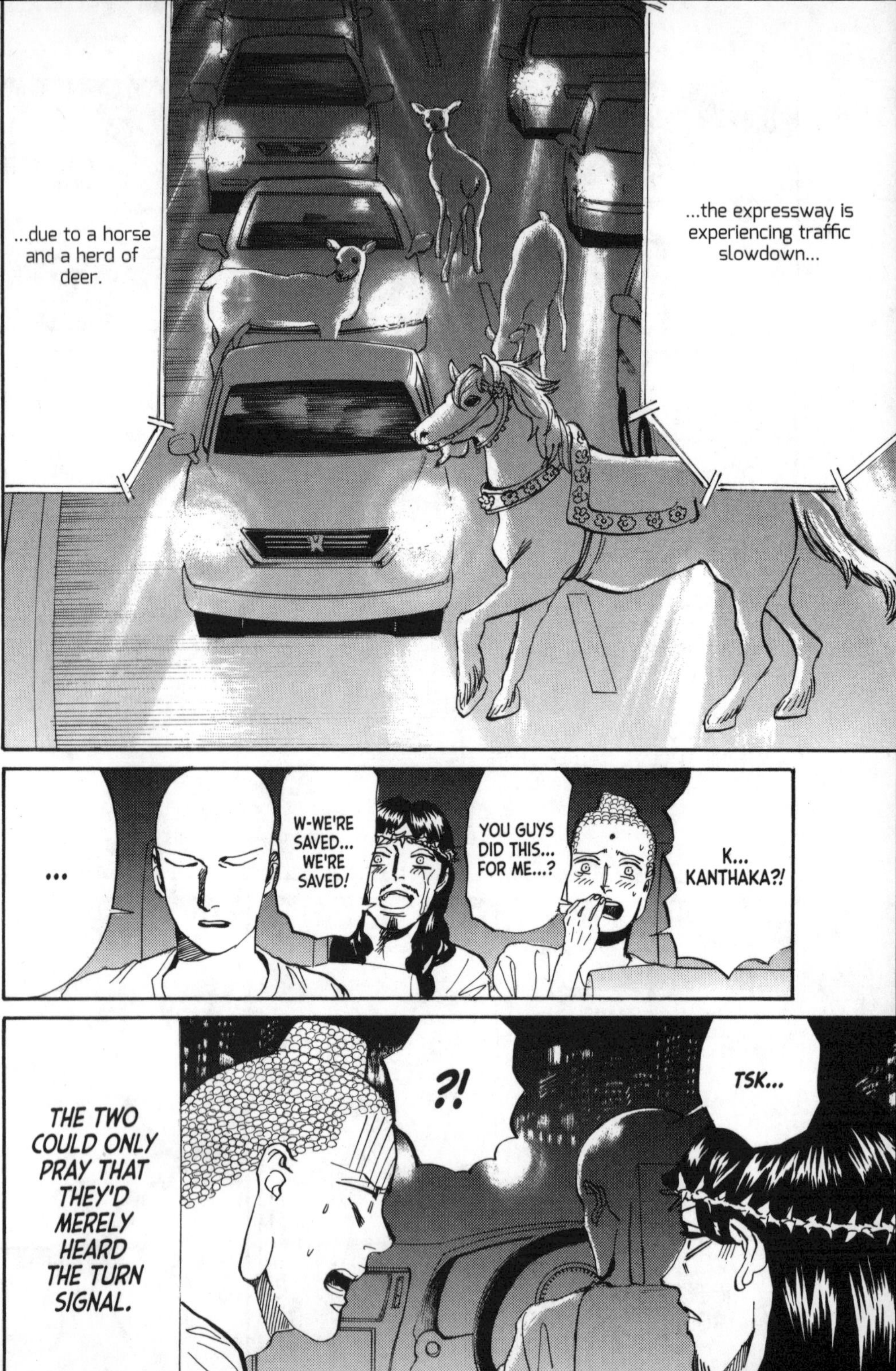
...the expressway is experiencing traffic slowdown...
...due to a horse and a herd of deer.
K... KANTHAKA?!
YOU GUYS DID THIS... FOR ME...?
W-WE'RE SAVED... WE'RE SAVED!
...
TSK...
?!
THE TWO COULD ONLY PRAY THAT THEY'D MERELY HEARD THE TURN SIGNAL.

SIDE BY SIDE WITH THE WIFE ALL THE WAY HOME

First a bicycle and now a car, Siddhartha-sama? Oh, I don't mind, though. If you love those rounded feet so much, so be it. But have you noticed what's happening here? Upon my back, you will never have to suffer the humiliation of waiting for traffic to move.

CLOP...
CLOP...

SAINT☆YOUNG MEN

CHAPTER 75 TRANSLATION NOTES

Sarira, page 33
The Sanskrit word for "body," referring to cremated remains. More specifically in Japanese, the translation (*shari*) is used to mean the remains of the Buddha himself.

Divine Comedy, page 33
The title of Dante's great work that contains *Inferno*, *Purgatorio*, and *Paradiso*, the story of Dante traveling through the various levels of Heaven, Purgatory, and Hell.

Red Hare, page 34
The name of the horse owned by the ancient Chinese warlord Lu Bu. It is described in *Romance of the Three Kingdoms* as being entirely red, and much like Lu Bu himself, one of the mightiest and quickest of its kind.

Funeral Midnight, page 34
This chapter's title is a pun on the famous street racing series *Wangan Midnight*, which is equivalent in influence to *Initial D*. The manga by Michiharu Kusunoki started in the early 1990s and has been running in various forms and sequels ever since.

Hearse, page 36
Traditional Japanese hearses in the age of the automobile resemble Western-style ones, but with the backseat area modified to allow for a massive, ornate temple-like box decoration. When Sariputra says that this is the ideal vehicle for the "departed," it replaces a joke about the word *hotoke-sama*, which can mean "Buddha," "holy person," or "deceased," depending on the context.

Rainbow Bridge, page 37
A double-decker suspension bridge in Tokyo Bay that connects the Minato ward of Tokyo to the manmade island of Odaiba.

Middle Path, page 39
The Middle Path or Middle Way is the teaching of Buddha to avoid extremes and practice moderation.

Initial D, page 40
Perhaps the most famous of all street racing manga/anime, created by Shuichi Shigeno in 1995. The anime in particular is famous for its Eurobeat soundtrack.

Flood, page 42
In the Book of Genesis, the story of Noah's Ark begins with a flood that God sends to the earth for forty days and nights in order to cleanse the corruption and violence plaguing mankind.

Gundam, page 45
In 2009, a large statue of the famous original Gundam mecha was constructed and placed outside of the DiverCity mall in Odaiba. At the time this manga was drawn, the original Gundam statue was still present, but in 2017, it was replaced with a more recent Unicorn Gundam model.

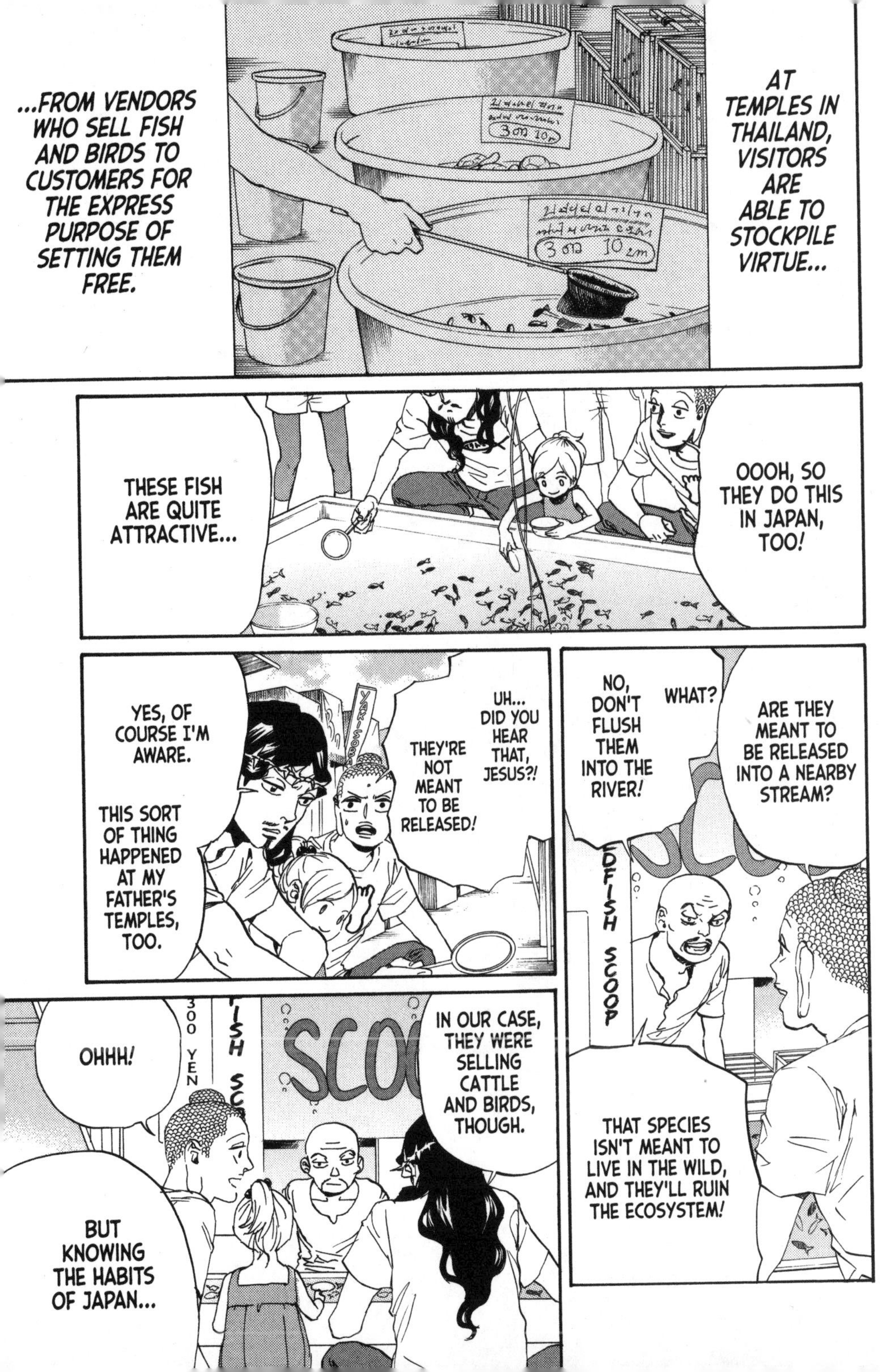
AT TEMPLES IN THAILAND, VISITORS ARE ABLE TO STOCKPILE VIRTUE...
...FROM VENDORS WHO SELL FISH AND BIRDS TO CUSTOMERS FOR THE EXPRESS PURPOSE OF SETTING THEM FREE.
OOOH, SO THEY DO THIS IN JAPAN, TOO!
THESE FISH ARE QUITE ATTRACTIVE...
ARE THEY MEANT TO BE RELEASED INTO A NEARBY STREAM?
WHAT?
NO, DON'T FLUSH THEM INTO THE RIVER!
THAT SPECIES ISN'T MEANT TO LIVE IN THE WILD, AND THEY'LL RUIN THE ECOSYSTEM!
UH... DID YOU HEAR THAT, JESUS?!
THEY'RE NOT MEANT TO BE RELEASED!
YES, OF COURSE I'M AWARE.
THIS SORT OF THING HAPPENED AT MY FATHER'S TEMPLES, TOO.
IN OUR CASE, THEY WERE SELLING CATTLE AND BIRDS, THOUGH.
OHHH!
300 YEN
BUT KNOWING THE HABITS OF JAPAN...

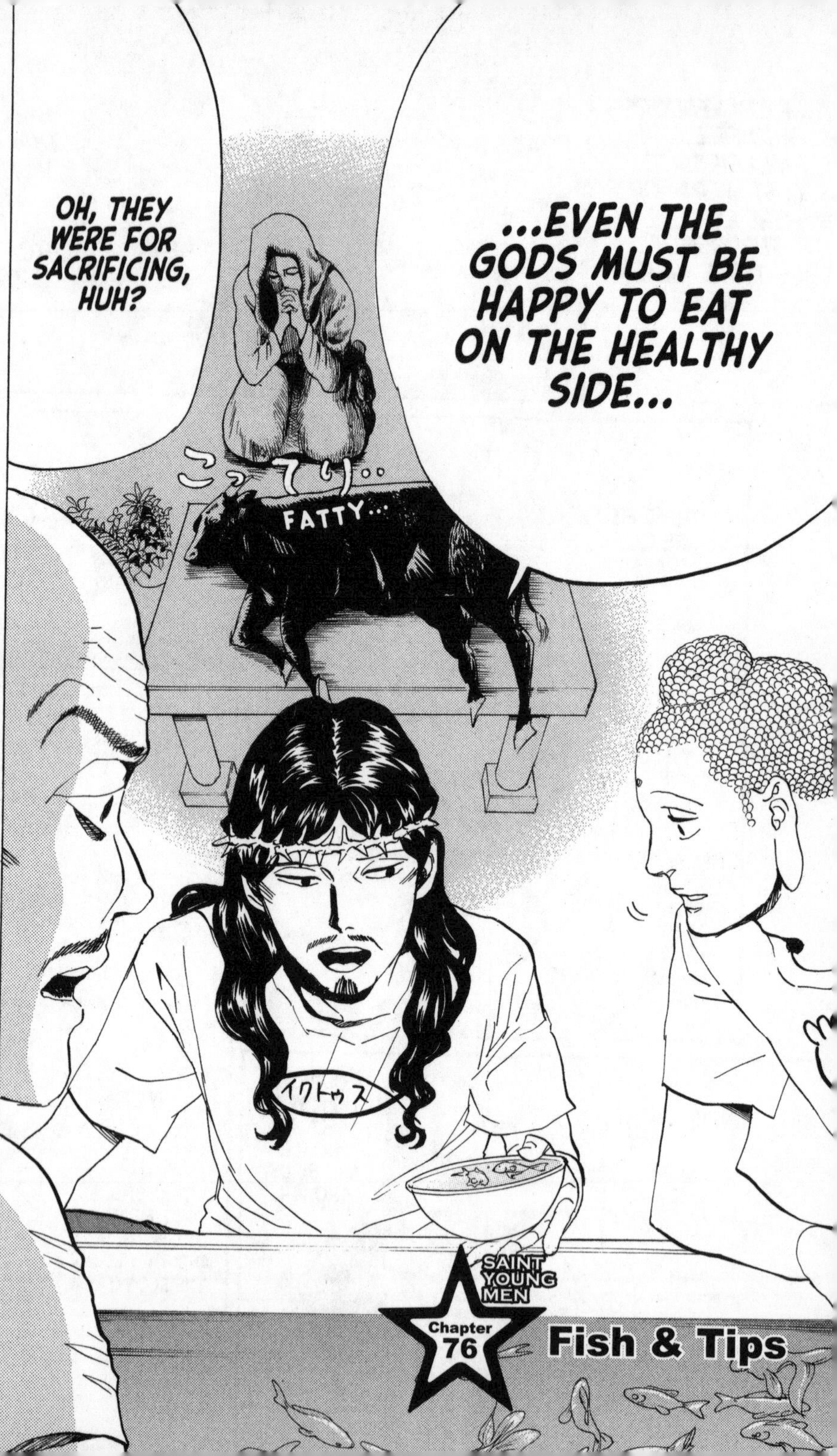
...EVEN THE GODS MUST BE HAPPY TO EAT ON THE HEALTHY SIDE...
OH, THEY WERE FOR SACRIFICING, HUH?
こってり‥
FATTY...
イクトゥス
SAINT YOUNG MEN
Chapter 76
Fish & Tips

JESUS'S DAD STARTS THE MEAL WITH NOTHING LESS THAN POULTRY.

JESUS'S SHIRT: ICHTHYS

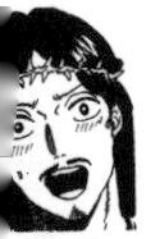

JESUS
SO MANY *YO-KAI WATCH* MERCHANDISE STANDS! HE ALSO SEES LOTS OF STANDS COVERED IN FROZEN ART, BUT WITH NO TITLE FOR THE BUSINESS. WHAT IS THAT ABOUT? IN THE SUMMER FESTIVALS OF 2014, THE HOTTEST TRENDS AMONG CHILDREN ARE ON DISPLAY.

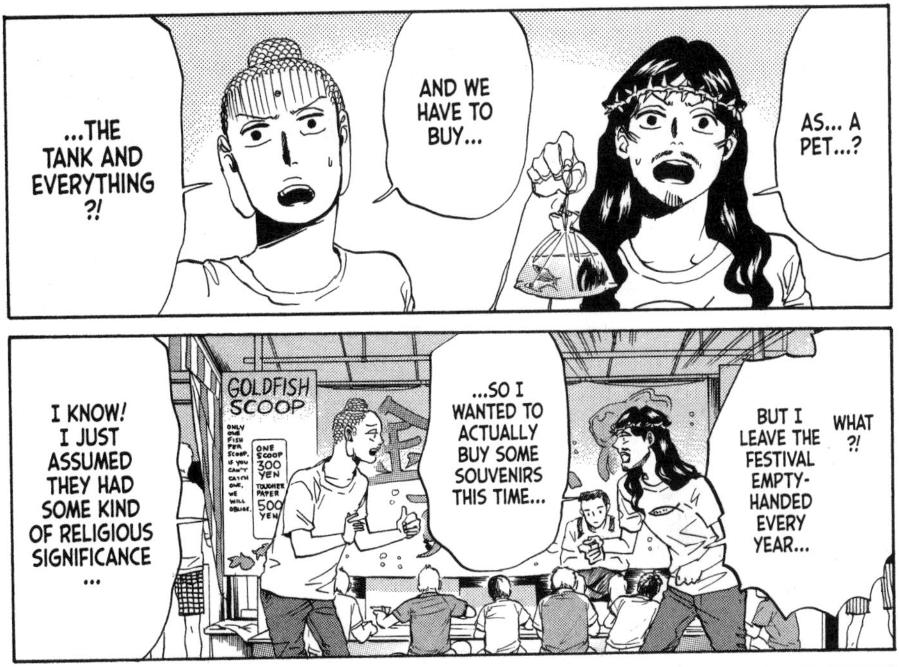
AS... A PET...?
AND WE HAVE TO BUY...
...THE TANK AND EVERYTHING?!
WHAT?!
BUT I LEAVE THE FESTIVAL EMPTY-HANDED EVERY YEAR...
...SO I WANTED TO ACTUALLY BUY SOME SOUVENIRS THIS TIME...
GOLDFISH SCOOP
ONLY ONE FISH PER SCOOP. IF YOU CAN'T CATCH ONE, WE WILL OBLIGE.
ONE SCOOP 300 YEN
TOUGHER PAPER 500 YEN
I KNOW! I JUST ASSUMED THEY HAD SOME KIND OF RELIGIOUS SIGNIFICANCE...

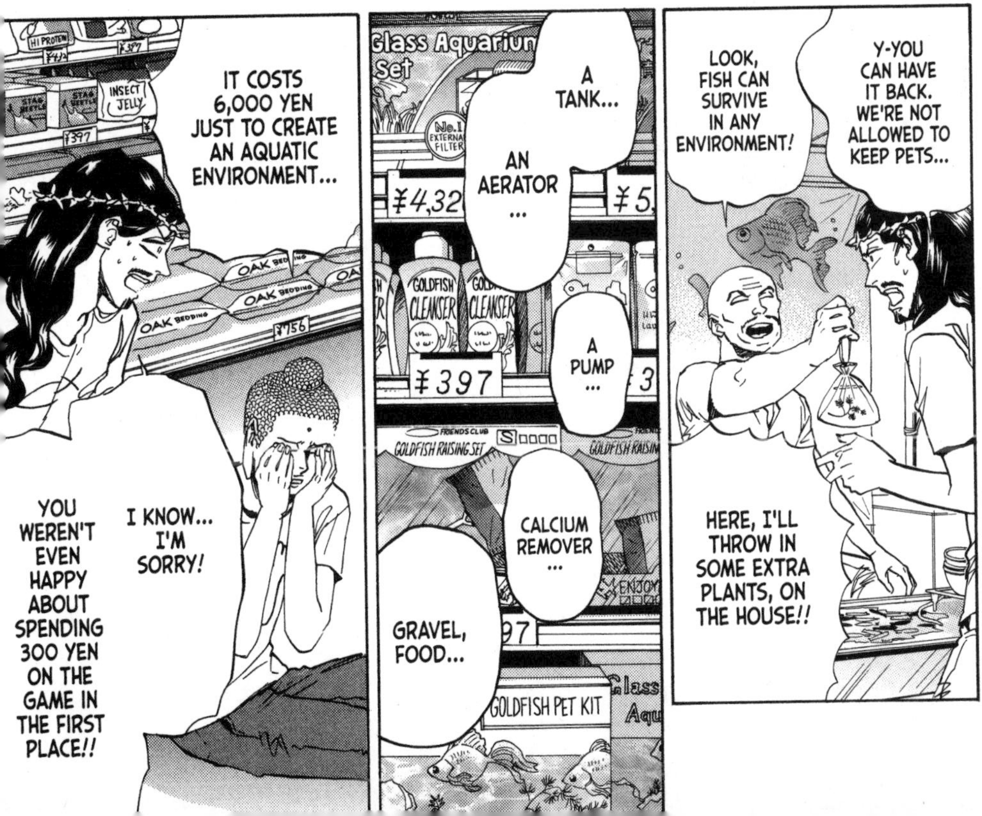
Y-YOU CAN HAVE IT BACK. WE'RE NOT ALLOWED TO KEEP PETS...
LOOK, FISH CAN SURVIVE IN ANY ENVIRONMENT!
HERE, I'LL THROW IN SOME EXTRA PLANTS, ON THE HOUSE!!
Glass Aquarium Set
No.1 EXTERNAL FILTER
A TANK...
AN AERATOR...
GOLDFISH CLEANSER
¥397
A PUMP...
GOLDFISH RAISING SET
CALCIUM REMOVER...
GRAVEL, FOOD...
GOLDFISH PET KIT
HI PROTEIN
INSECT JELLY
OAK BEDDING
¥756
IT COSTS 6,000 YEN JUST TO CREATE AN AQUATIC ENVIRONMENT...
I KNOW... I'M SORRY!
YOU WEREN'T EVEN HAPPY ABOUT SPENDING 300 YEN ON THE GAME IN THE FIRST PLACE!!

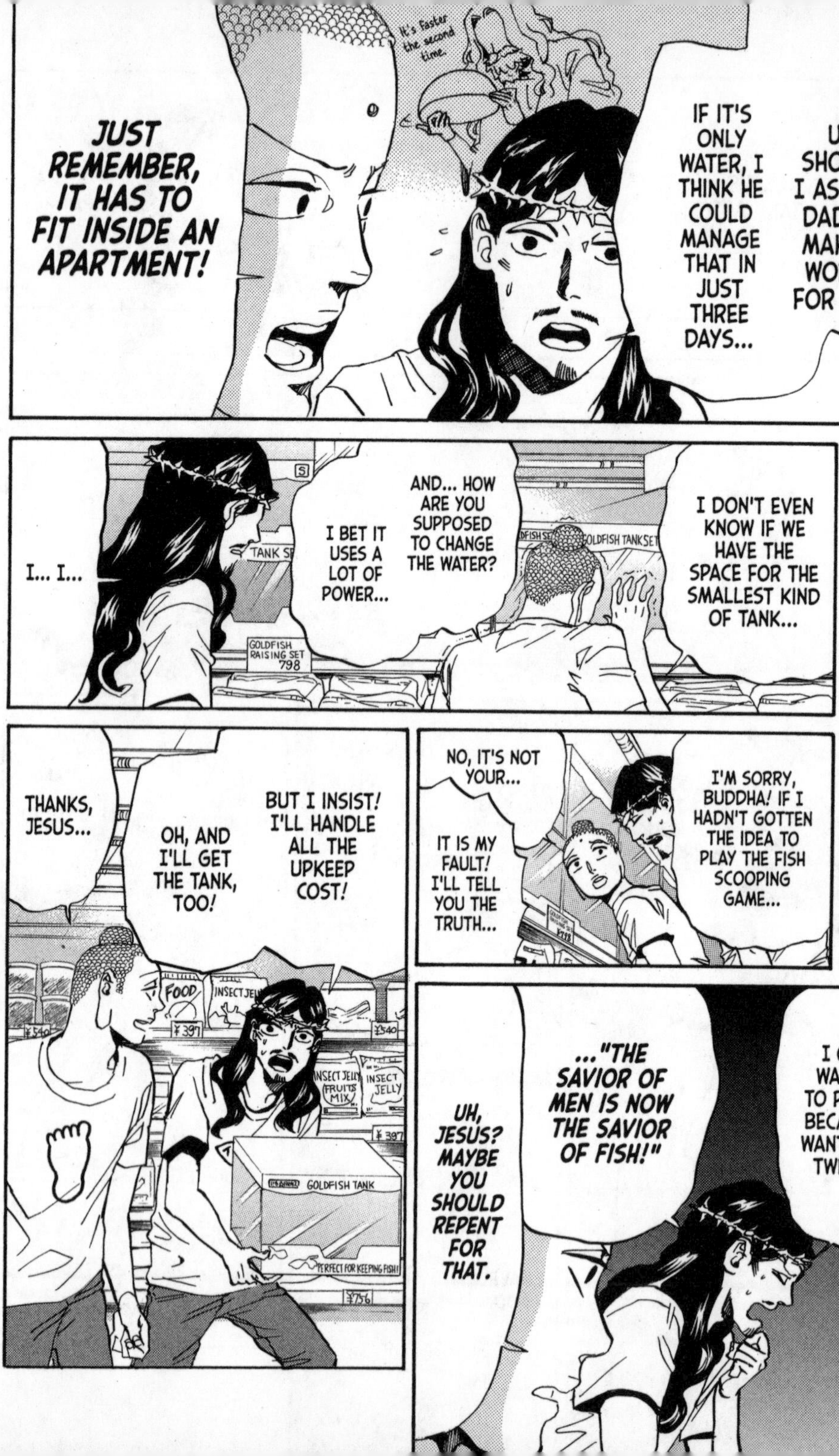
UH, SHOULD I ASK MY DAD TO MAKE A WORLD FOR US?!
IF IT'S ONLY WATER, I THINK HE COULD MANAGE THAT IN JUST THREE DAYS...
It's faster the second time.
JUST REMEMBER, IT HAS TO FIT INSIDE AN APARTMENT!
I DON'T EVEN KNOW IF WE HAVE THE SPACE FOR THE SMALLEST KIND OF TANK...
GOLDFISH TANK SET
AND... HOW ARE YOU SUPPOSED TO CHANGE THE WATER?
I BET IT USES A LOT OF POWER...
GOLDFISH RAISING SET 798
I... I...
I'M SORRY, BUDDHA! IF I HADN'T GOTTEN THE IDEA TO PLAY THE FISH SCOOPING GAME...
NO, IT'S NOT YOUR...
IT IS MY FAULT! I'LL TELL YOU THE TRUTH...
I ONLY WANTED TO PLAY IT BECAUSE I WANTED TO TWEET...
..."THE SAVIOR OF MEN IS NOW THE SAVIOR OF FISH!"
UH, JESUS? MAYBE YOU SHOULD REPENT FOR THAT.
BUT I INSIST! I'LL HANDLE ALL THE UPKEEP COST!
OH, AND I'LL GET THE TANK, TOO!
THANKS, JESUS...
FOOD
INSECT JELLY
INSECT JELLY (FRUITS MIX)
INSECT JELLY
¥540
¥397
¥540
¥397
GOLDFISH TANK
PERFECT FOR KEEPING FISH!
¥756

BUDDHA THERE ISN'T MUCH HE CAN EAT, SO THE ROASTED CORN SELLERS ARE VERY WELCOME. HE'S ALSO GRATEFUL FOR THE RECENT TREND OF WHOLE CUCUMBER PICKLES. APPARENTLY YOU CAN ORDER TAKOYAKI WITHOUT THE OCTOPUS AT THE SUMMER FESTIVALS OF 2014, BUT HE'S TOO SCARED TO TRY.

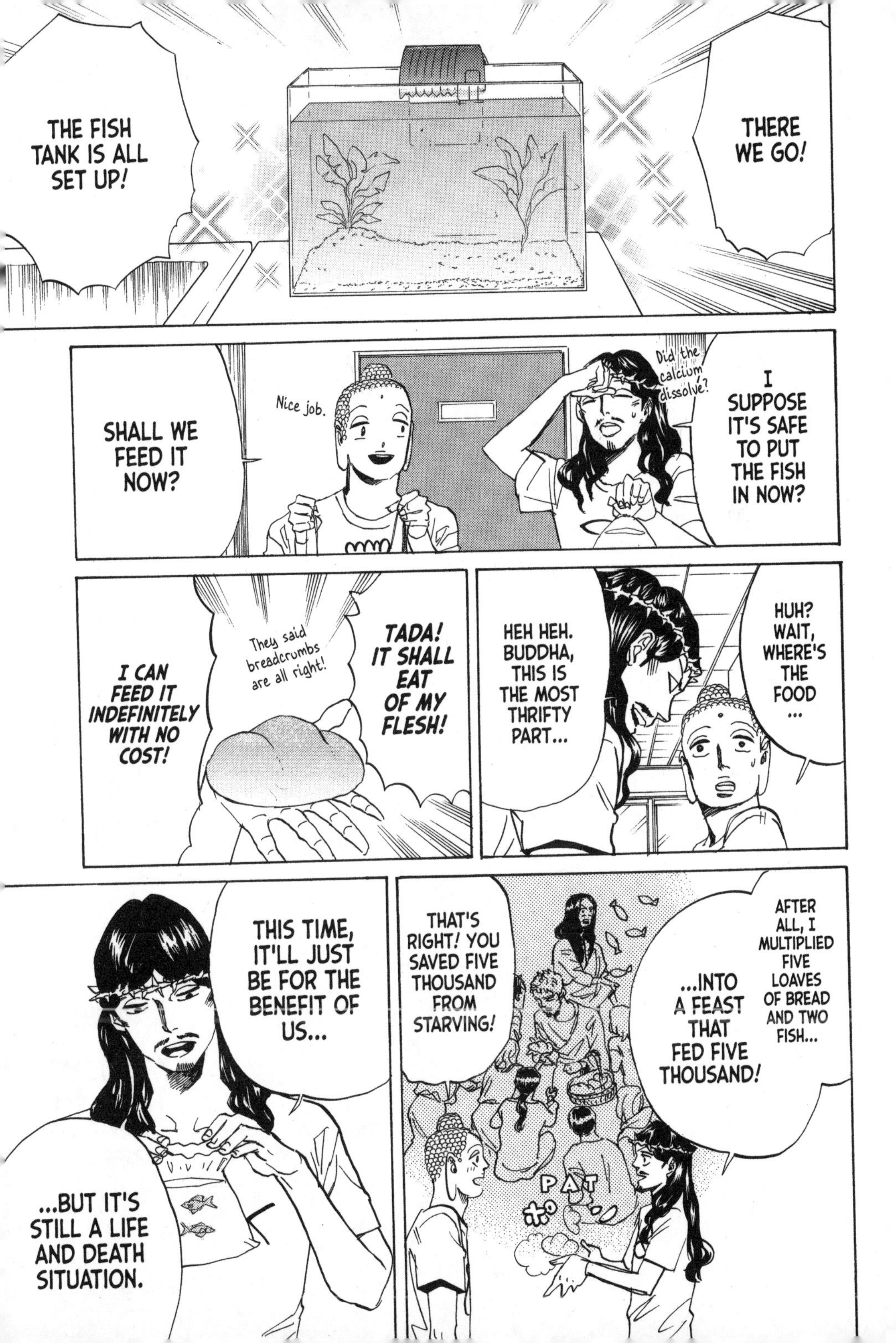
THERE WE GO!
THE FISH TANK IS ALL SET UP!
Did the calcium dissolve?
I SUPPOSE IT'S SAFE TO PUT THE FISH IN NOW?
Nice job.
SHALL WE FEED IT NOW?
HUH? WAIT, WHERE'S THE FOOD ...
HEH HEH. BUDDHA, THIS IS THE MOST THRIFTY PART...
TADA! IT SHALL EAT OF MY FLESH!
They said breadcrumbs are all right!
I CAN FEED IT INDEFINITELY WITH NO COST!
AFTER ALL, I MULTIPLIED FIVE LOAVES OF BREAD AND TWO FISH...
...INTO A FEAST THAT FED FIVE THOUSAND!
THAT'S RIGHT! YOU SAVED FIVE THOUSAND FROM STARVING!
PAT
ポ
THIS TIME, IT'LL JUST BE FOR THE BENEFIT OF US...
...BUT IT'S STILL A LIFE AND DEATH SITUATION.

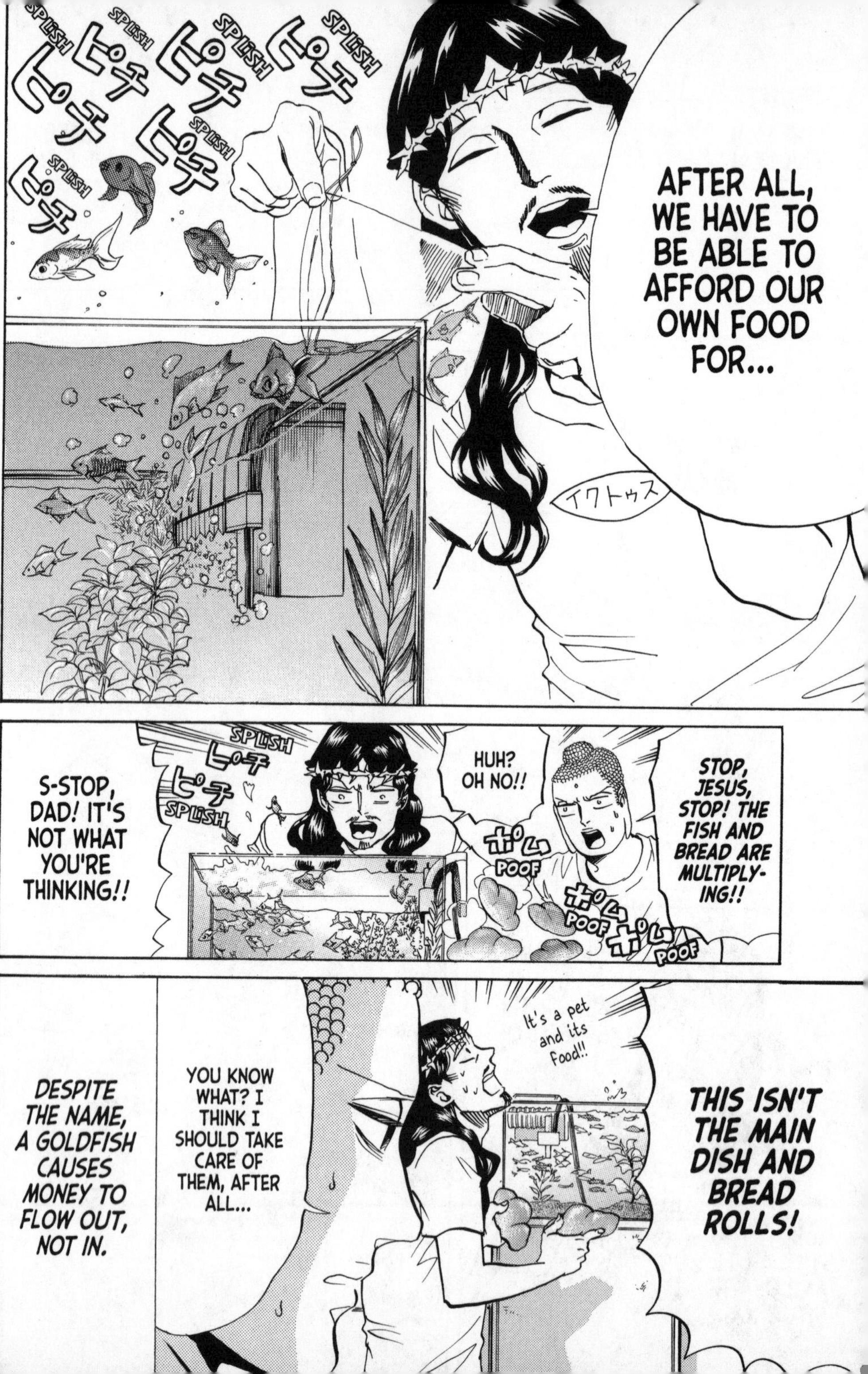
AFTER ALL, WE HAVE TO BE ABLE TO AFFORD OUR OWN FOOD FOR...
イクトゥス
ピチ SPLISH
ピチ SPLISH
ピチ SPLISH
ピチ SPLISH
ピチ SPLISH
STOP, JESUS, STOP! THE FISH AND BREAD ARE MULTIPLY-ING!!
HUH? OH NO!!
ポム POOF
ポム POOF
ポム POOF
ピチ SPLISH
ピチ SPLISH
S-STOP, DAD! IT'S NOT WHAT YOU'RE THINKING!!
THIS ISN'T THE MAIN DISH AND BREAD ROLLS!
It's a pet and its food!!
YOU KNOW WHAT? I THINK I SHOULD TAKE CARE OF THEM, AFTER ALL...
DESPITE THE NAME, A GOLDFISH CAUSES MONEY TO FLOW OUT, NOT IN.

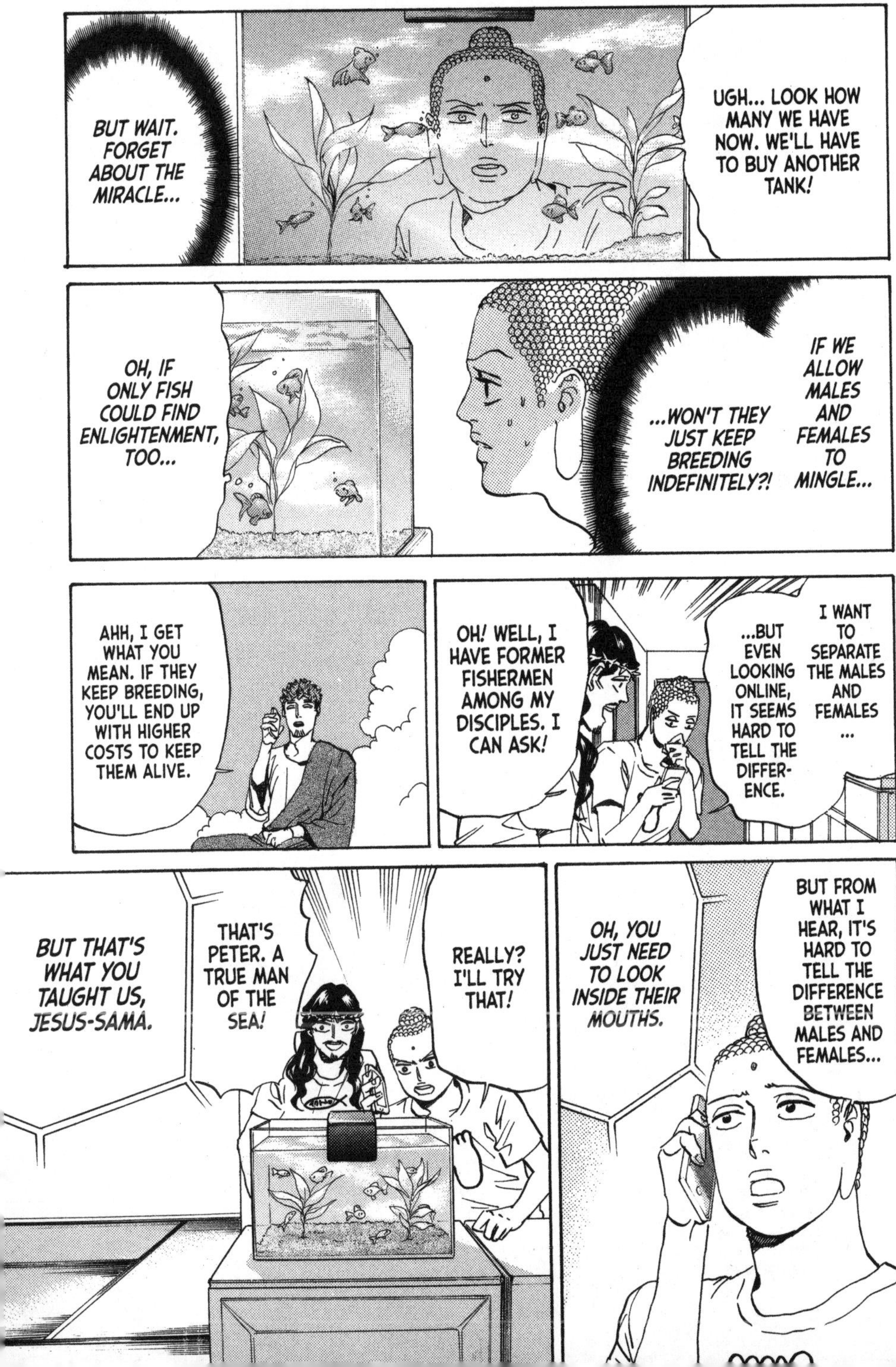
UGH... LOOK HOW MANY WE HAVE NOW. WE'LL HAVE TO BUY ANOTHER TANK!
BUT WAIT. FORGET ABOUT THE MIRACLE...
IF WE ALLOW MALES AND FEMALES TO MINGLE...
...WON'T THEY JUST KEEP BREEDING INDEFINITELY?!
OH, IF ONLY FISH COULD FIND ENLIGHTENMENT, TOO...
I WANT TO SEPARATE THE MALES AND FEMALES ...
...BUT EVEN LOOKING ONLINE, IT SEEMS HARD TO TELL THE DIFFER-ENCE.
OH! WELL, I HAVE FORMER FISHERMEN AMONG MY DISCIPLES. I CAN ASK!
AHH, I GET WHAT YOU MEAN. IF THEY KEEP BREEDING, YOU'LL END UP WITH HIGHER COSTS TO KEEP THEM ALIVE.
BUT FROM WHAT I HEAR, IT'S HARD TO TELL THE DIFFERENCE BETWEEN MALES AND FEMALES...
OH, YOU JUST NEED TO LOOK INSIDE THEIR MOUTHS.
REALLY? I'LL TRY THAT!
THAT'S PETER. A TRUE MAN OF THE SEA!
BUT THAT'S WHAT YOU TAUGHT US, JESUS-SAMA.

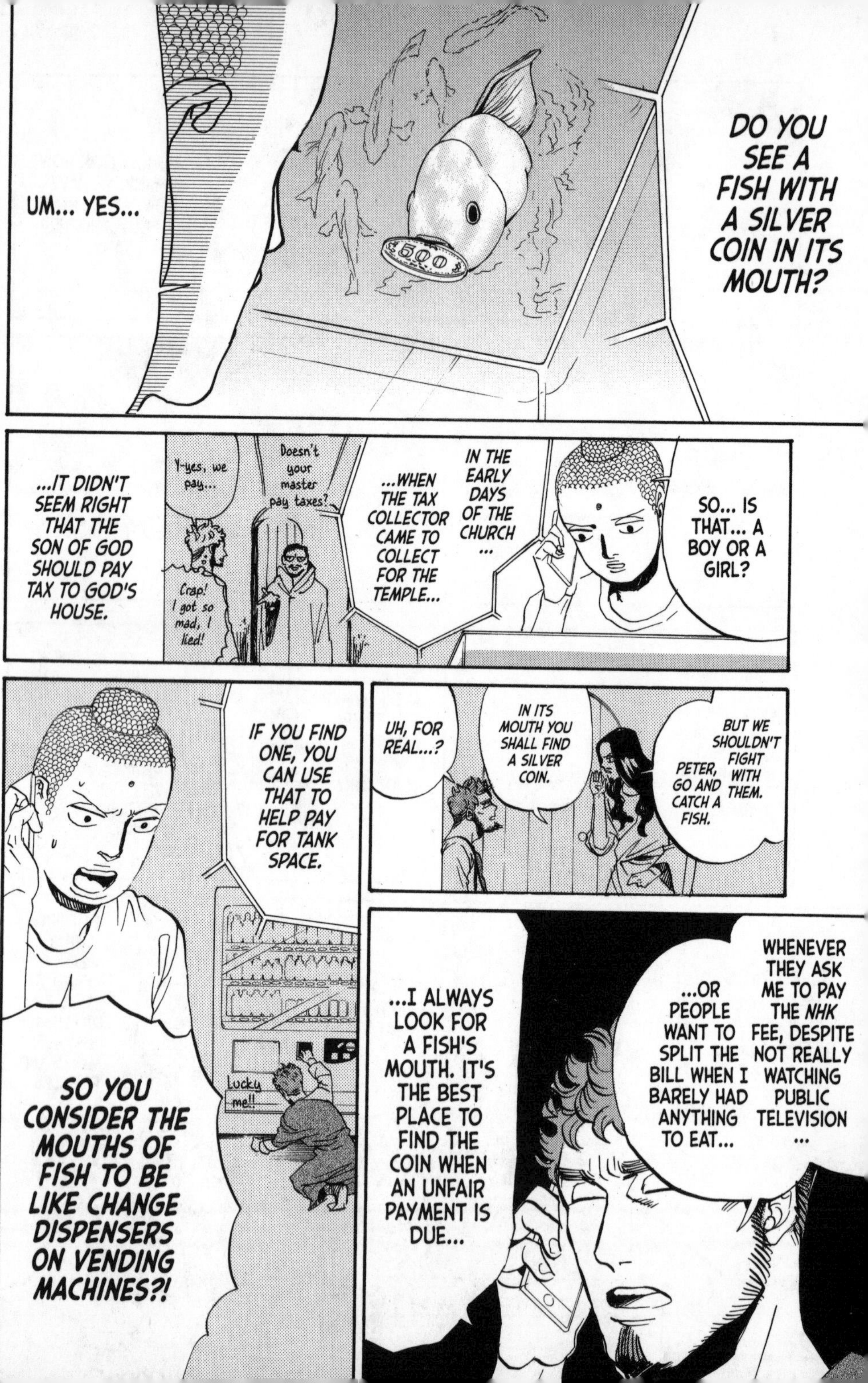
DO YOU SEE A FISH WITH A SILVER COIN IN ITS MOUTH?
500
UM... YES...
SO... IS THAT... A BOY OR A GIRL?
IN THE EARLY DAYS OF THE CHURCH...
...WHEN THE TAX COLLECTOR CAME TO COLLECT FOR THE TEMPLE...
Doesn't your master pay taxes?
Y-yes, we pay...
Crap! I got so mad, I lied!
...IT DIDN'T SEEM RIGHT THAT THE SON OF GOD SHOULD PAY TAX TO GOD'S HOUSE.
BUT WE SHOULDN'T FIGHT WITH THEM.
PETER, GO AND CATCH A FISH.
IN ITS MOUTH YOU SHALL FIND A SILVER COIN.
UH, FOR REAL...?
WHENEVER THEY ASK ME TO PAY THE *NHK* FEE, DESPITE NOT REALLY WATCHING PUBLIC TELEVISION...
...OR PEOPLE WANT TO SPLIT THE BILL WHEN I BARELY HAD ANYTHING TO EAT...
...I ALWAYS LOOK FOR A FISH'S MOUTH. IT'S THE BEST PLACE TO FIND THE COIN WHEN AN UNFAIR PAYMENT IS DUE...
IF YOU FIND ONE, YOU CAN USE THAT TO HELP PAY FOR TANK SPACE.
Lucky me!!
SO YOU CONSIDER THE MOUTHS OF FISH TO BE LIKE CHANGE DISPENSERS ON VENDING MACHINES?!

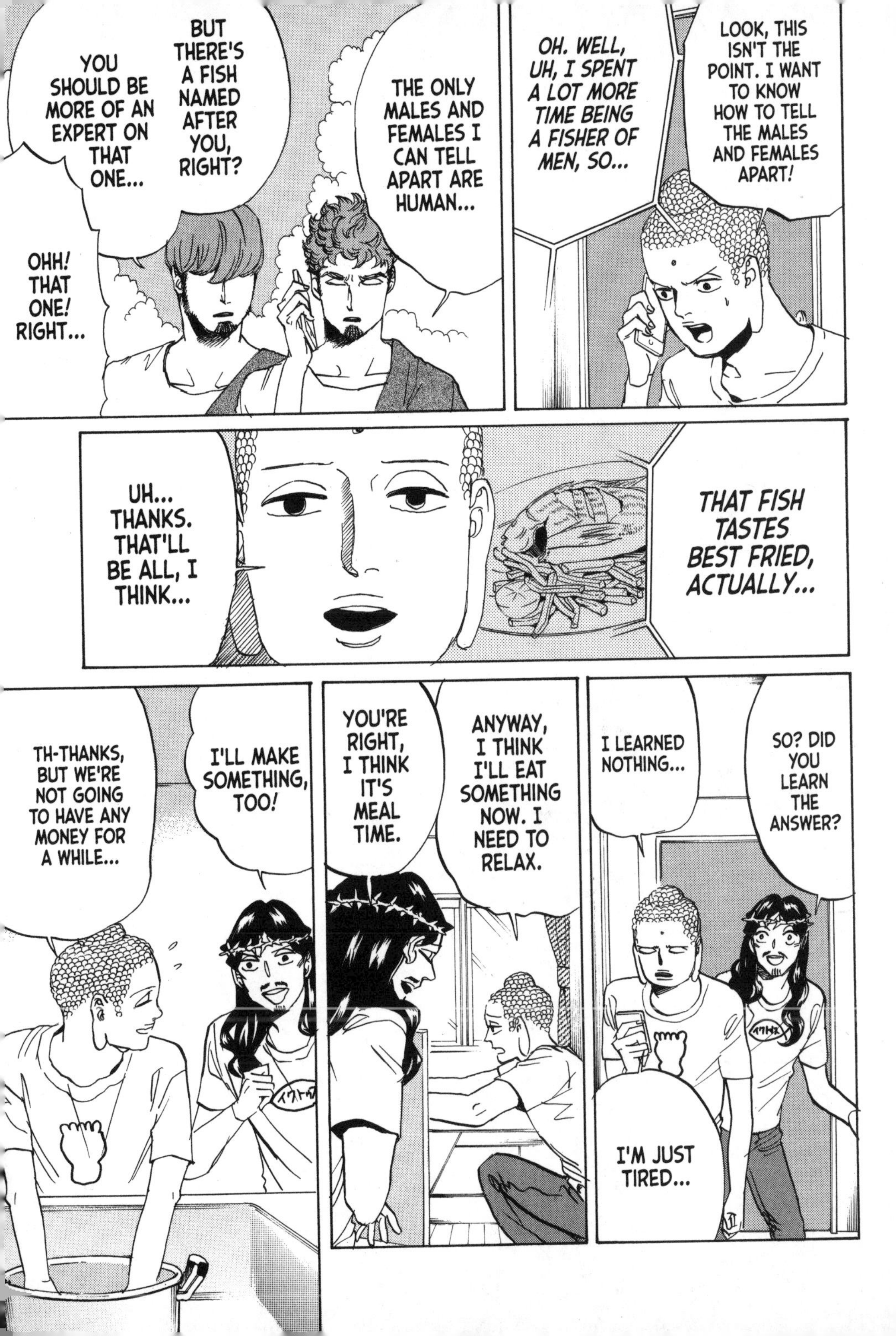
LOOK, THIS ISN'T THE POINT. I WANT TO KNOW HOW TO TELL THE MALES AND FEMALES APART!
OH. WELL, UH, I SPENT A LOT MORE TIME BEING A FISHER OF MEN, SO...
THE ONLY MALES AND FEMALES I CAN TELL APART ARE HUMAN...
BUT THERE'S A FISH NAMED AFTER YOU, RIGHT?
YOU SHOULD BE MORE OF AN EXPERT ON THAT ONE...
OHH! THAT ONE! RIGHT...
THAT FISH TASTES BEST FRIED, ACTUALLY...
UH... THANKS. THAT'LL BE ALL, I THINK...
SO? DID YOU LEARN THE ANSWER?
I LEARNED NOTHING...
I'M JUST TIRED...
ANYWAY, I THINK I'LL EAT SOMETHING NOW. I NEED TO RELAX.
YOU'RE RIGHT, I THINK IT'S MEAL TIME.
I'LL MAKE SOMETHING, TOO!
TH-THANKS, BUT WE'RE NOT GOING TO HAVE ANY MONEY FOR A WHILE...

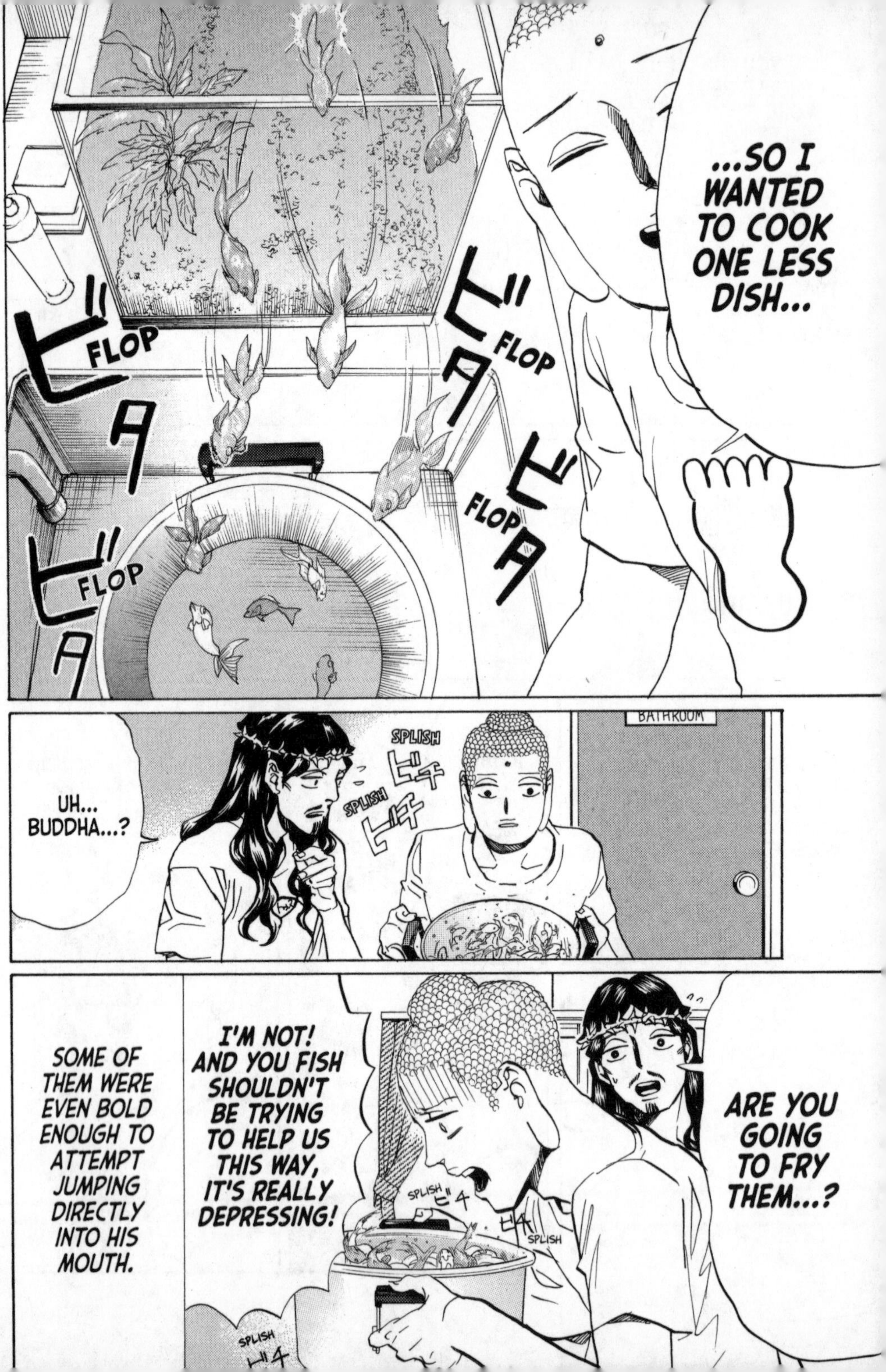

...SO I WANTED TO COOK ONE LESS DISH...
ビタ FLOP
ビタ FLOP
ビタ FLOP
ビタ FLOP
BATHROOM
SPLISH
SPLISH
UH... BUDDHA...?
ARE YOU GOING TO FRY THEM...?
I'M NOT! AND YOU FISH SHOULDN'T BE TRYING TO HELP US THIS WAY, IT'S REALLY DEPRESSING!
SPLISH
SPLISH
SPLISH
SOME OF THEM WERE EVEN BOLD ENOUGH TO ATTEMPT JUMPING DIRECTLY INTO HIS MOUTH.

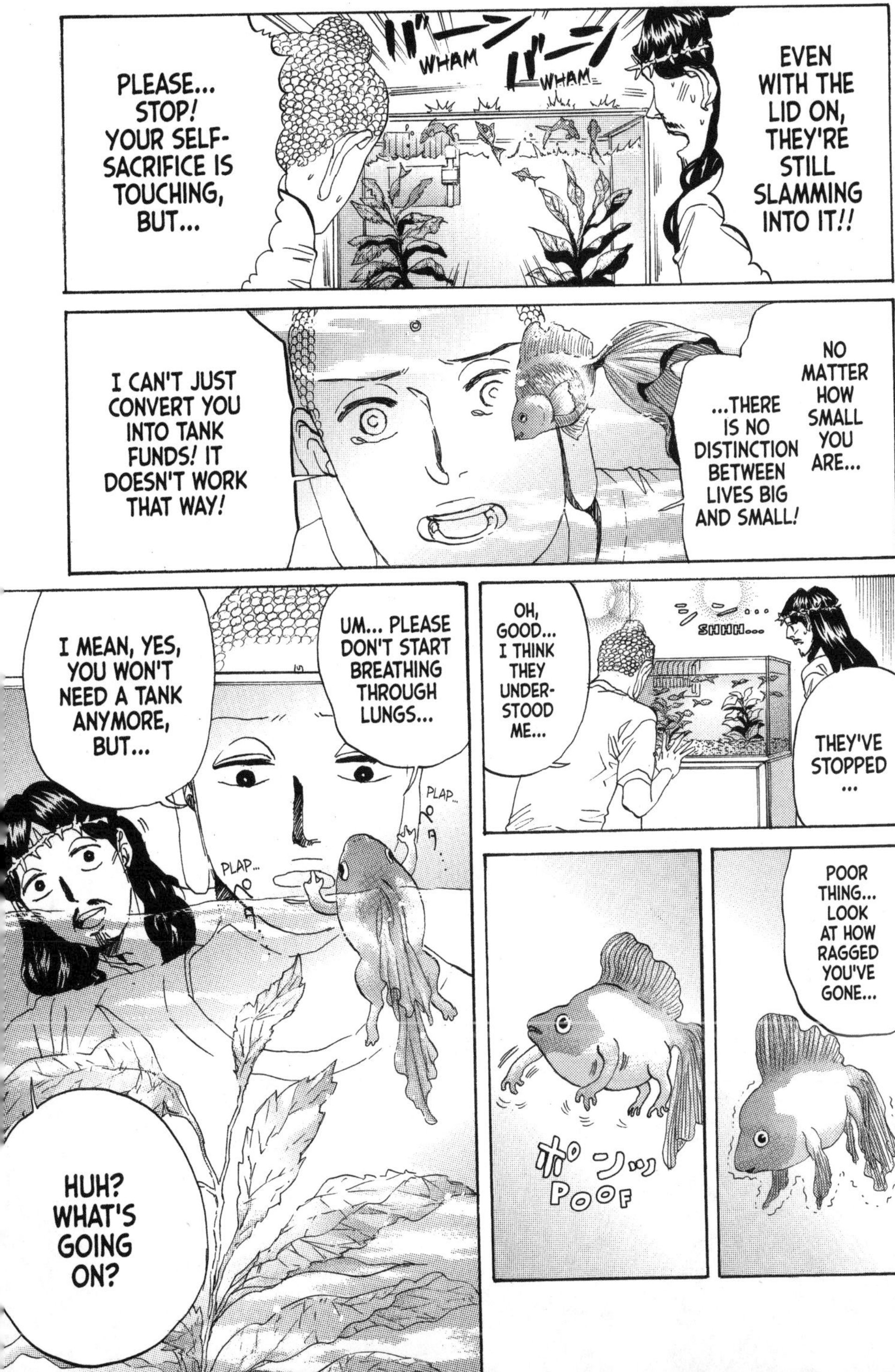
EVEN WITH THE LID ON, THEY'RE STILL SLAMMING INTO IT!!
バーン WHAM
バーン WHAM
PLEASE... STOP! YOUR SELF-SACRIFICE IS TOUCHING, BUT...
NO MATTER HOW SMALL YOU ARE...
...THERE IS NO DISTINCTION BETWEEN LIVES BIG AND SMALL!
I CAN'T JUST CONVERT YOU INTO TANK FUNDS! IT DOESN'T WORK THAT WAY!
SHHH...
THEY'VE STOPPED ...
OH, GOOD... I THINK THEY UNDERSTOOD ME...
POOR THING... LOOK AT HOW RAGGED YOU'VE GONE...
ポンッ POOF
UM... PLEASE DON'T START BREATHING THROUGH LUNGS...
PLAP...
PLAP...
I MEAN, YES, YOU WON'T NEED A TANK ANYMORE, BUT...
HUH? WHAT'S GOING ON?

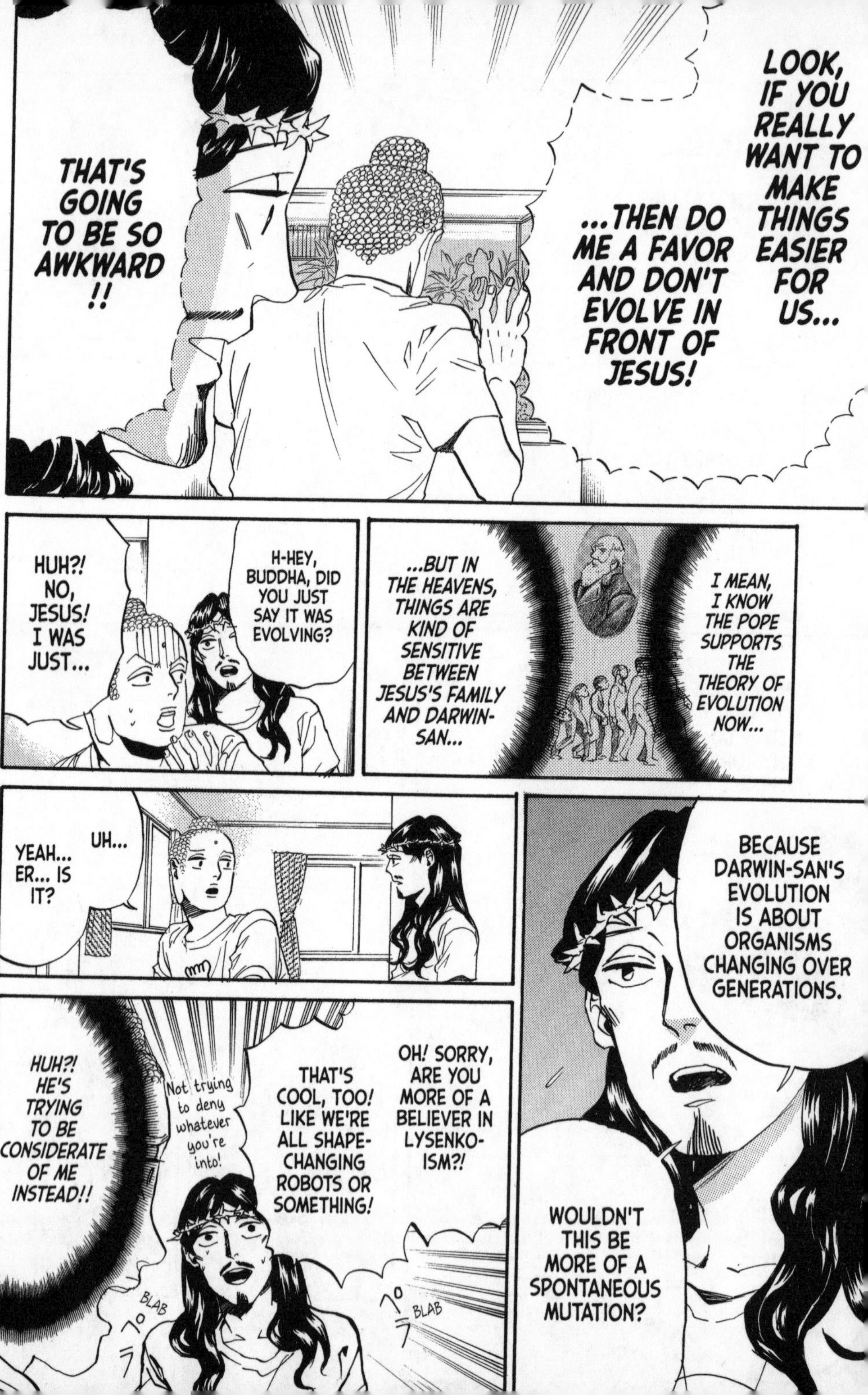
LOOK, IF YOU REALLY WANT TO MAKE THINGS EASIER FOR US...
...THEN DO ME A FAVOR AND DON'T EVOLVE IN FRONT OF JESUS!
THAT'S GOING TO BE SO AWKWARD!!
I MEAN, I KNOW THE POPE SUPPORTS THE THEORY OF EVOLUTION NOW...
...BUT IN THE HEAVENS, THINGS ARE KIND OF SENSITIVE BETWEEN JESUS'S FAMILY AND DARWIN-SAN...
H-HEY, BUDDHA, DID YOU JUST SAY IT WAS EVOLVING?
HUH?! NO, JESUS! I WAS JUST...
BECAUSE DARWIN-SAN'S EVOLUTION IS ABOUT ORGANISMS CHANGING OVER GENERATIONS.
WOULDN'T THIS BE MORE OF A SPONTANEOUS MUTATION?
UH...
YEAH... ER... IS IT?
OH! SORRY, ARE YOU MORE OF A BELIEVER IN LYSENKO-ISM?!
THAT'S COOL, TOO! LIKE WE'RE ALL SHAPE-CHANGING ROBOTS OR SOMETHING!
Not trying to deny whatever you're into!
BLAB
BLAB
HUH?! HE'S TRYING TO BE CONSIDERATE OF ME INSTEAD!!

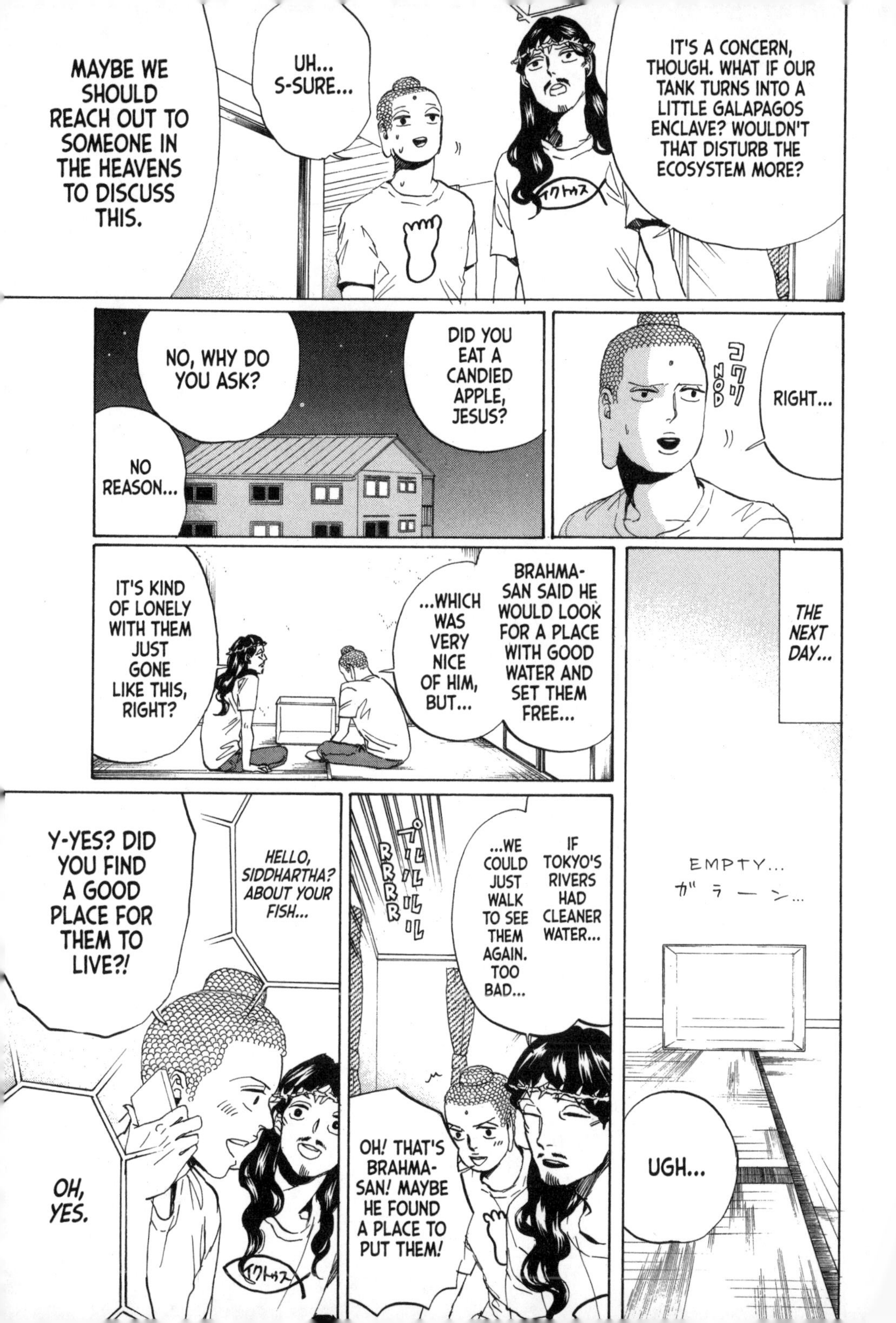

IT'S A CONCERN, THOUGH. WHAT IF OUR TANK TURNS INTO A LITTLE GALAPAGOS ENCLAVE? WOULDN'T THAT DISTURB THE ECOSYSTEM MORE?
UH... S-SURE...
MAYBE WE SHOULD REACH OUT TO SOMEONE IN THE HEAVENS TO DISCUSS THIS.
コクリ
NOD
RIGHT...
DID YOU EAT A CANDIED APPLE, JESUS?
NO, WHY DO YOU ASK?
NO REASON...
THE NEXT DAY...
EMPTY...
ガラーン...
UGH...
BRAHMA-SAN SAID HE WOULD LOOK FOR A PLACE WITH GOOD WATER AND SET THEM FREE...
...WHICH WAS VERY NICE OF HIM, BUT...
IT'S KIND OF LONELY WITH THEM JUST GONE LIKE THIS, RIGHT?
IF TOKYO'S RIVERS HAD CLEANER WATER...
...WE COULD JUST WALK TO SEE THEM AGAIN. TOO BAD...
プルルルル
RRRR
OH! THAT'S BRAHMA-SAN! MAYBE HE FOUND A PLACE TO PUT THEM!
HELLO, SIDDHARTHA? ABOUT YOUR FISH...
Y-YES? DID YOU FIND A GOOD PLACE FOR THEM TO LIVE?!
OH, YES.

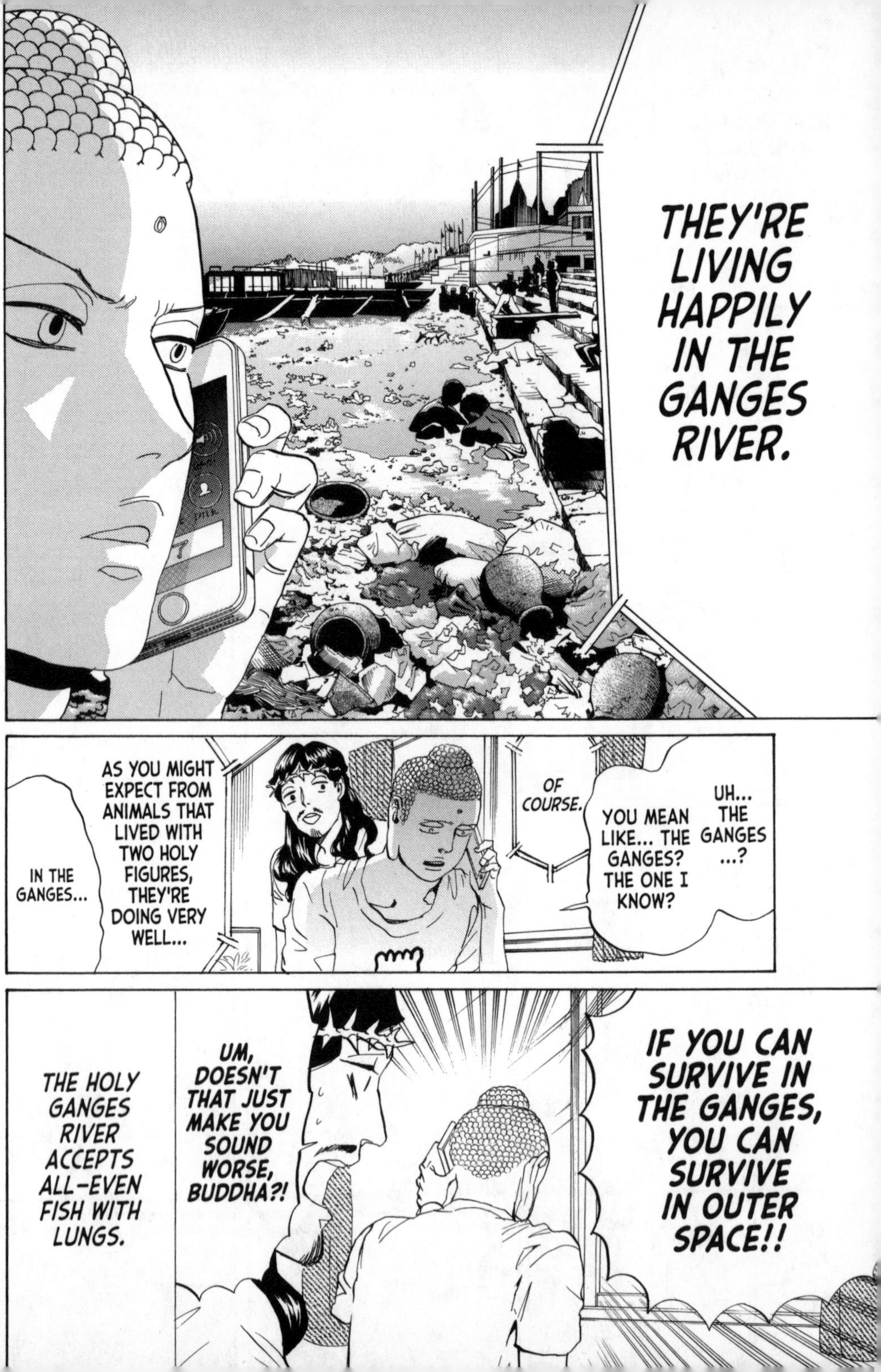
THEY'RE LIVING HAPPILY IN THE GANGES RIVER.
UH... THE GANGES ...?
YOU MEAN LIKE... THE GANGES? THE ONE I KNOW?
OF COURSE.
AS YOU MIGHT EXPECT FROM ANIMALS THAT LIVED WITH TWO HOLY FIGURES, THEY'RE DOING VERY WELL...
IN THE GANGES...
IF YOU CAN SURVIVE IN THE GANGES, YOU CAN SURVIVE IN OUTER SPACE!!
UM, DOESN'T THAT JUST MAKE YOU SOUND WORSE, BUDDHA?!
THE HOLY GANGES RIVER ACCEPTS ALL—EVEN FISH WITH LUNGS.

Three days after arriving at the Ganges

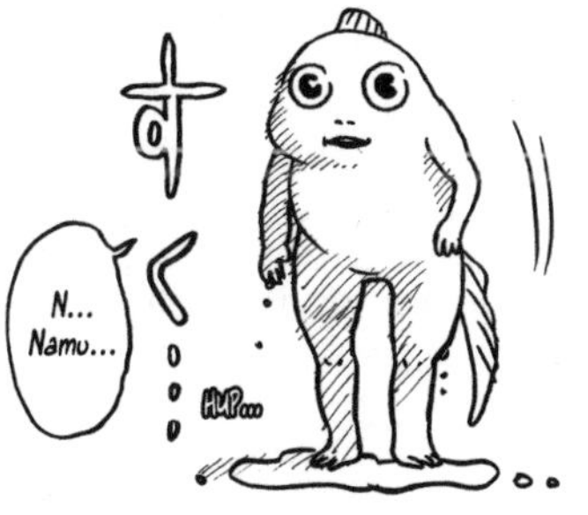
すく
N... Namu...
HUP...

SAINT ☆ YOUNG MEN

CHAPTER 76 TRANSLATION NOTES

Goldfish scooping, page 49
A type of game known in Japanese as kingyo-sukui, and played at traditional festivals. Typically, the scoops have a paper layer over the hoop that will quickly weaken and break in water, increasing the difficulty of supporting a goldfish's weight.

Ichthys, page 50
The early Christian symbol of the fish, dating back to the 2nd century AD.

Yo-kai Watch, page 51
An intensely popular children's franchise based on a series of handheld video games. *Yo-kai Watch* combines the "catch them all" RPG structure of Pokemon with Japanese *yôkai* folklore monsters.

The Feeding of the Five Thousand, page 53
One of the miracles of Jesus, described in all four gospels. Jesus is followed by a large crowd that will soon go hungry. In order to feed the people, he breaks five loaves and two fish and hands them to the disciples to distribute among the crowd, who all eat to contentment.

Coin in the Fish's Mouth, page 56
A miracle of Jesus described in the Gospel of Matthew. As shown in the manga here, a tax collector asks for a temple tax. Jesus instructs Peter to go catch a fish, open its mouth, and find a coin there to pay the tax. Although not named specifically in the story, tilapia are also called "St. Peter's fish."

NHK, page 56
Japan's public broadcasting network is NHK (*Nihon Hôsô Kyôkai*) or Japan Broadcasting Corporation. It receives its funding from reception fees which are collected from every household with a TV capable of receiving NHK signals, to a cost of somewhere between $100-$200 per year. However, there is no punitive measure for refusing to pay, so many people avoid doing so--and as a result, the collectors who go door to door canvassing for NHK reception fees can be rather pushy and unpleasant.

Lysenkoism, page 60
A Soviet scientific argument brought forth by Trofim Lysenko that claimed changes in the body of organisms during life can alter hereditary characteristics passed down to offspring, allowing for the "development" of desirable traits. Lysenko's work was mainly based on grafting different kinds of trees together. The Soviet government chose to push Lysenkoism as a state science for ideological reasons, and the name has since become synonymous with deliberately distorted science that furthers the aims of authority figures for their own political gains.

Namu, page 63
An abbreviation of the phrase *Namu Amida Butsu*, the Japanese version of a common Buddhist recitation. It translates roughly to "Hail to the Amitabha Buddha." It is often repeated while meditating, and as a simple repetitive part of faith, plays a similar role to the "Hail Mary" prayer of the Catholic Church.

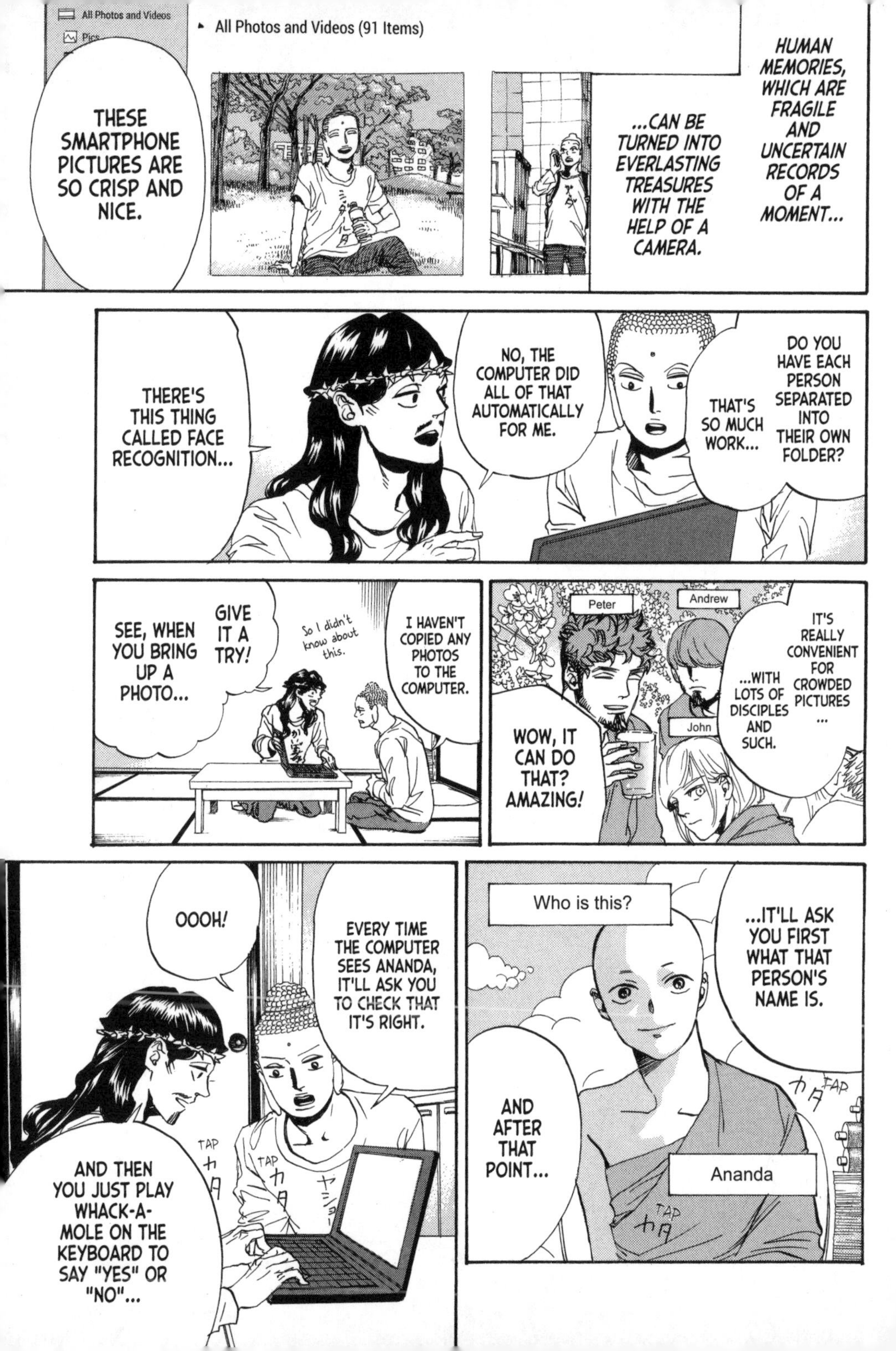
HUMAN MEMORIES, WHICH ARE FRAGILE AND UNCERTAIN RECORDS OF A MOMENT...
...CAN BE TURNED INTO EVERLASTING TREASURES WITH THE HELP OF A CAMERA.
All Photos and Videos (91 Items)
All Photos and Videos
Pics
THESE SMARTPHONE PICTURES ARE SO CRISP AND NICE.
DO YOU HAVE EACH PERSON SEPARATED INTO THEIR OWN FOLDER?
THAT'S SO MUCH WORK...
NO, THE COMPUTER DID ALL OF THAT AUTOMATICALLY FOR ME.
THERE'S THIS THING CALLED FACE RECOGNITION...
Andrew
Peter
IT'S REALLY CONVENIENT FOR CROWDED PICTURES...
...WITH LOTS OF DISCIPLES AND SUCH.
John
WOW, IT CAN DO THAT? AMAZING!
I HAVEN'T COPIED ANY PHOTOS TO THE COMPUTER.
So I didn't know about this.
GIVE IT A TRY!
SEE, WHEN YOU BRING UP A PHOTO...
...IT'LL ASK YOU FIRST WHAT THAT PERSON'S NAME IS.
Who is this?
TAP
AND AFTER THAT POINT...
Ananda
TAP
EVERY TIME THE COMPUTER SEES ANANDA, IT'LL ASK YOU TO CHECK THAT IT'S RIGHT.
OOOH!
TAP
TAP
AND THEN YOU JUST PLAY WHACK-A-MOLE ON THE KEYBOARD TO SAY "YES" OR "NO"...

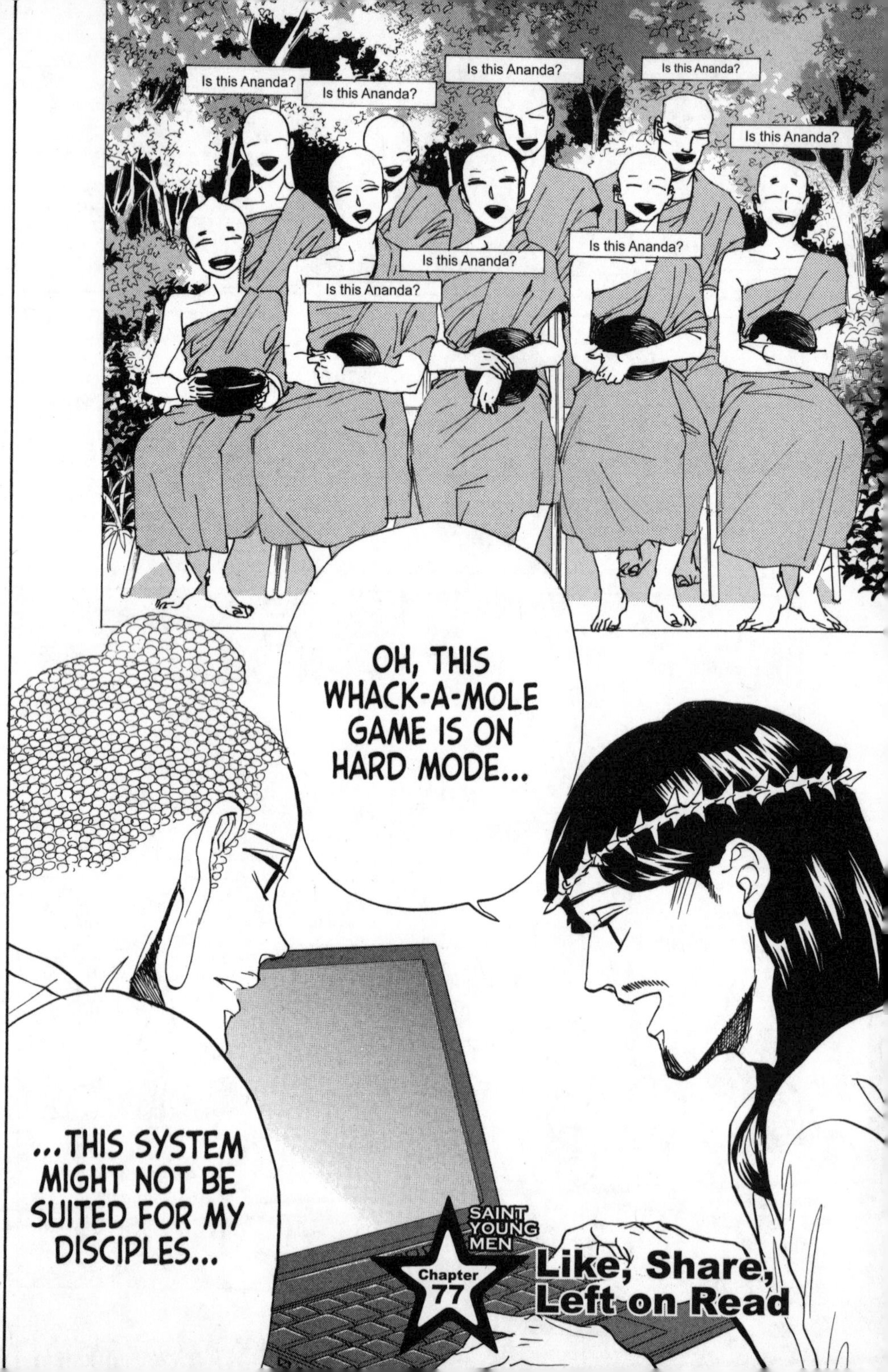
Is this Ananda?
Is this Ananda?
Is this Ananda?
Is this Ananda?
Is this Ananda?
Is this Ananda?
Is this Ananda?
Is this Ananda?
OH, THIS WHACK-A-MOLE GAME IS ON HARD MODE...
...THIS SYSTEM MIGHT NOT BE SUITED FOR MY DISCIPLES...
SAINT YOUNG MEN
Chapter 77
Like, Share, Left on Read

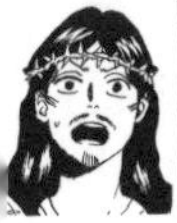

JESUS FOUND OUT THERE'S A KIND OF TRIPOD CALLED A MONOPOD. IT'S ALREADY EXCITING ENOUGH WITH SINGLE AND DUAL-LENS! WHAT KIND OF MONSTER IS THIS?!

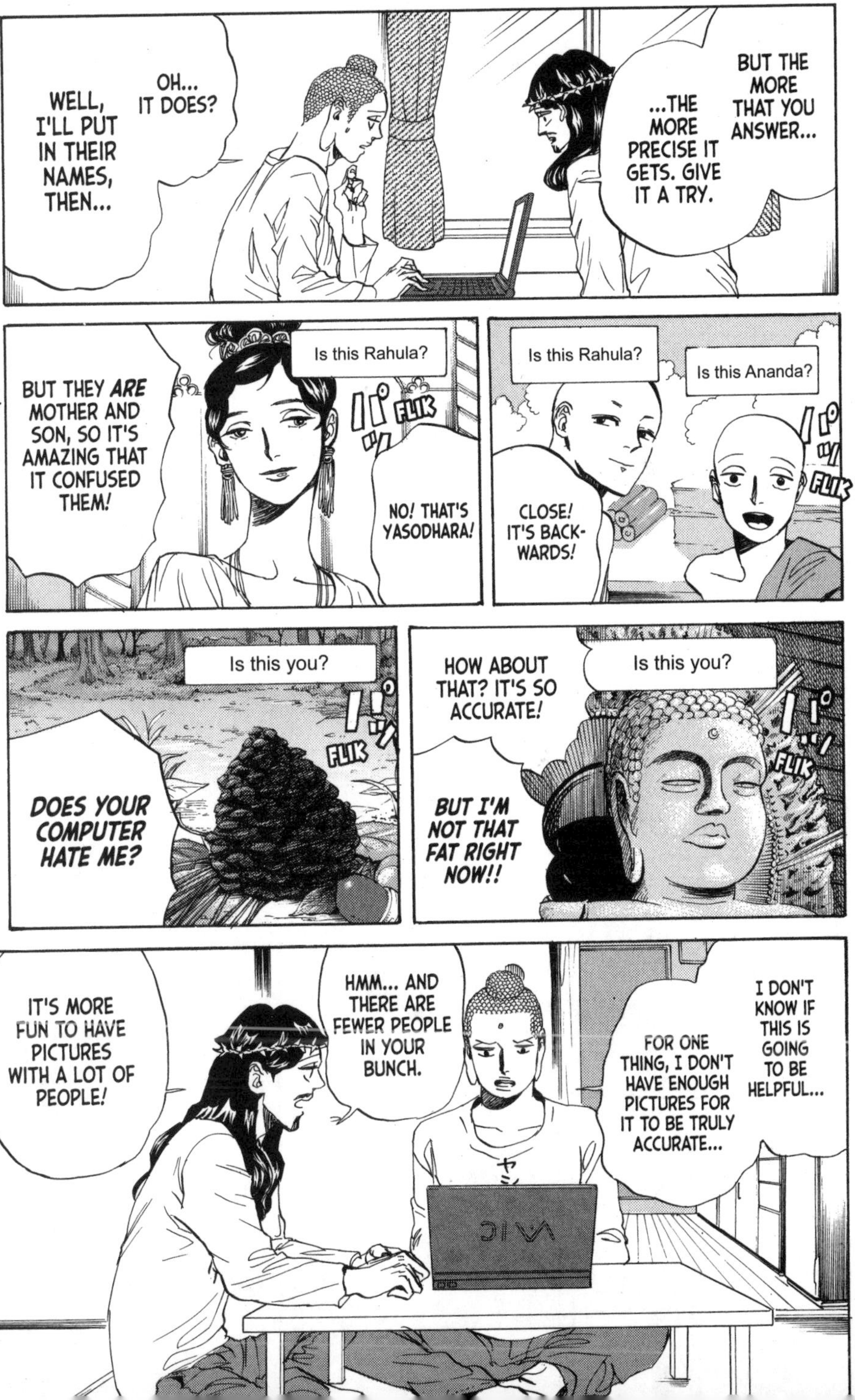
BUT THE MORE THAT YOU ANSWER...
...THE MORE PRECISE IT GETS. GIVE IT A TRY.
OH... IT DOES?
WELL, I'LL PUT IN THEIR NAMES, THEN...
Is this Rahula?
Is this Ananda?
FLIK
CLOSE! IT'S BACKWARDS!
Is this Rahula?
FLIK
NO! THAT'S YASODHARA!
BUT THEY ARE MOTHER AND SON, SO IT'S AMAZING THAT IT CONFUSED THEM!
Is this you?
FLIK
HOW ABOUT THAT? IT'S SO ACCURATE!
BUT I'M NOT THAT FAT RIGHT NOW!!
Is this you?
FLIK
DOES YOUR COMPUTER HATE ME?
I DON'T KNOW IF THIS IS GOING TO BE HELPFUL...
FOR ONE THING, I DON'T HAVE ENOUGH PICTURES FOR IT TO BE TRULY ACCURATE...
HMM... AND THERE ARE FEWER PEOPLE IN YOUR BUNCH.
IT'S MORE FUN TO HAVE PICTURES WITH A LOT OF PEOPLE!

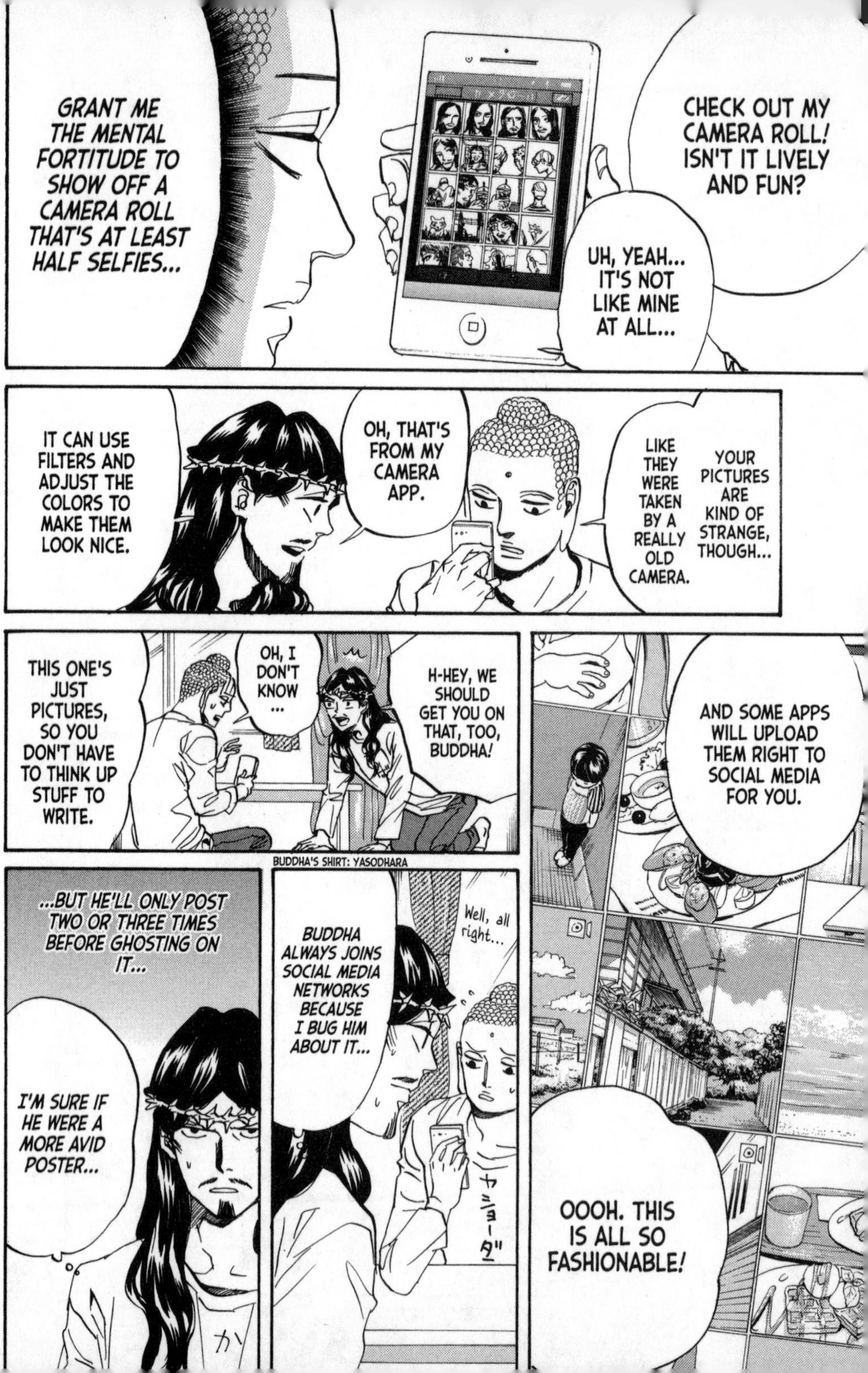
CHECK OUT MY CAMERA ROLL! ISN'T IT LIVELY AND FUN?
UH, YEAH... IT'S NOT LIKE MINE AT ALL...
GRANT ME THE MENTAL FORTITUDE TO SHOW OFF A CAMERA ROLL THAT'S AT LEAST HALF SELFIES...
YOUR PICTURES ARE KIND OF STRANGE, THOUGH...
LIKE THEY WERE TAKEN BY A REALLY OLD CAMERA.
OH, THAT'S FROM MY CAMERA APP.
IT CAN USE FILTERS AND ADJUST THE COLORS TO MAKE THEM LOOK NICE.
AND SOME APPS WILL UPLOAD THEM RIGHT TO SOCIAL MEDIA FOR YOU.
OOOH. THIS IS ALL SO FASHIONABLE!
H-HEY, WE SHOULD GET YOU ON THAT, TOO, BUDDHA!
OH, I DON'T KNOW ...
THIS ONE'S JUST PICTURES, SO YOU DON'T HAVE TO THINK UP STUFF TO WRITE.
BUDDHA'S SHIRT: YASODHARA
Well, all right...
BUDDHA ALWAYS JOINS SOCIAL MEDIA NETWORKS BECAUSE I BUG HIM ABOUT IT...
ヤショーダ
...BUT HE'LL ONLY POST TWO OR THREE TIMES BEFORE GHOSTING ON IT...
I'M SURE IF HE WERE A MORE AVID POSTER...
か

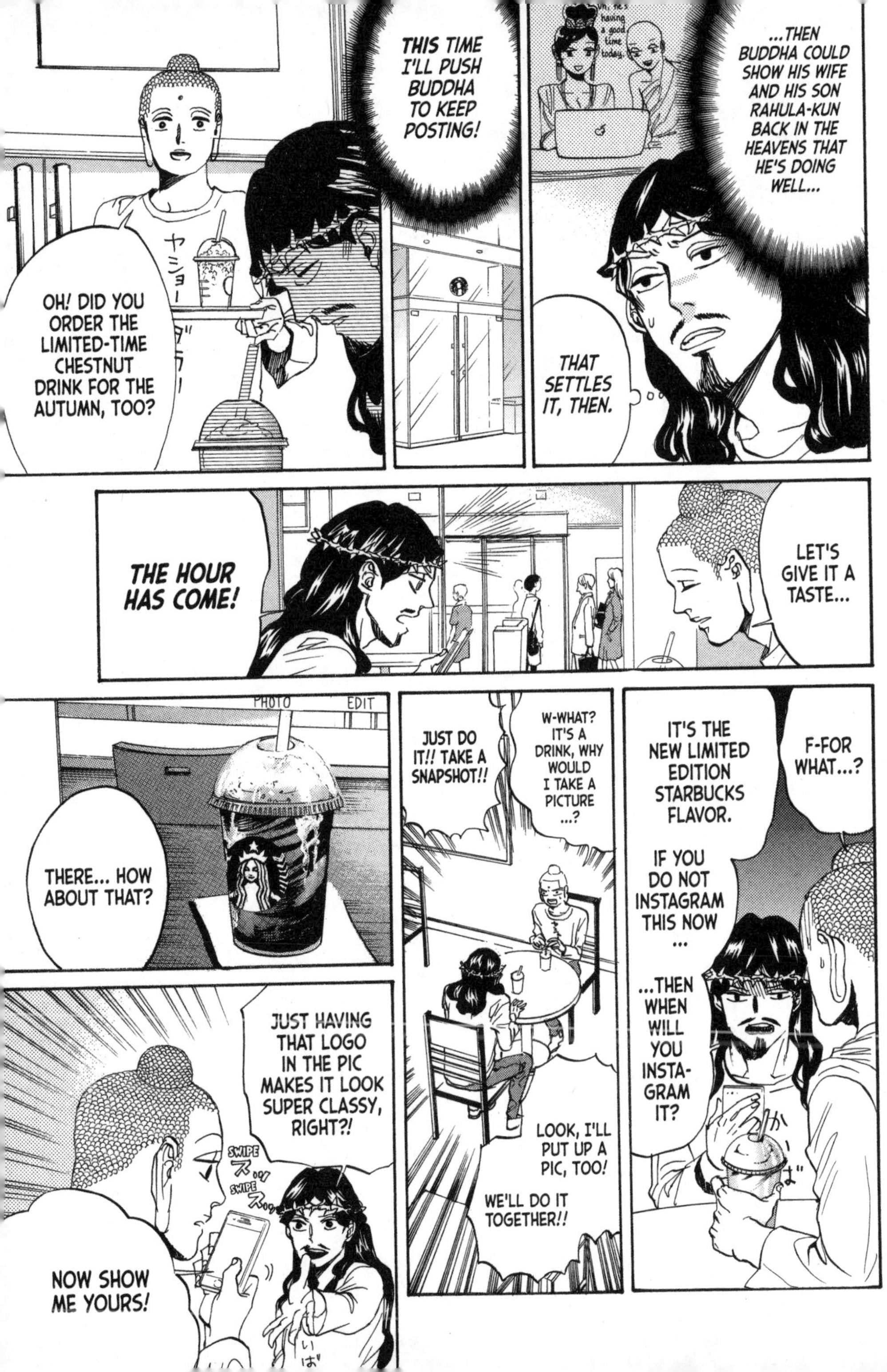
having a good time today.
...THEN BUDDHA COULD SHOW HIS WIFE AND HIS SON RAHULA-KUN BACK IN THE HEAVENS THAT HE'S DOING WELL...
THAT SETTLES IT, THEN.
THIS TIME I'LL PUSH BUDDHA TO KEEP POSTING!
OH! DID YOU ORDER THE LIMITED-TIME CHESTNUT DRINK FOR THE AUTUMN, TOO?
LET'S GIVE IT A TASTE...
THE HOUR HAS COME!
F-FOR WHAT...?
IT'S THE NEW LIMITED EDITION STARBUCKS FLAVOR.
IF YOU DO NOT INSTAGRAM THIS NOW ...
...THEN WHEN WILL YOU INSTA-GRAM IT?
W-WHAT? IT'S A DRINK, WHY WOULD I TAKE A PICTURE ...?
JUST DO IT!! TAKE A SNAPSHOT!!
LOOK, I'LL PUT UP A PIC, TOO!
WE'LL DO IT TOGETHER!!
PHOTO
EDIT
THERE... HOW ABOUT THAT?
JUST HAVING THAT LOGO IN THE PIC MAKES IT LOOK SUPER CLASSY, RIGHT?!
SWIPE
SWIPE
NOW SHOW ME YOURS!

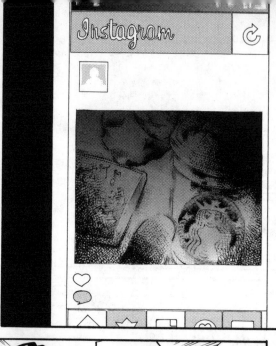

Instagram
WHERE DID YOU TAKE THIS, THE STARBUCKS IN HELL?!
HUH? W-WHY DO YOU SAY THAT?
WHY IS IT SO DARK?!
YOUR FINGER'S IN THE FRAME!
GET THAT TISSUE OUT OF THERE!!
ヤショーダ
KTHUNK
ガタタ
BETWEEN THE BLURRINESS AND LACK OF FOCUS, THE STARBUCKS MERMAID LOOKS LIKE A HORROR MOVIE LOGO!!
JESUS'S SHIRT: MANGER
YOU REALLY DON'T TAKE PHOTOS, DO YOU...?
ACTUALLY, I'VE BEEN MUCH MORE ACTIVE LATELY!
かいばおけ
YOU SAID THAT I SHOULD UPLOAD PICTURES OF MY COOKING...
OH, YOU DID LIKE I SAID!
YES. I'VE GOT A FAIR NUMBER OF FOLLOWERS, ACTUALLY...
I GUESS THAT PICTURES OF HOME-COOKED MEALS ARE PRETTY POPULAR.
PLUS, YOUR COOKING IS VEGE-TARIAN...
...SO I'M SURE IT GETS A BIG BOOST FROM THE ORGANIC CROWD...

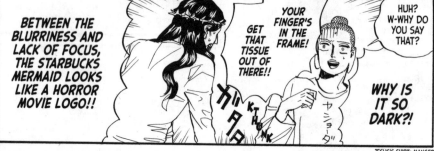

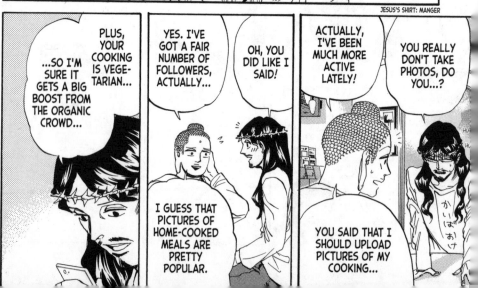

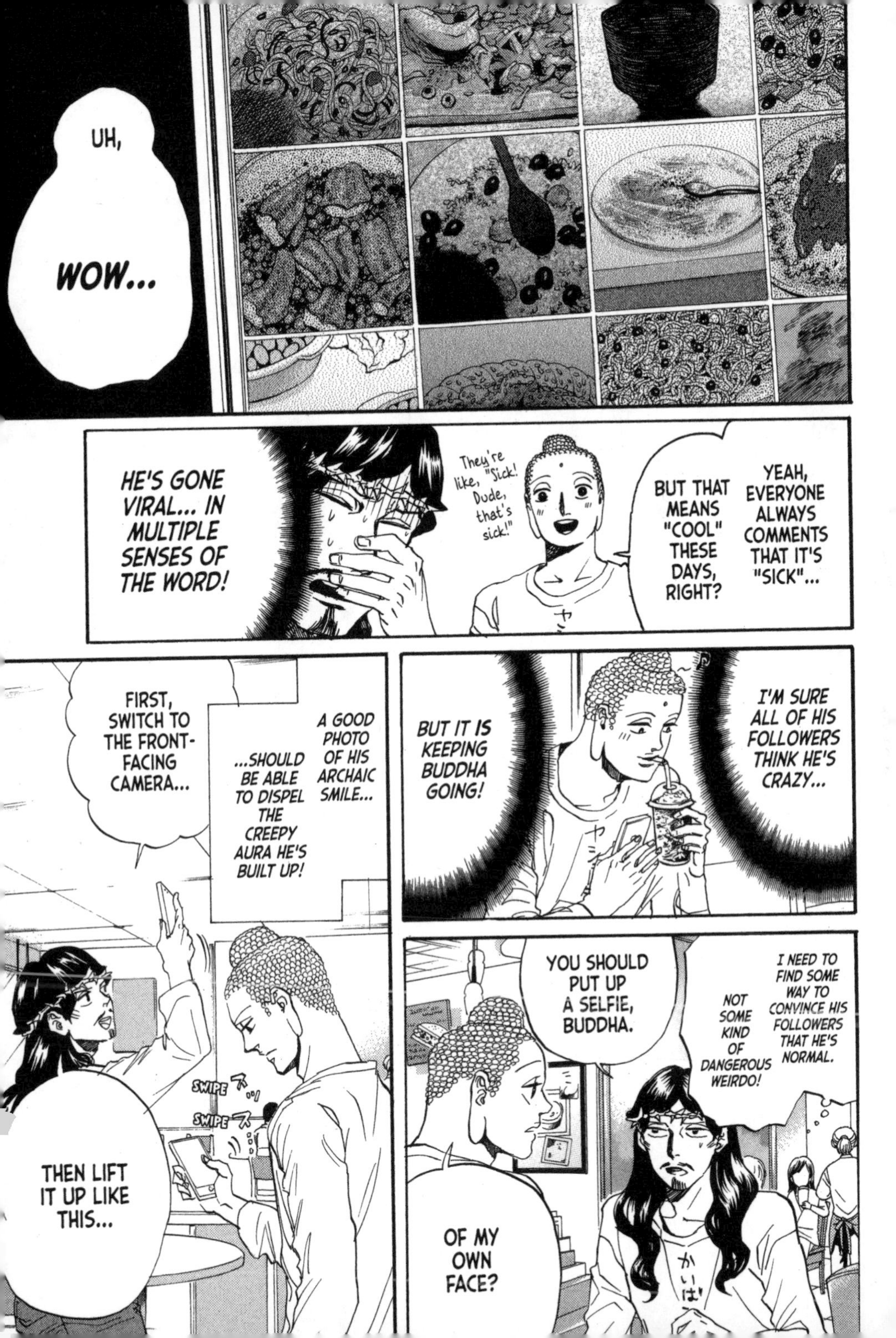
UH,
WOW...
YEAH, EVERYONE ALWAYS COMMENTS THAT IT'S "SICK"...
BUT THAT MEANS "COOL" THESE DAYS, RIGHT?
They're like, "Sick! Dude, that's sick!"
HE'S GONE VIRAL... IN MULTIPLE SENSES OF THE WORD!
I'M SURE ALL OF HIS FOLLOWERS THINK HE'S CRAZY...
BUT IT IS KEEPING BUDDHA GOING!
I NEED TO FIND SOME WAY TO CONVINCE HIS FOLLOWERS THAT HE'S NORMAL.
NOT SOME KIND OF DANGEROUS WEIRDO!
YOU SHOULD PUT UP A SELFIE, BUDDHA.
OF MY OWN FACE?
A GOOD PHOTO OF HIS ARCHAIC SMILE...
...SHOULD BE ABLE TO DISPEL THE CREEPY AURA HE'S BUILT UP!
FIRST, SWITCH TO THE FRONT-FACING CAMERA...
SWIPE
SWIPE
THEN LIFT IT UP LIKE THIS...

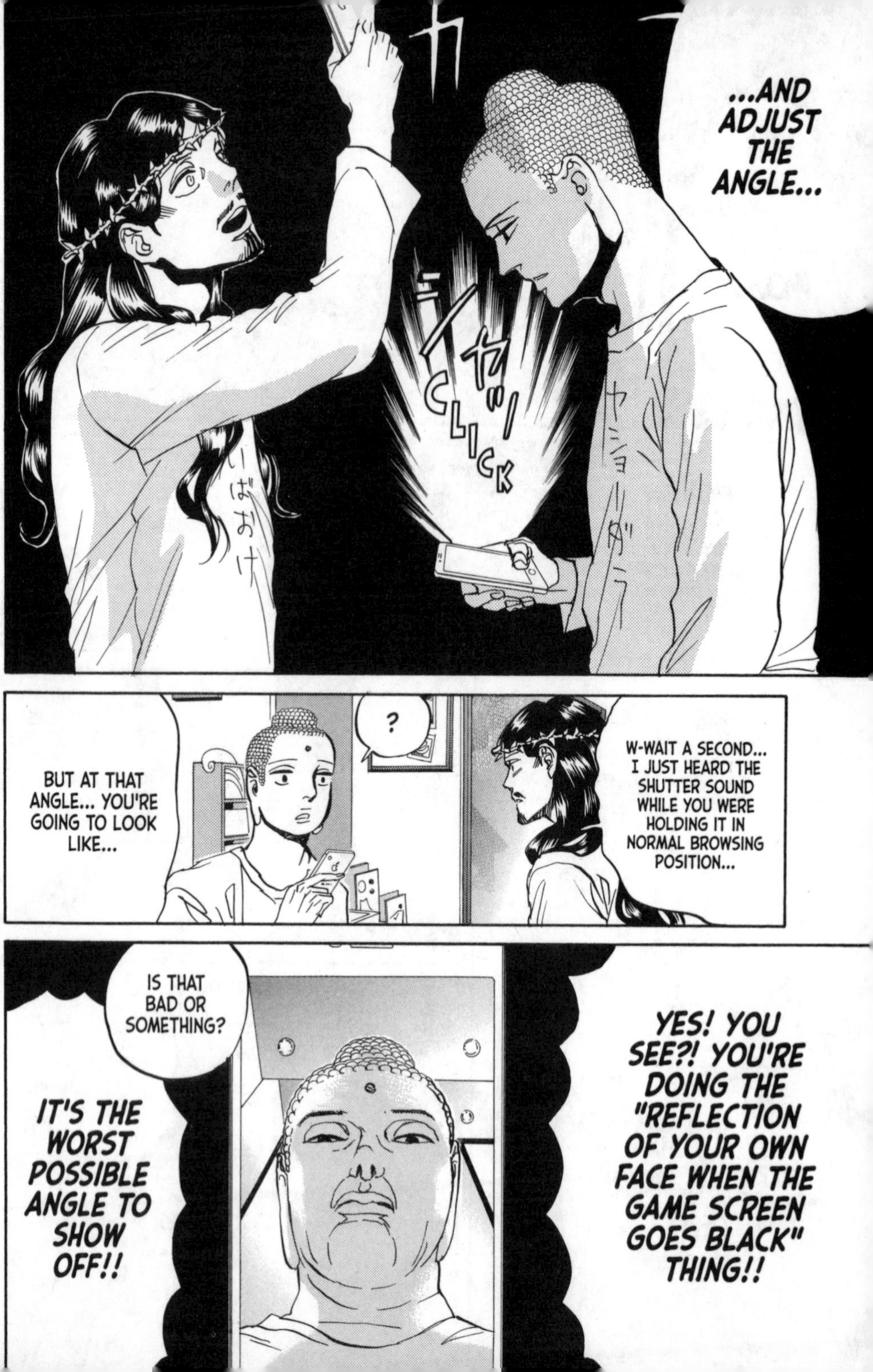
...AND ADJUST THE ANGLE...
CLICK
W-WAIT A SECOND... I JUST HEARD THE SHUTTER SOUND WHILE YOU WERE HOLDING IT IN NORMAL BROWSING POSITION...
?
BUT AT THAT ANGLE... YOU'RE GOING TO LOOK LIKE...
YES! YOU SEE?! YOU'RE DOING THE "REFLECTION OF YOUR OWN FACE WHEN THE GAME SCREEN GOES BLACK" THING!!
IS THAT BAD OR SOMETHING?
IT'S THE WORST POSSIBLE ANGLE TO SHOW OFF!!

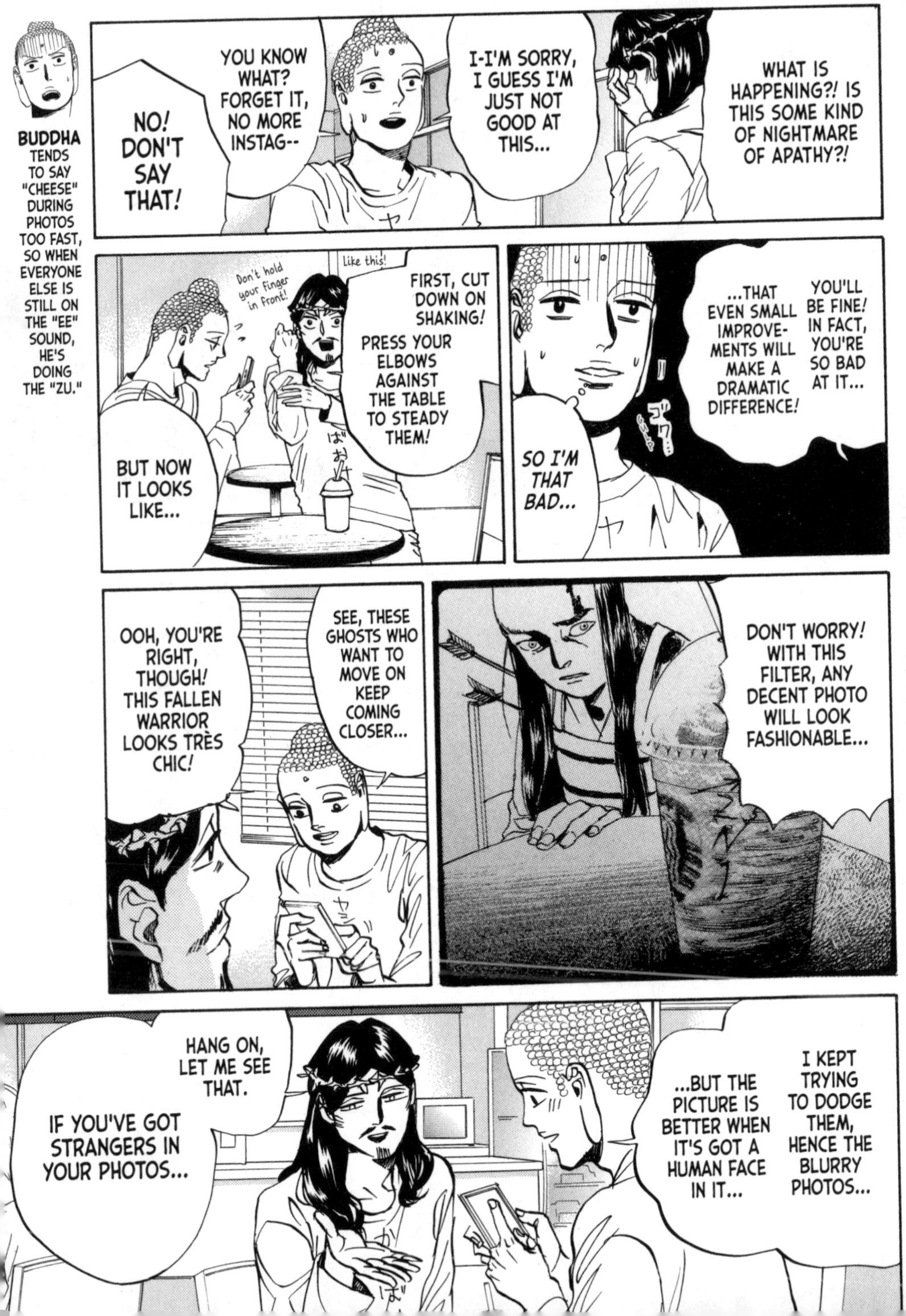
WHAT IS HAPPENING?! IS THIS SOME KIND OF NIGHTMARE OF APATHY?!
I-I'M SORRY, I GUESS I'M JUST NOT GOOD AT THIS...
YOU KNOW WHAT? FORGET IT, NO MORE INSTAG--
NO! DON'T SAY THAT!
YOU'LL BE FINE! IN FACT, YOU'RE SO BAD AT IT...
...THAT EVEN SMALL IMPROVE- MENTS WILL MAKE A DRAMATIC DIFFERENCE!
SO I'M THAT BAD...
Like this!
FIRST, CUT DOWN ON SHAKING!
PRESS YOUR ELBOWS AGAINST THE TABLE TO STEADY THEM!
Don't hold your finger in Front!
BUT NOW IT LOOKS LIKE...
DON'T WORRY! WITH THIS FILTER, ANY DECENT PHOTO WILL LOOK FASHIONABLE...
SEE, THESE GHOSTS WHO WANT TO MOVE ON KEEP COMING CLOSER...
OOH, YOU'RE RIGHT, THOUGH! THIS FALLEN WARRIOR LOOKS TRÈS CHIC!
I KEPT TRYING TO DODGE THEM, HENCE THE BLURRY PHOTOS...
...BUT THE PICTURE IS BETTER WHEN IT'S GOT A HUMAN FACE IN IT...
HANG ON, LET ME SEE THAT.
IF YOU'VE GOT STRANGERS IN YOUR PHOTOS...
BUDDHA TENDS TO SAY "CHEESE" DURING PHOTOS TOO FAST, SO WHEN EVERYONE ELSE IS STILL ON THE "EE" SOUND, HE'S DOING THE "ZU."

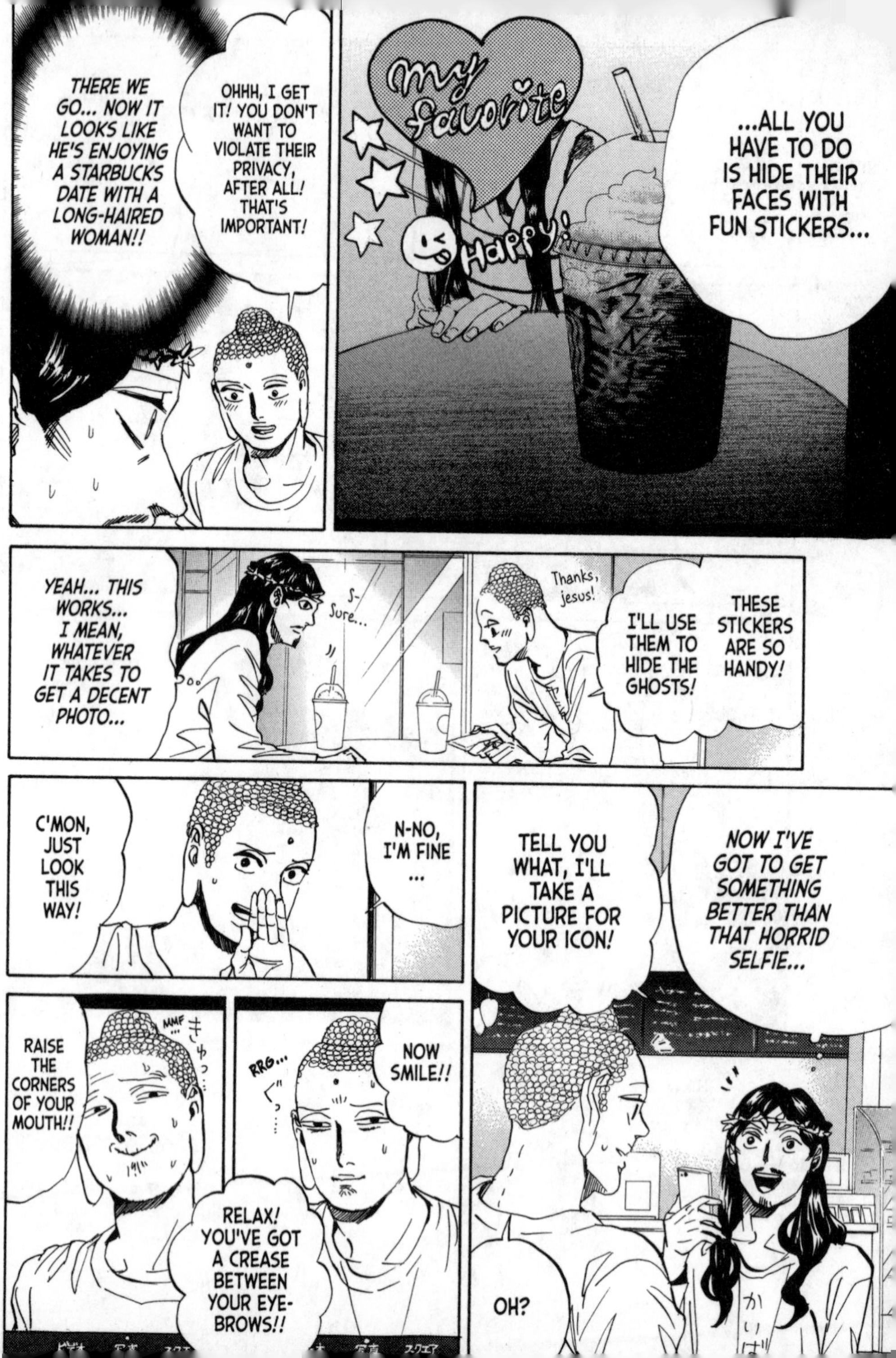
...ALL YOU HAVE TO DO IS HIDE THEIR FACES WITH FUN STICKERS...
my favorite
Happy!
OHHH, I GET IT! YOU DON'T WANT TO VIOLATE THEIR PRIVACY, AFTER ALL! THAT'S IMPORTANT!
THERE WE GO... NOW IT LOOKS LIKE HE'S ENJOYING A STARBUCKS DATE WITH A LONG-HAIRED WOMAN!!
THESE STICKERS ARE SO HANDY!
I'LL USE THEM TO HIDE THE GHOSTS!
Thanks, jesus!
S-Sure...
YEAH... THIS WORKS... I MEAN, WHATEVER IT TAKES TO GET A DECENT PHOTO...
NOW I'VE GOT TO GET SOMETHING BETTER THAN THAT HORRID SELFIE...
TELL YOU WHAT, I'LL TAKE A PICTURE FOR YOUR ICON!
OH?
N-NO, I'M FINE ...
C'MON, JUST LOOK THIS WAY!
NOW SMILE!!
RRG...
RELAX! YOU'VE GOT A CREASE BETWEEN YOUR EYE-BROWS!!
MMF...
RAISE THE CORNERS OF YOUR MOUTH!!

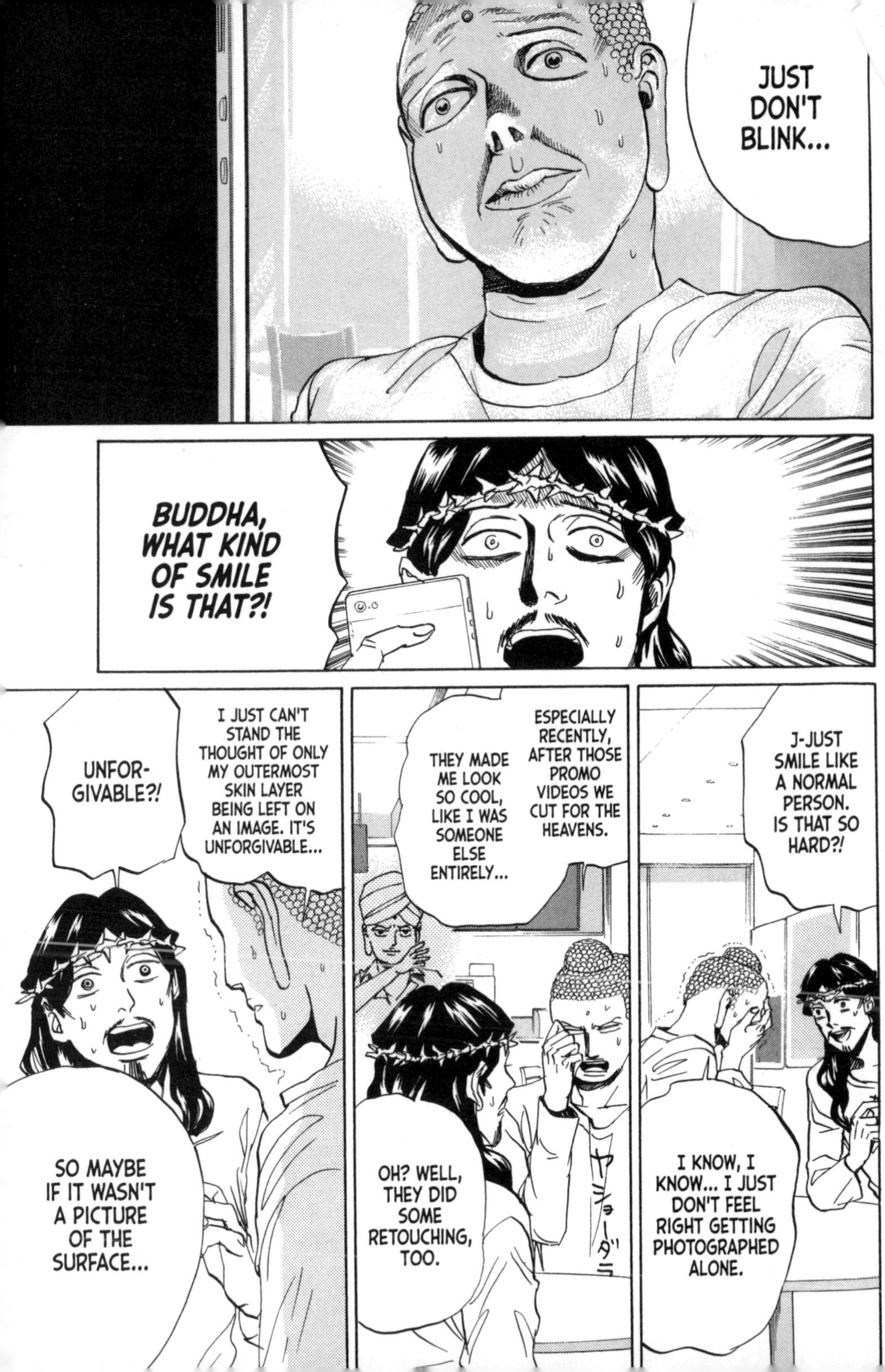
JUST DON'T BLINK...
BUDDHA, WHAT KIND OF SMILE IS THAT?!
J-JUST SMILE LIKE A NORMAL PERSON. IS THAT SO HARD?!
I KNOW, I KNOW... I JUST DON'T FEEL RIGHT GETTING PHOTOGRAPHED ALONE.
ESPECIALLY RECENTLY, AFTER THOSE PROMO VIDEOS WE CUT FOR THE HEAVENS.
THEY MADE ME LOOK SO COOL, LIKE I WAS SOMEONE ELSE ENTIRELY...
OH? WELL, THEY DID SOME RETOUCHING, TOO.
ヤショーダラ
I JUST CAN'T STAND THE THOUGHT OF ONLY MY OUTERMOST SKIN LAYER BEING LEFT ON AN IMAGE. IT'S UNFORGIVABLE...
UNFOR-GIVABLE?!
SO MAYBE IF IT WASN'T A PICTURE OF THE SURFACE...

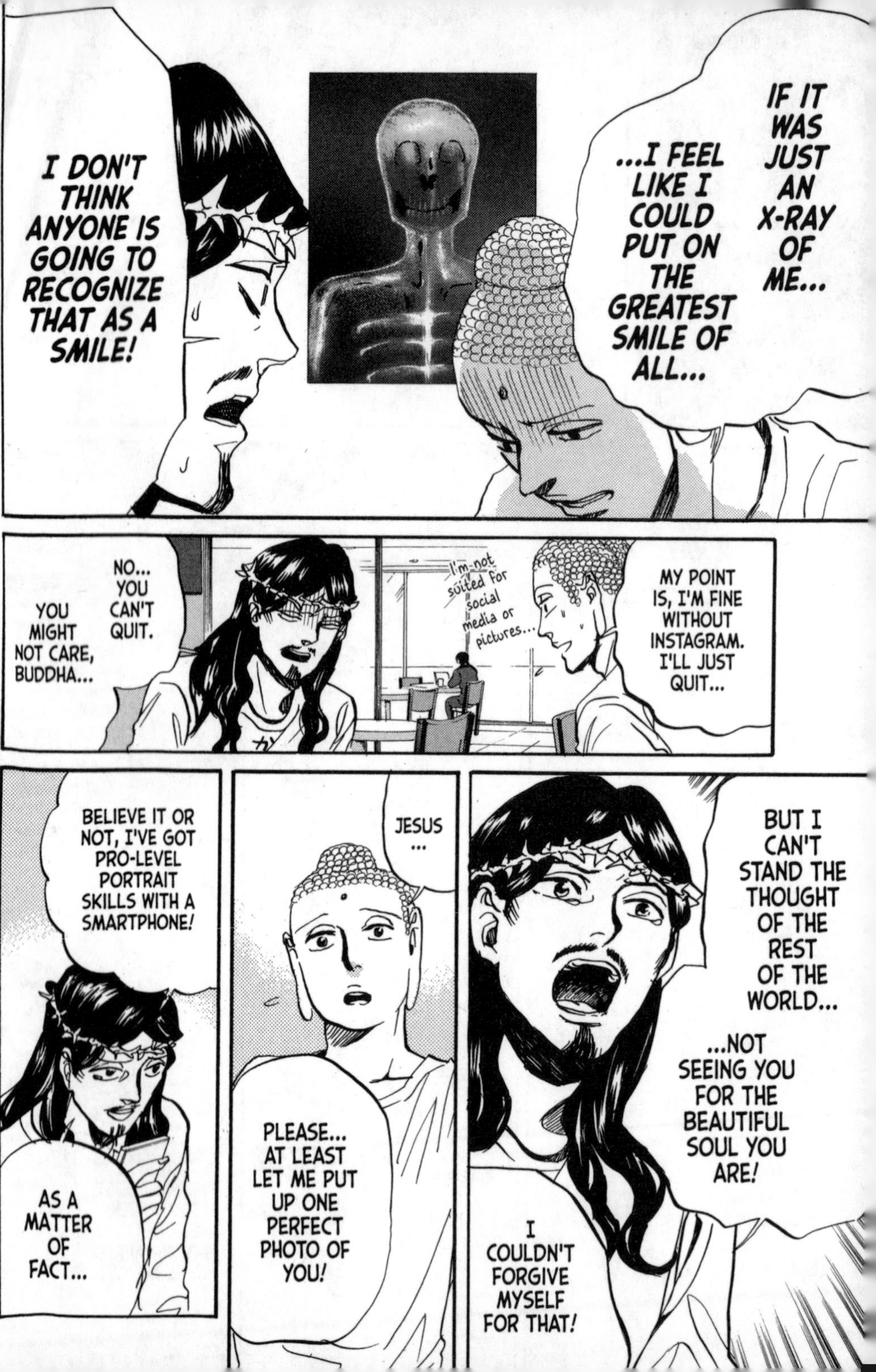
IF IT WAS JUST AN X-RAY OF ME...
...I FEEL LIKE I COULD PUT ON THE GREATEST SMILE OF ALL...
I DON'T THINK ANYONE IS GOING TO RECOGNIZE THAT AS A SMILE!
MY POINT IS, I'M FINE WITHOUT INSTAGRAM. I'LL JUST QUIT...
I'm not suited for social media or pictures...
NO... YOU CAN'T QUIT.
YOU MIGHT NOT CARE, BUDDHA...
BUT I CAN'T STAND THE THOUGHT OF THE REST OF THE WORLD...
...NOT SEEING YOU FOR THE BEAUTIFUL SOUL YOU ARE!
I COULDN'T FORGIVE MYSELF FOR THAT!
JESUS ...
PLEASE... AT LEAST LET ME PUT UP ONE PERFECT PHOTO OF YOU!
BELIEVE IT OR NOT, I'VE GOT PRO-LEVEL PORTRAIT SKILLS WITH A SMARTPHONE!
AS A MATTER OF FACT...

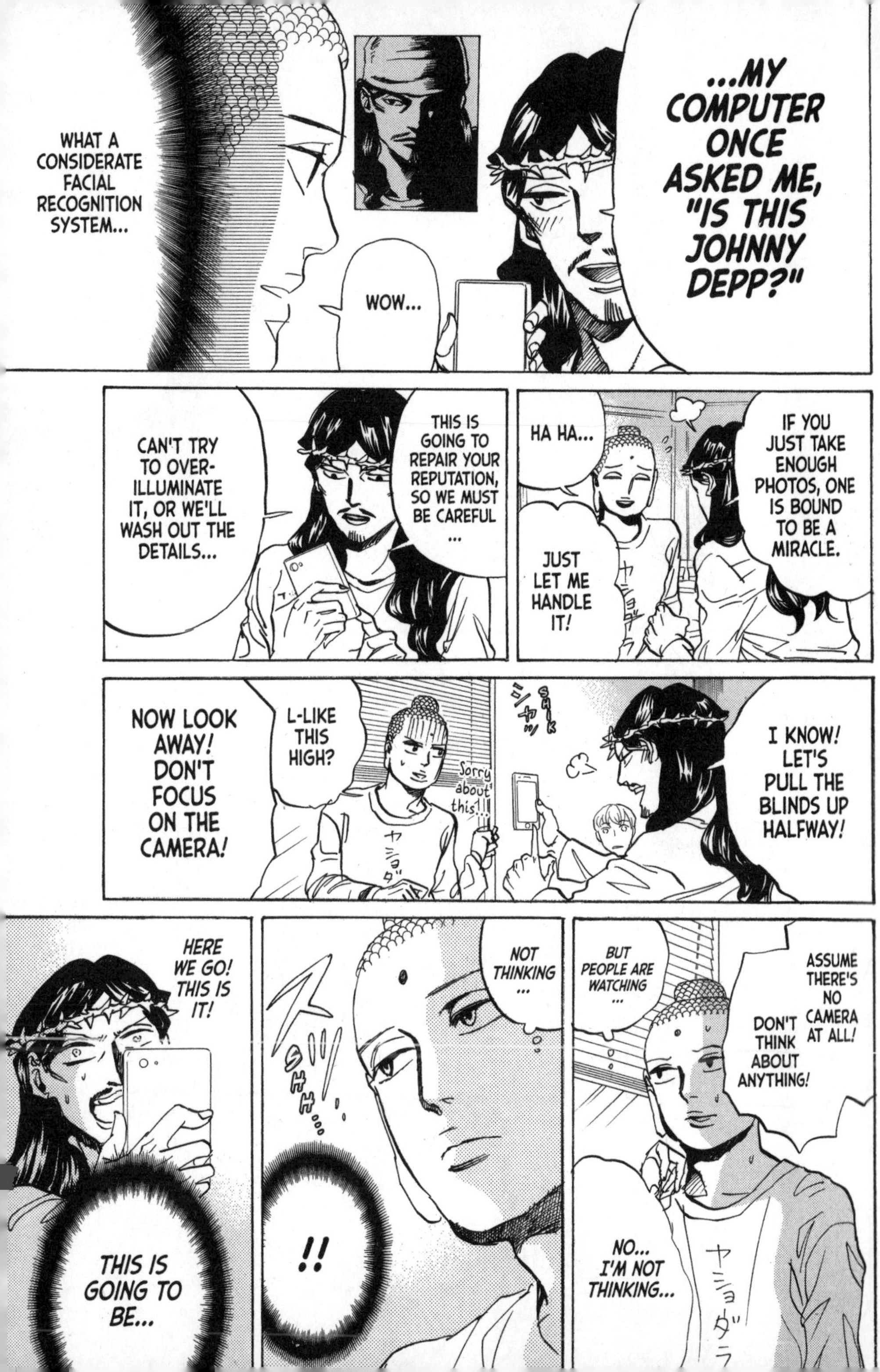
...MY COMPUTER ONCE ASKED ME, "IS THIS JOHNNY DEPP?"
WOW...
WHAT A CONSIDERATE FACIAL RECOGNITION SYSTEM...
IF YOU JUST TAKE ENOUGH PHOTOS, ONE IS BOUND TO BE A MIRACLE.
HA HA...
JUST LET ME HANDLE IT!
THIS IS GOING TO REPAIR YOUR REPUTATION, SO WE MUST BE CAREFUL ...
CAN'T TRY TO OVER-ILLUMINATE IT, OR WE'LL WASH OUT THE DETAILS...
SHIK
I KNOW! LET'S PULL THE BLINDS UP HALFWAY!
L-LIKE THIS HIGH?
Sorry about this!!
NOW LOOK AWAY! DON'T FOCUS ON THE CAMERA!
ASSUME THERE'S NO CAMERA AT ALL!
DON'T THINK ABOUT ANYTHING!
BUT PEOPLE ARE WATCHING ...
NO... I'M NOT THINKING...
NOT THINKING ...
SHH...
!!
HERE WE GO! THIS IS IT!
THIS IS GOING TO BE...

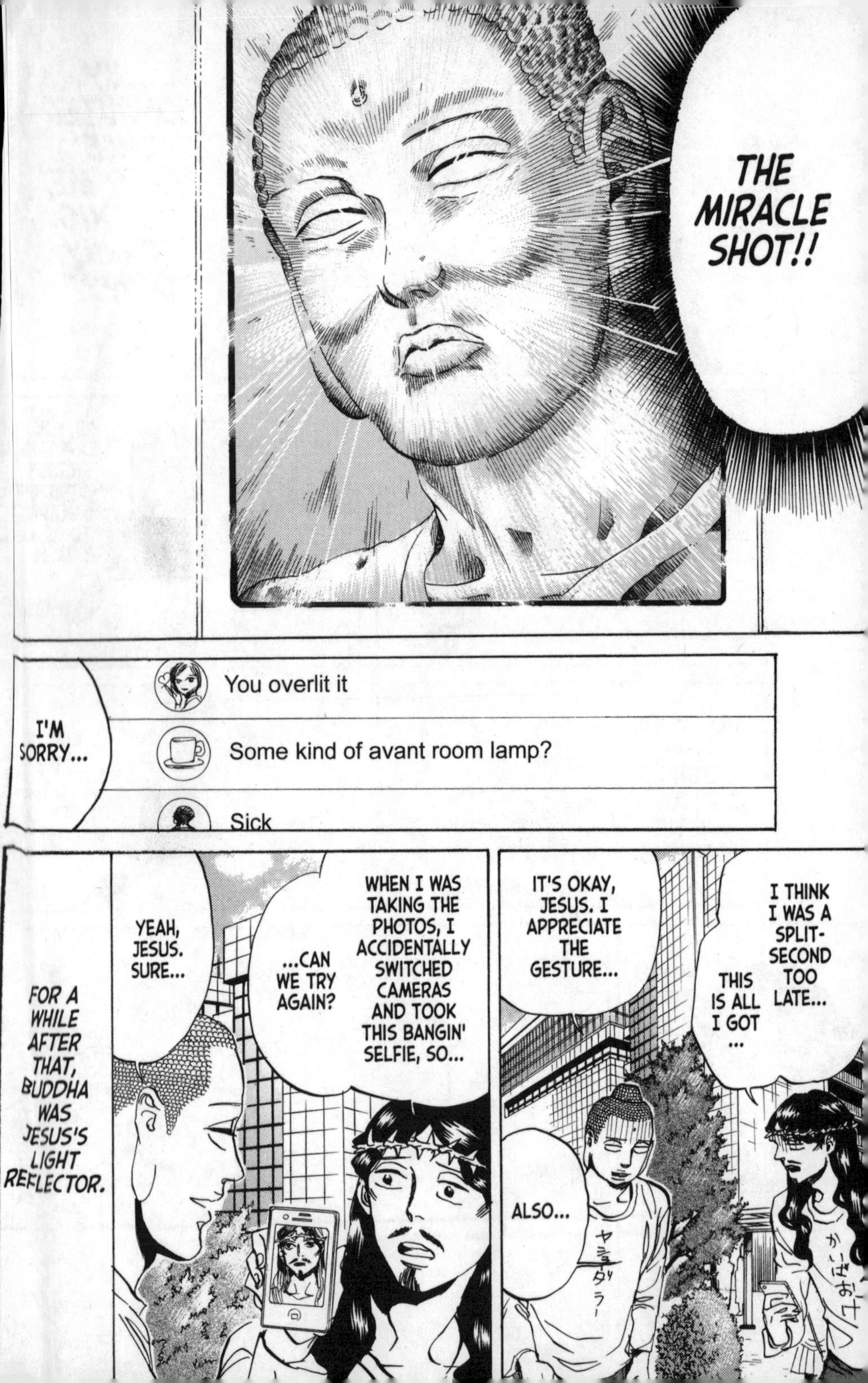
THE MIRACLE SHOT!!
You overlit it
Some kind of avant room lamp?
Sick
I'M SORRY...
I THINK I WAS A SPLIT-SECOND TOO LATE...
THIS IS ALL I GOT ...
IT'S OKAY, JESUS. I APPRECIATE THE GESTURE...
ALSO...
WHEN I WAS TAKING THE PHOTOS, I ACCIDENTALLY SWITCHED CAMERAS AND TOOK THIS BANGIN' SELFIE, SO...
...CAN WE TRY AGAIN?
YEAH, JESUS. SURE...
FOR A WHILE AFTER THAT, BUDDHA WAS JESUS'S LIGHT REFLECTOR.

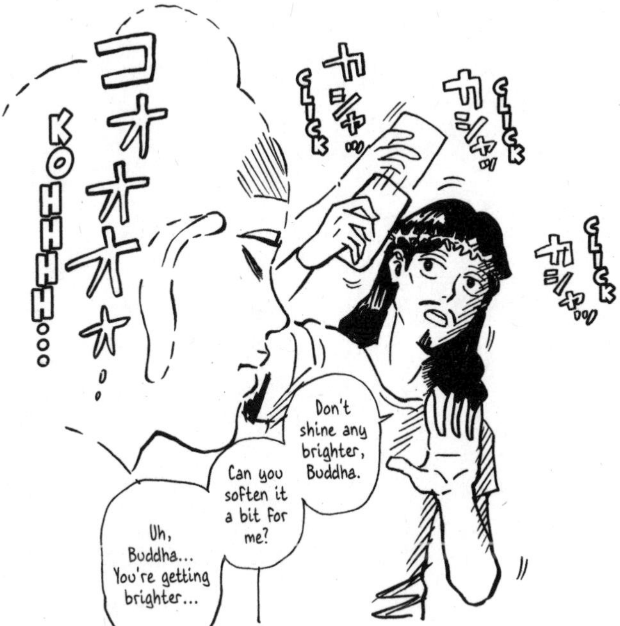
CLICK
カシャッ
CLICK
カシャッ
カシャッ
CLICK
コォオオォ…
KOHHHH…
Don't shine any brighter, Buddha.
Can you soften it a bit for me?
Uh, Buddha… You're getting brighter…

The ascetic trial of being forced to served as a light reflector for someone else's selfies

SAINT☆YOUNG MEN

CHAPTER 77 TRANSLATION NOTES

Yasodhara, page 67
The wife of Gautama Buddha, and the mother of Rahula, their son.

Archaic smile, page 71
The archaic smile is the name of a type of facial expression often seen on ancient Greek sculpture.

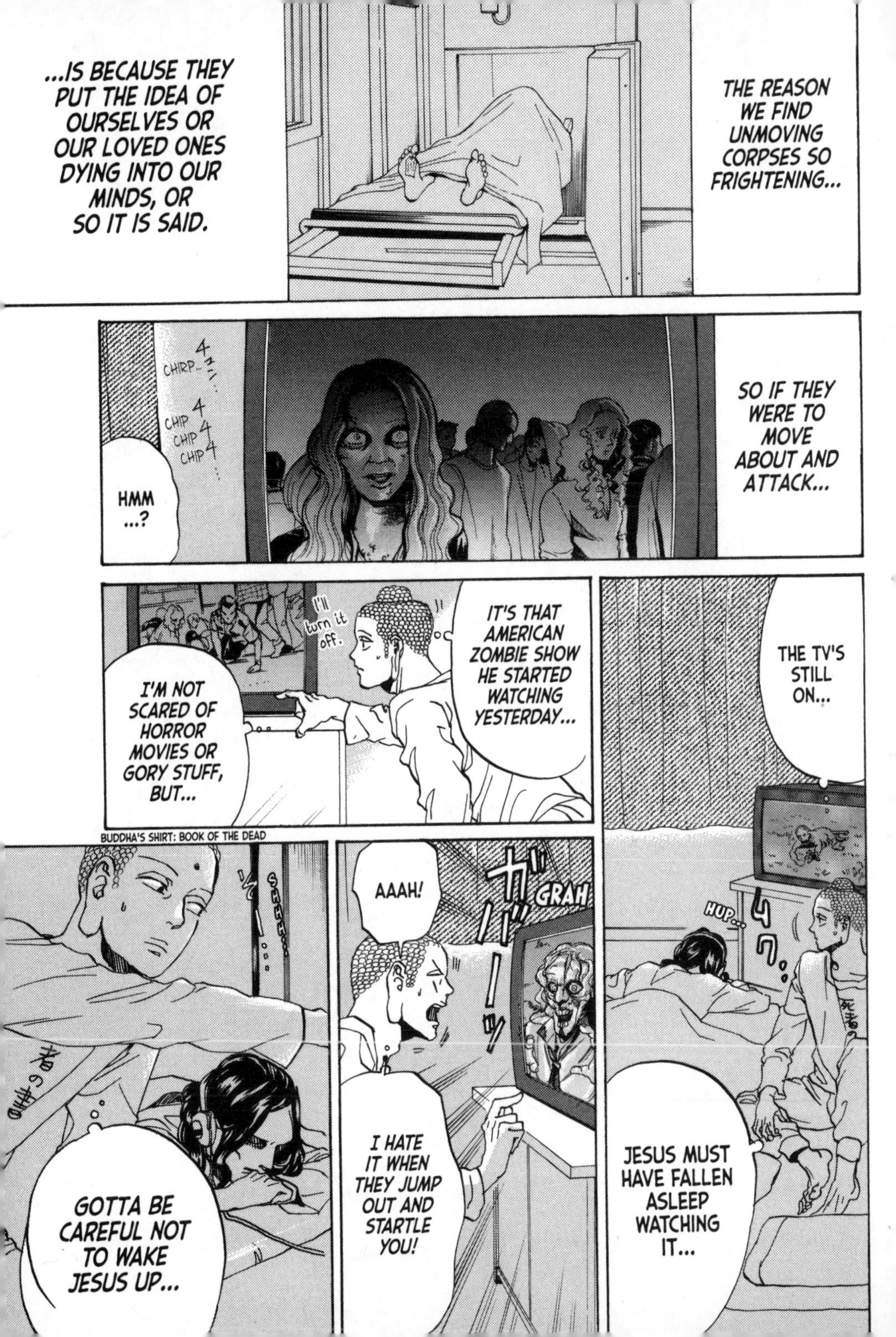
THE REASON WE FIND UNMOVING CORPSES SO FRIGHTENING...
...IS BECAUSE THEY PUT THE IDEA OF OURSELVES OR OUR LOVED ONES DYING INTO OUR MINDS, OR SO IT IS SAID.
SO IF THEY WERE TO MOVE ABOUT AND ATTACK...
CHIRP...
CHIP CHIP CHIP
HMM ...?
THE TV'S STILL ON...
HUP...
JESUS MUST HAVE FALLEN ASLEEP WATCHING IT...
IT'S THAT AMERICAN ZOMBIE SHOW HE STARTED WATCHING YESTERDAY...
I'll turn it off.
I'M NOT SCARED OF HORROR MOVIES OR GORY STUFF, BUT...
BUDDHA'S SHIRT: BOOK OF THE DEAD
AAAH!
GRAH
I HATE IT WHEN THEY JUMP OUT AND STARTLE YOU!
SHHH...
GOTTA BE CAREFUL NOT TO WAKE JESUS UP...

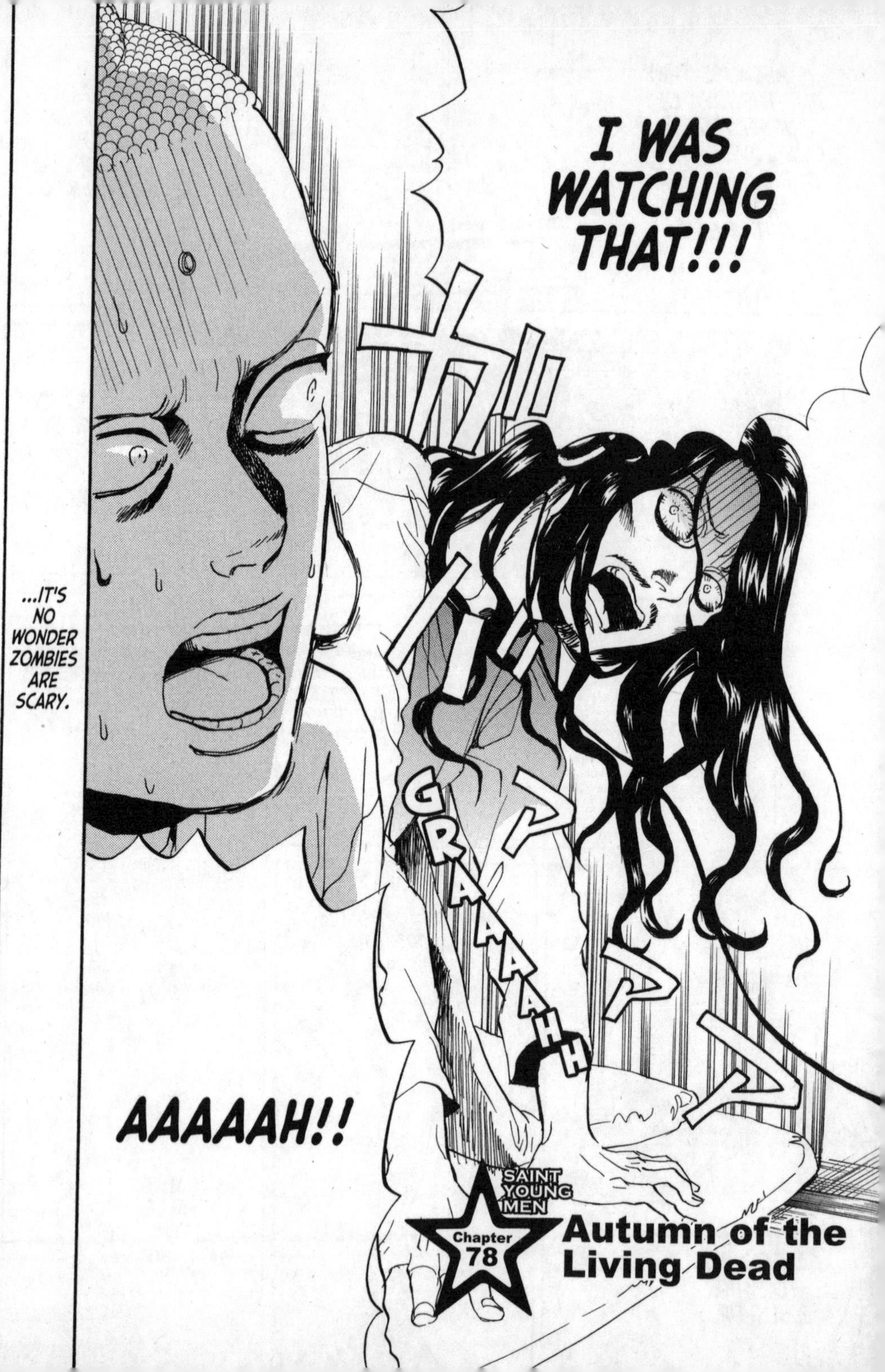
I WAS WATCHING THAT!!!
GRAAAAAHH
...IT'S NO WONDER ZOMBIES ARE SCARY.
AAAAAH!!
SAINT YOUNG MEN
Chapter 78
Autumn of the Living Dead

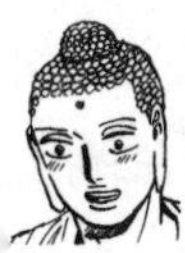

BUDDHA
ALL THE MOVIES AND TV SHOWS YOU CAN WATCH, FOR ONE SIMPLE PRICE A MONTH?! THAT'S A STEAL! BUT WITH THE WAY JESUS GOT SUCKED INTO IT, BUDDHA REALIZED THAT THE POWER BILL COULD BE HUGE.

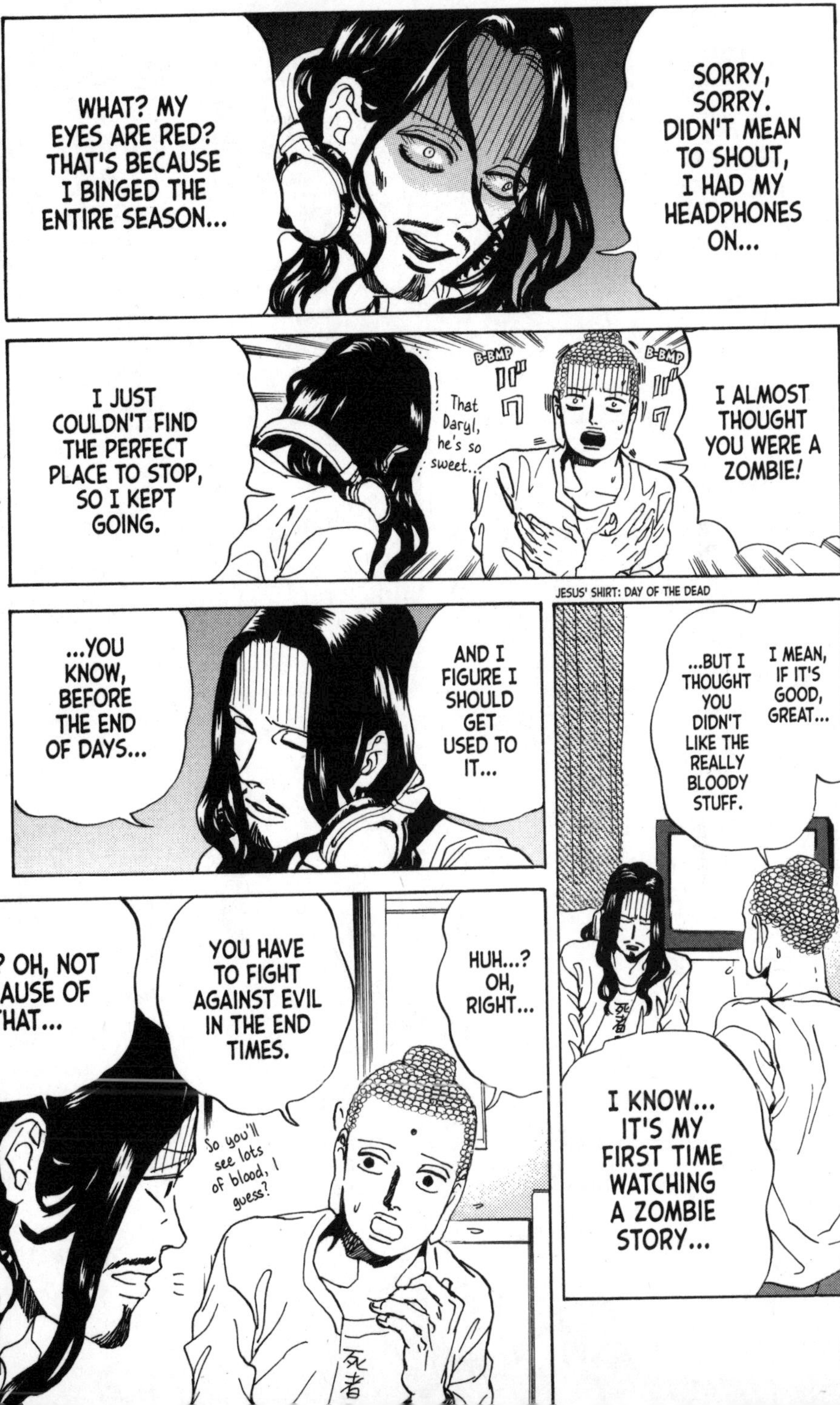
SORRY, SORRY. DIDN'T MEAN TO SHOUT, I HAD MY HEADPHONES ON...
WHAT? MY EYES ARE RED? THAT'S BECAUSE I BINGED THE ENTIRE SEASON...
I ALMOST THOUGHT YOU WERE A ZOMBIE!
B-BMP
B-BMP
That Daryl, he's so sweet...
I JUST COULDN'T FIND THE PERFECT PLACE TO STOP, SO I KEPT GOING.
JESUS' SHIRT: DAY OF THE DEAD
I MEAN, IF IT'S GOOD, GREAT...
...BUT I THOUGHT YOU DIDN'T LIKE THE REALLY BLOODY STUFF.
I KNOW... IT'S MY FIRST TIME WATCHING A ZOMBIE STORY...
AND I FIGURE I SHOULD GET USED TO IT...
...YOU KNOW, BEFORE THE END OF DAYS...
HUH...? OH, RIGHT...
So you'll see lots of blood, I guess?
YOU HAVE TO FIGHT AGAINST EVIL IN THE END TIMES.
HUH? OH, NOT BECAUSE OF THAT...

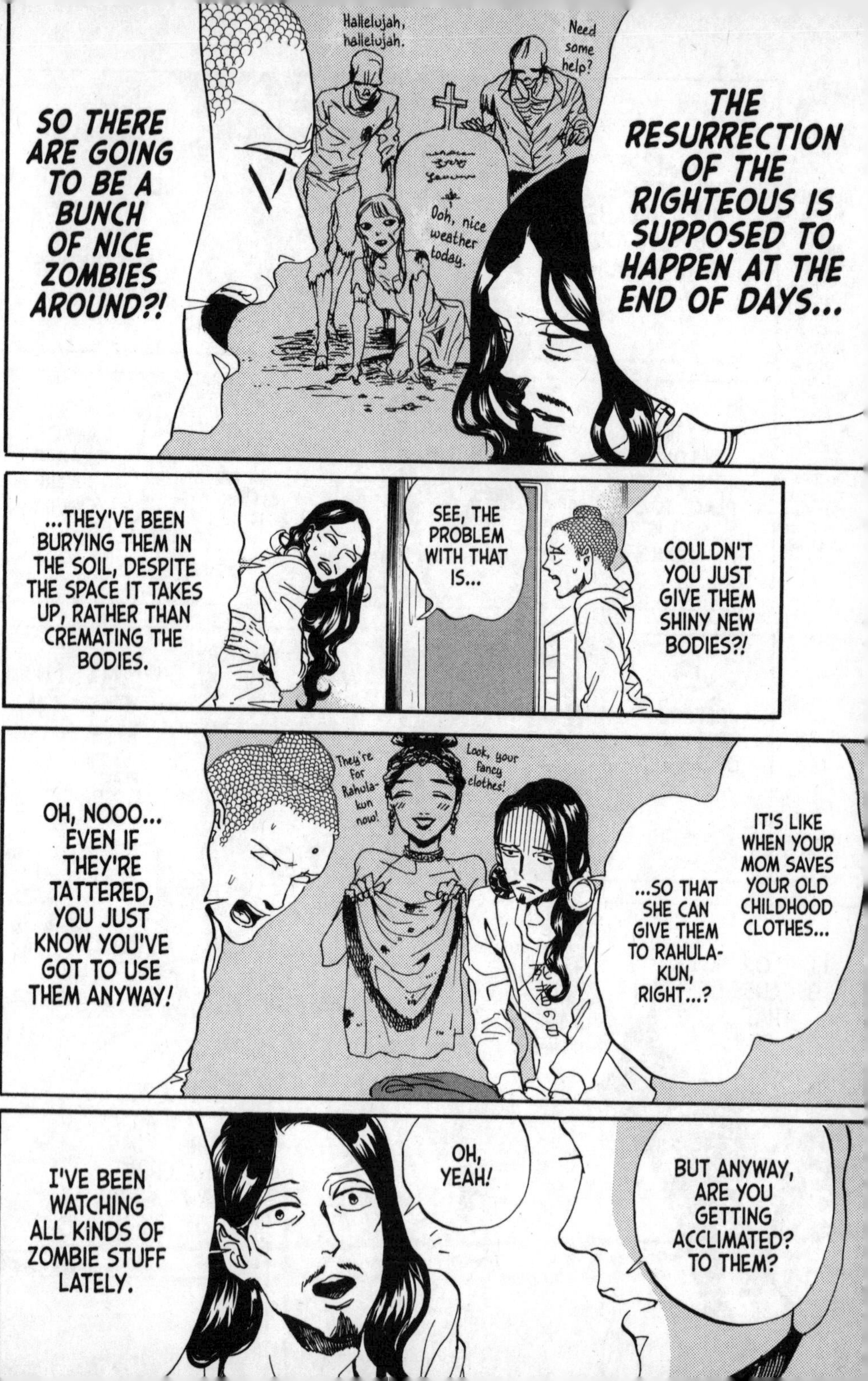
THE RESURRECTION OF THE RIGHTEOUS IS SUPPOSED TO HAPPEN AT THE END OF DAYS...
Need some help?
Hallelujah, hallelujah.
Ooh, nice weather today.
SO THERE ARE GOING TO BE A BUNCH OF NICE ZOMBIES AROUND?!
COULDN'T YOU JUST GIVE THEM SHINY NEW BODIES?!
SEE, THE PROBLEM WITH THAT IS...
...THEY'VE BEEN BURYING THEM IN THE SOIL, DESPITE THE SPACE IT TAKES UP, RATHER THAN CREMATING THE BODIES.
IT'S LIKE WHEN YOUR MOM SAVES YOUR OLD CHILDHOOD CLOTHES...
...SO THAT SHE CAN GIVE THEM TO RAHULA-KUN, RIGHT...?
Look, your fancy clothes!
They're for Rahula-kun now!
OH, NOOO... EVEN IF THEY'RE TATTERED, YOU JUST KNOW YOU'VE GOT TO USE THEM ANYWAY!
BUT ANYWAY, ARE YOU GETTING ACCLIMATED? TO THEM?
OH, YEAH!
I'VE BEEN WATCHING ALL KINDS OF ZOMBIE STUFF LATELY.

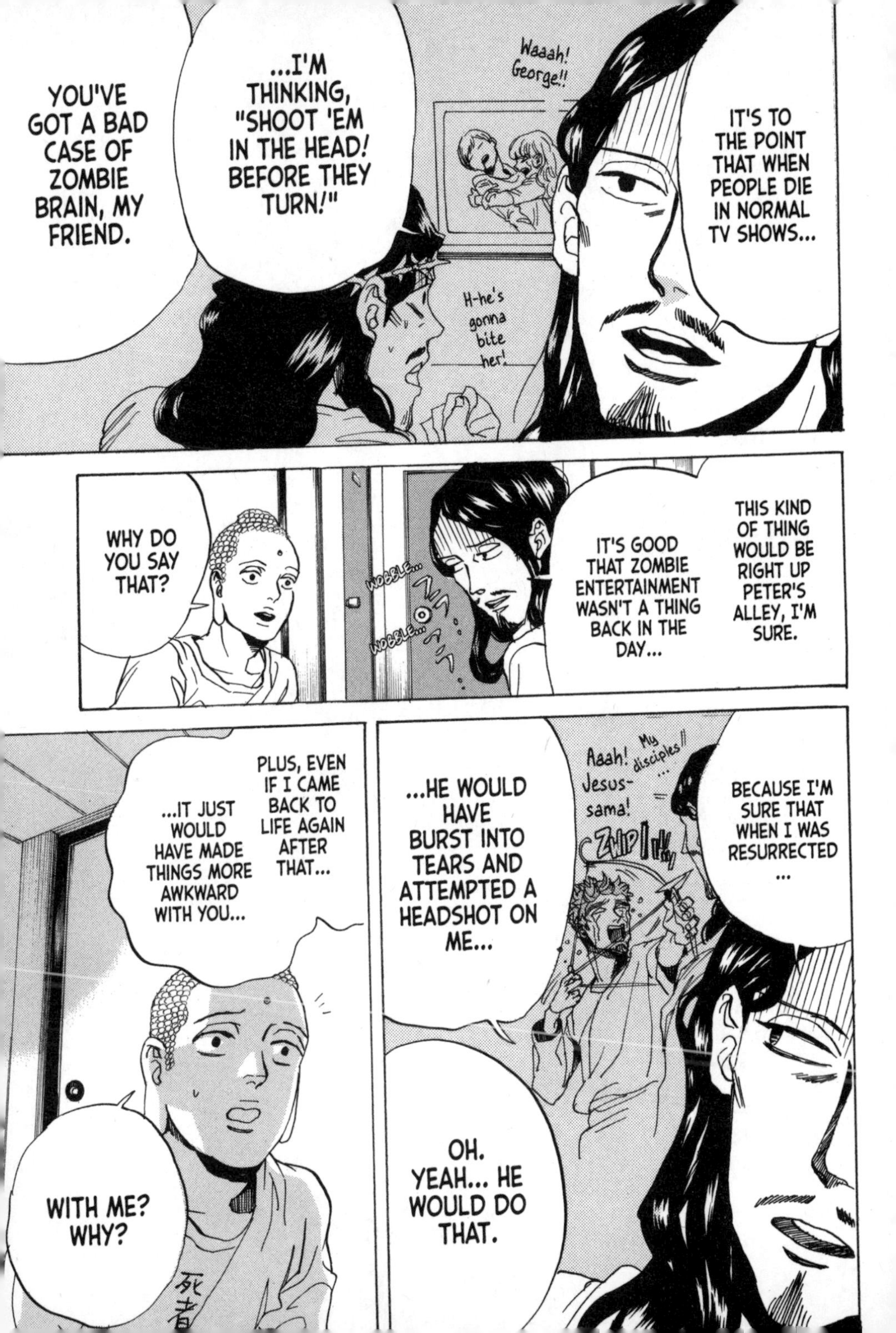
IT'S TO THE POINT THAT WHEN PEOPLE DIE IN NORMAL TV SHOWS...
Waaah! George!!
...I'M THINKING, "SHOOT 'EM IN THE HEAD! BEFORE THEY TURN!"
H-he's gonna bite her!
YOU'VE GOT A BAD CASE OF ZOMBIE BRAIN, MY FRIEND.
THIS KIND OF THING WOULD BE RIGHT UP PETER'S ALLEY, I'M SURE.
IT'S GOOD THAT ZOMBIE ENTERTAINMENT WASN'T A THING BACK IN THE DAY...
WOBBLE...
WOBBLE...
WHY DO YOU SAY THAT?
BECAUSE I'M SURE THAT WHEN I WAS RESURRECTED ...
My disciples!! ...
Aaah! Jesus-sama!
ZWIP
...HE WOULD HAVE BURST INTO TEARS AND ATTEMPTED A HEADSHOT ON ME...
OH. YEAH... HE WOULD DO THAT.
PLUS, EVEN IF I CAME BACK TO LIFE AGAIN AFTER THAT...
...IT JUST WOULD HAVE MADE THINGS MORE AWKWARD WITH YOU...
WITH ME? WHY?
死者

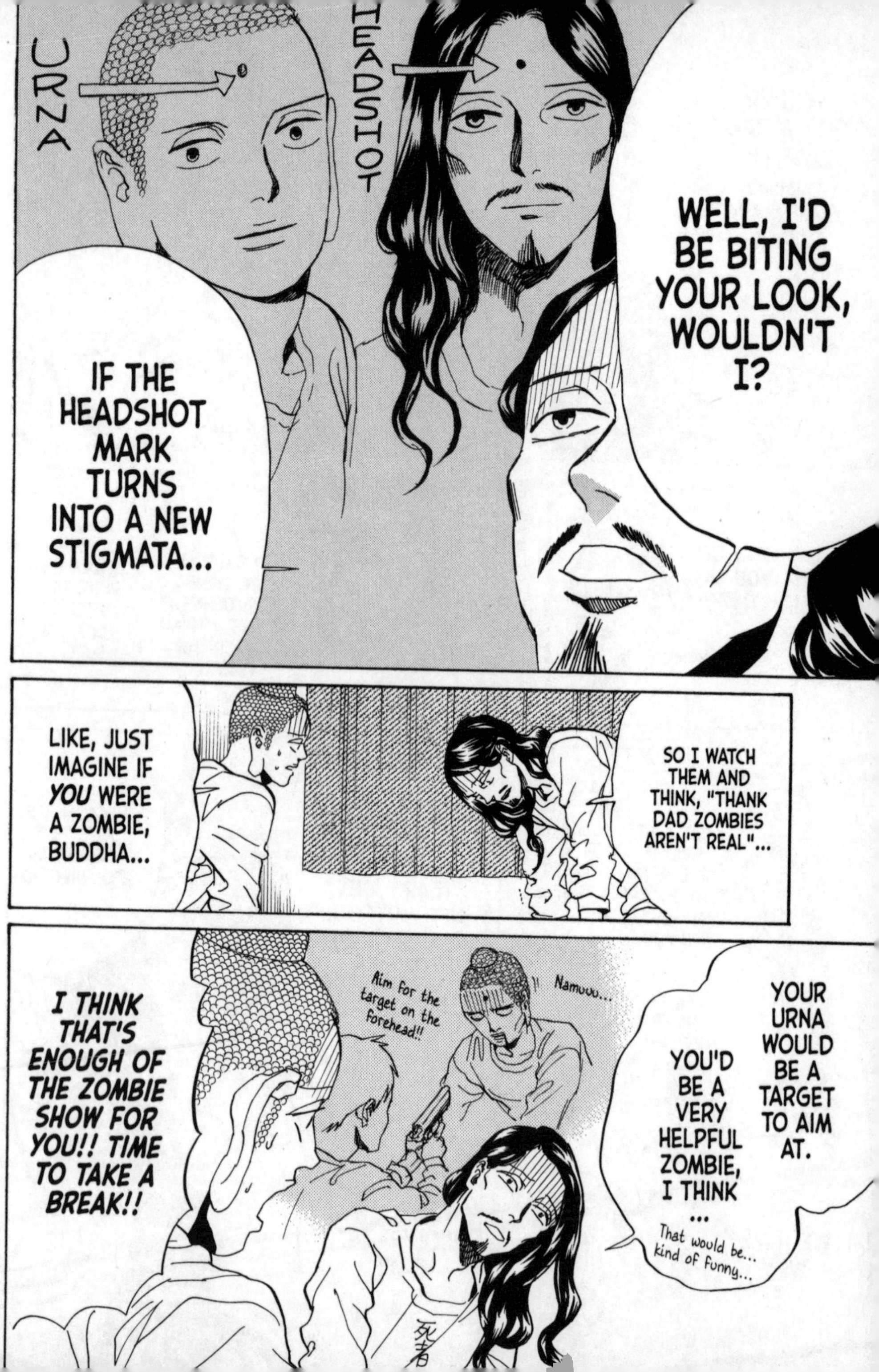
HEADSHOT
URNA
WELL, I'D BE BITING YOUR LOOK, WOULDN'T I?
IF THE HEADSHOT MARK TURNS INTO A NEW STIGMATA...
SO I WATCH THEM AND THINK, "THANK DAD ZOMBIES AREN'T REAL"...
LIKE, JUST IMAGINE IF *YOU* WERE A ZOMBIE, BUDDHA...
YOUR URNA WOULD BE A TARGET TO AIM AT.
YOU'D BE A VERY HELPFUL ZOMBIE, I THINK ...
That would be... kind of funny...
Namuuu...
Aim for the target on the forehead!!
I THINK THAT'S ENOUGH OF THE ZOMBIE SHOW FOR YOU!! TIME TO TAKE A BREAK!!
死者

JESUS
THEY'RE EVOLVING AS FAST AS SMART-PHONES THESE DAYS--RUNNING, OBSERVING TARGETS, TURNING EVEN WITHOUT A BITE. IF THEY COULD USE SMART-PHONES, THAT WOULD BE THE WORST OF ALL.

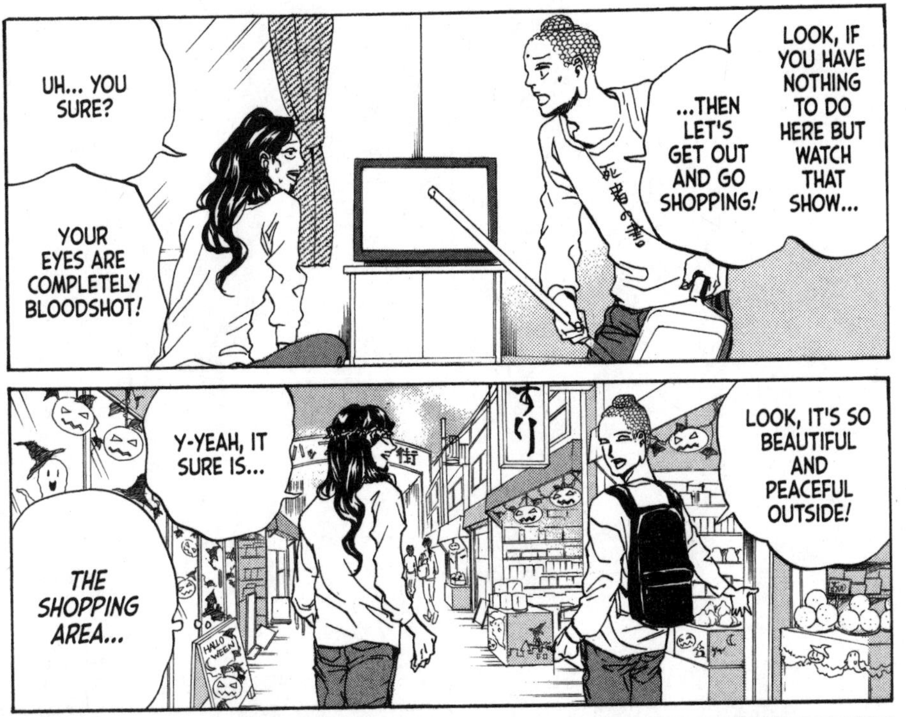
LOOK, IF YOU HAVE NOTHING TO DO HERE BUT WATCH THAT SHOW...
...THEN LET'S GET OUT AND GO SHOPPING!
UH... YOU SURE?
YOUR EYES ARE COMPLETELY BLOODSHOT!
LOOK, IT'S SO BEAUTIFUL AND PEACEFUL OUTSIDE!
Y-YEAH, IT SURE IS...
THE SHOPPING AREA...
HALLO WEEN

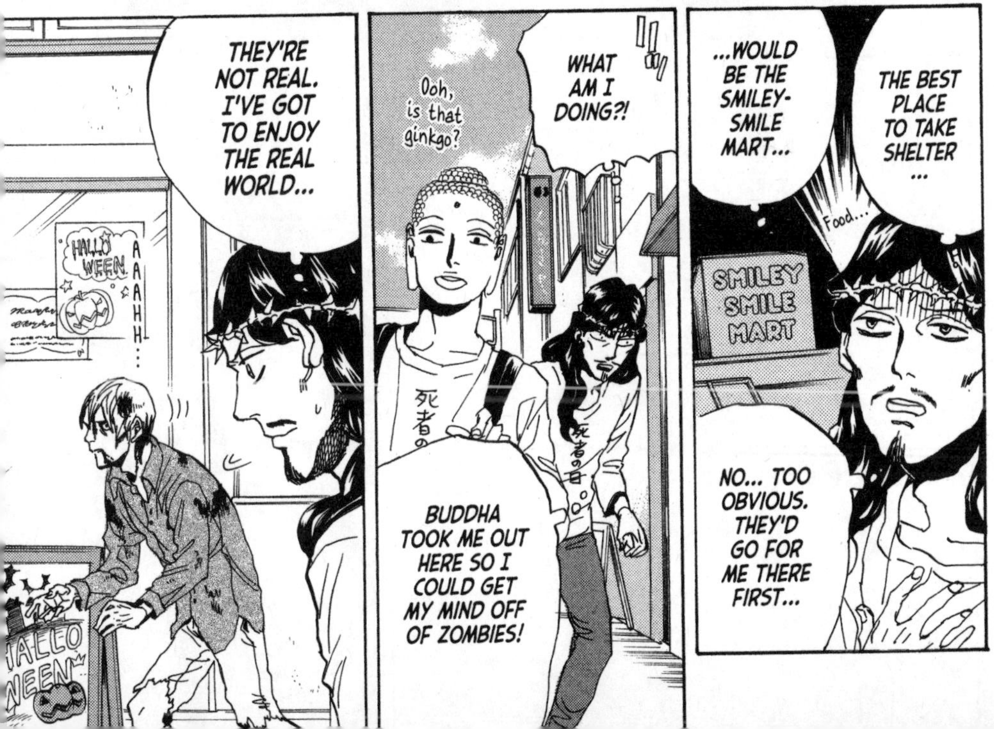
THE BEST PLACE TO TAKE SHELTER ...
...WOULD BE THE SMILEY-SMILE MART...
Food...
SMILEY SMILE MART
NO... TOO OBVIOUS. THEY'D GO FOR ME THERE FIRST...
WHAT AM I DOING?!
Ooh, is that ginkgo?
BUDDHA TOOK ME OUT HERE SO I COULD GET MY MIND OFF OF ZOMBIES!
THEY'RE NOT REAL. I'VE GOT TO ENJOY THE REAL WORLD...
HALLO WEEN
AAAHH...
HALLO WEEN

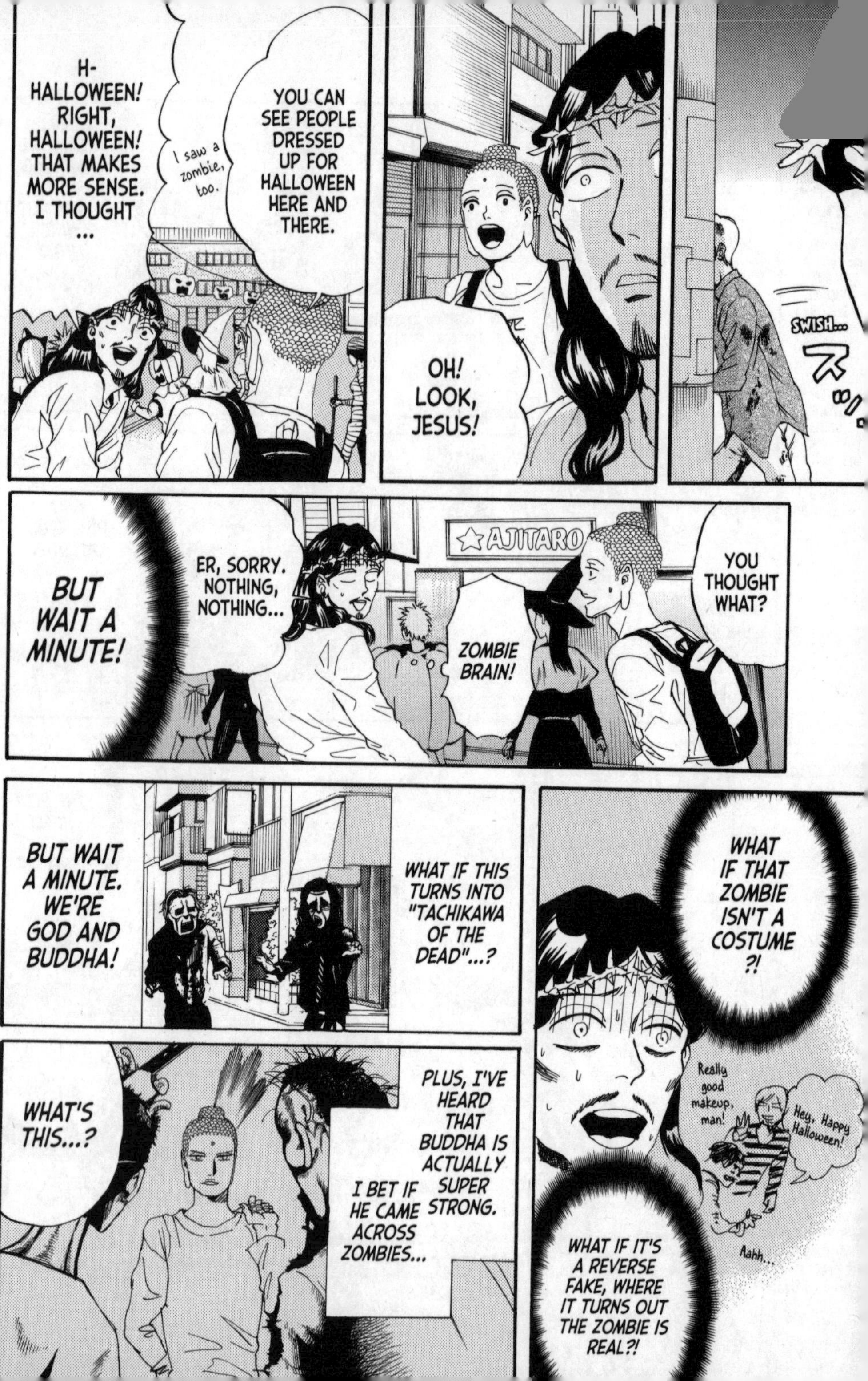
SWISH...
OH! LOOK, JESUS!
YOU CAN SEE PEOPLE DRESSED UP FOR HALLOWEEN HERE AND THERE.
I saw a zombie, too.
H-HALLOWEEN! RIGHT, HALLOWEEN! THAT MAKES MORE SENSE. I THOUGHT ...
YOU THOUGHT WHAT?
AJITARO
ZOMBIE BRAIN!
ER, SORRY. NOTHING, NOTHING...
BUT WAIT A MINUTE!
WHAT IF THAT ZOMBIE ISN'T A COSTUME?!
Hey, Happy Halloween!
Really good makeup, man!
Aahh...
WHAT IF IT'S A REVERSE FAKE, WHERE IT TURNS OUT THE ZOMBIE IS REAL?!
WHAT IF THIS TURNS INTO "TACHIKAWA OF THE DEAD"...?
BUT WAIT A MINUTE. WE'RE GOD AND BUDDHA!
PLUS, I'VE HEARD THAT BUDDHA IS ACTUALLY SUPER STRONG.
I BET IF HE CAME ACROSS ZOMBIES...
WHAT'S THIS...?

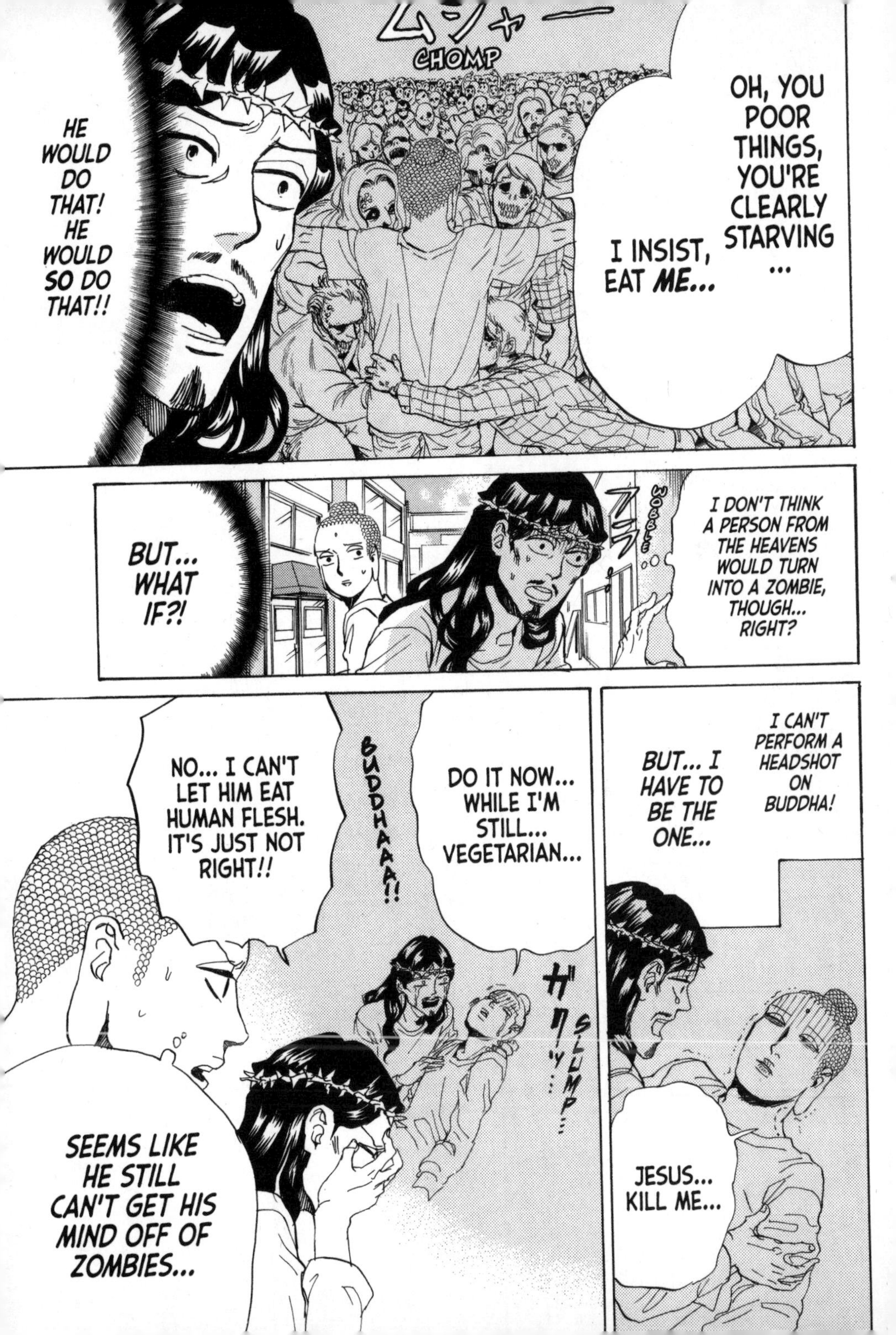
OH, YOU POOR THINGS, YOU'RE CLEARLY STARVING...
I INSIST, EAT ME...
ムシャー
CHOMP
HE WOULD DO THAT! HE WOULD SO DO THAT!!
I DON'T THINK A PERSON FROM THE HEAVENS WOULD TURN INTO A ZOMBIE, THOUGH... RIGHT?
WOBBLE
BUT... WHAT IF?!
I CAN'T PERFORM A HEADSHOT ON BUDDHA!
BUT... I HAVE TO BE THE ONE...
JESUS... KILL ME...
DO IT NOW... WHILE I'M STILL... VEGETARIAN...
BUDDHAAA!!
SLUMP...
NO... I CAN'T LET HIM EAT HUMAN FLESH. IT'S JUST NOT RIGHT!!
SEEMS LIKE HE STILL CAN'T GET HIS MIND OFF OF ZOMBIES...

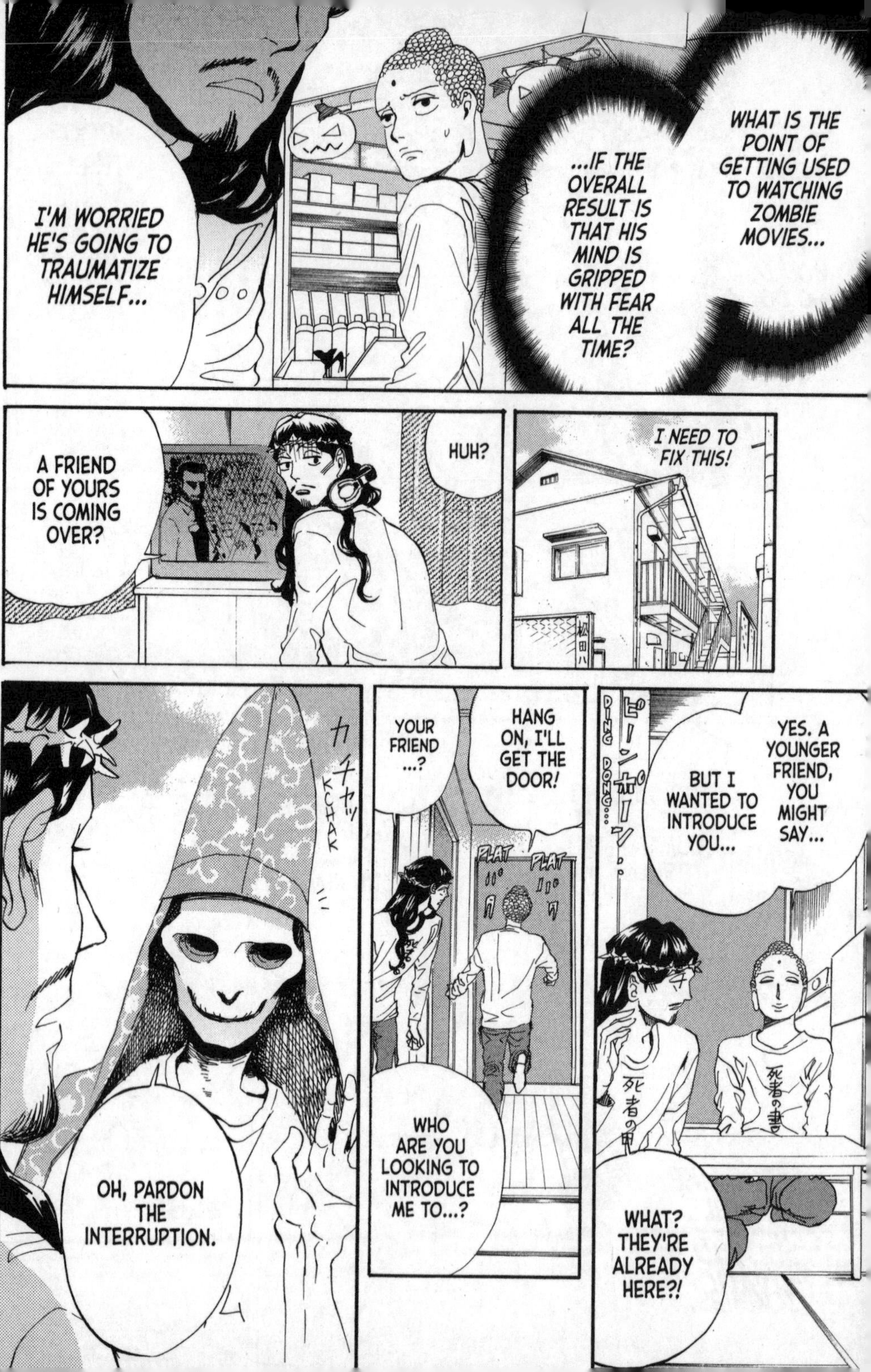
WHAT IS THE POINT OF GETTING USED TO WATCHING ZOMBIE MOVIES...
...IF THE OVERALL RESULT IS THAT HIS MIND IS GRIPPED WITH FEAR ALL THE TIME?
I'M WORRIED HE'S GOING TO TRAUMATIZE HIMSELF...
I NEED TO FIX THIS!
HUH?
A FRIEND OF YOURS IS COMING OVER?
YES. A YOUNGER FRIEND, YOU MIGHT SAY...
BUT I WANTED TO INTRODUCE YOU...
ピンポーン。。
DING DONG...
WHAT? THEY'RE ALREADY HERE?!
HANG ON, I'LL GET THE DOOR!
YOUR FRIEND ...?
パタパタ
PLAT PLAT
WHO ARE YOU LOOKING TO INTRODUCE ME TO...?
カチャッ
KCHAK
OH, PARDON THE INTERRUPTION.

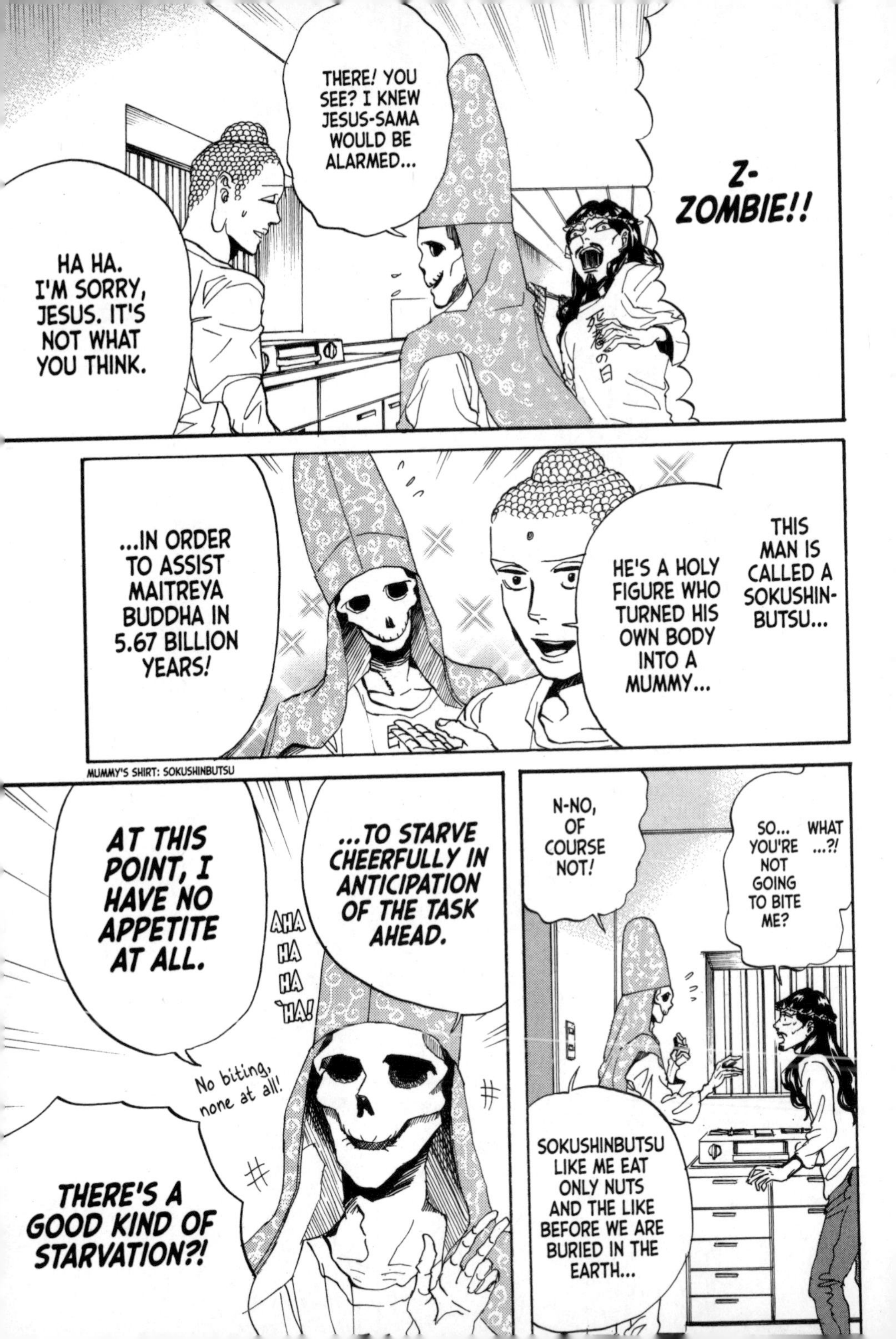
Z-ZOMBIE!!
THERE! YOU SEE? I KNEW JESUS-SAMA WOULD BE ALARMED...
HA HA. I'M SORRY, JESUS. IT'S NOT WHAT YOU THINK.
THIS MAN IS CALLED A SOKUSHIN-BUTSU...
HE'S A HOLY FIGURE WHO TURNED HIS OWN BODY INTO A MUMMY...
...IN ORDER TO ASSIST MAITREYA BUDDHA IN 5.67 BILLION YEARS!
MUMMY'S SHIRT: SOKUSHINBUTSU
WHAT ...?!
SO... YOU'RE NOT GOING TO BITE ME?
N-NO, OF COURSE NOT!
SOKUSHINBUTSU LIKE ME EAT ONLY NUTS AND THE LIKE BEFORE WE ARE BURIED IN THE EARTH...
...TO STARVE CHEERFULLY IN ANTICIPATION OF THE TASK AHEAD.
AT THIS POINT, I HAVE NO APPETITE AT ALL.
AHA HA HA HA!
No biting, none at all!
THERE'S A GOOD KIND OF STARVATION?!

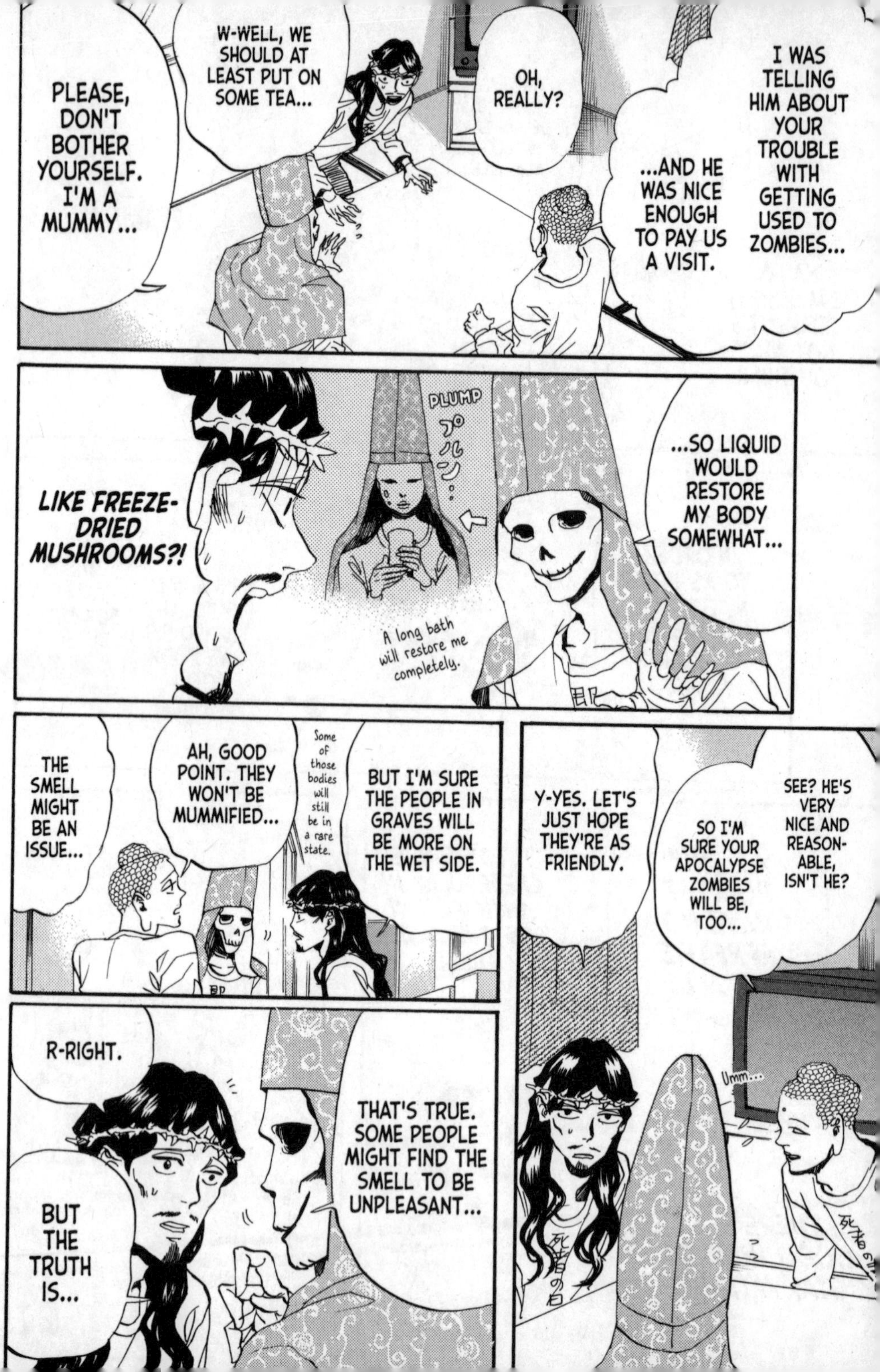
I WAS TELLING HIM ABOUT YOUR TROUBLE WITH GETTING USED TO ZOMBIES...
...AND HE WAS NICE ENOUGH TO PAY US A VISIT.
OH, REALLY?
W-WELL, WE SHOULD AT LEAST PUT ON SOME TEA...
PLEASE, DON'T BOTHER YOURSELF. I'M A MUMMY...
...SO LIQUID WOULD RESTORE MY BODY SOMEWHAT...
PLUMP
A long bath will restore me completely.
LIKE FREEZE-DRIED MUSHROOMS?!
SEE? HE'S VERY NICE AND REASON-ABLE, ISN'T HE?
SO I'M SURE YOUR APOCALYPSE ZOMBIES WILL BE, TOO...
Y-YES. LET'S JUST HOPE THEY'RE AS FRIENDLY.
Umm...
BUT I'M SURE THE PEOPLE IN GRAVES WILL BE MORE ON THE WET SIDE.
Some of those bodies will still be in a rare state.
AH, GOOD POINT. THEY WON'T BE MUMMIFIED...
THE SMELL MIGHT BE AN ISSUE...
THAT'S TRUE. SOME PEOPLE MIGHT FIND THE SMELL TO BE UNPLEASANT...
R-RIGHT.
BUT THE TRUTH IS...

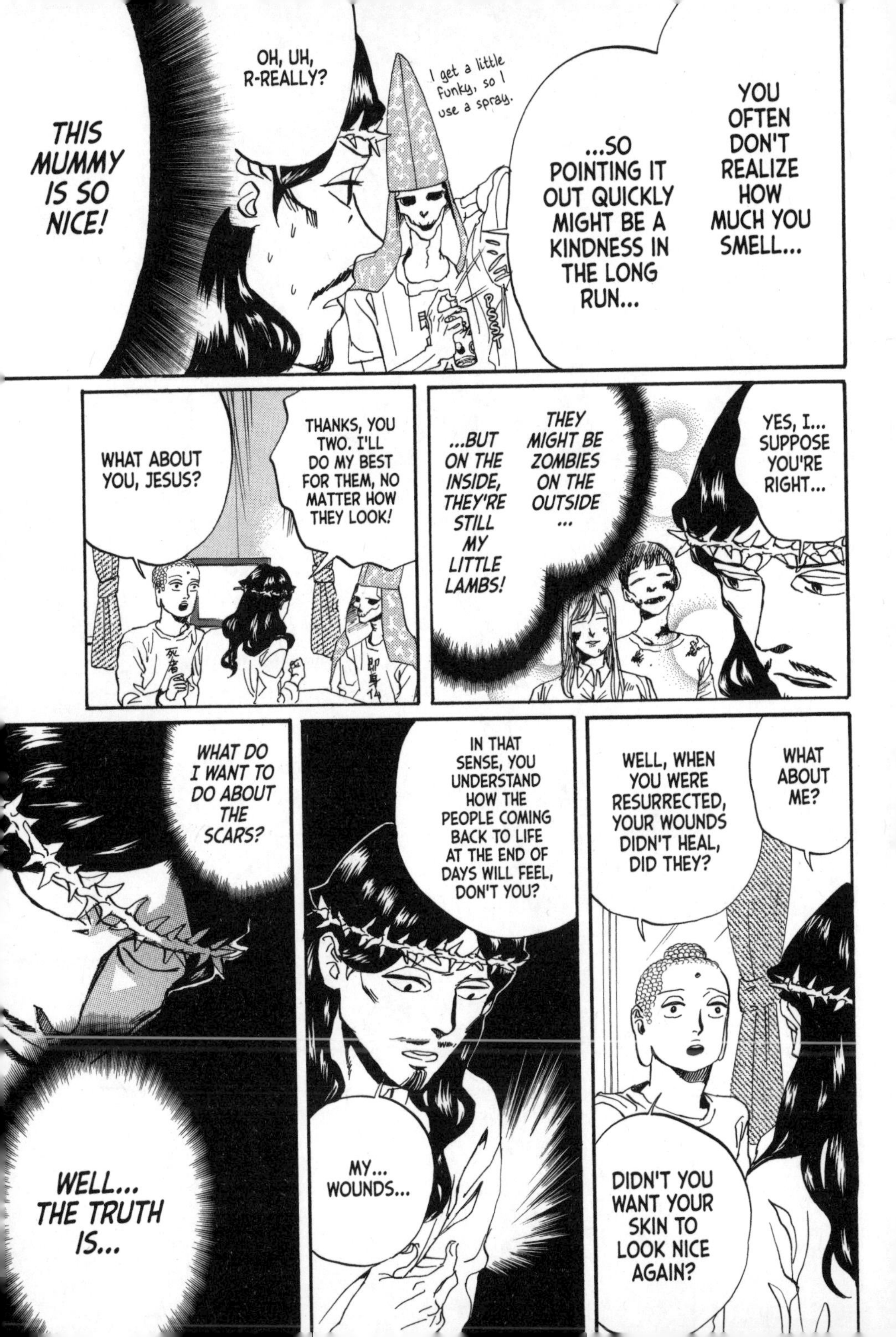
YOU OFTEN DON'T REALIZE HOW MUCH YOU SMELL...
...SO POINTING IT OUT QUICKLY MIGHT BE A KINDNESS IN THE LONG RUN...
I get a little funky, so I use a spray.
PSSST
OH, UH, R-REALLY?
THIS MUMMY IS SO NICE!
YES, I... SUPPOSE YOU'RE RIGHT...
THEY MIGHT BE ZOMBIES ON THE OUTSIDE ...
...BUT ON THE INSIDE, THEY'RE STILL MY LITTLE LAMBS!
THANKS, YOU TWO. I'LL DO MY BEST FOR THEM, NO MATTER HOW THEY LOOK!
WHAT ABOUT YOU, JESUS?
WHAT ABOUT ME?
WELL, WHEN YOU WERE RESURRECTED, YOUR WOUNDS DIDN'T HEAL, DID THEY?
DIDN'T YOU WANT YOUR SKIN TO LOOK NICE AGAIN?
IN THAT SENSE, YOU UNDERSTAND HOW THE PEOPLE COMING BACK TO LIFE AT THE END OF DAYS WILL FEEL, DON'T YOU?
MY... WOUNDS...
WHAT DO I WANT TO DO ABOUT THE SCARS?
WELL... THE TRUTH IS...

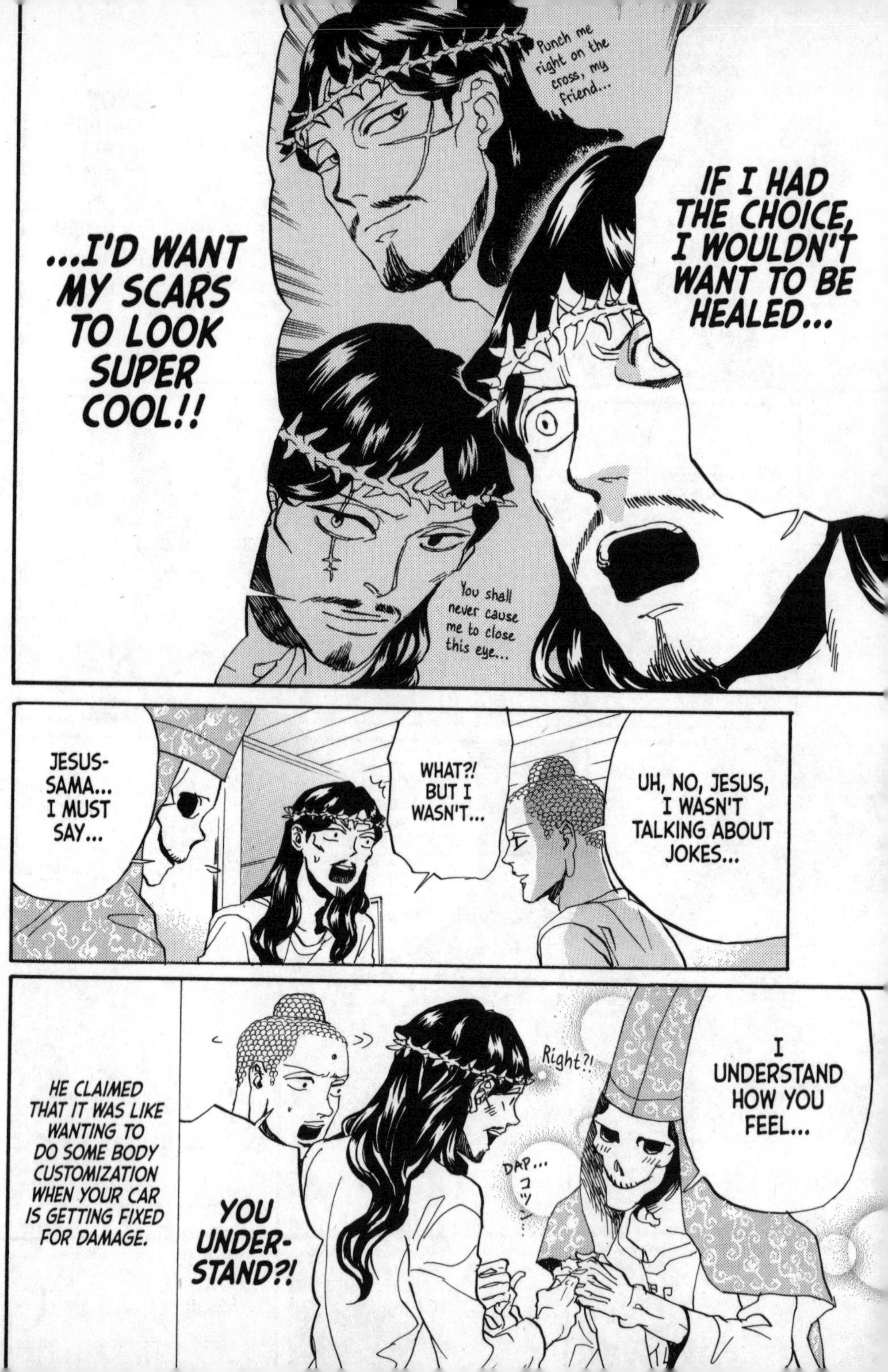
IF I HAD THE CHOICE, I WOULDN'T WANT TO BE HEALED...
Punch me right on the cross, my friend...
...I'D WANT MY SCARS TO LOOK SUPER COOL!!
You shall never cause me to close this eye...
UH, NO, JESUS, I WASN'T TALKING ABOUT JOKES...
WHAT?! BUT I WASN'T...
JESUS-SAMA... I MUST SAY...
I UNDERSTAND HOW YOU FEEL...
Right?!
DAP...
YOU UNDER-STAND?!
HE CLAIMED THAT IT WAS LIKE WANTING TO DO SOME BODY CUSTOMIZATION WHEN YOUR CAR IS GETTING FIXED FOR DAMAGE.

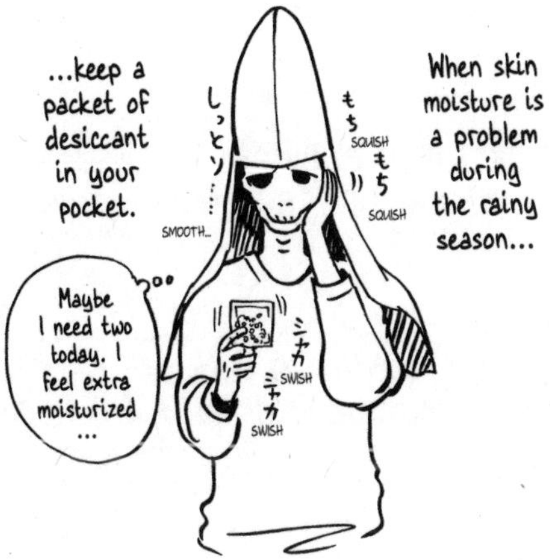
When skin moisture is a problem during the rainy season...
もち SQUISH もち SQUISH
しっとり…… SMOOTH...
...keep a packet of desiccant in your pocket.
シャカ SWISH シャカ SWISH
Maybe I need two today. I feel extra moisturized ...

CHAPTER 78 TRANSLATION NOTES

Book of the Dead, page 81

While there is an Egyptian Book of the Dead, the reference on Buddha's shirt is most likely to the Tibetan Book of the Dead, supposedly written in the 8th century. It mainly details the experiences one must go through after death to prepare for the next life to come.

Day of the Dead, page 83

Most explicitly, this would seem to reference the Mexican Dia de Muertos, a holiday for remembering dead loved ones held in early November. Although the colorful traditions associated with Dia de Muertos are Mexican in origin, the practice of observing a day to remember the dead is practiced by Catholic cultures all over, often as "All Souls' Day."

Urna, page 86

The dot on Buddha's forehead is a symbolic representation of his third eye, which gives him vision beyond the mundane world into the realm of the divine.

Mummy, page 91

A practice called *sokushinbutsu*, which refers to monks and ascetics who die (reach enlightenment) while meditating, and whose bodies are left in that state without preservatives.

Maitreya Buddha, page 91

The name of a future buddha who is said to come and usher in a new age of teaching, taking over for the current buddha of Gautama, 5.6 billion years after his death.

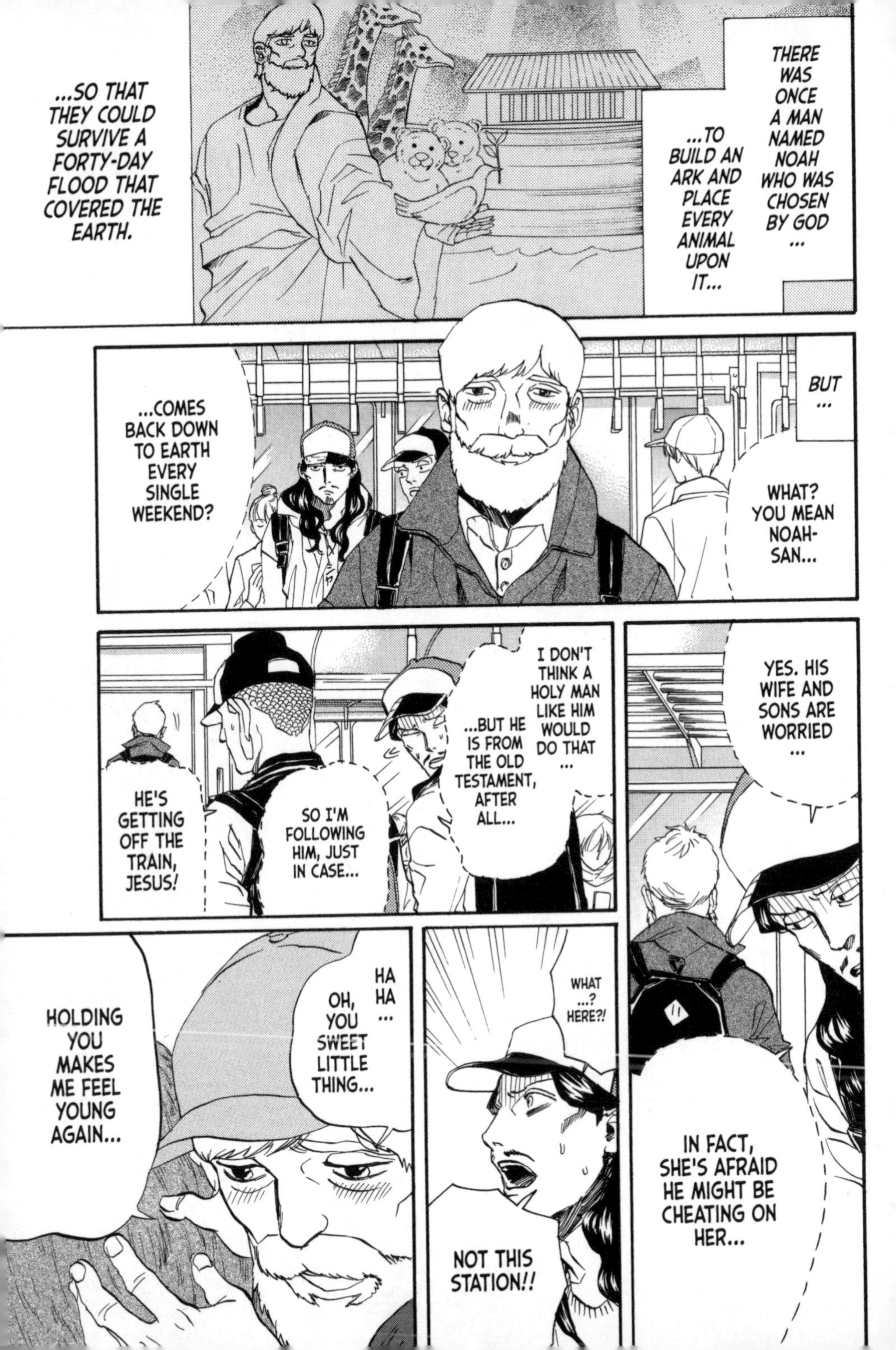
THERE WAS ONCE A MAN NAMED NOAH WHO WAS CHOSEN BY GOD ...
...TO BUILD AN ARK AND PLACE EVERY ANIMAL UPON IT...
...SO THAT THEY COULD SURVIVE A FORTY-DAY FLOOD THAT COVERED THE EARTH.
BUT ...
WHAT? YOU MEAN NOAH-SAN...
...COMES BACK DOWN TO EARTH EVERY SINGLE WEEKEND?
YES. HIS WIFE AND SONS ARE WORRIED ...
IN FACT, SHE'S AFRAID HE MIGHT BE CHEATING ON HER...
I DON'T THINK A HOLY MAN LIKE HIM WOULD DO THAT ...
...BUT HE IS FROM THE OLD TESTAMENT, AFTER ALL...
SO I'M FOLLOWING HIM, JUST IN CASE...
HE'S GETTING OFF THE TRAIN, JESUS!
WHAT ...? HERE?!
NOT THIS STATION!!
HA HA ...
OH, YOU SWEET LITTLE THING...
HOLDING YOU MAKES ME FEEL YOUNG AGAIN...

JESUS'S SHIRT: MESSIAH BUDDHA'S SHIRT: SHAKYAMUNI

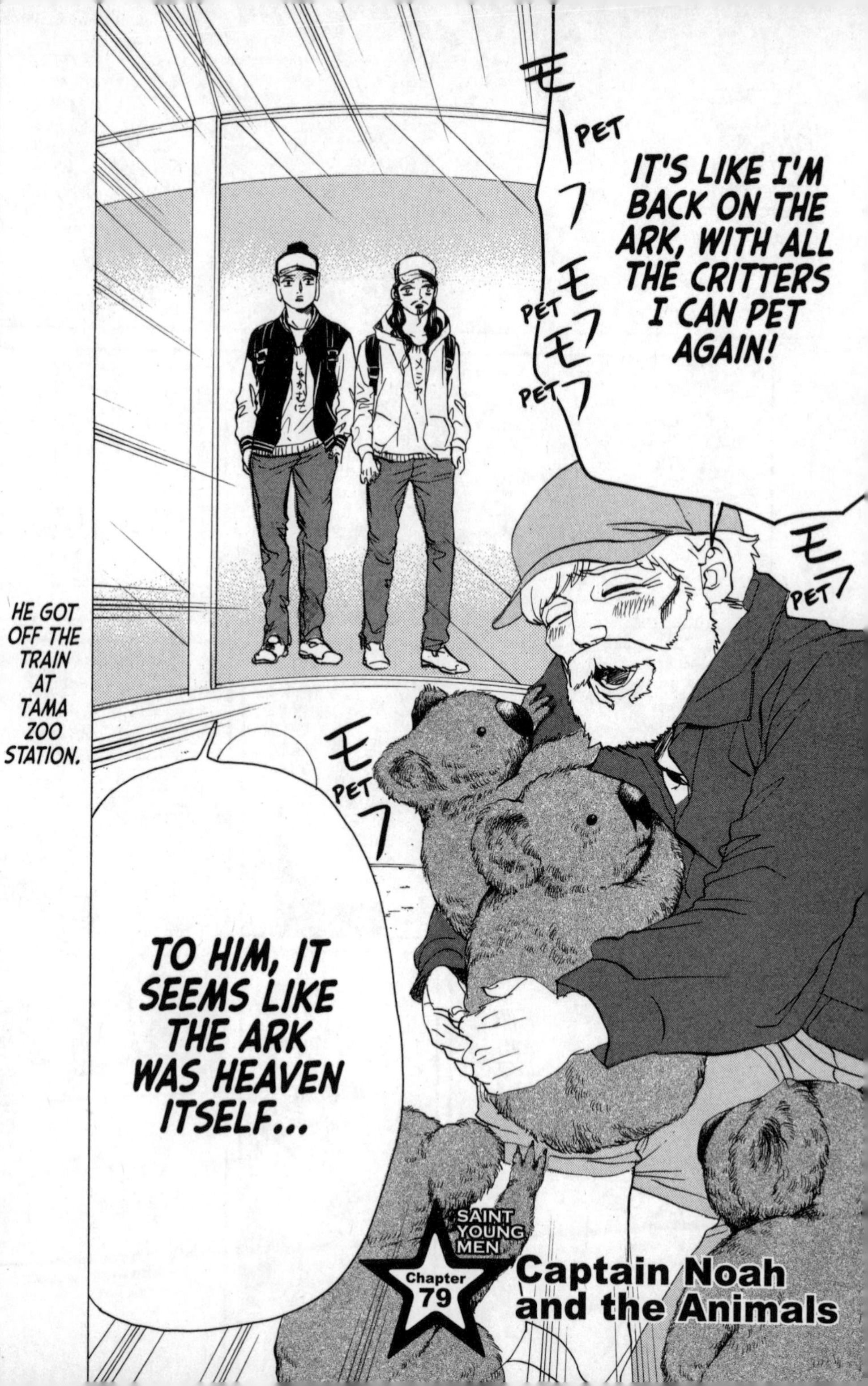

モーフ PET
モフ PET
モフ PET
IT'S LIKE I'M BACK ON THE ARK, WITH ALL THE CRITTERS I CAN PET AGAIN!
モフ PET
モフ PET
TO HIM, IT SEEMS LIKE THE ARK WAS HEAVEN ITSELF...
HE GOT OFF THE TRAIN AT TAMA ZOO STATION.
SAINT YOUNG MEN
Chapter 79
Captain Noah and the Animals

BUDDHA
HUH? PEOPLE CAN EAT THESE? JUST LIKE "DEER CRACKERS," THERE'S A SPECIAL FOOD WITH A VERY MISLEADING NAME. ANIMAL COOKIES! THEY'RE TASTY!

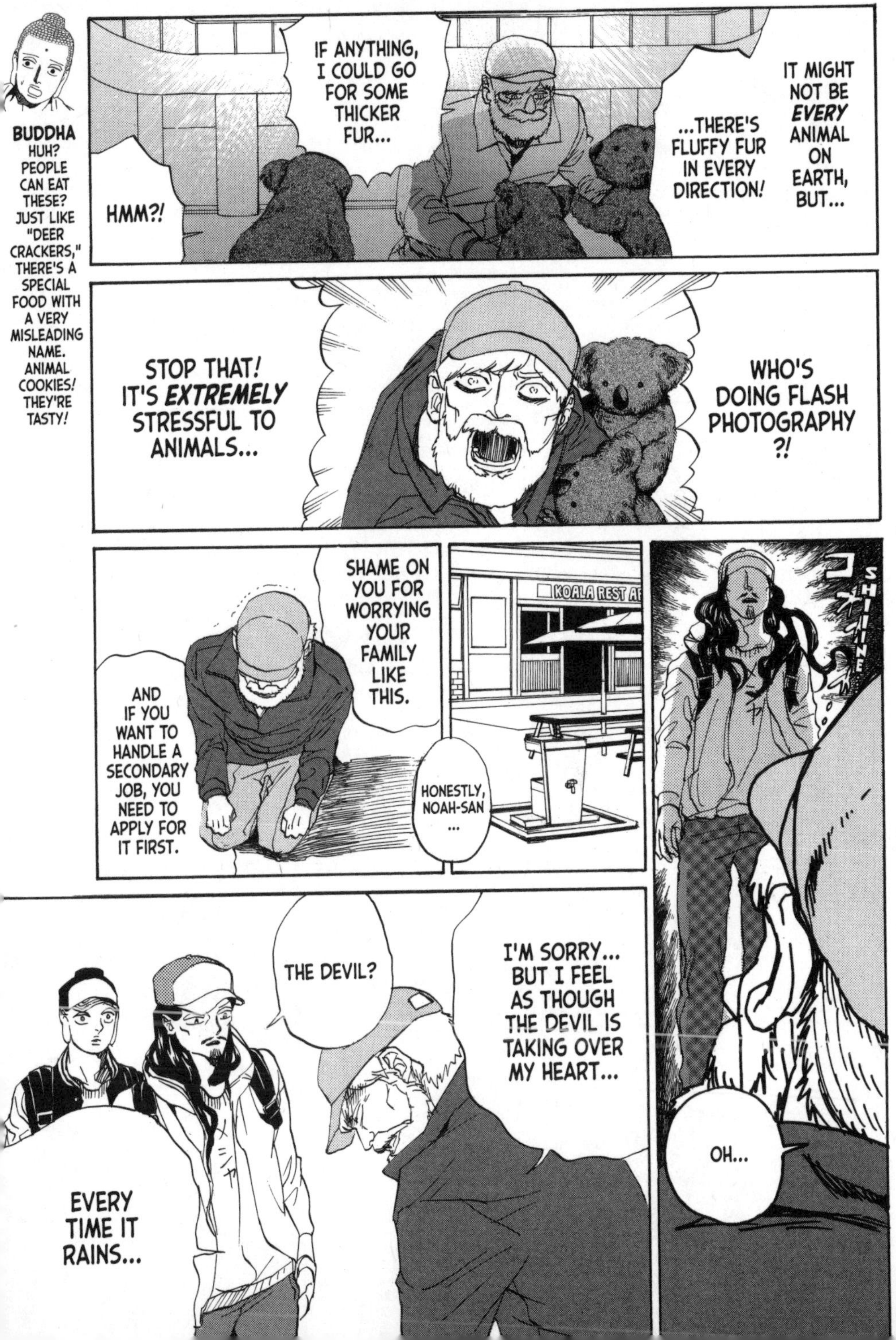

IT MIGHT NOT BE *EVERY* ANIMAL ON EARTH, BUT...
...THERE'S FLUFFY FUR IN EVERY DIRECTION!
IF ANYTHING, I COULD GO FOR SOME THICKER FUR...
HMM?!
WHO'S DOING FLASH PHOTOGRAPHY ?!
STOP THAT! IT'S *EXTREMELY* STRESSFUL TO ANIMALS...
SHIIINE
OH...
KOALA REST AR
HONESTLY, NOAH-SAN ...
SHAME ON YOU FOR WORRYING YOUR FAMILY LIKE THIS.
AND IF YOU WANT TO HANDLE A SECONDARY JOB, YOU NEED TO APPLY FOR IT FIRST.
I'M SORRY... BUT I FEEL AS THOUGH THE DEVIL IS TAKING OVER MY HEART...
THE DEVIL?
EVERY TIME IT RAINS...

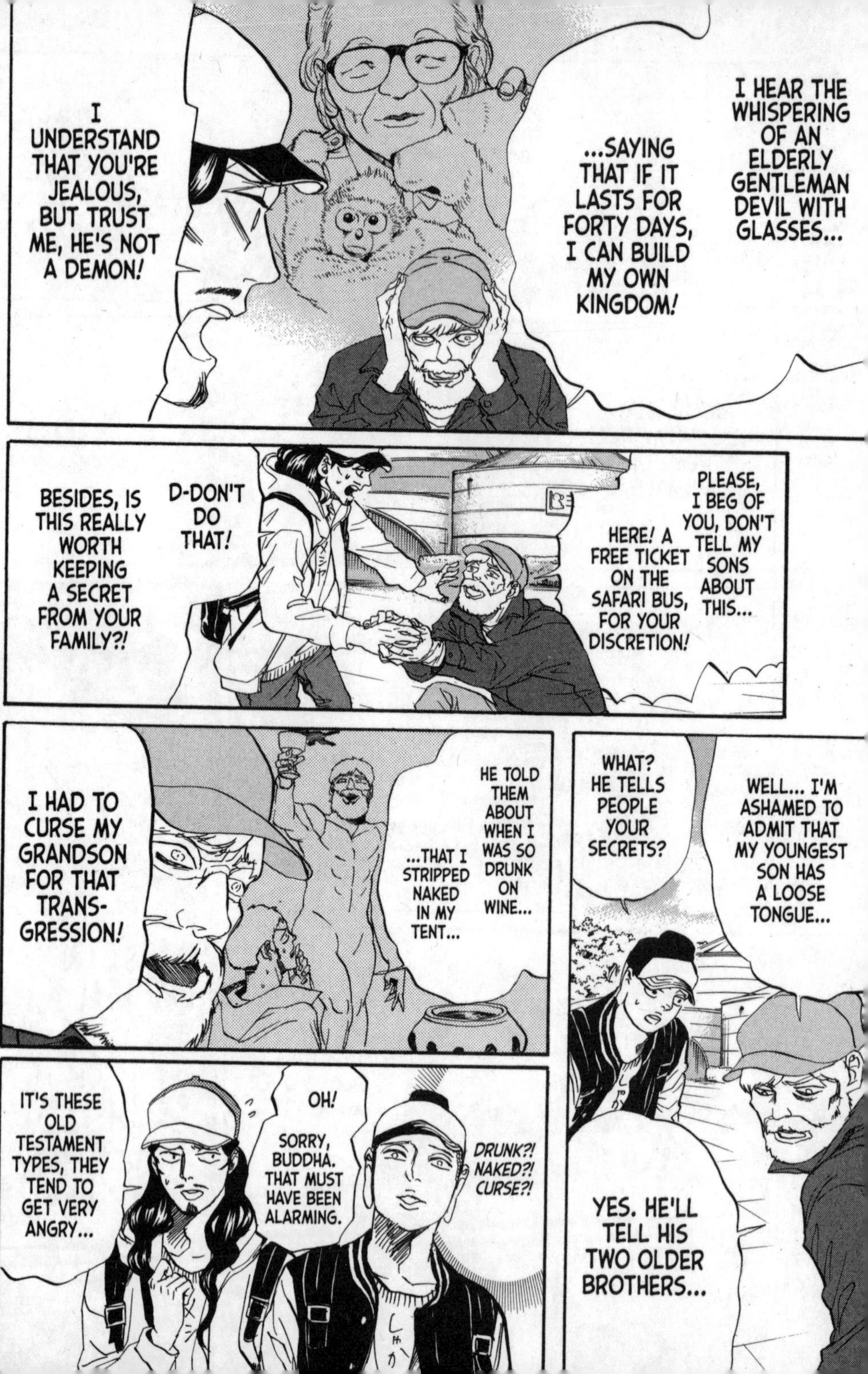

I HEAR THE WHISPERING OF AN ELDERLY GENTLEMAN DEVIL WITH GLASSES...
...SAYING THAT IF IT LASTS FOR FORTY DAYS, I CAN BUILD MY OWN KINGDOM!
I UNDERSTAND THAT YOU'RE JEALOUS, BUT TRUST ME, HE'S NOT A DEMON!
PLEASE, I BEG OF YOU, DON'T TELL MY SONS ABOUT THIS...
HERE! A FREE TICKET ON THE SAFARI BUS, FOR YOUR DISCRETION!
D-DON'T DO THAT!
BESIDES, IS THIS REALLY WORTH KEEPING A SECRET FROM YOUR FAMILY?!
WELL... I'M ASHAMED TO ADMIT THAT MY YOUNGEST SON HAS A LOOSE TONGUE...
WHAT? HE TELLS PEOPLE YOUR SECRETS?
YES. HE'LL TELL HIS TWO OLDER BROTHERS...
HE TOLD THEM ABOUT WHEN I WAS SO DRUNK ON WINE...
...THAT I STRIPPED NAKED IN MY TENT...
I HAD TO CURSE MY GRANDSON FOR THAT TRANSGRESSION!
DRUNK?! NAKED?! CURSE?!
OH!
SORRY, BUDDHA. THAT MUST HAVE BEEN ALARMING.
IT'S THESE OLD TESTAMENT TYPES, THEY TEND TO GET VERY ANGRY...

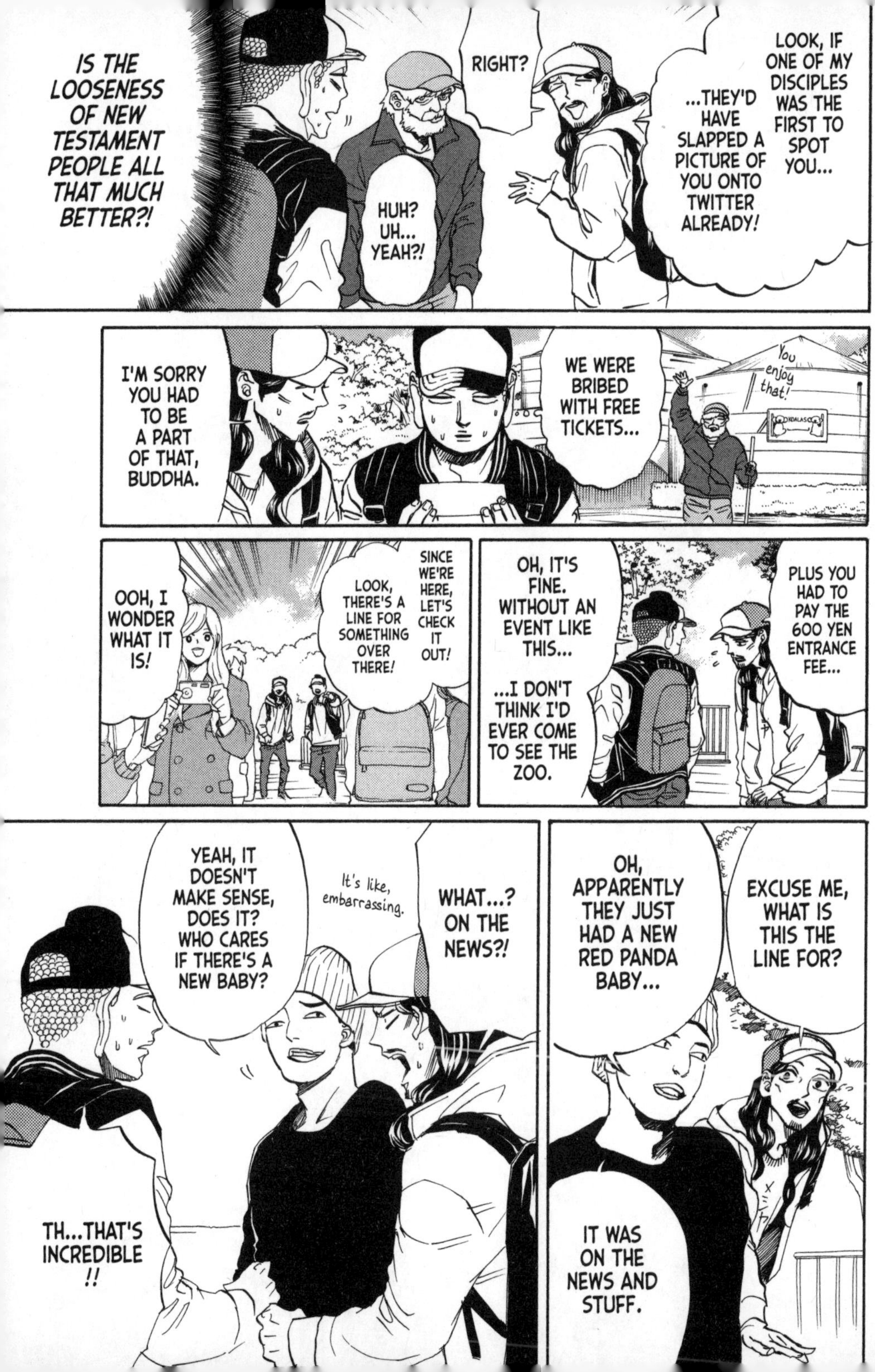
LOOK, IF ONE OF MY DISCIPLES WAS THE FIRST TO SPOT YOU...
...THEY'D HAVE SLAPPED A PICTURE OF YOU ONTO TWITTER ALREADY!
RIGHT?
HUH? UH... YEAH?!
IS THE LOOSENESS OF NEW TESTAMENT PEOPLE ALL THAT MUCH BETTER?!
You enjoy that!
WE WERE BRIBED WITH FREE TICKETS...
I'M SORRY YOU HAD TO BE A PART OF THAT, BUDDHA.
PLUS YOU HAD TO PAY THE 600 YEN ENTRANCE FEE...
OH, IT'S FINE. WITHOUT AN EVENT LIKE THIS...
...I DON'T THINK I'D EVER COME TO SEE THE ZOO.
SINCE WE'RE HERE, LET'S CHECK IT OUT!
LOOK, THERE'S A LINE FOR SOMETHING OVER THERE!
OOH, I WONDER WHAT IT IS!
EXCUSE ME, WHAT IS THIS THE LINE FOR?
OH, APPARENTLY THEY JUST HAD A NEW RED PANDA BABY...
IT WAS ON THE NEWS AND STUFF.
WHAT...? ON THE NEWS?!
It's like, embarrassing.
YEAH, IT DOESN'T MAKE SENSE, DOES IT? WHO CARES IF THERE'S A NEW BABY?
TH...THAT'S INCREDIBLE!!

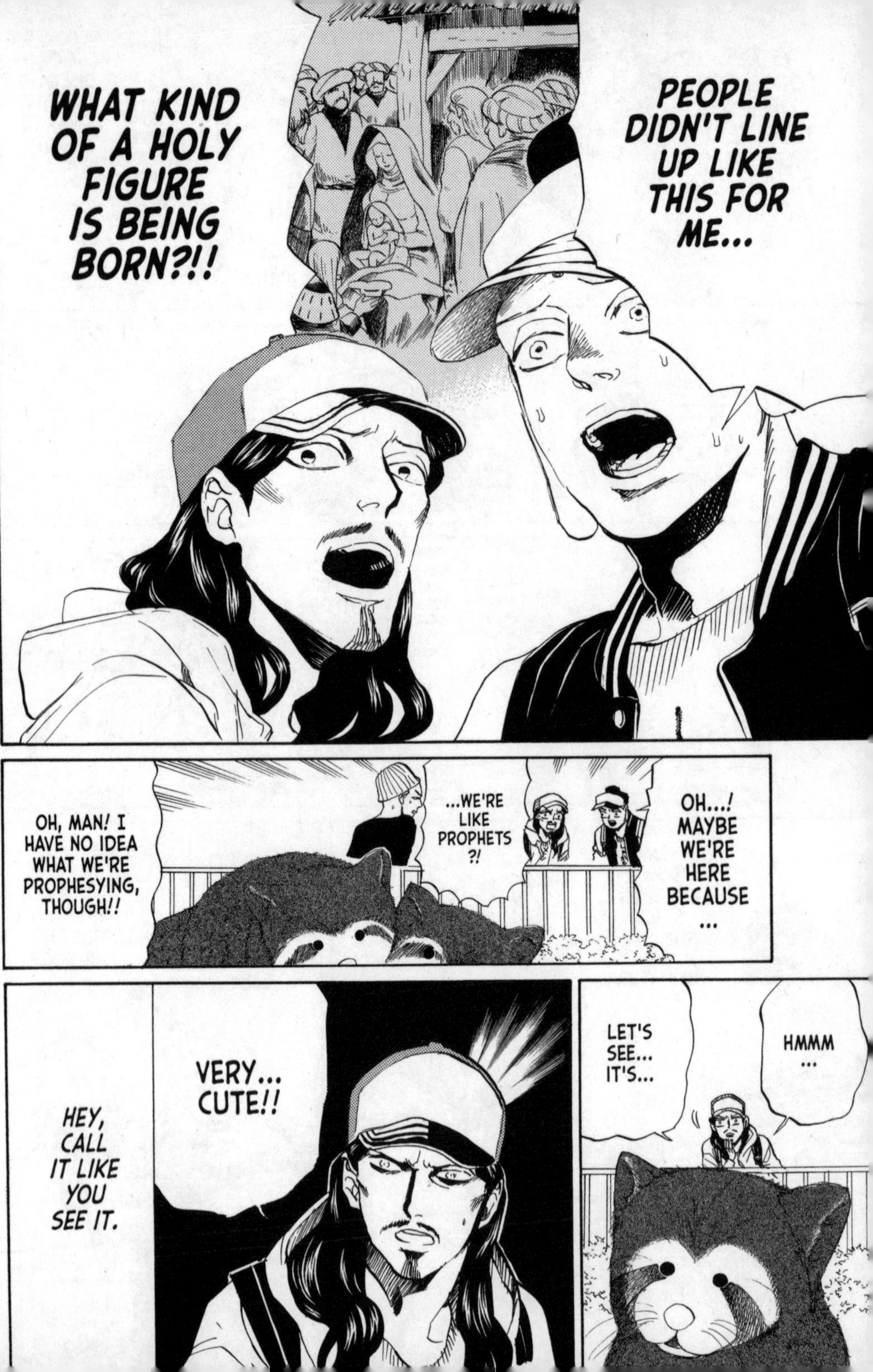
PEOPLE DIDN'T LINE UP LIKE THIS FOR ME...
WHAT KIND OF A HOLY FIGURE IS BEING BORN?!!
OH...! MAYBE WE'RE HERE BECAUSE ...
...WE'RE LIKE PROPHETS ?!
OH, MAN! I HAVE NO IDEA WHAT WE'RE PROPHESYING, THOUGH!!
HMMM ...
LET'S SEE... IT'S...
VERY... CUTE!!
HEY, CALL IT LIKE YOU SEE IT.

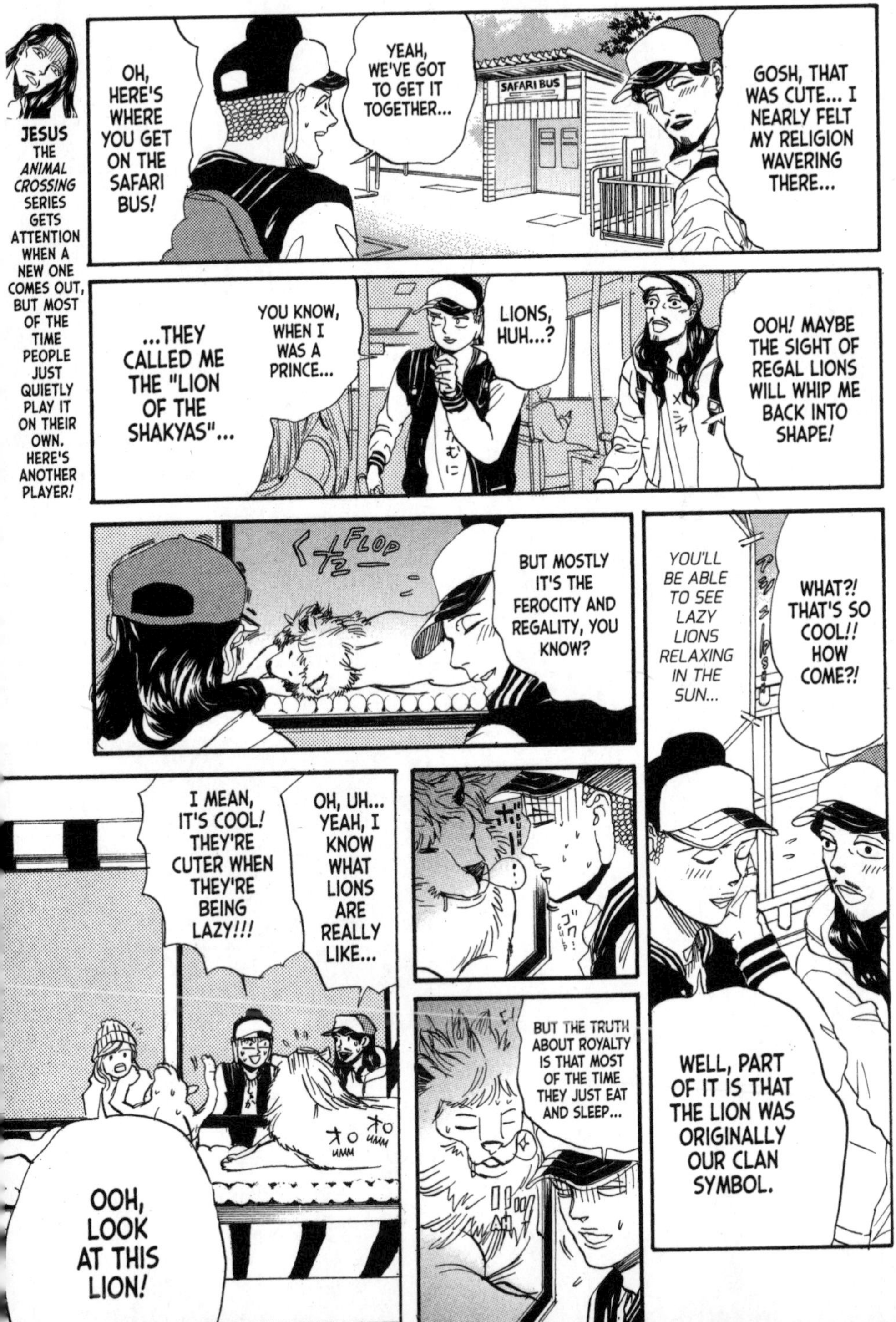
GOSH, THAT WAS CUTE... I NEARLY FELT MY RELIGION WAVERING THERE...
YEAH, WE'VE GOT TO GET IT TOGETHER...
SAFARI BUS
OH, HERE'S WHERE YOU GET ON THE SAFARI BUS!
OOH! MAYBE THE SIGHT OF REGAL LIONS WILL WHIP ME BACK INTO SHAPE!
LIONS, HUH...?
YOU KNOW, WHEN I WAS A PRINCE...
...THEY CALLED ME THE "LION OF THE SHAKYAS"...
WHAT?! THAT'S SO COOL!! HOW COME?!
YOU'LL BE ABLE TO SEE LAZY LIONS RELAXING IN THE SUN...
BUT MOSTLY IT'S THE FEROCITY AND REGALITY, YOU KNOW?
FLOP
WELL, PART OF IT IS THAT THE LION WAS ORIGINALLY OUR CLAN SYMBOL.
OH, UH... YEAH, I KNOW WHAT LIONS ARE REALLY LIKE...
BUNN
GULP
BUT THE TRUTH ABOUT ROYALTY IS THAT MOST OF THE TIME THEY JUST EAT AND SLEEP...
AH
I MEAN, IT'S COOL! THEY'RE CUTER WHEN THEY'RE BEING LAZY!!!
UMM
UMM
OOH, LOOK AT THIS LION!
JESUS
THE *ANIMAL CROSSING* SERIES GETS ATTENTION WHEN A NEW ONE COMES OUT, BUT MOST OF THE TIME PEOPLE JUST QUIETLY PLAY IT ON THEIR OWN. HERE'S ANOTHER PLAYER!

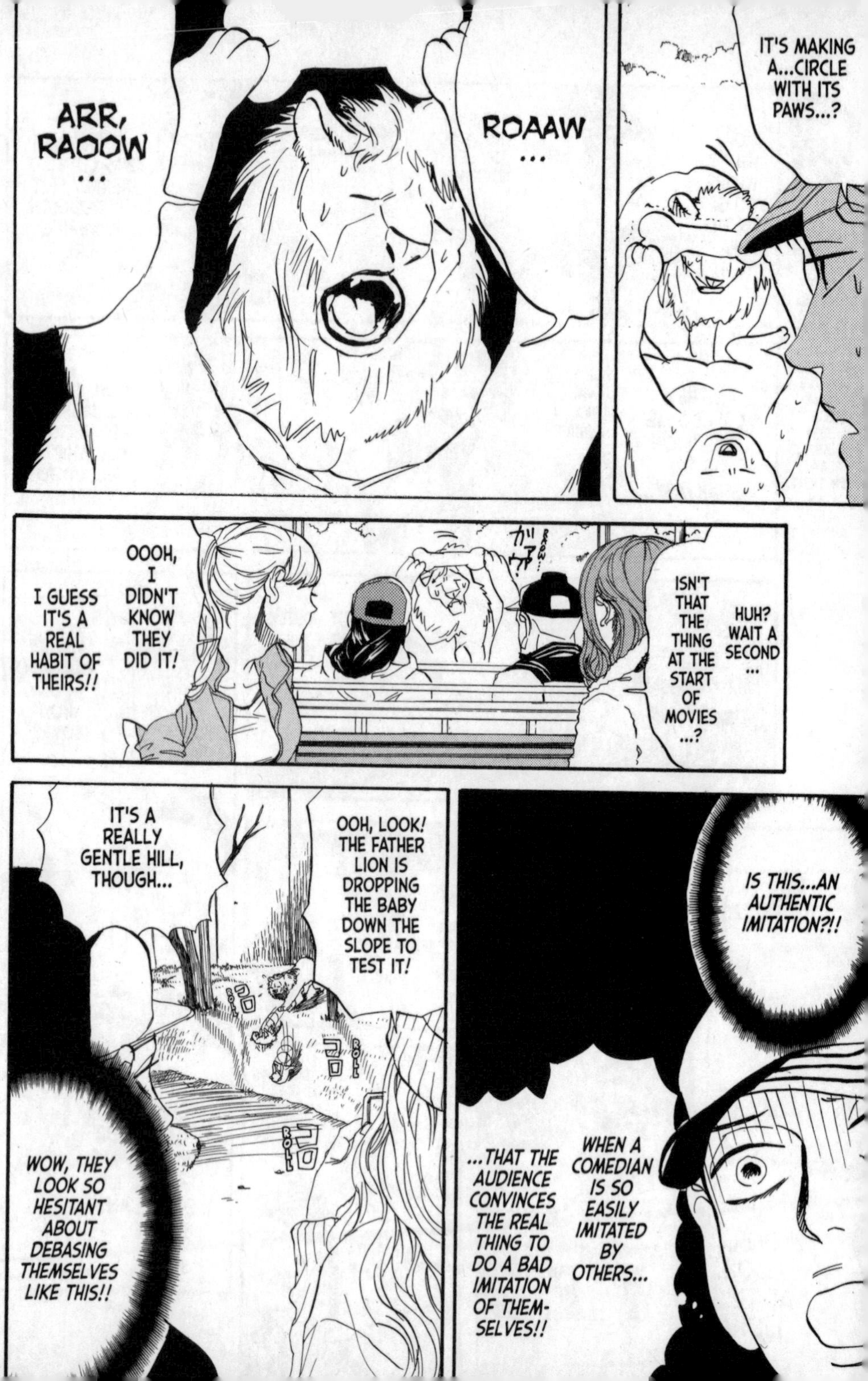
IT'S MAKING A...CIRCLE WITH ITS PAWS...?
ROAAW ...
ARR, RAOOW ...
HUH? WAIT A SECOND...
ISN'T THAT THE THING AT THE START OF MOVIES...?
RAOW...
OOOH, I DIDN'T KNOW THEY DID IT!
I GUESS IT'S A REAL HABIT OF THEIRS!!
IS THIS...AN AUTHENTIC IMITATION?!!
WHEN A COMEDIAN IS SO EASILY IMITATED BY OTHERS...
...THAT THE AUDIENCE CONVINCES THE REAL THING TO DO A BAD IMITATION OF THEM-SELVES!!
OOH, LOOK! THE FATHER LION IS DROPPING THE BABY DOWN THE SLOPE TO TEST IT!
IT'S A REALLY GENTLE HILL, THOUGH...
ROLL
ROLL
ROLL
WOW, THEY LOOK SO HESITANT ABOUT DEBASING THEMSELVES LIKE THIS!!

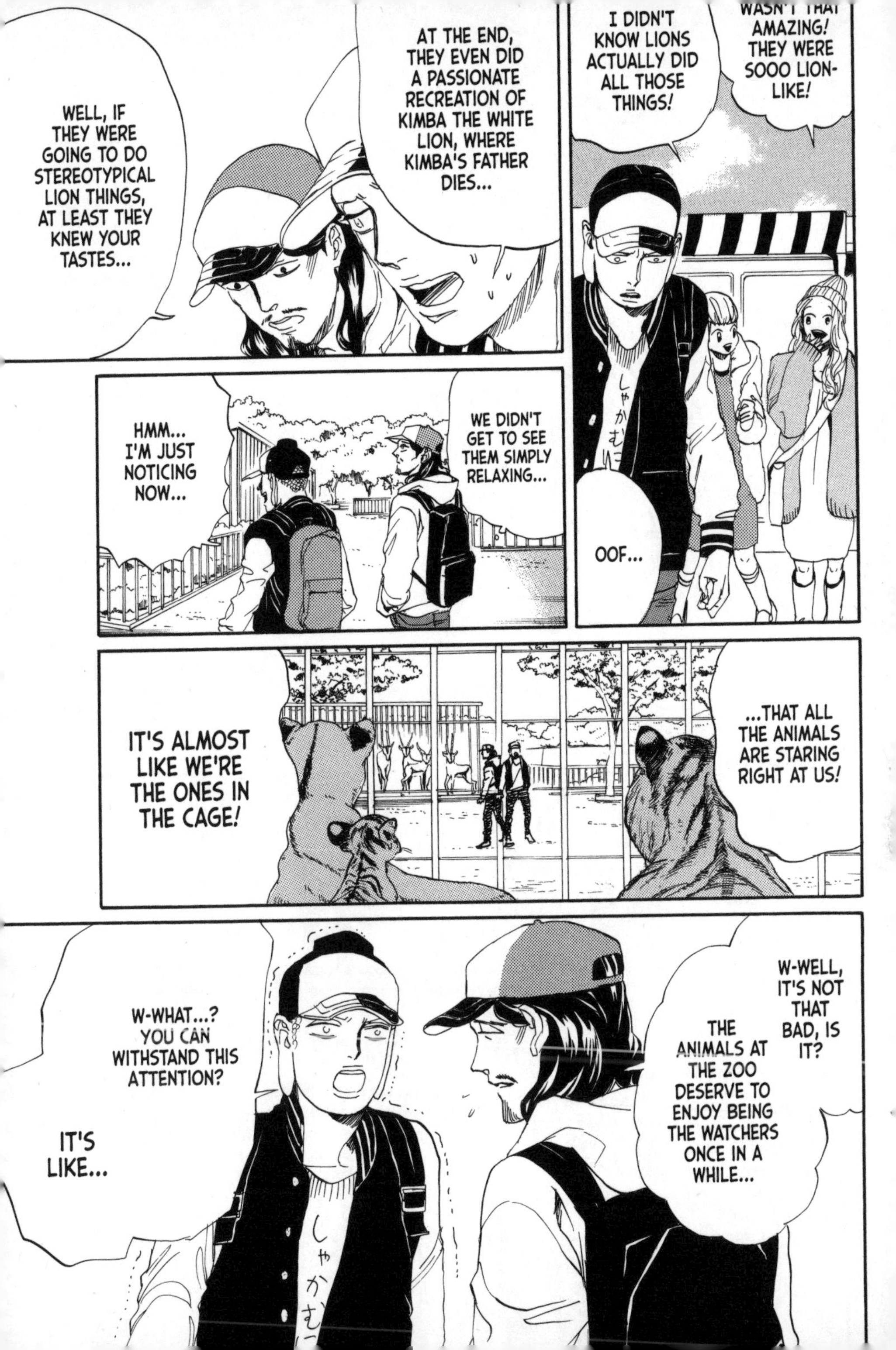
WASN'T THAT AMAZING! THEY WERE SOOO LION-LIKE!
I DIDN'T KNOW LIONS ACTUALLY DID ALL THOSE THINGS!
OOF...
AT THE END, THEY EVEN DID A PASSIONATE RECREATION OF KIMBA THE WHITE LION, WHERE KIMBA'S FATHER DIES...
WELL, IF THEY WERE GOING TO DO STEREOTYPICAL LION THINGS, AT LEAST THEY KNEW YOUR TASTES...
WE DIDN'T GET TO SEE THEM SIMPLY RELAXING...
HMM... I'M JUST NOTICING NOW...
...THAT ALL THE ANIMALS ARE STARING RIGHT AT US!
IT'S ALMOST LIKE WE'RE THE ONES IN THE CAGE!
W-WELL, IT'S NOT THAT BAD, IS IT?
THE ANIMALS AT THE ZOO DESERVE TO ENJOY BEING THE WATCHERS ONCE IN A WHILE...
W-WHAT...? YOU CAN WITHSTAND THIS ATTENTION?
IT'S LIKE...

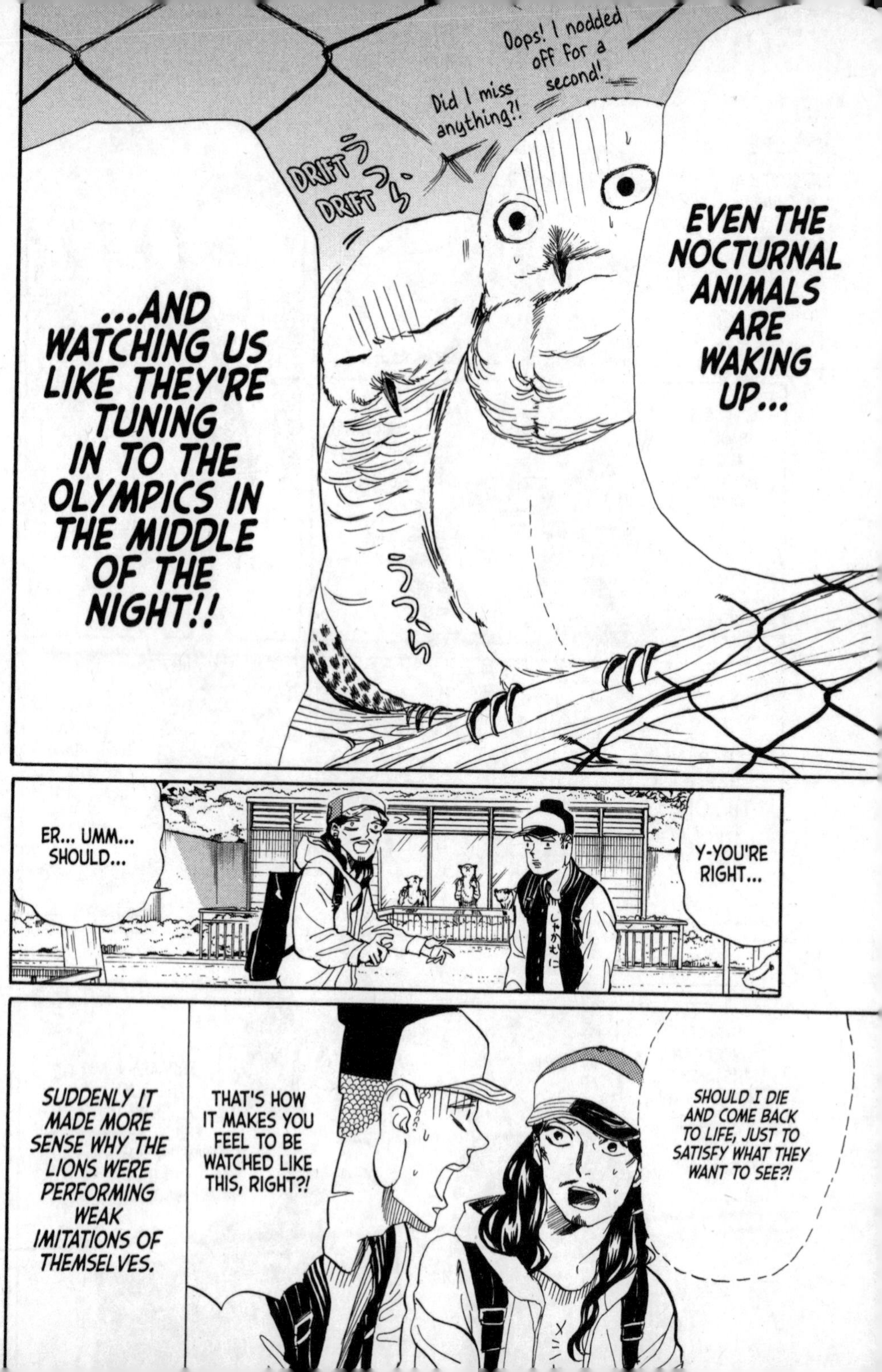
Oops! I nodded off for a second!
Did I miss anything?!
DRIFT
DRIFT
EVEN THE NOCTURNAL ANIMALS ARE WAKING UP...
...AND WATCHING US LIKE THEY'RE TUNING IN TO THE OLYMPICS IN THE MIDDLE OF THE NIGHT!!
Y-YOU'RE RIGHT...
ER... UMM... SHOULD...
SHOULD I DIE AND COME BACK TO LIFE, JUST TO SATISFY WHAT THEY WANT TO SEE?!
THAT'S HOW IT MAKES YOU FEEL TO BE WATCHED LIKE THIS, RIGHT?!
SUDDENLY IT MADE MORE SENSE WHY THE LIONS WERE PERFORMING WEAK IMITATIONS OF THEMSELVES.

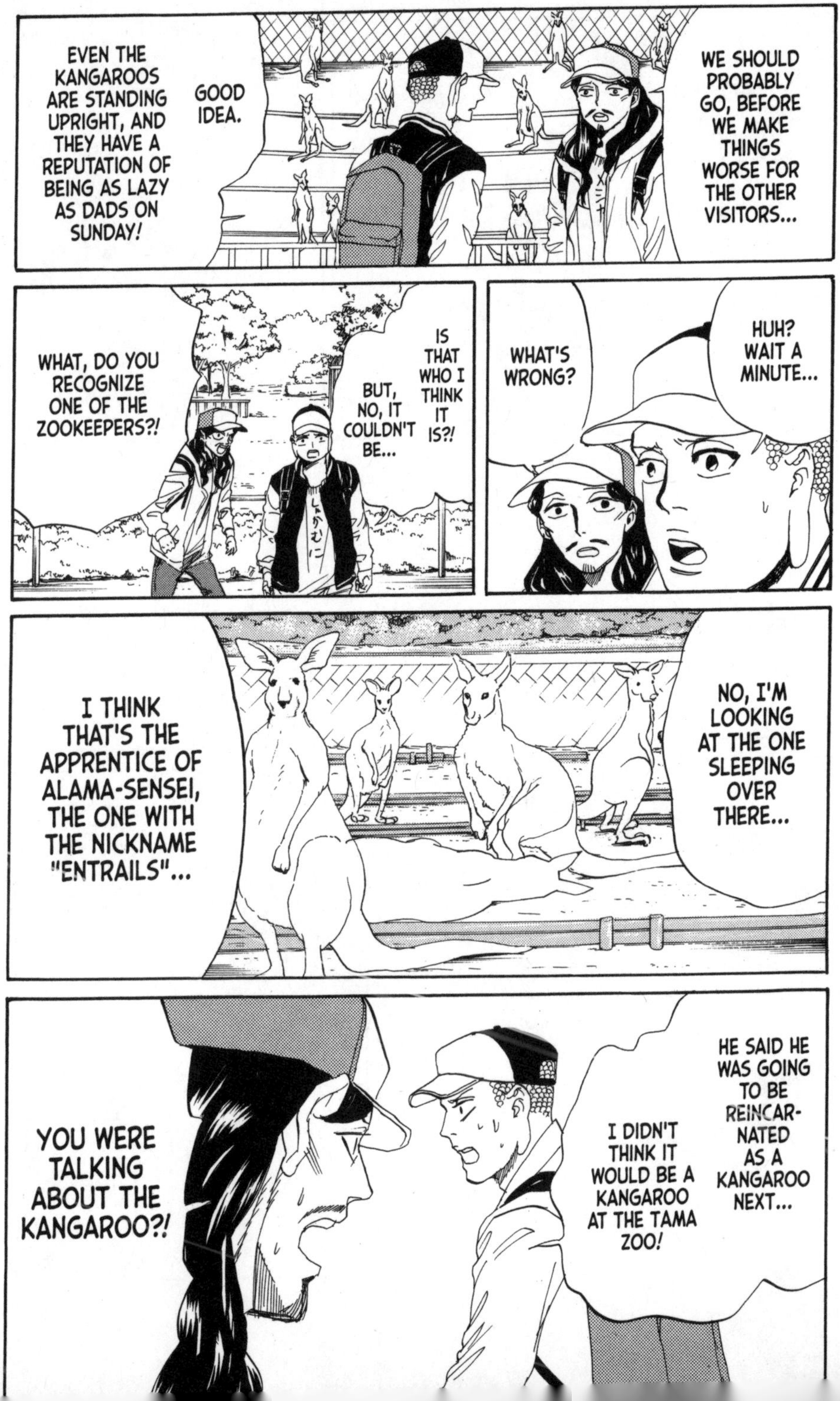
WE SHOULD PROBABLY GO, BEFORE WE MAKE THINGS WORSE FOR THE OTHER VISITORS...
GOOD IDEA.
EVEN THE KANGAROOS ARE STANDING UPRIGHT, AND THEY HAVE A REPUTATION OF BEING AS LAZY AS DADS ON SUNDAY!
HUH? WAIT A MINUTE...
WHAT'S WRONG?
IS THAT WHO I THINK IT IS?!
BUT, NO, IT COULDN'T BE...
WHAT, DO YOU RECOGNIZE ONE OF THE ZOOKEEPERS?!
NO, I'M LOOKING AT THE ONE SLEEPING OVER THERE...
I THINK THAT'S THE APPRENTICE OF ALAMA-SENSEI, THE ONE WITH THE NICKNAME "ENTRAILS"...
HE SAID HE WAS GOING TO BE REINCAR-NATED AS A KANGAROO NEXT...
I DIDN'T THINK IT WOULD BE A KANGAROO AT THE TAMA ZOO!
YOU WERE TALKING ABOUT THE KANGAROO?!

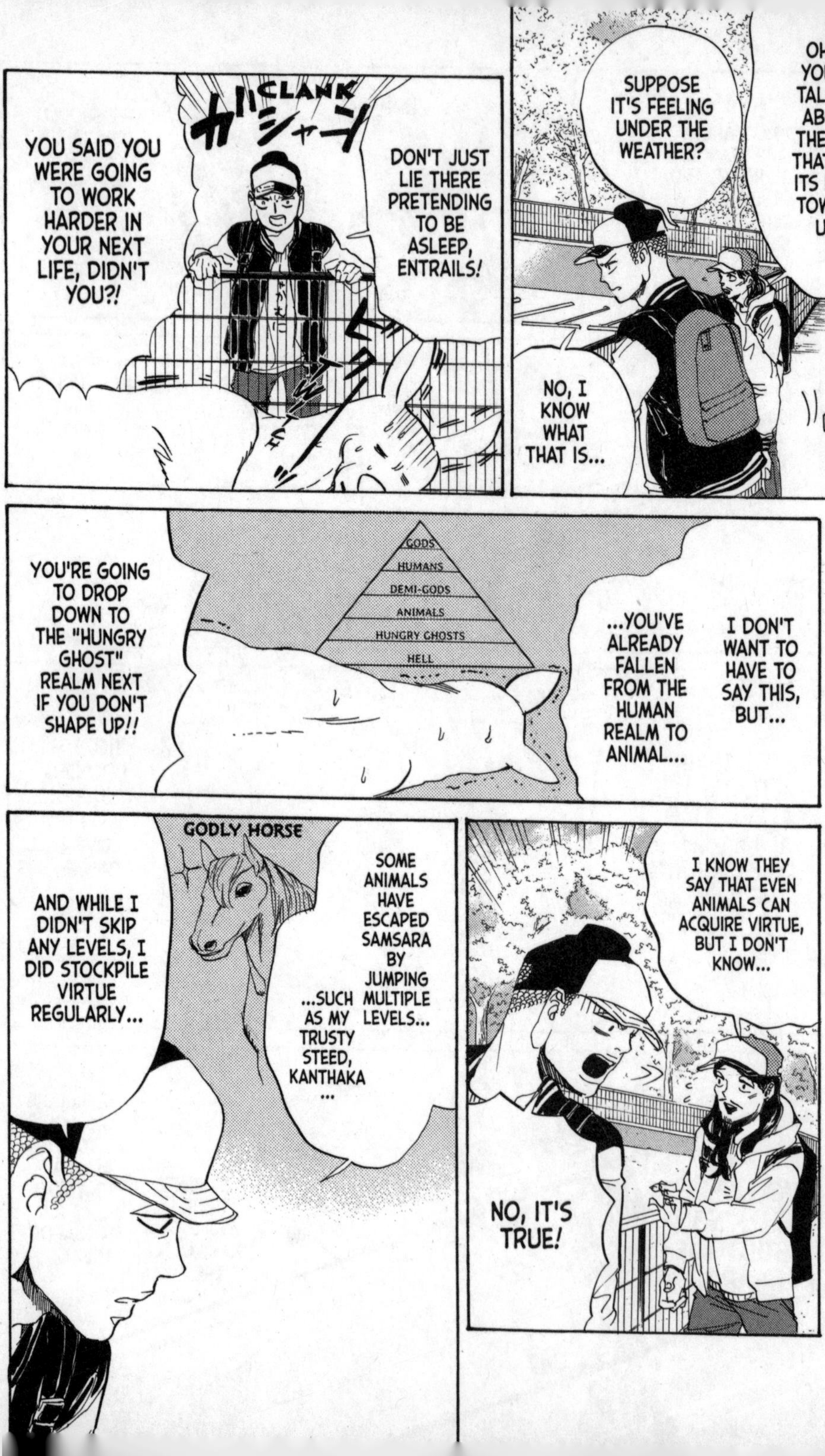
OHHH, YOU'RE TALKING ABOUT THE ONE THAT HAS ITS BACK TOWARD US?
SUPPOSE IT'S FEELING UNDER THE WEATHER?
NO, I KNOW WHAT THAT IS...
STOMP
STOMP
CLANK
DON'T JUST LIE THERE PRETENDING TO BE ASLEEP, ENTRAILS!
YOU SAID YOU WERE GOING TO WORK HARDER IN YOUR NEXT LIFE, DIDN'T YOU?!
I DON'T WANT TO HAVE TO SAY THIS, BUT...
...YOU'VE ALREADY FALLEN FROM THE HUMAN REALM TO ANIMAL...
GODS
HUMANS
DEMI-GODS
ANIMALS
HUNGRY GHOSTS
HELL
YOU'RE GOING TO DROP DOWN TO THE "HUNGRY GHOST" REALM NEXT IF YOU DON'T SHAPE UP!!
I KNOW THEY SAY THAT EVEN ANIMALS CAN ACQUIRE VIRTUE, BUT I DON'T KNOW...
NO, IT'S TRUE!
GODLY HORSE
SOME ANIMALS HAVE ESCAPED SAMSARA BY JUMPING MULTIPLE LEVELS...
...SUCH AS MY TRUSTY STEED, KANTHAKA...
AND WHILE I DIDN'T SKIP ANY LEVELS, I DID STOCKPILE VIRTUE REGULARLY...

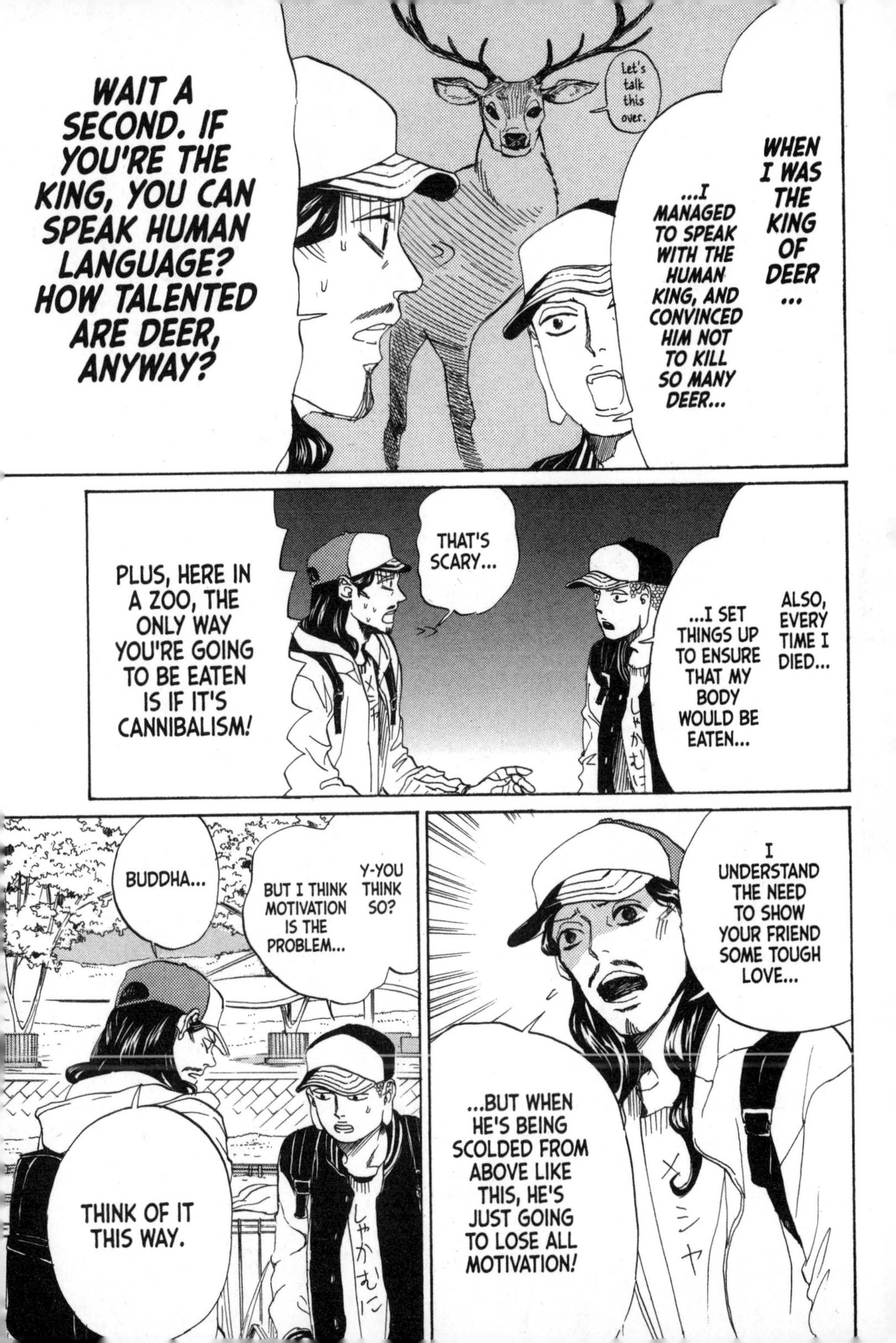
WHEN I WAS THE KING OF DEER...
...I MANAGED TO SPEAK WITH THE HUMAN KING, AND CONVINCED HIM NOT TO KILL SO MANY DEER...
Let's talk this over.
WAIT A SECOND. IF YOU'RE THE KING, YOU CAN SPEAK HUMAN LANGUAGE? HOW TALENTED ARE DEER, ANYWAY?
ALSO, EVERY TIME I DIED...
...I SET THINGS UP TO ENSURE THAT MY BODY WOULD BE EATEN...
THAT'S SCARY...
PLUS, HERE IN A ZOO, THE ONLY WAY YOU'RE GOING TO BE EATEN IS IF IT'S CANNIBALISM!
I UNDERSTAND THE NEED TO SHOW YOUR FRIEND SOME TOUGH LOVE...
...BUT WHEN HE'S BEING SCOLDED FROM ABOVE LIKE THIS, HE'S JUST GOING TO LOSE ALL MOTIVATION!
Y-YOU THINK SO?
BUT I THINK MOTIVATION IS THE PROBLEM...
BUDDHA...
THINK OF IT THIS WAY.

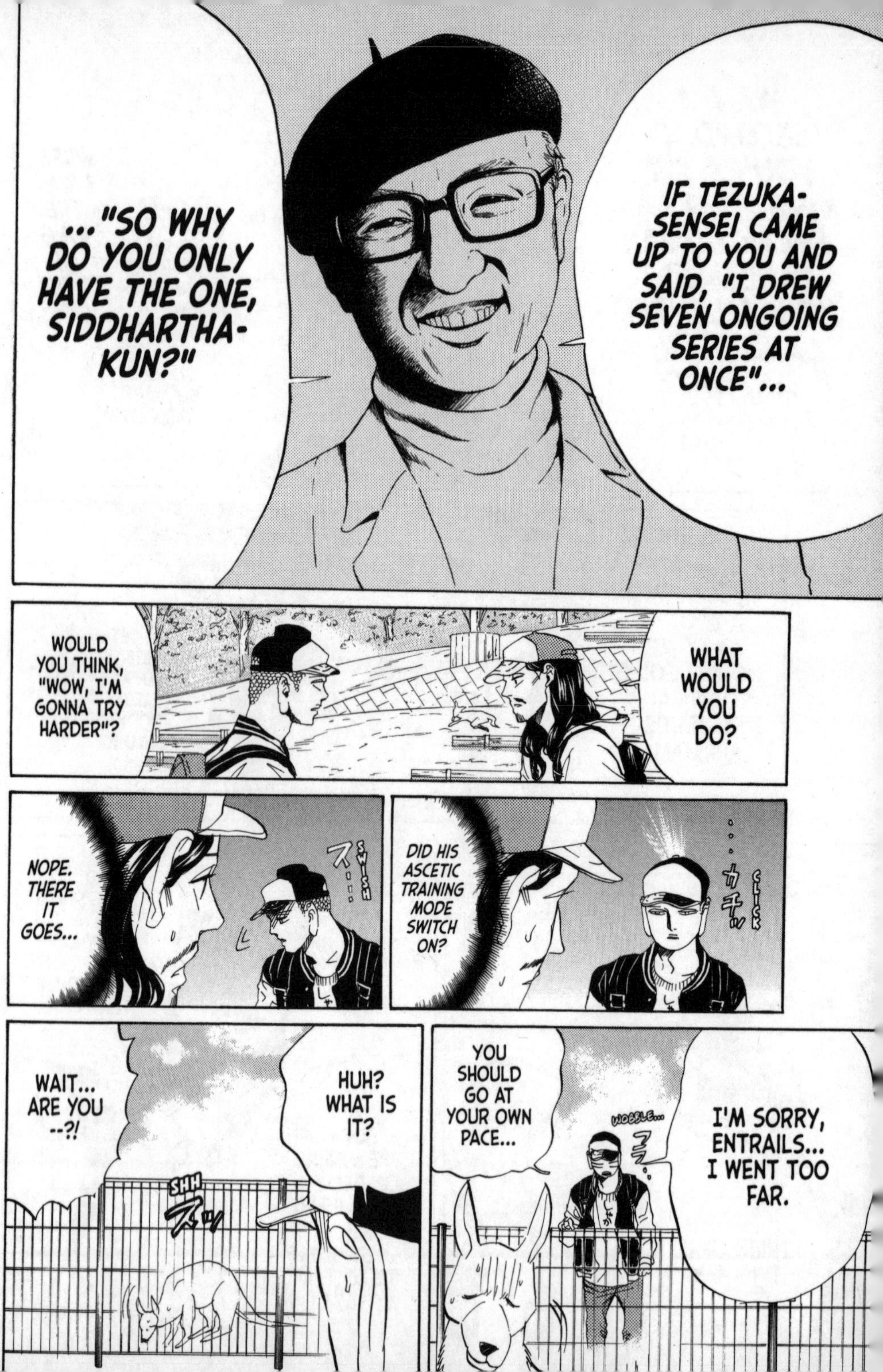
IF TEZUKA-SENSEI CAME UP TO YOU AND SAID, "I DREW SEVEN ONGOING SERIES AT ONCE"...
..."SO WHY DO YOU ONLY HAVE THE ONE, SIDDHARTHA-KUN?"
WHAT WOULD YOU DO?
WOULD YOU THINK, "WOW, I'M GONNA TRY HARDER"?
...
CLICK
DID HIS ASCETIC TRAINING MODE SWITCH ON?
SWISH
NOPE. THERE IT GOES...
I'M SORRY, ENTRAILS... I WENT TOO FAR.
WOBBLE...
YOU SHOULD GO AT YOUR OWN PACE...
HUH? WHAT IS IT?
SHH
WAIT... ARE YOU --?!

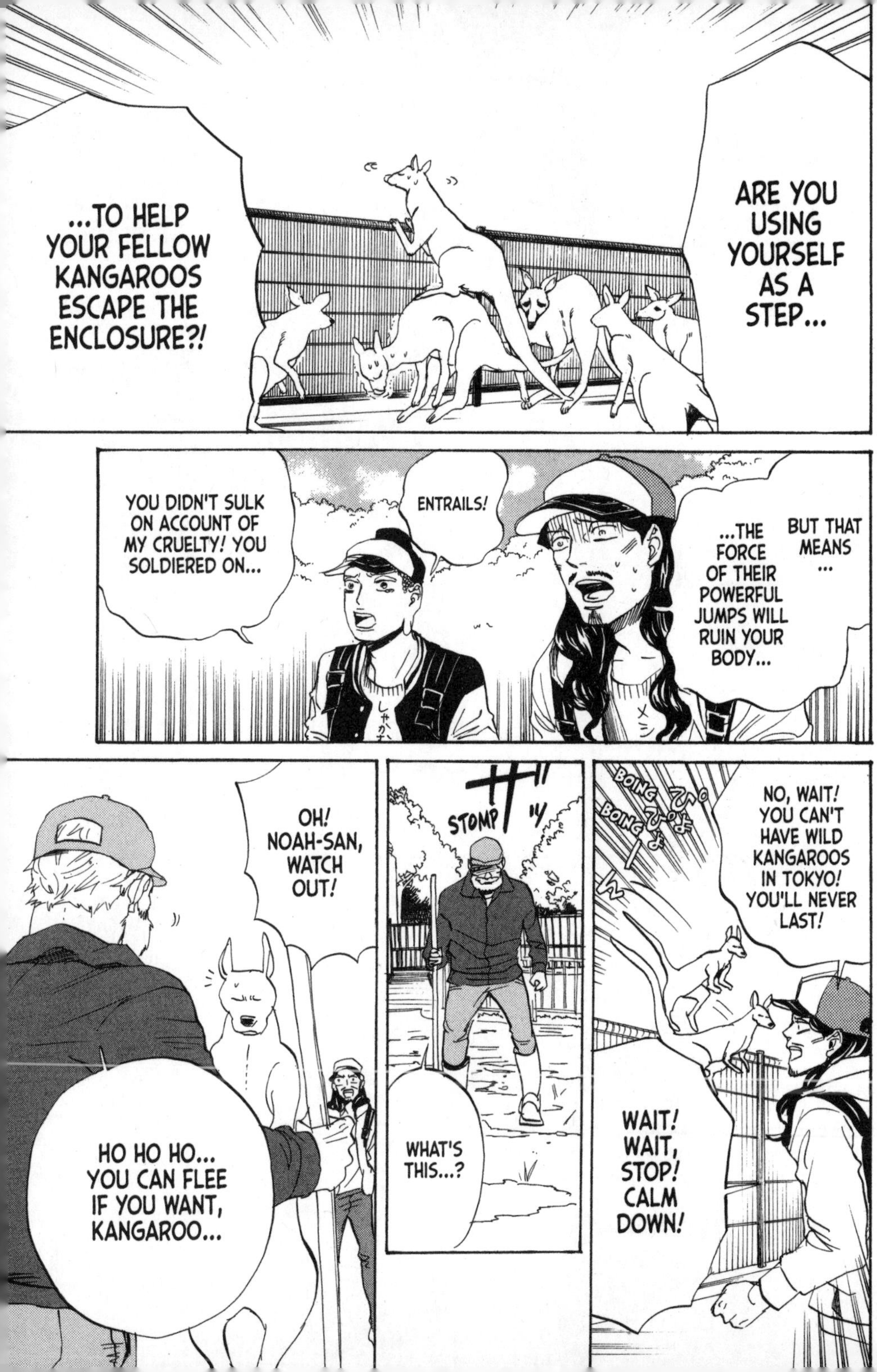
ARE YOU USING YOURSELF AS A STEP...
...TO HELP YOUR FELLOW KANGAROOS ESCAPE THE ENCLOSURE?!
BUT THAT MEANS ...
...THE FORCE OF THEIR POWERFUL JUMPS WILL RUIN YOUR BODY...
ENTRAILS!
YOU DIDN'T SULK ON ACCOUNT OF MY CRUELTY! YOU SOLDIERED ON...
BOING
BOING
NO, WAIT! YOU CAN'T HAVE WILD KANGAROOS IN TOKYO! YOU'LL NEVER LAST!
WAIT! WAIT, STOP! CALM DOWN!
STOMP
WHAT'S THIS...?
OH! NOAH-SAN, WATCH OUT!
HO HO HO... YOU CAN FLEE IF YOU WANT, KANGAROO...

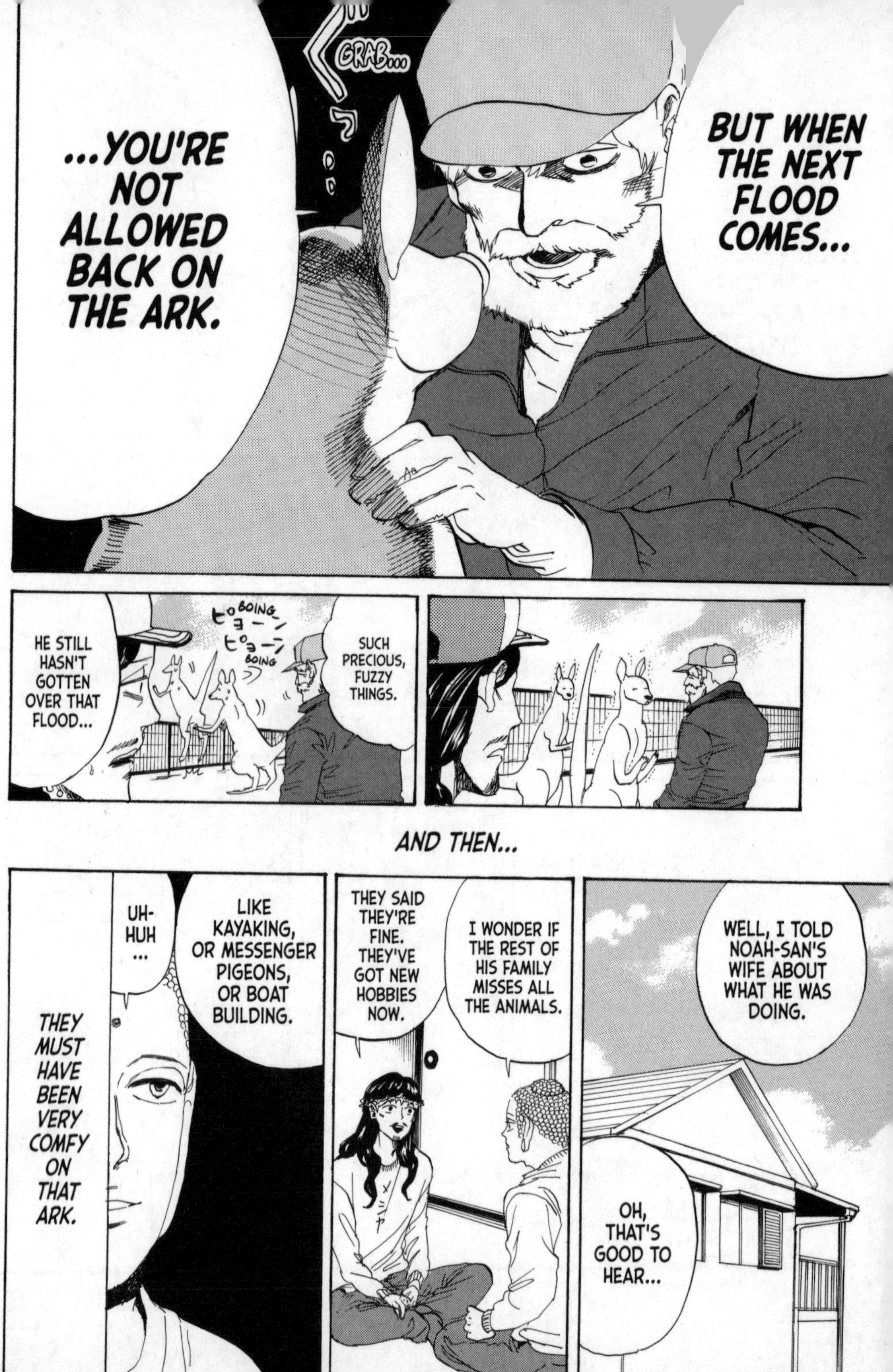
BUT WHEN THE NEXT FLOOD COMES...
GRAB...
...YOU'RE NOT ALLOWED BACK ON THE ARK.
SUCH PRECIOUS, FUZZY THINGS.
ピョーン ピョーン BOING BOING
HE STILL HASN'T GOTTEN OVER THAT FLOOD...
AND THEN...
WELL, I TOLD NOAH-SAN'S WIFE ABOUT WHAT HE WAS DOING.
OH, THAT'S GOOD TO HEAR...
I WONDER IF THE REST OF HIS FAMILY MISSES ALL THE ANIMALS.
THEY SAID THEY'RE FINE. THEY'VE GOT NEW HOBBIES NOW.
LIKE KAYAKING, OR MESSENGER PIGEONS, OR BOAT BUILDING.
UH-HUH...
THEY MUST HAVE BEEN VERY COMFY ON THAT ARK.

Growing your own fuzz to pet

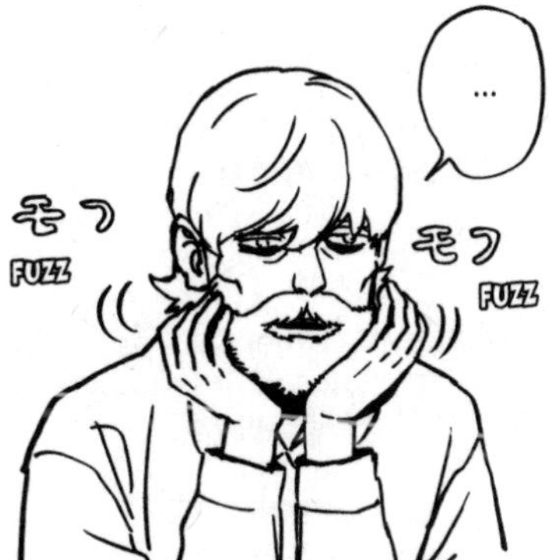
...
モフ
FUZZ
モフ
FUZZ

SAINT ☆ YOUNG MEN

CHAPTER 79 TRANSLATION NOTES

Shakyamuni, page 98
A title given to the Buddha that means "Sage of the Shakyas," referring to his clan.

Mutsugoro, page 100
Mutsugoro is the stage name of a famous Japanese writer and personality known for his love of animals. He is often seen on variety shows with an animal theme. He built a nature preserve in Hokkaido in the 1970s called Mutsugoro Animal Kingdom to allow visitors to come into contact with nature. In the West he is also known for his involvement in the *Milo & Otis* movie.

Noah's curse, page 100
In the Book of Genesis, following the flood, Noah plants grapes and creates wine, which then develops into a tendency toward drunkenness. When he is seen naked by his youngest son Ham, who tells his brothers Shem and Japheth, Noah grows so angry that he curses Ham's son Canaan. This story is commonly believed to explain why the Canaanites (his descendents) should be subjects to the Israelites, the descendents of Shem.

Lion cubs, page 104
A well-known saying in Japan is that a grown lion tosses its cubs over a cliff to see which ones are strong enough to climb back up and survive.

Kimba the White Lion, page 105
One of Osamu Tezuka's classic works, originally titled *Jungle Emperor* (or *Jungle Emperor Leo*) in Japan. It was adapted into an animated TV series that was released in English in the 1960s. Later, there was a controversy when Disney's 'The Lion King' showed many similarities to Tezuka's classic story of a lion cub who loses his father to tragic circumstances.

Samsara, page 108
The cycle of rebirth takes places through six realms of existence, as seen here. The karma of one's actions will have an influence on the status of the next life, going from the good realms (the first three) to the evil realms (the latter three).

Deer King, page 109
This comes from a story of one of the Buddha's previous lives. He was a golden deer king whose herd lived in a human king's hunting grounds. The deer king sacrificed himself when the human king was going to hunt a pregnant doe, and upon seeing this, the human king outlawed hunting.

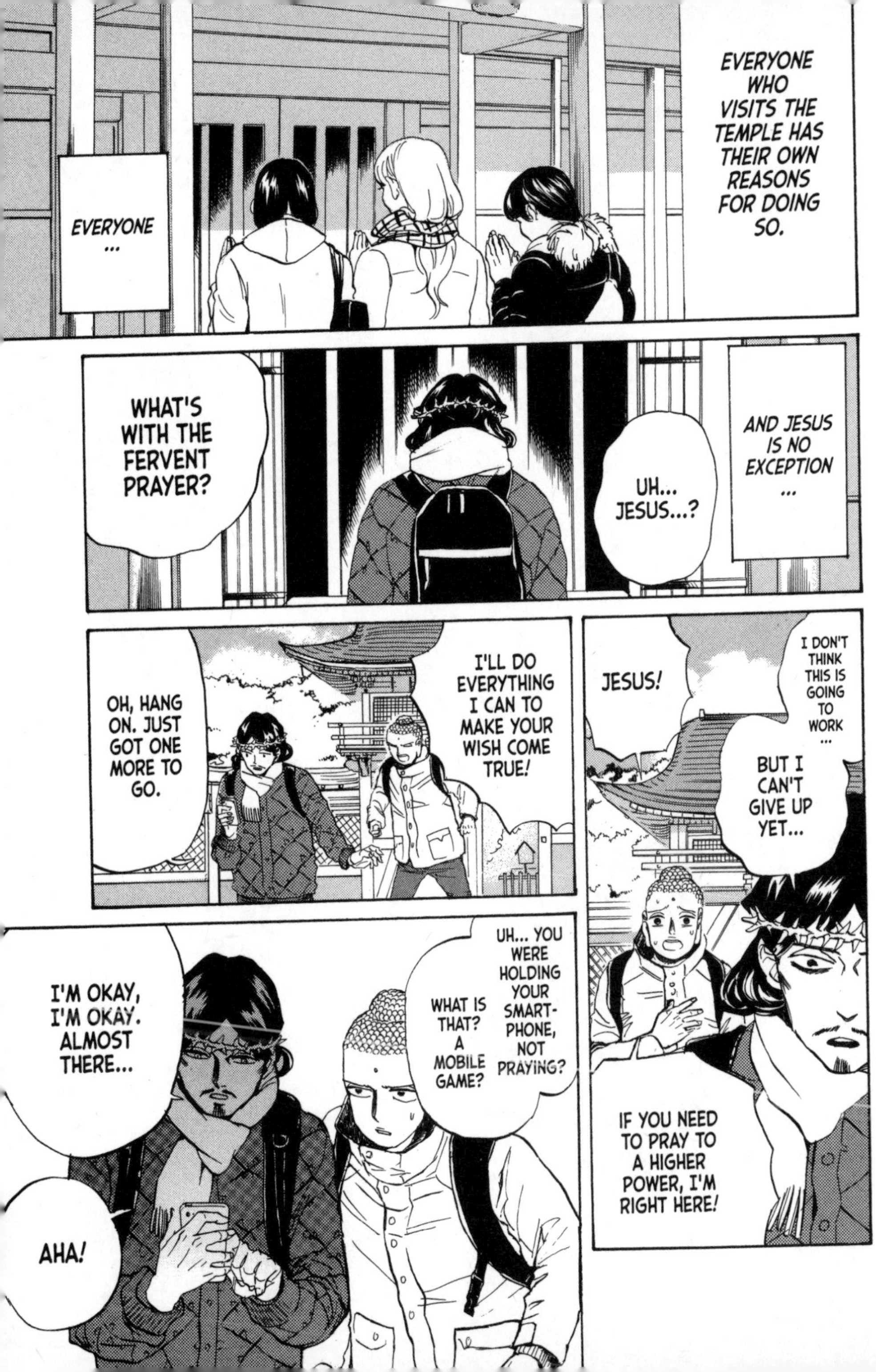
EVERYONE WHO VISITS THE TEMPLE HAS THEIR OWN REASONS FOR DOING SO.
EVERYONE ...
AND JESUS IS NO EXCEPTION ...
UH... JESUS...?
WHAT'S WITH THE FERVENT PRAYER?
I DON'T THINK THIS IS GOING TO WORK ...
JESUS!
BUT I CAN'T GIVE UP YET...
IF YOU NEED TO PRAY TO A HIGHER POWER, I'M RIGHT HERE!
I'LL DO EVERYTHING I CAN TO MAKE YOUR WISH COME TRUE!
OH, HANG ON. JUST GOT ONE MORE TO GO.
UH... YOU WERE HOLDING YOUR SMART-PHONE, NOT PRAYING?
WHAT IS THAT? A MOBILE GAME?
I'M OKAY, I'M OKAY. ALMOST THERE...
AHA!

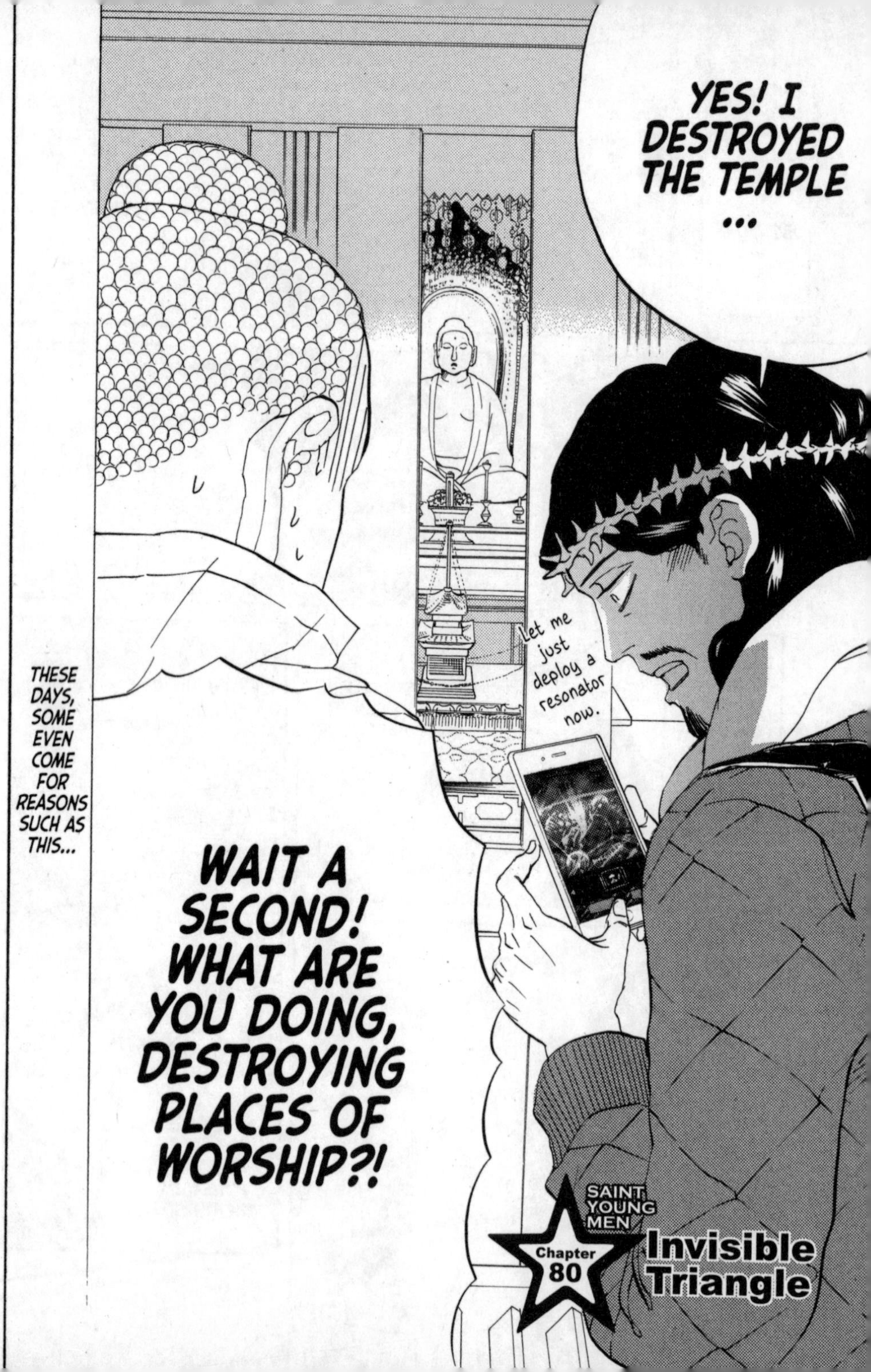
YES! I DESTROYED THE TEMPLE ...
Let me just deploy a resonator now.
WAIT A SECOND! WHAT ARE YOU DOING, DESTROYING PLACES OF WORSHIP?!
THESE DAYS, SOME EVEN COME FOR REASONS SUCH AS THIS...
SAINT YOUNG MEN
Chapter 80
Invisible Triangle

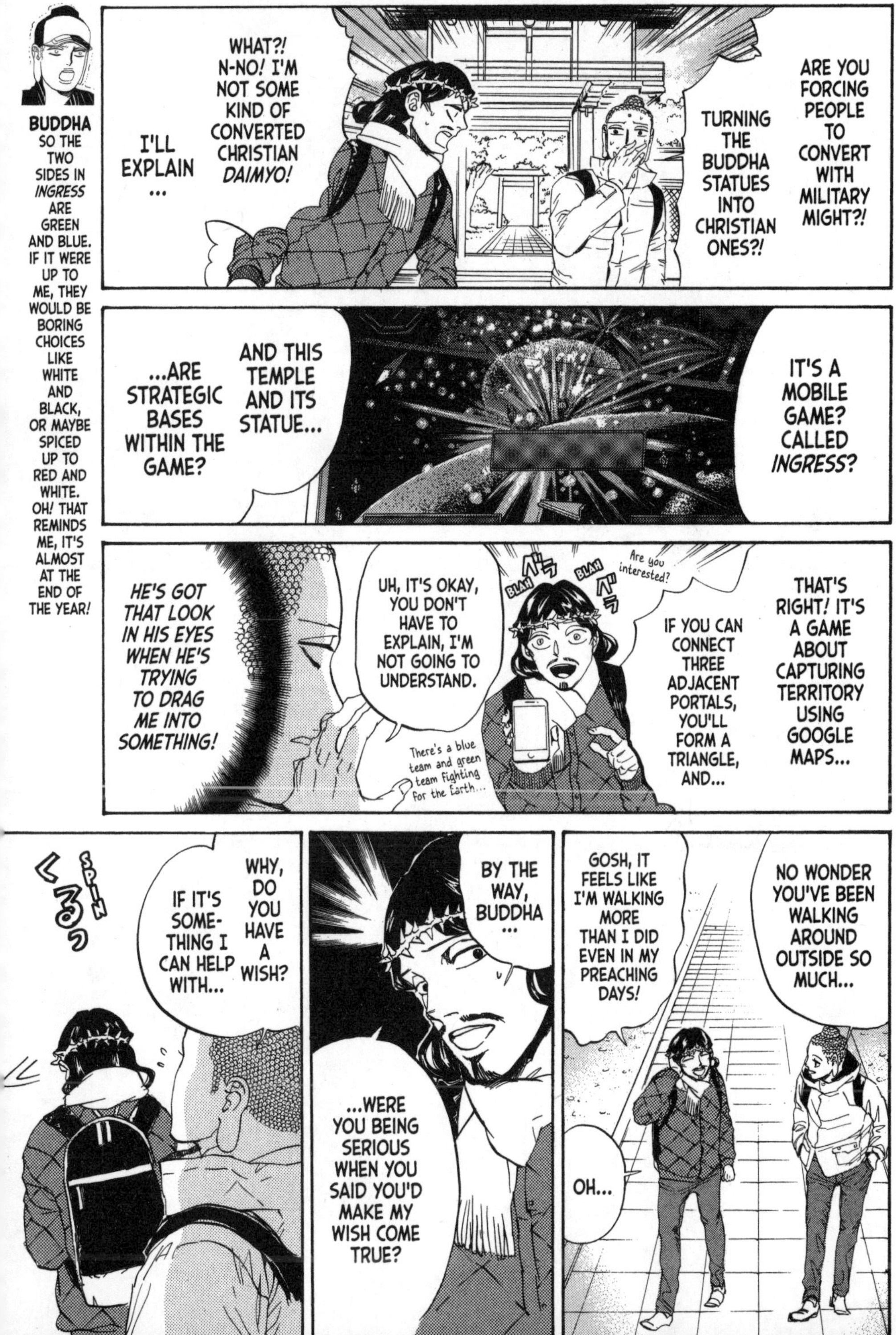
ARE YOU FORCING PEOPLE TO CONVERT WITH MILITARY MIGHT?!
TURNING THE BUDDHA STATUES INTO CHRISTIAN ONES?!
WHAT?! N-NO! I'M NOT SOME KIND OF CONVERTED CHRISTIAN *DAIMYO!*
I'LL EXPLAIN ...
IT'S A MOBILE GAME? CALLED *INGRESS?*
AND THIS TEMPLE AND ITS STATUE...
...ARE STRATEGIC BASES WITHIN THE GAME?
THAT'S RIGHT! IT'S A GAME ABOUT CAPTURING TERRITORY USING GOOGLE MAPS...
IF YOU CAN CONNECT THREE ADJACENT PORTALS, YOU'LL FORM A TRIANGLE, AND...
Are you interested?
BLAH
BLAH
There's a blue team and green team fighting for the Earth...
UH, IT'S OKAY, YOU DON'T HAVE TO EXPLAIN, I'M NOT GOING TO UNDERSTAND.
HE'S GOT THAT LOOK IN HIS EYES WHEN HE'S TRYING TO DRAG ME INTO SOMETHING!
NO WONDER YOU'VE BEEN WALKING AROUND OUTSIDE SO MUCH...
GOSH, IT FEELS LIKE I'M WALKING MORE THAN I DID EVEN IN MY PREACHING DAYS!
OH...
BY THE WAY, BUDDHA ...
...WERE YOU BEING SERIOUS WHEN YOU SAID YOU'D MAKE MY WISH COME TRUE?
WHY, DO YOU HAVE A WISH?
IF IT'S SOMETHING I CAN HELP WITH...
SPIN

BUDDHA SO THE TWO SIDES IN *INGRESS* ARE GREEN AND BLUE. IF IT WERE UP TO ME, THEY WOULD BE BORING CHOICES LIKE WHITE AND BLACK, OR MAYBE SPICED UP TO RED AND WHITE. OH! THAT REMINDS ME, IT'S ALMOST AT THE END OF THE YEAR!

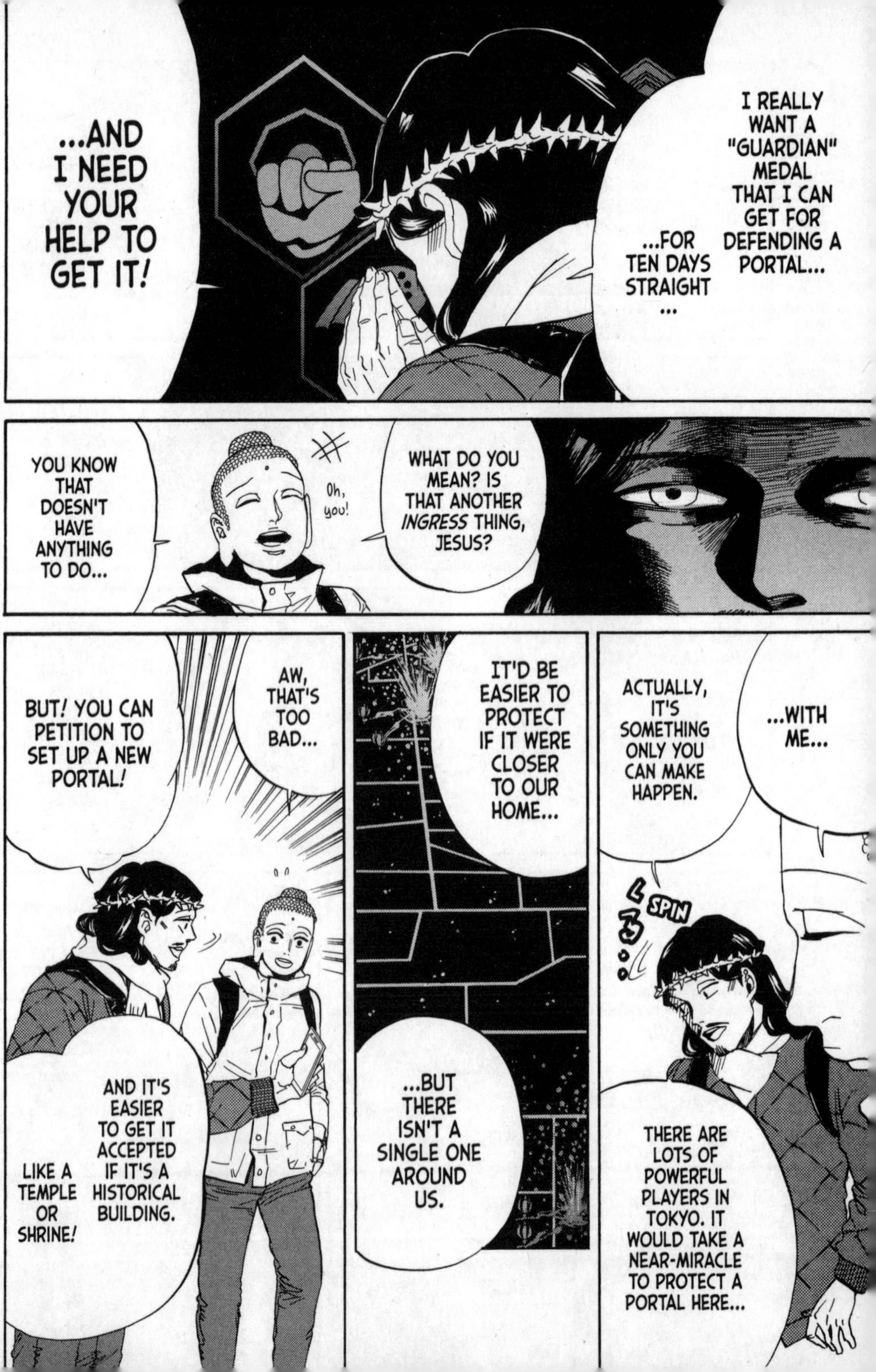
I REALLY WANT A "GUARDIAN" MEDAL THAT I CAN GET FOR DEFENDING A PORTAL...
...FOR TEN DAYS STRAIGHT ...
...AND I NEED YOUR HELP TO GET IT!
WHAT DO YOU MEAN? IS THAT ANOTHER *INGRESS* THING, JESUS?
Oh, you!
YOU KNOW THAT DOESN'T HAVE ANYTHING TO DO...
...WITH ME...
ACTUALLY, IT'S SOMETHING ONLY YOU CAN MAKE HAPPEN.
SPIN
THERE ARE LOTS OF POWERFUL PLAYERS IN TOKYO. IT WOULD TAKE A NEAR-MIRACLE TO PROTECT A PORTAL HERE...
IT'D BE EASIER TO PROTECT IF IT WERE CLOSER TO OUR HOME...
...BUT THERE ISN'T A SINGLE ONE AROUND US.
AW, THAT'S TOO BAD...
BUT! YOU CAN PETITION TO SET UP A NEW PORTAL!
AND IT'S EASIER TO GET IT ACCEPTED IF IT'S A HISTORICAL BUILDING.
LIKE A TEMPLE OR SHRINE!

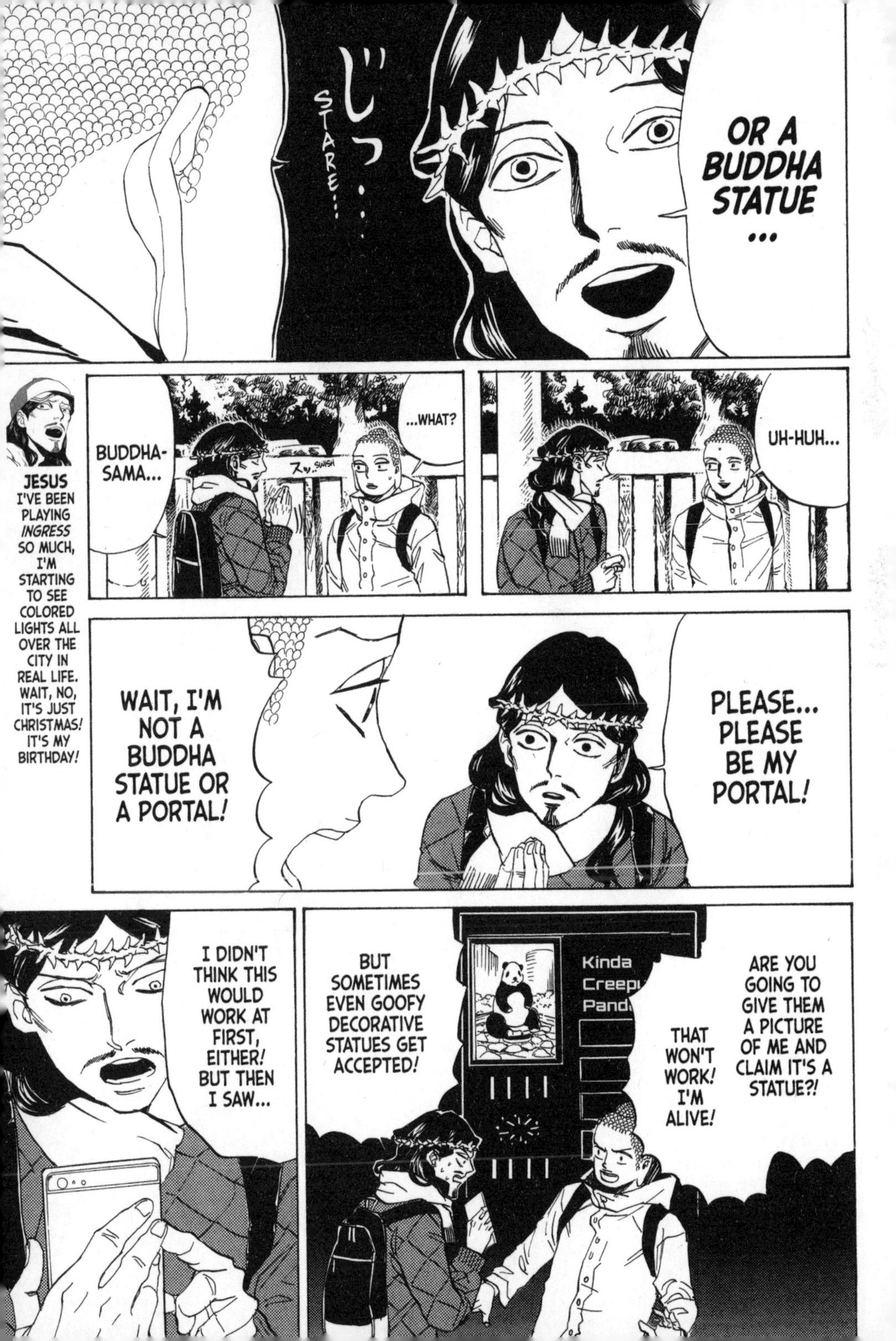
OR A BUDDHA STATUE ...
じっ…
STARE…
UH-HUH...
...WHAT?
BUDDHA-SAMA...
スッ
SWISH
PLEASE... PLEASE BE MY PORTAL!
WAIT, I'M NOT A BUDDHA STATUE OR A PORTAL!
ARE YOU GOING TO GIVE THEM A PICTURE OF ME AND CLAIM IT'S A STATUE?!
THAT WON'T WORK! I'M ALIVE!
BUT SOMETIMES EVEN GOOFY DECORATIVE STATUES GET ACCEPTED!
Kinda Creep Pand
I DIDN'T THINK THIS WOULD WORK AT FIRST, EITHER! BUT THEN I SAW...
JESUS
I'VE BEEN PLAYING *INGRESS* SO MUCH, I'M STARTING TO SEE COLORED LIGHTS ALL OVER THE CITY IN REAL LIFE. WAIT, NO, IT'S JUST CHRISTMAS! IT'S MY BIRTHDAY!

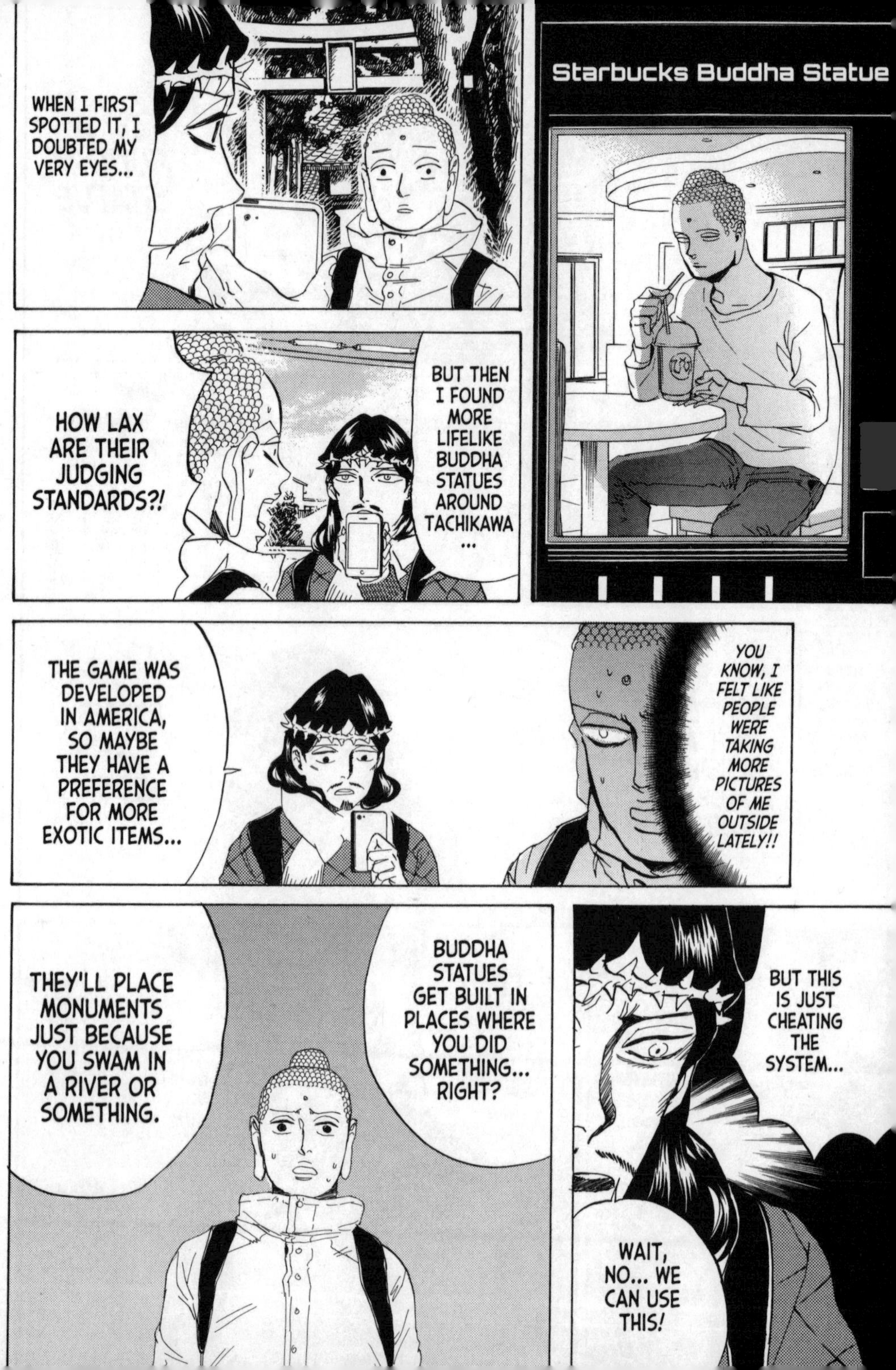
Starbucks Buddha Statue
WHEN I FIRST SPOTTED IT, I DOUBTED MY VERY EYES...
BUT THEN I FOUND MORE LIFELIKE BUDDHA STATUES AROUND TACHIKAWA ...
HOW LAX ARE THEIR JUDGING STANDARDS?!
YOU KNOW, I FELT LIKE PEOPLE WERE TAKING MORE PICTURES OF ME OUTSIDE LATELY!!
THE GAME WAS DEVELOPED IN AMERICA, SO MAYBE THEY HAVE A PREFERENCE FOR MORE EXOTIC ITEMS...
BUT THIS IS JUST CHEATING THE SYSTEM...
WAIT, NO... WE CAN USE THIS!
BUDDHA STATUES GET BUILT IN PLACES WHERE YOU DID SOMETHING... RIGHT?
THEY'LL PLACE MONUMENTS JUST BECAUSE YOU SWAM IN A RIVER OR SOMETHING.

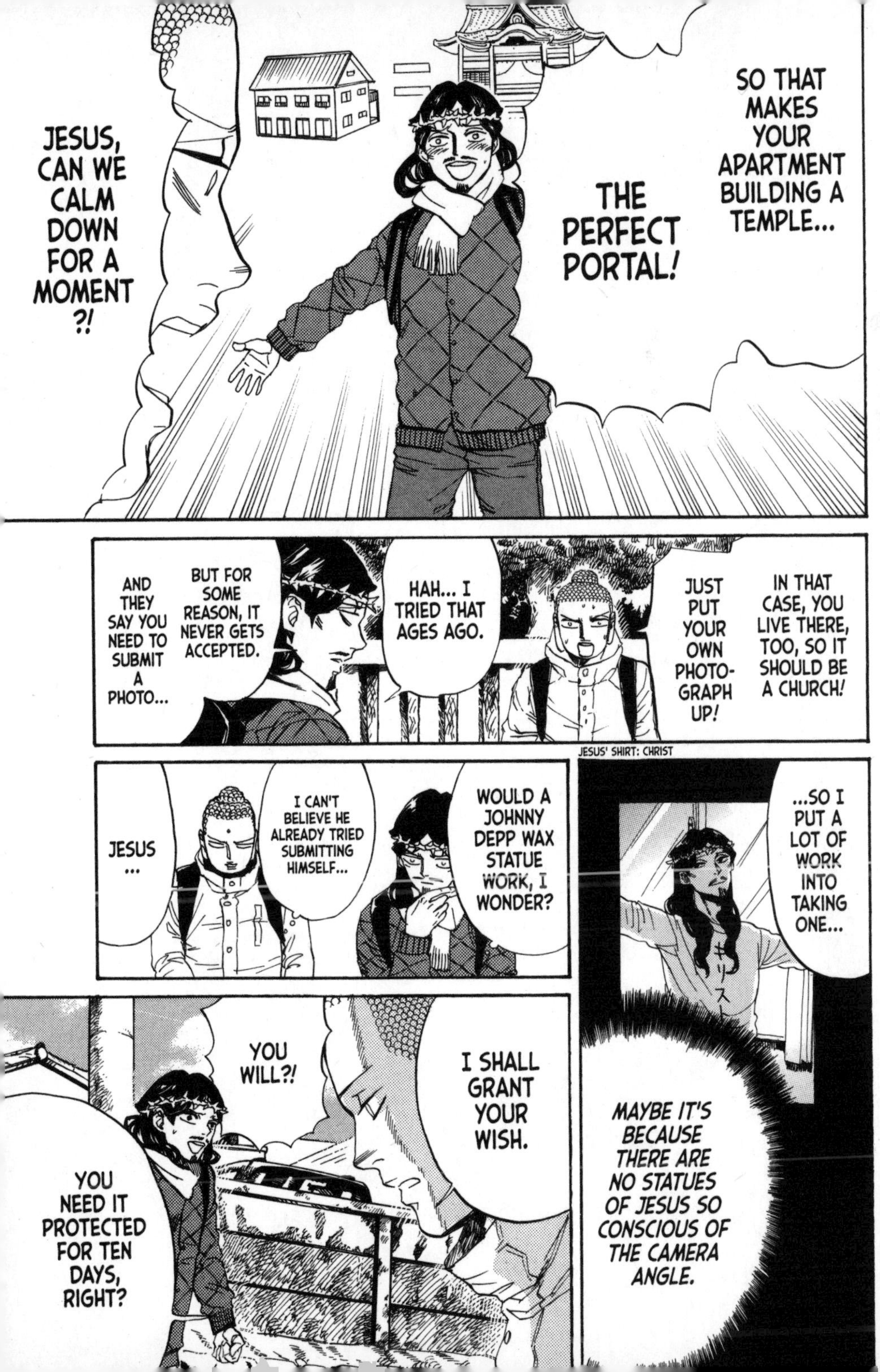
SO THAT MAKES YOUR APARTMENT BUILDING A TEMPLE...
THE PERFECT PORTAL!
JESUS, CAN WE CALM DOWN FOR A MOMENT?!
IN THAT CASE, YOU LIVE THERE, TOO, SO IT SHOULD BE A CHURCH!
JUST PUT YOUR OWN PHOTOGRAPH UP!
HAH... I TRIED THAT AGES AGO.
BUT FOR SOME REASON, IT NEVER GETS ACCEPTED.
AND THEY SAY YOU NEED TO SUBMIT A PHOTO...
JESUS' SHIRT: CHRIST
...SO I PUT A LOT OF WORK INTO TAKING ONE...
MAYBE IT'S BECAUSE THERE ARE NO STATUES OF JESUS SO CONSCIOUS OF THE CAMERA ANGLE.
WOULD A JOHNNY DEPP WAX STATUE WORK, I WONDER?
I CAN'T BELIEVE HE ALREADY TRIED SUBMITTING HIMSELF...
JESUS...
I SHALL GRANT YOUR WISH.
YOU WILL?!
YOU NEED IT PROTECTED FOR TEN DAYS, RIGHT?

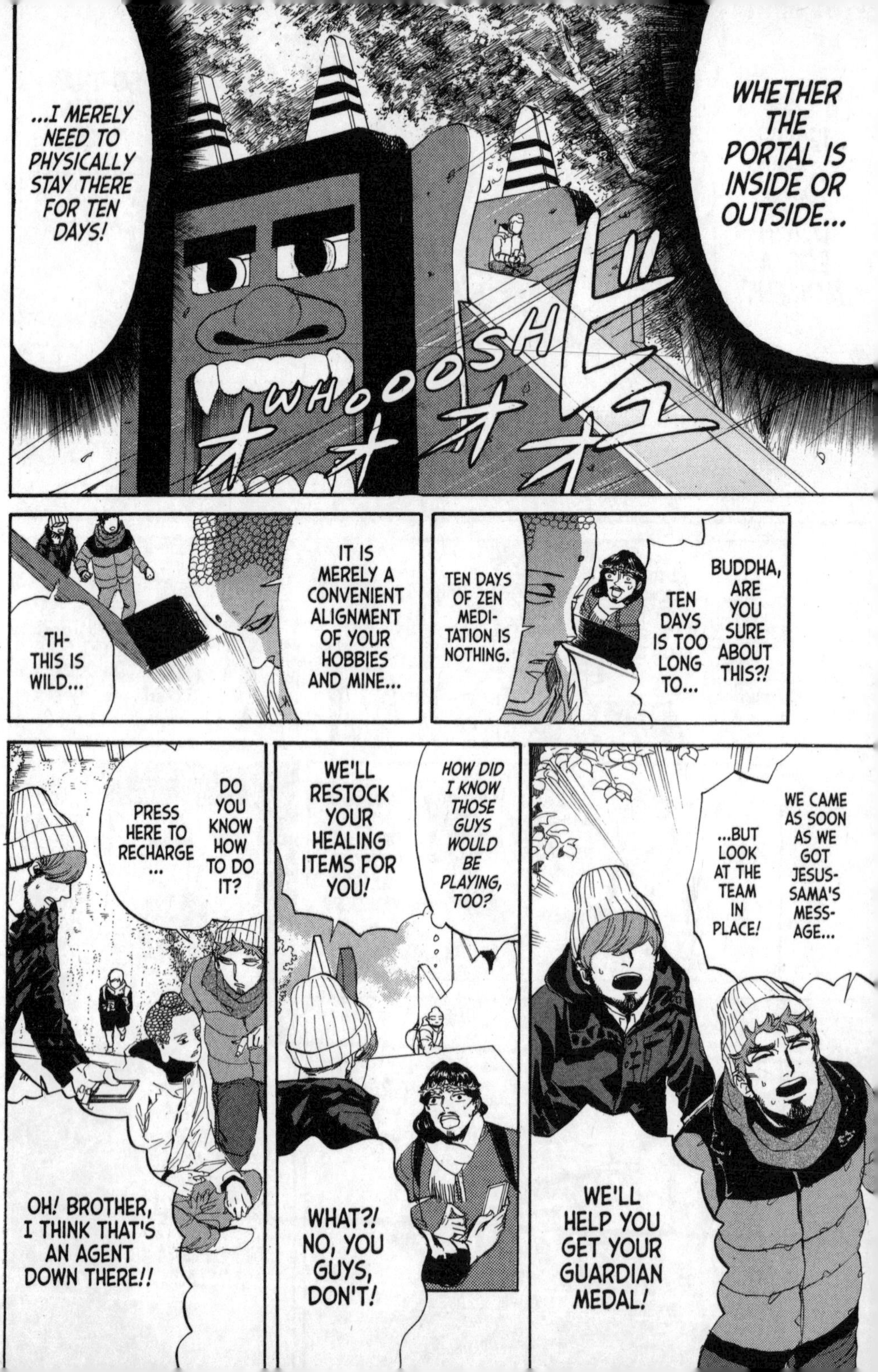
WHETHER THE PORTAL IS INSIDE OR OUTSIDE...
...I MERELY NEED TO PHYSICALLY STAY THERE FOR TEN DAYS!
WHOOOSH
ビュオオオオ
BUDDHA, ARE YOU SURE ABOUT THIS?!
TEN DAYS IS TOO LONG TO...
TEN DAYS OF ZEN MEDITATION IS NOTHING.
IT IS MERELY A CONVENIENT ALIGNMENT OF YOUR HOBBIES AND MINE...
TH- THIS IS WILD...
WE CAME AS SOON AS WE GOT JESUS-SAMA'S MESSAGE...
...BUT LOOK AT THE TEAM IN PLACE!
WE'LL HELP YOU GET YOUR GUARDIAN MEDAL!
HOW DID I KNOW THOSE GUYS WOULD BE PLAYING, TOO?
WE'LL RESTOCK YOUR HEALING ITEMS FOR YOU!
WHAT?! NO, YOU GUYS, DON'T!
DO YOU KNOW HOW TO DO IT?
PRESS HERE TO RECHARGE...
OH! BROTHER, I THINK THAT'S AN AGENT DOWN THERE!!

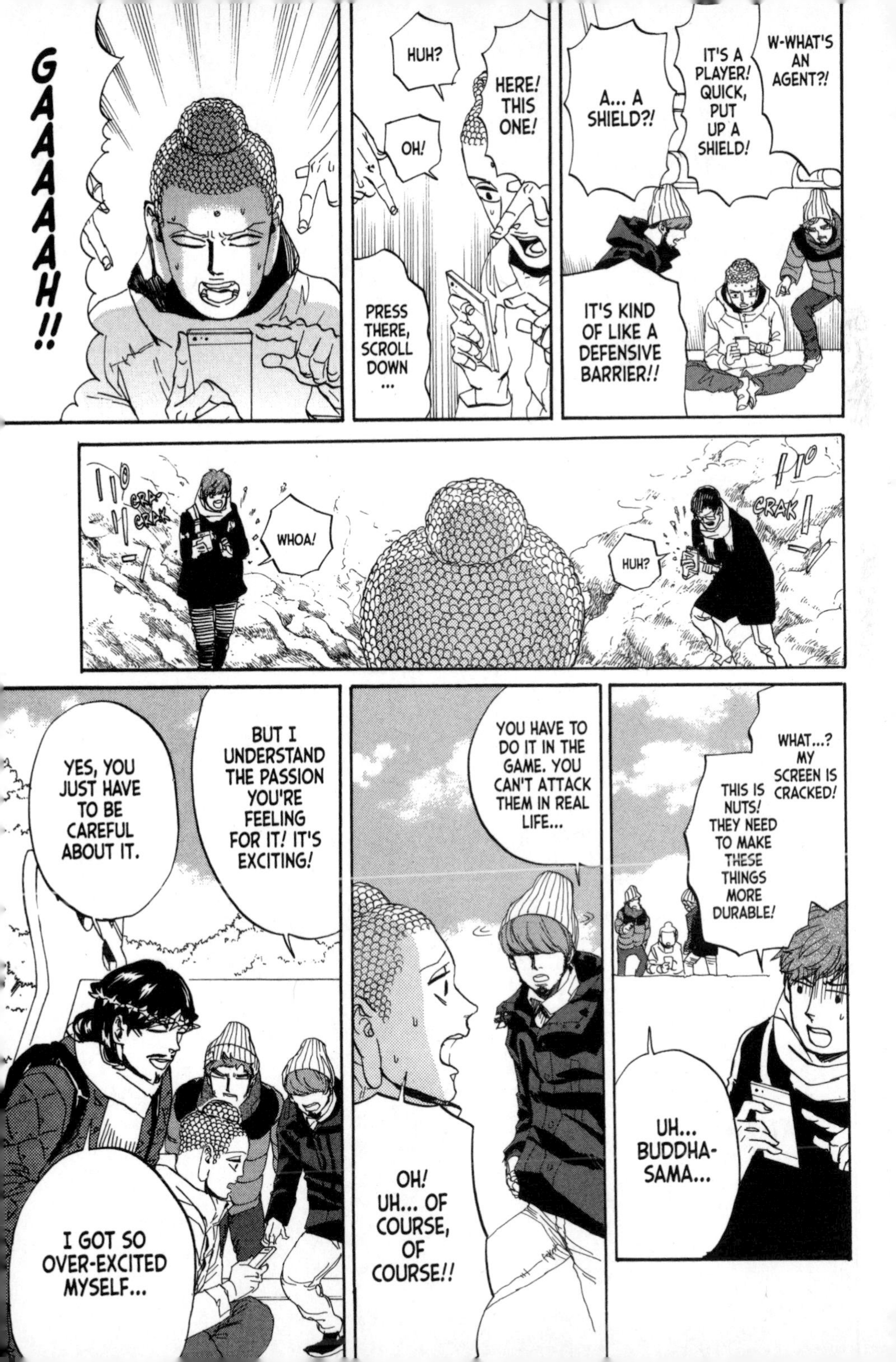
W-WHAT'S AN AGENT?!
IT'S A PLAYER! QUICK, PUT UP A SHIELD!
A... A SHIELD?!
IT'S KIND OF LIKE A DEFENSIVE BARRIER!!
HERE! THIS ONE!
HUH?
OH!
PRESS THERE, SCROLL DOWN ...
GAAAAAAH!!
CRAK
HUH?
WHOA!
WHAT...? MY SCREEN IS CRACKED!
THIS IS NUTS! THEY NEED TO MAKE THESE THINGS MORE DURABLE!
UH... BUDDHA-SAMA...
YOU HAVE TO DO IT IN THE GAME. YOU CAN'T ATTACK THEM IN REAL LIFE...
OH! UH... OF COURSE, OF COURSE!!
BUT I UNDERSTAND THE PASSION YOU'RE FEELING FOR IT! IT'S EXCITING!
YES, YOU JUST HAVE TO BE CAREFUL ABOUT IT.
I GOT SO OVER-EXCITED MYSELF...

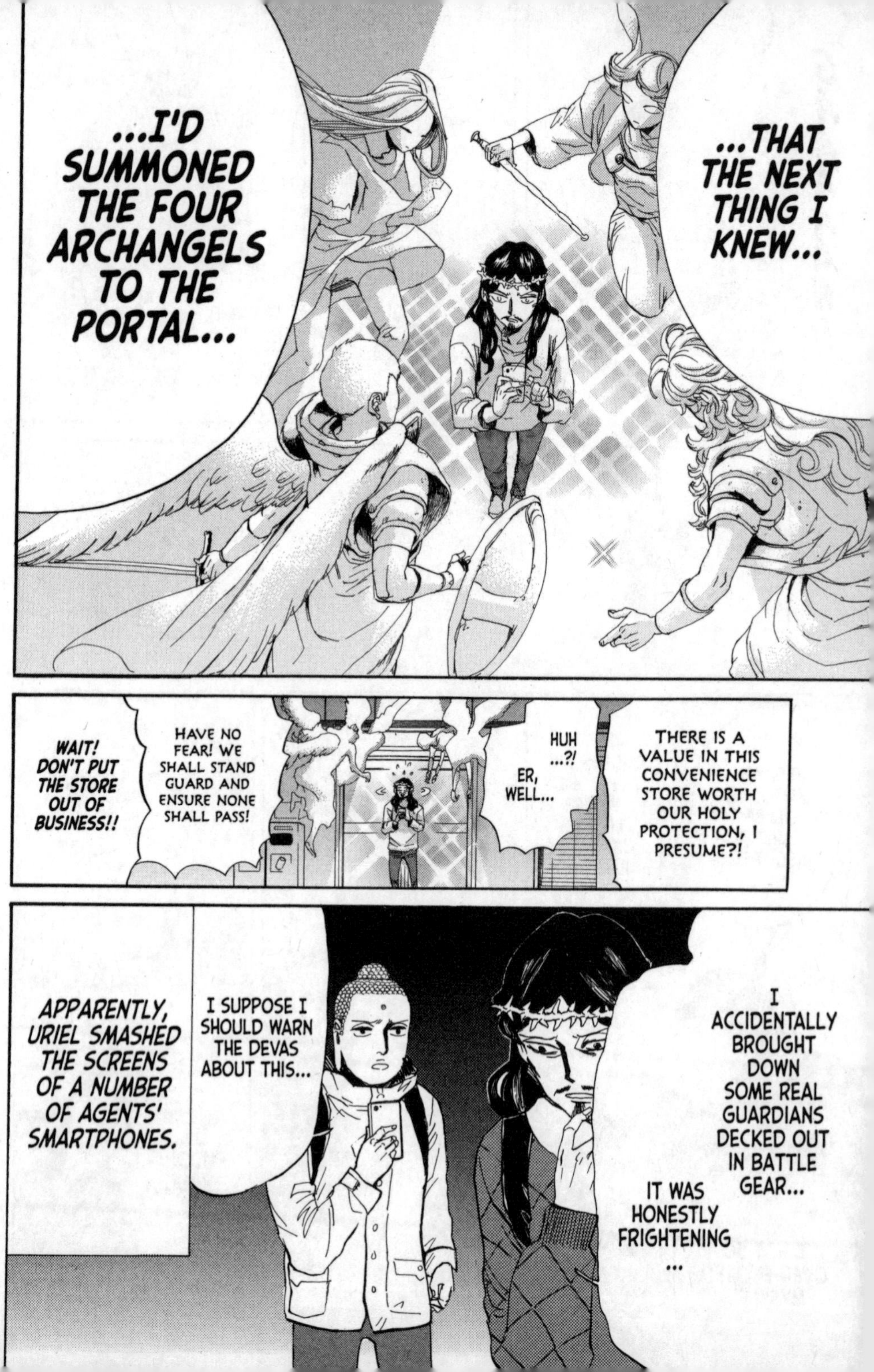
...I'D SUMMONED THE FOUR ARCHANGELS TO THE PORTAL...
...THAT THE NEXT THING I KNEW...
THERE IS A VALUE IN THIS CONVENIENCE STORE WORTH OUR HOLY PROTECTION, I PRESUME?!
HUH ...?!
ER, WELL...
HAVE NO FEAR! WE SHALL STAND GUARD AND ENSURE NONE SHALL PASS!
WAIT! DON'T PUT THE STORE OUT OF BUSINESS!!
I ACCIDENTALLY BROUGHT DOWN SOME REAL GUARDIANS DECKED OUT IN BATTLE GEAR...
IT WAS HONESTLY FRIGHTENING...
I SUPPOSE I SHOULD WARN THE DEVAS ABOUT THIS...
APPARENTLY, URIEL SMASHED THE SCREENS OF A NUMBER OF AGENTS' SMARTPHONES.

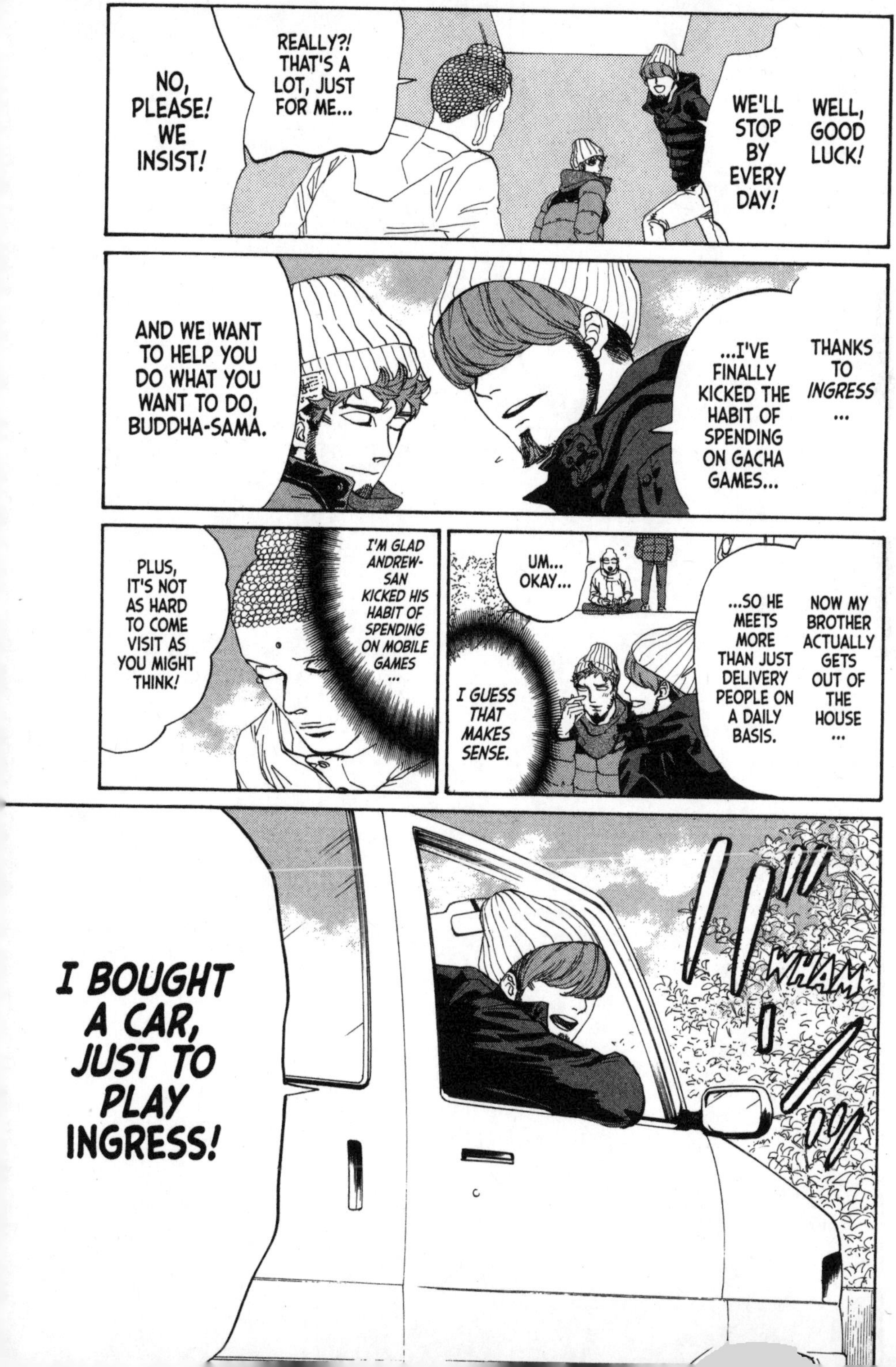
WELL, GOOD LUCK!
WE'LL STOP BY EVERY DAY!
REALLY?! THAT'S A LOT, JUST FOR ME...
NO, PLEASE! WE INSIST!
THANKS TO *INGRESS*...
...I'VE FINALLY KICKED THE HABIT OF SPENDING ON GACHA GAMES...
AND WE WANT TO HELP YOU DO WHAT YOU WANT TO DO, BUDDHA-SAMA.
NOW MY BROTHER ACTUALLY GETS OUT OF THE HOUSE...
...SO HE MEETS MORE THAN JUST DELIVERY PEOPLE ON A DAILY BASIS.
UM... OKAY...
I GUESS THAT MAKES SENSE.
I'M GLAD ANDREW-SAN KICKED HIS HABIT OF SPENDING ON MOBILE GAMES...
PLUS, IT'S NOT AS HARD TO COME VISIT AS YOU MIGHT THINK!
WHAM
I BOUGHT A CAR, JUST TO PLAY INGRESS!

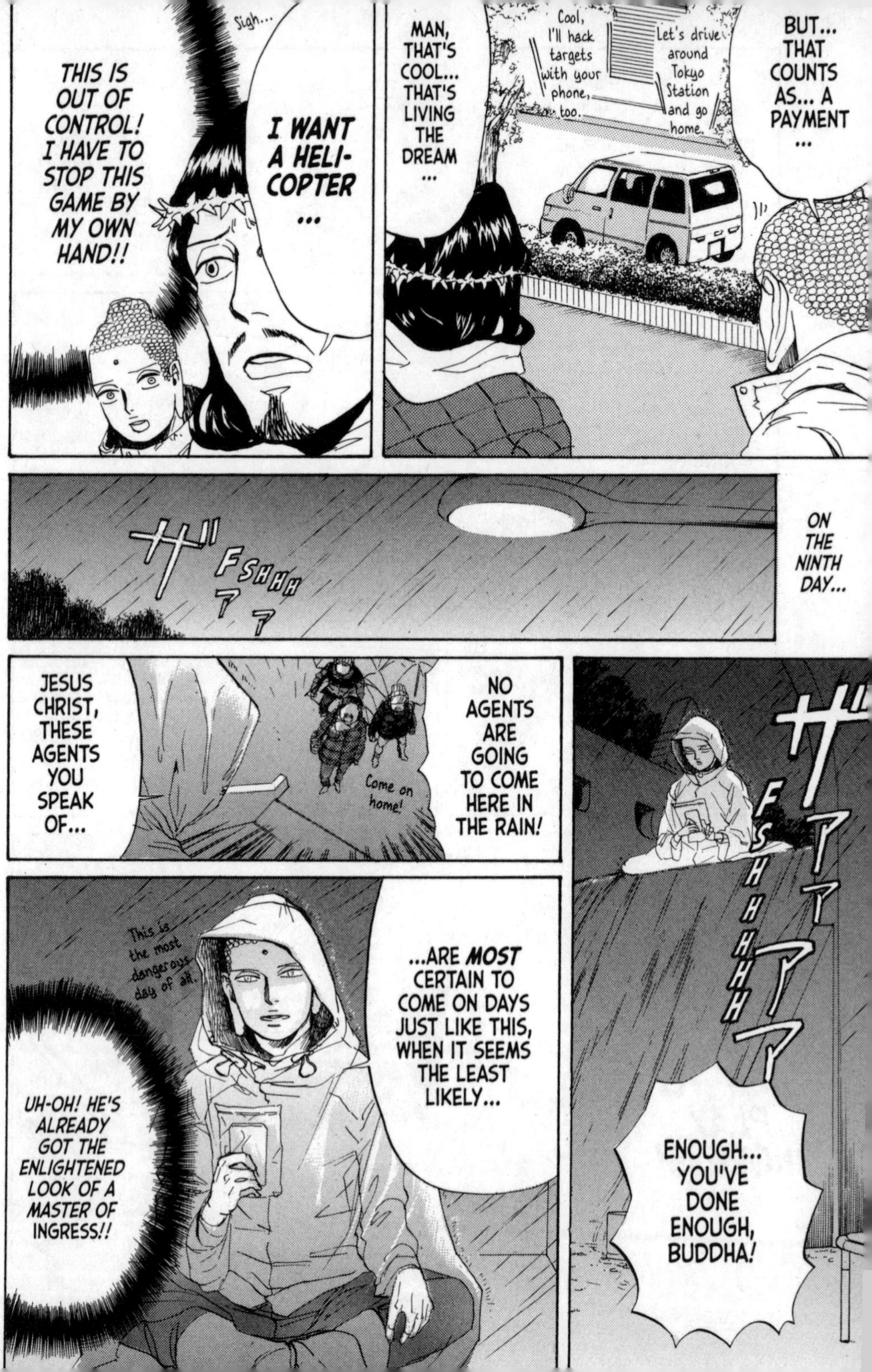

BUT... THAT COUNTS AS... A PAYMENT...
Let's drive around Tokyo Station and go home.
Cool, I'll hack targets with your phone, too.
MAN, THAT'S COOL... THAT'S LIVING THE DREAM...
Sigh...
I WANT A HELICOPTER...
THIS IS OUT OF CONTROL! I HAVE TO STOP THIS GAME BY MY OWN HAND!!
ON THE NINTH DAY...
FSHHHH
FSHHHHHH
ENOUGH... YOU'VE DONE ENOUGH, BUDDHA!
NO AGENTS ARE GOING TO COME HERE IN THE RAIN!
Come on home!
JESUS CHRIST, THESE AGENTS YOU SPEAK OF...
...ARE MOST CERTAIN TO COME ON DAYS JUST LIKE THIS, WHEN IT SEEMS THE LEAST LIKELY...
This is the most dangerous day of all.
UH-OH! HE'S ALREADY GOT THE ENLIGHTENED LOOK OF A MASTER OF INGRESS!!

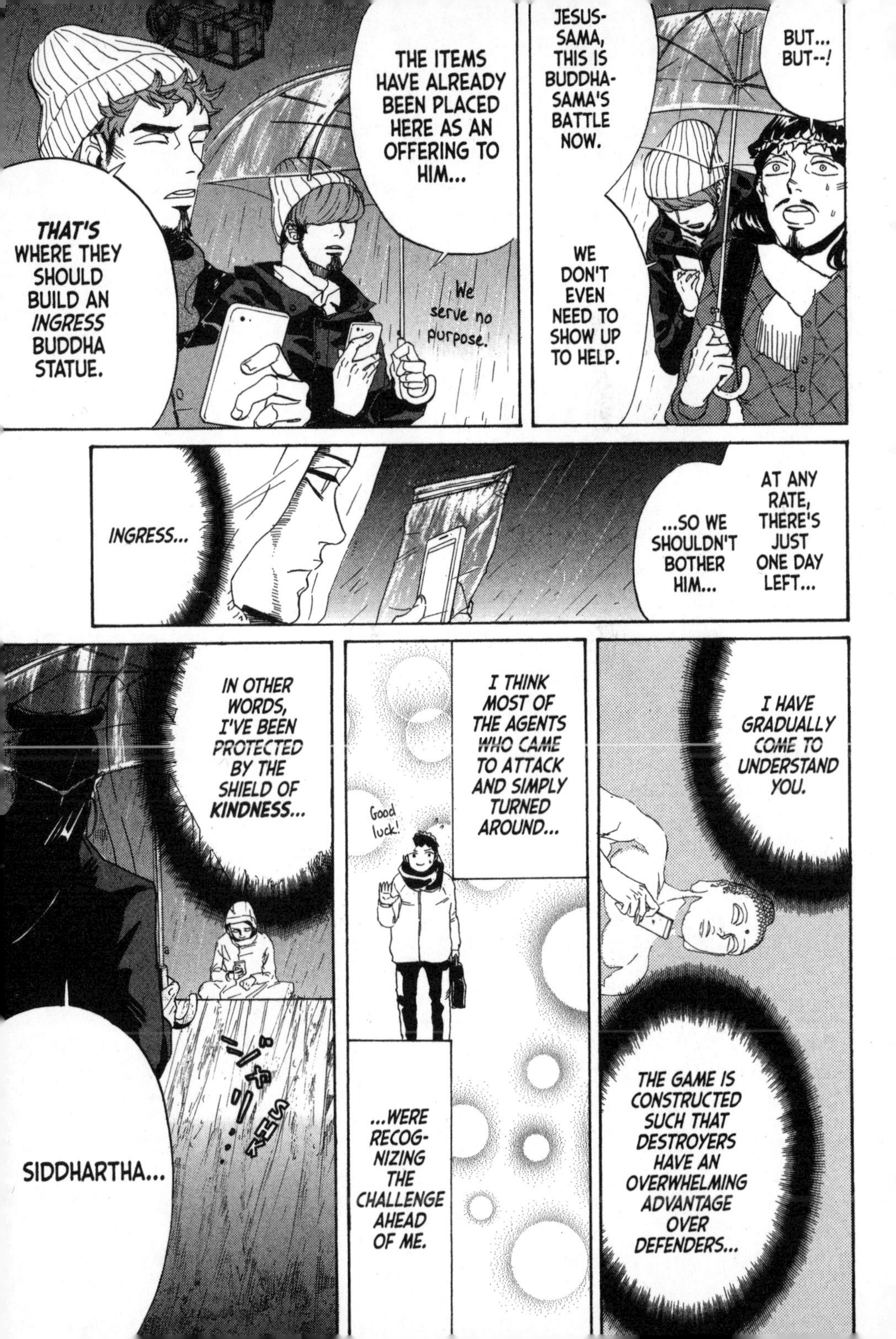
BUT... BUT--!
JESUS-SAMA, THIS IS BUDDHA-SAMA'S BATTLE NOW.
WE DON'T EVEN NEED TO SHOW UP TO HELP.
THE ITEMS HAVE ALREADY BEEN PLACED HERE AS AN OFFERING TO HIM...
We serve no purpose.
THAT'S WHERE THEY SHOULD BUILD AN *INGRESS* BUDDHA STATUE.
AT ANY RATE, THERE'S JUST ONE DAY LEFT...
...SO WE SHOULDN'T BOTHER HIM...
INGRESS...
I HAVE GRADUALLY COME TO UNDERSTAND YOU.
THE GAME IS CONSTRUCTED SUCH THAT DESTROYERS HAVE AN OVERWHELMING ADVANTAGE OVER DEFENDERS...
I THINK MOST OF THE AGENTS WHO CAME TO ATTACK AND SIMPLY TURNED AROUND...
Good luck!
...WERE RECOGNIZING THE CHALLENGE AHEAD OF ME.
IN OTHER WORDS, I'VE BEEN PROTECTED BY THE SHIELD OF ***KINDNESS...***
SIDDHARTHA...

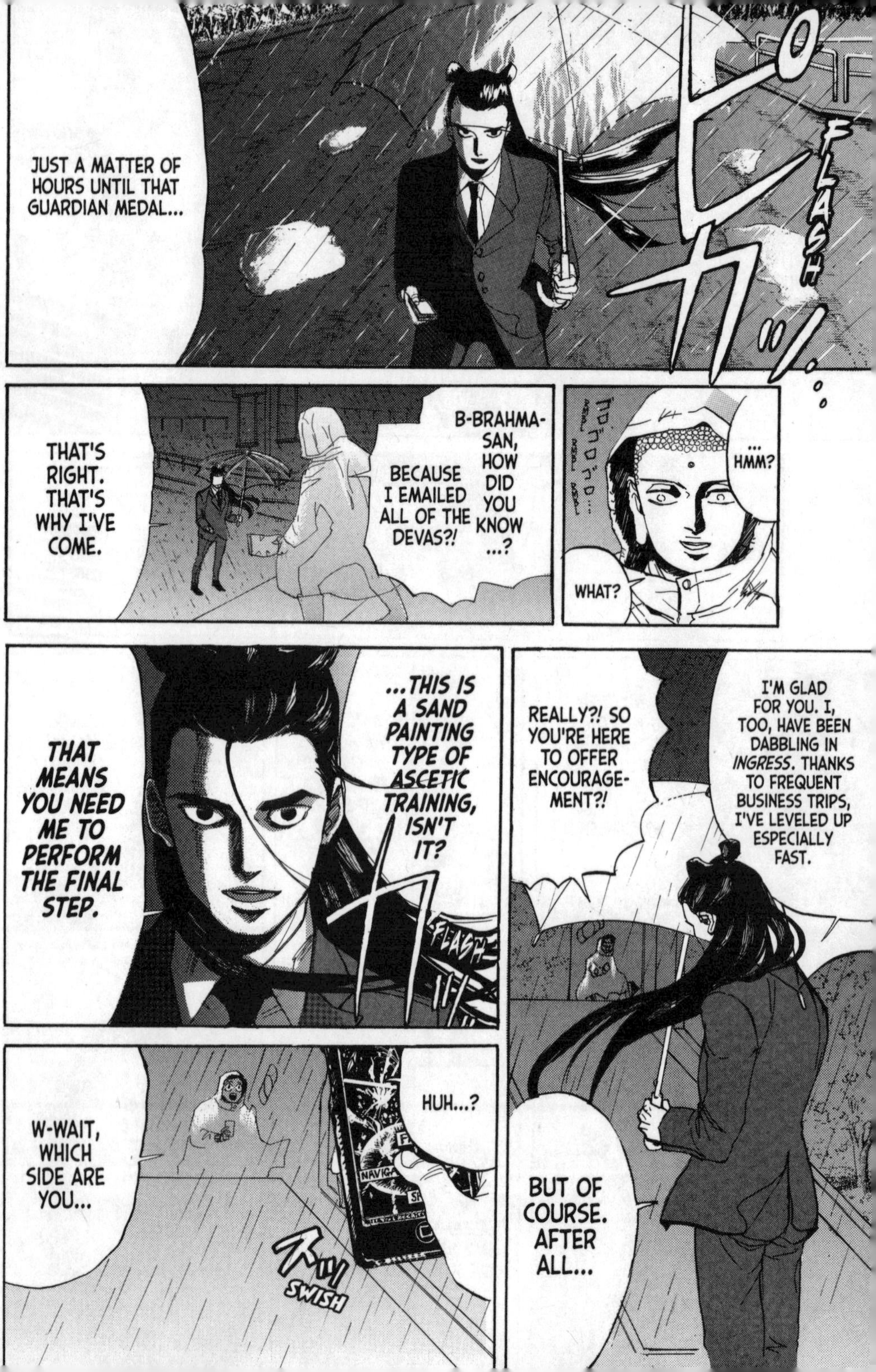
FLASH
JUST A MATTER OF HOURS UNTIL THAT GUARDIAN MEDAL...
...HMM?
RMBL RMBL
WHAT?
B-BRAHMA-SAN, HOW DID YOU KNOW ...?
BECAUSE I EMAILED ALL OF THE DEVAS?!
THAT'S RIGHT. THAT'S WHY I'VE COME.
I'M GLAD FOR YOU. I, TOO, HAVE BEEN DABBLING IN *INGRESS*. THANKS TO FREQUENT BUSINESS TRIPS, I'VE LEVELED UP ESPECIALLY FAST.
REALLY?! SO YOU'RE HERE TO OFFER ENCOURAGE-MENT?!
BUT OF COURSE. AFTER ALL...
...THIS IS A SAND PAINTING TYPE OF ASCETIC TRAINING, ISN'T IT?
THAT MEANS YOU NEED ME TO PERFORM THE FINAL STEP.
FLASH
HUH...?
W-WAIT, WHICH SIDE ARE YOU...
SWISH

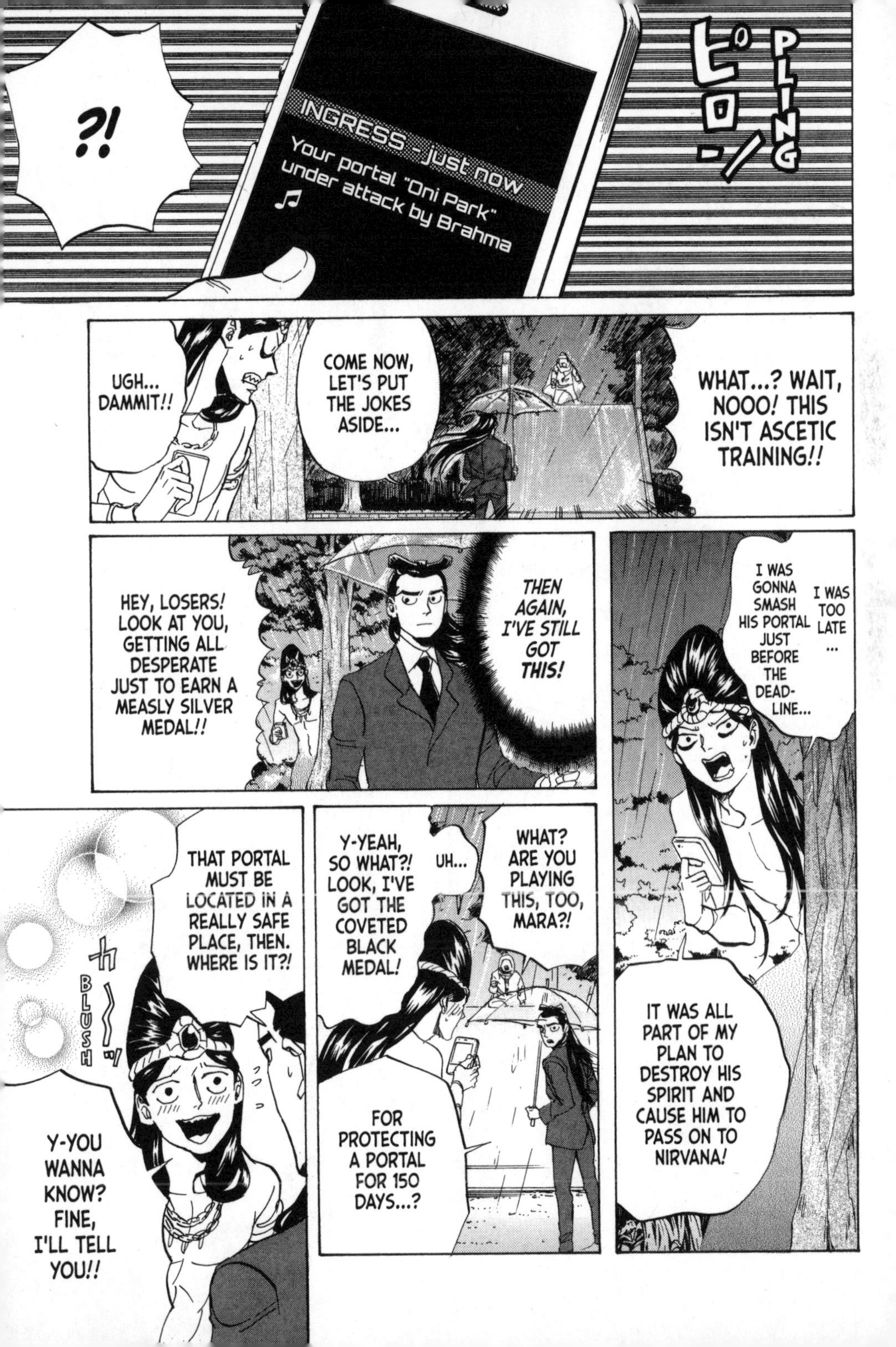
PLING
INGRESS - just now
Your portal "Oni Park" under attack by Brahma
?!
WHAT...? WAIT, NOOO! THIS ISN'T ASCETIC TRAINING!!
COME NOW, LET'S PUT THE JOKES ASIDE...
UGH... DAMMIT!!
I WAS TOO LATE...
I WAS GONNA SMASH HIS PORTAL JUST BEFORE THE DEAD-LINE...
IT WAS ALL PART OF MY PLAN TO DESTROY HIS SPIRIT AND CAUSE HIM TO PASS ON TO NIRVANA!
THEN AGAIN, I'VE STILL GOT THIS!
HEY, LOSERS! LOOK AT YOU, GETTING ALL DESPERATE JUST TO EARN A MEASLY SILVER MEDAL!!
WHAT? ARE YOU PLAYING THIS, TOO, MARA?!
UH...
Y-YEAH, SO WHAT?! LOOK, I'VE GOT THE COVETED BLACK MEDAL!
FOR PROTECTING A PORTAL FOR 150 DAYS...?
THAT PORTAL MUST BE LOCATED IN A REALLY SAFE PLACE, THEN. WHERE IS IT?!
BLUSH
Y-YOU WANNA KNOW? FINE, I'LL TELL YOU!!

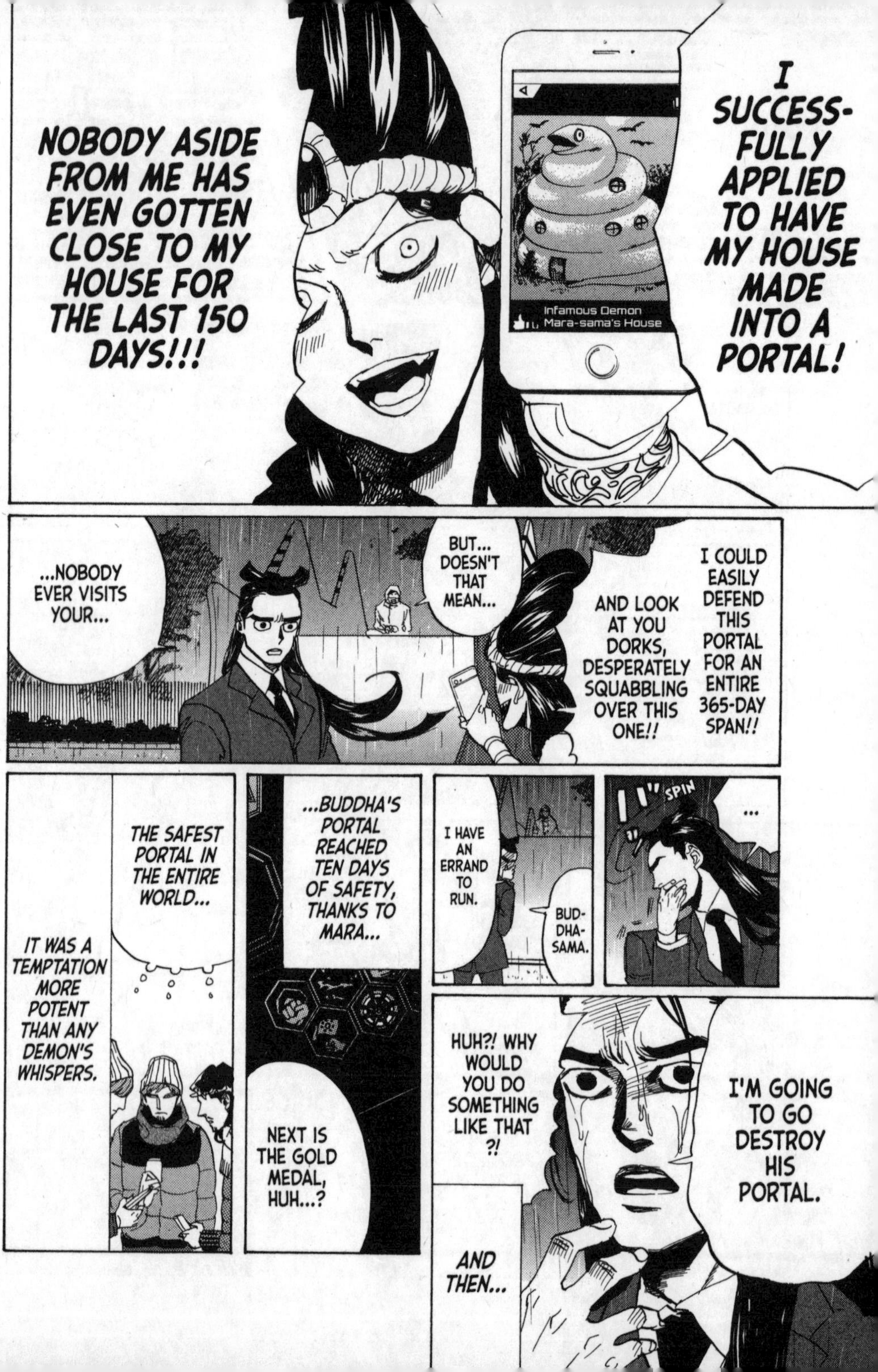

I SUCCESSFULLY APPLIED TO HAVE MY HOUSE MADE INTO A PORTAL!
Infamous Demon Mara-sama's House
NOBODY ASIDE FROM ME HAS EVEN GOTTEN CLOSE TO MY HOUSE FOR THE LAST 150 DAYS!!!
I COULD EASILY DEFEND THIS PORTAL FOR AN ENTIRE 365-DAY SPAN!!
AND LOOK AT YOU DORKS, DESPERATELY SQUABBLING OVER THIS ONE!!
BUT... DOESN'T THAT MEAN...
...NOBODY EVER VISITS YOUR...
SPIN
...
I HAVE AN ERRAND TO RUN.
BUDDHA-SAMA.
I'M GOING TO GO DESTROY HIS PORTAL.
HUH?! WHY WOULD YOU DO SOMETHING LIKE THAT?!
AND THEN...
...BUDDHA'S PORTAL REACHED TEN DAYS OF SAFETY, THANKS TO MARA...
NEXT IS THE GOLD MEDAL, HUH...?
THE SAFEST PORTAL IN THE ENTIRE WORLD...
IT WAS A TEMPTATION MORE POTENT THAN ANY DEMON'S WHISPERS.

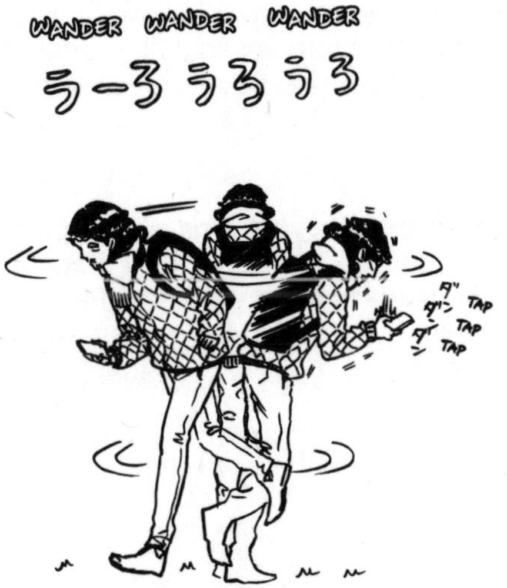
WANDER WANDER WANDER
うーろうろうろ
ダン TAP
ダン TAP
ダン TAP

Playing Ingress

CHAPTER 80 TRANSLATION NOTES

Red and white, page 117

The word *kôhaku* means "red and white," and these are considered the default colors for two teams in competition. On its own, this word is usually shorthand for the "*Kôhaku* Song Competition," a New Year's Eve TV extravaganza that is consistently the most popular televised event of the year. On it, singers, actors, and other popular celebrities appear to sing hit songs of the present and past to round out the year. The female participants make up the red team and the male participants the white, with the winning team being chosen by a combination of judges and audience voting.

Christian *daimyo*, page 117

In the early days of the Portuguese missionaries' attempts to bring Christianity to Japan, they quickly found support among some daimyo lords, many of whom eagerly (or forcefully) converted their subjects as well, and appropriated Buddhist icons into Christian ones. These lords were called "*Kirishitan daimyo*" during this period.

Ingress, page 117

As explained in the manga, Ingress is a real mobile game by Niantic that was first released to the public in 2013, and utilized public Google Maps data to generate "territory" to be fought over by players. It served as a proof of concept that GPS data and local points of interest could be turned into gameplay elements, and is now a footnote to Niantic's success with their wildly popular follow-up game, *Pokémon Go*.

Sand painting, page 128

A Tibetan Buddhist tradition of creating mandala patterns out of special colored sand, painstakingly crafted using special hollow tools that are rubbed to cause the sand to trickle out of the holes at the end. When the mandala is complete, it is then ritually destroyed to symbolize the impermanence of being.

SAINT☆YOUNG MEN

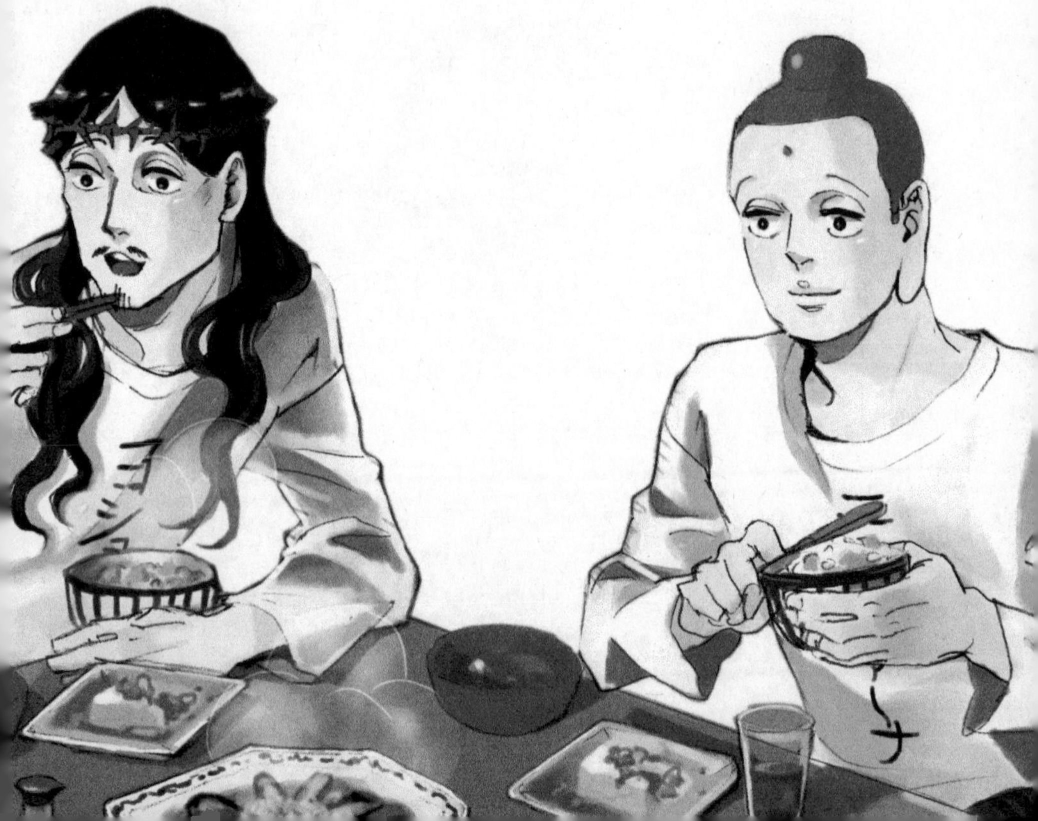

SAINT☆YOUNG MEN

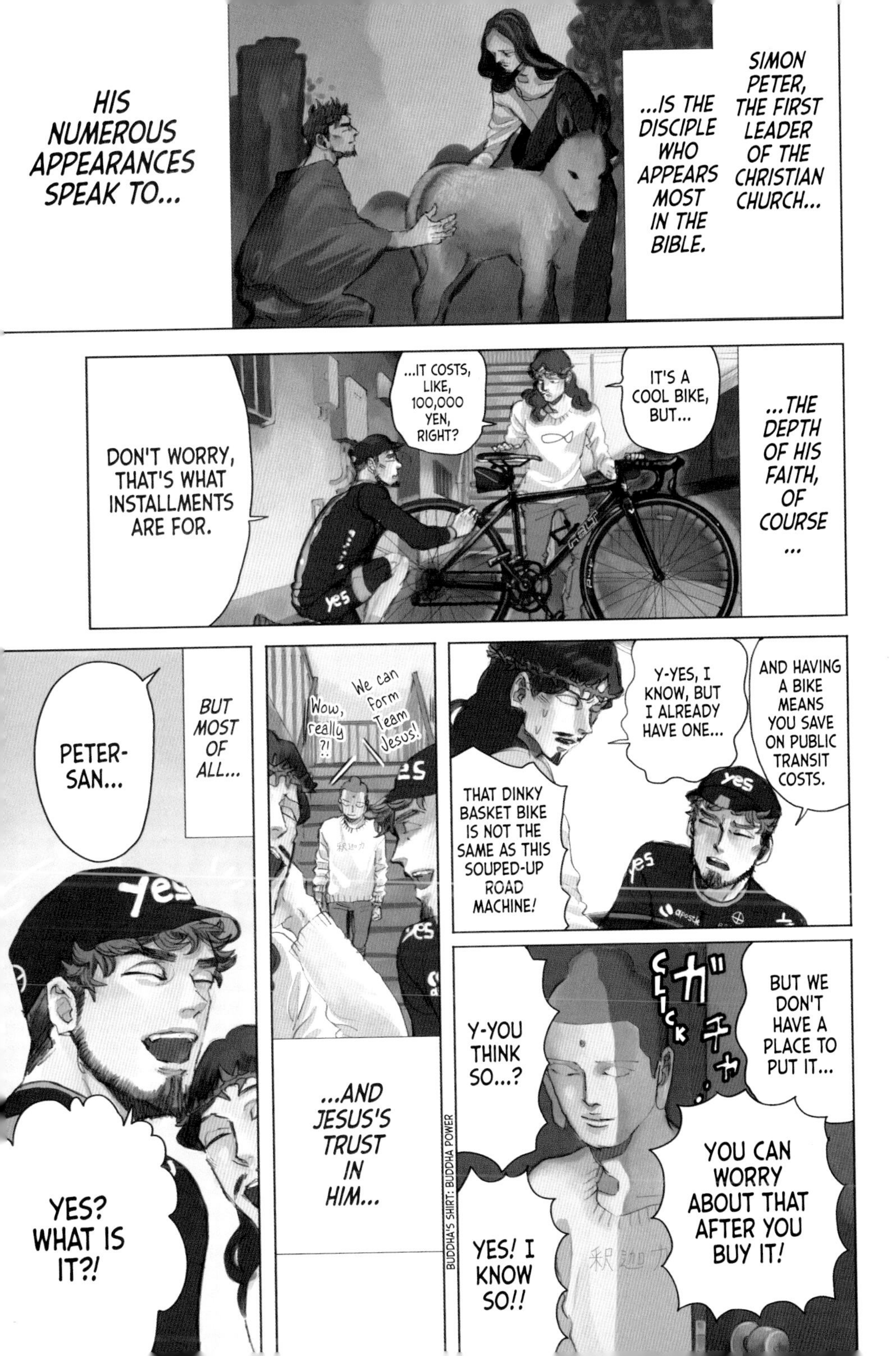
SIMON PETER, THE FIRST LEADER OF THE CHRISTIAN CHURCH...
...IS THE DISCIPLE WHO APPEARS MOST IN THE BIBLE.
HIS NUMEROUS APPEARANCES SPEAK TO...
...THE DEPTH OF HIS FAITH, OF COURSE...
IT'S A COOL BIKE, BUT...
...IT COSTS, LIKE, 100,000 YEN, RIGHT?
DON'T WORRY, THAT'S WHAT INSTALLMENTS ARE FOR.
AND HAVING A BIKE MEANS YOU SAVE ON PUBLIC TRANSIT COSTS.
Y-YES, I KNOW, BUT I ALREADY HAVE ONE...
THAT DINKY BASKET BIKE IS NOT THE SAME AS THIS SOUPED-UP ROAD MACHINE!
BUT WE DON'T HAVE A PLACE TO PUT IT...
CLICK
Y-YOU THINK SO...?
YOU CAN WORRY ABOUT THAT AFTER YOU BUY IT!
YES! I KNOW SO!!
We can form Team Jesus!
Wow, really?!
BUDDHA'S SHIRT: BUDDHA POWER
...AND JESUS'S TRUST IN HIM...
BUT MOST OF ALL...
PETER-SAN...
YES? WHAT IS IT?!

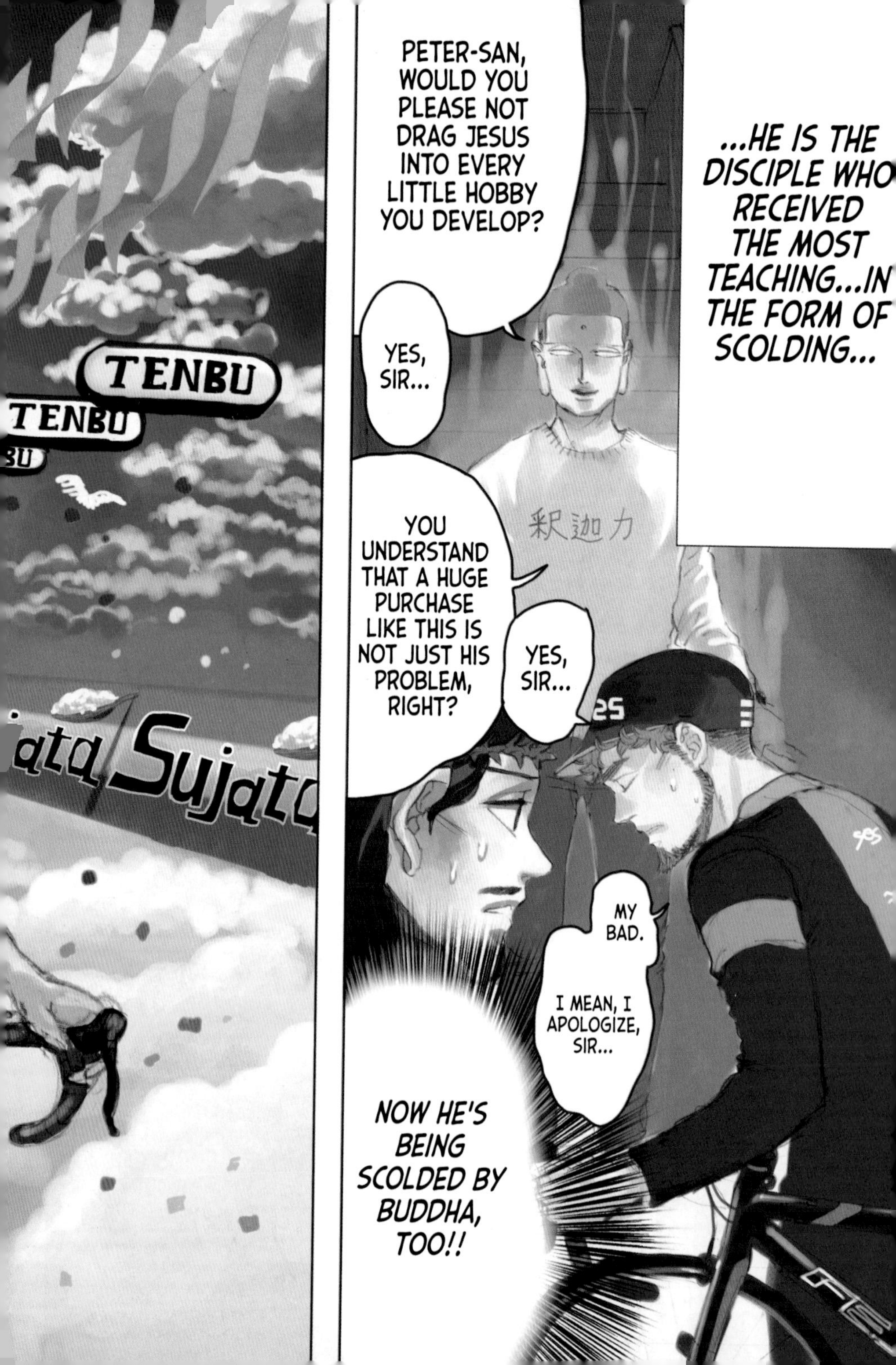
...HE IS THE DISCIPLE WHO RECEIVED THE MOST TEACHING...IN THE FORM OF SCOLDING...
PETER-SAN, WOULD YOU PLEASE NOT DRAG JESUS INTO EVERY LITTLE HOBBY YOU DEVELOP?
YES, SIR...
釈迦力
YOU UNDERSTAND THAT A HUGE PURCHASE LIKE THIS IS NOT JUST HIS PROBLEM, RIGHT?
YES, SIR...
MY BAD.
I MEAN, I APOLOGIZE, SIR...
NOW HE'S BEING SCOLDED BY BUDDHA, TOO!!
TENBU
TENBU

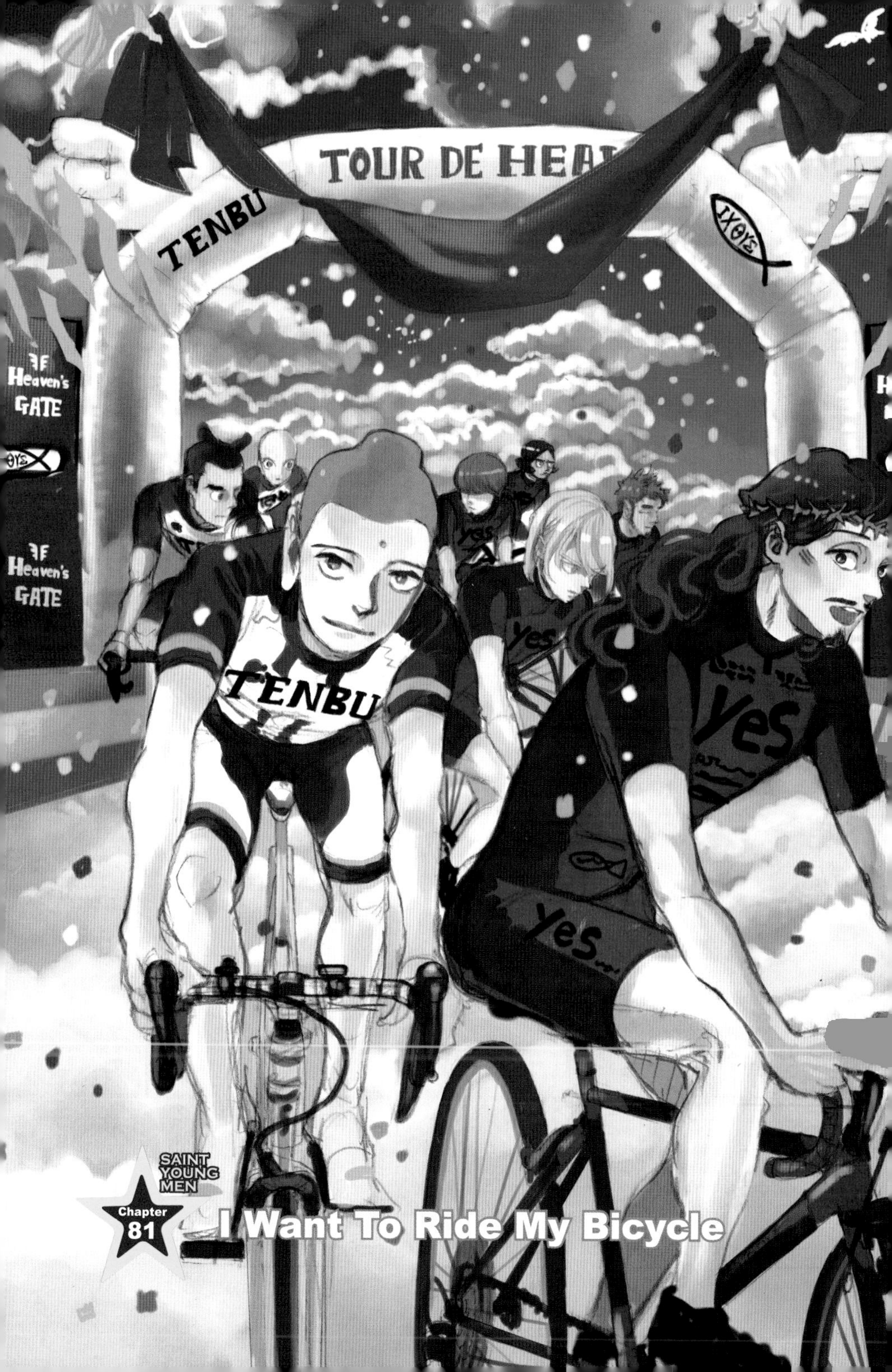
TOUR DE HEA
TENBU
Heaven's GATE
Heaven's GATE
TENBU
yes
yes
SAINT YOUNG MEN
Chapter 81
I Want To Ride My Bicycle

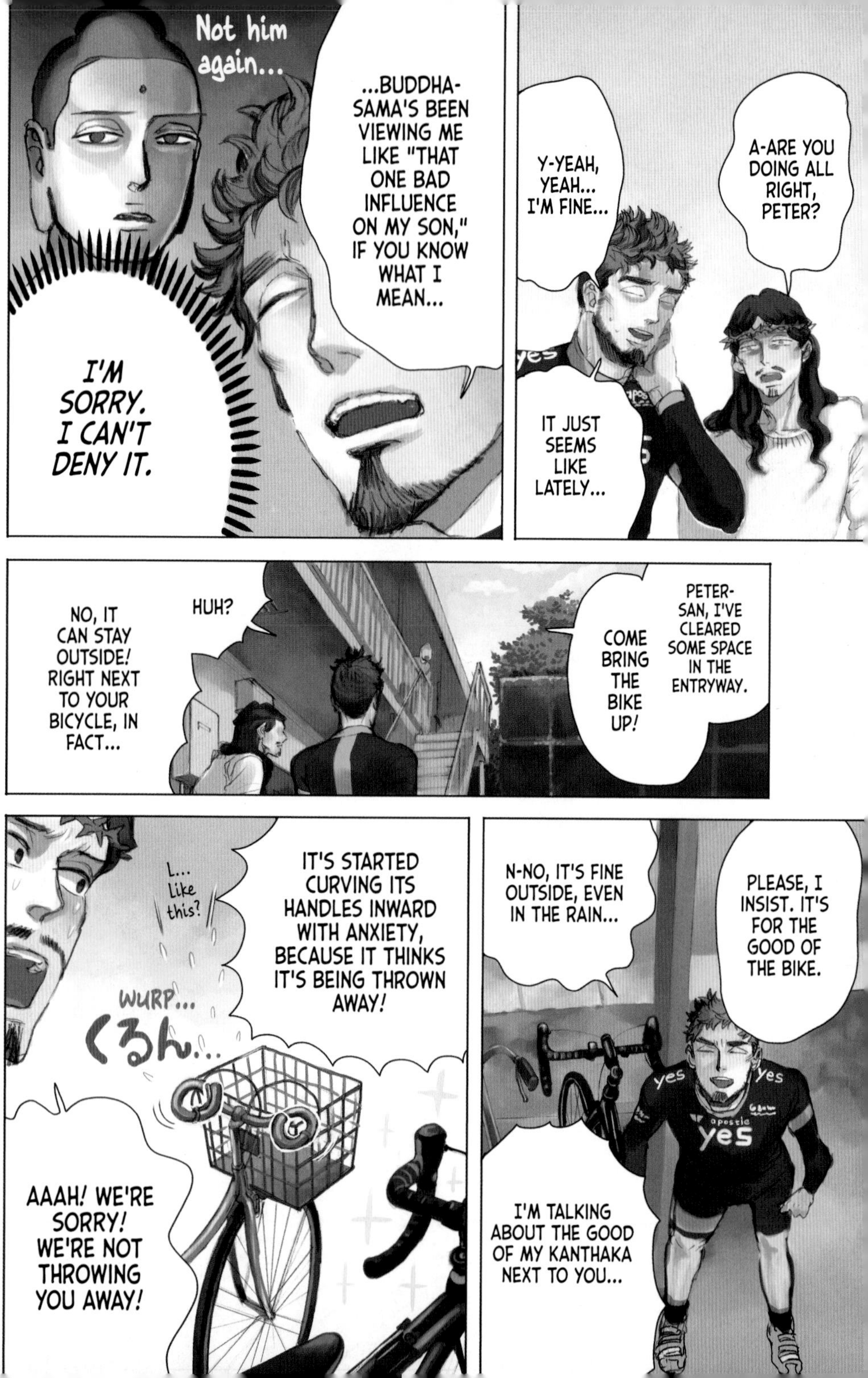
A-ARE YOU DOING ALL RIGHT, PETER?
Y-YEAH, YEAH... I'M FINE...
IT JUST SEEMS LIKE LATELY...
...BUDDHA-SAMA'S BEEN VIEWING ME LIKE "THAT ONE BAD INFLUENCE ON MY SON," IF YOU KNOW WHAT I MEAN...
Not him again...
I'M SORRY. I CAN'T DENY IT.
PETER-SAN, I'VE CLEARED SOME SPACE IN THE ENTRYWAY.
COME BRING THE BIKE UP!
HUH?
NO, IT CAN STAY OUTSIDE! RIGHT NEXT TO YOUR BICYCLE, IN FACT...
PLEASE, I INSIST. IT'S FOR THE GOOD OF THE BIKE.
N-NO, IT'S FINE OUTSIDE, EVEN IN THE RAIN...
I'M TALKING ABOUT THE GOOD OF MY KANTHAKA NEXT TO YOU...
IT'S STARTED CURVING ITS HANDLES INWARD WITH ANXIETY, BECAUSE IT THINKS IT'S BEING THROWN AWAY!
L... Like this?
WURP...
くるん...
AAAH! WE'RE SORRY! WE'RE NOT THROWING YOU AWAY!

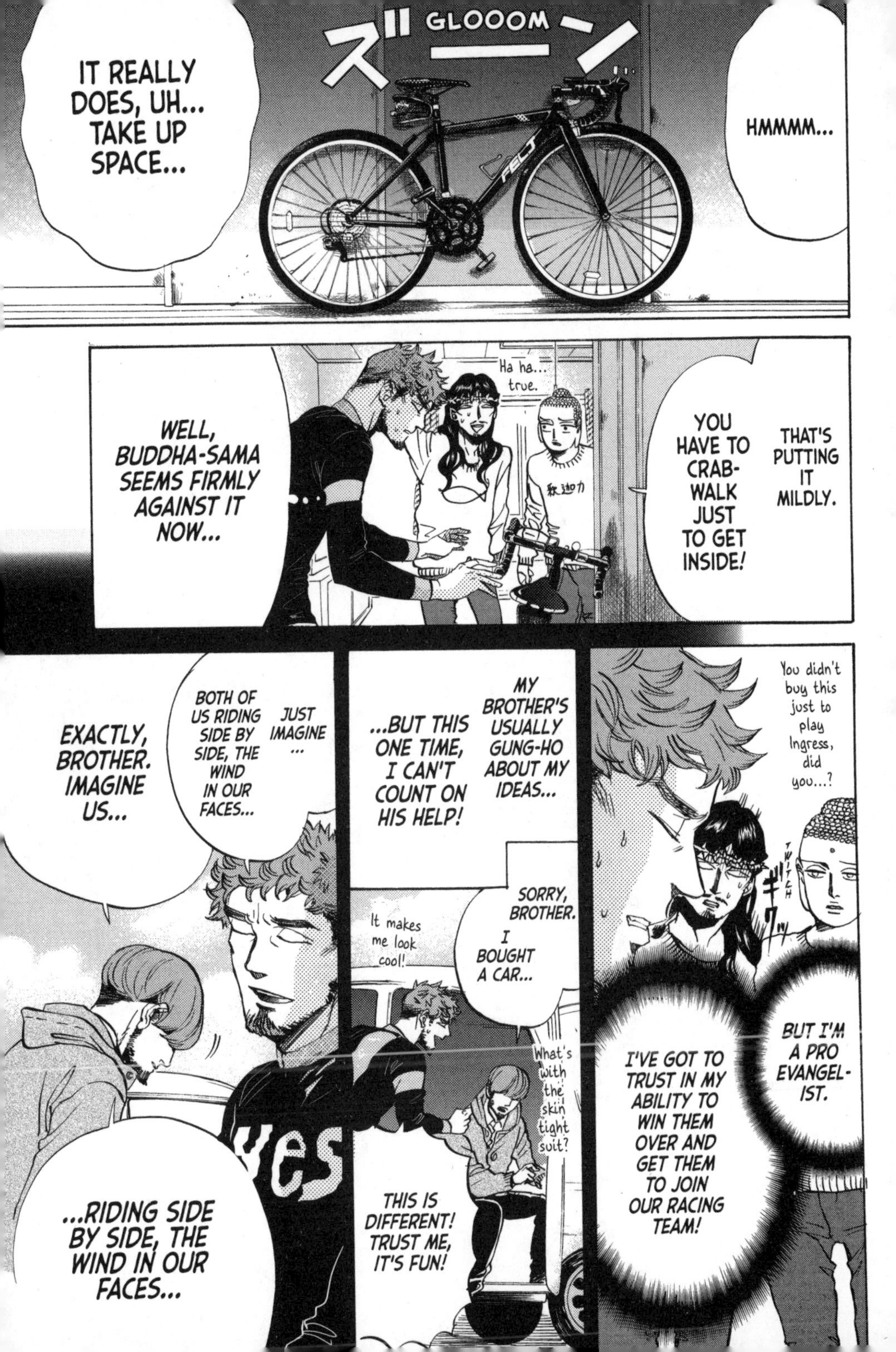
GLOOOM
HMMMM...
IT REALLY DOES, UH... TAKE UP SPACE...
THAT'S PUTTING IT MILDLY.
YOU HAVE TO CRAB-WALK JUST TO GET INSIDE!
Ha ha... true.
WELL, BUDDHA-SAMA SEEMS FIRMLY AGAINST IT NOW...
You didn't buy this just to play Ingress, did you...?
TWITCH
BUT I'M A PRO EVANGEL-IST.
I'VE GOT TO TRUST IN MY ABILITY TO WIN THEM OVER AND GET THEM TO JOIN OUR RACING TEAM!
MY BROTHER'S USUALLY GUNG-HO ABOUT MY IDEAS...
...BUT THIS ONE TIME, I CAN'T COUNT ON HIS HELP!
SORRY, BROTHER. I BOUGHT A CAR...
It makes me look cool!
What's with the skin tight suit?
THIS IS DIFFERENT! TRUST ME, IT'S FUN!
JUST IMAGINE...
BOTH OF US RIDING SIDE BY SIDE, THE WIND IN OUR FACES...
EXACTLY, BROTHER. IMAGINE US...
...RIDING SIDE BY SIDE, THE WIND IN OUR FACES...

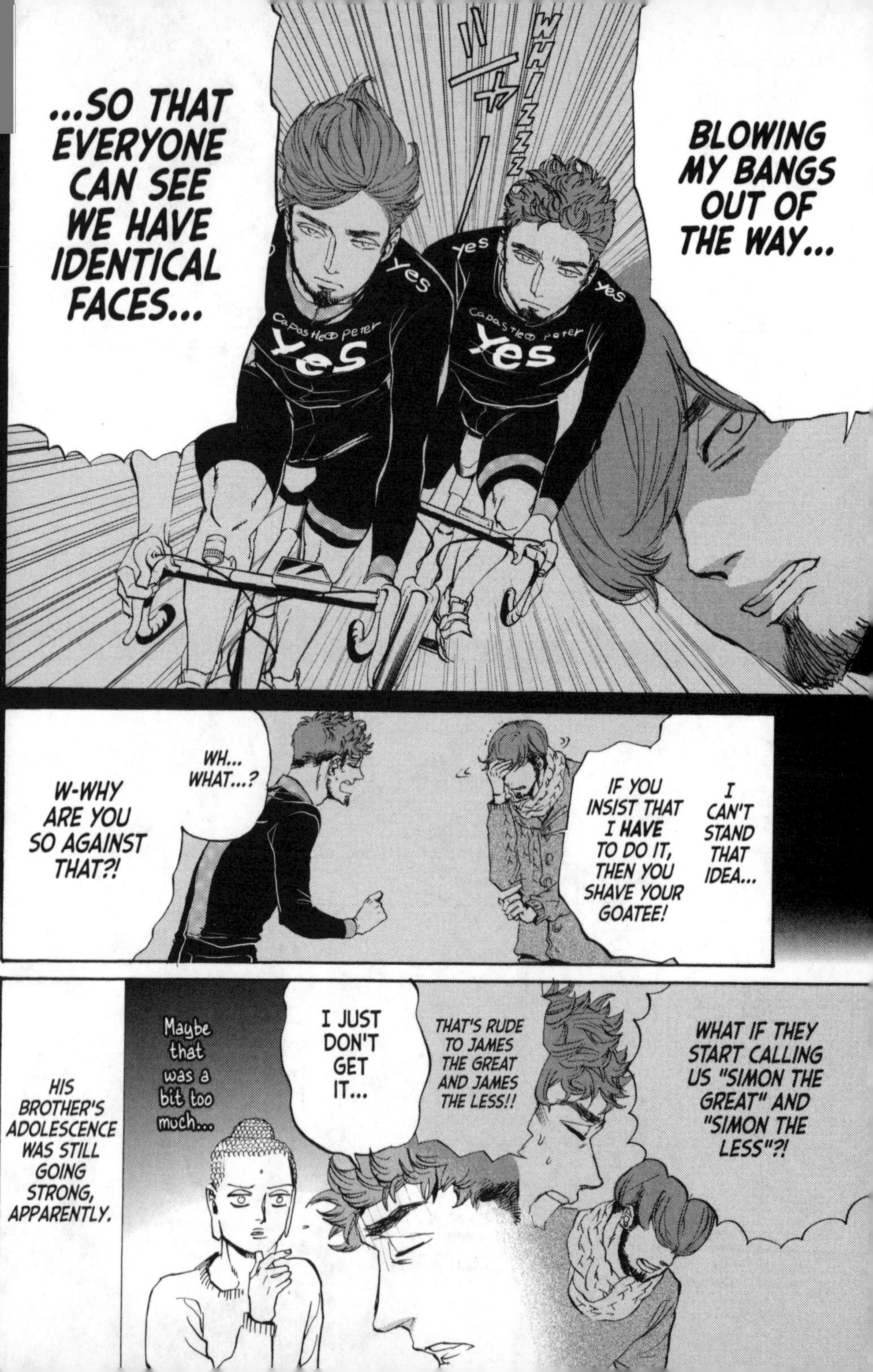
BLOWING MY BANGS OUT OF THE WAY...
WHIZZZ
...SO THAT EVERYONE CAN SEE WE HAVE IDENTICAL FACES...
I CAN'T STAND THAT IDEA...
IF YOU INSIST THAT I HAVE TO DO IT, THEN YOU SHAVE YOUR GOATEE!
WH... WHAT...?
W-WHY ARE YOU SO AGAINST THAT?!
WHAT IF THEY START CALLING US "SIMON THE GREAT" AND "SIMON THE LESS"?!
THAT'S RUDE TO JAMES THE GREAT AND JAMES THE LESS!!
I JUST DON'T GET IT...
Maybe that was a bit too much...
HIS BROTHER'S ADOLESCENCE WAS STILL GOING STRONG, APPARENTLY.

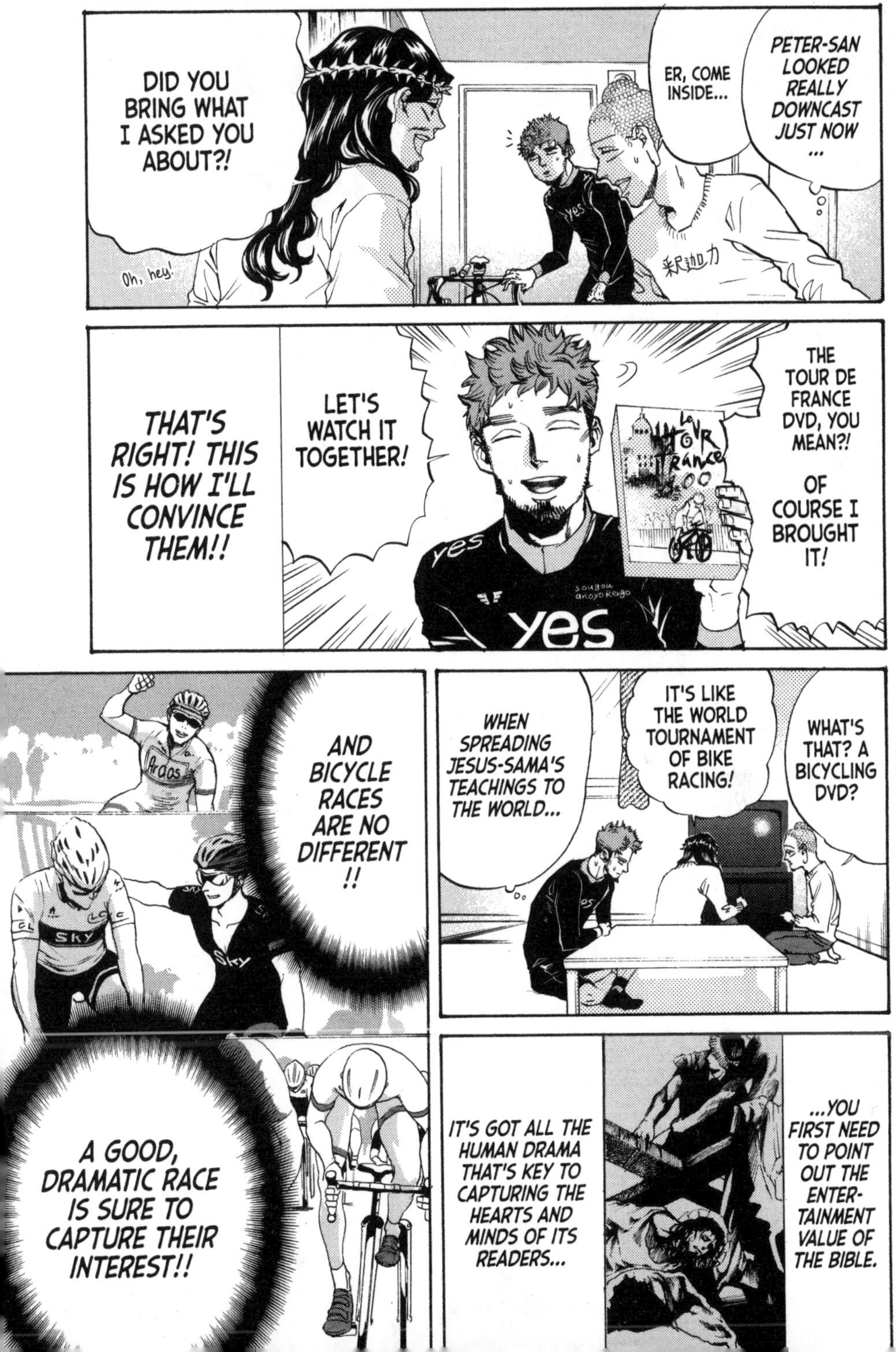
PETER-SAN LOOKED REALLY DOWNCAST JUST NOW ...
ER, COME INSIDE...
DID YOU BRING WHAT I ASKED YOU ABOUT?!
Oh, hey!
THE TOUR DE FRANCE DVD, YOU MEAN?!
OF COURSE I BROUGHT IT!
LET'S WATCH IT TOGETHER!
THAT'S RIGHT! THIS IS HOW I'LL CONVINCE THEM!!
WHAT'S THAT? A BICYCLING DVD?
IT'S LIKE THE WORLD TOURNAMENT OF BIKE RACING!
WHEN SPREADING JESUS-SAMA'S TEACHINGS TO THE WORLD...
AND BICYCLE RACES ARE NO DIFFERENT!!
...YOU FIRST NEED TO POINT OUT THE ENTER-TAINMENT VALUE OF THE BIBLE.
IT'S GOT ALL THE HUMAN DRAMA THAT'S KEY TO CAPTURING THE HEARTS AND MINDS OF ITS READERS...
A GOOD, DRAMATIC RACE IS SURE TO CAPTURE THEIR INTEREST!!

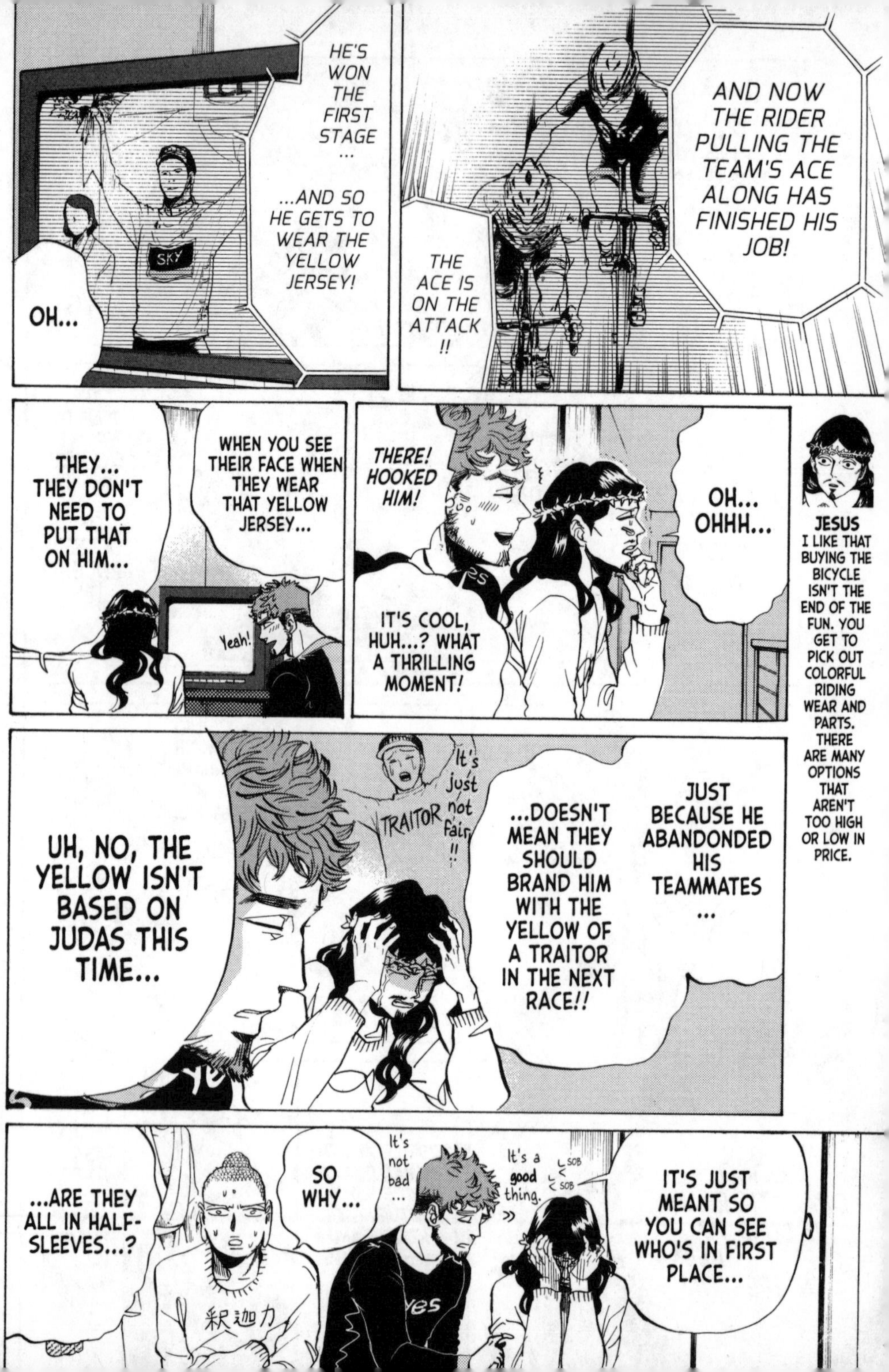
AND NOW THE RIDER PULLING THE TEAM'S ACE ALONG HAS FINISHED HIS JOB!
THE ACE IS ON THE ATTACK !!
HE'S WON THE FIRST STAGE ...
...AND SO HE GETS TO WEAR THE YELLOW JERSEY!
SKY
OH...
OH... OHHH...
THERE! HOOKED HIM!
IT'S COOL, HUH...? WHAT A THRILLING MOMENT!
WHEN YOU SEE THEIR FACE WHEN THEY WEAR THAT YELLOW JERSEY...
Yeah!
THEY... THEY DON'T NEED TO PUT THAT ON HIM...
JUST BECAUSE HE ABANDONDED HIS TEAMMATES ...
...DOESN'T MEAN THEY SHOULD BRAND HIM WITH THE YELLOW OF A TRAITOR IN THE NEXT RACE!!
It's just not fair !!
TRAITOR
UH, NO, THE YELLOW ISN'T BASED ON JUDAS THIS TIME...
IT'S JUST MEANT SO YOU CAN SEE WHO'S IN FIRST PLACE...
SOB SOB
It's a good thing.
It's not bad ...
SO WHY...
...ARE THEY ALL IN HALF-SLEEVES...?
yes
釈迦力
JESUS
I LIKE THAT BUYING THE BICYCLE ISN'T THE END OF THE FUN. YOU GET TO PICK OUT COLORFUL RIDING WEAR AND PARTS. THERE ARE MANY OPTIONS THAT AREN'T TOO HIGH OR LOW IN PRICE.

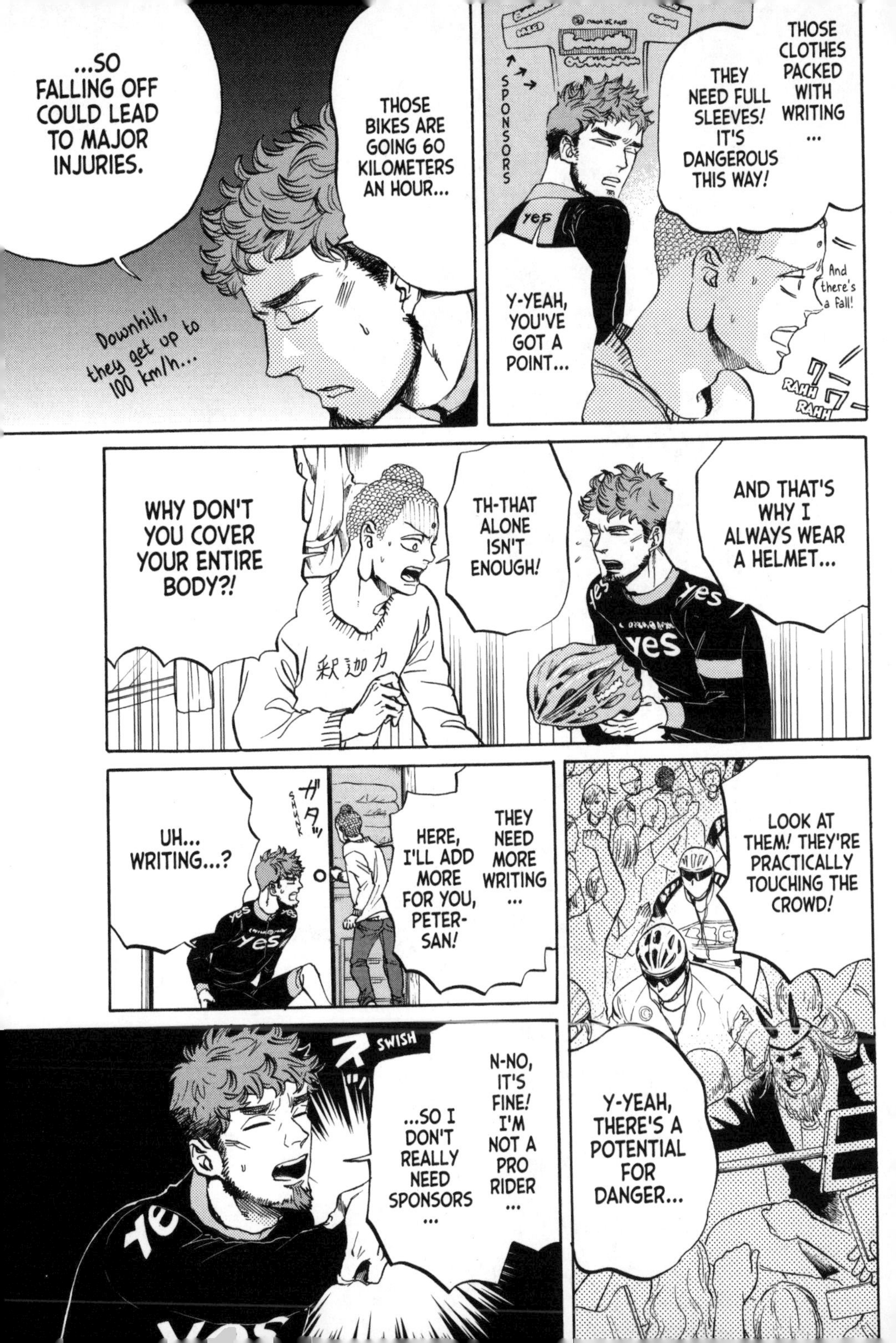
THOSE CLOTHES PACKED WITH WRITING ...
THEY NEED FULL SLEEVES! IT'S DANGEROUS THIS WAY!
SPONSORS
And there's a fall!
RAHH RAHH
Y-YEAH, YOU'VE GOT A POINT...
THOSE BIKES ARE GOING 60 KILOMETERS AN HOUR...
...SO FALLING OFF COULD LEAD TO MAJOR INJURIES.
Downhill, they get up to 100 km/h...
AND THAT'S WHY I ALWAYS WEAR A HELMET...
TH-THAT ALONE ISN'T ENOUGH!
WHY DON'T YOU COVER YOUR ENTIRE BODY?!
釈迦力
LOOK AT THEM! THEY'RE PRACTICALLY TOUCHING THE CROWD!
Y-YEAH, THERE'S A POTENTIAL FOR DANGER...
THEY NEED MORE WRITING ...
HERE, I'LL ADD MORE FOR YOU, PETER-SAN!
ガタッ SHUNK
UH... WRITING...?
スッ SWISH
N-NO, IT'S FINE! I'M NOT A PRO RIDER ...
...SO I DON'T REALLY NEED SPONSORS ...

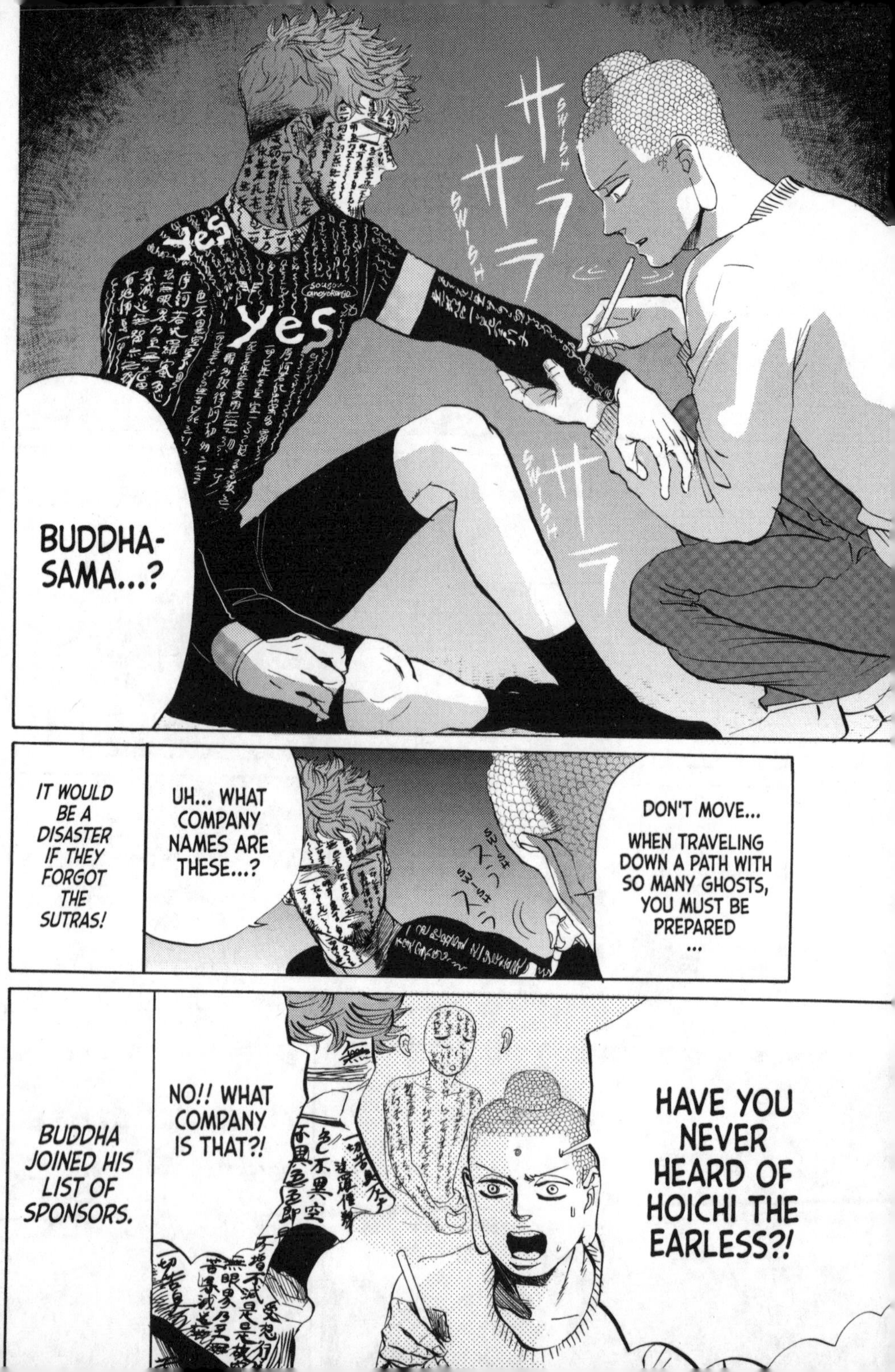
SWISH
SWISH
SWISH
BUDDHA-SAMA...?
DON'T MOVE...
WHEN TRAVELING DOWN A PATH WITH SO MANY GHOSTS, YOU MUST BE PREPARED ...
UH... WHAT COMPANY NAMES ARE THESE...?
IT WOULD BE A DISASTER IF THEY FORGOT THE SUTRAS!
HAVE YOU NEVER HEARD OF HOICHI THE EARLESS?!
NO!! WHAT COMPANY IS THAT?!
BUDDHA JOINED HIS LIST OF SPONSORS.

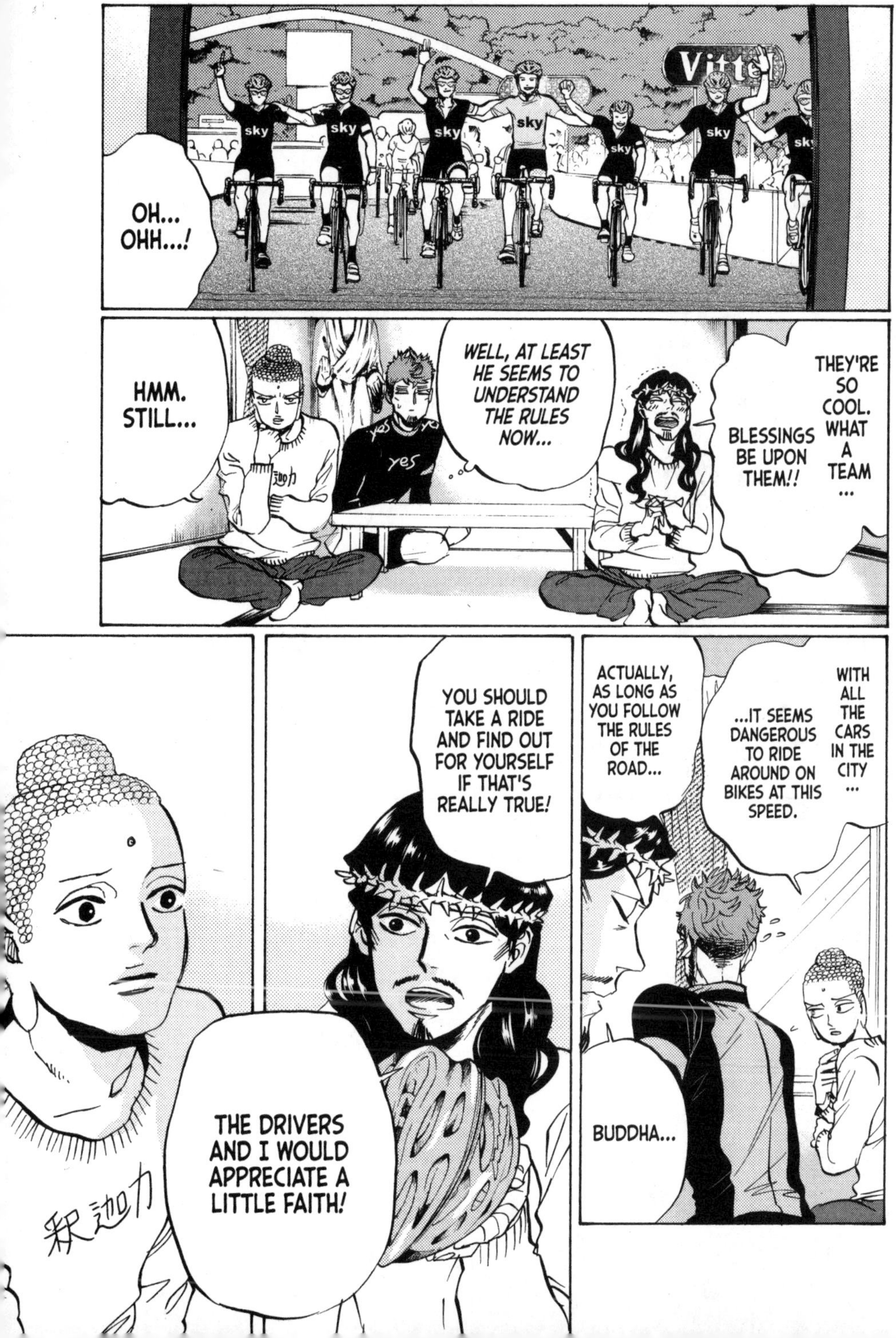
OH... OHH...!
THEY'RE SO COOL. WHAT A TEAM...
BLESSINGS BE UPON THEM!!
WELL, AT LEAST HE SEEMS TO UNDERSTAND THE RULES NOW...
HMM. STILL...
WITH ALL THE CARS IN THE CITY...
...IT SEEMS DANGEROUS TO RIDE AROUND ON BIKES AT THIS SPEED.
ACTUALLY, AS LONG AS YOU FOLLOW THE RULES OF THE ROAD...
BUDDHA...
YOU SHOULD TAKE A RIDE AND FIND OUT FOR YOURSELF IF THAT'S REALLY TRUE!
THE DRIVERS AND I WOULD APPRECIATE A LITTLE FAITH!
釈迦力

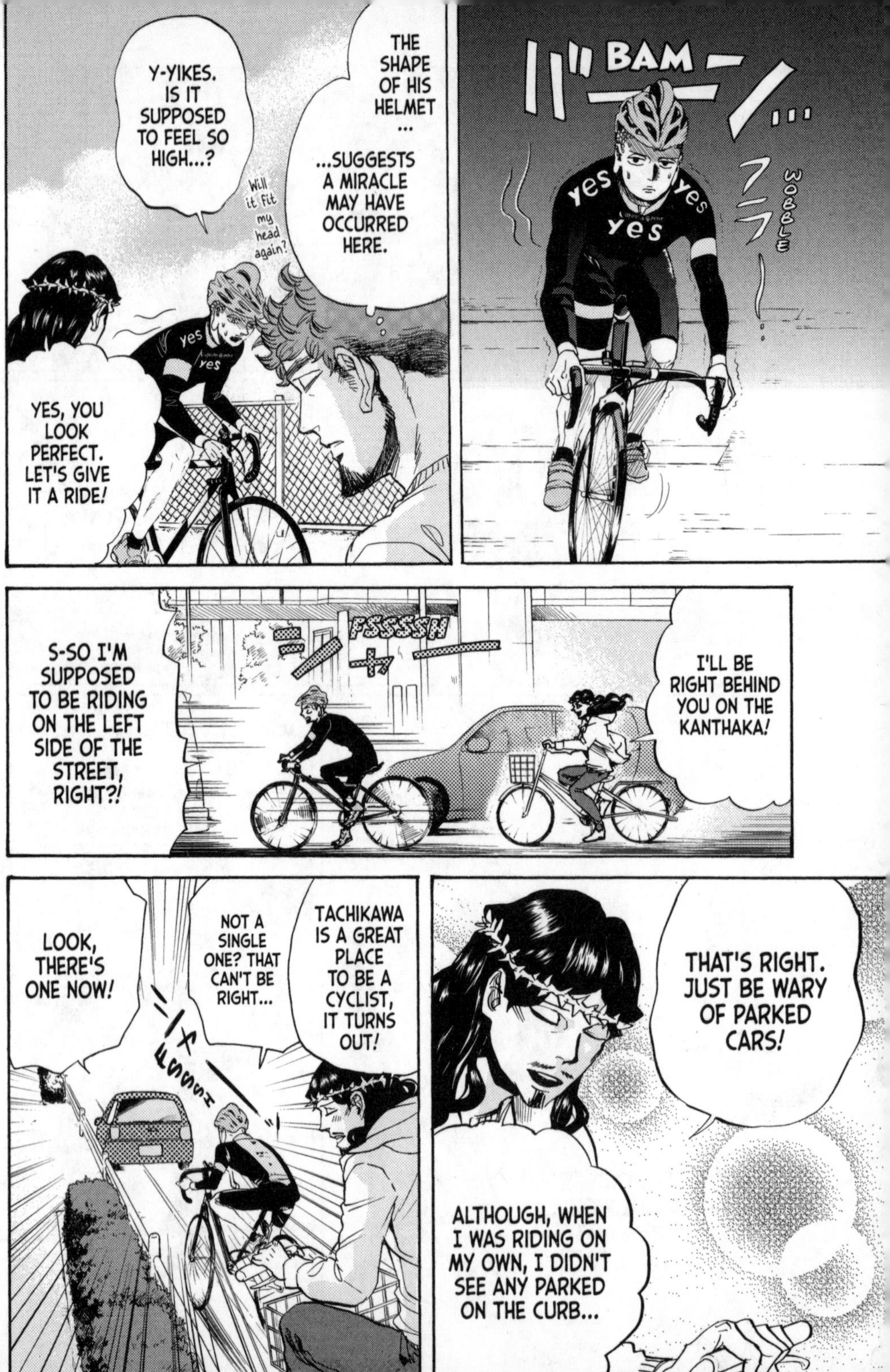
BAM
WOBBLE
THE SHAPE OF HIS HELMET ...
...SUGGESTS A MIRACLE MAY HAVE OCCURRED HERE.
Will it fit my head again?
Y-YIKES. IS IT SUPPOSED TO FEEL SO HIGH...?
YES, YOU LOOK PERFECT. LET'S GIVE IT A RIDE!
I'LL BE RIGHT BEHIND YOU ON THE KANTHAKA!
FSSSSH
S-SO I'M SUPPOSED TO BE RIDING ON THE LEFT SIDE OF THE STREET, RIGHT?!
THAT'S RIGHT. JUST BE WARY OF PARKED CARS!
ALTHOUGH, WHEN I WAS RIDING ON MY OWN, I DIDN'T SEE ANY PARKED ON THE CURB...
TACHIKAWA IS A GREAT PLACE TO BE A CYCLIST, IT TURNS OUT!
NOT A SINGLE ONE? THAT CAN'T BE RIGHT...
LOOK, THERE'S ONE NOW!

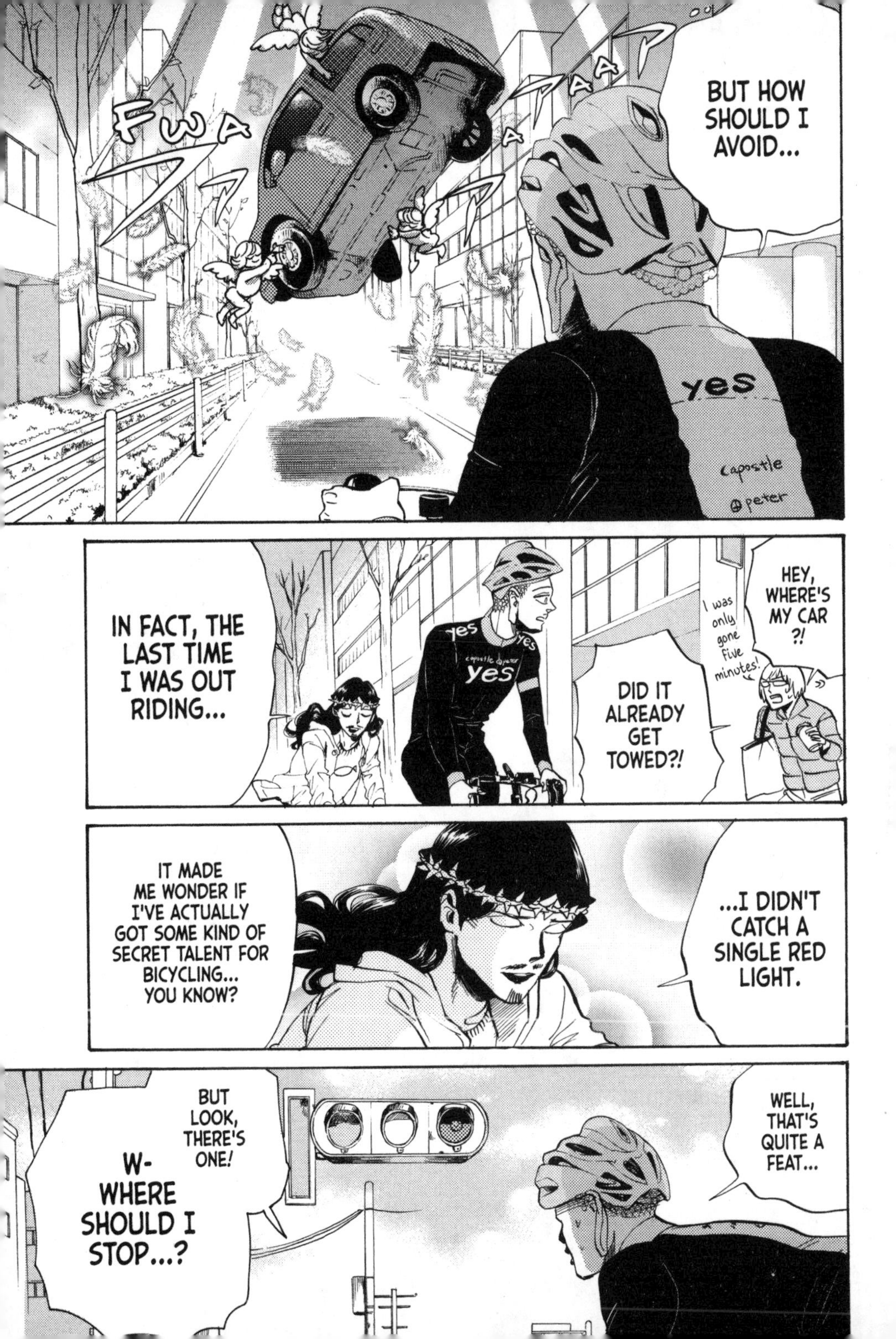
BUT HOW SHOULD I AVOID...
FWAAAAP
yes
capostle @peter
HEY, WHERE'S MY CAR ?!
I was only gone five minutes!
DID IT ALREADY GET TOWED?!
IN FACT, THE LAST TIME I WAS OUT RIDING...
...I DIDN'T CATCH A SINGLE RED LIGHT.
IT MADE ME WONDER IF I'VE ACTUALLY GOT SOME KIND OF SECRET TALENT FOR BICYCLING... YOU KNOW?
WELL, THAT'S QUITE A FEAT...
BUT LOOK, THERE'S ONE!
W- WHERE SHOULD I STOP...?

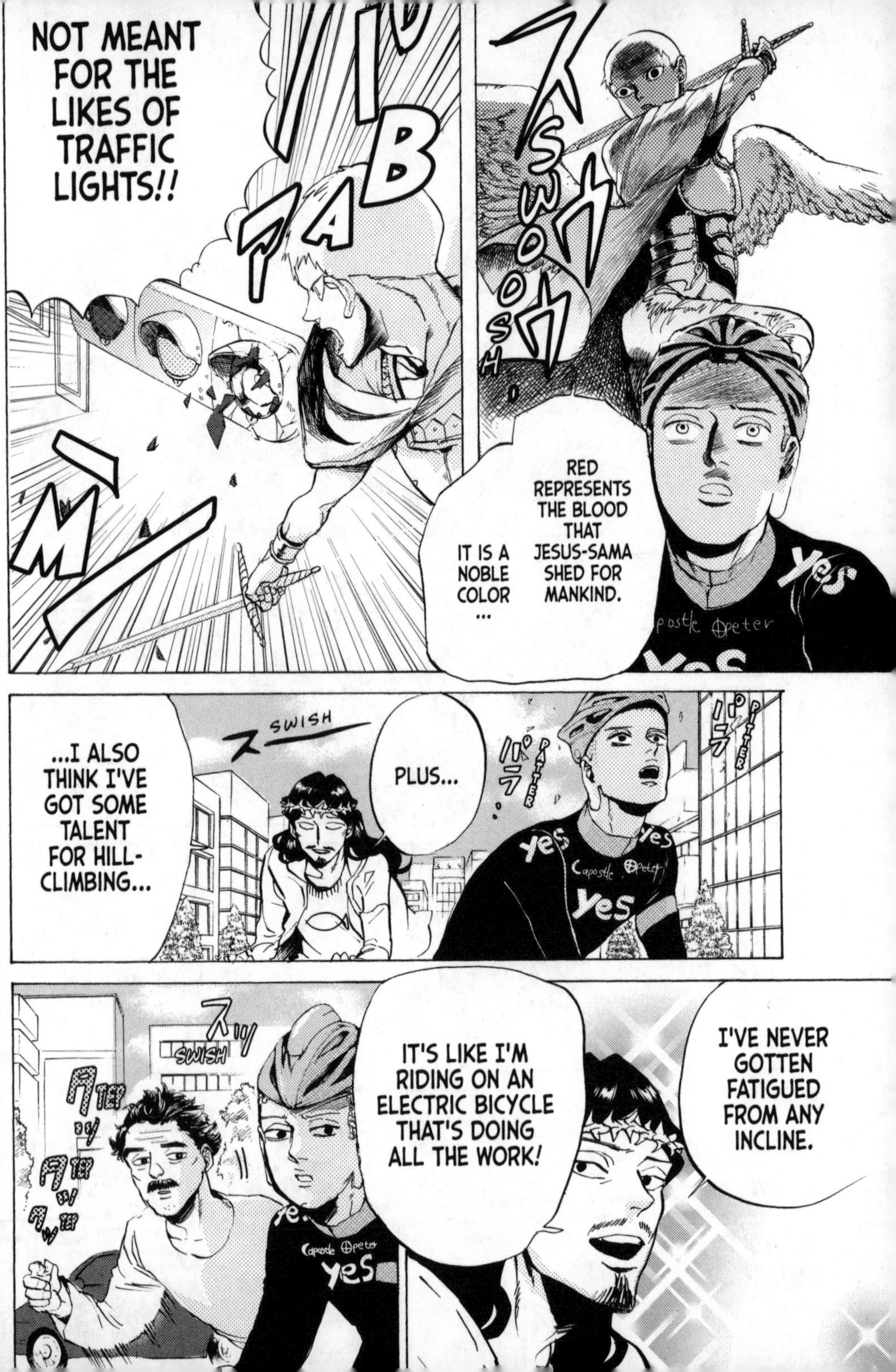
SWOOSH
RED REPRESENTS THE BLOOD THAT JESUS-SAMA SHED FOR MANKIND.
IT IS A NOBLE COLOR ...
BAM
NOT MEANT FOR THE LIKES OF TRAFFIC LIGHTS!!
PITTER
PATTER
PLUS...
SWISH
...I ALSO THINK I'VE GOT SOME TALENT FOR HILL-CLIMBING...
I'VE NEVER GOTTEN FATIGUED FROM ANY INCLINE.
IT'S LIKE I'M RIDING ON AN ELECTRIC BICYCLE THAT'S DOING ALL THE WORK!
SWISH

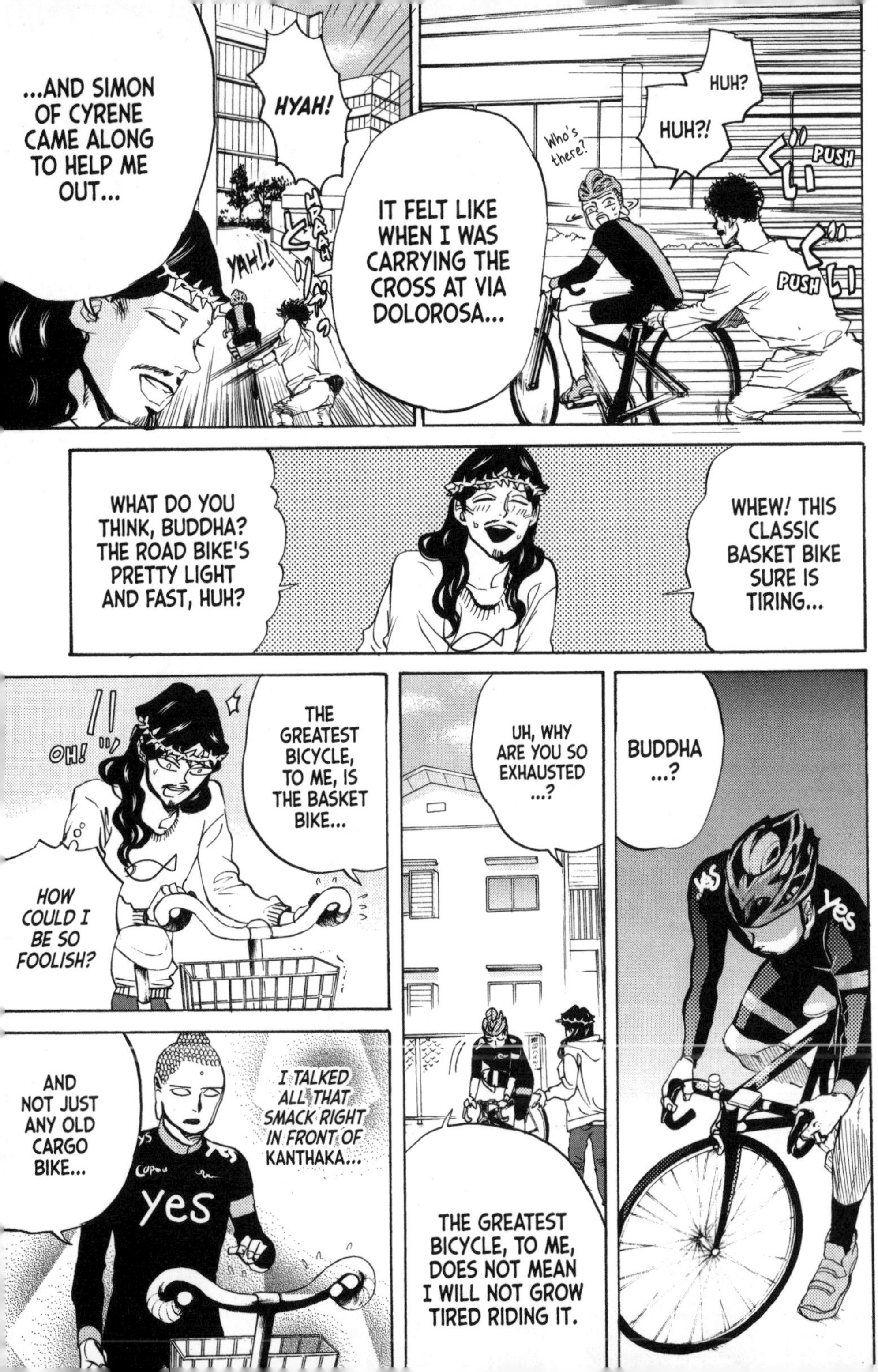
HUH?
HUH?!
Who's there?
PUSH
PUSH
HYAH!
IT FELT LIKE WHEN I WAS CARRYING THE CROSS AT VIA DOLOROSA...
...AND SIMON OF CYRENE CAME ALONG TO HELP ME OUT...
YAH!!
WHEW! THIS CLASSIC BASKET BIKE SURE IS TIRING...
WHAT DO YOU THINK, BUDDHA? THE ROAD BIKE'S PRETTY LIGHT AND FAST, HUH?
BUDDHA ...?
UH, WHY ARE YOU SO EXHAUSTED ...?
THE GREATEST BICYCLE, TO ME, DOES NOT MEAN I WILL NOT GROW TIRED RIDING IT.
THE GREATEST BICYCLE, TO ME, IS THE BASKET BIKE...
OH!
HOW COULD I BE SO FOOLISH?
I TALKED ALL THAT SMACK RIGHT IN FRONT OF KANTHAKA...
AND NOT JUST ANY OLD CARGO BIKE...
yes

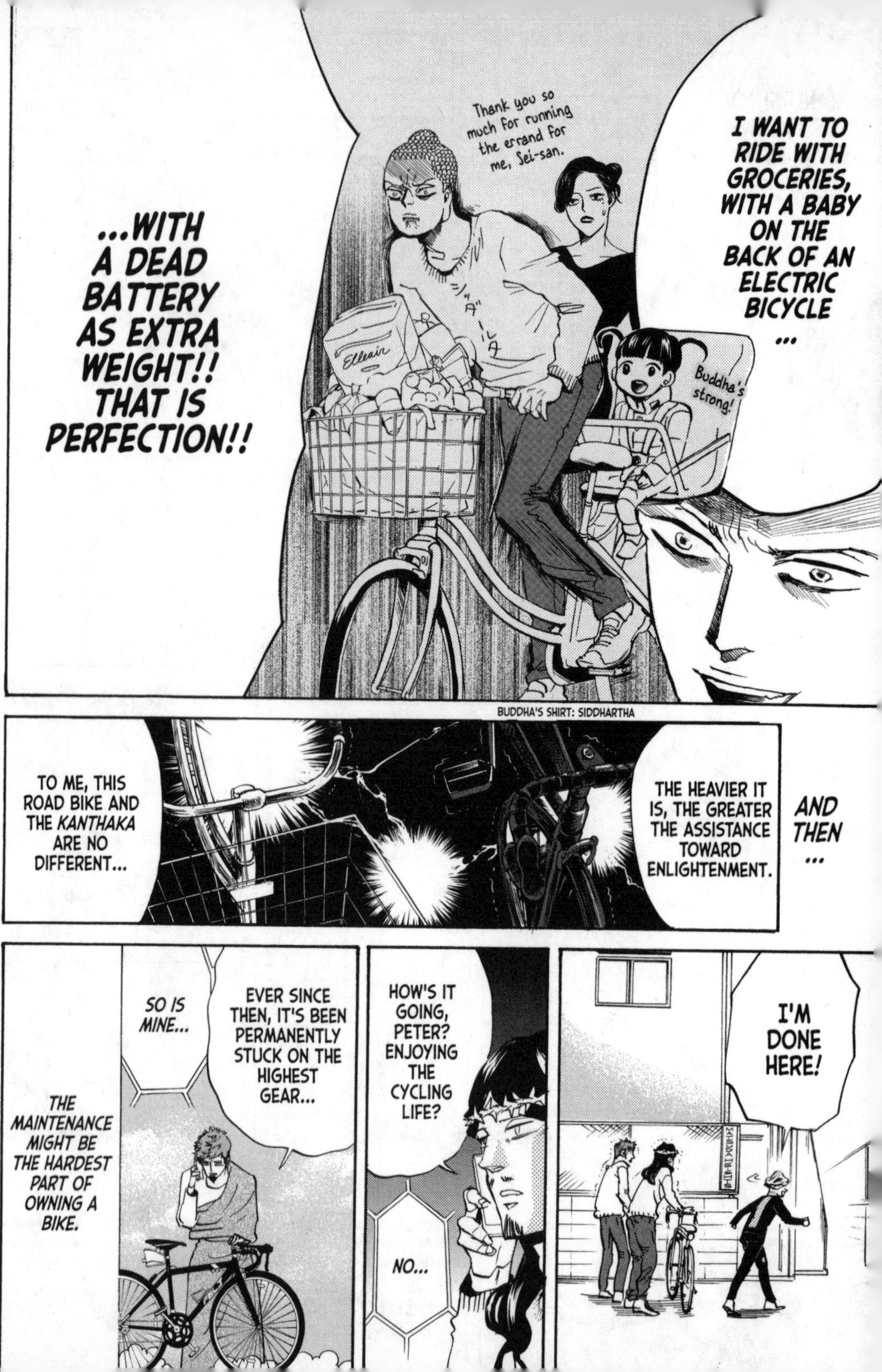
I WANT TO RIDE WITH GROCERIES, WITH A BABY ON THE BACK OF AN ELECTRIC BICYCLE ...
Thank you so much for running the errand for me, Sei-san.
Buddha's strong!
Elleair
...WITH A DEAD BATTERY AS EXTRA WEIGHT!! THAT IS PERFECTION!!
BUDDHA'S SHIRT: SIDDHARTHA
AND THEN ...
THE HEAVIER IT IS, THE GREATER THE ASSISTANCE TOWARD ENLIGHTENMENT.
TO ME, THIS ROAD BIKE AND THE *KANTHAKA* ARE NO DIFFERENT...
I'M DONE HERE!
HOW'S IT GOING, PETER? ENJOYING THE CYCLING LIFE?
NO...
EVER SINCE THEN, IT'S BEEN PERMANENTLY STUCK ON THE HIGHEST GEAR...
SO IS MINE...
THE MAINTENANCE MIGHT BE THE HARDEST PART OF OWNING A BIKE.

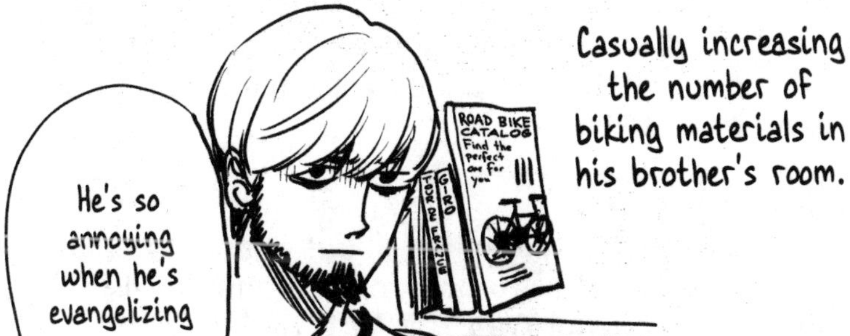
Casually increasing the number of biking materials in his brother's room.
He's so annoying when he's evangelizing ...
ROAD BIKE CATALOG Find the perfect one for you
TOUR DE FRANCE
GIRO
JUMP

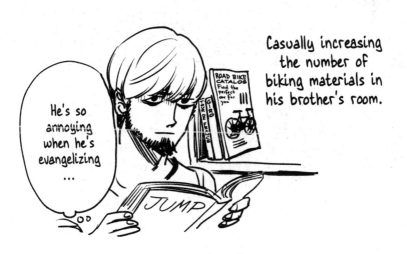

CHAPTER 81 TRANSLATION NOTES

James the Great, page 6
St. James the Great and James the Less are two of the Twelve Apostles, given their epithets to distinguish them from each other. The "greater" and "lesser" adjectives were only meant in terms of height or age, and not commentary on their personalities.

Yes, page 6
The name of the riding team ("Yes") is a play on the Japanese pronunciation of the name Jesus, which is *iesu*, a homonym of the English word "yes."

Hoichi the Earless, page 10
A folklore tale about a blind performer named Hoichi. When he is approached by the ghost of a samurai who asks him to play his *biwa* lute in a cemetery, he agrees. The priest of the temple decides to protect Hoichi from the ghost by painting his body with the the Heart Sutra, and instructs him to ignore the ghost's call. When the ghost returns, Hoichi survives the ordeal, but loses his ears to the ghost, because they were the one part of his body not covered by the sutra.

Via Dolorosa, page 15
The name of the route in Jerusalem that Jesus is said to have walked through on the way to his crucifixion. The name Via Dolorosa is Latin for "Sorrowful Way," or "Way of Suffering." Simon of Cyrene was a man in the crowd whom the Roman soldiers compelled to help Jesus carry the cross for a time along the route.

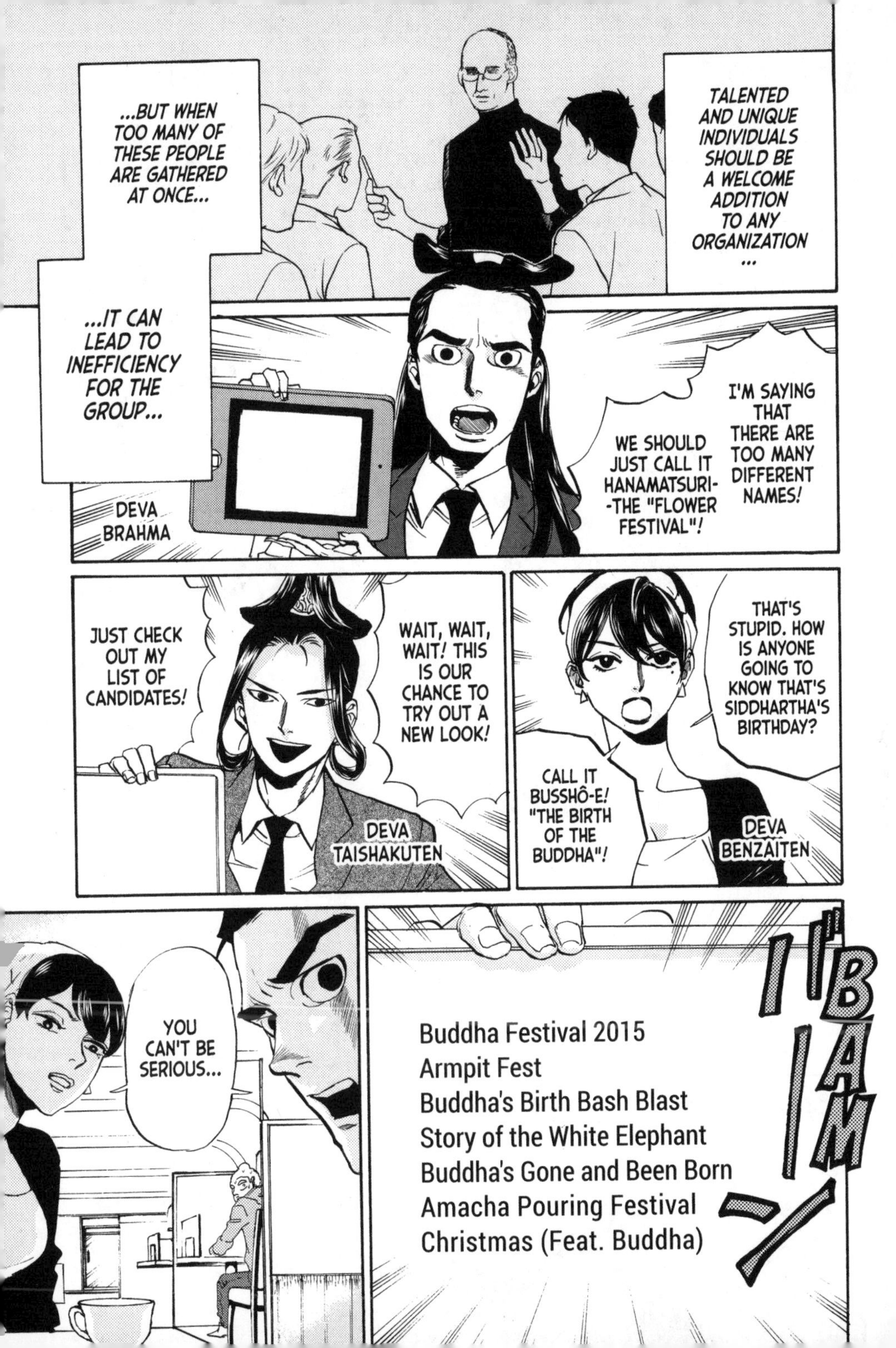
TALENTED AND UNIQUE INDIVIDUALS SHOULD BE A WELCOME ADDITION TO ANY ORGANIZATION ...
...BUT WHEN TOO MANY OF THESE PEOPLE ARE GATHERED AT ONCE...
...IT CAN LEAD TO INEFFICIENCY FOR THE GROUP...
I'M SAYING THAT THERE ARE TOO MANY DIFFERENT NAMES!
WE SHOULD JUST CALL IT HANAMATSURI--THE "FLOWER FESTIVAL"!
DEVA BRAHMA
THAT'S STUPID. HOW IS ANYONE GOING TO KNOW THAT'S SIDDHARTHA'S BIRTHDAY?
CALL IT BUSSHÔ-E! "THE BIRTH OF THE BUDDHA"!
DEVA BENZAITEN
WAIT, WAIT, WAIT! THIS IS OUR CHANCE TO TRY OUT A NEW LOOK!
JUST CHECK OUT MY LIST OF CANDIDATES!
DEVA TAISHAKUTEN
BAM
Buddha Festival 2015
Armpit Fest
Buddha's Birth Bash Blast
Story of the White Elephant
Buddha's Gone and Been Born
Amacha Pouring Festival
Christmas (Feat. Buddha)
YOU CAN'T BE SERIOUS...

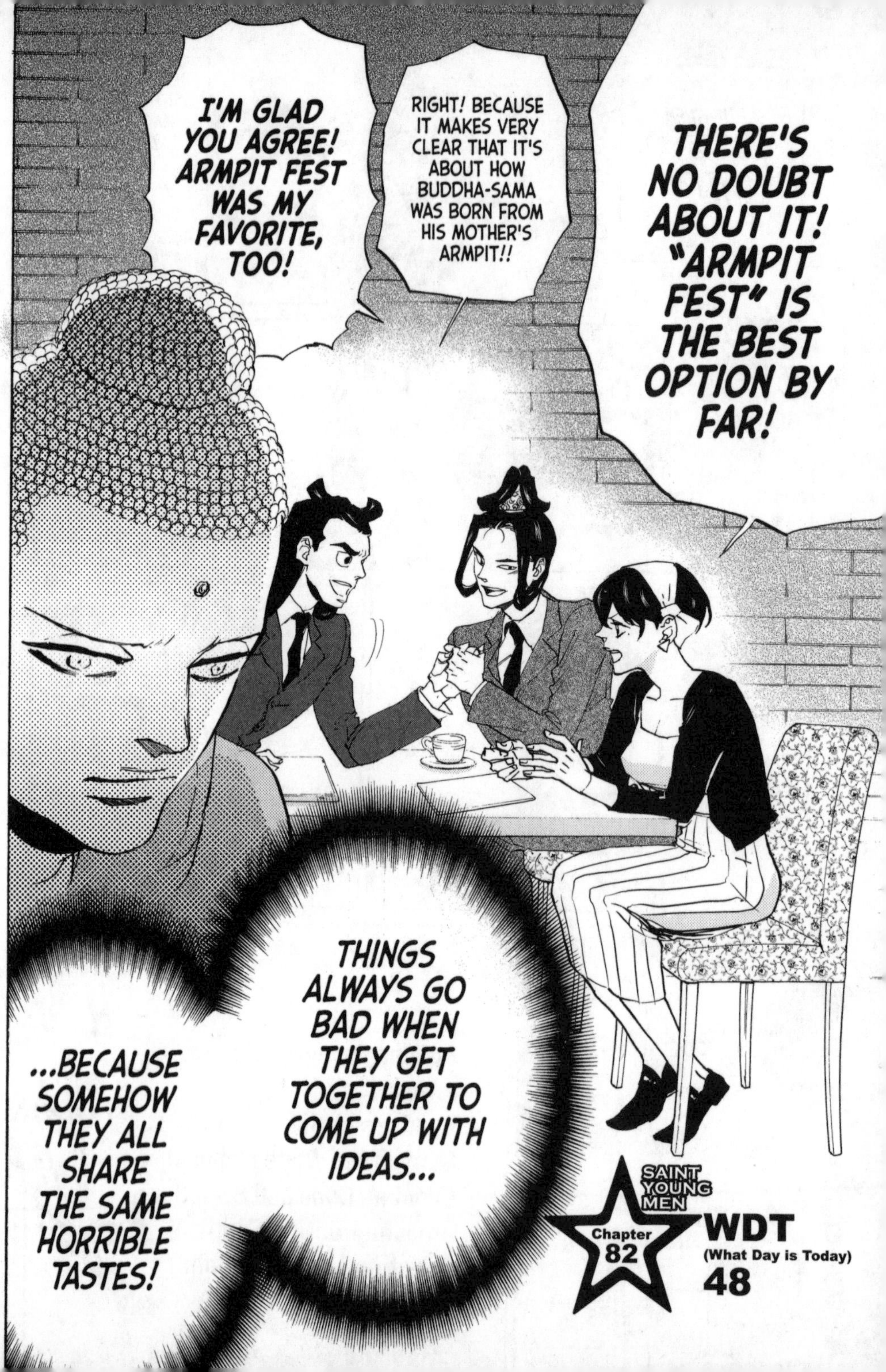
THERE'S NO DOUBT ABOUT IT! "ARMPIT FEST" IS THE BEST OPTION BY FAR!
RIGHT! BECAUSE IT MAKES VERY CLEAR THAT IT'S ABOUT HOW BUDDHA-SAMA WAS BORN FROM HIS MOTHER'S ARMPIT!!
I'M GLAD YOU AGREE! ARMPIT FEST WAS MY FAVORITE, TOO!
THINGS ALWAYS GO BAD WHEN THEY GET TOGETHER TO COME UP WITH IDEAS...
...BECAUSE SOMEHOW THEY ALL SHARE THE SAME HORRIBLE TASTES!
SAINT YOUNG MEN
Chapter 82
WDT
(What Day is Today)
48

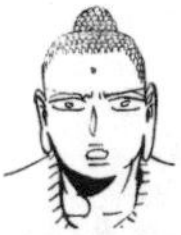

BUDDHA
EVERYBODY SAYS, "DIDN'T I JUST SEE YOU ON TV?" BUT I MUST BE CLEAR: THAT WAS NOT ME AT THE END OF THE TALE OF THE PRINCESS KAGUYA. WHEN WILL THEY FINISH THE STAGE PLAY OF TEZUKA'S *BUDDHA*, BY THE WAY?

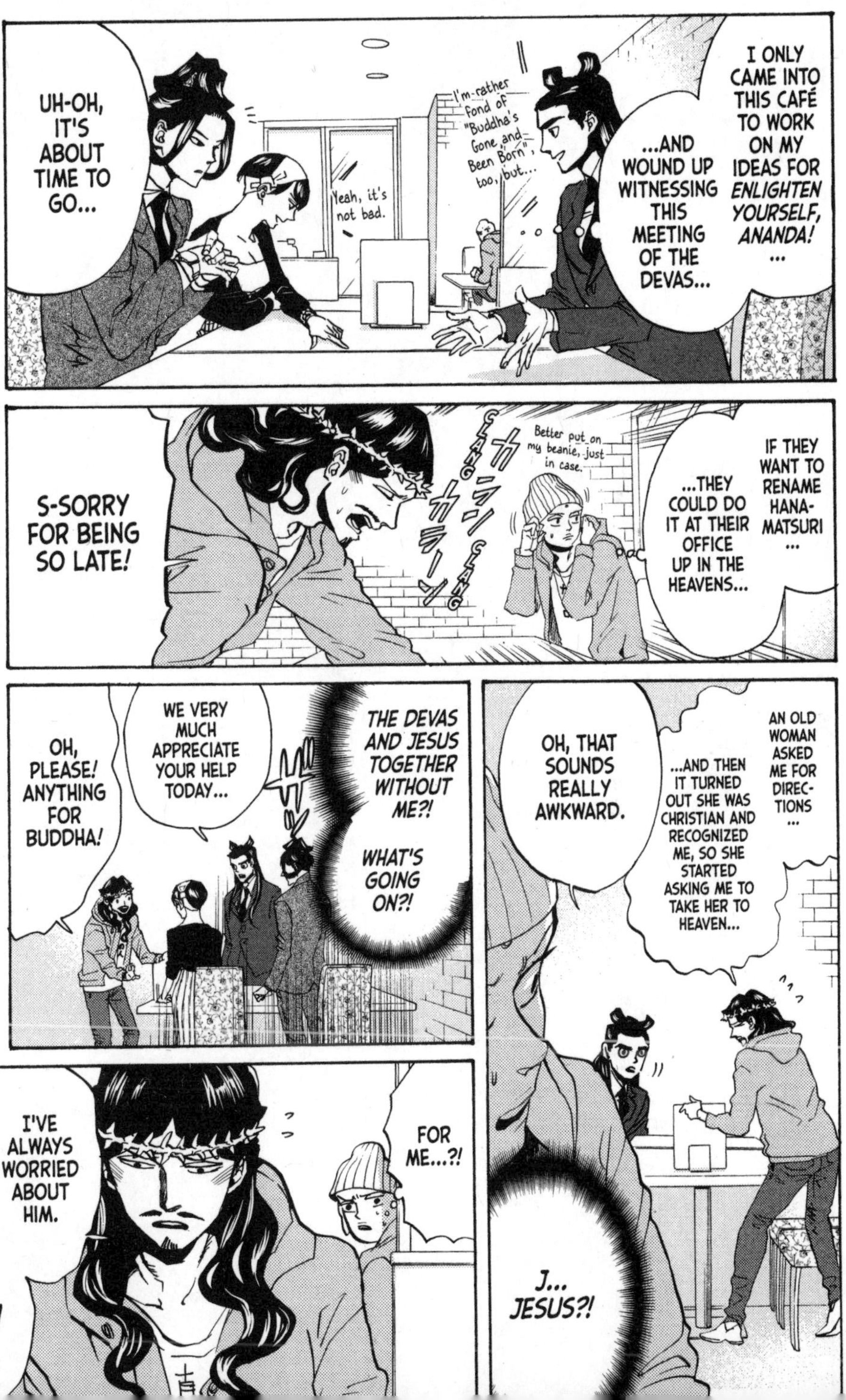
I ONLY CAME INTO THIS CAFÉ TO WORK ON MY IDEAS FOR ENLIGHTEN YOURSELF, ANANDA! ...
...AND WOUND UP WITNESSING THIS MEETING OF THE DEVAS...
I'm rather fond of "Buddha's Gone and Been Born", too, but...
Yeah, it's not bad.
UH-OH, IT'S ABOUT TIME TO GO...
IF THEY WANT TO RENAME HANA-MATSURI ...
...THEY COULD DO IT AT THEIR OFFICE UP IN THE HEAVENS...
Better put on my beanie, just in case.
CLANG
CLANG
S-SORRY FOR BEING SO LATE!
AN OLD WOMAN ASKED ME FOR DIRECTIONS ...
...AND THEN IT TURNED OUT SHE WAS CHRISTIAN AND RECOGNIZED ME, SO SHE STARTED ASKING ME TO TAKE HER TO HEAVEN...
OH, THAT SOUNDS REALLY AWKWARD.
J... JESUS?!
THE DEVAS AND JESUS TOGETHER WITHOUT ME?!
WHAT'S GOING ON?!
WE VERY MUCH APPRECIATE YOUR HELP TODAY...
OH, PLEASE! ANYTHING FOR BUDDHA!
FOR ME...?!
I'VE ALWAYS WORRIED ABOUT HIM.
YOU KNOW ...

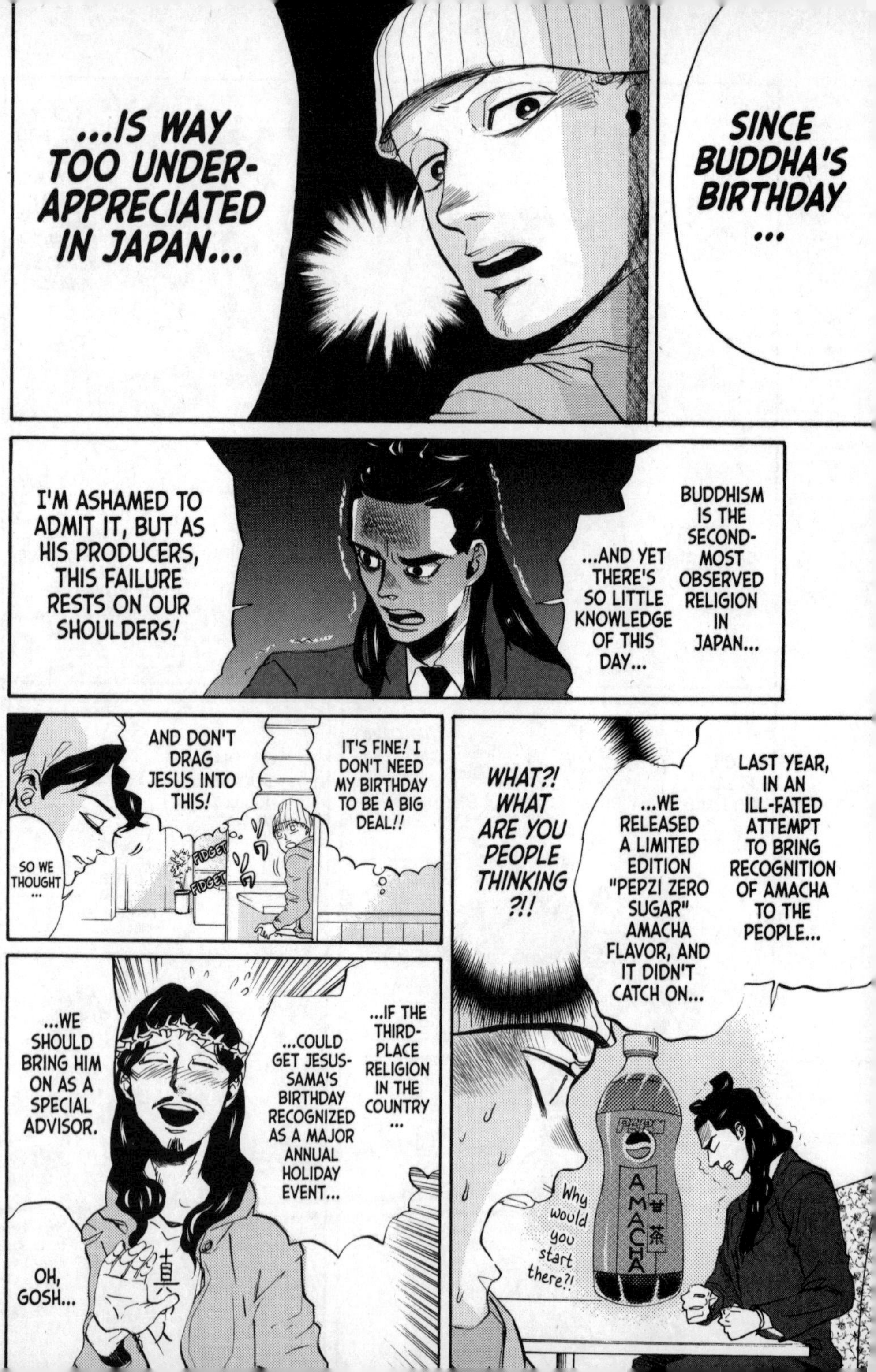
SINCE BUDDHA'S BIRTHDAY ...
...IS WAY TOO UNDER-APPRECIATED IN JAPAN...
BUDDHISM IS THE SECOND-MOST OBSERVED RELIGION IN JAPAN...
...AND YET THERE'S SO LITTLE KNOWLEDGE OF THIS DAY...
I'M ASHAMED TO ADMIT IT, BUT AS HIS PRODUCERS, THIS FAILURE RESTS ON OUR SHOULDERS!
LAST YEAR, IN AN ILL-FATED ATTEMPT TO BRING RECOGNITION OF AMACHA TO THE PEOPLE...
...WE RELEASED A LIMITED EDITION "PEPZI ZERO SUGAR" AMACHA FLAVOR, AND IT DIDN'T CATCH ON...
WHAT?! WHAT ARE YOU PEOPLE THINKING?!!
AMACHA 甘茶
Why would you start there?!
IT'S FINE! I DON'T NEED MY BIRTHDAY TO BE A BIG DEAL!!
FIDGET FIDGET
AND DON'T DRAG JESUS INTO THIS!
SO WE THOUGHT ...
...IF THE THIRD-PLACE RELIGION IN THE COUNTRY ...
...COULD GET JESUS-SAMA'S BIRTHDAY RECOGNIZED AS A MAJOR ANNUAL HOLIDAY EVENT...
...WE SHOULD BRING HIM ON AS A SPECIAL ADVISOR.
OH, GOSH...

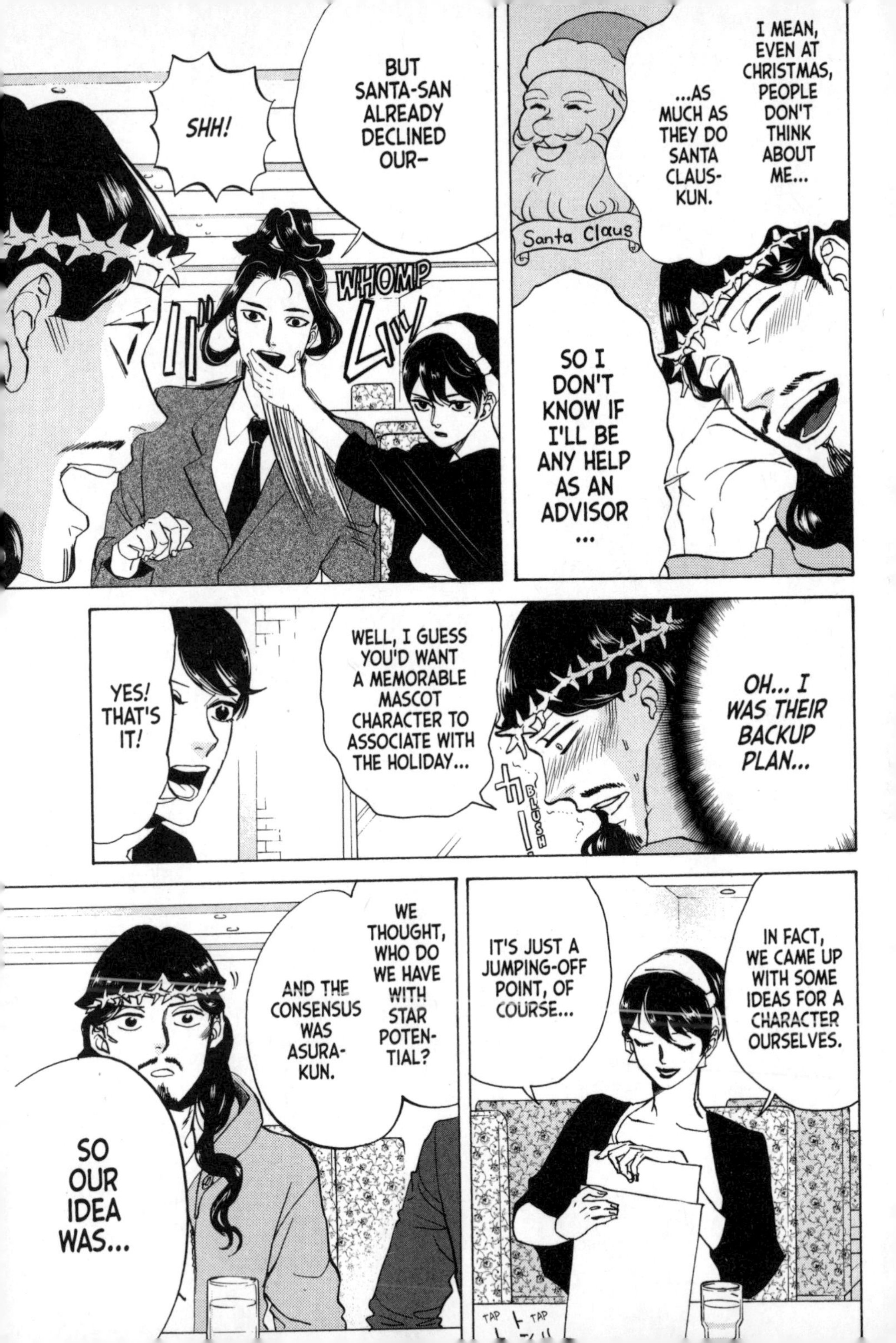
I MEAN, EVEN AT CHRISTMAS, PEOPLE DON'T THINK ABOUT ME...
...AS MUCH AS THEY DO SANTA CLAUS-KUN.
Santa Claus
SO I DON'T KNOW IF I'LL BE ANY HELP AS AN ADVISOR...
BUT SANTA-SAN ALREADY DECLINED OUR–
SHH!
WHOMP
OH... I WAS THEIR BACKUP PLAN...
BLUSH
WELL, I GUESS YOU'D WANT A MEMORABLE MASCOT CHARACTER TO ASSOCIATE WITH THE HOLIDAY...
YES! THAT'S IT!
IN FACT, WE CAME UP WITH SOME IDEAS FOR A CHARACTER OURSELVES.
IT'S JUST A JUMPING-OFF POINT, OF COURSE...
TAP TAP
WE THOUGHT, WHO DO WE HAVE WITH STAR POTENTIAL?
AND THE CONSENSUS WAS ASURA-KUN.
SO OUR IDEA WAS...

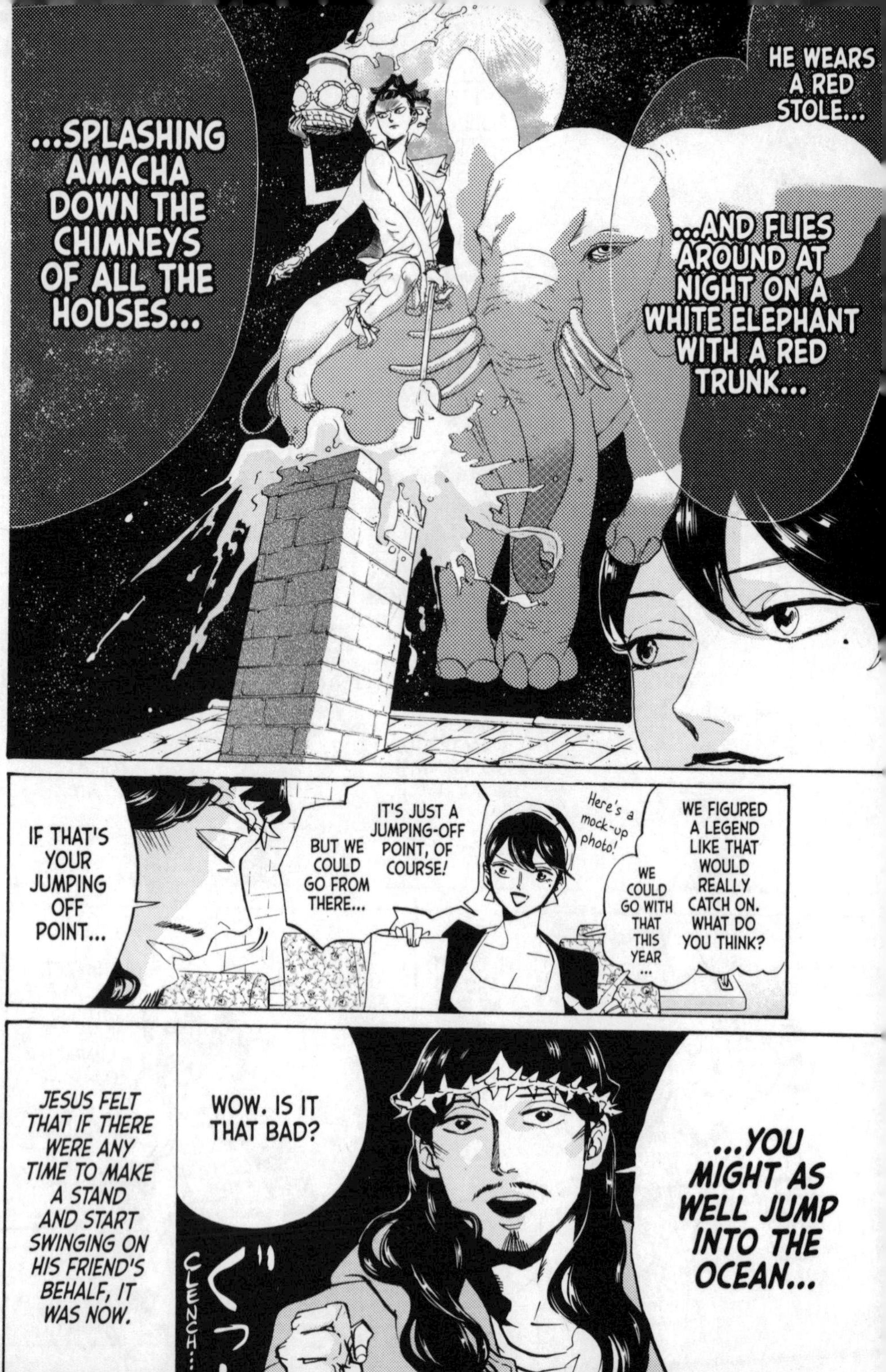
HE WEARS A RED STOLE...
...AND FLIES AROUND AT NIGHT ON A WHITE ELEPHANT WITH A RED TRUNK...
...SPLASHING AMACHA DOWN THE CHIMNEYS OF ALL THE HOUSES...
WE FIGURED A LEGEND LIKE THAT WOULD REALLY CATCH ON. WHAT DO YOU THINK?
Here's a mock-up photo!
WE COULD GO WITH THAT THIS YEAR...
IT'S JUST A JUMPING-OFF POINT, OF COURSE!
BUT WE COULD GO FROM THERE...
IF THAT'S YOUR JUMPING OFF POINT...
...YOU MIGHT AS WELL JUMP INTO THE OCEAN...
WOW. IS IT THAT BAD?
CLENCH...
JESUS FELT THAT IF THERE WERE ANY TIME TO MAKE A STAND AND START SWINGING ON HIS FRIEND'S BEHALF, IT WAS NOW.

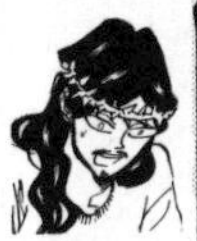

JESUS
I WAS PHOTOGRAPHED INSIDE THE NORTHERN LIGHTS? UM...THAT'S MORE OF AN AGENCY MATTER. YOU'D WANT TO CONTACT THE HEAVENLY PUBLIC RELATIONS DEPARTMENT. THERE'S A LUPIN EPISODE ABOUT STEALING THE CHRIST THE REDEEMER STATUE IN RIO THAT I LOVE FOR ITS SHEER GALL.

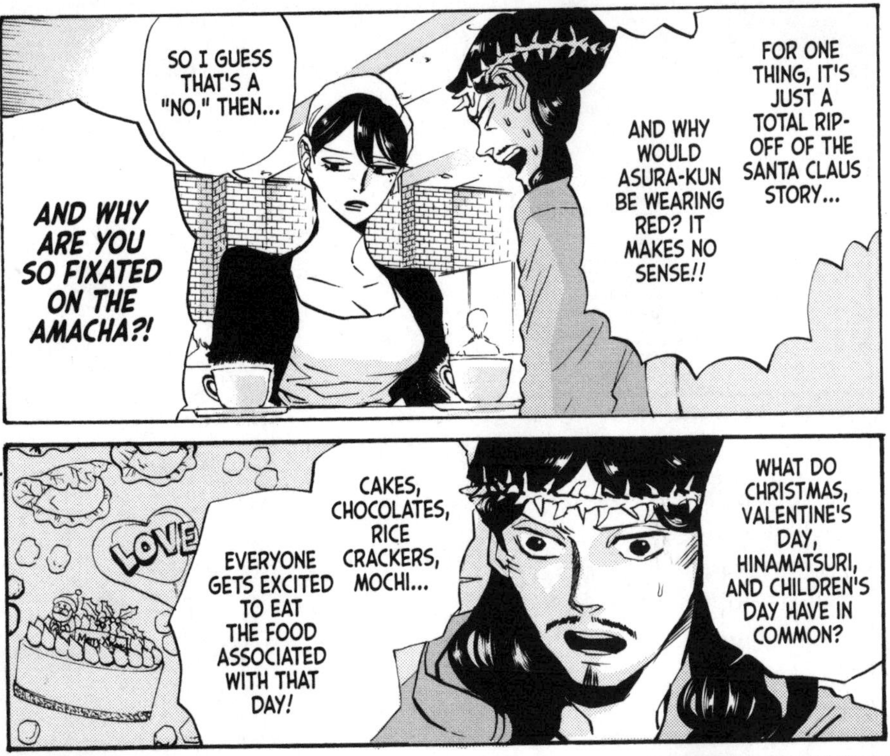
FOR ONE THING, IT'S JUST A TOTAL RIP-OFF OF THE SANTA CLAUS STORY...
AND WHY WOULD ASURA-KUN BE WEARING RED? IT MAKES NO SENSE!!
SO I GUESS THAT'S A "NO," THEN...
AND WHY ARE YOU SO FIXATED ON THE AMACHA?!
WHAT DO CHRISTMAS, VALENTINE'S DAY, HINAMATSURI, AND CHILDREN'S DAY HAVE IN COMMON?
CAKES, CHOCOLATES, RICE CRACKERS, MOCHI...
EVERYONE GETS EXCITED TO EAT THE FOOD ASSOCIATED WITH THAT DAY!
LOVE

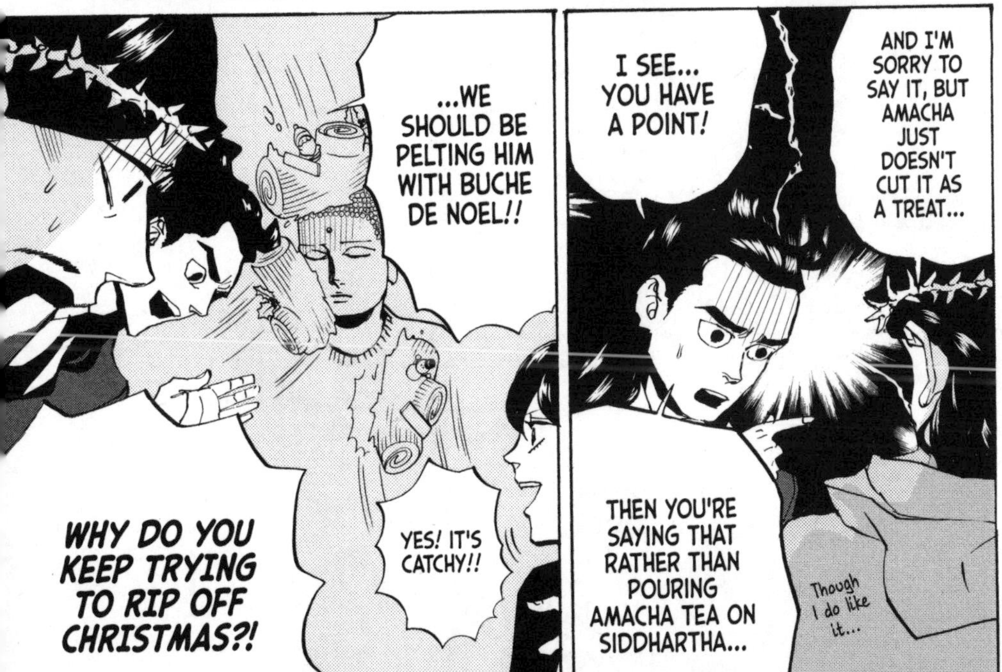
AND I'M SORRY TO SAY IT, BUT AMACHA JUST DOESN'T CUT IT AS A TREAT...
I SEE... YOU HAVE A POINT!
Though I do like it...
THEN YOU'RE SAYING THAT RATHER THAN POURING AMACHA TEA ON SIDDHARTHA...
...WE SHOULD BE PELTING HIM WITH BUCHE DE NOEL!!
YES! IT'S CATCHY!!
WHY DO YOU KEEP TRYING TO RIP OFF CHRISTMAS?!

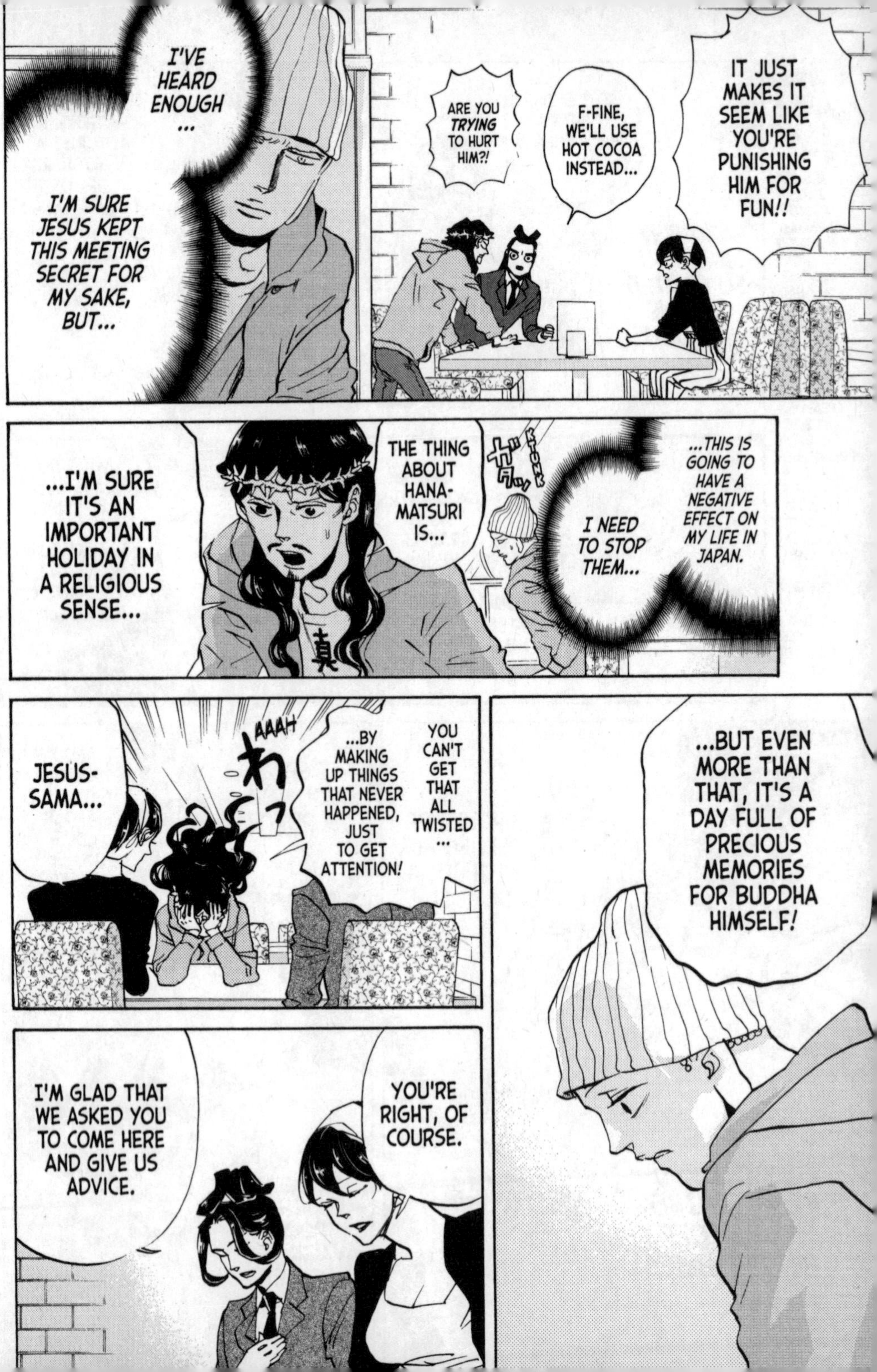
IT JUST MAKES IT SEEM LIKE YOU'RE PUNISHING HIM FOR FUN!!
F-FINE, WE'LL USE HOT COCOA INSTEAD...
ARE YOU *TRYING* TO HURT HIM?!
I'VE HEARD ENOUGH...
I'M SURE JESUS KEPT THIS MEETING SECRET FOR MY SAKE, BUT...
...THIS IS GOING TO HAVE A NEGATIVE EFFECT ON MY LIFE IN JAPAN.
I NEED TO STOP THEM...
ガタッ KTUNK
THE THING ABOUT HANA-MATSURI IS...
...I'M SURE IT'S AN IMPORTANT HOLIDAY IN A RELIGIOUS SENSE...
...BUT EVEN MORE THAN THAT, IT'S A DAY FULL OF PRECIOUS MEMORIES FOR BUDDHA HIMSELF!
YOU CAN'T GET THAT ALL TWISTED...
...BY MAKING UP THINGS THAT NEVER HAPPENED, JUST TO GET ATTENTION!
わっ AAAH
JESUS-SAMA...
YOU'RE RIGHT, OF COURSE.
I'M GLAD THAT WE ASKED YOU TO COME HERE AND GIVE US ADVICE.

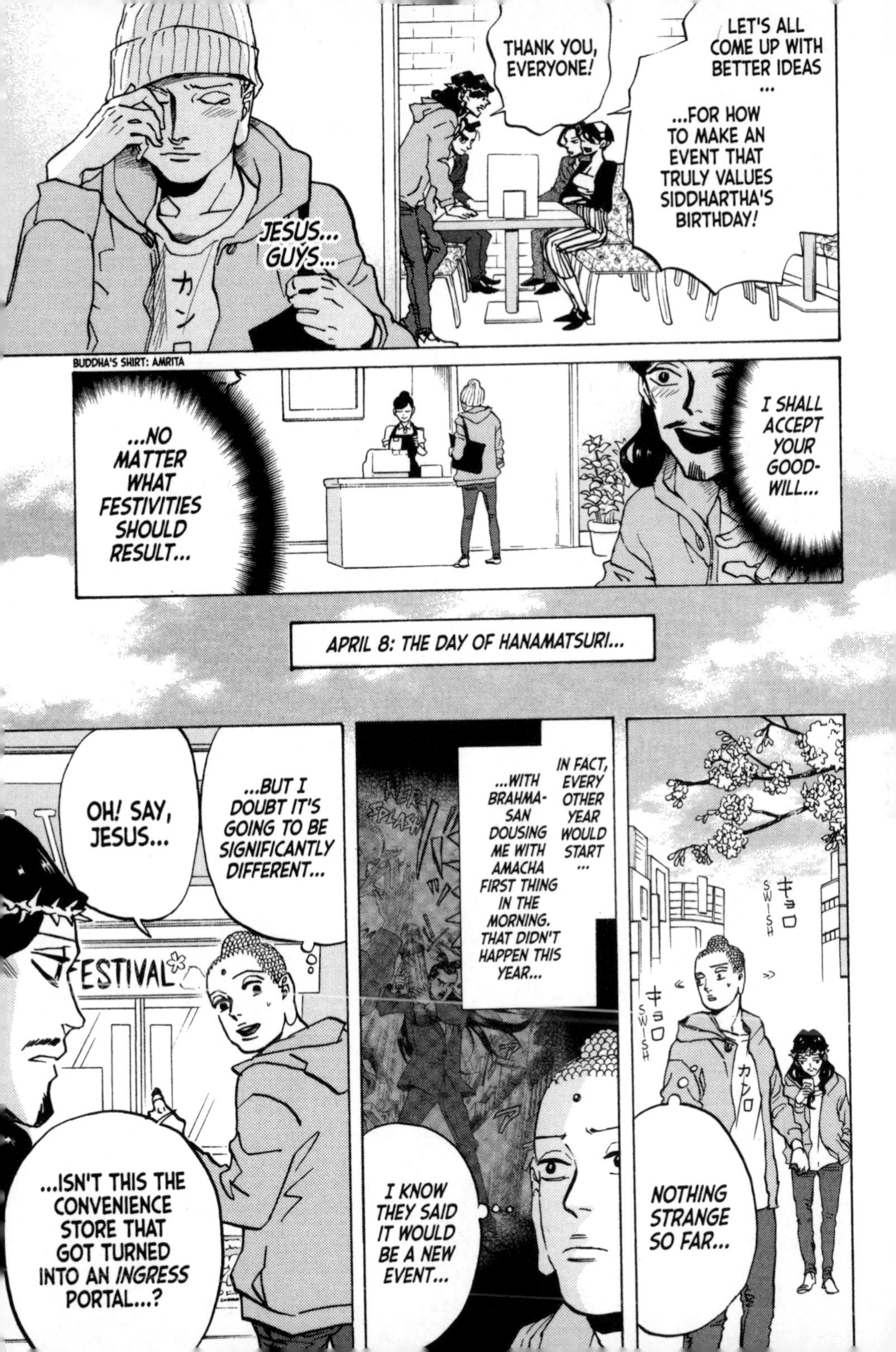
LET'S ALL COME UP WITH BETTER IDEAS ...
...FOR HOW TO MAKE AN EVENT THAT TRULY VALUES SIDDHARTHA'S BIRTHDAY!
THANK YOU, EVERYONE!
JESUS... GUYS...
BUDDHA'S SHIRT: AMRITA
I SHALL ACCEPT YOUR GOOD-WILL...
...NO MATTER WHAT FESTIVITIES SHOULD RESULT...
APRIL 8: THE DAY OF HANAMATSURI...
キョロ SWISH
キョロ SWISH
NOTHING STRANGE SO FAR...
IN FACT, EVERY OTHER YEAR WOULD START ...
...WITH BRAHMA-SAN DOUSING ME WITH AMACHA FIRST THING IN THE MORNING. THAT DIDN'T HAPPEN THIS YEAR...
I KNOW THEY SAID IT WOULD BE A NEW EVENT...
...BUT I DOUBT IT'S GOING TO BE SIGNIFICANTLY DIFFERENT...
OH! SAY, JESUS...
FESTIVAL
...ISN'T THIS THE CONVENIENCE STORE THAT GOT TURNED INTO AN INGRESS PORTAL...?

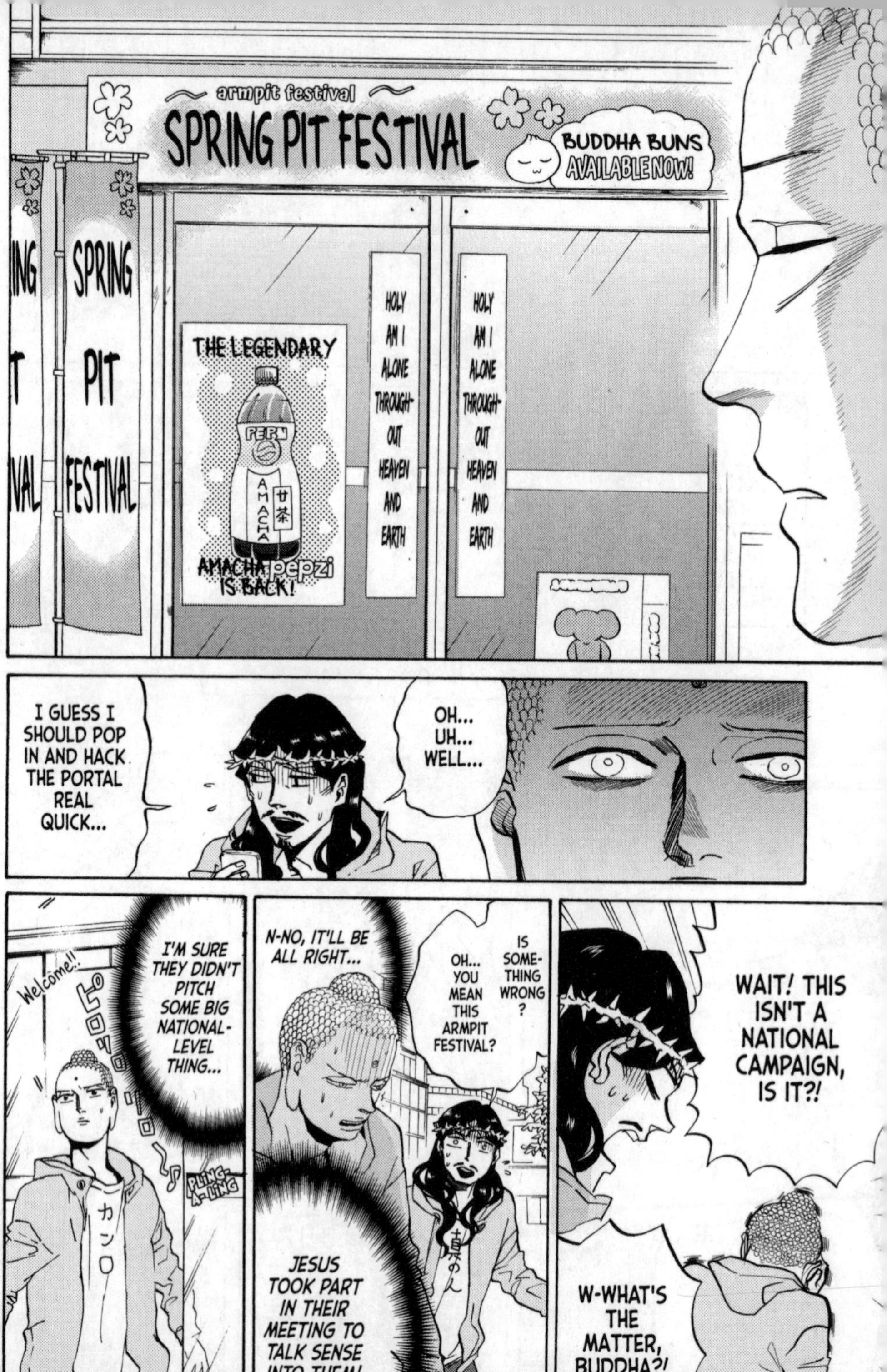
armpit festival
SPRING PIT FESTIVAL
BUDDHA BUNS AVAILABLE NOW!
SPRING PIT FESTIVAL
HOLY AM I ALONE THROUGHOUT HEAVEN AND EARTH
HOLY AM I ALONE THROUGHOUT HEAVEN AND EARTH
THE LEGENDARY
AMACHA
甘茶
AMACHA pepzi IS BACK!
OH... UH... WELL...
I GUESS I SHOULD POP IN AND HACK THE PORTAL REAL QUICK...
WAIT! THIS ISN'T A NATIONAL CAMPAIGN, IS IT?!
W-WHAT'S THE MATTER, BUDDHA?!
IS SOMETHING WRONG?
OH... YOU MEAN THIS ARMPIT FESTIVAL?
N-NO, IT'LL BE ALL RIGHT...
JESUS TOOK PART IN THEIR MEETING TO TALK SENSE INTO THEM!
I'M SURE THEY DIDN'T PITCH SOME BIG NATIONAL-LEVEL THING...
Welcome!!
ピロリロリロ
PLING-A-LING
カンロ

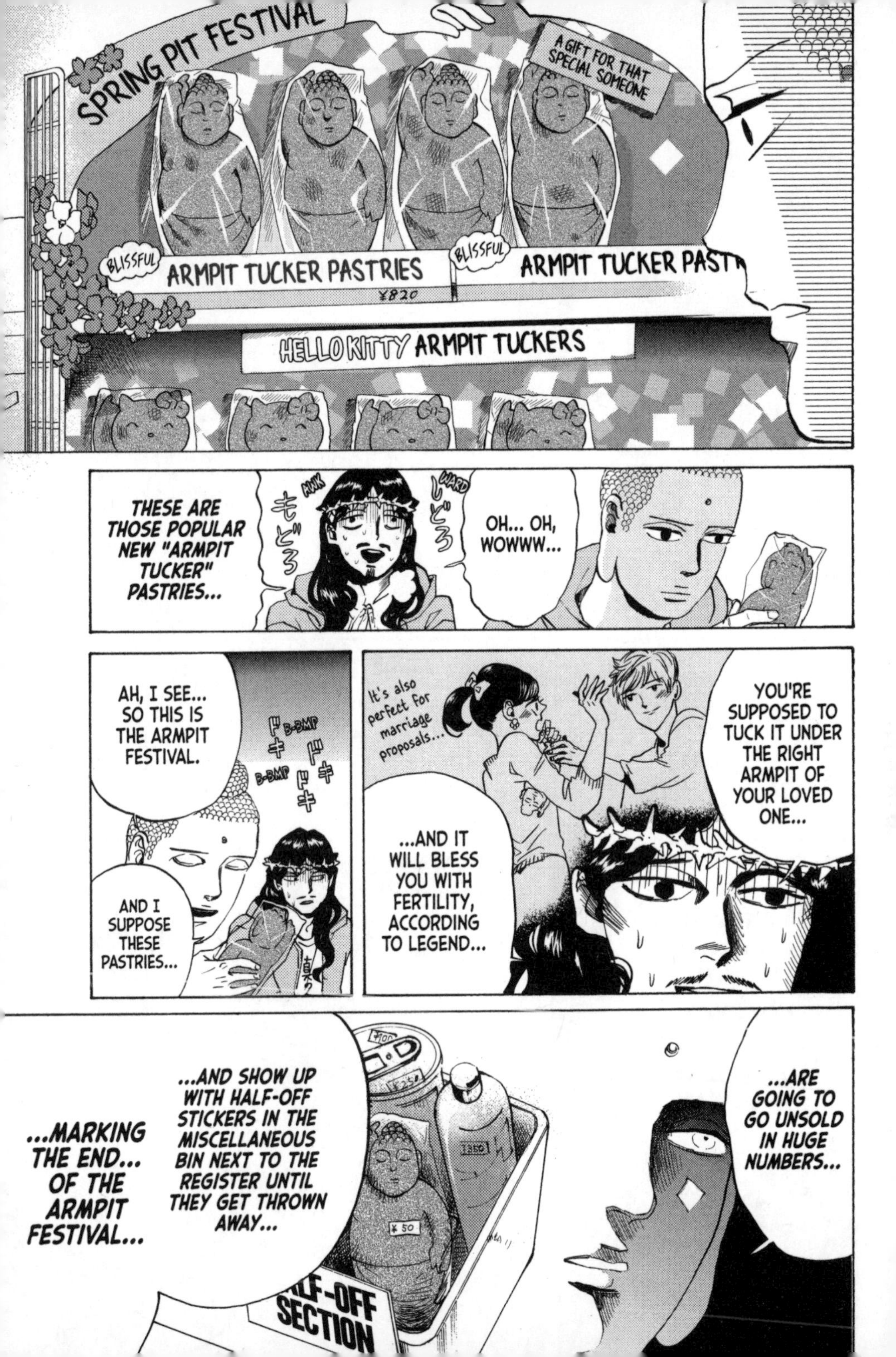
SPRING PIT FESTIVAL
A GIFT FOR THAT SPECIAL SOMEONE
BLISSFUL
ARMPIT TUCKER PAST
BLISSFUL
ARMPIT TUCKER PASTRIES
¥820
HELLO KITTY ARMPIT TUCKERS
OH... OH, WOWWW...
じどろ HARD
もどろ HNK
THESE ARE THOSE POPULAR NEW "ARMPIT TUCKER" PASTRIES...
YOU'RE SUPPOSED TO TUCK IT UNDER THE RIGHT ARMPIT OF YOUR LOVED ONE...
It's also perfect for marriage proposals...
...AND IT WILL BLESS YOU WITH FERTILITY, ACCORDING TO LEGEND...
AH, I SEE... SO THIS IS THE ARMPIT FESTIVAL.
ドキ B-BMP
ドキドキ B-BMP
AND I SUPPOSE THESE PASTRIES...
...ARE GOING TO GO UNSOLD IN HUGE NUMBERS...
...AND SHOW UP WITH HALF-OFF STICKERS IN THE MISCELLANEOUS BIN NEXT TO THE REGISTER UNTIL THEY GET THROWN AWAY...
...MARKING THE END... OF THE ARMPIT FESTIVAL...
¥50
HALF-OFF SECTION

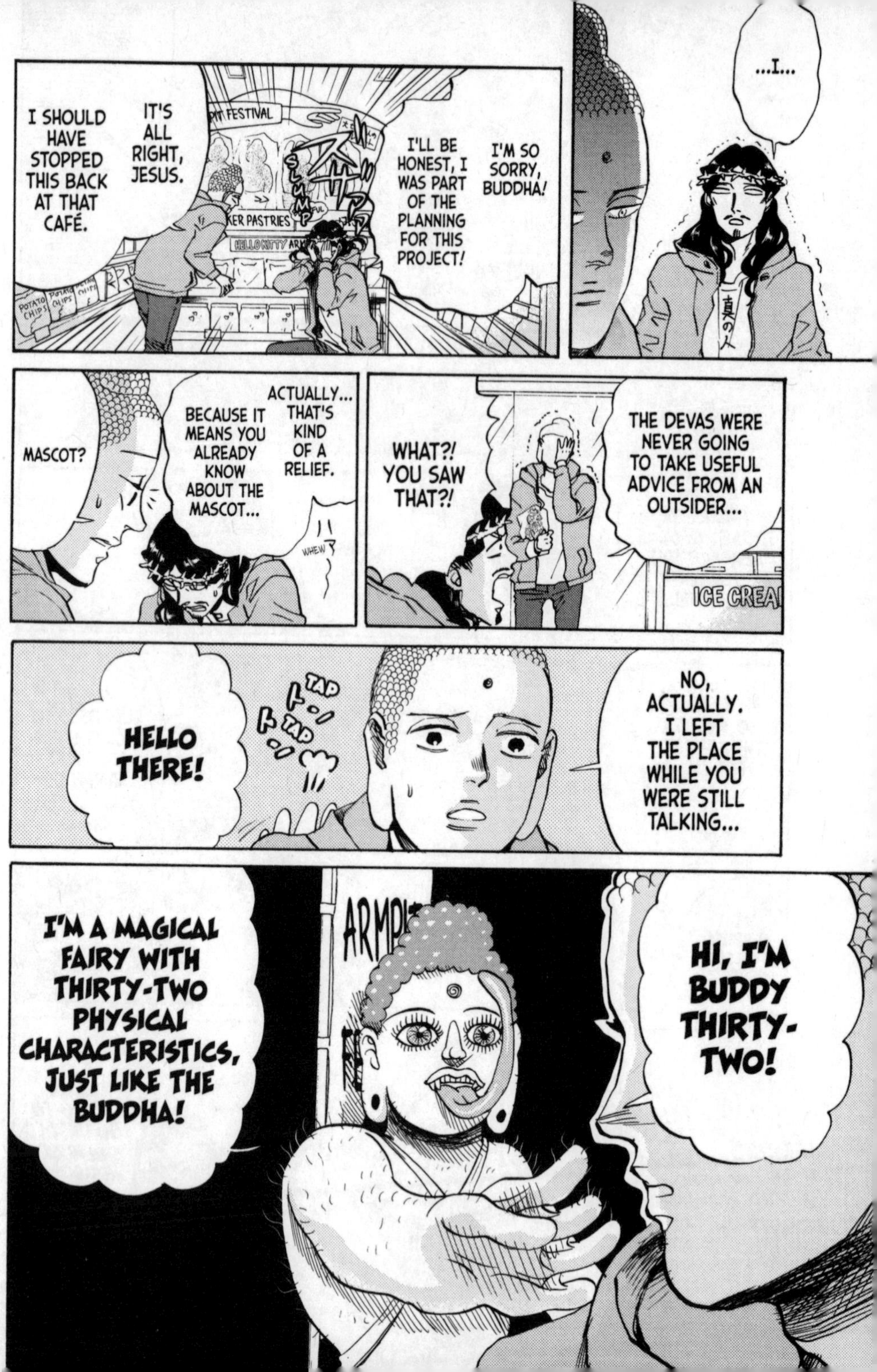
...I...
I'M SO SORRY, BUDDHA!
I'LL BE HONEST, I WAS PART OF THE PLANNING FOR THIS PROJECT!
SLUMP
IT'S ALL RIGHT, JESUS.
I SHOULD HAVE STOPPED THIS BACK AT THAT CAFÉ.
POTATO CHIPS
THE DEVAS WERE NEVER GOING TO TAKE USEFUL ADVICE FROM AN OUTSIDER...
WHAT?! YOU SAW THAT?!
ACTUALLY... THAT'S KIND OF A RELIEF.
BECAUSE IT MEANS YOU ALREADY KNOW ABOUT THE MASCOT...
WHEW
MASCOT?
NO, ACTUALLY. I LEFT THE PLACE WHILE YOU WERE STILL TALKING...
TAP TAP
HELLO THERE!
HI, I'M BUDDY THIRTY-TWO!
I'M A MAGICAL FAIRY WITH THIRTY-TWO PHYSICAL CHARACTERISTICS, JUST LIKE THE BUDDHA!

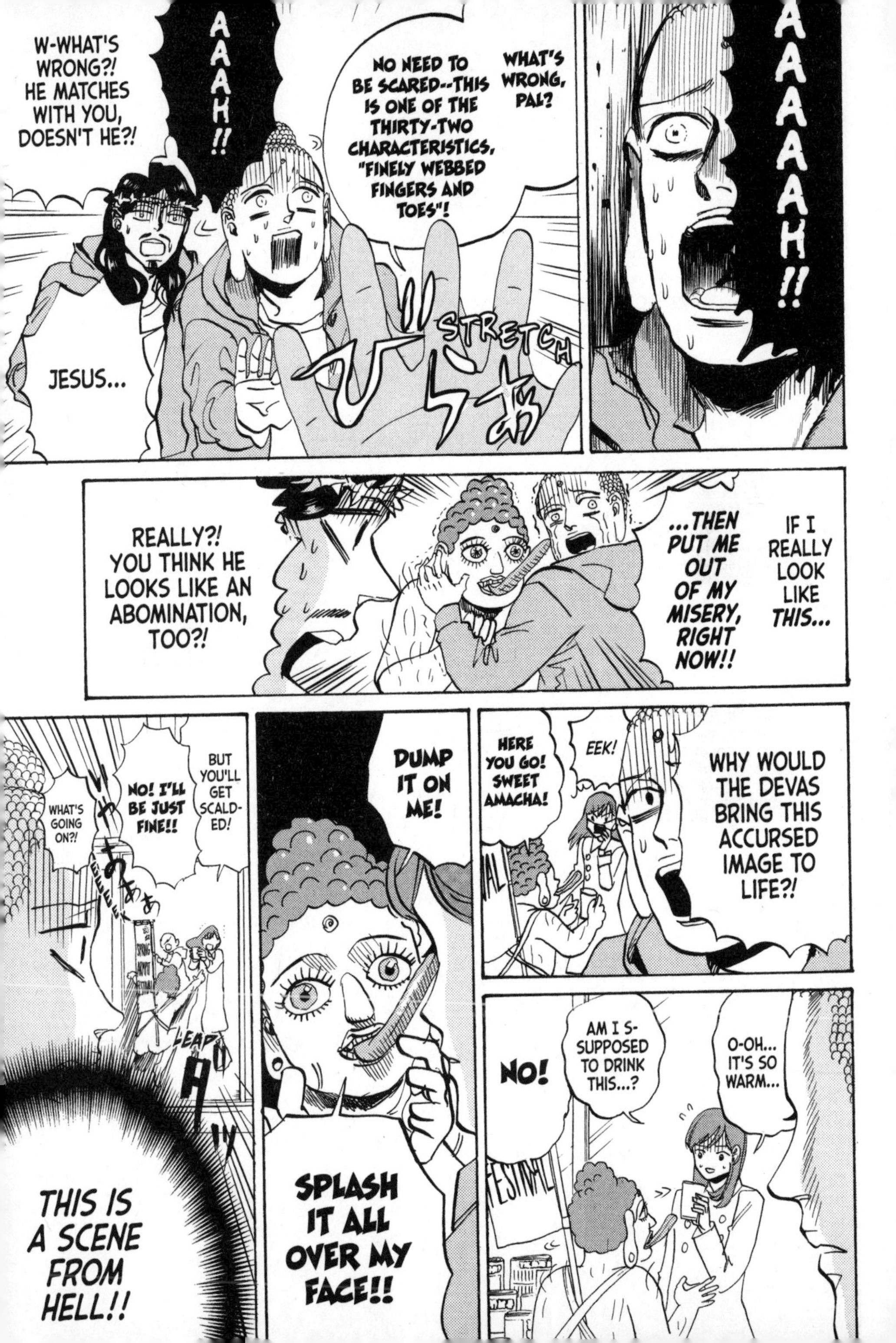
AAAAAH!!
WHAT'S WRONG, PAL?
NO NEED TO BE SCARED--THIS IS ONE OF THE THIRTY-TWO CHARACTERISTICS, "FINELY WEBBED FINGERS AND TOES"!
AAAH!!
W-WHAT'S WRONG?! HE MATCHES WITH YOU, DOESN'T HE?!
STRETCH
JESUS...
IF I REALLY LOOK LIKE THIS...
...THEN PUT ME OUT OF MY MISERY, RIGHT NOW!!
REALLY?! YOU THINK HE LOOKS LIKE AN ABOMINATION, TOO?!
WHY WOULD THE DEVAS BRING THIS ACCURSED IMAGE TO LIFE?!
EEK!
HERE YOU GO! SWEET AMACHA!
O-OH... IT'S SO WARM...
AM I S-SUPPOSED TO DRINK THIS...?
NO!
DUMP IT ON ME!
SPLASH IT ALL OVER MY FACE!!
BUT YOU'LL GET SCALD-ED!
NO! I'LL BE JUST FINE!!
WHAT'S GOING ON?!
LEAP
THIS IS A SCENE FROM HELL!!

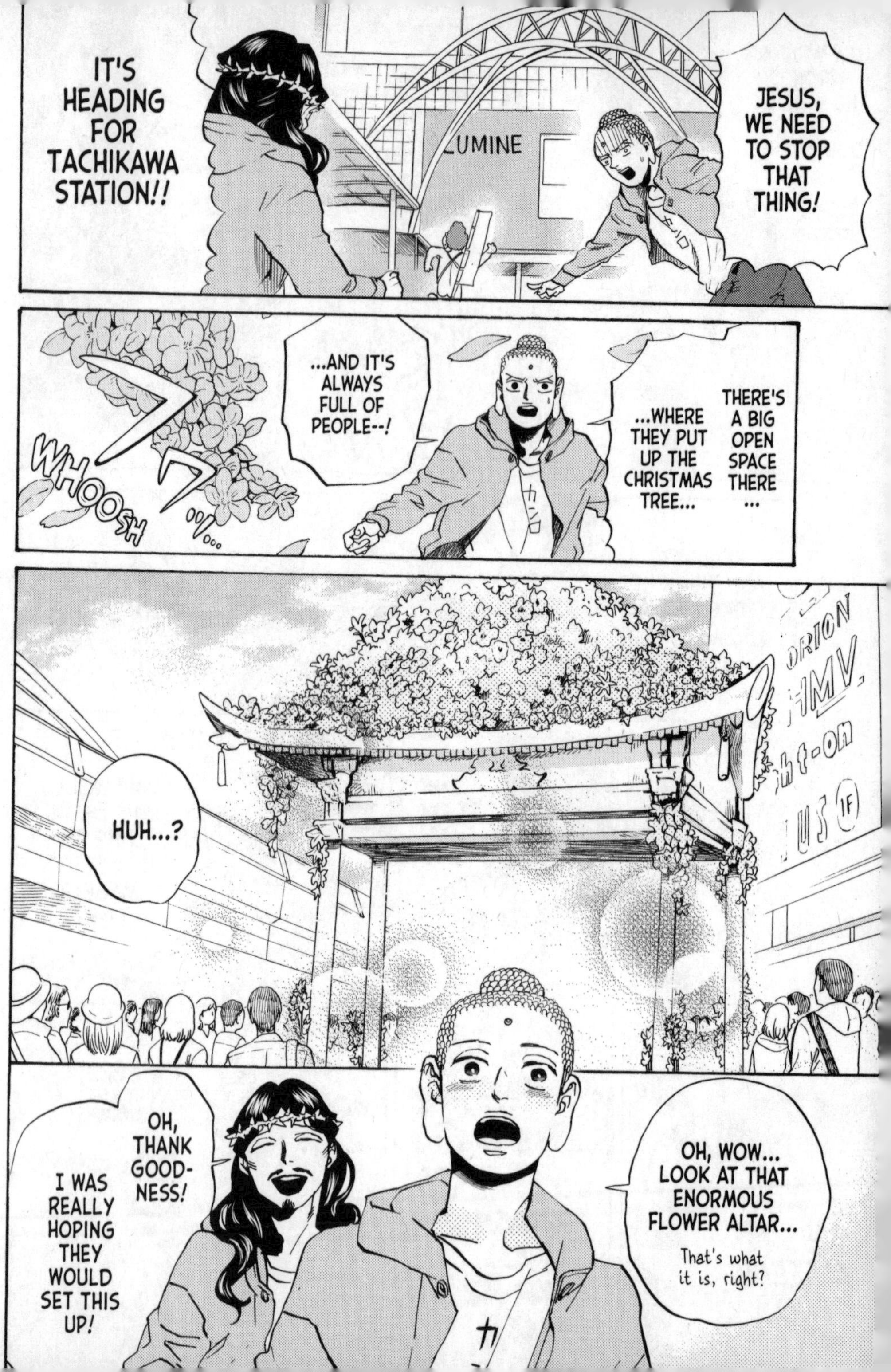
JESUS, WE NEED TO STOP THAT THING!
LUMINE
IT'S HEADING FOR TACHIKAWA STATION!!
THERE'S A BIG OPEN SPACE THERE...
...WHERE THEY PUT UP THE CHRISTMAS TREE...
...AND IT'S ALWAYS FULL OF PEOPLE--!
WHOOSH
ORION
HMV
HUH...?
OH, WOW... LOOK AT THAT ENORMOUS FLOWER ALTAR...
That's what it is, right?
OH, THANK GOODNESS!
I WAS REALLY HOPING THEY WOULD SET THIS UP!

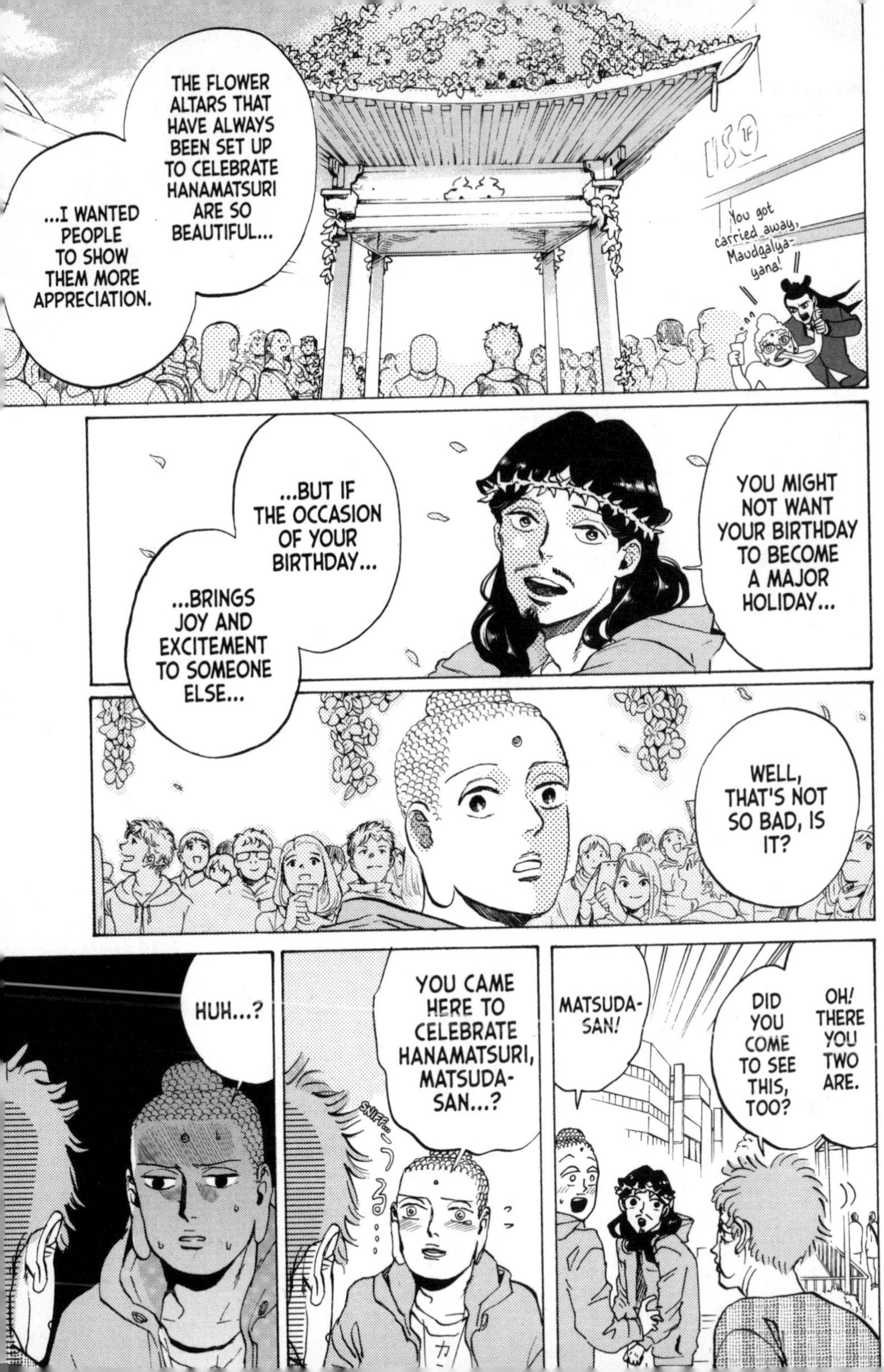
THE FLOWER ALTARS THAT HAVE ALWAYS BEEN SET UP TO CELEBRATE HANAMATSURI ARE SO BEAUTIFUL...
...I WANTED PEOPLE TO SHOW THEM MORE APPRECIATION.
You got carried away, Maudgalyayana!
YOU MIGHT NOT WANT YOUR BIRTHDAY TO BECOME A MAJOR HOLIDAY...
...BUT IF THE OCCASION OF YOUR BIRTHDAY...
...BRINGS JOY AND EXCITEMENT TO SOMEONE ELSE...
WELL, THAT'S NOT SO BAD, IS IT?
OH! THERE YOU TWO ARE.
DID YOU COME TO SEE THIS, TOO?
MATSUDA-SAN!
YOU CAME HERE TO CELEBRATE HANAMATSURI, MATSUDA-SAN...?
SNIFF...
HUH...?

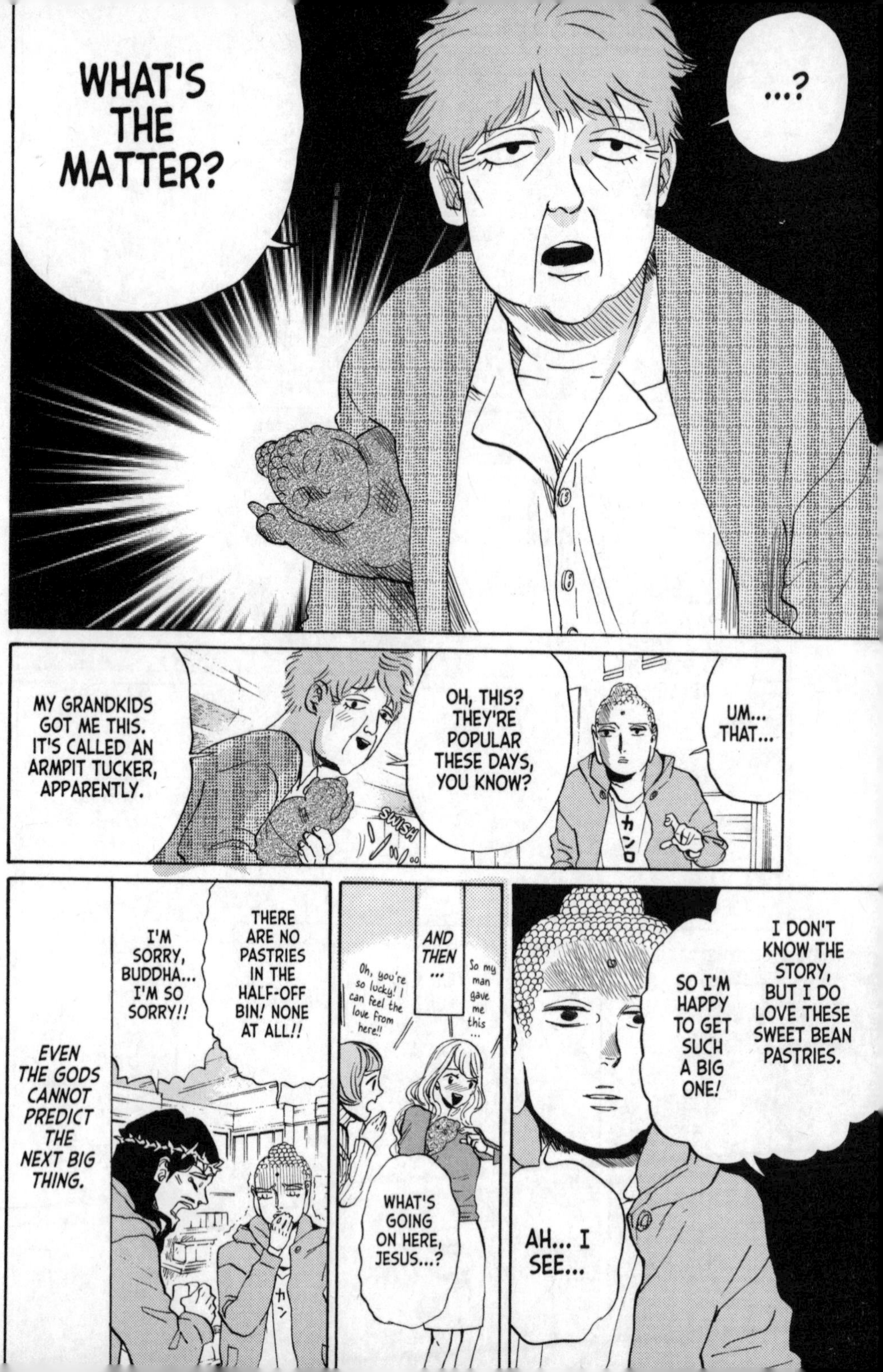

...?
WHAT'S THE MATTER?
UM... THAT...
OH, THIS? THEY'RE POPULAR THESE DAYS, YOU KNOW?
MY GRANDKIDS GOT ME THIS. IT'S CALLED AN ARMPIT TUCKER, APPARENTLY.
SWISH
カンロ
I DON'T KNOW THE STORY, BUT I DO LOVE THESE SWEET BEAN PASTRIES.
SO I'M HAPPY TO GET SUCH A BIG ONE!
AH... I SEE...
AND THEN ...
So my man gave me this ...
Oh, you're so lucky! I can feel the love from here!!
WHAT'S GOING ON HERE, JESUS...?
THERE ARE NO PASTRIES IN THE HALF-OFF BIN! NONE AT ALL!!
I'M SORRY, BUDDHA... I'M SO SORRY!!
EVEN THE GODS CANNOT PREDICT THE NEXT BIG THING.

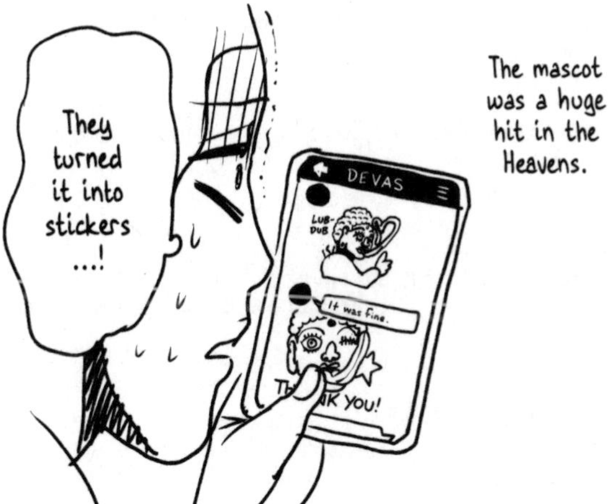
The mascot was a huge hit in the Heavens.
They turned it into stickers ....!
DEVAS
LUB-DUB
It was fine.

SAINT☆YOUNG MEN

CHAPTER 82 TRANSLATION NOTES

Amacha, page 19
Amacha literally means "sweet tea," and is brewed from the naturally sweet fermented leaves of a species of hydrangea. On Buddha's Birthday (April 8), normally called Hanamatsuri or "Flower Festival" in Japan, amacha is ceremonially poured on small Buddha statues to mimic bathing a newborn. It is not related to the "sweet tea" popular in the American South.

WDT 48, page 20
A parody of the template for the pop idol group AKB48, short for Akihabara 48, referring to the "home ground" of the group, and the number of members it contains. Many other affiliated groups under the same management were formed, following the same pattern of a three-letter anagram and the number 48.

The Tale of the Princess Kaguya, page 21
A 2013 Ghibli animated film, directed by Isao Takahata (*Grave of the Fireflies, Pom Poko*). An adaptation of the famous story, The Tale of the Bamboo Cutter, it revolves around Princess Kaguya, a being that was found in a bamboo shoot, but was originally from the moon.. At the climax of the film, a procession of celestial beings comes down to take her away, led by a figure (the king of the moon) drawn to resemble the Buddha.

Children's Day, page 25
A holiday observed on May 5, and previously known as "Boys' Day," as a counterpart to "Girls' Day" (*Hinamatsuri*). As a customary part of the holiday, rice cakes filled with *anko* (sweet bean paste) and wrapped in *kashiwa* (oak) leaves called *kashiwa mochi* are eaten. These can be seen in the upper left corner of the panel.

Buche de Noel, page 25
A kind of Christmas cake made in France and other primarily French-speaking countries. It is a sponge cake that is rolled and decorated to look like a Yule log. It is also well known in Japan.

Amrita, page 27
A Sanskrit word meaning "immortality" that refers to a kind of drink in Indian mythology that confers immortality upon whoever drinks it. In Japanese this is written kanro, meaning "sweet dew."

Thirty-Two, page 30
A series of characteristics called "Signs of a Great Man" that were used as a description of the Buddha in early Buddhist art. These include features such as "finely webbed fingers and toes" and "a tongue long and broad."

Flower altar, page 32
A special altar for displaying flowers on Hanamatsuri, the day of observing Buddha's birth. Usually they resemble miniature gazebo shrines about the size of a small table, with the flowers adorning the roof of the structure and a tiny Buddha statue below, upon which visitors pour the amacha.

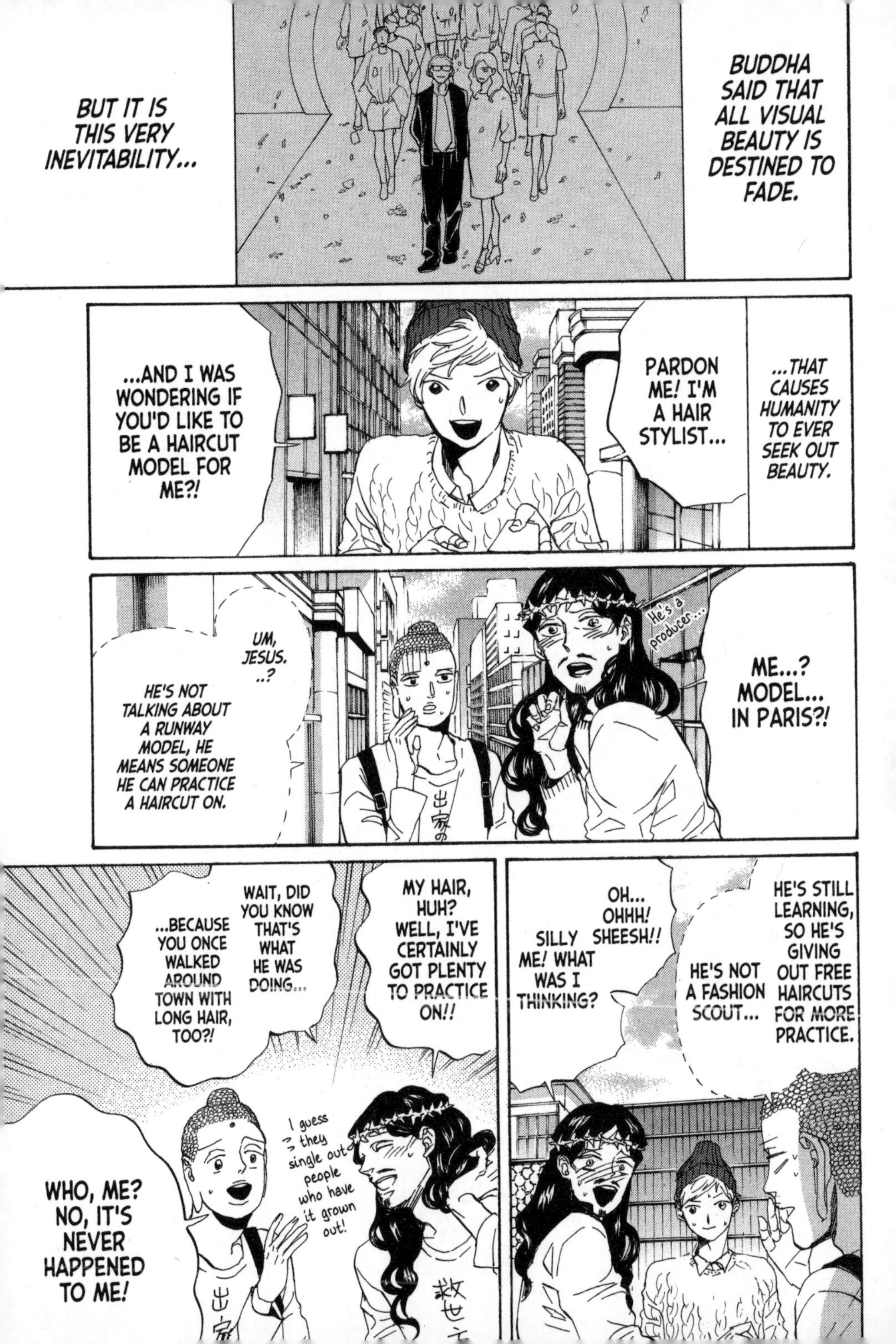
BUDDHA SAID THAT ALL VISUAL BEAUTY IS DESTINED TO FADE.
BUT IT IS THIS VERY INEVITABILITY...
...THAT CAUSES HUMANITY TO EVER SEEK OUT BEAUTY.
PARDON ME! I'M A HAIR STYLIST...
...AND I WAS WONDERING IF YOU'D LIKE TO BE A HAIRCUT MODEL FOR ME?!
ME...? MODEL... IN PARIS?!
He's a producer...
UM, JESUS. ..?
HE'S NOT TALKING ABOUT A RUNWAY MODEL, HE MEANS SOMEONE HE CAN PRACTICE A HAIRCUT ON.
HE'S STILL LEARNING, SO HE'S GIVING OUT FREE HAIRCUTS FOR MORE PRACTICE.
HE'S NOT A FASHION SCOUT...
OH... OHHH! SHEESH!!
SILLY ME! WHAT WAS I THINKING?
MY HAIR, HUH? WELL, I'VE CERTAINLY GOT PLENTY TO PRACTICE ON!!
WAIT, DID YOU KNOW THAT'S WHAT HE WAS DOING...
...BECAUSE YOU ONCE WALKED AROUND TOWN WITH LONG HAIR, TOO?!
I guess they single out people who have it grown out!
WHO, ME? NO, IT'S NEVER HAPPENED TO ME!

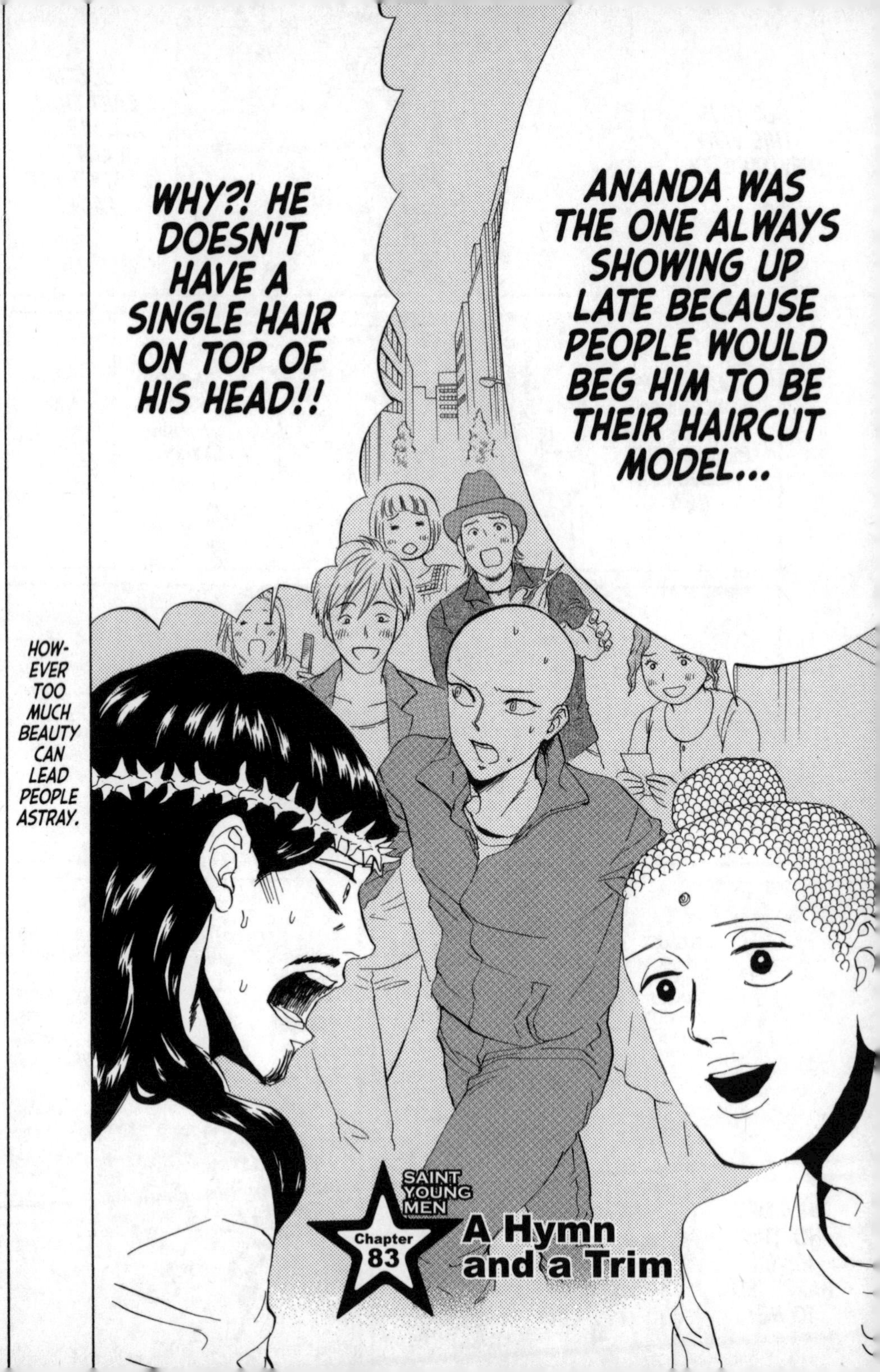
ANANDA WAS THE ONE ALWAYS SHOWING UP LATE BECAUSE PEOPLE WOULD BEG HIM TO BE THEIR HAIRCUT MODEL...
WHY?! HE DOESN'T HAVE A SINGLE HAIR ON TOP OF HIS HEAD!!
HOW-EVER TOO MUCH BEAUTY CAN LEAD PEOPLE ASTRAY.
SAINT YOUNG MEN
Chapter 83
A Hymn and a Trim

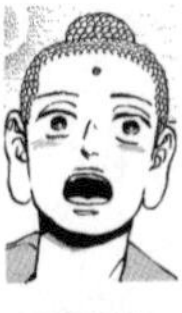

BUDDHA
I ALWAYS WONDERED WHY PEOPLE GET SO DRESSED UP IN THE SPRING. TURNS OUT IT'S ALL THE NEW COMPANY HIRES AND COLLEGE STUDENTS. I'M SURE IT'S STRESSFUL MAKING IMPRESSIONS ON ALL THOSE NEW PEOPLE, BUT YOU'LL GET USED TO IT SOON!

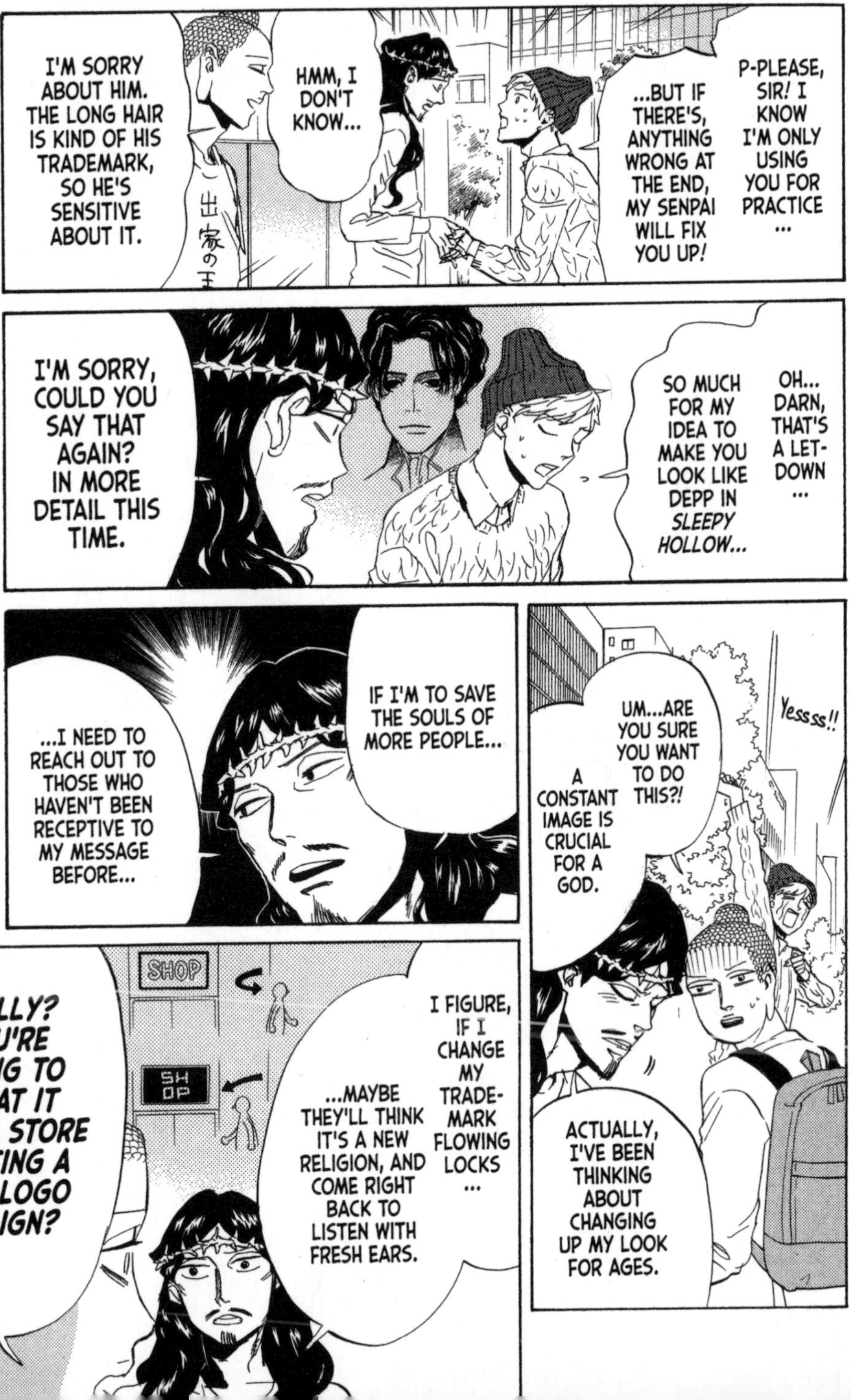
P-PLEASE, SIR! I KNOW I'M ONLY USING YOU FOR PRACTICE ...
...BUT IF THERE'S, ANYTHING WRONG AT THE END, MY SENPAI WILL FIX YOU UP!
HMM, I DON'T KNOW...
I'M SORRY ABOUT HIM. THE LONG HAIR IS KIND OF HIS TRADEMARK, SO HE'S SENSITIVE ABOUT IT.
出家の王
OH... DARN, THAT'S A LET-DOWN ...
SO MUCH FOR MY IDEA TO MAKE YOU LOOK LIKE DEPP IN SLEEPY HOLLOW...
I'M SORRY, COULD YOU SAY THAT AGAIN? IN MORE DETAIL THIS TIME.
Yessss!!
UM...ARE YOU SURE YOU WANT TO DO THIS?!
A CONSTANT IMAGE IS CRUCIAL FOR A GOD.
ACTUALLY, I'VE BEEN THINKING ABOUT CHANGING UP MY LOOK FOR AGES.
IF I'M TO SAVE THE SOULS OF MORE PEOPLE...
...I NEED TO REACH OUT TO THOSE WHO HAVEN'T BEEN RECEPTIVE TO MY MESSAGE BEFORE...
I FIGURE, IF I CHANGE MY TRADE-MARK FLOWING LOCKS ...
...MAYBE THEY'LL THINK IT'S A NEW RELIGION, AND COME RIGHT BACK TO LISTEN WITH FRESH EARS.
SHOP
SH OP
REALLY? YOU'RE GOING TO TREAT IT LIKE A STORE GETTING A NEW LOGO DESIGN?

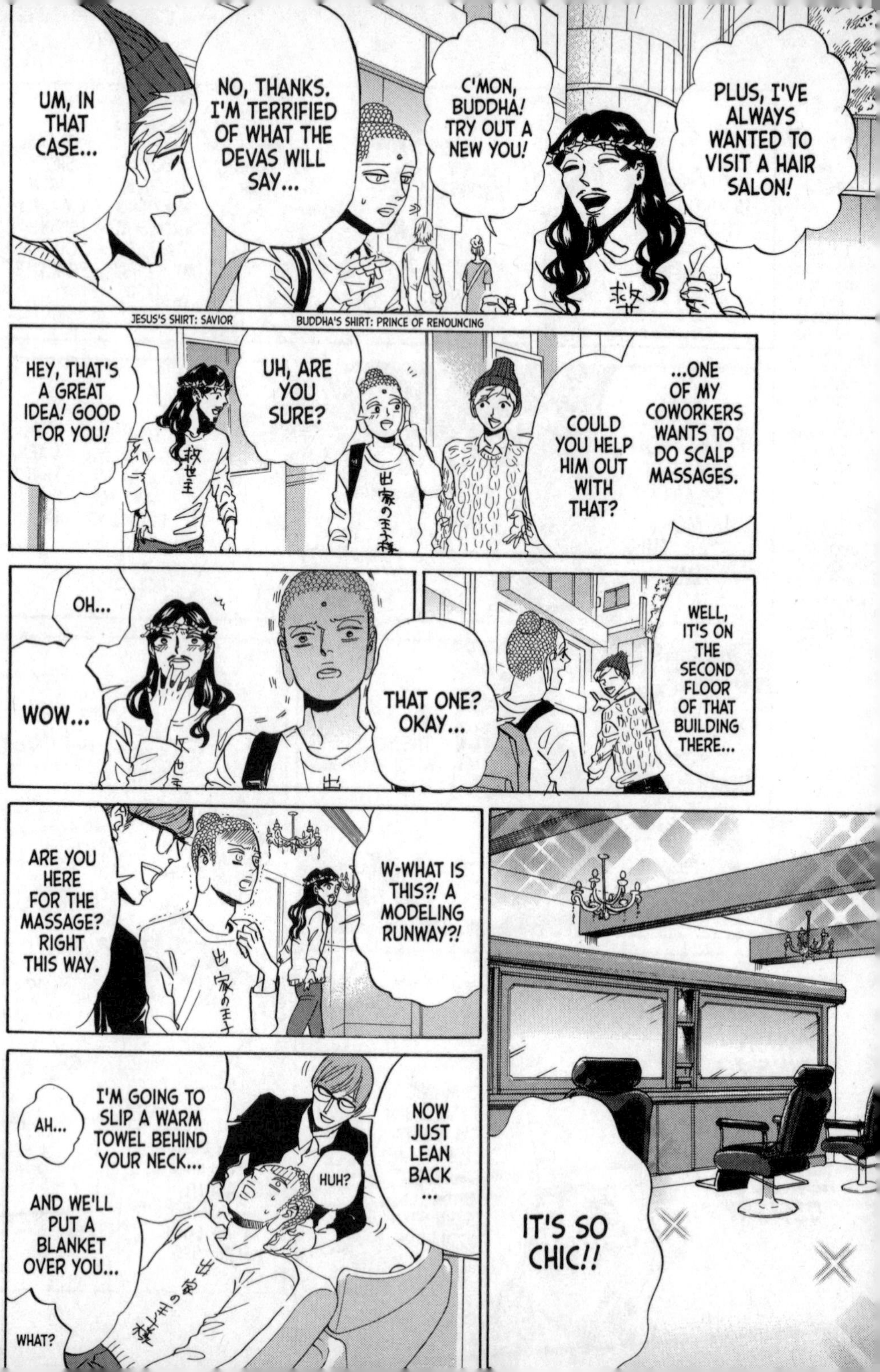
PLUS, I'VE ALWAYS WANTED TO VISIT A HAIR SALON!
C'MON, BUDDHA! TRY OUT A NEW YOU!
NO, THANKS. I'M TERRIFIED OF WHAT THE DEVAS WILL SAY...
UM, IN THAT CASE...
BUDDHA'S SHIRT: PRINCE OF RENOUNCING
JESUS'S SHIRT: SAVIOR
...ONE OF MY COWORKERS WANTS TO DO SCALP MASSAGES.
COULD YOU HELP HIM OUT WITH THAT?
UH, ARE YOU SURE?
HEY, THAT'S A GREAT IDEA! GOOD FOR YOU!
WELL, IT'S ON THE SECOND FLOOR OF THAT BUILDING THERE...
THAT ONE? OKAY...
OH...
WOW...
IT'S SO CHIC!!
W-WHAT IS THIS?! A MODELING RUNWAY?!
ARE YOU HERE FOR THE MASSAGE? RIGHT THIS WAY.
NOW JUST LEAN BACK ...
HUH?
I'M GOING TO SLIP A WARM TOWEL BEHIND YOUR NECK...
AH...
AND WE'LL PUT A BLANKET OVER YOU...
WHAT?

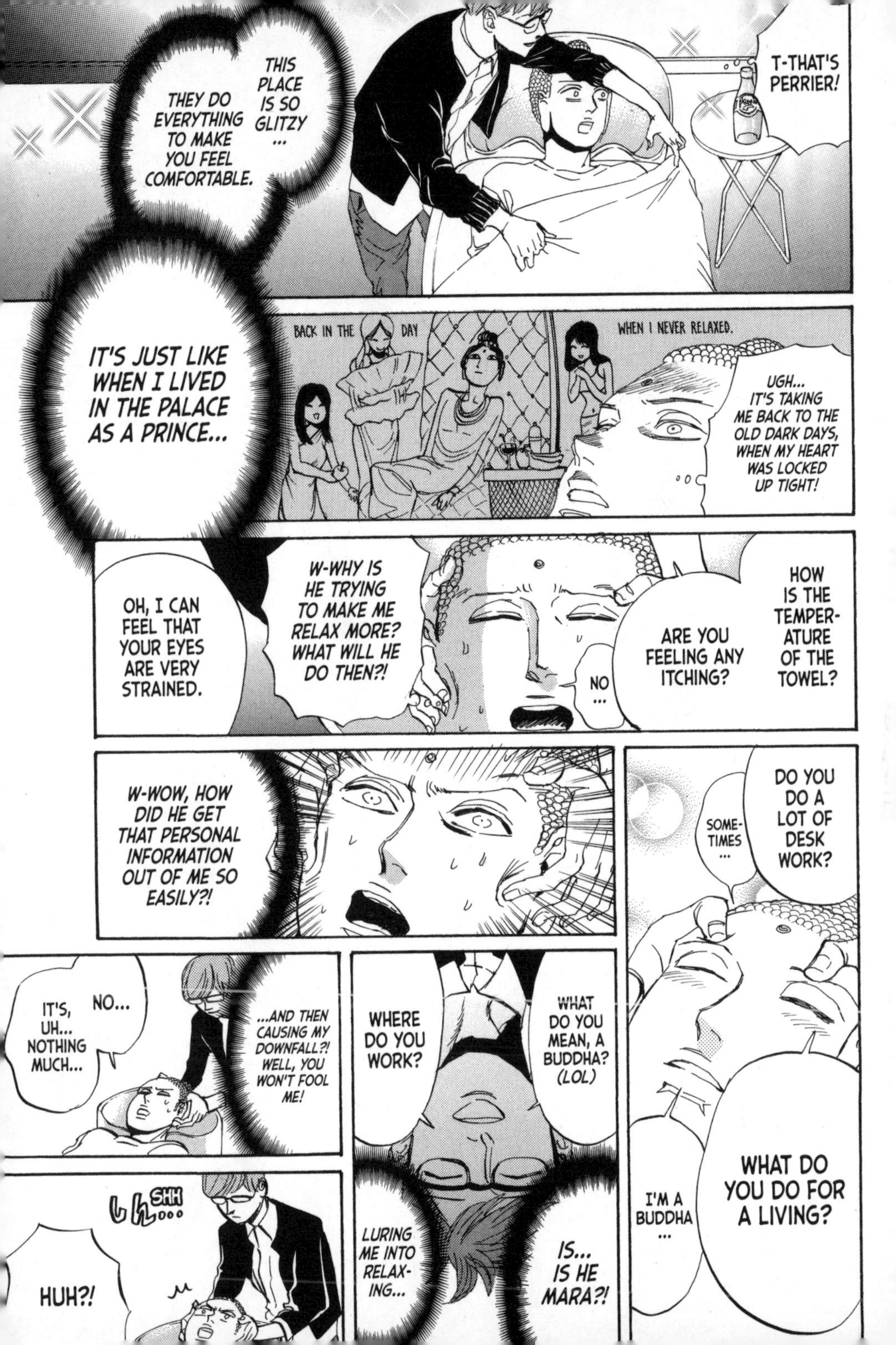

T-THAT'S PERRIER!
THIS PLACE IS SO GLITZY...
THEY DO EVERYTHING TO MAKE YOU FEEL COMFORTABLE.
IT'S JUST LIKE WHEN I LIVED IN THE PALACE AS A PRINCE...
UGH... IT'S TAKING ME BACK TO THE OLD DARK DAYS, WHEN MY HEART WAS LOCKED UP TIGHT!
BACK IN THE DAY
WHEN I NEVER RELAXED.
HOW IS THE TEMPER-ATURE OF THE TOWEL?
ARE YOU FEELING ANY ITCHING?
NO...
W-WHY IS HE TRYING TO MAKE ME RELAX MORE? WHAT WILL HE DO THEN?!
OH, I CAN FEEL THAT YOUR EYES ARE VERY STRAINED.
DO YOU DO A LOT OF DESK WORK?
SOME-TIMES...
WHAT DO YOU DO FOR A LIVING?
I'M A BUDDHA...
W-WOW, HOW DID HE GET THAT PERSONAL INFORMATION OUT OF ME SO EASILY?!
WHAT DO YOU MEAN, A BUDDHA? (LOL)
WHERE DO YOU WORK?
LURING ME INTO RELAX-ING...
IS... IS HE MARA?!
...AND THEN CAUSING MY DOWNFALL?! WELL, YOU WON'T FOOL ME!
NO...
IT'S, UH... NOTHING MUCH...
SHH
HUH?!

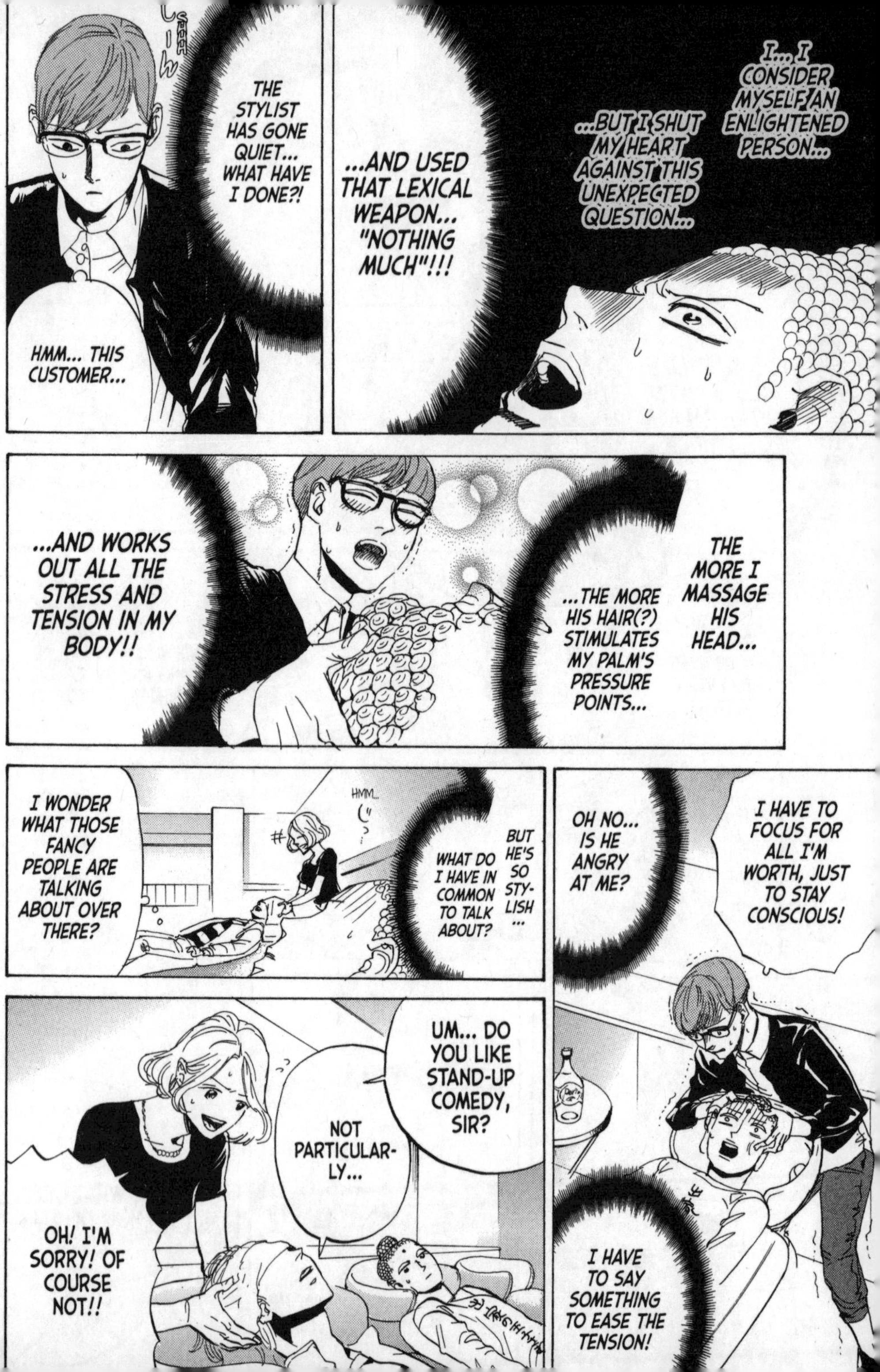
I... I CONSIDER MYSELF AN ENLIGHTENED PERSON...
...BUT I SHUT MY HEART AGAINST THIS UNEXPECTED QUESTION...
...AND USED THAT LEXICAL WEAPON... "NOTHING MUCH"!!!
SHHH
THE STYLIST HAS GONE QUIET... WHAT HAVE I DONE?!
HMM... THIS CUSTOMER...
THE MORE I MASSAGE HIS HEAD...
...THE MORE HIS HAIR(?) STIMULATES MY PALM'S PRESSURE POINTS...
...AND WORKS OUT ALL THE STRESS AND TENSION IN MY BODY!!
I HAVE TO FOCUS FOR ALL I'M WORTH, JUST TO STAY CONSCIOUS!
OH NO... IS HE ANGRY AT ME?
I HAVE TO SAY SOMETHING TO EASE THE TENSION!
BUT HE'S SO STY-LISH...
WHAT DO I HAVE IN COMMON TO TALK ABOUT?
HMM...
I WONDER WHAT THOSE FANCY PEOPLE ARE TALKING ABOUT OVER THERE?
UM... DO YOU LIKE STAND-UP COMEDY, SIR?
NOT PARTICULAR-LY...
OH! I'M SORRY! OF COURSE NOT!!

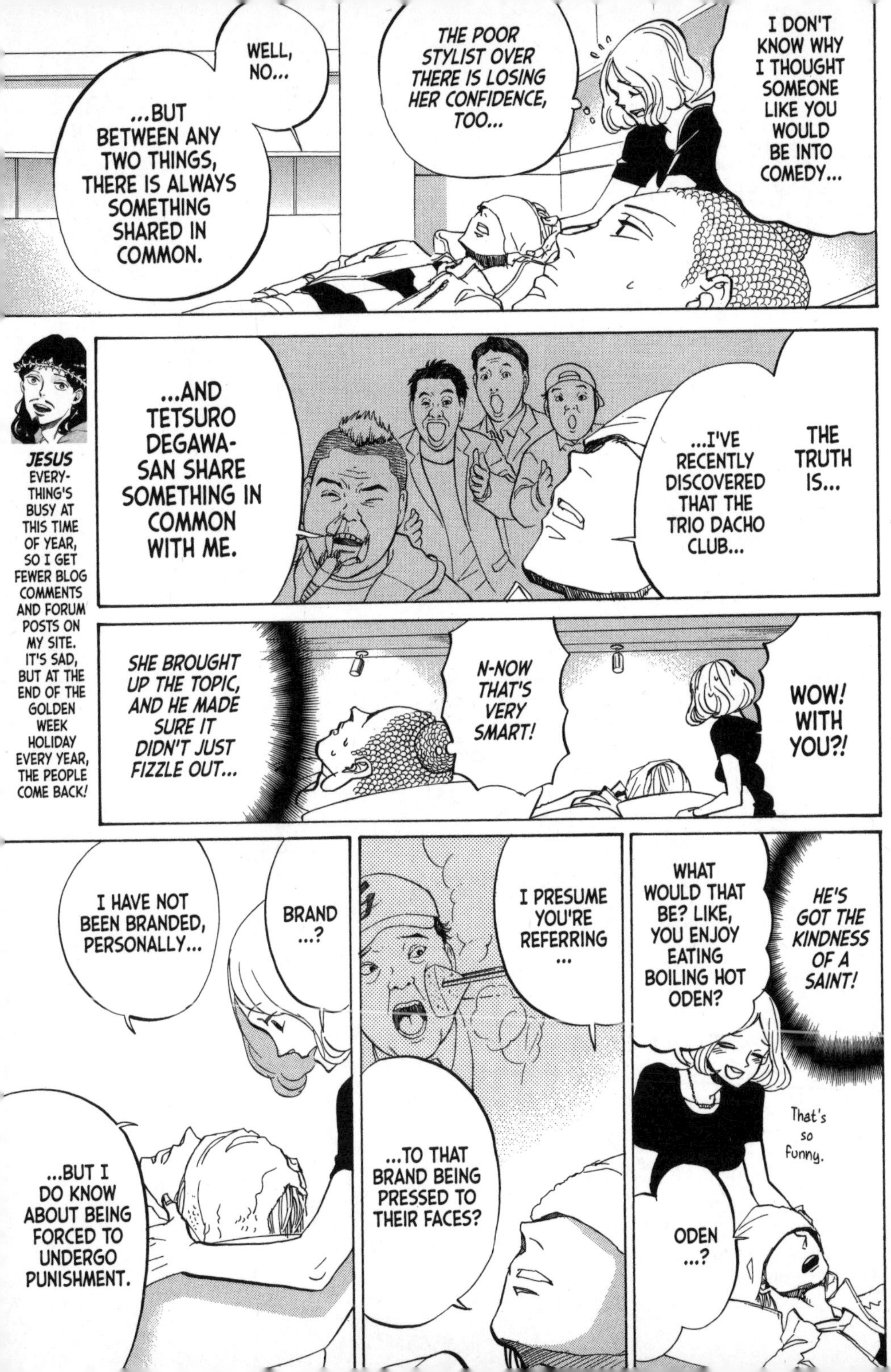
I DON'T KNOW WHY I THOUGHT SOMEONE LIKE YOU WOULD BE INTO COMEDY...
THE POOR STYLIST OVER THERE IS LOSING HER CONFIDENCE, TOO...
WELL, NO...
...BUT BETWEEN ANY TWO THINGS, THERE IS ALWAYS SOMETHING SHARED IN COMMON.
THE TRUTH IS...
...I'VE RECENTLY DISCOVERED THAT THE TRIO DACHO CLUB...
...AND TETSURO DEGAWA-SAN SHARE SOMETHING IN COMMON WITH ME.
WOW! WITH YOU?!
N-NOW THAT'S VERY SMART!
SHE BROUGHT UP THE TOPIC, AND HE MADE SURE IT DIDN'T JUST FIZZLE OUT...
HE'S GOT THE KINDNESS OF A SAINT!
WHAT WOULD THAT BE? LIKE, YOU ENJOY EATING BOILING HOT ODEN?
That's so funny.
ODEN ...?
I PRESUME YOU'RE REFERRING ...
...TO THAT BRAND BEING PRESSED TO THEIR FACES?
BRAND ...?
I HAVE NOT BEEN BRANDED, PERSONALLY...
...BUT I DO KNOW ABOUT BEING FORCED TO UNDERGO PUNISHMENT.
JESUS
EVERYTHING'S BUSY AT THIS TIME OF YEAR, SO I GET FEWER BLOG COMMENTS AND FORUM POSTS ON MY SITE. IT'S SAD, BUT AT THE END OF THE GOLDEN WEEK HOLIDAY EVERY YEAR, THE PEOPLE COME BACK!

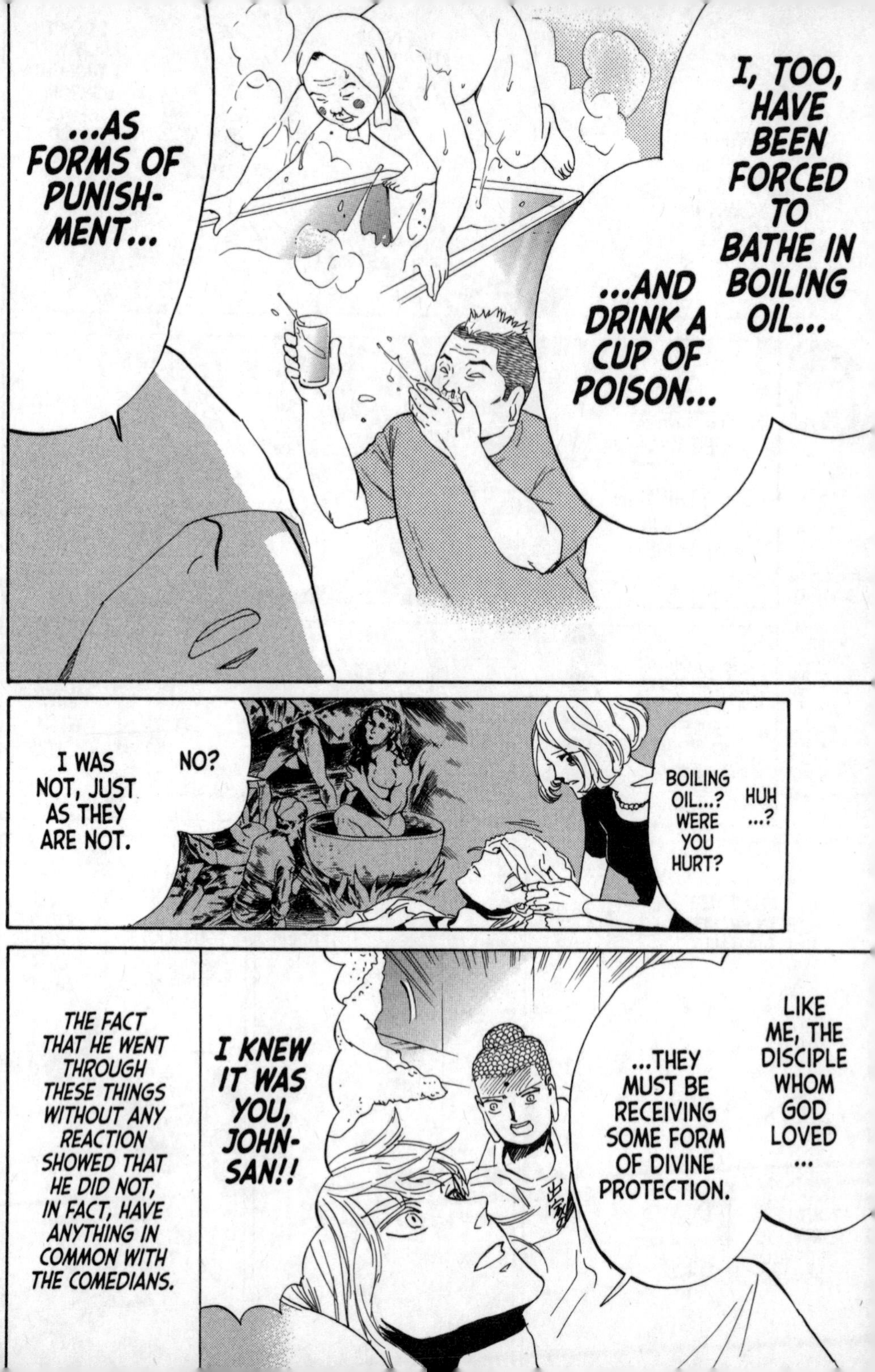
I, TOO, HAVE BEEN FORCED TO BATHE IN BOILING OIL...
...AND DRINK A CUP OF POISON...
...AS FORMS OF PUNISHMENT...
HUH ...?
BOILING OIL...? WERE YOU HURT?
NO?
I WAS NOT, JUST AS THEY ARE NOT.
LIKE ME, THE DISCIPLE WHOM GOD LOVED ...
...THEY MUST BE RECEIVING SOME FORM OF DIVINE PROTECTION.
I KNEW IT WAS YOU, JOHN-SAN!!
THE FACT THAT HE WENT THROUGH THESE THINGS WITHOUT ANY REACTION SHOWED THAT HE DID NOT, IN FACT, HAVE ANYTHING IN COMMON WITH THE COMEDIANS.

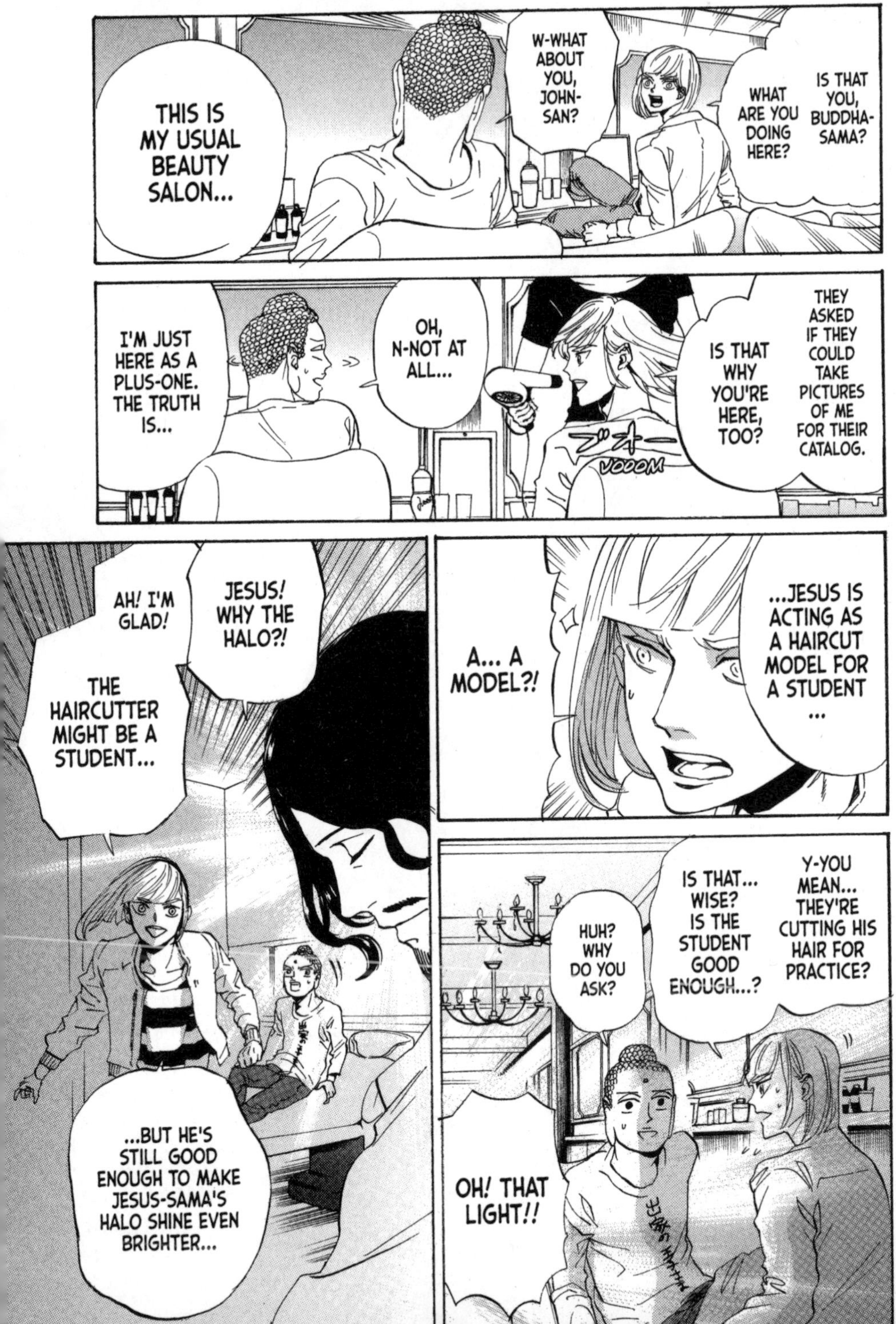
IS THAT YOU, BUDDHA-SAMA?
WHAT ARE YOU DOING HERE?
W-WHAT ABOUT YOU, JOHN-SAN?
THIS IS MY USUAL BEAUTY SALON...
THEY ASKED IF THEY COULD TAKE PICTURES OF ME FOR THEIR CATALOG.
IS THAT WHY YOU'RE HERE, TOO?
ブオー
VOOOM
OH, N-NOT AT ALL...
I'M JUST HERE AS A PLUS-ONE. THE TRUTH IS...
...JESUS IS ACTING AS A HAIRCUT MODEL FOR A STUDENT ...
A... A MODEL?!
Y-YOU MEAN... THEY'RE CUTTING HIS HAIR FOR PRACTICE?
IS THAT... WISE? IS THE STUDENT GOOD ENOUGH...?
HUH? WHY DO YOU ASK?
OH! THAT LIGHT!!
JESUS! WHY THE HALO?!
AH! I'M GLAD!
THE HAIRCUTTER MIGHT BE A STUDENT...
...BUT HE'S STILL GOOD ENOUGH TO MAKE JESUS-SAMA'S HALO SHINE EVEN BRIGHTER...

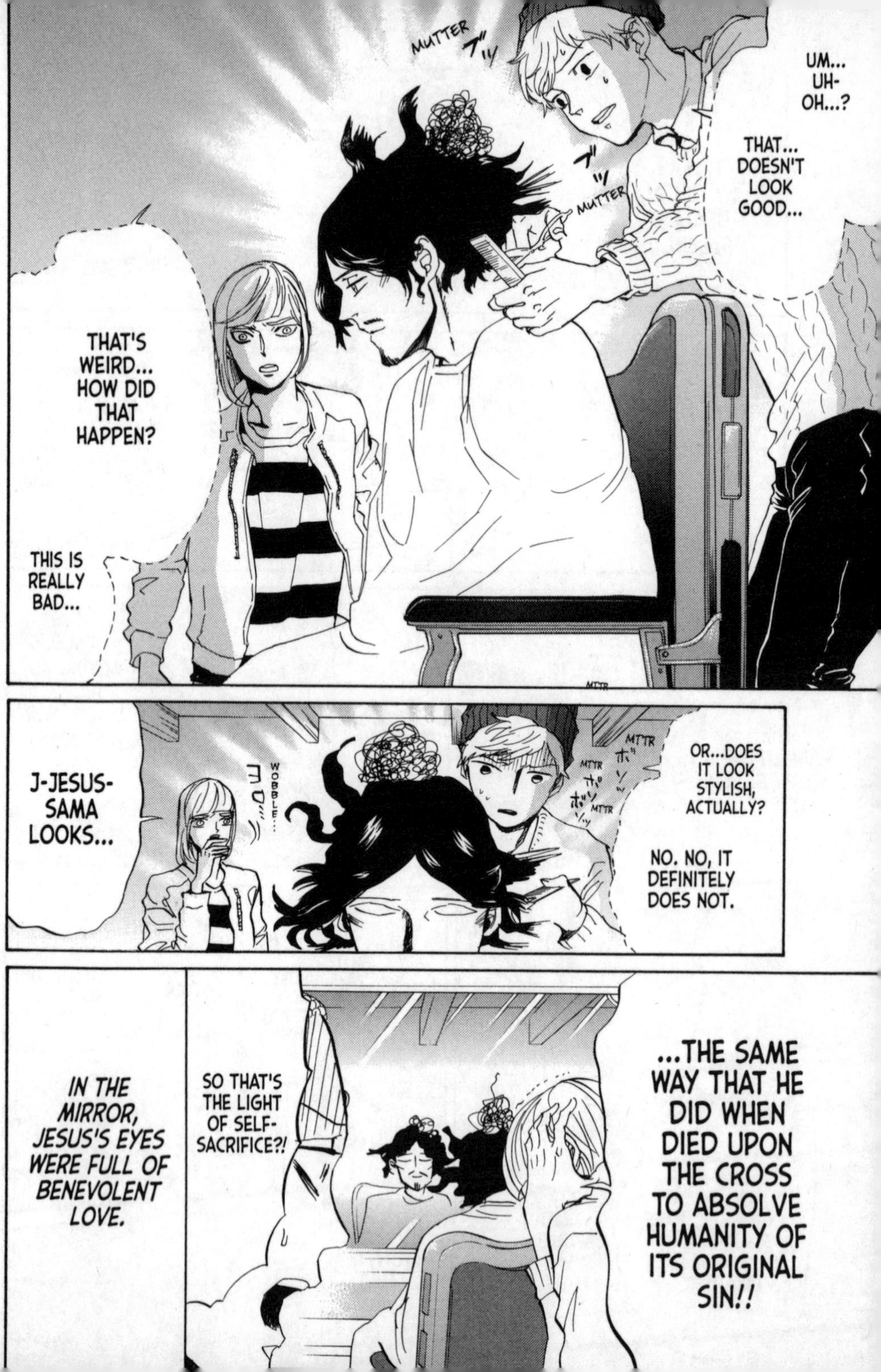
MUTTER
UM... UH-OH...?
THAT... DOESN'T LOOK GOOD...
MUTTER
THAT'S WEIRD... HOW DID THAT HAPPEN?
THIS IS REALLY BAD...
MTTR
OR...DOES IT LOOK STYLISH, ACTUALLY?
NO. NO, IT DEFINITELY DOES NOT.
MTTR
MTTR
MTTR
WOBBLE...
J-JESUS-SAMA LOOKS...
...THE SAME WAY THAT HE DID WHEN DIED UPON THE CROSS TO ABSOLVE HUMANITY OF ITS ORIGINAL SIN!!
SO THAT'S THE LIGHT OF SELF-SACRIFICE?!
IN THE MIRROR, JESUS'S EYES WERE FULL OF BENEVOLENT LOVE.

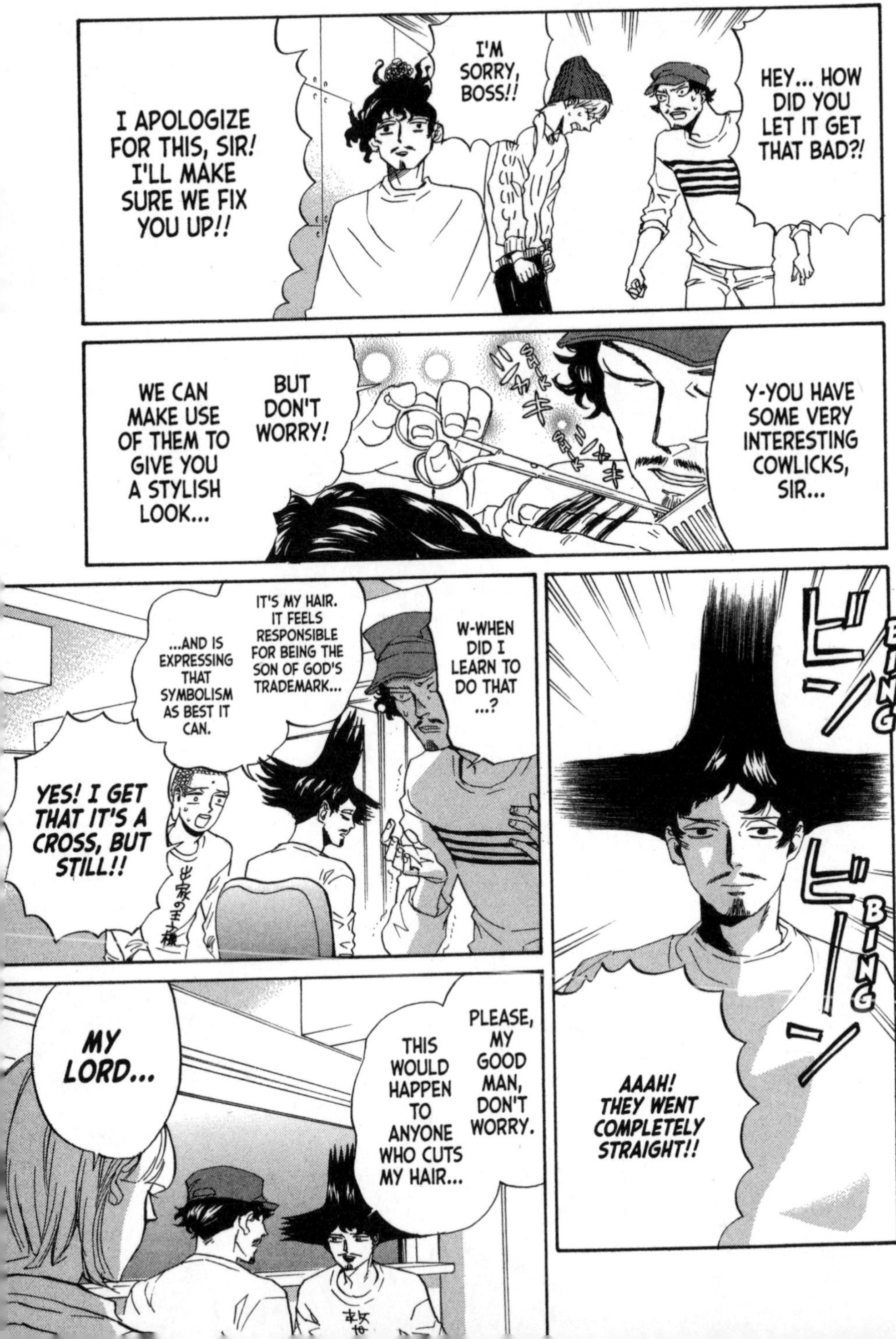
HEY... HOW DID YOU LET IT GET THAT BAD?!
I'M SORRY, BOSS!!
I APOLOGIZE FOR THIS, SIR! I'LL MAKE SURE WE FIX YOU UP!!
Y-YOU HAVE SOME VERY INTERESTING COWLICKS, SIR...
BUT DON'T WORRY!
WE CAN MAKE USE OF THEM TO GIVE YOU A STYLISH LOOK...
BING
BING
AAAH! THEY WENT COMPLETELY STRAIGHT!!
W-WHEN DID I LEARN TO DO THAT ...?
IT'S MY HAIR. IT FEELS RESPONSIBLE FOR BEING THE SON OF GOD'S TRADEMARK...
...AND IS EXPRESSING THAT SYMBOLISM AS BEST IT CAN.
YES! I GET THAT IT'S A CROSS, BUT STILL!!
PLEASE, MY GOOD MAN, DON'T WORRY.
THIS WOULD HAPPEN TO ANYONE WHO CUTS MY HAIR...
MY LORD...

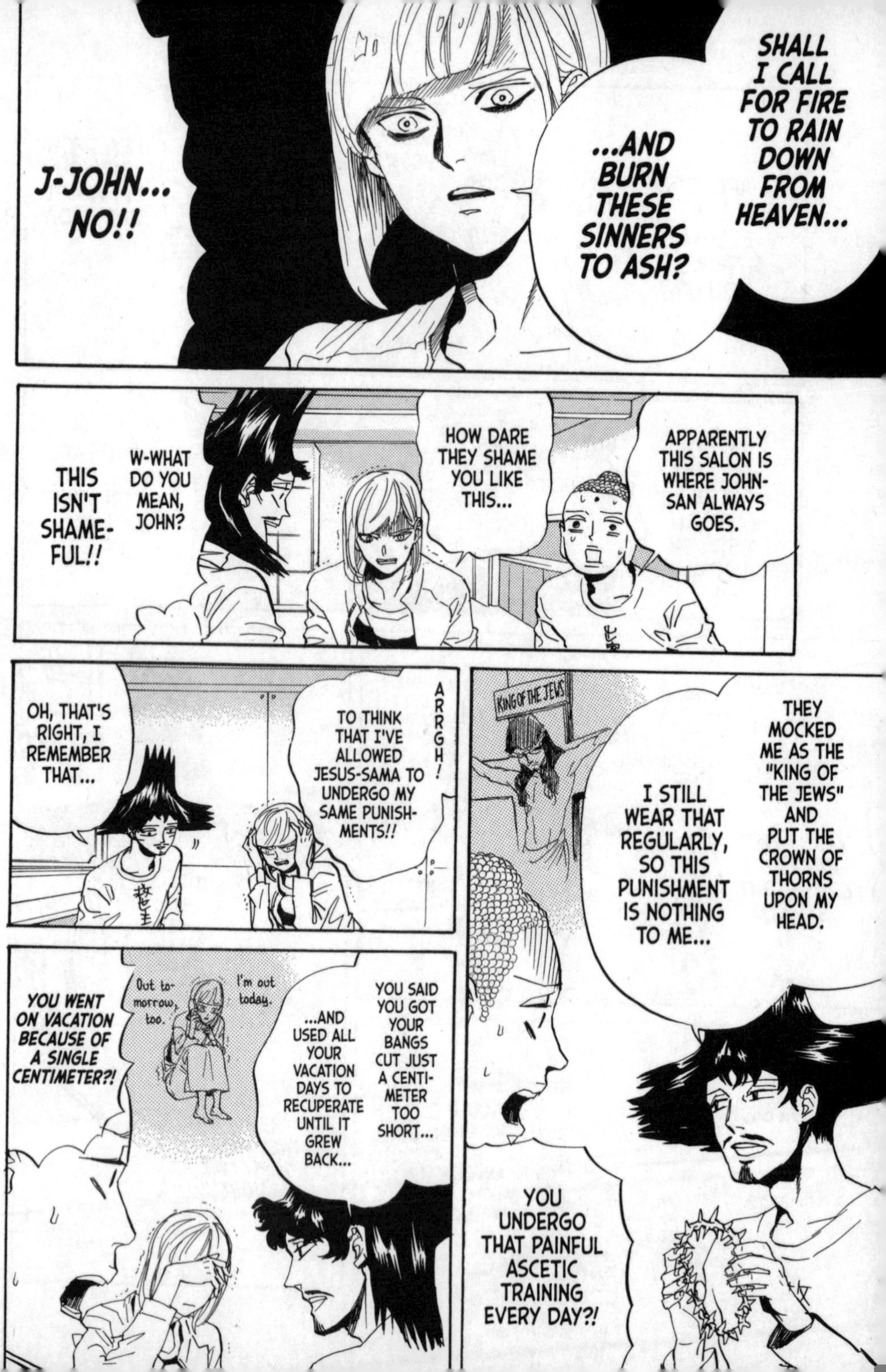
SHALL I CALL FOR FIRE TO RAIN DOWN FROM HEAVEN...
...AND BURN THESE SINNERS TO ASH?
J-JOHN... NO!!
APPARENTLY THIS SALON IS WHERE JOHN-SAN ALWAYS GOES.
HOW DARE THEY SHAME YOU LIKE THIS...
W-WHAT DO YOU MEAN, JOHN?
THIS ISN'T SHAME-FUL!!
KING OF THE JEWS
THEY MOCKED ME AS THE "KING OF THE JEWS" AND PUT THE CROWN OF THORNS UPON MY HEAD.
I STILL WEAR THAT REGULARLY, SO THIS PUNISHMENT IS NOTHING TO ME...
YOU UNDERGO THAT PAINFUL ASCETIC TRAINING EVERY DAY?!
ARRGH!
TO THINK THAT I'VE ALLOWED JESUS-SAMA TO UNDERGO MY SAME PUNISH-MENTS!!
OH, THAT'S RIGHT, I REMEMBER THAT...
YOU SAID YOU GOT YOUR BANGS CUT JUST A CENTI-METER TOO SHORT...
...AND USED ALL YOUR VACATION DAYS TO RECUPERATE UNTIL IT GREW BACK...
I'm out today.
Out to-morrow, too.
YOU WENT ON VACATION BECAUSE OF A SINGLE CENTIMETER?!

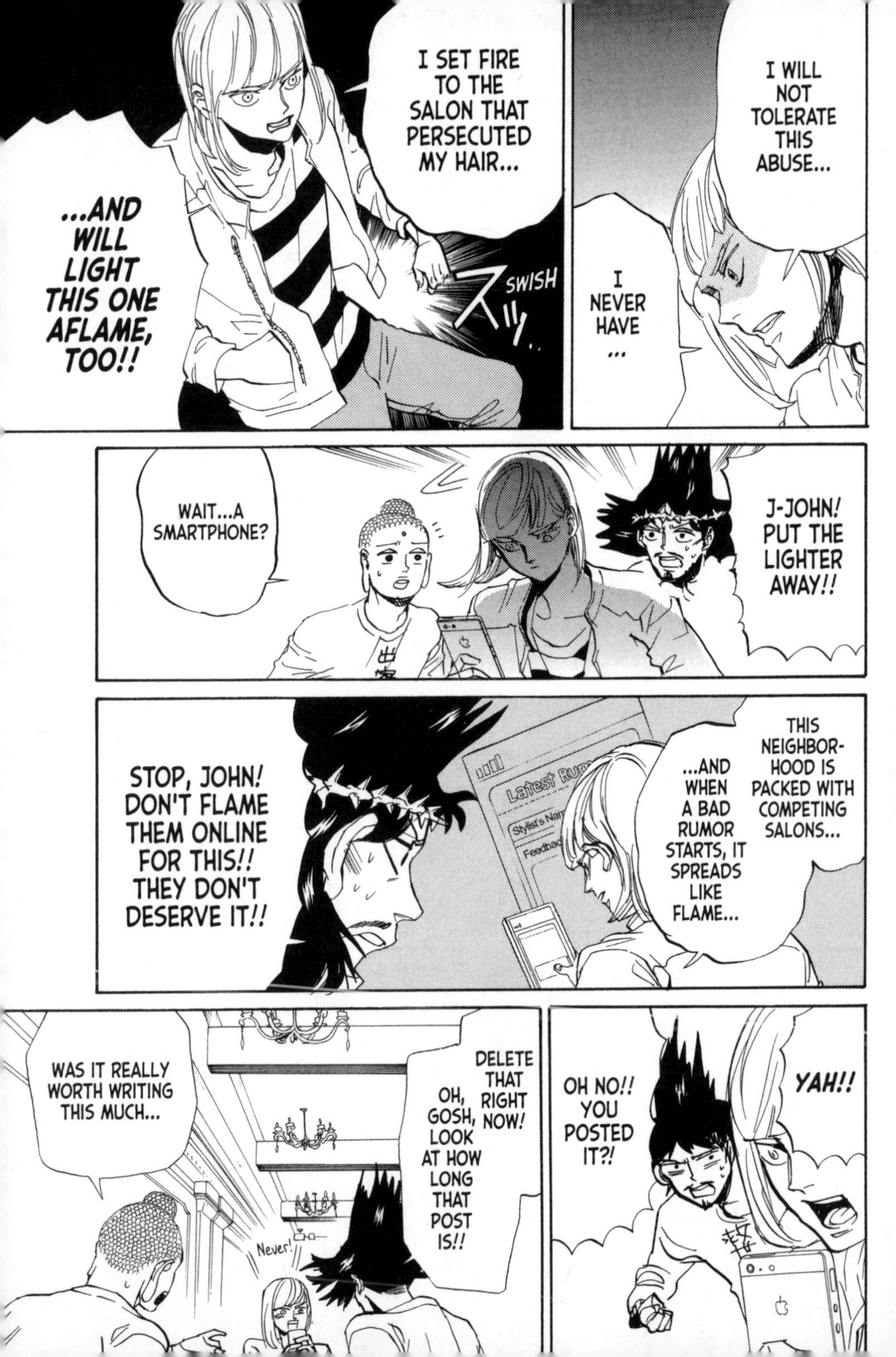
I WILL NOT TOLERATE THIS ABUSE...
I NEVER HAVE ...
I SET FIRE TO THE SALON THAT PERSECUTED MY HAIR...
...AND WILL LIGHT THIS ONE AFLAME, TOO!!
SWISH
J-JOHN! PUT THE LIGHTER AWAY!!
WAIT...A SMARTPHONE?
THIS NEIGHBOR-HOOD IS PACKED WITH COMPETING SALONS...
...AND WHEN A BAD RUMOR STARTS, IT SPREADS LIKE FLAME...
STOP, JOHN! DON'T FLAME THEM ONLINE FOR THIS!! THEY DON'T DESERVE IT!!
YAH!!
OH NO!! YOU POSTED IT?!
DELETE THAT RIGHT NOW!
OH, GOSH, LOOK AT HOW LONG THAT POST IS!!
WAS IT REALLY WORTH WRITING THIS MUCH...
Never!

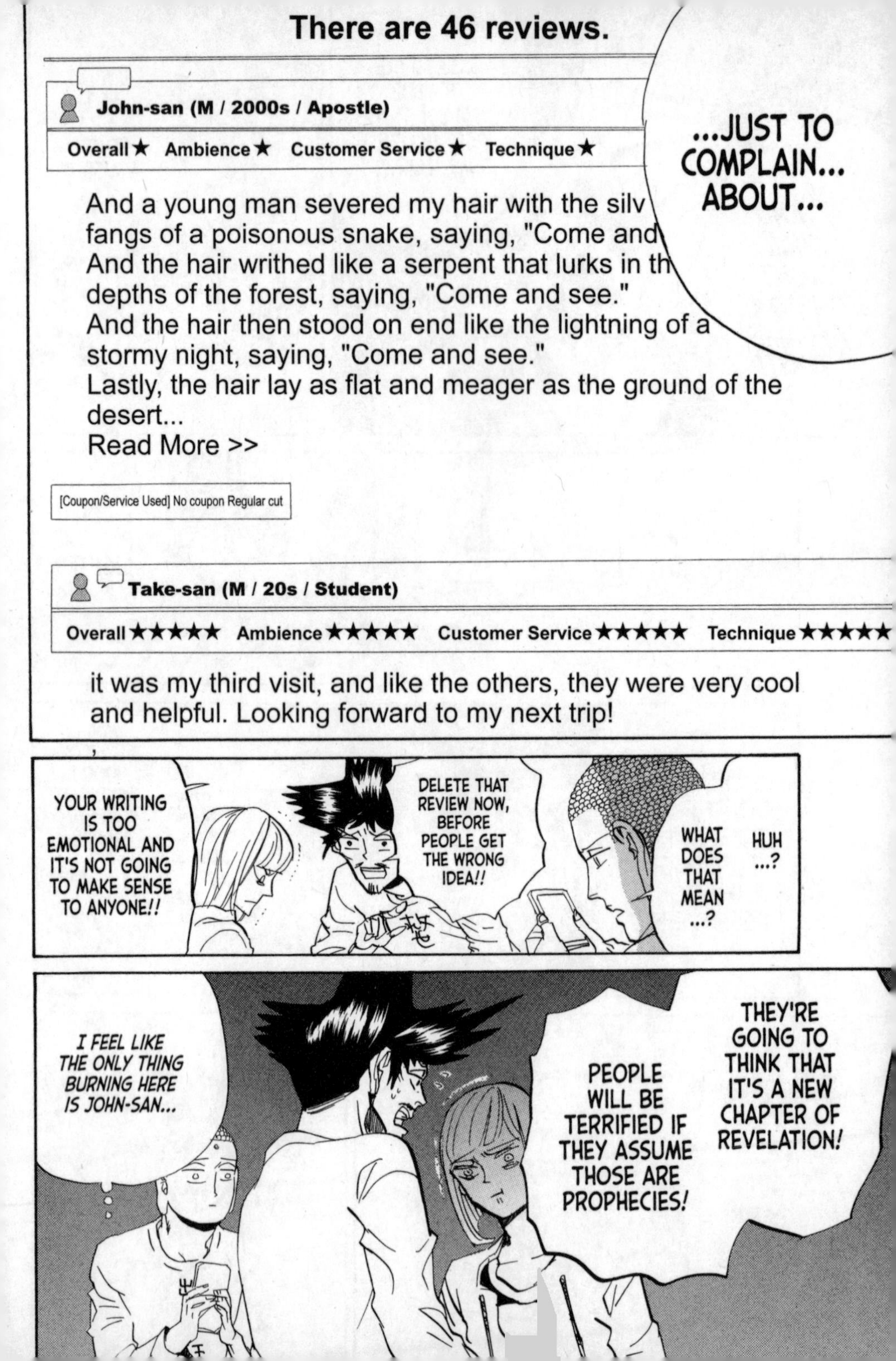
...JUST TO COMPLAIN... ABOUT...
There are 46 reviews.
John-san (M / 2000s / Apostle)
Overall★ Ambience★ Customer Service★ Technique★
And a young man severed my hair with the silv
fangs of a poisonous snake, saying, "Come and
And the hair writhed like a serpent that lurks in th
depths of the forest, saying, "Come and see."
And the hair then stood on end like the lightning of a stormy night, saying, "Come and see."
Lastly, the hair lay as flat and meager as the ground of the desert...
Read More >>
[Coupon/Service Used] No coupon Regular cut
Take-san (M / 20s / Student)
Overall★★★★★ Ambience★★★★★ Customer Service★★★★★ Technique★★★★★
it was my third visit, and like the others, they were very cool and helpful. Looking forward to my next trip!
HUH ...?
WHAT DOES THAT MEAN ...?
DELETE THAT REVIEW NOW, BEFORE PEOPLE GET THE WRONG IDEA!!
YOUR WRITING IS TOO EMOTIONAL AND IT'S NOT GOING TO MAKE SENSE TO ANYONE!!
THEY'RE GOING TO THINK THAT IT'S A NEW CHAPTER OF REVELATION!
PEOPLE WILL BE TERRIFIED IF THEY ASSUME THOSE ARE PROPHECIES!
I FEEL LIKE THE ONLY THING BURNING HERE IS JOHN-SAN...

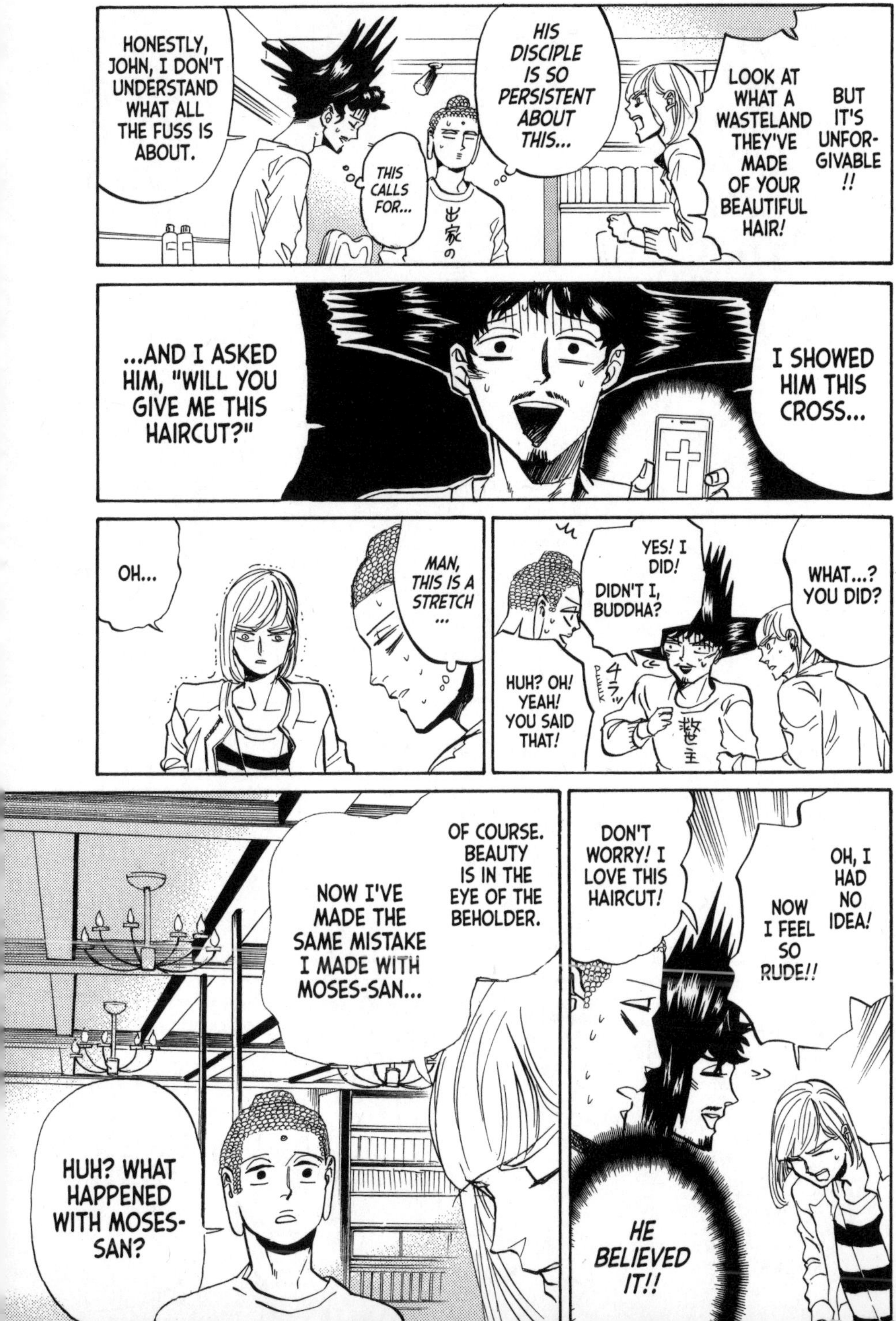
BUT IT'S UNFORGIVABLE!!
LOOK AT WHAT A WASTELAND THEY'VE MADE OF YOUR BEAUTIFUL HAIR!
HIS DISCIPLE IS SO PERSISTENT ABOUT THIS...
HONESTLY, JOHN, I DON'T UNDERSTAND WHAT ALL THE FUSS IS ABOUT.
THIS CALLS FOR...
I SHOWED HIM THIS CROSS...
...AND I ASKED HIM, "WILL YOU GIVE ME THIS HAIRCUT?"
WHAT...? YOU DID?
YES! I DID! DIDN'T I, BUDDHA?
HUH? OH! YEAH! YOU SAID THAT!
MAN, THIS IS A STRETCH...
OH...
OH, I HAD NO IDEA!
NOW I FEEL SO RUDE!!
DON'T WORRY! I LOVE THIS HAIRCUT!
HE BELIEVED IT!!
OF COURSE. BEAUTY IS IN THE EYE OF THE BEHOLDER.
NOW I'VE MADE THE SAME MISTAKE I MADE WITH MOSES-SAN...
HUH? WHAT HAPPENED WITH MOSES-SAN?

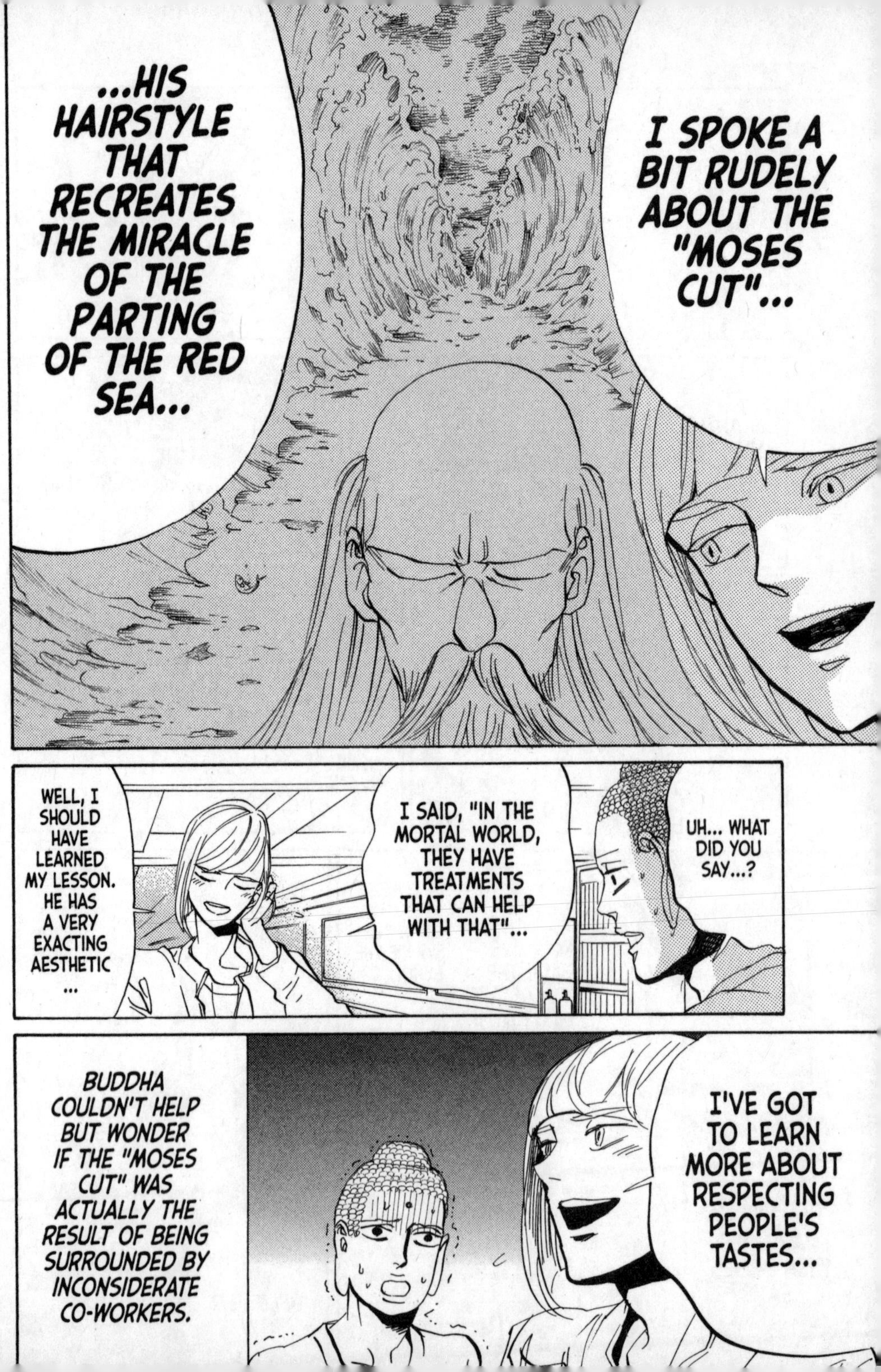
I SPOKE A BIT RUDELY ABOUT THE "MOSES CUT"...
...HIS HAIRSTYLE THAT RECREATES THE MIRACLE OF THE PARTING OF THE RED SEA...
UH... WHAT DID YOU SAY...?
I SAID, "IN THE MORTAL WORLD, THEY HAVE TREATMENTS THAT CAN HELP WITH THAT"...
WELL, I SHOULD HAVE LEARNED MY LESSON. HE HAS A VERY EXACTING AESTHETIC ...
I'VE GOT TO LEARN MORE ABOUT RESPECTING PEOPLE'S TASTES...
BUDDHA COULDN'T HELP BUT WONDER IF THE "MOSES CUT" WAS ACTUALLY THE RESULT OF BEING SURROUNDED BY INCONSIDERATE CO-WORKERS.

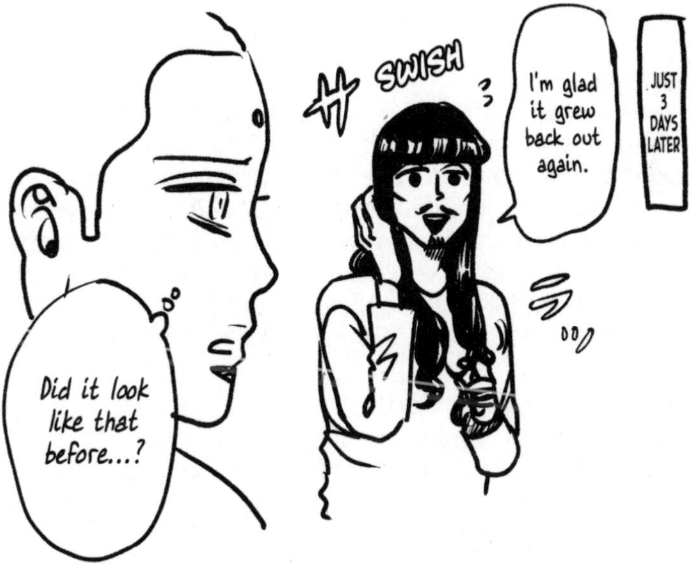
JUST 3 DAYS LATER
I'm glad it grew back out again.
SWISH
Did it look like that before...?

CHAPTER 83 TRANSLATION NOTES

Dacho Club and Tetsuro Degawa, page 43

These are two examples of veteran comedians who are known for their outlandish reactions to pranks or stunts (reaction *geinin*). Many of their televised acts are based around undertaking painful punishments, such as being pinched by lobsters, being forced to eat extremely hot dishes like boiled oden (a seasonal hot pot assortment), or trying not to fall into a tub of very hot water.

Boiling oil and poison, page 44

In apocryphal traditions outside of Biblical sources, it is said that John was plunged into boiling oil in Rome, and emerged miraculously unscathed, which supposedly converted everyone who witnessed the act to Christianity. Some other writings tell a story of John drinking poison to demonstrate his faith.

Revelation, page 50

The Book of Revelation is the final book of the Bible, and is written by a "John" whom early sources (and this manga) considered to be John the Apostle. As an apocalyptic book describing future events, Revelation is famous for its fantastical imagery describing the Second Coming of Jesus, including such figures as the Four Horsemen of the Apocalypse, the Beast, and the Seven Angelic Trumpeters. Pertinent to this scene in particular is the sixth chapter, which features four "beasts" who each repeat the phrase "Come and see."

Parting of the Red Sea, page 52

Moses was chosen to lead the Israelite slaves out of Egypt into Canaan. With the Egyptians pursuing them to the edge of the Red Sea, Moses raised his staff and called upon the power of God to part the Red Sea so that the Israelites could pass safely.

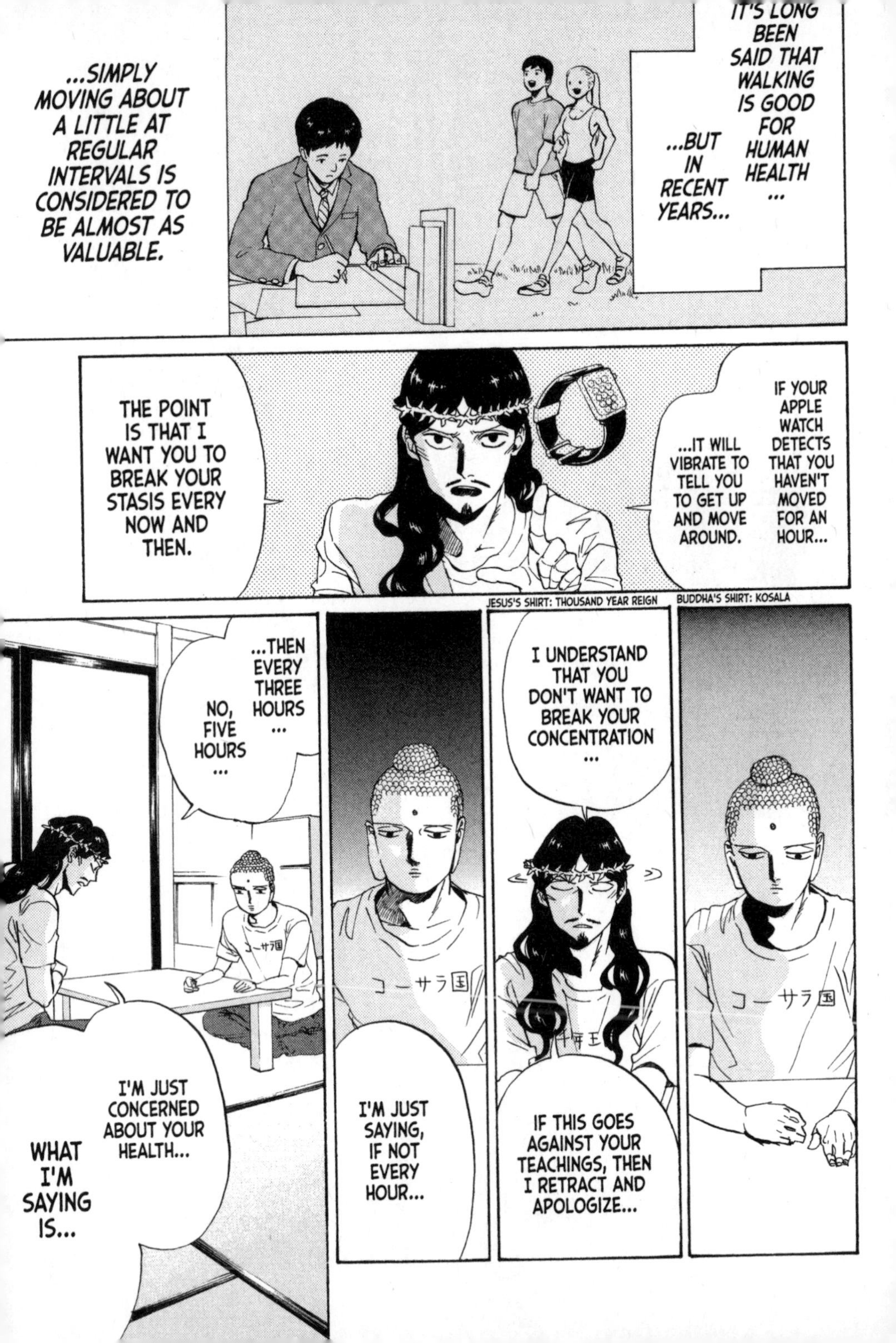

IT'S LONG BEEN SAID THAT WALKING IS GOOD FOR HUMAN HEALTH...
...BUT IN RECENT YEARS...
...SIMPLY MOVING ABOUT A LITTLE AT REGULAR INTERVALS IS CONSIDERED TO BE ALMOST AS VALUABLE.
IF YOUR APPLE WATCH DETECTS THAT YOU HAVEN'T MOVED FOR AN HOUR...
...IT WILL VIBRATE TO TELL YOU TO GET UP AND MOVE AROUND.
THE POINT IS THAT I WANT YOU TO BREAK YOUR STASIS EVERY NOW AND THEN.
BUDDHA'S SHIRT: KOSALA
JESUS'S SHIRT: THOUSAND YEAR REIGN
I UNDERSTAND THAT YOU DON'T WANT TO BREAK YOUR CONCENTRATION...
IF THIS GOES AGAINST YOUR TEACHINGS, THEN I RETRACT AND APOLOGIZE...
I'M JUST SAYING, IF NOT EVERY HOUR...
...THEN EVERY THREE HOURS...
NO, FIVE HOURS...
I'M JUST CONCERNED ABOUT YOUR HEALTH...
WHAT I'M SAYING IS...

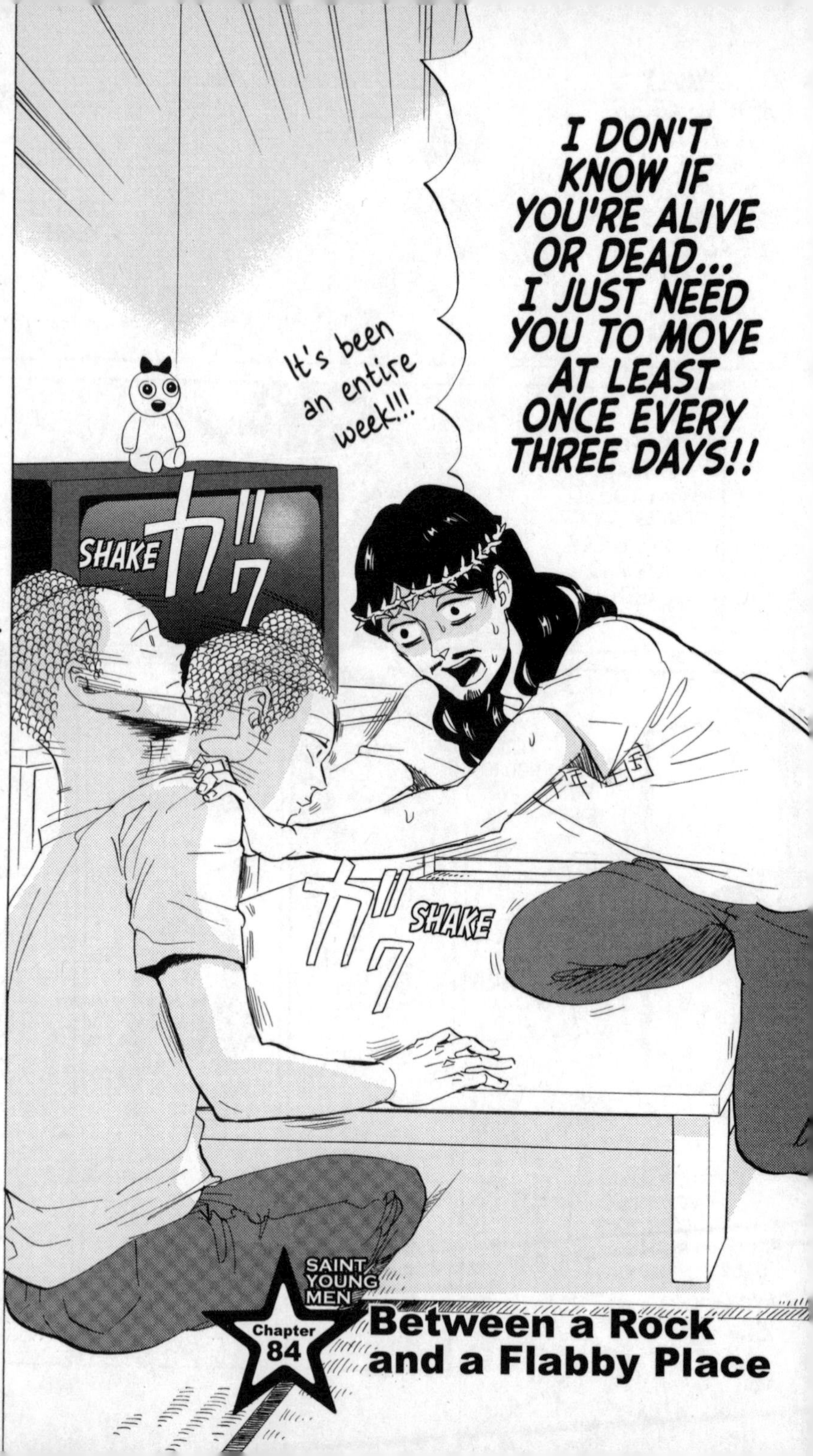

I DON'T KNOW IF YOU'RE ALIVE OR DEAD... I JUST NEED YOU TO MOVE AT LEAST ONCE EVERY THREE DAYS!!
It's been an entire week!!!
IT'S SAID THAT AFTER HIS ENLIGHT-ENMENT, BUDDHA KEPT MEDI-TATING FOR 21 DAYS.
SHAKE ガク
SHAKE ガク
SAINT YOUNG MEN
Chapter 84
Between a Rock and a Flabby Place

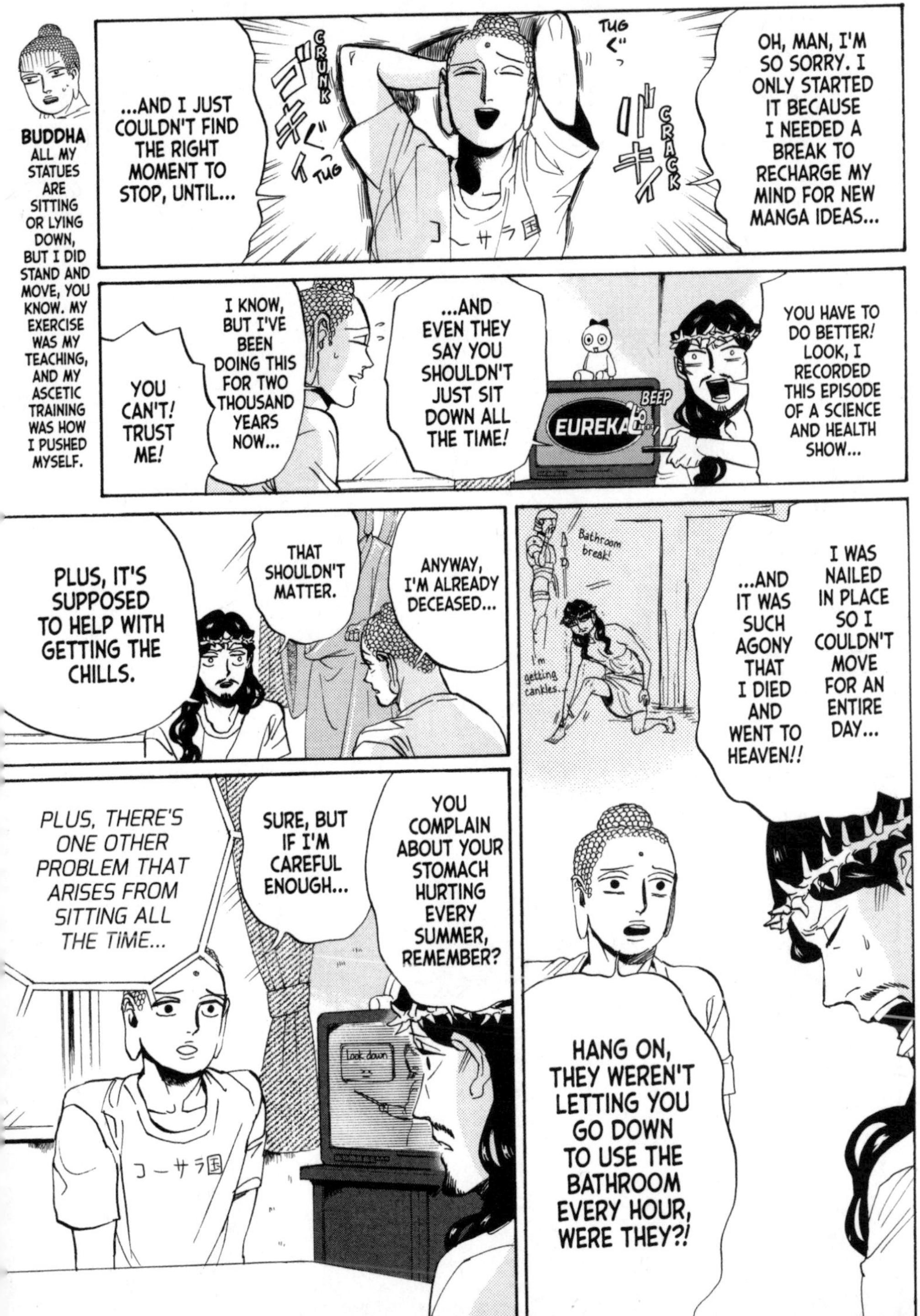
OH, MAN, I'M SO SORRY. I ONLY STARTED IT BECAUSE I NEEDED A BREAK TO RECHARGE MY MIND FOR NEW MANGA IDEAS...
CRACK
TUG
CRUNK
TUG
...AND I JUST COULDN'T FIND THE RIGHT MOMENT TO STOP, UNTIL...
BUDDHA
ALL MY STATUES ARE SITTING OR LYING DOWN, BUT I DID STAND AND MOVE, YOU KNOW. MY EXERCISE WAS MY TEACHING, AND MY ASCETIC TRAINING WAS HOW I PUSHED MYSELF.
YOU HAVE TO DO BETTER! LOOK, I RECORDED THIS EPISODE OF A SCIENCE AND HEALTH SHOW...
BEEP
EUREKA
...AND EVEN THEY SAY YOU SHOULDN'T JUST SIT DOWN ALL THE TIME!
I KNOW, BUT I'VE BEEN DOING THIS FOR TWO THOUSAND YEARS NOW...
YOU CAN'T! TRUST ME!
I WAS NAILED IN PLACE SO I COULDN'T MOVE FOR AN ENTIRE DAY...
...AND IT WAS SUCH AGONY THAT I DIED AND WENT TO HEAVEN!!
Bathroom break!
I'm getting cankles...
HANG ON, THEY WEREN'T LETTING YOU GO DOWN TO USE THE BATHROOM EVERY HOUR, WERE THEY?!
ANYWAY, I'M ALREADY DECEASED...
THAT SHOULDN'T MATTER.
PLUS, IT'S SUPPOSED TO HELP WITH GETTING THE CHILLS.
YOU COMPLAIN ABOUT YOUR STOMACH HURTING EVERY SUMMER, REMEMBER?
SURE, BUT IF I'M CAREFUL ENOUGH...
PLUS, THERE'S ONE OTHER PROBLEM THAT ARISES FROM SITTING ALL THE TIME...
Look down

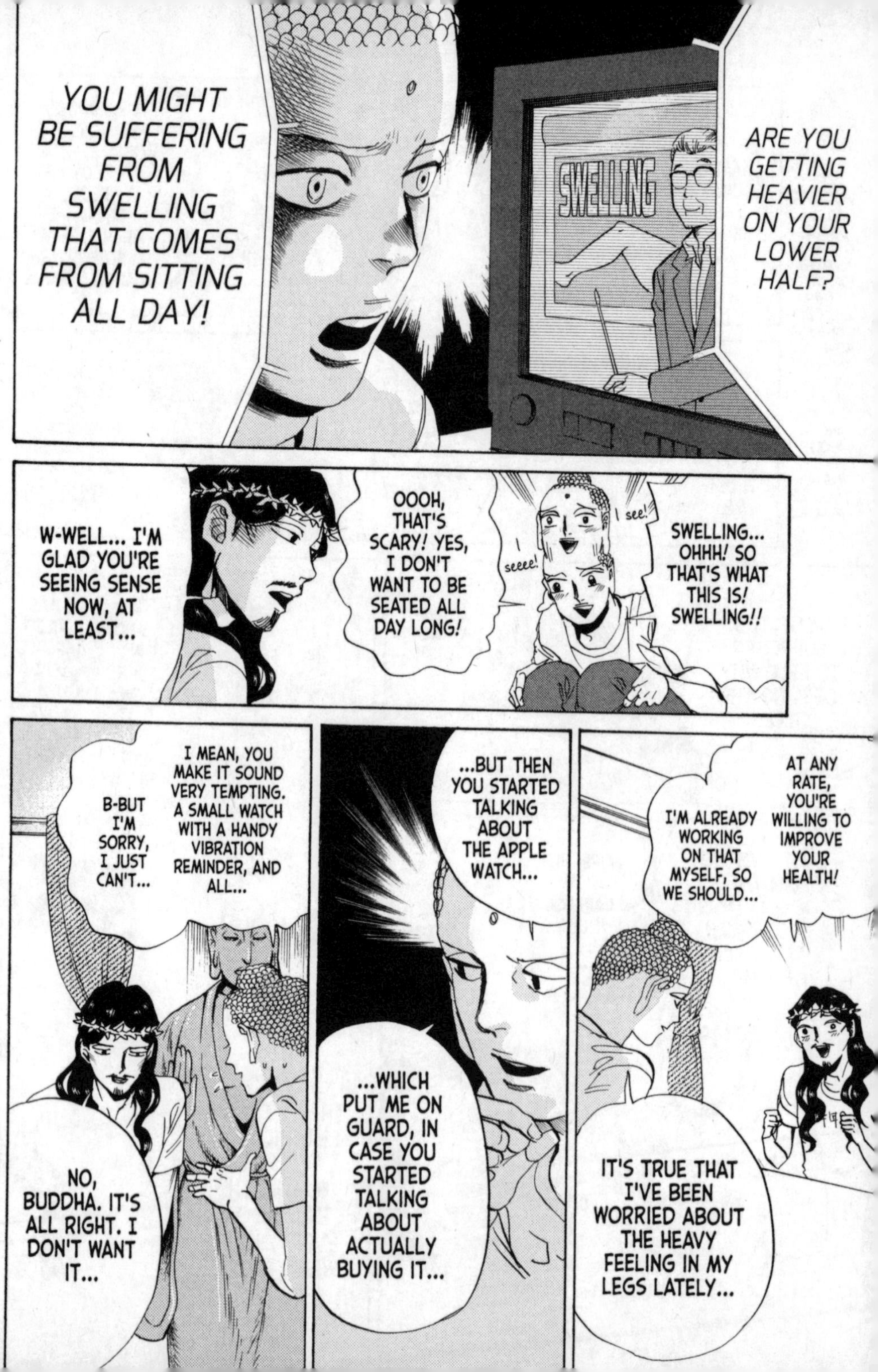
ARE YOU GETTING HEAVIER ON YOUR LOWER HALF?
SWELLING
YOU MIGHT BE SUFFERING FROM SWELLING THAT COMES FROM SITTING ALL DAY!
SWELLING... OHHH! SO THAT'S WHAT THIS IS! SWELLING!!
I see!
I seeee!
OOOH, THAT'S SCARY! YES, I DON'T WANT TO BE SEATED ALL DAY LONG!
W-WELL... I'M GLAD YOU'RE SEEING SENSE NOW, AT LEAST...
AT ANY RATE, YOU'RE WILLING TO IMPROVE YOUR HEALTH!
I'M ALREADY WORKING ON THAT MYSELF, SO WE SHOULD...
IT'S TRUE THAT I'VE BEEN WORRIED ABOUT THE HEAVY FEELING IN MY LEGS LATELY...
...BUT THEN YOU STARTED TALKING ABOUT THE APPLE WATCH...
...WHICH PUT ME ON GUARD, IN CASE YOU STARTED TALKING ABOUT ACTUALLY BUYING IT...
I MEAN, YOU MAKE IT SOUND VERY TEMPTING. A SMALL WATCH WITH A HANDY VIBRATION REMINDER, AND ALL...
B-BUT I'M SORRY, I JUST CAN'T...
NO, BUDDHA. IT'S ALL RIGHT. I DON'T WANT IT...

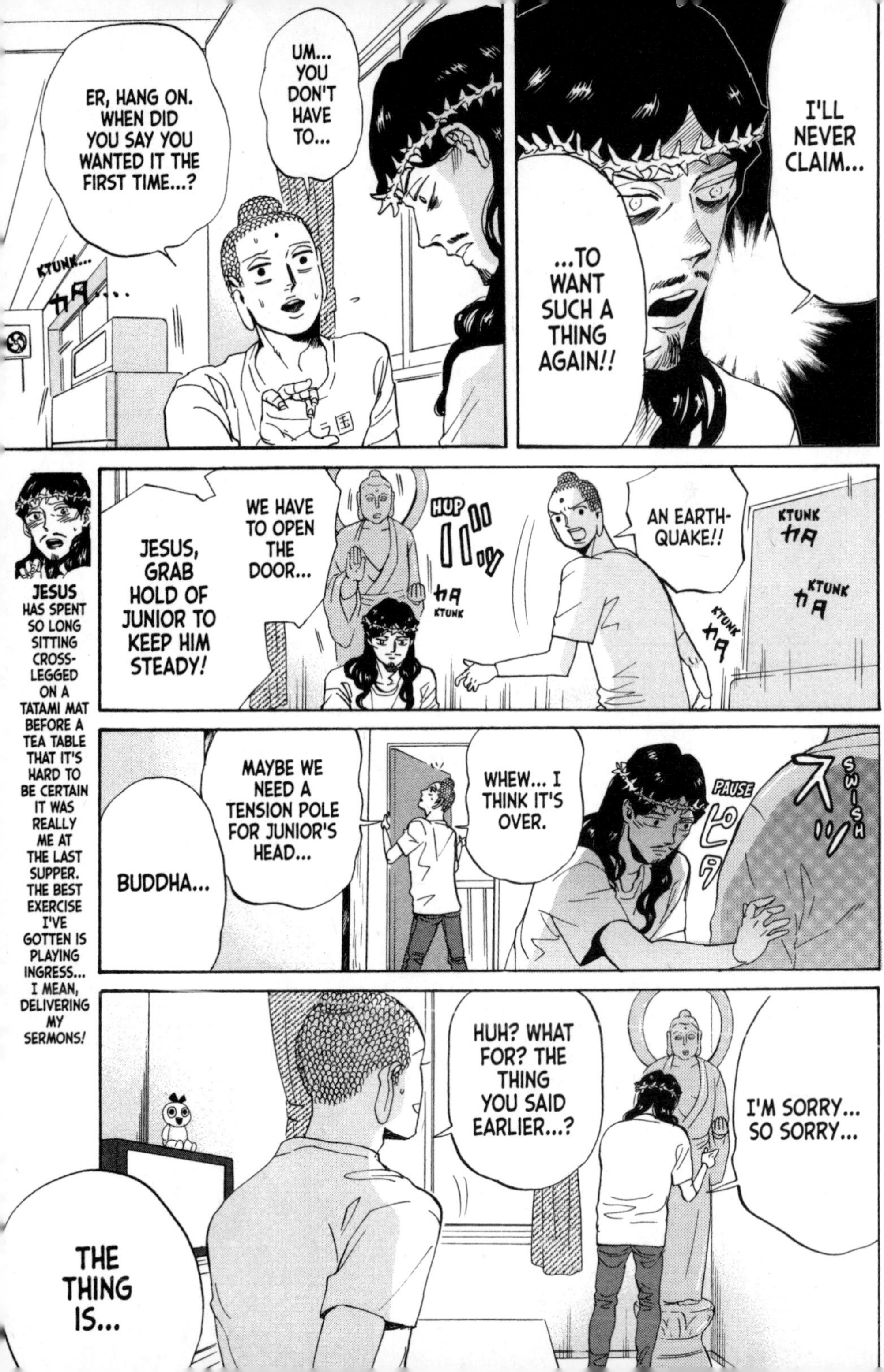
I'LL NEVER CLAIM...
...TO WANT SUCH A THING AGAIN!!
UM... YOU DON'T HAVE TO...
ER, HANG ON. WHEN DID YOU SAY YOU WANTED IT THE FIRST TIME...?
KTUNK...
カタ....
AN EARTH-QUAKE!!
KTUNK
カタ
KTUNK
カタ
KTUNK
カタ
HUP
KTUNK
カタ
WE HAVE TO OPEN THE DOOR...
JESUS, GRAB HOLD OF JUNIOR TO KEEP HIM STEADY!
SWISH
PAUSE
WHEW... I THINK IT'S OVER.
MAYBE WE NEED A TENSION POLE FOR JUNIOR'S HEAD...
BUDDHA...
I'M SORRY... SO SORRY...
HUH? WHAT FOR? THE THING YOU SAID EARLIER...?
THE THING IS...
JESUS HAS SPENT SO LONG SITTING CROSS-LEGGED ON A TATAMI MAT BEFORE A TEA TABLE THAT IT'S HARD TO BE CERTAIN IT WAS REALLY ME AT THE LAST SUPPER. THE BEST EXERCISE I'VE GOTTEN IS PLAYING INGRESS... I MEAN, DELIVERING MY SERMONS!

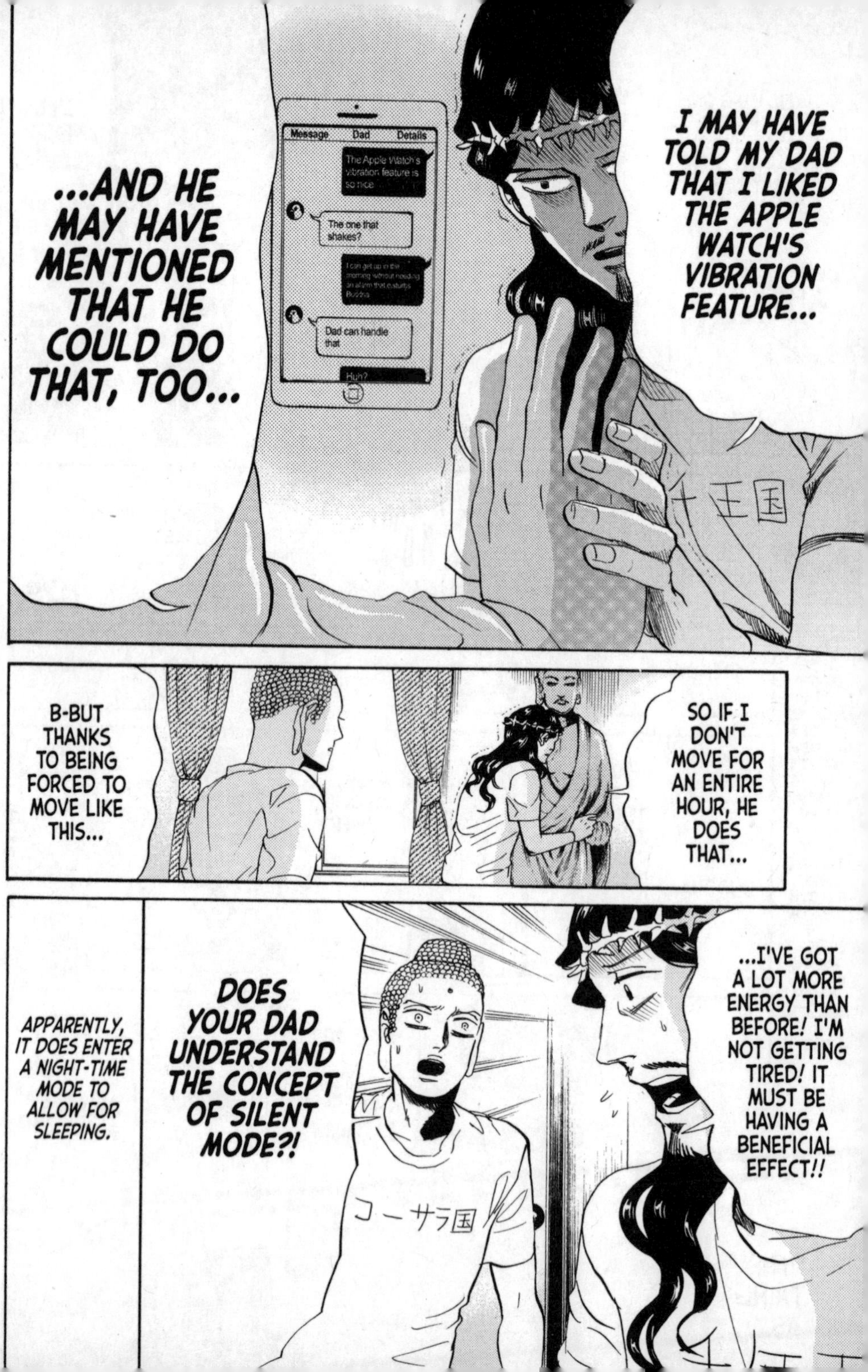
I MAY HAVE TOLD MY DAD THAT I LIKED THE APPLE WATCH'S VIBRATION FEATURE...
...AND HE MAY HAVE MENTIONED THAT HE COULD DO THAT, TOO...
Message
Dad
Details
The Apple Watch's vibration feature is so nice
The one that shakes?
I can get up in the morning without needing an alarm that disturbs Buddha.
Dad can handle that
Huh?
SO IF I DON'T MOVE FOR AN ENTIRE HOUR, HE DOES THAT...
B-BUT THANKS TO BEING FORCED TO MOVE LIKE THIS...
...I'VE GOT A LOT MORE ENERGY THAN BEFORE! I'M NOT GETTING TIRED! IT MUST BE HAVING A BENEFICIAL EFFECT!!
DOES YOUR DAD UNDERSTAND THE CONCEPT OF SILENT MODE?!
コーサラ国
APPARENTLY, IT DOES ENTER A NIGHT-TIME MODE TO ALLOW FOR SLEEPING.

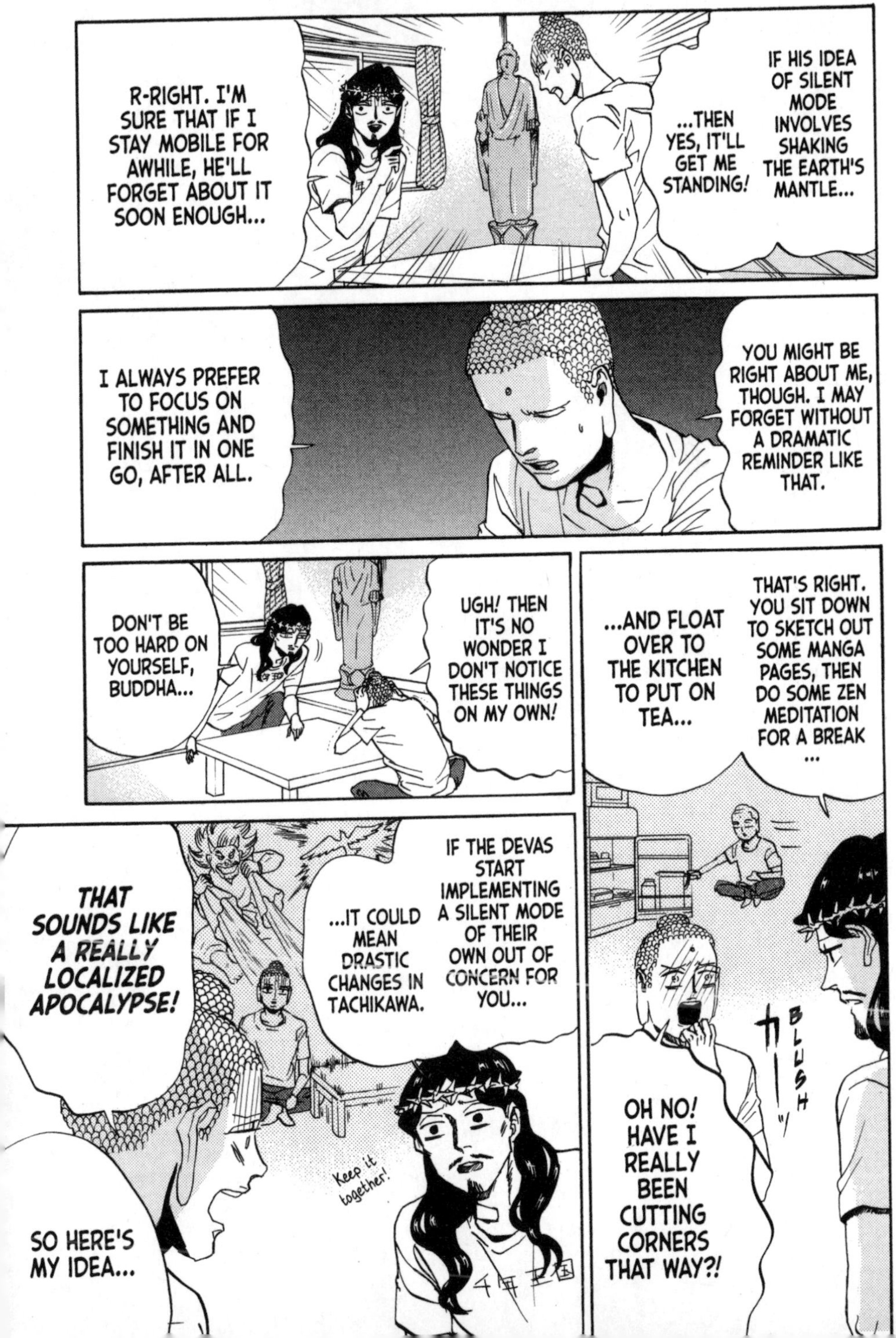
IF HIS IDEA OF SILENT MODE INVOLVES SHAKING THE EARTH'S MANTLE...
...THEN YES, IT'LL GET ME STANDING!
R-RIGHT. I'M SURE THAT IF I STAY MOBILE FOR AWHILE, HE'LL FORGET ABOUT IT SOON ENOUGH...
YOU MIGHT BE RIGHT ABOUT ME, THOUGH. I MAY FORGET WITHOUT A DRAMATIC REMINDER LIKE THAT.
I ALWAYS PREFER TO FOCUS ON SOMETHING AND FINISH IT IN ONE GO, AFTER ALL.
THAT'S RIGHT. YOU SIT DOWN TO SKETCH OUT SOME MANGA PAGES, THEN DO SOME ZEN MEDITATION FOR A BREAK ...
...AND FLOAT OVER TO THE KITCHEN TO PUT ON TEA...
BLUSH
OH NO! HAVE I REALLY BEEN CUTTING CORNERS THAT WAY?!
UGH! THEN IT'S NO WONDER I DON'T NOTICE THESE THINGS ON MY OWN!
DON'T BE TOO HARD ON YOURSELF, BUDDHA...
IF THE DEVAS START IMPLEMENTING A SILENT MODE OF THEIR OWN OUT OF CONCERN FOR YOU...
...IT COULD MEAN DRASTIC CHANGES IN TACHIKAWA.
THAT SOUNDS LIKE A REALLY LOCALIZED APOCALYPSE!
Keep it together!
SO HERE'S MY IDEA...

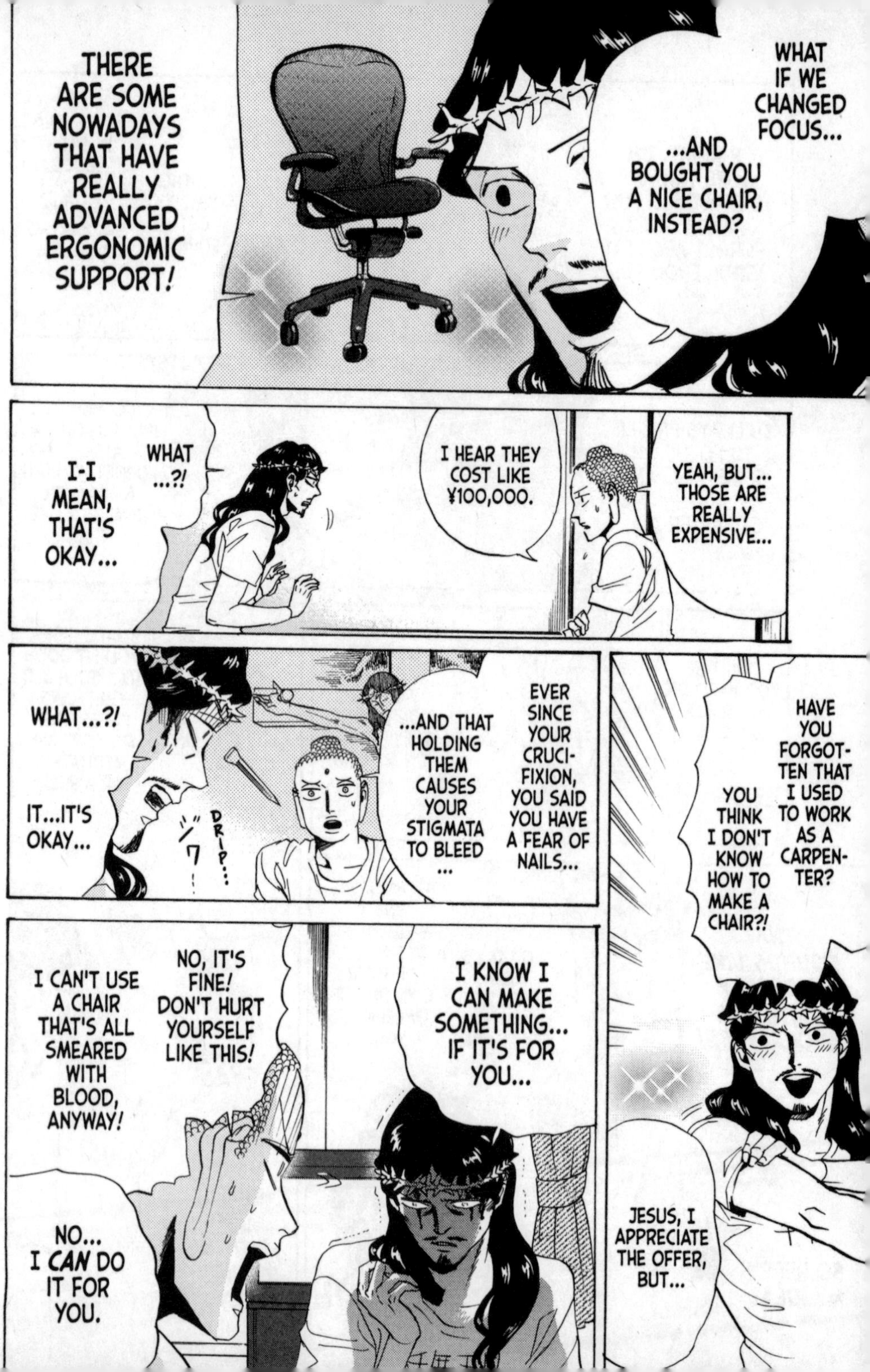
WHAT IF WE CHANGED FOCUS...
...AND BOUGHT YOU A NICE CHAIR, INSTEAD?
THERE ARE SOME NOWADAYS THAT HAVE REALLY ADVANCED ERGONOMIC SUPPORT!
YEAH, BUT... THOSE ARE REALLY EXPENSIVE...
I HEAR THEY COST LIKE ¥100,000.
WHAT ...?!
I-I MEAN, THAT'S OKAY...
HAVE YOU FORGOT-TEN THAT I USED TO WORK AS A CARPEN-TER?
YOU THINK I DON'T KNOW HOW TO MAKE A CHAIR?!
JESUS, I APPRECIATE THE OFFER, BUT...
EVER SINCE YOUR CRUCI-FIXION, YOU SAID YOU HAVE A FEAR OF NAILS...
...AND THAT HOLDING THEM CAUSES YOUR STIGMATA TO BLEED ...
WHAT...?!
IT...IT'S OKAY...
DRIP...
I KNOW I CAN MAKE SOMETHING... IF IT'S FOR YOU...
NO, IT'S FINE! DON'T HURT YOURSELF LIKE THIS!
I CAN'T USE A CHAIR THAT'S ALL SMEARED WITH BLOOD, ANYWAY!
NO... I *CAN* DO IT FOR YOU.

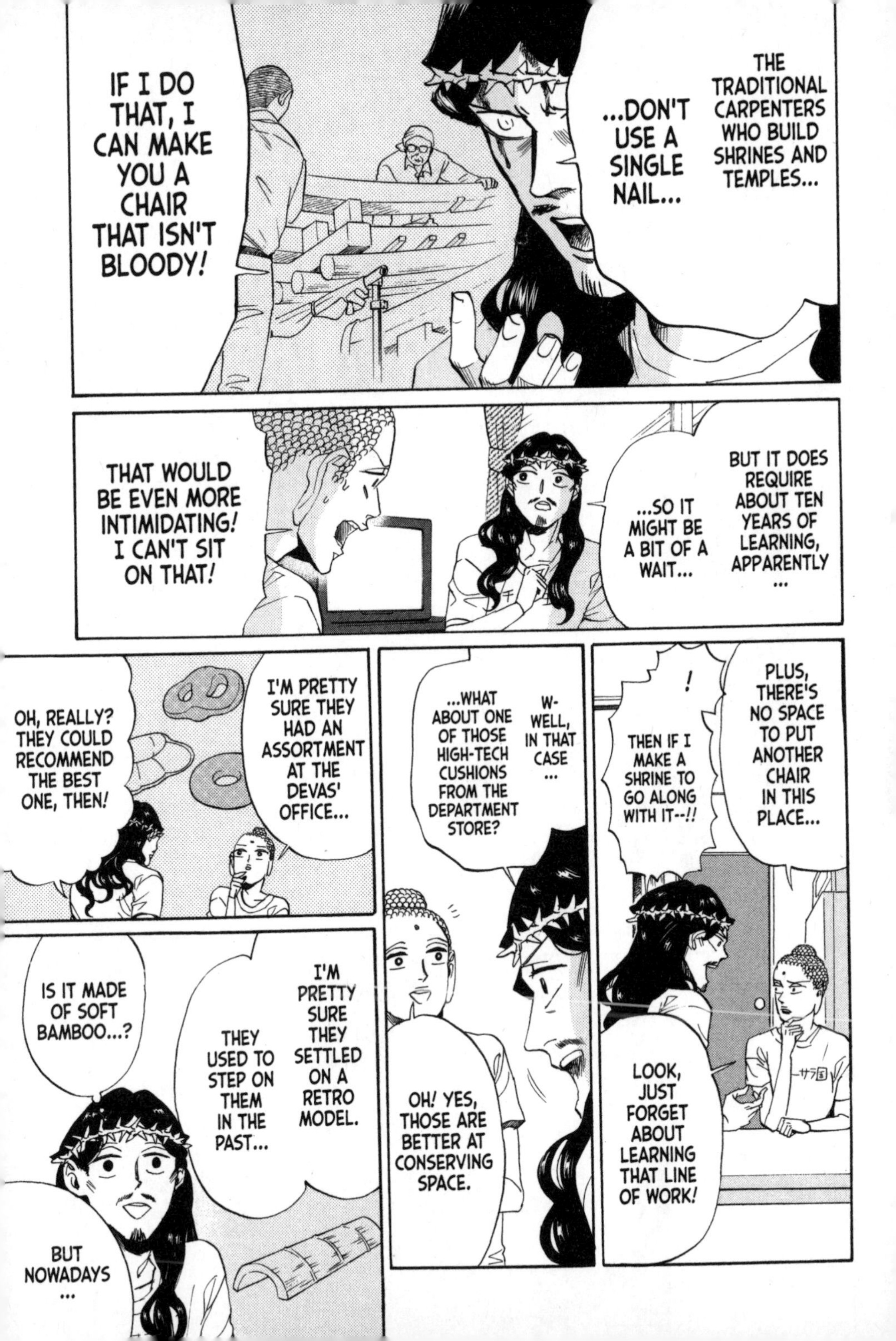
THE TRADITIONAL CARPENTERS WHO BUILD SHRINES AND TEMPLES...
...DON'T USE A SINGLE NAIL...
IF I DO THAT, I CAN MAKE YOU A CHAIR THAT ISN'T BLOODY!
BUT IT DOES REQUIRE ABOUT TEN YEARS OF LEARNING, APPARENTLY...
...SO IT MIGHT BE A BIT OF A WAIT...
THAT WOULD BE EVEN MORE INTIMIDATING! I CAN'T SIT ON THAT!
PLUS, THERE'S NO SPACE TO PUT ANOTHER CHAIR IN THIS PLACE...
!
THEN IF I MAKE A SHRINE TO GO ALONG WITH IT--!!
LOOK, JUST FORGET ABOUT LEARNING THAT LINE OF WORK!
W-WELL, IN THAT CASE...
...WHAT ABOUT ONE OF THOSE HIGH-TECH CUSHIONS FROM THE DEPARTMENT STORE?
OH! YES, THOSE ARE BETTER AT CONSERVING SPACE.
I'M PRETTY SURE THEY HAD AN ASSORTMENT AT THE DEVAS' OFFICE...
OH, REALLY? THEY COULD RECOMMEND THE BEST ONE, THEN!
I'M PRETTY SURE THEY SETTLED ON A RETRO MODEL.
THEY USED TO STEP ON THEM IN THE PAST...
IS IT MADE OF SOFT BAMBOO...?
BUT NOWADAYS...

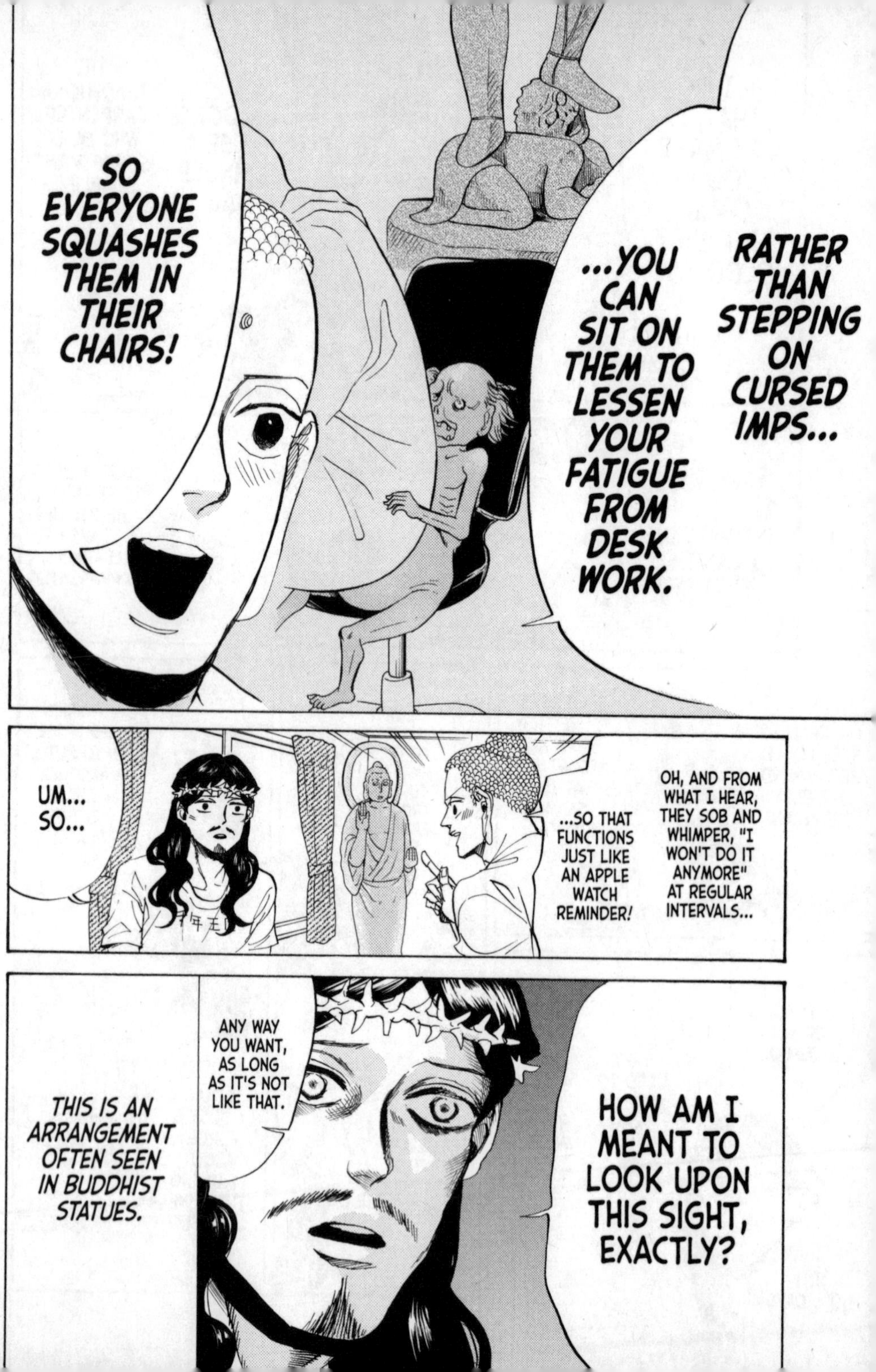
RATHER THAN STEPPING ON CURSED IMPS...
...YOU CAN SIT ON THEM TO LESSEN YOUR FATIGUE FROM DESK WORK.
SO EVERYONE SQUASHES THEM IN THEIR CHAIRS!
OH, AND FROM WHAT I HEAR, THEY SOB AND WHIMPER, "I WON'T DO IT ANYMORE" AT REGULAR INTERVALS...
...SO THAT FUNCTIONS JUST LIKE AN APPLE WATCH REMINDER!
UM... SO...
HOW AM I MEANT TO LOOK UPON THIS SIGHT, EXACTLY?
ANY WAY YOU WANT, AS LONG AS IT'S NOT LIKE THAT.
THIS IS AN ARRANGEMENT OFTEN SEEN IN BUDDHIST STATUES.

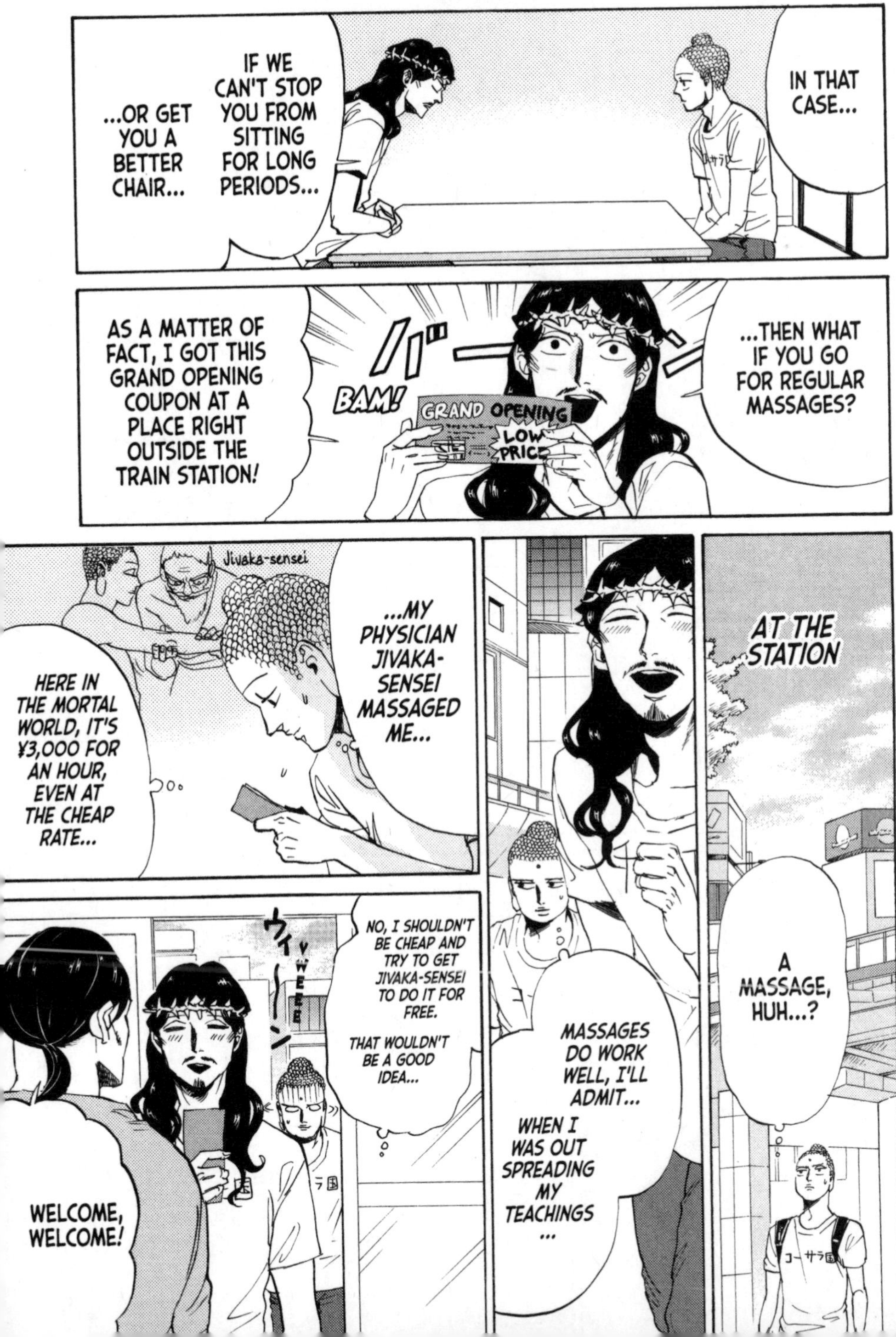
IN THAT CASE...
IF WE CAN'T STOP YOU FROM SITTING FOR LONG PERIODS...
...OR GET YOU A BETTER CHAIR...
...THEN WHAT IF YOU GO FOR REGULAR MASSAGES?
バ
BAM!
GRAND OPENING
LOW PRICE
AS A MATTER OF FACT, I GOT THIS GRAND OPENING COUPON AT A PLACE RIGHT OUTSIDE THE TRAIN STATION!
AT THE STATION
A MASSAGE, HUH...?
MASSAGES DO WORK WELL, I'LL ADMIT...
WHEN I WAS OUT SPREADING MY TEACHINGS ...
...MY PHYSICIAN JIVAKA-SENSEI MASSAGED ME...
Jivaka-sensei
HERE IN THE MORTAL WORLD, IT'S ¥3,000 FOR AN HOUR, EVEN AT THE CHEAP RATE...
NO, I SHOULDN'T BE CHEAP AND TRY TO GET JIVAKA-SENSEI TO DO IT FOR FREE.
THAT WOULDN'T BE A GOOD IDEA...
ウィーン
WEEE
WELCOME, WELCOME!

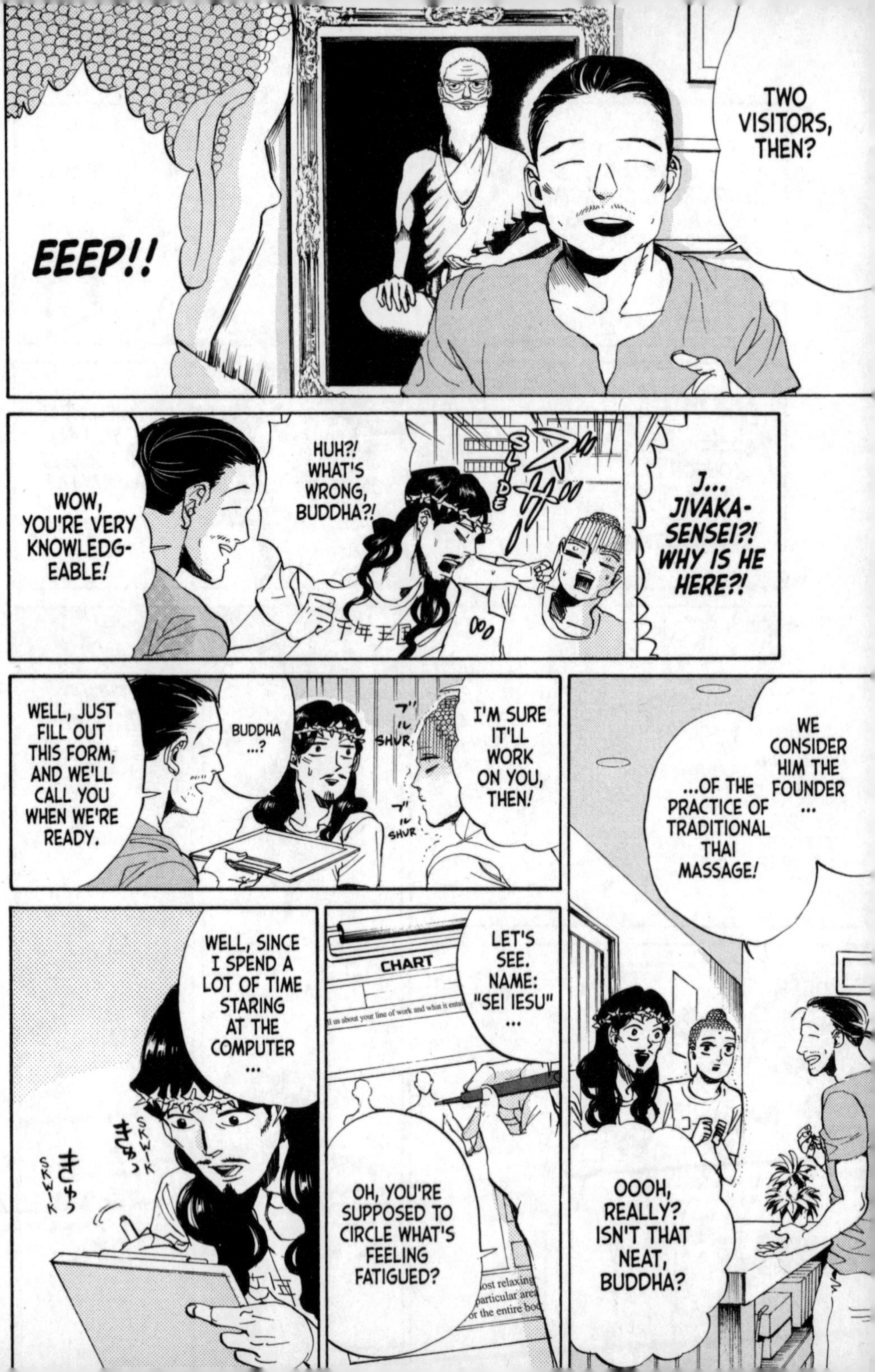
TWO VISITORS, THEN?
EEEP!!
J... JIVAKA-SENSEI?! WHY IS HE HERE?!
SLIDE
HUH?! WHAT'S WRONG, BUDDHA?!
WOW, YOU'RE VERY KNOWLEDG-EABLE!
WE CONSIDER HIM THE FOUNDER ...
...OF THE PRACTICE OF TRADITIONAL THAI MASSAGE!
I'M SURE IT'LL WORK ON YOU, THEN!
SHUR
SHUR
BUDDHA ...?
WELL, JUST FILL OUT THIS FORM, AND WE'LL CALL YOU WHEN WE'RE READY.
OOOH, REALLY? ISN'T THAT NEAT, BUDDHA?
LET'S SEE. NAME: "SEI IESU" ...
CHART
OH, YOU'RE SUPPOSED TO CIRCLE WHAT'S FEELING FATIGUED?
WELL, SINCE I SPEND A LOT OF TIME STARING AT THE COMPUTER ...
SKWIK
SKWIK

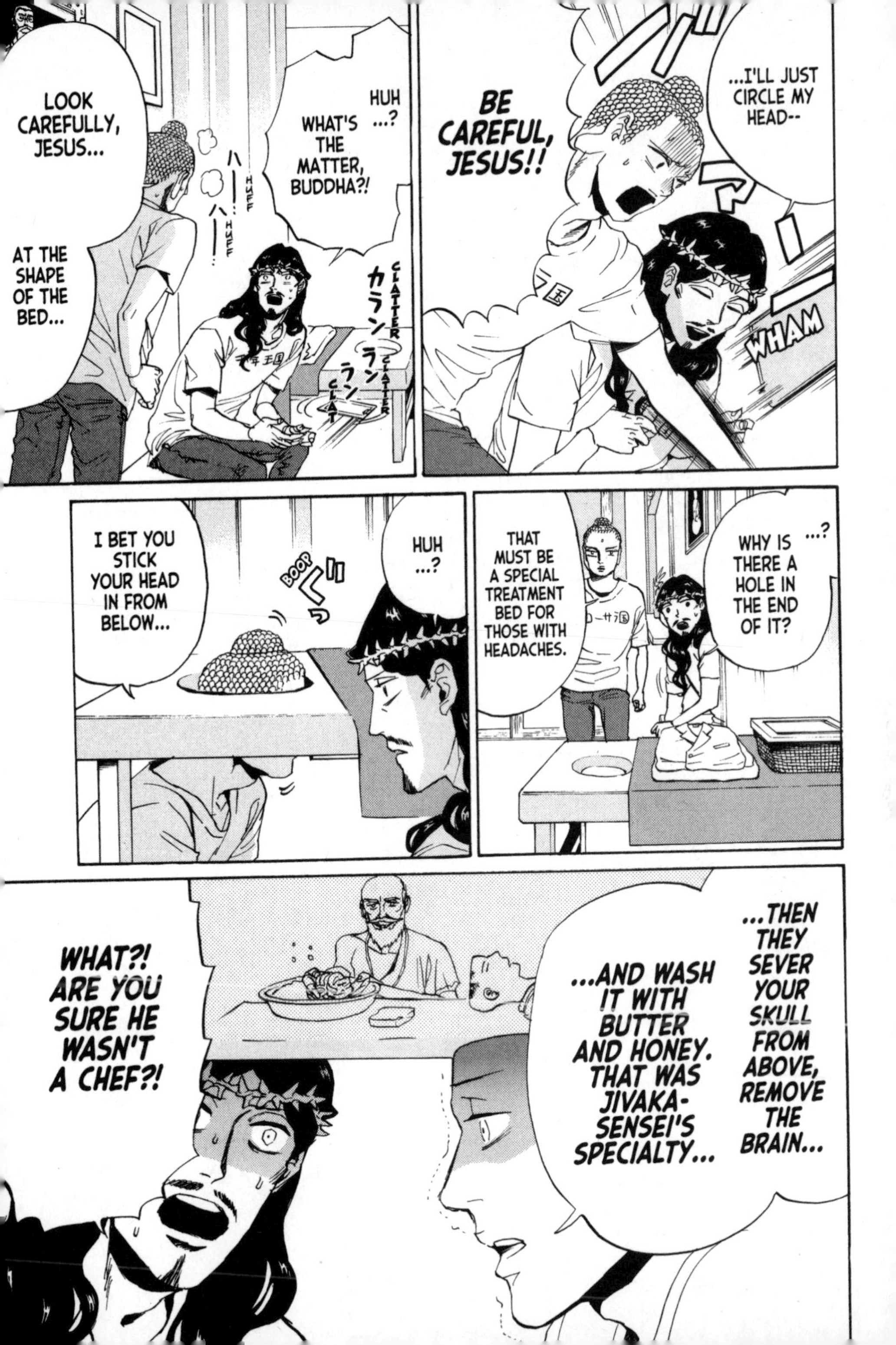
...I'LL JUST CIRCLE MY HEAD--
BE CAREFUL, JESUS!!
WHAM
HUH ...?
WHAT'S THE MATTER, BUDDHA?!
ハー!! HUFF
ハー!! HUFF
カラン CLATTER
ラン CLATTER
ラン CLAT
LOOK CAREFULLY, JESUS...
AT THE SHAPE OF THE BED...
...?
WHY IS THERE A HOLE IN THE END OF IT?
THAT MUST BE A SPECIAL TREATMENT BED FOR THOSE WITH HEADACHES.
HUH ...?
BOOP
I BET YOU STICK YOUR HEAD IN FROM BELOW...
...THEN THEY SEVER YOUR SKULL FROM ABOVE, REMOVE THE BRAIN...
...AND WASH IT WITH BUTTER AND HONEY. THAT WAS JIVAKA-SENSEI'S SPECIALTY...
WHAT?! ARE YOU SURE HE WASN'T A CHEF?!

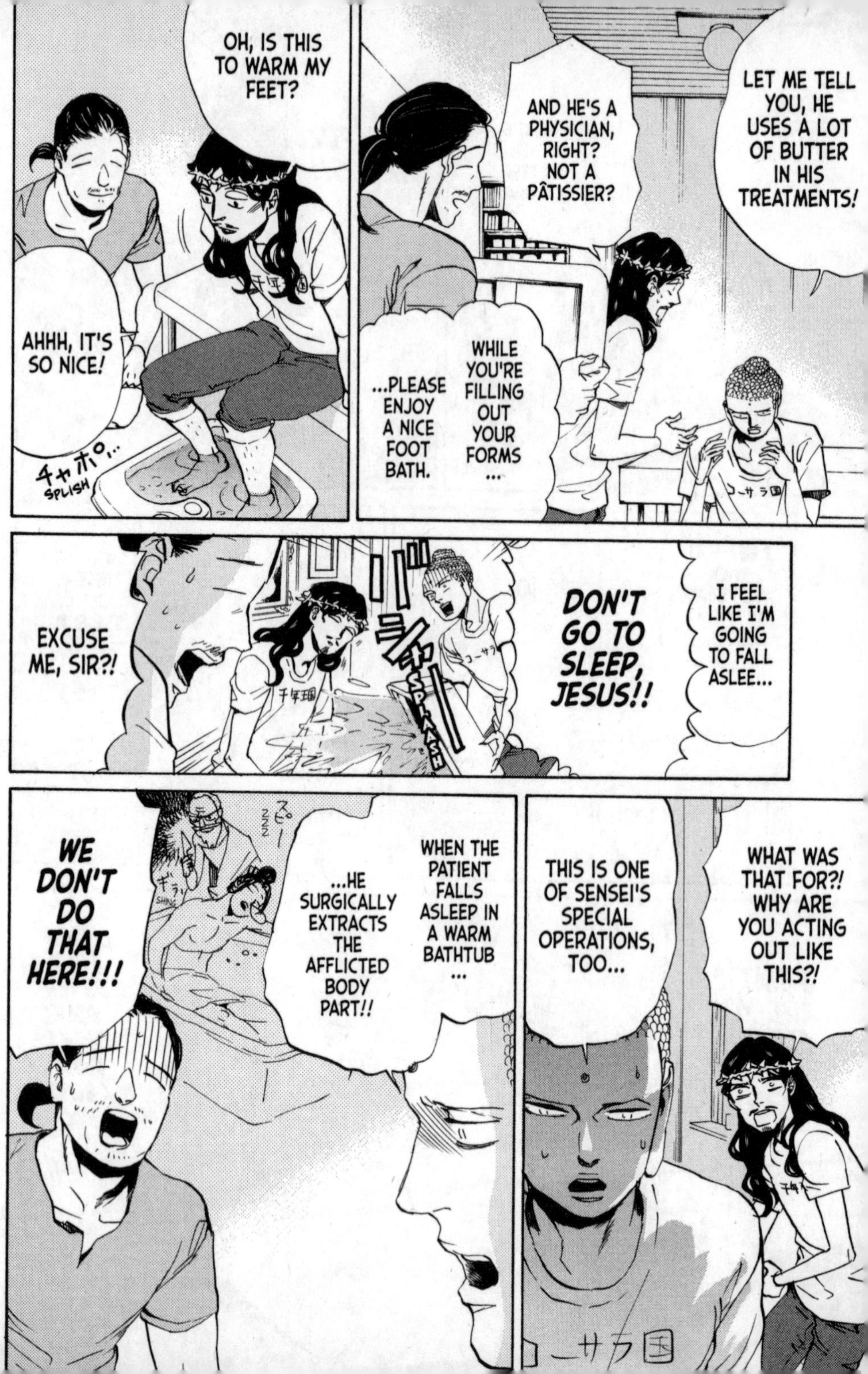
LET ME TELL YOU, HE USES A LOT OF BUTTER IN HIS TREATMENTS!
AND HE'S A PHYSICIAN, RIGHT? NOT A PÂTISSIER?
WHILE YOU'RE FILLING OUT YOUR FORMS ...
...PLEASE ENJOY A NICE FOOT BATH.
OH, IS THIS TO WARM MY FEET?
AHHH, IT'S SO NICE!
SPLISH
I FEEL LIKE I'M GOING TO FALL ASLEE...
DON'T GO TO SLEEP, JESUS!!
SPLASH
EXCUSE ME, SIR?!
WHAT WAS THAT FOR?! WHY ARE YOU ACTING OUT LIKE THIS?!
THIS IS ONE OF SENSEI'S SPECIAL OPERATIONS, TOO...
WHEN THE PATIENT FALLS ASLEEP IN A WARM BATHTUB ...
...HE SURGICALLY EXTRACTS THE AFFLICTED BODY PART!!
SHING
WE DON'T DO THAT HERE!!!

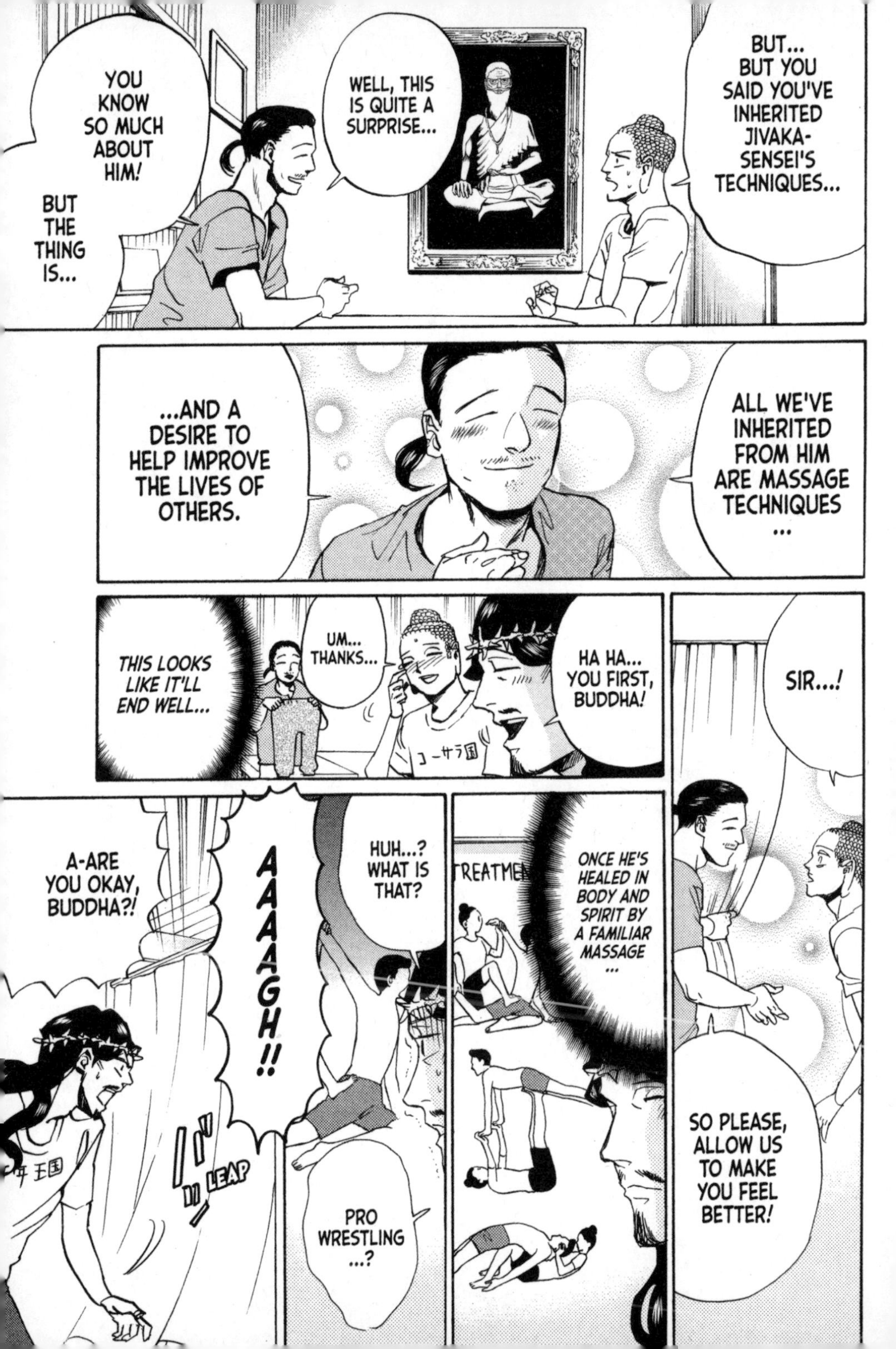
BUT... BUT YOU SAID YOU'VE INHERITED JIVAKA-SENSEI'S TECHNIQUES...
WELL, THIS IS QUITE A SURPRISE...
YOU KNOW SO MUCH ABOUT HIM!
BUT THE THING IS...
ALL WE'VE INHERITED FROM HIM ARE MASSAGE TECHNIQUES ...
...AND A DESIRE TO HELP IMPROVE THE LIVES OF OTHERS.
SIR...!
SO PLEASE, ALLOW US TO MAKE YOU FEEL BETTER!
HA HA... YOU FIRST, BUDDHA!
UM... THANKS...
コーサラ国
THIS LOOKS LIKE IT'LL END WELL...
ONCE HE'S HEALED IN BODY AND SPIRIT BY A FAMILIAR MASSAGE ...
TREATMEN
HUH...? WHAT IS THAT?
PRO WRESTLING ...?
AAAAAGH!!
LEAP
A-ARE YOU OKAY, BUDDHA?!

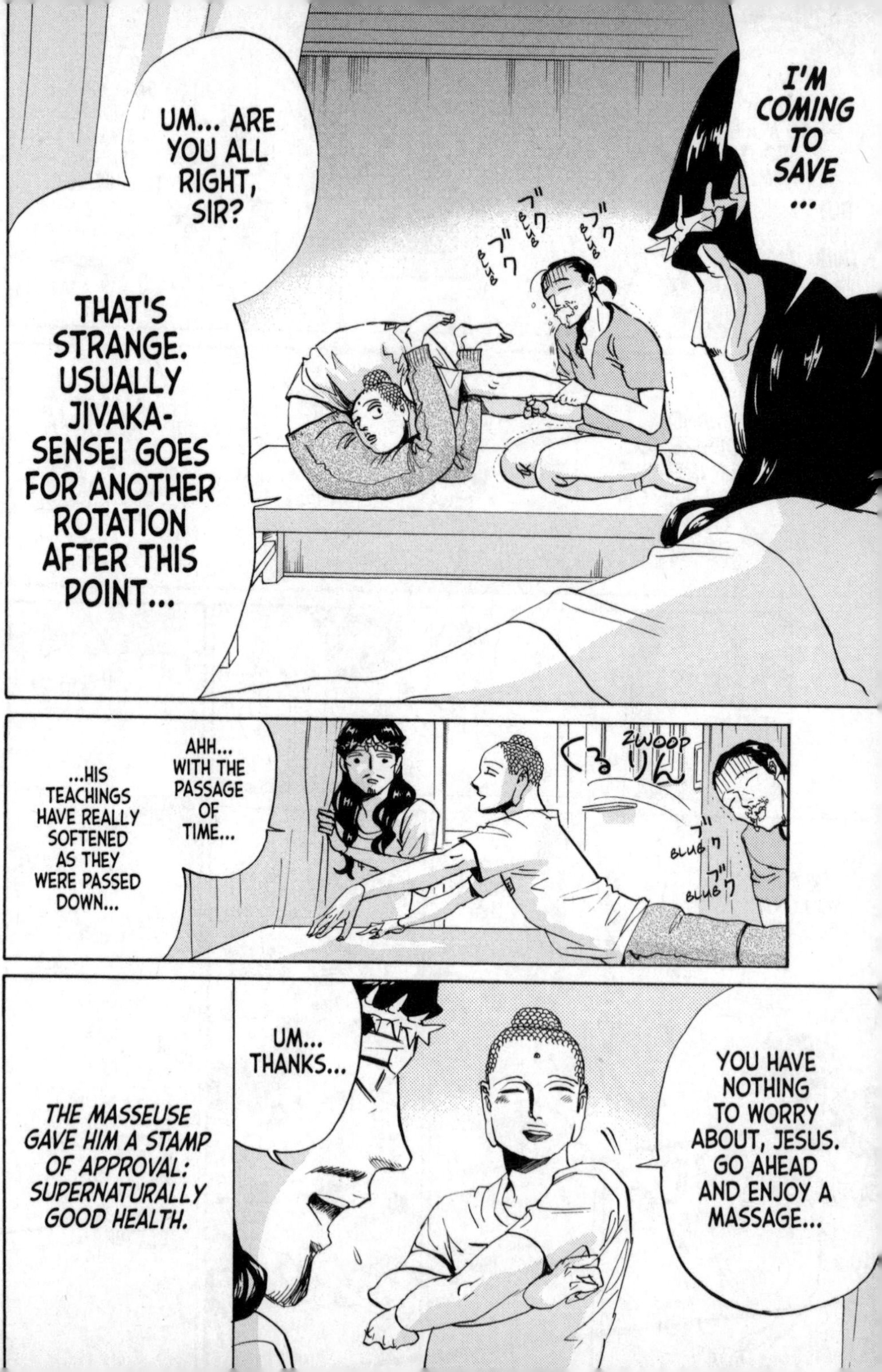

I'M COMING TO SAVE ...
ブク BLUB ブク BLUB
ブク BLUB
UM... ARE YOU ALL RIGHT, SIR?
THAT'S STRANGE. USUALLY JIVAKA-SENSEI GOES FOR ANOTHER ROTATION AFTER THIS POINT...
くるりん ZWOOP
ブク BLUB
ブク BLUB
AHH... WITH THE PASSAGE OF TIME...
...HIS TEACHINGS HAVE REALLY SOFTENED AS THEY WERE PASSED DOWN...
YOU HAVE NOTHING TO WORRY ABOUT, JESUS. GO AHEAD AND ENJOY A MASSAGE...
UM... THANKS...
THE MASSEUSE GAVE HIM A STAMP OF APPROVAL: SUPERNATURALLY GOOD HEALTH.

How Jivaka-sensei would do it...

SAINT☆YOUNG MEN

CHAPTER 84 TRANSLATION NOTES

Kosala, page 55

The name of a kingdom in ancient India that was positioned adjacent to the territory of the Shakyas, the people who gave birth to Gautama Buddha. A king of Kosala at the time of the Buddha's life, Virudhaka, was born to a servant of the Shakyas, and is said to have been the one who later invaded and wiped out the clan.

Thousand Year Reign, page 55

In the Book of Revelation, it is stated that after Christ's return, the souls of the faithful who were killed for being faithful to him shall be resurrected and join Christ in a thousand-year reign over the earth, after which the rest of the souls of the dead will be revived.

Tameshite Gatten!, page 57

A long-running television show on NHK, Japan's public broadcaster. Translating to roughly "Try It and Eureka!" the program provides a look at common-sense knowledge about science and lifestyle news (nowadays they might be called "life hacks") to improve the lives of viewers. The show's famous pose and logo iconography is a raised fist over a flat palm, to imitate the palm-smacking "Oh!" moment of understanding.

Cursed imps, page 64

Called *preta* in Sanskrit or *gaki* in Japanese, and sometimes translated as "hungry ghost," these creatures are often thought to be the souls of those who were greedy or deceitful in a previous life, and are cursed to be starving. In some Buddhist art, figures such as the Four Heavenly Kings or the Niô guardian statues that stand at the gates of temples are depicted stepping upon these imps, which are believed to be so ravenous that they absorb one's physical pain and fatigue.

Jivaka, page 65

The personal doctor of Gautama Buddha in life. Jivaka took on a reputation as a great healer and wise physician, and is revered in many traditions as a kind of Buddhist saint of healing.

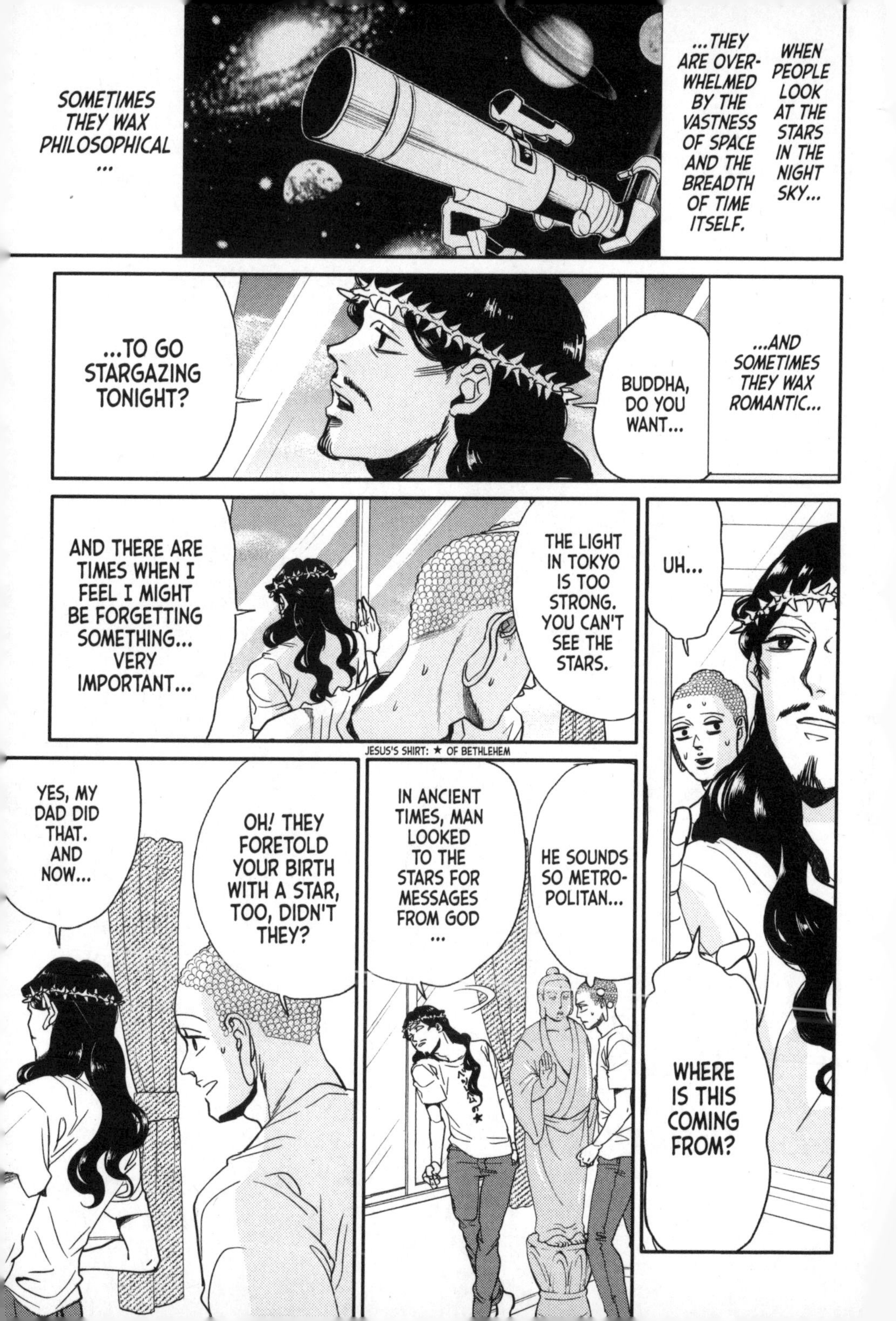
WHEN PEOPLE LOOK AT THE STARS IN THE NIGHT SKY...
...THEY ARE OVER-WHELMED BY THE VASTNESS OF SPACE AND THE BREADTH OF TIME ITSELF.
SOMETIMES THEY WAX PHILOSOPHICAL ...
...AND SOMETIMES THEY WAX ROMANTIC...
BUDDHA, DO YOU WANT...
...TO GO STARGAZING TONIGHT?
UH...
WHERE IS THIS COMING FROM?
THE LIGHT IN TOKYO IS TOO STRONG. YOU CAN'T SEE THE STARS.
AND THERE ARE TIMES WHEN I FEEL I MIGHT BE FORGETTING SOMETHING... VERY IMPORTANT...
JESUS'S SHIRT: ★ OF BETHLEHEM
HE SOUNDS SO METRO-POLITAN...
IN ANCIENT TIMES, MAN LOOKED TO THE STARS FOR MESSAGES FROM GOD ...
OH! THEY FORETOLD YOUR BIRTH WITH A STAR, TOO, DIDN'T THEY?
YES, MY DAD DID THAT. AND NOW...

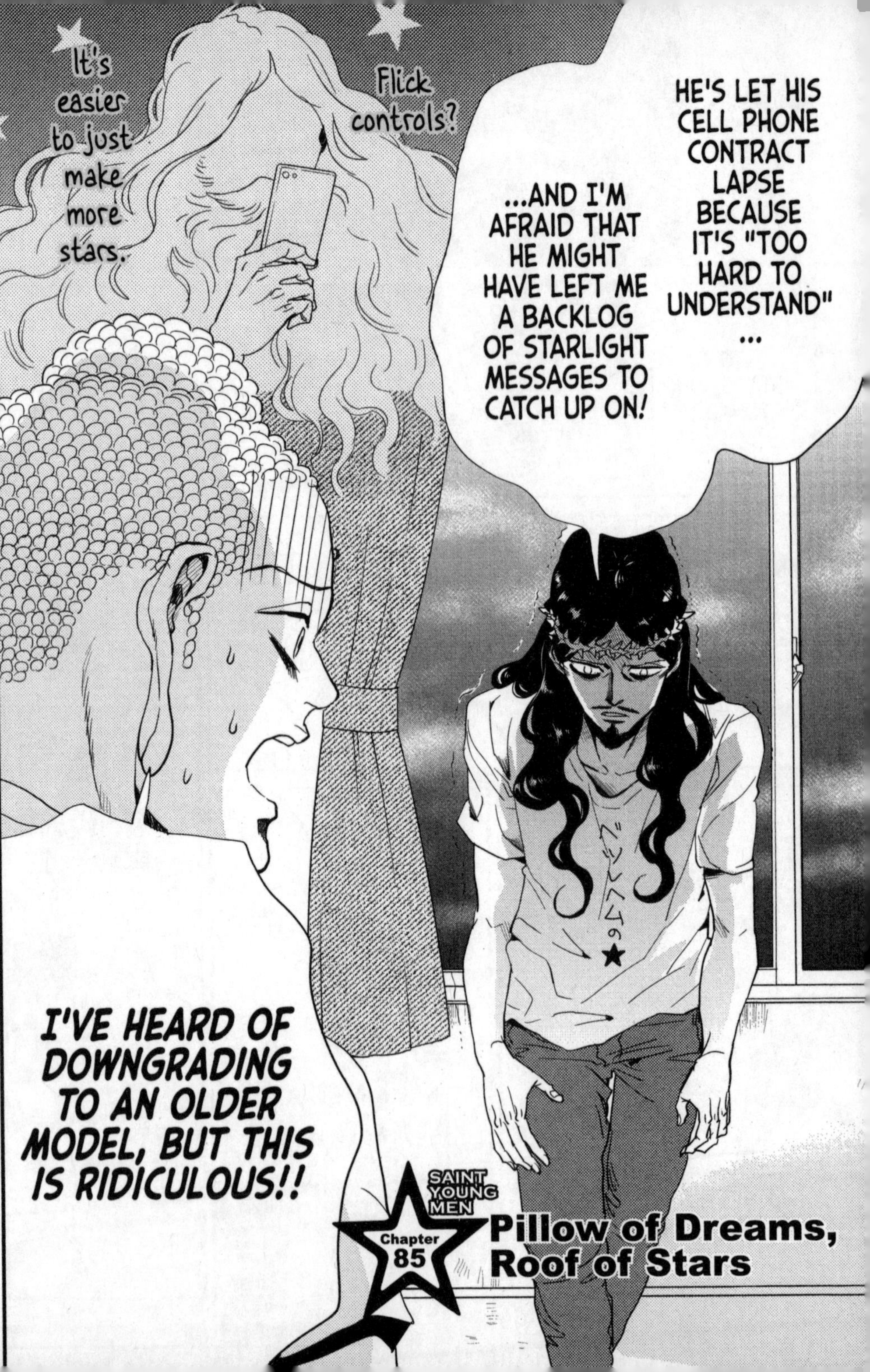
HE'S LET HIS CELL PHONE CONTRACT LAPSE BECAUSE IT'S "TOO HARD TO UNDERSTAND" ...
...AND I'M AFRAID THAT HE MIGHT HAVE LEFT ME A BACKLOG OF STARLIGHT MESSAGES TO CATCH UP ON!
Flick controls?
It's easier to just make more stars.
I'VE HEARD OF DOWNGRADING TO AN OLDER MODEL, BUT THIS IS RIDICULOUS!!
SAINT YOUNG MEN
Chapter 85
Pillow of Dreams, Roof of Stars

JESUS THE INDOOR TYPE, SO HE DOESN'T MIND THE RAINY SEASON. BUT IT HURTS NOT TO BE ABLE TO GO TO THE VIDEO STORE OR MINI MART. HOPEFULLY IT LETS UP SOON.

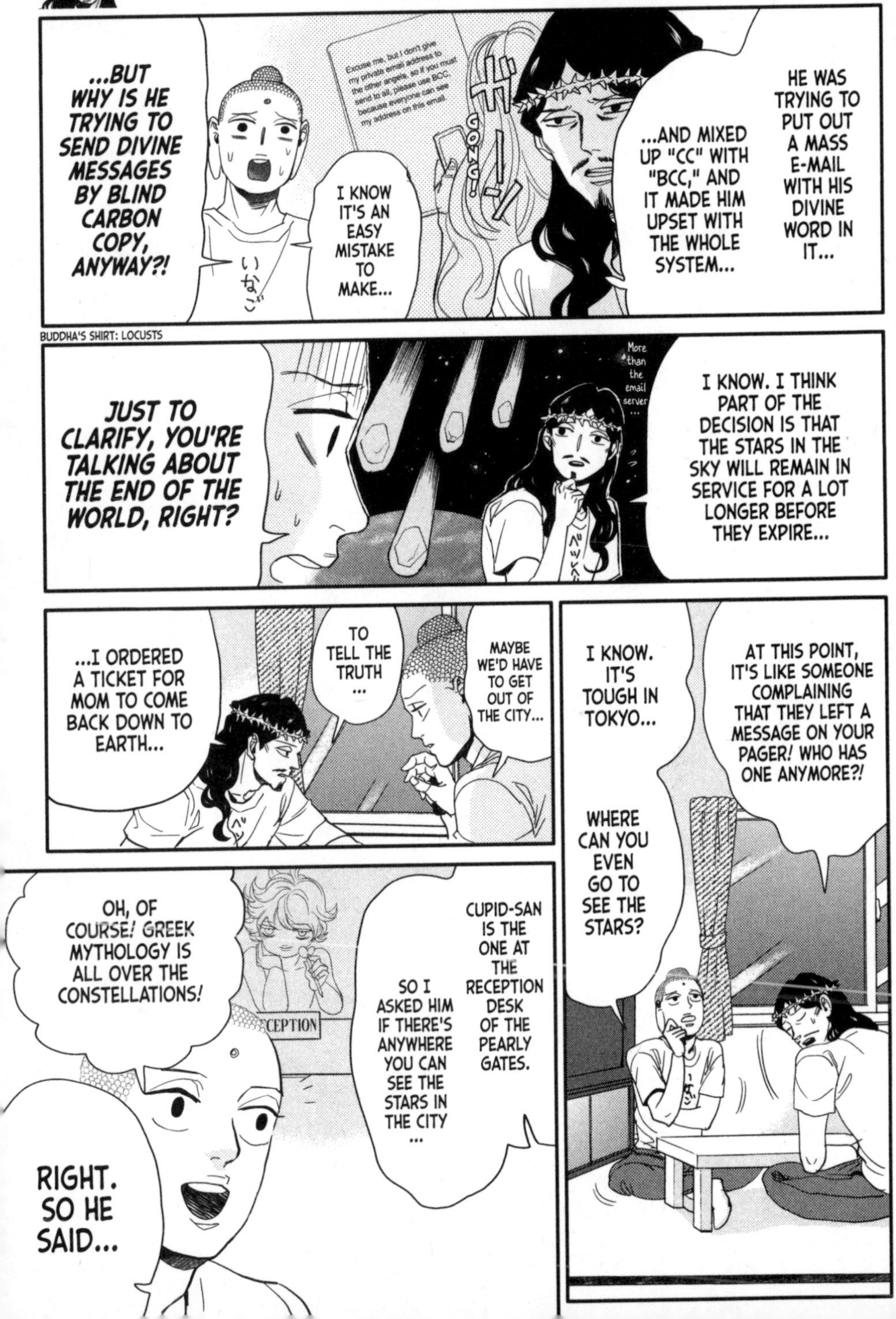

HE WAS TRYING TO PUT OUT A MASS E-MAIL WITH HIS DIVINE WORD IN IT...
...AND MIXED UP "CC" WITH "BCC," AND IT MADE HIM UPSET WITH THE WHOLE SYSTEM...
GONG!
Excuse me, but I don't give my private email address to the other angels, so if you must send to all, please use BCC, because everyone can see my address on this email.
I KNOW IT'S AN EASY MISTAKE TO MAKE...
...BUT WHY IS HE TRYING TO SEND DIVINE MESSAGES BY BLIND CARBON COPY, ANYWAY?!
いなご
BUDDHA'S SHIRT: LOCUSTS
I KNOW. I THINK PART OF THE DECISION IS THAT THE STARS IN THE SKY WILL REMAIN IN SERVICE FOR A LOT LONGER BEFORE THEY EXPIRE...
More than the email server...
JUST TO CLARIFY, YOU'RE TALKING ABOUT THE END OF THE WORLD, RIGHT?
AT THIS POINT, IT'S LIKE SOMEONE COMPLAINING THAT THEY LEFT A MESSAGE ON YOUR PAGER! WHO HAS ONE ANYMORE?!
I KNOW. IT'S TOUGH IN TOKYO...
WHERE CAN YOU EVEN GO TO SEE THE STARS?
MAYBE WE'D HAVE TO GET OUT OF THE CITY...
TO TELL THE TRUTH ...
...I ORDERED A TICKET FOR MOM TO COME BACK DOWN TO EARTH...
CUPID-SAN IS THE ONE AT THE RECEPTION DESK OF THE PEARLY GATES.
SO I ASKED HIM IF THERE'S ANYWHERE YOU CAN SEE THE STARS IN THE CITY ...
CEPTION
OH, OF COURSE! GREEK MYTHOLOGY IS ALL OVER THE CONSTELLATIONS!
RIGHT. SO HE SAID...

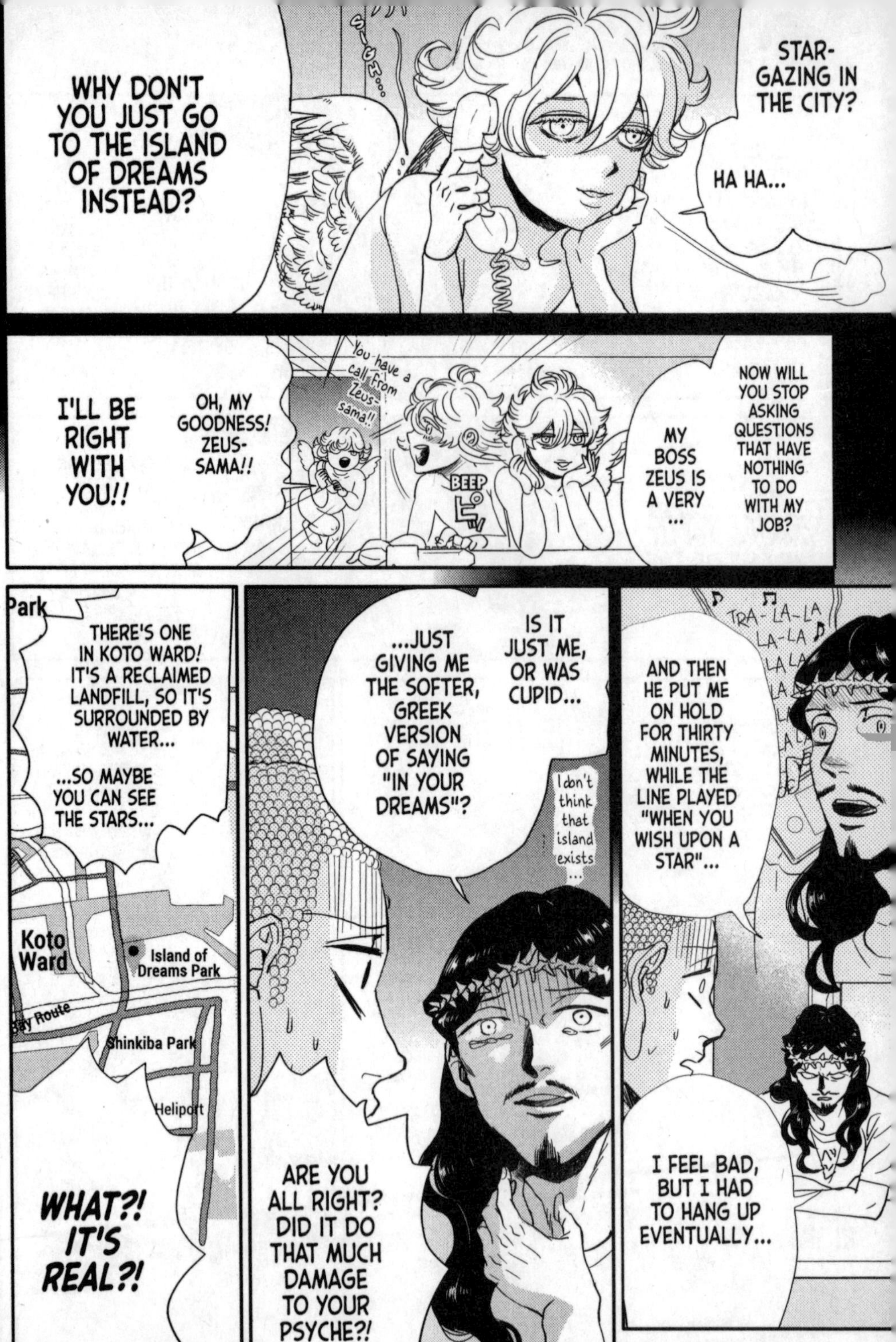
STAR-GAZING IN THE CITY?
HA HA...
SIGH...
WHY DON'T YOU JUST GO TO THE ISLAND OF DREAMS INSTEAD?
NOW WILL YOU STOP ASKING QUESTIONS THAT HAVE NOTHING TO DO WITH MY JOB?
MY BOSS ZEUS IS A VERY ...
You-have a call from Zeus-sama!!
BEEP
OH, MY GOODNESS! ZEUS-SAMA!!
I'LL BE RIGHT WITH YOU!!
TRA-LA-LA LA-LA
AND THEN HE PUT ME ON HOLD FOR THIRTY MINUTES, WHILE THE LINE PLAYED "WHEN YOU WISH UPON A STAR"...
I FEEL BAD, BUT I HAD TO HANG UP EVENTUALLY...
IS IT JUST ME, OR WAS CUPID...
...JUST GIVING ME THE SOFTER, GREEK VERSION OF SAYING "IN YOUR DREAMS"?
I don't think that island exists...
ARE YOU ALL RIGHT? DID IT DO THAT MUCH DAMAGE TO YOUR PSYCHE?!
THERE'S ONE IN KOTO WARD! IT'S A RECLAIMED LANDFILL, SO IT'S SURROUNDED BY WATER...
...SO MAYBE YOU CAN SEE THE STARS...
Park
Koto Ward
Island of Dreams Park
Bay Route
Shinkiba Park
Heliport
WHAT?! IT'S REAL?!

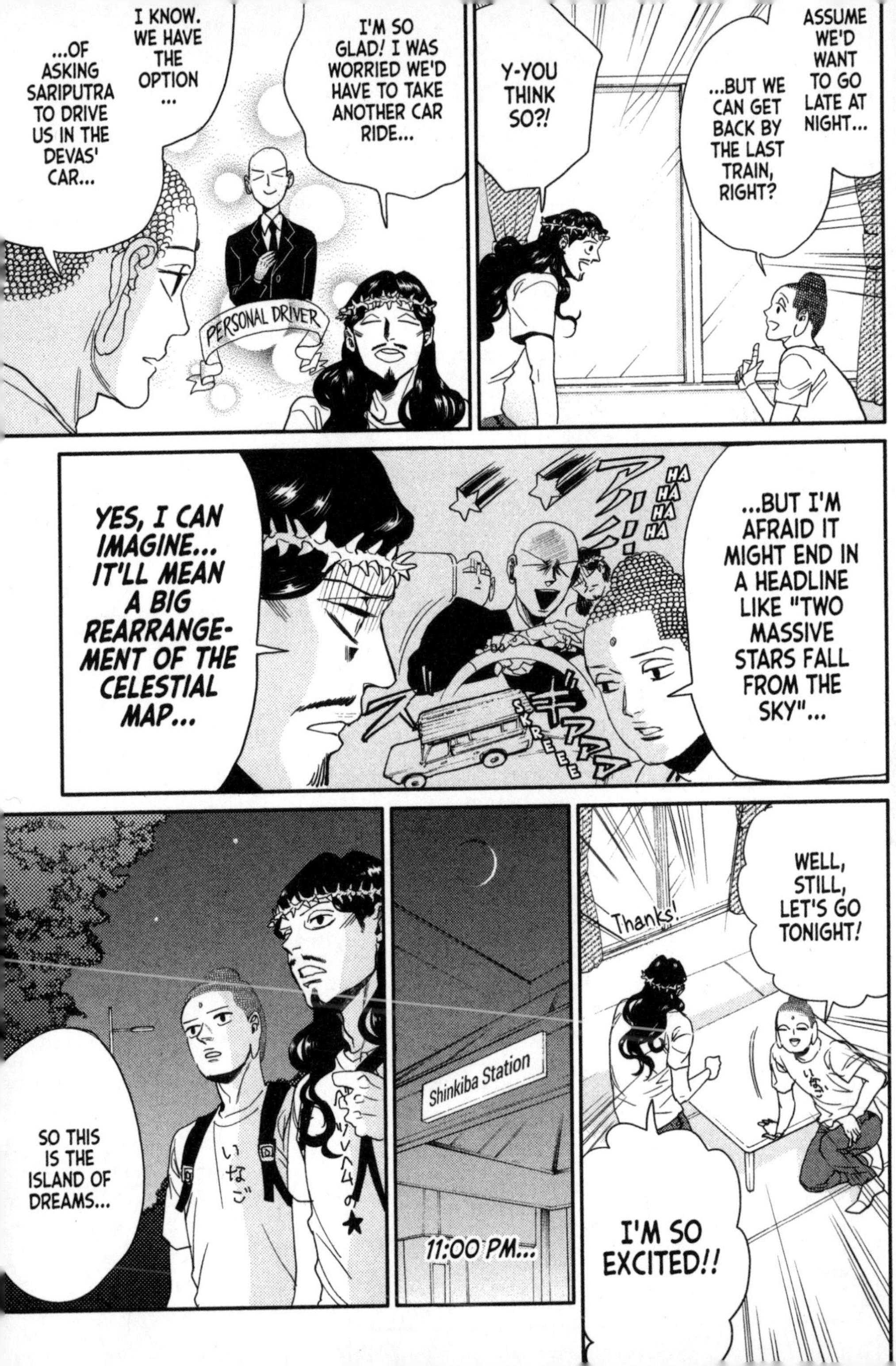
ASSUME WE'D WANT TO GO LATE AT NIGHT...
...BUT WE CAN GET BACK BY THE LAST TRAIN, RIGHT?
Y-YOU THINK SO?!
I'M SO GLAD! I WAS WORRIED WE'D HAVE TO TAKE ANOTHER CAR RIDE...
PERSONAL DRIVER
I KNOW. WE HAVE THE OPTION ...
...OF ASKING SARIPUTRA TO DRIVE US IN THE DEVAS' CAR...
...BUT I'M AFRAID IT MIGHT END IN A HEADLINE LIKE "TWO MASSIVE STARS FALL FROM THE SKY"...
HA HA HA HA
SKREEEE
YES, I CAN IMAGINE... IT'LL MEAN A BIG REARRANGEMENT OF THE CELESTIAL MAP...
WELL, STILL, LET'S GO TONIGHT!
Thanks!
I'M SO EXCITED!!
Shinkiba Station
11:00 PM...
SO THIS IS THE ISLAND OF DREAMS...

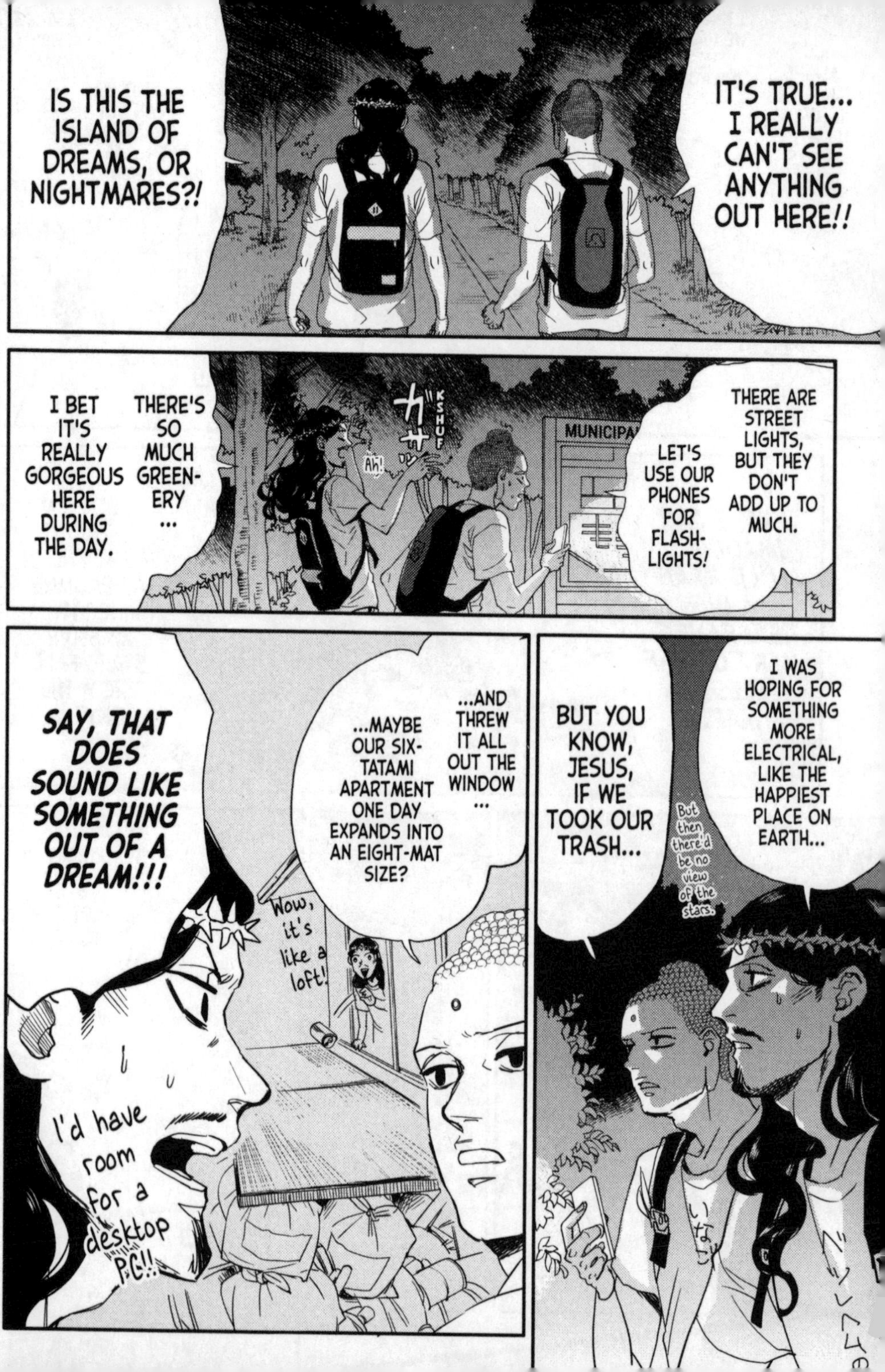
IT'S TRUE... I REALLY CAN'T SEE ANYTHING OUT HERE!!
IS THIS THE ISLAND OF DREAMS, OR NIGHTMARES?!
THERE ARE STREET LIGHTS, BUT THEY DON'T ADD UP TO MUCH.
LET'S USE OUR PHONES FOR FLASH-LIGHTS!
KSHUF
Ah!
THERE'S SO MUCH GREEN-ERY...
I BET IT'S REALLY GORGEOUS HERE DURING THE DAY.
I WAS HOPING FOR SOMETHING MORE ELECTRICAL, LIKE THE HAPPIEST PLACE ON EARTH...
But then there'd be no view of the stars.
BUT YOU KNOW, JESUS, IF WE TOOK OUR TRASH...
...AND THREW IT ALL OUT THE WINDOW...
...MAYBE OUR SIX-TATAMI APARTMENT ONE DAY EXPANDS INTO AN EIGHT-MAT SIZE?
Wow, it's like a loft!
SAY, THAT DOES SOUND LIKE SOMETHING OUT OF A DREAM!!!
I'd have room for a desktop PC!!

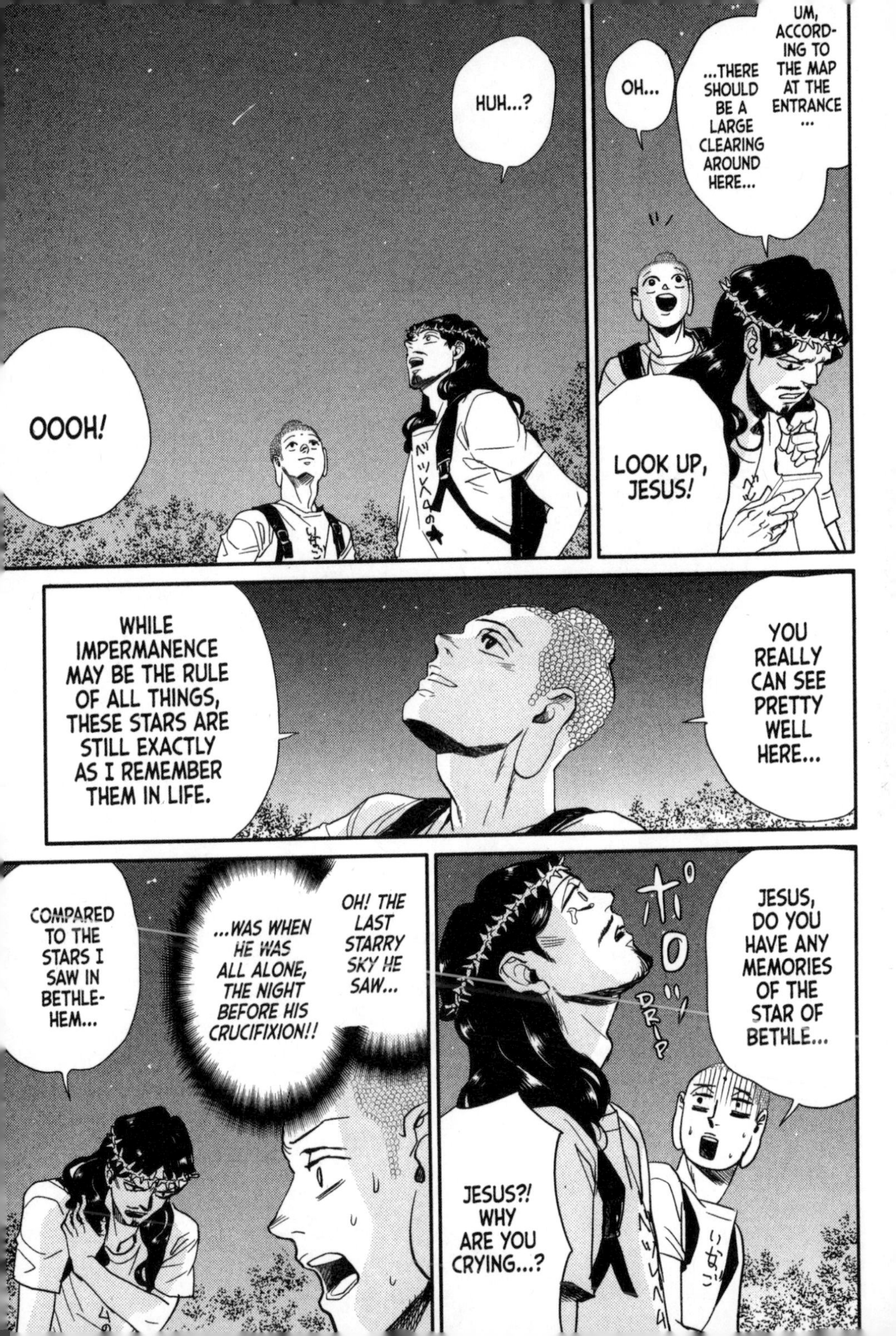
UM, ACCORDING TO THE MAP AT THE ENTRANCE...
...THERE SHOULD BE A LARGE CLEARING AROUND HERE...
OH...
LOOK UP, JESUS!
HUH...?
OOOH!
YOU REALLY CAN SEE PRETTY WELL HERE...
WHILE IMPERMANENCE MAY BE THE RULE OF ALL THINGS, THESE STARS ARE STILL EXACTLY AS I REMEMBER THEM IN LIFE.
JESUS, DO YOU HAVE ANY MEMORIES OF THE STAR OF BETHLE...
ポロ
DRIP
JESUS?! WHY ARE YOU CRYING...?
OH! THE LAST STARRY SKY HE SAW...
...WAS WHEN HE WAS ALL ALONE, THE NIGHT BEFORE HIS CRUCIFIXION!!
COMPARED TO THE STARS I SAW IN BETHLEHEM...

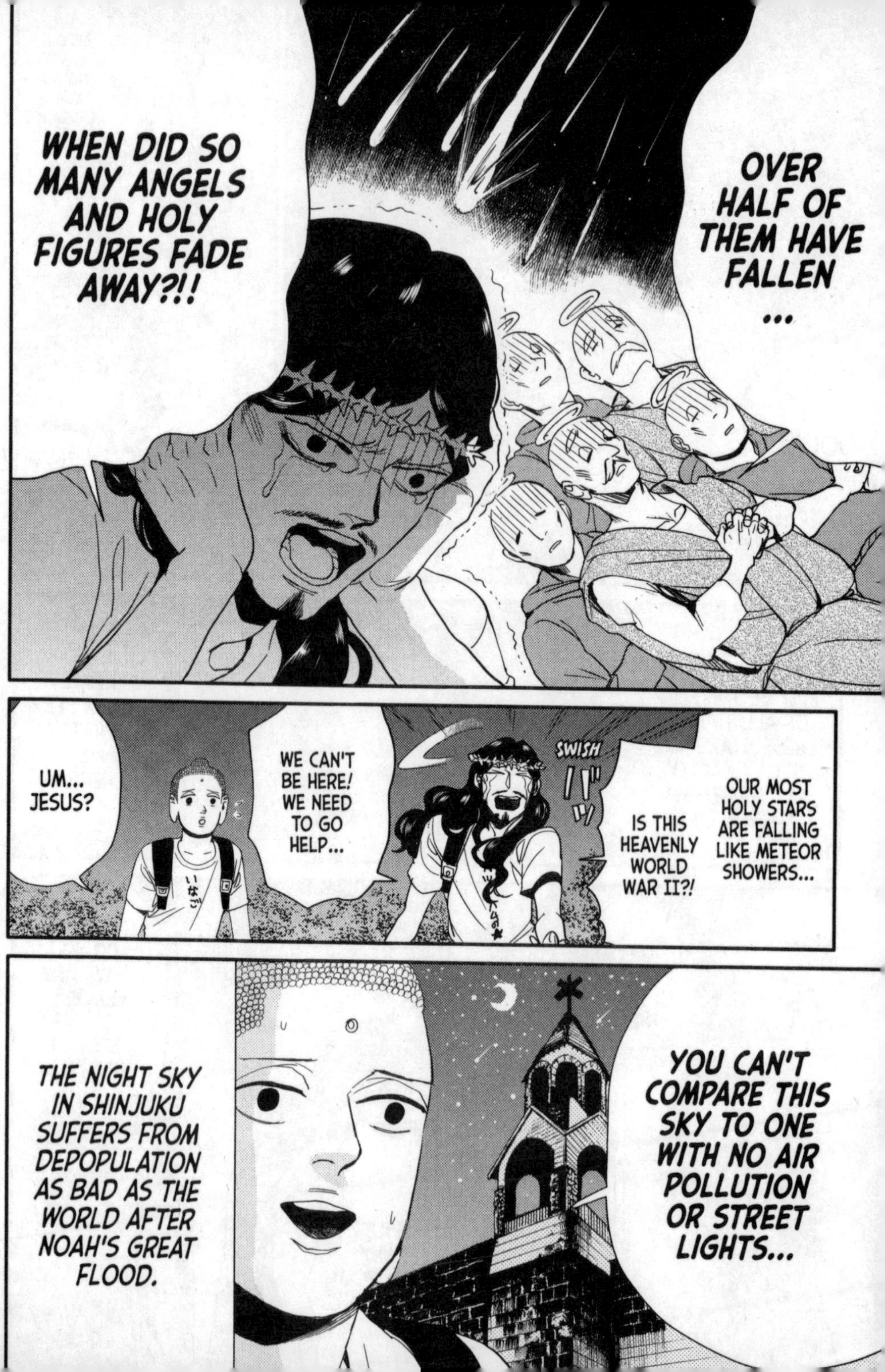
OVER HALF OF THEM HAVE FALLEN ...
WHEN DID SO MANY ANGELS AND HOLY FIGURES FADE AWAY?!!
OUR MOST HOLY STARS ARE FALLING LIKE METEOR SHOWERS...
IS THIS HEAVENLY WORLD WAR II?!
SWISH
WE CAN'T BE HERE! WE NEED TO GO HELP...
UM... JESUS?
YOU CAN'T COMPARE THIS SKY TO ONE WITH NO AIR POLLUTION OR STREET LIGHTS...
THE NIGHT SKY IN SHINJUKU SUFFERS FROM DEPOPULATION AS BAD AS THE WORLD AFTER NOAH'S GREAT FLOOD.

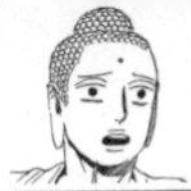

BUDDHA TRIES TO GET THROUGH THE RAINY SEASON WITH COOKING AND MEDITATION. BUT THE FOOD GOES BAD, SO HE CAN'T STOCKPILE IT, WHICH MAKES IT IMPOSSIBLE TO STAY FOCUSED.

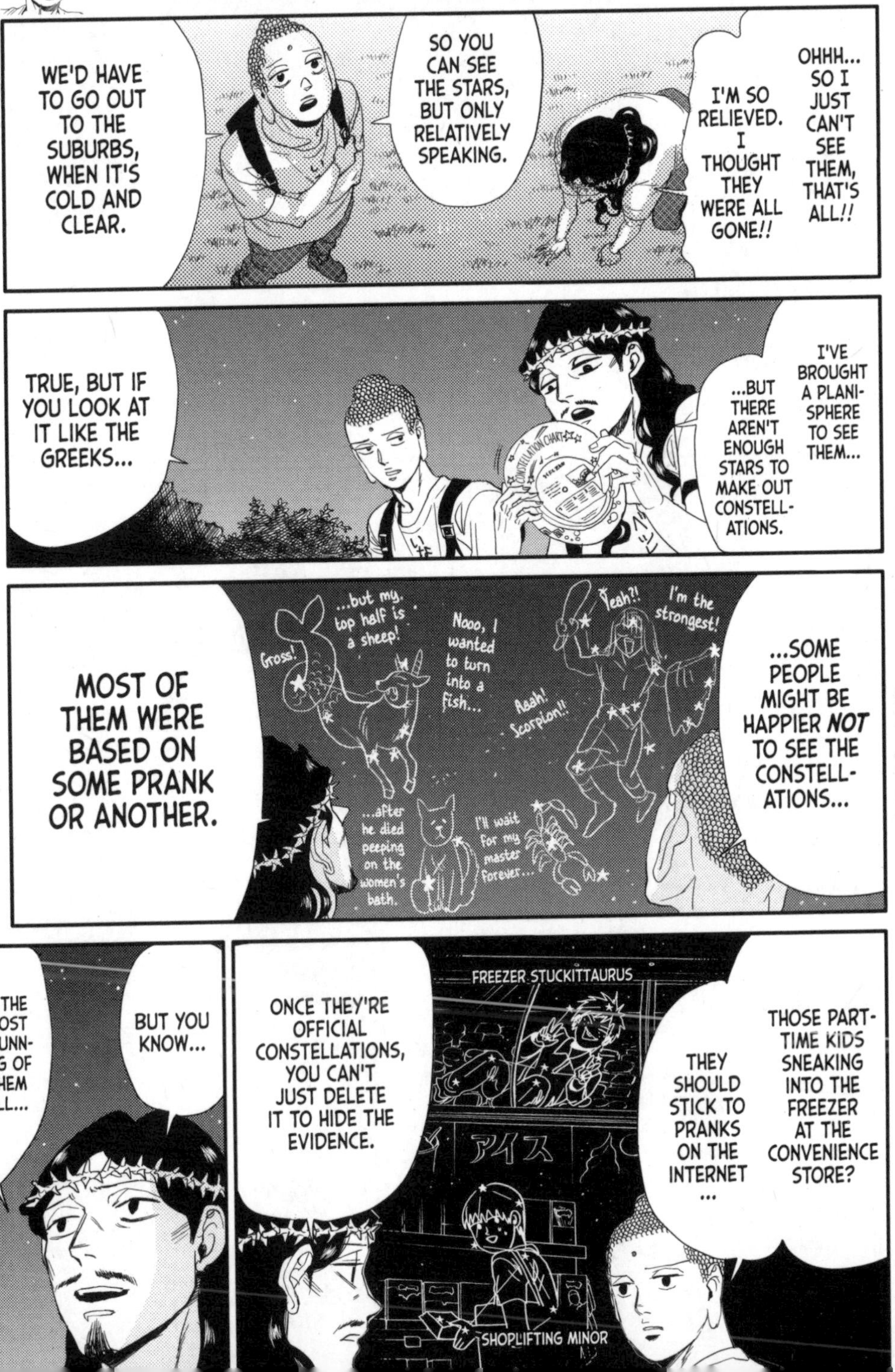
OHHH... SO I JUST CAN'T SEE THEM, THAT'S ALL!!
I'M SO RELIEVED. I THOUGHT THEY WERE ALL GONE!!
SO YOU CAN SEE THE STARS, BUT ONLY RELATIVELY SPEAKING.
WE'D HAVE TO GO OUT TO THE SUBURBS, WHEN IT'S COLD AND CLEAR.
I'VE BROUGHT A PLANISPHERE TO SEE THEM...
...BUT THERE AREN'T ENOUGH STARS TO MAKE OUT CONSTELLATIONS.
CONSTELLATION CHART
TRUE, BUT IF YOU LOOK AT IT LIKE THE GREEKS...
...SOME PEOPLE MIGHT BE HAPPIER *NOT* TO SEE THE CONSTELLATIONS...
I'm the strongest!
Yeah?!
Aaah! Scorpion!!
I'll wait for my master forever...
Nooo, I wanted to turn into a fish...
...but my top half is a sheep!
Gross!
...after he died peeping on the women's bath.
MOST OF THEM WERE BASED ON SOME PRANK OR ANOTHER.
THOSE PART-TIME KIDS SNEAKING INTO THE FREEZER AT THE CONVENIENCE STORE?
THEY SHOULD STICK TO PRANKS ON THE INTERNET...
FREEZER STUCKITTAURUS
ONCE THEY'RE OFFICIAL CONSTELLATIONS, YOU CAN'T JUST DELETE IT TO HIDE THE EVIDENCE.
アイス
SHOPLIFTING MINOR
BUT YOU KNOW...
...THE MOST STUNNING OF THEM ALL...

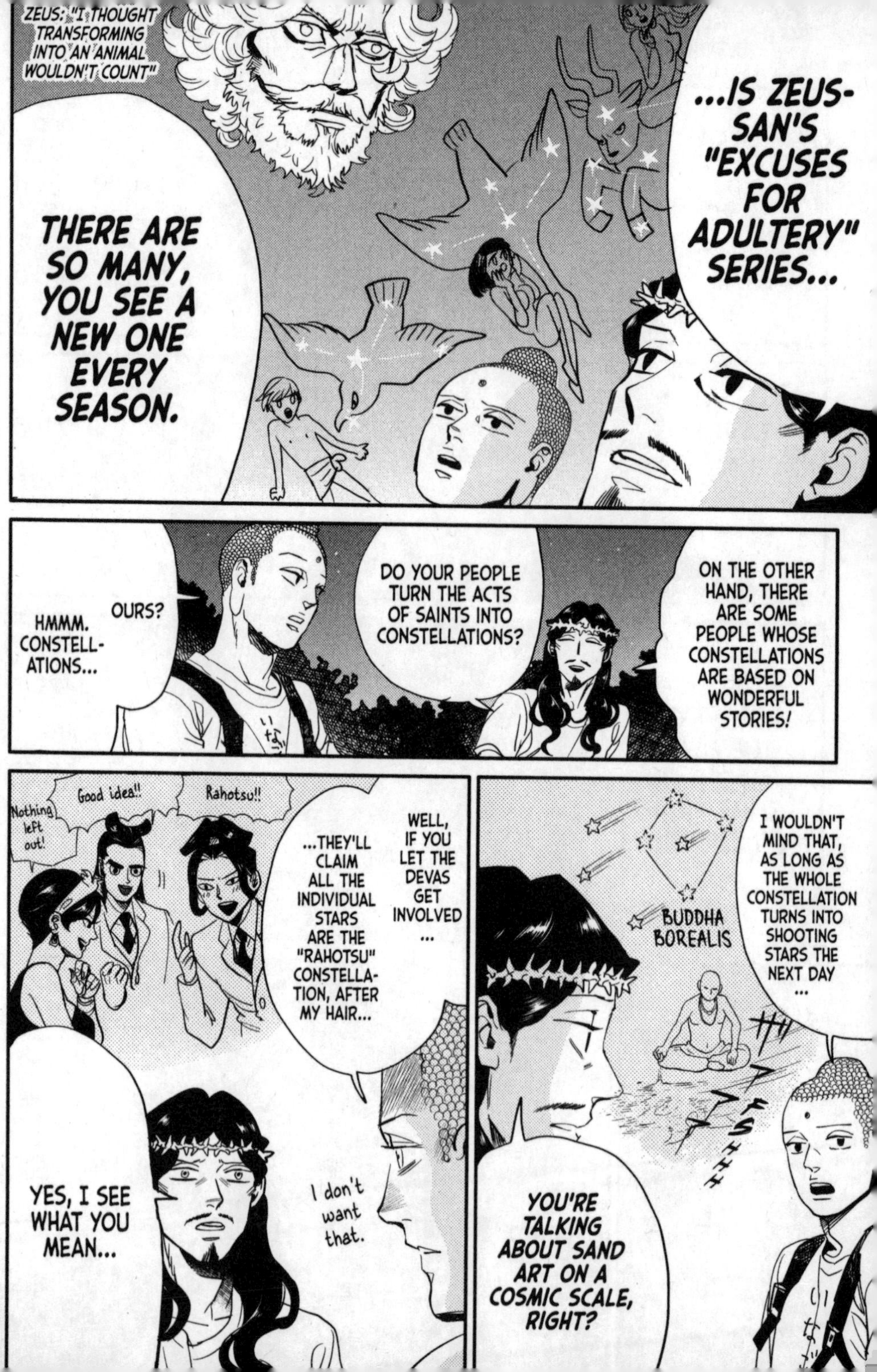

...IS ZEUS-SAN'S "EXCUSES FOR ADULTERY" SERIES...
ZEUS: "I THOUGHT TRANSFORMING INTO AN ANIMAL WOULDN'T COUNT"
THERE ARE SO MANY, YOU SEE A NEW ONE EVERY SEASON.
ON THE OTHER HAND, THERE ARE SOME PEOPLE WHOSE CONSTELLATIONS ARE BASED ON WONDERFUL STORIES!
DO YOUR PEOPLE TURN THE ACTS OF SAINTS INTO CONSTELLATIONS?
OURS?
HMMM. CONSTELL-ATIONS...
I WOULDN'T MIND THAT, AS LONG AS THE WHOLE CONSTELLATION TURNS INTO SHOOTING STARS THE NEXT DAY ...
BUDDHA BOREALIS
YOU'RE TALKING ABOUT SAND ART ON A COSMIC SCALE, RIGHT?
WELL, IF YOU LET THE DEVAS GET INVOLVED ...
...THEY'LL CLAIM ALL THE INDIVIDUAL STARS ARE THE "RAHOTSU" CONSTELLA-TION, AFTER MY HAIR...
Rahotsu!!
Good idea!!
Nothing left out!
I don't want that.
YES, I SEE WHAT YOU MEAN...

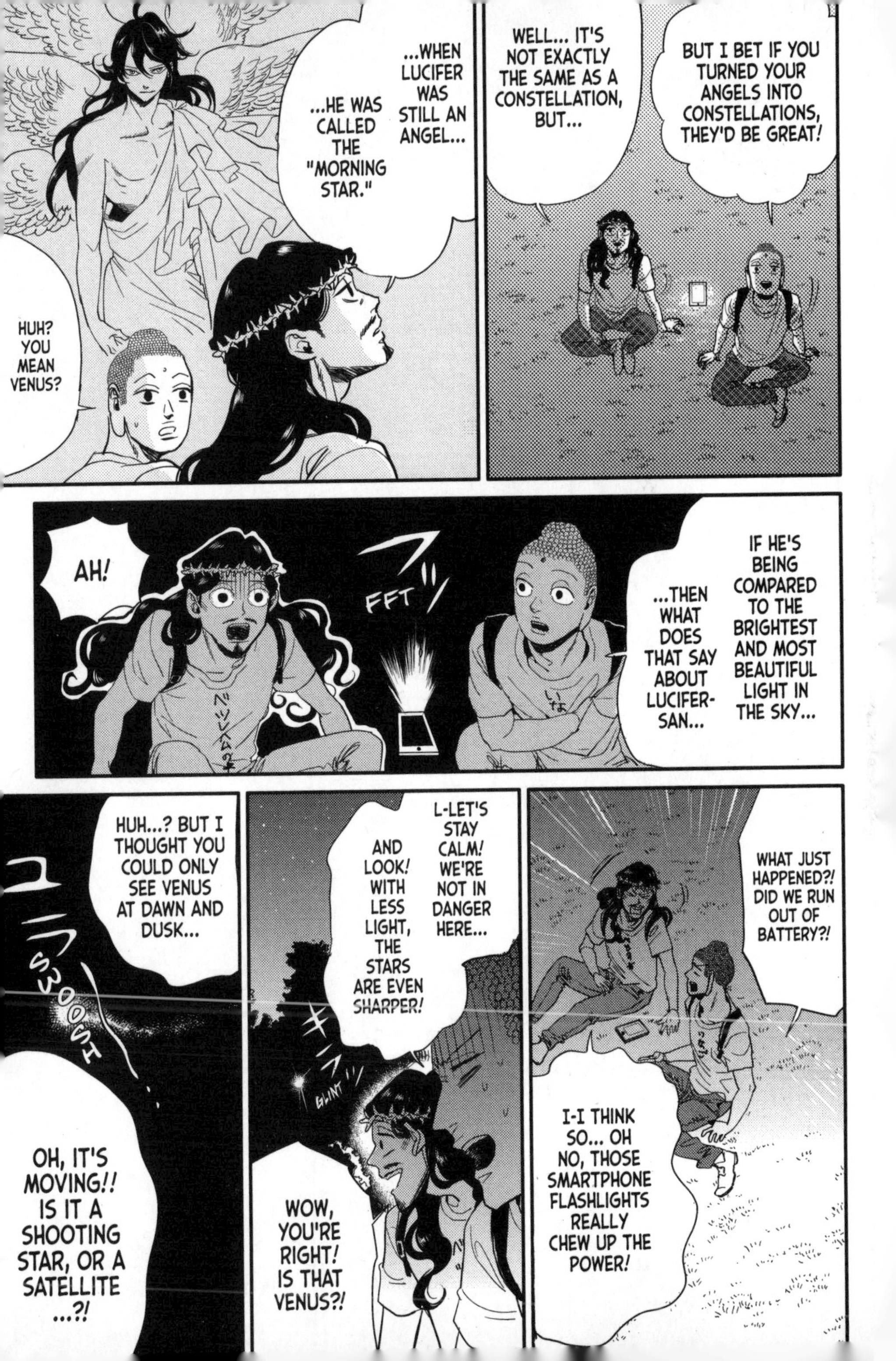
BUT I BET IF YOU TURNED YOUR ANGELS INTO CONSTELLATIONS, THEY'D BE GREAT!
WELL... IT'S NOT EXACTLY THE SAME AS A CONSTELLATION, BUT...
...WHEN LUCIFER WAS STILL AN ANGEL...
...HE WAS CALLED THE "MORNING STAR."
HUH? YOU MEAN VENUS?
IF HE'S BEING COMPARED TO THE BRIGHTEST AND MOST BEAUTIFUL LIGHT IN THE SKY...
...THEN WHAT DOES THAT SAY ABOUT LUCIFER-SAN...
FFT
AH!
WHAT JUST HAPPENED?! DID WE RUN OUT OF BATTERY?!
I-I THINK SO... OH NO, THOSE SMARTPHONE FLASHLIGHTS REALLY CHEW UP THE POWER!
L-LET'S STAY CALM! WE'RE NOT IN DANGER HERE...
AND LOOK! WITH LESS LIGHT, THE STARS ARE EVEN SHARPER!
GLINT
WOW, YOU'RE RIGHT! IS THAT VENUS?!
HUH...? BUT I THOUGHT YOU COULD ONLY SEE VENUS AT DAWN AND DUSK...
SWOOSH
OH, IT'S MOVING!! IS IT A SHOOTING STAR, OR A SATELLITE ...?!

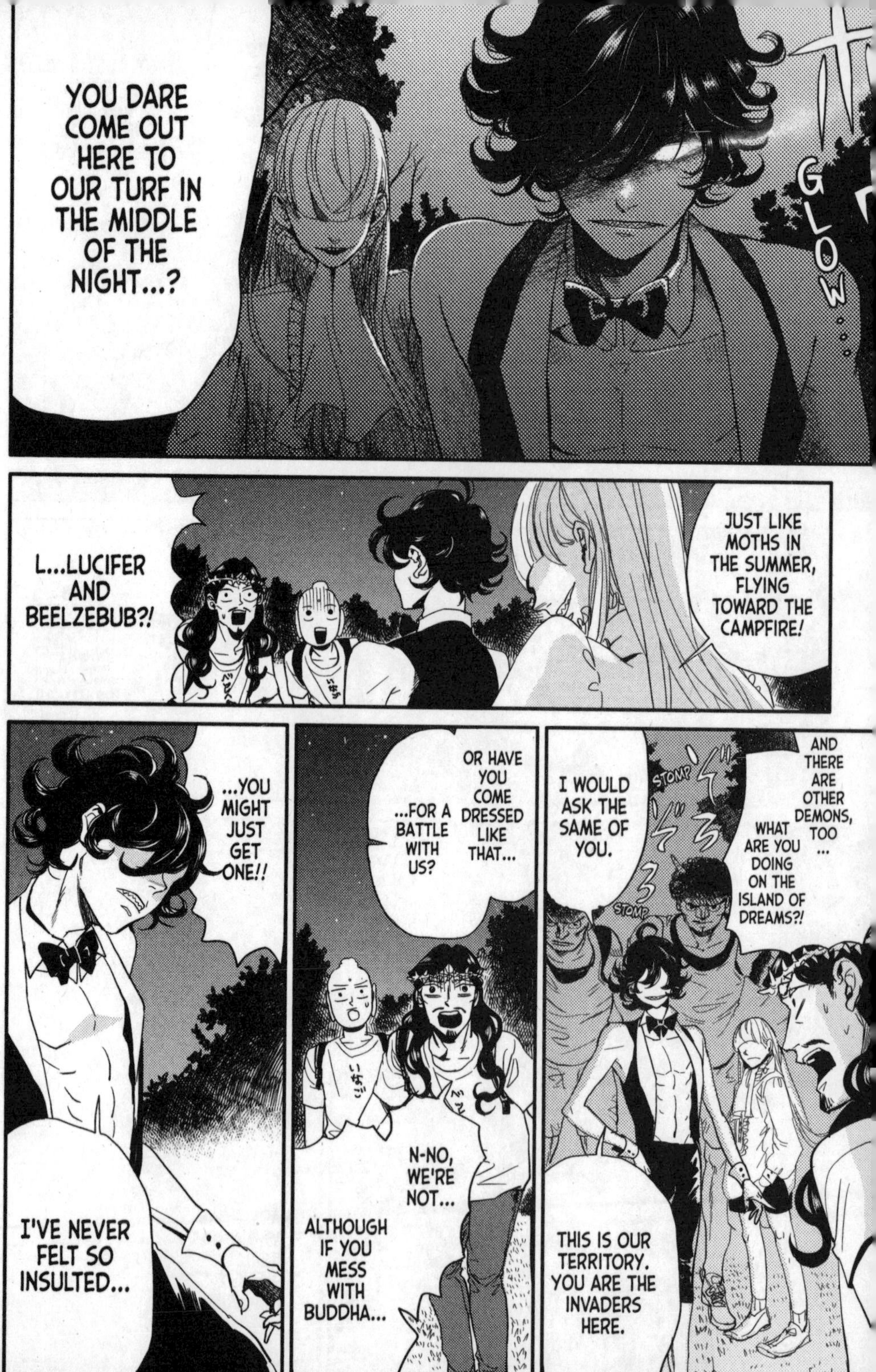
GLOW...
YOU DARE COME OUT HERE TO OUR TURF IN THE MIDDLE OF THE NIGHT...?
JUST LIKE MOTHS IN THE SUMMER, FLYING TOWARD THE CAMPFIRE!
L...LUCIFER AND BEELZEBUB?!
AND THERE ARE OTHER DEMONS, TOO...
WHAT ARE YOU DOING ON THE ISLAND OF DREAMS?!
STOMP
STOMP
I WOULD ASK THE SAME OF YOU.
THIS IS OUR TERRITORY. YOU ARE THE INVADERS HERE.
OR HAVE YOU COME DRESSED LIKE THAT...
...FOR A BATTLE WITH US?
N-NO, WE'RE NOT...
ALTHOUGH IF YOU MESS WITH BUDDHA...
...YOU MIGHT JUST GET ONE!!
I'VE NEVER FELT SO INSULTED...

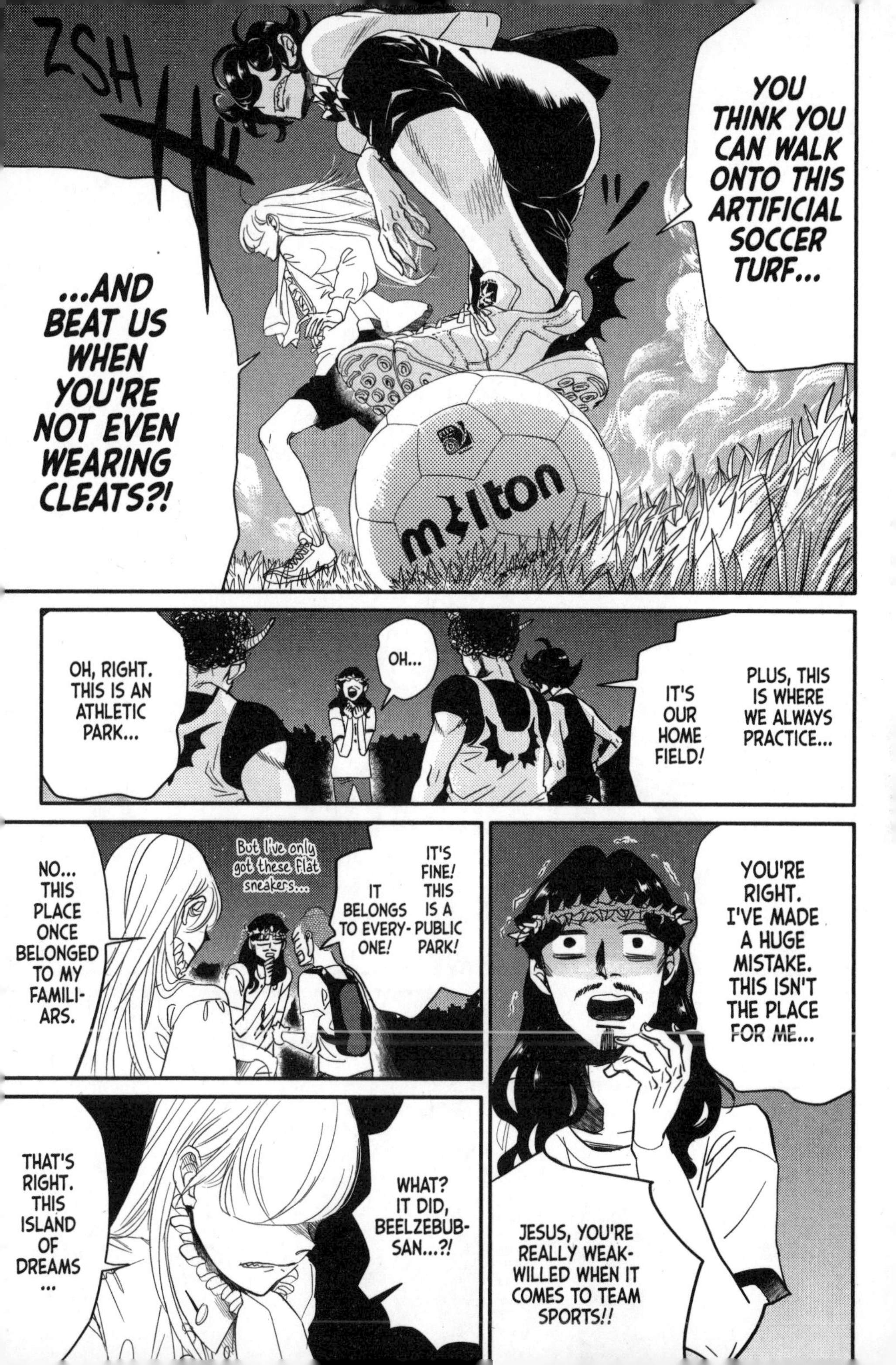
YOU THINK YOU CAN WALK ONTO THIS ARTIFICIAL SOCCER TURF...
...AND BEAT US WHEN YOU'RE NOT EVEN WEARING CLEATS?!
PLUS, THIS IS WHERE WE ALWAYS PRACTICE...
IT'S OUR HOME FIELD!
OH...
OH, RIGHT. THIS IS AN ATHLETIC PARK...
YOU'RE RIGHT. I'VE MADE A HUGE MISTAKE. THIS ISN'T THE PLACE FOR ME...
JESUS, YOU'RE REALLY WEAK-WILLED WHEN IT COMES TO TEAM SPORTS!!
IT'S FINE! THIS IS A PUBLIC PARK!
IT BELONGS TO EVERY-ONE!
But I've only got these flat sneakers...
NO... THIS PLACE ONCE BELONGED TO MY FAMILI-ARS.
WHAT? IT DID, BEELZEBUB-SAN...?!
THAT'S RIGHT. THIS ISLAND OF DREAMS ...

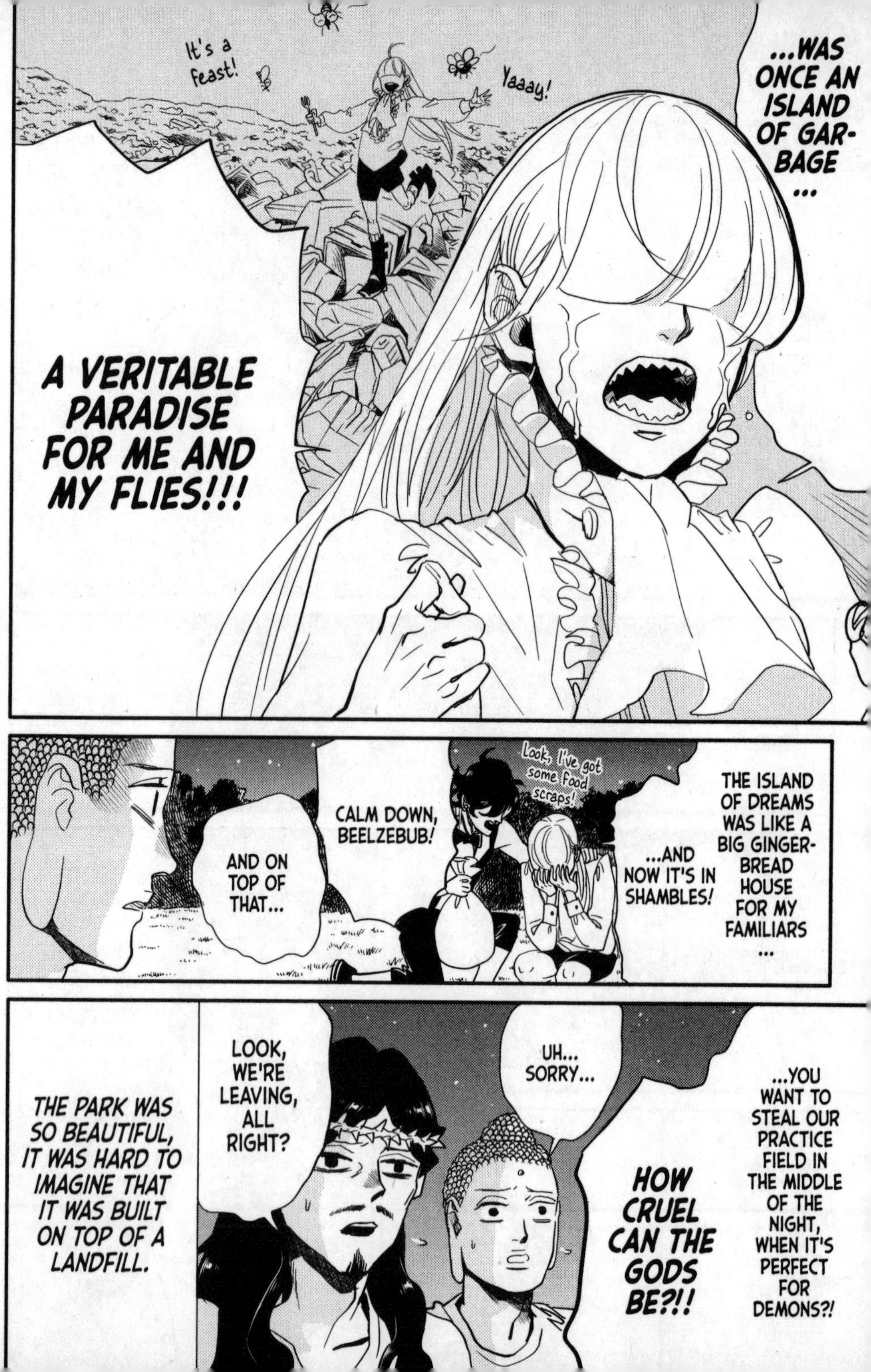
...WAS ONCE AN ISLAND OF GARBAGE...
Yaaay!
It's a feast!
A VERITABLE PARADISE FOR ME AND MY FLIES!!!
THE ISLAND OF DREAMS WAS LIKE A BIG GINGERBREAD HOUSE FOR MY FAMILIARS...
...AND NOW IT'S IN SHAMBLES!
Look, I've got some food scraps!
CALM DOWN, BEELZEBUB!
AND ON TOP OF THAT...
...YOU WANT TO STEAL OUR PRACTICE FIELD IN THE MIDDLE OF THE NIGHT, WHEN IT'S PERFECT FOR DEMONS?!
HOW CRUEL CAN THE GODS BE?!!
UH... SORRY...
LOOK, WE'RE LEAVING, ALL RIGHT?
THE PARK WAS SO BEAUTIFUL, IT WAS HARD TO IMAGINE THAT IT WAS BUILT ON TOP OF A LANDFILL.

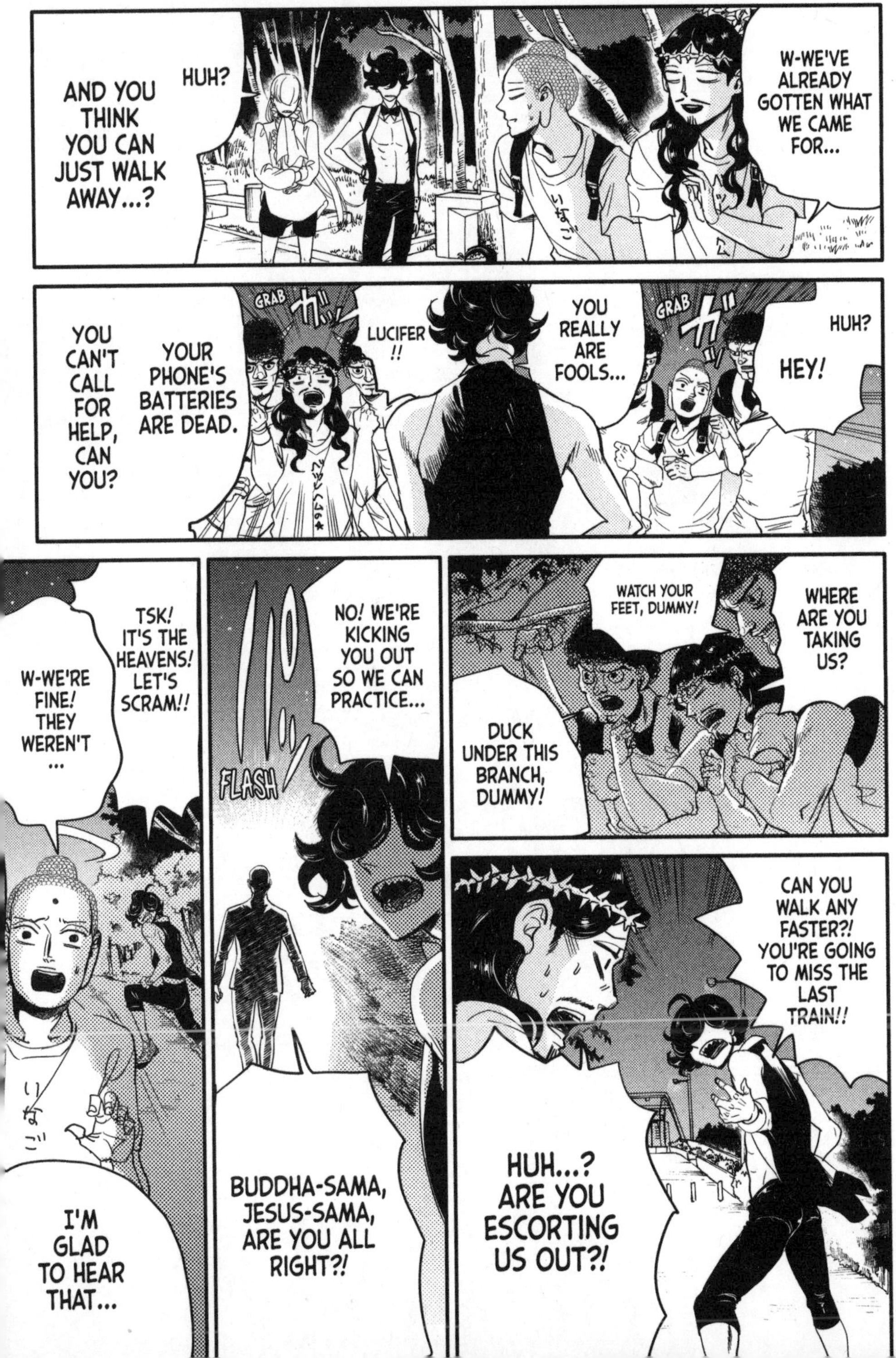
W-WE'VE ALREADY GOTTEN WHAT WE CAME FOR...
いなご
HUH?
AND YOU THINK YOU CAN JUST WALK AWAY...?
HUH?
HEY!
GRAB
YOU REALLY ARE FOOLS...
LUCIFER!!
GRAB
YOUR PHONE'S BATTERIES ARE DEAD.
YOU CAN'T CALL FOR HELP, CAN YOU?
WHERE ARE YOU TAKING US?
WATCH YOUR FEET, DUMMY!
DUCK UNDER THIS BRANCH, DUMMY!
CAN YOU WALK ANY FASTER?! YOU'RE GOING TO MISS THE LAST TRAIN!!
HUH...? ARE YOU ESCORTING US OUT?!
NO! WE'RE KICKING YOU OUT SO WE CAN PRACTICE...
FLASH
BUDDHA-SAMA, JESUS-SAMA, ARE YOU ALL RIGHT?!
TSK! IT'S THE HEAVENS! LET'S SCRAM!!
W-WE'RE FINE! THEY WEREN'T ...
いなご
I'M GLAD TO HEAR THAT...

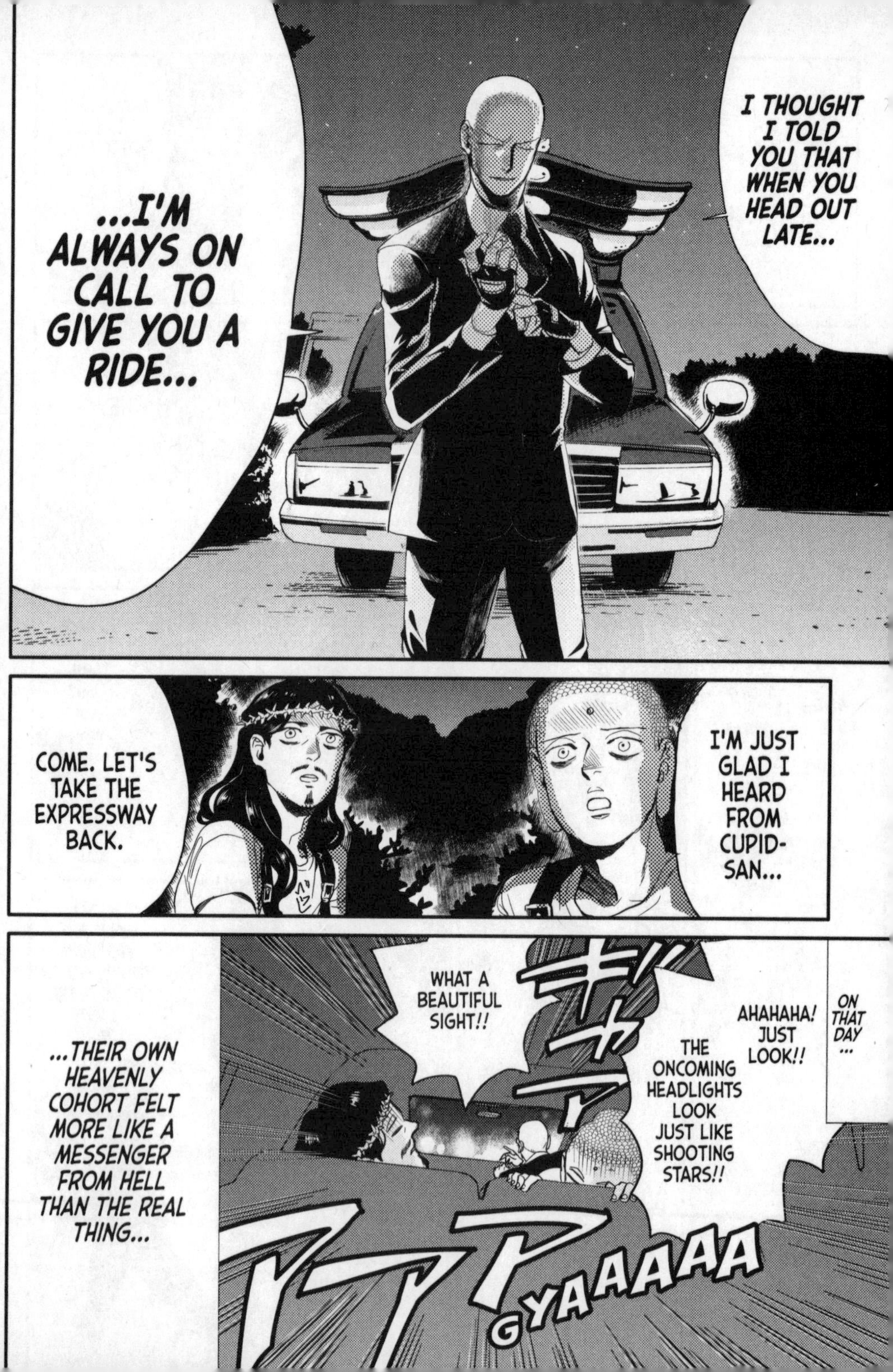
I THOUGHT I TOLD YOU THAT WHEN YOU HEAD OUT LATE...
...I'M ALWAYS ON CALL TO GIVE YOU A RIDE...
I'M JUST GLAD I HEARD FROM CUPID-SAN...
COME. LET'S TAKE THE EXPRESSWAY BACK.
ON THAT DAY...
AHAHAHA! JUST LOOK!!
THE ONCOMING HEADLIGHTS LOOK JUST LIKE SHOOTING STARS!!
WHAT A BEAUTIFUL SIGHT!!
GYAAAAAA
...THEIR OWN HEAVENLY COHORT FELT MORE LIKE A MESSENGER FROM HELL THAN THE REAL THING...

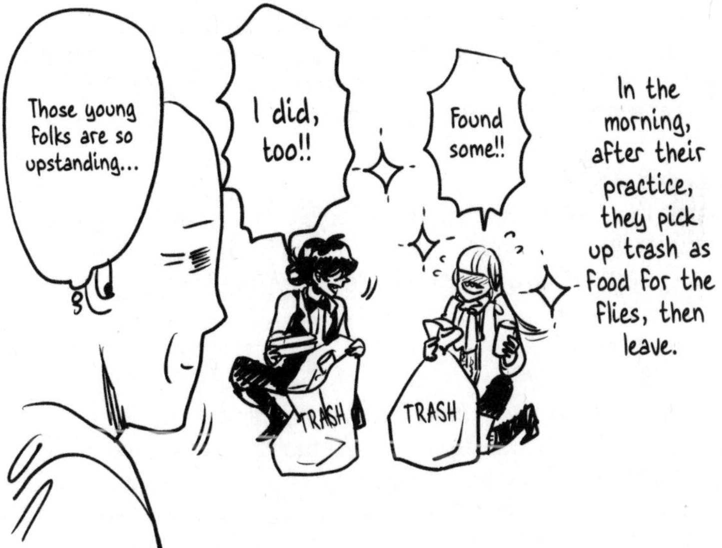
In the morning, after their practice, they pick up trash as food for the flies, then leave.
Found some!!
TRASH
I did, too!!
TRASH
Those young folks are so upstanding...

SAINT ☆ YOUNG MEN

CHAPTER 85 TRANSLATION NOTES

Star of Bethlehem, page 73
In the Gospel of Matthew, the Star of Bethlehem is a guiding star that led the three wise men from the east toward Jerusalem to be present for the birth of Jesus. It eventually guided them to Bethlehem, where the birth took place.

Locusts, page 75
In the manga series *Buddha* by Osamu Tezuka (a favorite of Buddha, the character) there is a memorable scene in the first volume depicting Siddhartha's youth that features a major swarm of locusts.

Island of Dreams, page 77
This area, known in Japanese as Yumenoshima, is an actual landfill island in Tokyo Bay. There is park space, a sports stadium, a botanical garden, and other attractions. Before it was postponed, the Tokyo Olympics were to hold their archery events here.

Tatami mats, page 78
In Japan, room size in apartments and homes is measured by tatami mats, which are typically around 0.9 meters by 1.75 meters in the Tokyo area, although elsewhere the standard size might be slightly larger.

Lucifer, page 83
The Latin name Lucifer, meaning "Light-Bringer," is traditionally associated with the planet Venus. Because Venus appears and disappears in the night sky, the name Lucifer was associated with Satan, the angel who fell from Heaven, although in the Bible it is generally agreed the original Hebrew refers to the morning star.

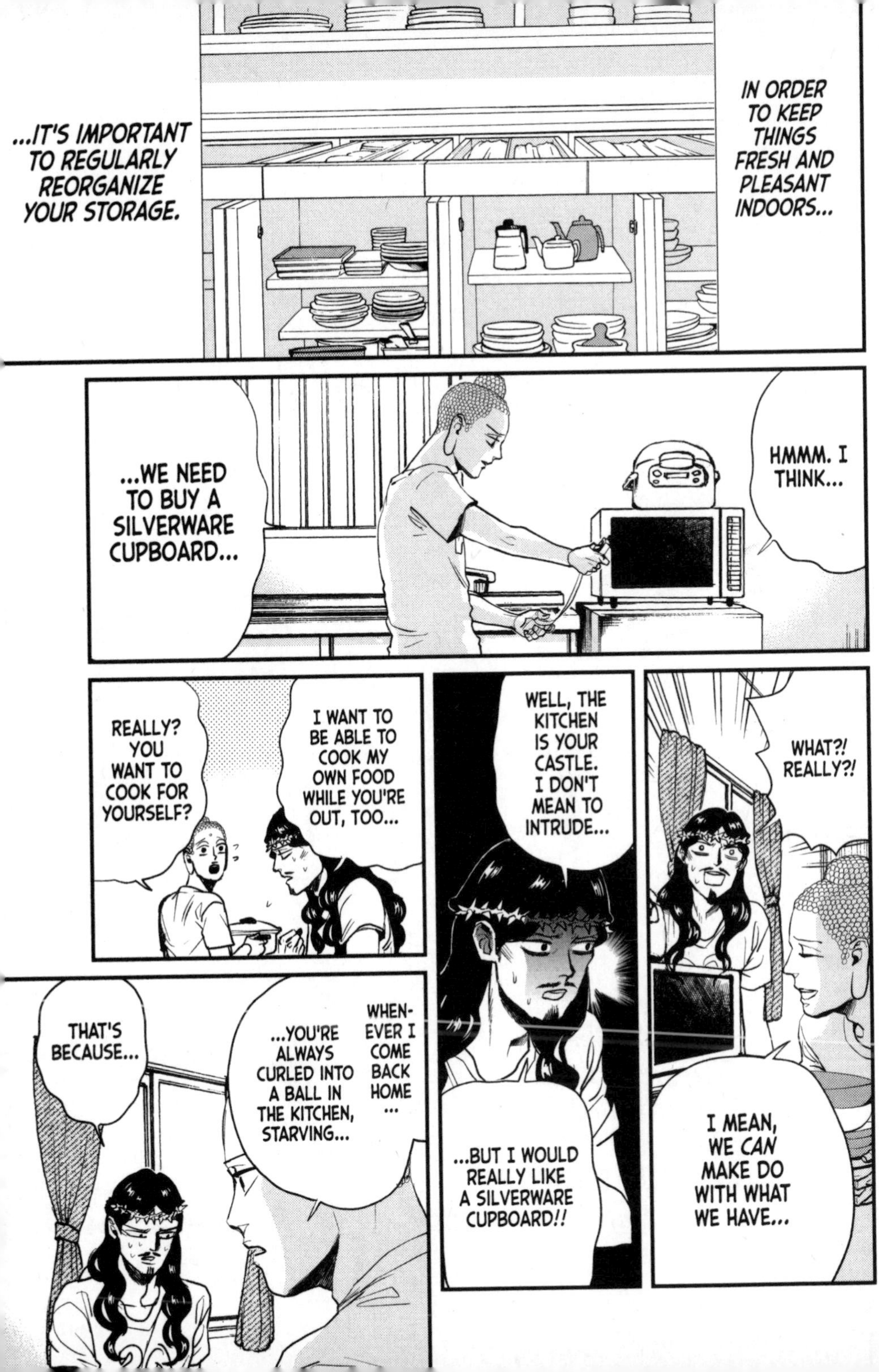
IN ORDER TO KEEP THINGS FRESH AND PLEASANT INDOORS...
...IT'S IMPORTANT TO REGULARLY REORGANIZE YOUR STORAGE.
HMMM. I THINK...
...WE NEED TO BUY A SILVERWARE CUPBOARD...
WHAT?! REALLY?!
I MEAN, WE CAN MAKE DO WITH WHAT WE HAVE...
WELL, THE KITCHEN IS YOUR CASTLE. I DON'T MEAN TO INTRUDE...
...BUT I WOULD REALLY LIKE A SILVERWARE CUPBOARD!!
I WANT TO BE ABLE TO COOK MY OWN FOOD WHILE YOU'RE OUT, TOO...
REALLY? YOU WANT TO COOK FOR YOURSELF?
WHENEVER I COME BACK HOME...
...YOU'RE ALWAYS CURLED INTO A BALL IN THE KITCHEN, STARVING...
THAT'S BECAUSE...

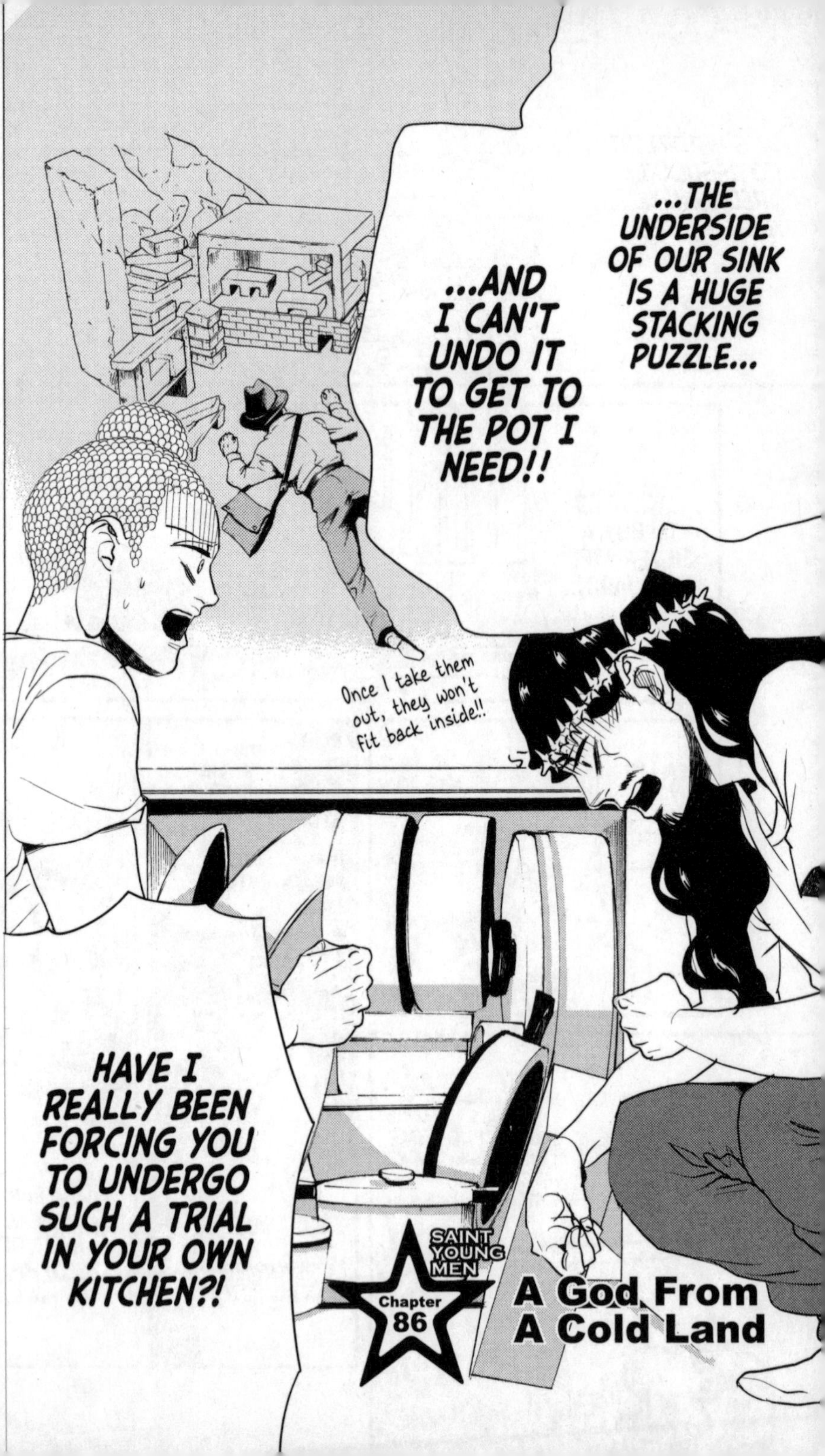
...THE UNDERSIDE OF OUR SINK IS A HUGE STACKING PUZZLE...
...AND I CAN'T UNDO IT TO GET TO THE POT I NEED!!
Once I take them out, they won't fit back inside!!
HAVE I REALLY BEEN FORCING YOU TO UNDERGO SUCH A TRIAL IN YOUR OWN KITCHEN?!
SUDDENLY, INDIANA JONES DOESN'T SEEM SO OUT-LANDISH.
SAINT YOUNG MEN
Chapter 86
A God From A Cold Land

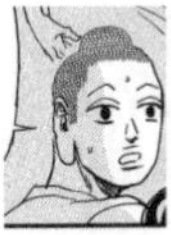

BUDDHA
THE AREA AROUND TACHIKAWA STATION IS GETTING REALLY DEVELOPED, WHICH MADE ME WONDER IF THE DEVAS OR ANGELS HAVE A HAND IN THAT. BUT WHEN I SEE HOW TIME IS FROZEN AROUND MATSUDA HEIGHTS, I REALIZE I'M JUST IMAGINING THINGS.

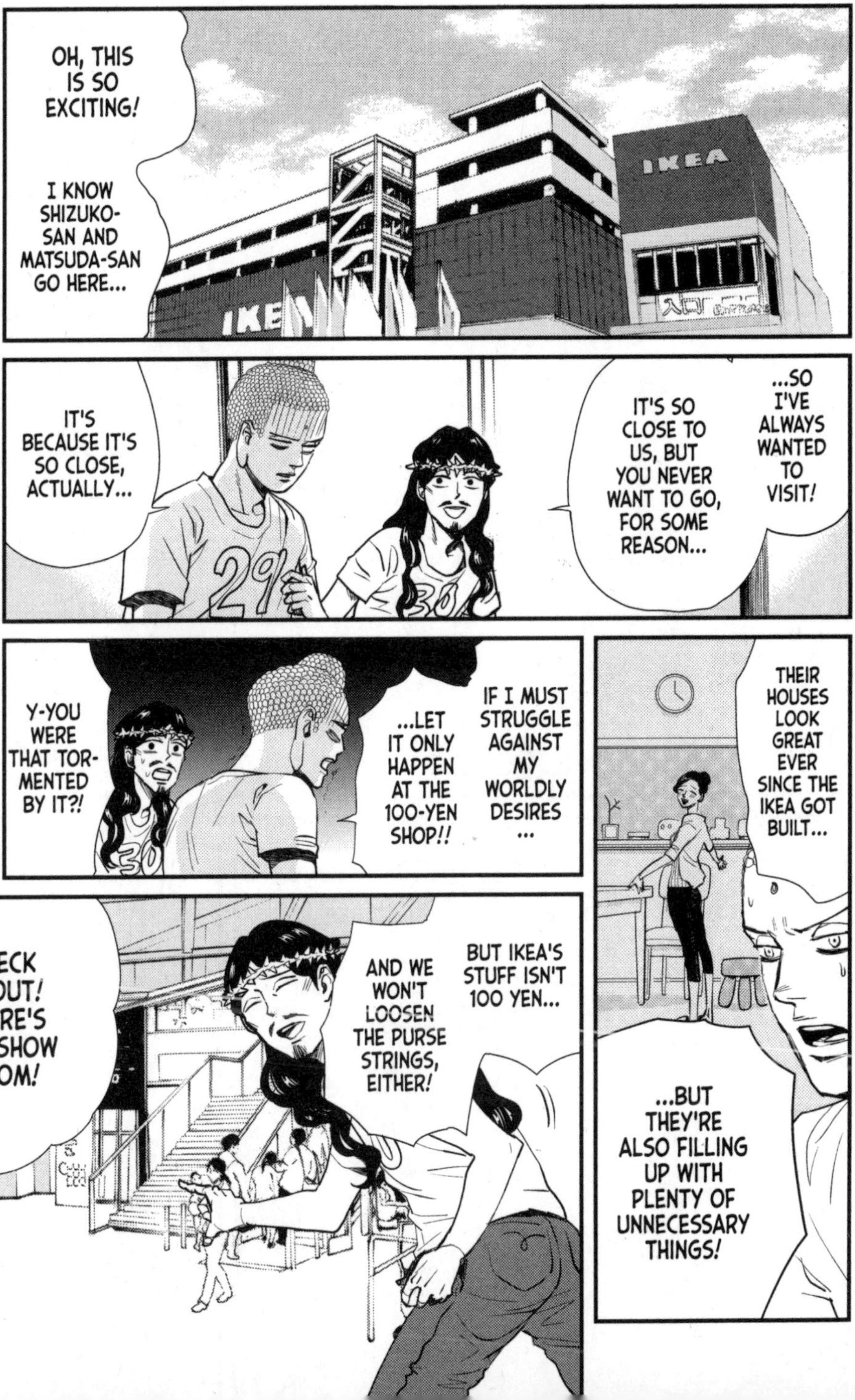
IKEA
OH, THIS IS SO EXCITING!
I KNOW SHIZUKO-SAN AND MATSUDA-SAN GO HERE...
...SO I'VE ALWAYS WANTED TO VISIT!
IT'S SO CLOSE TO US, BUT YOU NEVER WANT TO GO, FOR SOME REASON...
IT'S BECAUSE IT'S SO CLOSE, ACTUALLY...
THEIR HOUSES LOOK GREAT EVER SINCE THE IKEA GOT BUILT...
...BUT THEY'RE ALSO FILLING UP WITH PLENTY OF UNNECESSARY THINGS!
IF I MUST STRUGGLE AGAINST MY WORLDLY DESIRES...
...LET IT ONLY HAPPEN AT THE 100-YEN SHOP!!
Y-YOU WERE THAT TOR-MENTED BY IT?!
BUT IKEA'S STUFF ISN'T 100 YEN...
AND WE WON'T LOOSEN THE PURSE STRINGS, EITHER!
CHECK IT OUT! THERE'S THE SHOW ROOM!

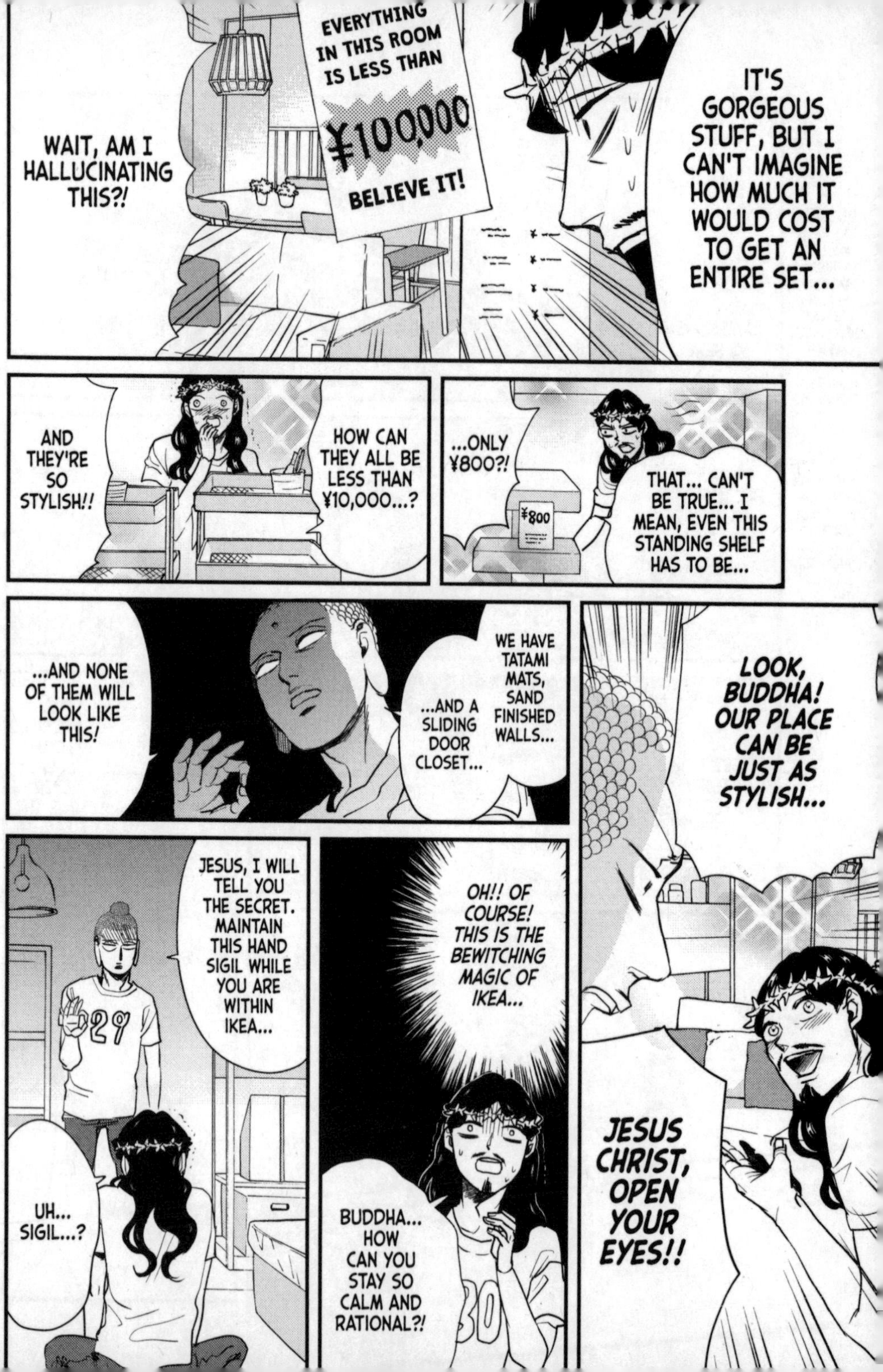
EVERYTHING IN THIS ROOM IS LESS THAN ¥100,000 BELIEVE IT!
IT'S GORGEOUS STUFF, BUT I CAN'T IMAGINE HOW MUCH IT WOULD COST TO GET AN ENTIRE SET...
WAIT, AM I HALLUCINATING THIS?!
THAT... CAN'T BE TRUE... I MEAN, EVEN THIS STANDING SHELF HAS TO BE...
¥800
...ONLY ¥800?!
HOW CAN THEY ALL BE LESS THAN ¥10,000...?
AND THEY'RE SO STYLISH!!
LOOK, BUDDHA! OUR PLACE CAN BE JUST AS STYLISH...
JESUS CHRIST, OPEN YOUR EYES!!
WE HAVE TATAMI MATS, SAND FINISHED WALLS...
...AND A SLIDING DOOR CLOSET...
...AND NONE OF THEM WILL LOOK LIKE THIS!
OH!! OF COURSE! THIS IS THE BEWITCHING MAGIC OF IKEA...
BUDDHA... HOW CAN YOU STAY SO CALM AND RATIONAL?!
JESUS, I WILL TELL YOU THE SECRET. MAINTAIN THIS HAND SIGIL WHILE YOU ARE WITHIN IKEA...
UH... SIGIL...?

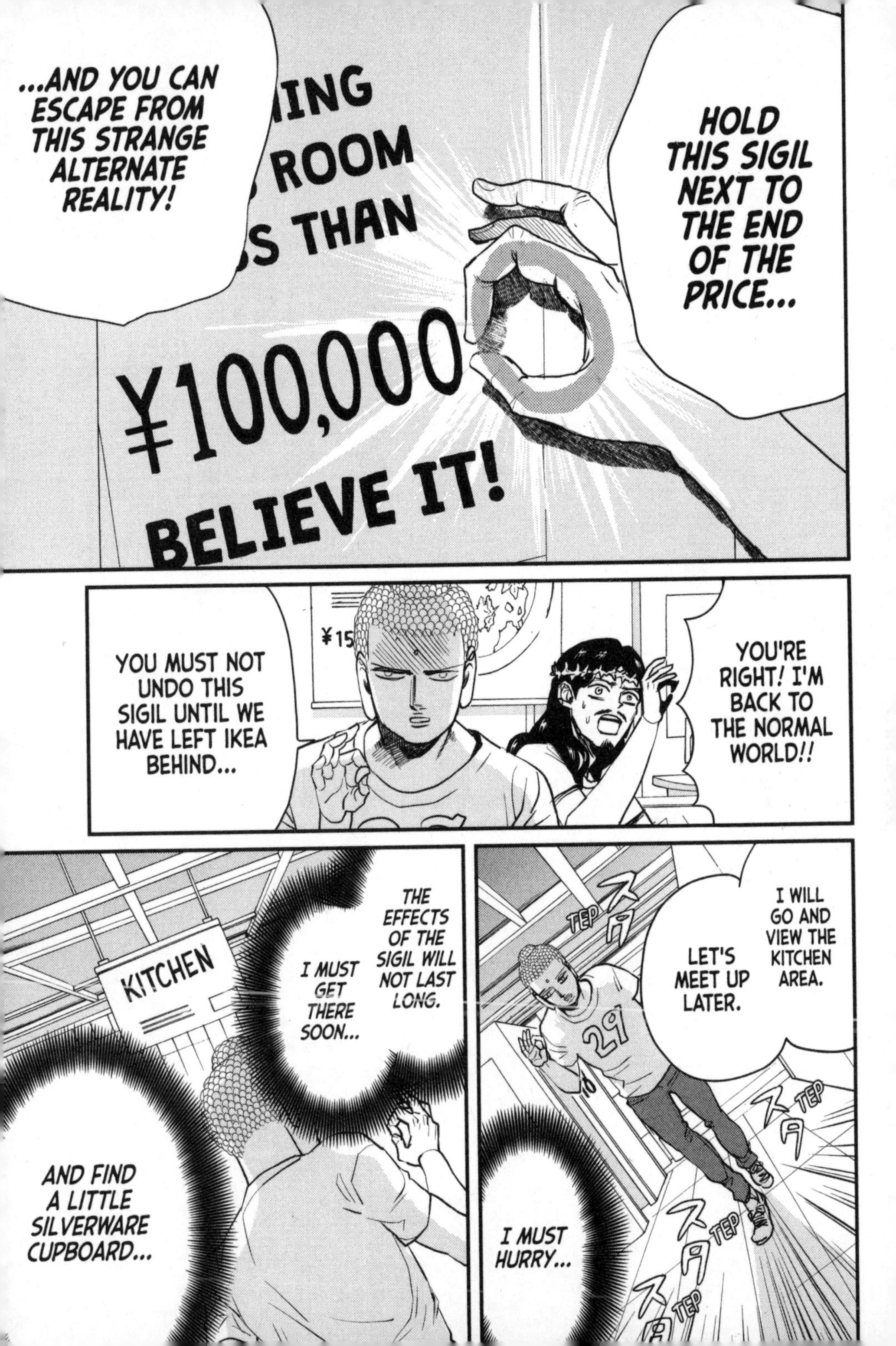
HOLD THIS SIGIL NEXT TO THE END OF THE PRICE...
...AND YOU CAN ESCAPE FROM THIS STRANGE ALTERNATE REALITY!
ROOM
¥100,000
BELIEVE IT!
YOU'RE RIGHT! I'M BACK TO THE NORMAL WORLD!!
YOU MUST NOT UNDO THIS SIGIL UNTIL WE HAVE LEFT IKEA BEHIND...
I WILL GO AND VIEW THE KITCHEN AREA.
LET'S MEET UP LATER.
TEP
29
TEP
TEP
TEP
I MUST HURRY...
THE EFFECTS OF THE SIGIL WILL NOT LAST LONG.
I MUST GET THERE SOON...
KITCHEN
AND FIND A LITTLE SILVERWARE CUPBOARD...

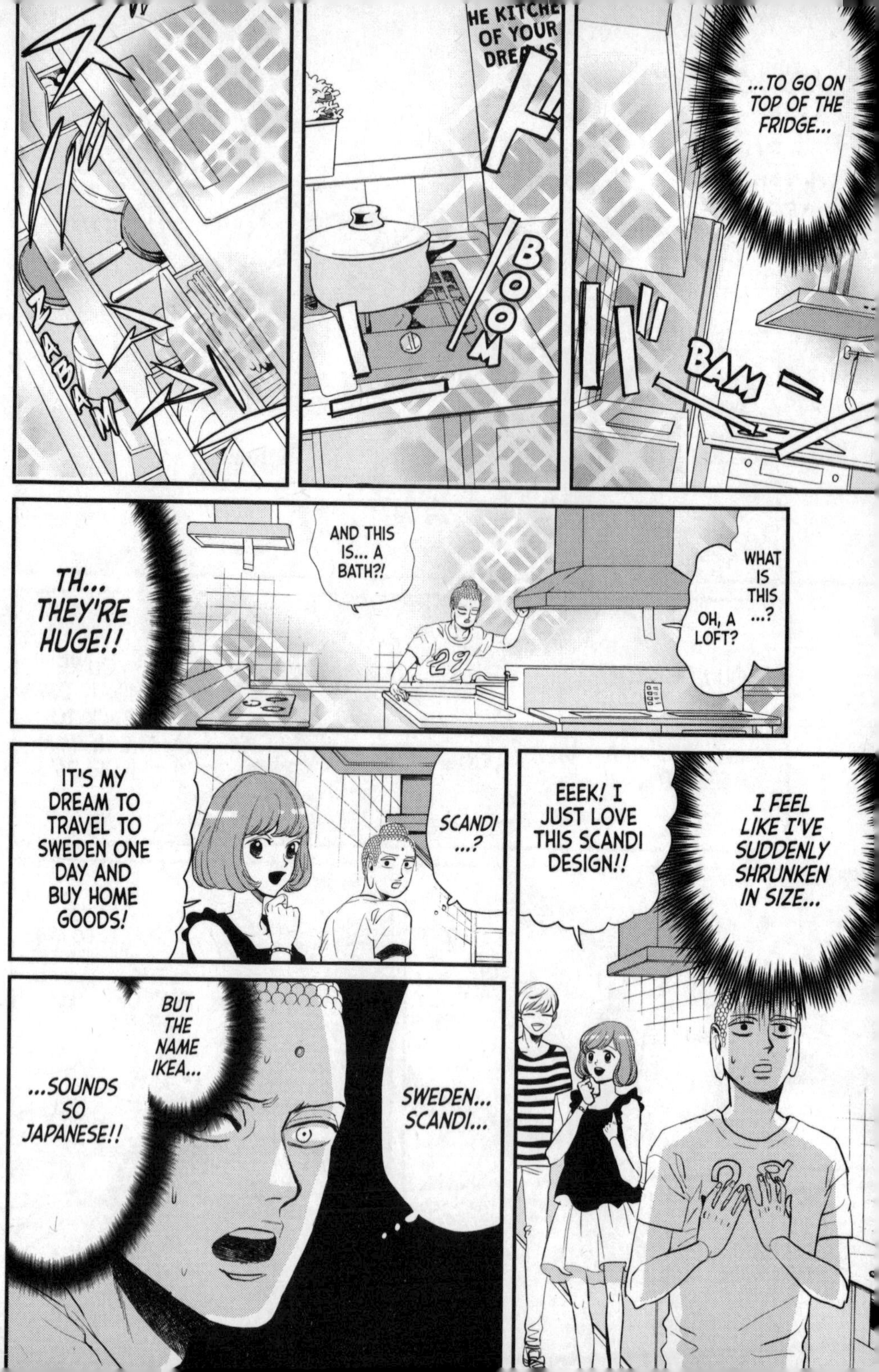
...TO GO ON TOP OF THE FRIDGE...
BAM
OF YOUR
BOOM
WHAT IS THIS ...?
OH, A LOFT?
AND THIS IS... A BATH?!
TH... THEY'RE HUGE!!
I FEEL LIKE I'VE SUDDENLY SHRUNKEN IN SIZE...
EEEK! I JUST LOVE THIS SCANDI DESIGN!!
SCANDI ...?
IT'S MY DREAM TO TRAVEL TO SWEDEN ONE DAY AND BUY HOME GOODS!
SWEDEN... SCANDI...
BUT THE NAME IKEA...
...SOUNDS SO JAPANESE!!

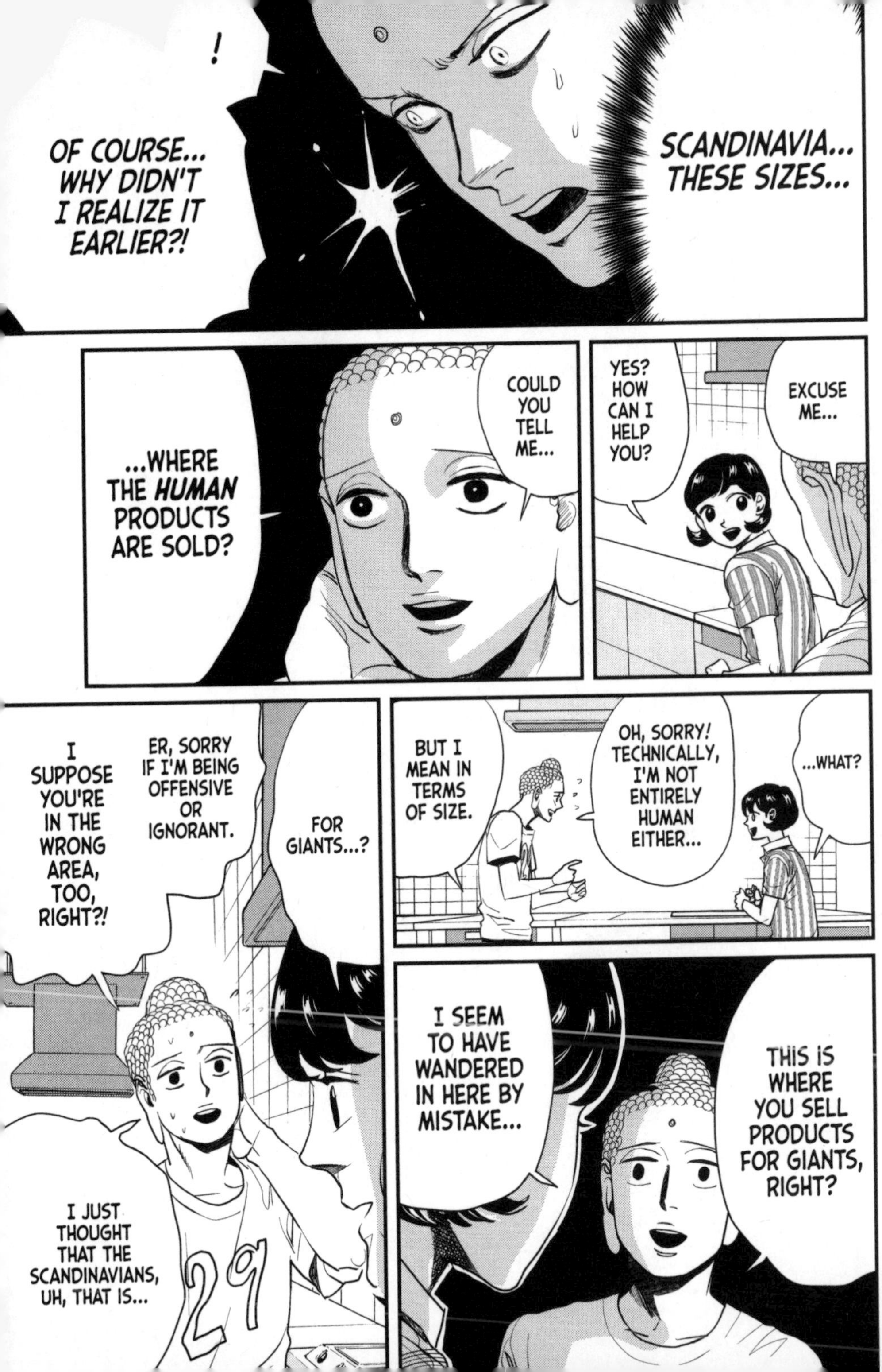
!
SCANDINAVIA... THESE SIZES...
OF COURSE... WHY DIDN'T I REALIZE IT EARLIER?!
EXCUSE ME...
YES? HOW CAN I HELP YOU?
COULD YOU TELL ME...
...WHERE THE *HUMAN* PRODUCTS ARE SOLD?
...WHAT?
OH, SORRY! TECHNICALLY, I'M NOT ENTIRELY HUMAN EITHER...
BUT I MEAN IN TERMS OF SIZE.
THIS IS WHERE YOU SELL PRODUCTS FOR GIANTS, RIGHT?
I SEEM TO HAVE WANDERED IN HERE BY MISTAKE...
FOR GIANTS...?
ER, SORRY IF I'M BEING OFFENSIVE OR IGNORANT.
I SUPPOSE YOU'RE IN THE WRONG AREA, TOO, RIGHT?!
I JUST THOUGHT THAT THE SCANDINAVIANS, UH, THAT IS...

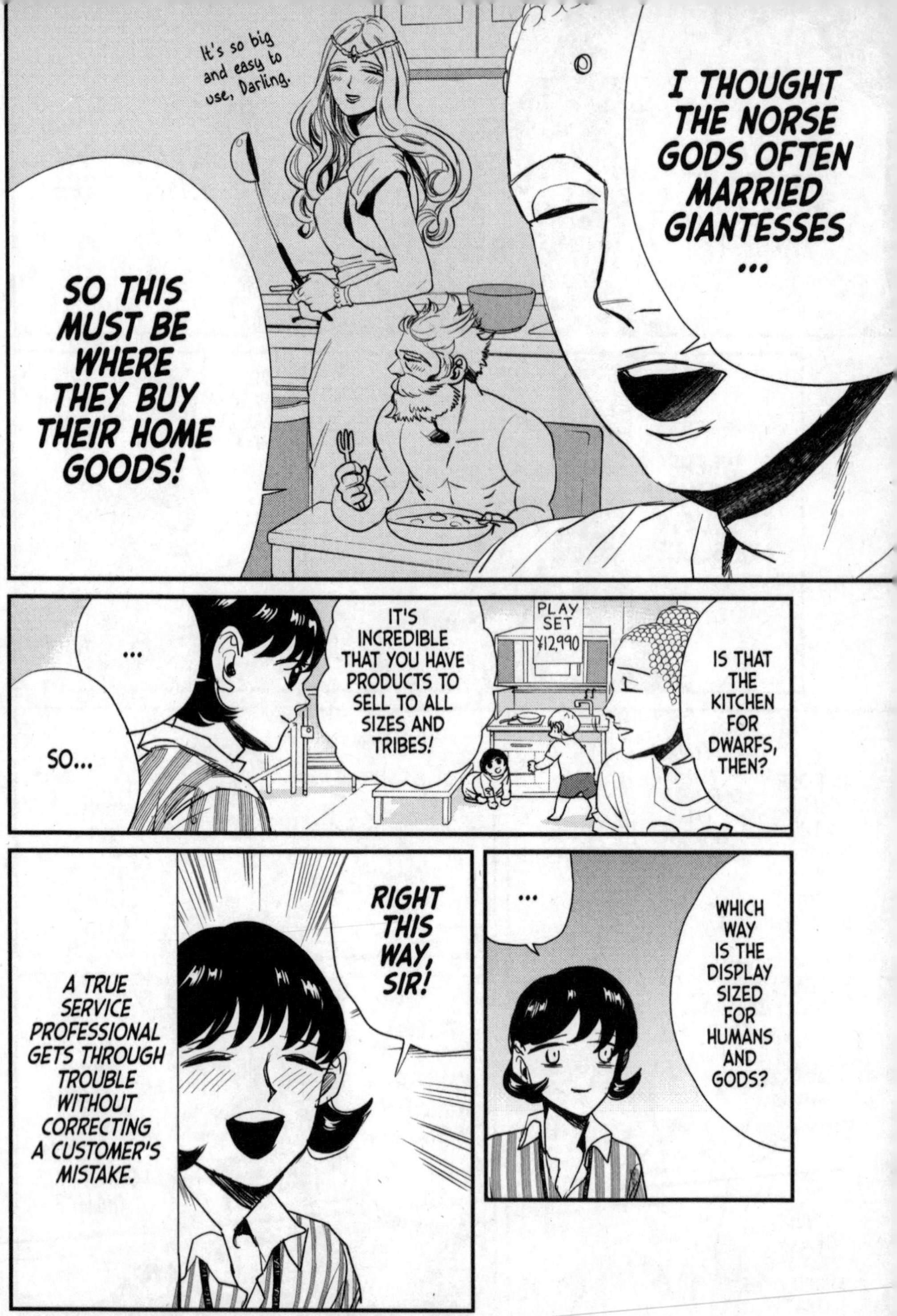
I THOUGHT THE NORSE GODS OFTEN MARRIED GIANTESSES ...
It's so big and easy to use, Darling.
SO THIS MUST BE WHERE THEY BUY THEIR HOME GOODS!
IS THAT THE KITCHEN FOR DWARFS, THEN?
PLAY SET ¥12,990
IT'S INCREDIBLE THAT YOU HAVE PRODUCTS TO SELL TO ALL SIZES AND TRIBES!
...
SO...
WHICH WAY IS THE DISPLAY SIZED FOR HUMANS AND GODS?
...
RIGHT THIS WAY, SIR!
A TRUE SERVICE PROFESSIONAL GETS THROUGH TROUBLE WITHOUT CORRECTING A CUSTOMER'S MISTAKE.

JESUS
I WAS WALKING A NICE PATH UNDER THE MONORAIL WHEN I SAW A THEATER ADVERTISING "DELUXE EXPLOSIVE SOUND." I WAS REALLY CURIOUS, BUT IT TURNED OUT TO BE *MAD MAX: FURY ROAD*. I WAS TOO WORRIED ABOUT WHAT PEOPLE MIGHT THINK OF ME.

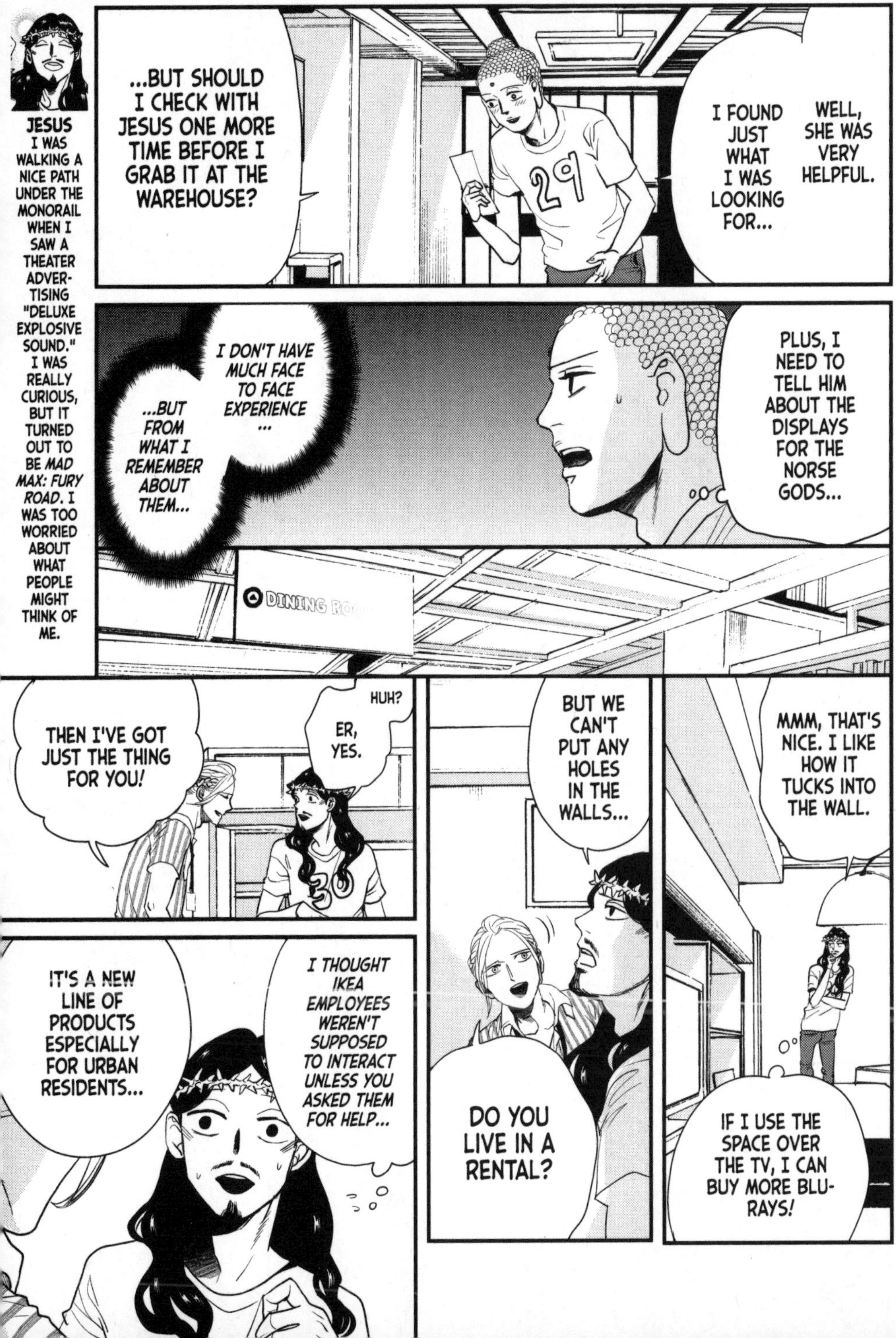
WELL, SHE WAS VERY HELPFUL.
I FOUND JUST WHAT I WAS LOOKING FOR...
...BUT SHOULD I CHECK WITH JESUS ONE MORE TIME BEFORE I GRAB IT AT THE WAREHOUSE?
PLUS, I NEED TO TELL HIM ABOUT THE DISPLAYS FOR THE NORSE GODS...
I DON'T HAVE MUCH FACE TO FACE EXPERIENCE...
...BUT FROM WHAT I REMEMBER ABOUT THEM...
DINING RO
MMM, THAT'S NICE. I LIKE HOW IT TUCKS INTO THE WALL.
IF I USE THE SPACE OVER THE TV, I CAN BUY MORE BLU-RAYS!
BUT WE CAN'T PUT ANY HOLES IN THE WALLS...
DO YOU LIVE IN A RENTAL?
HUH?
ER, YES.
THEN I'VE GOT JUST THE THING FOR YOU!
I THOUGHT IKEA EMPLOYEES WEREN'T SUPPOSED TO INTERACT UNLESS YOU ASKED THEM FOR HELP...
IT'S A NEW LINE OF PRODUCTS ESPECIALLY FOR URBAN RESIDENTS...

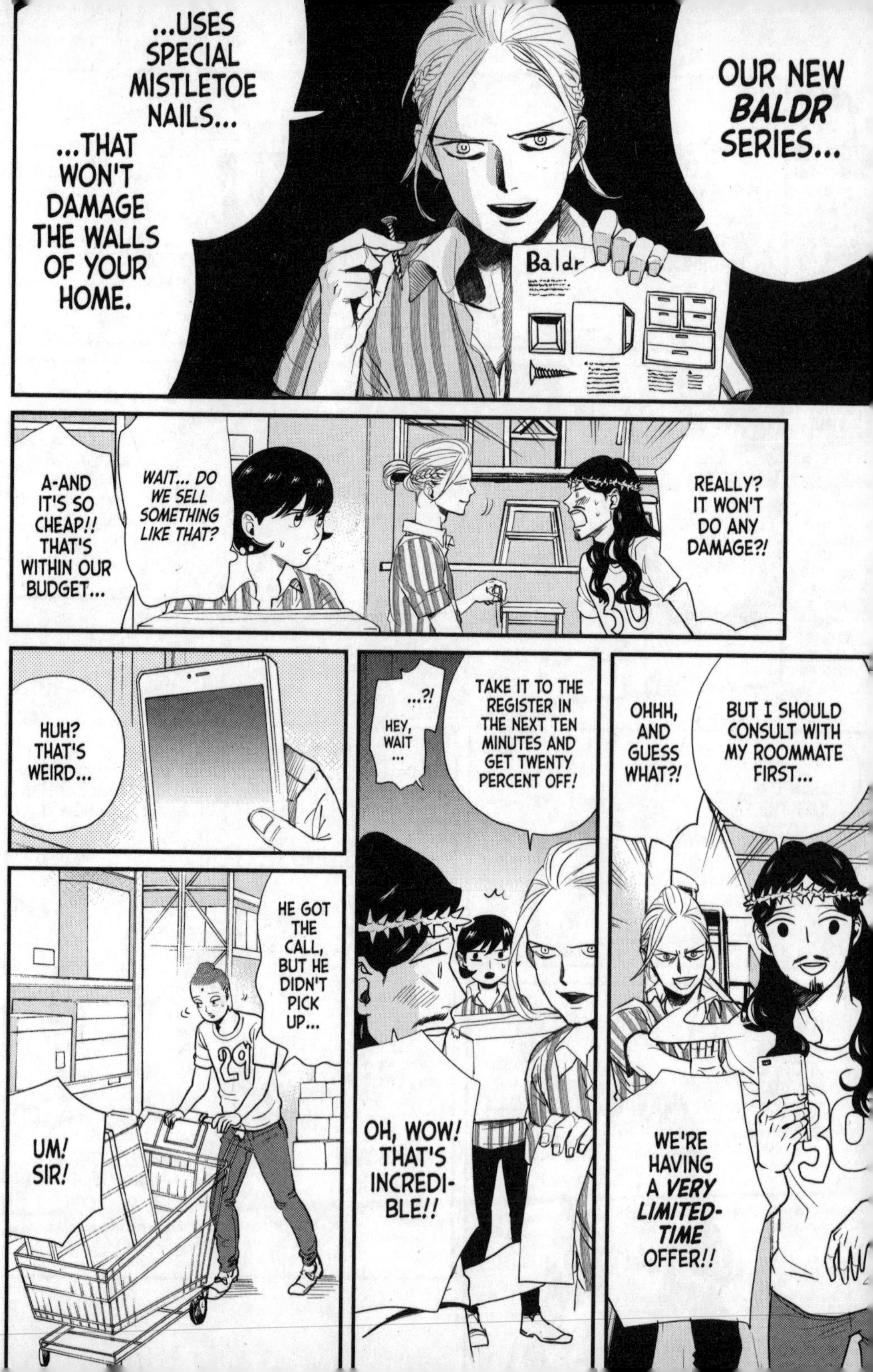
OUR NEW *BALDR* SERIES...
...USES SPECIAL MISTLETOE NAILS...
...THAT WON'T DAMAGE THE WALLS OF YOUR HOME.
Baldr
REALLY? IT WON'T DO ANY DAMAGE?!
WAIT... DO WE SELL SOMETHING LIKE THAT?
A-AND IT'S SO CHEAP!! THAT'S WITHIN OUR BUDGET...
BUT I SHOULD CONSULT WITH MY ROOMMATE FIRST...
OHHH, AND GUESS WHAT?!
WE'RE HAVING A *VERY LIMITED-TIME* OFFER!!
TAKE IT TO THE REGISTER IN THE NEXT TEN MINUTES AND GET TWENTY PERCENT OFF!
...?!
HEY, WAIT ...
OH, WOW! THAT'S INCREDI-BLE!!
HUH? THAT'S WEIRD...
HE GOT THE CALL, BUT HE DIDN'T PICK UP...
UM! SIR!

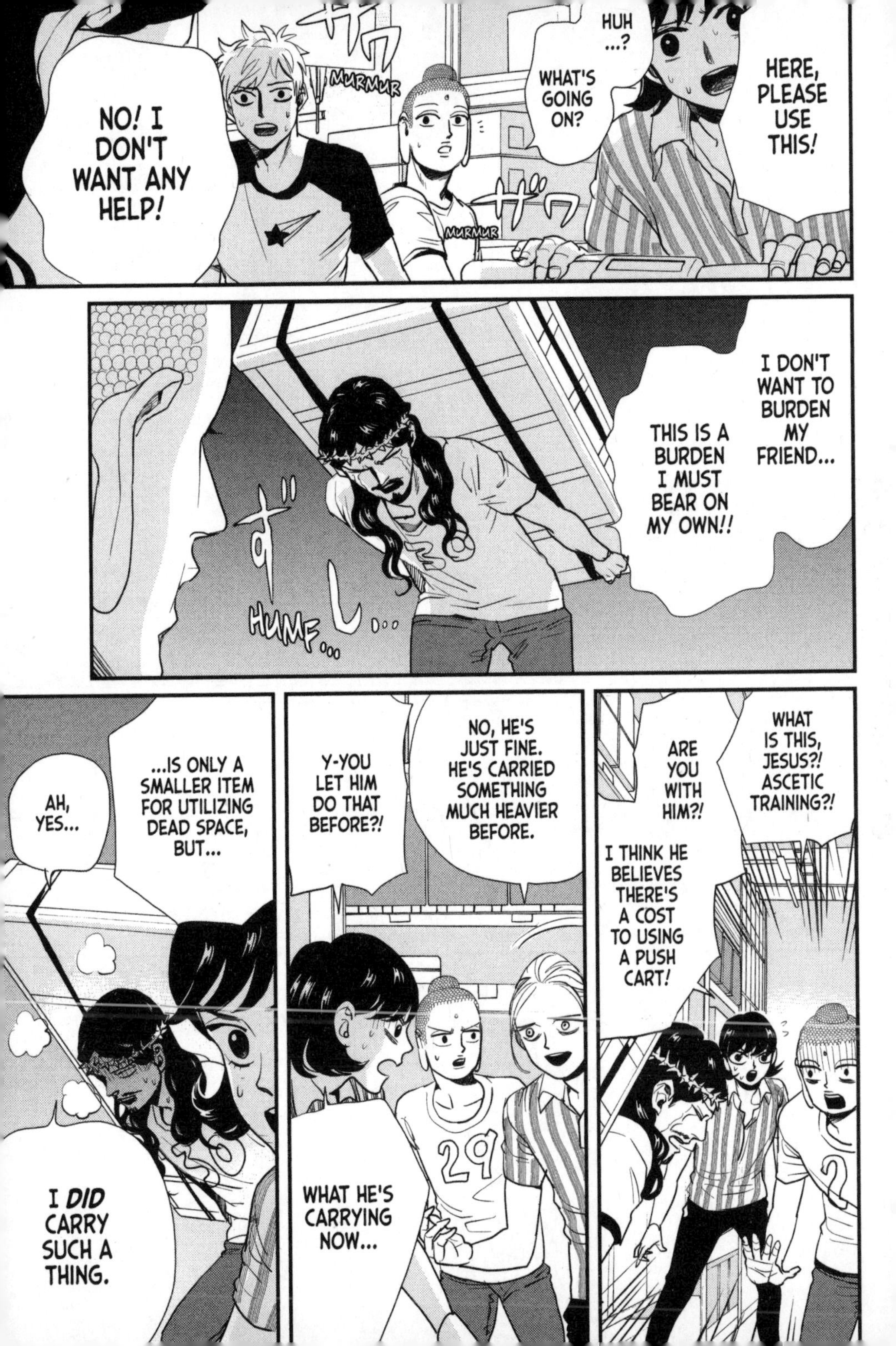
HERE, PLEASE USE THIS!
HUH ...?
WHAT'S GOING ON?
ザワ
MURMUR
ザワ
MURMUR
NO! I DON'T WANT ANY HELP!
I DON'T WANT TO BURDEN MY FRIEND...
THIS IS A BURDEN I MUST BEAR ON MY OWN!!
ずし...
HUMF...
WHAT IS THIS, JESUS?! ASCETIC TRAINING?!
ARE YOU WITH HIM?!
I THINK HE BELIEVES THERE'S A COST TO USING A PUSH CART!
NO, HE'S JUST FINE. HE'S CARRIED SOMETHING MUCH HEAVIER BEFORE.
Y-YOU LET HIM DO THAT BEFORE?!
WHAT HE'S CARRYING NOW...
...IS ONLY A SMALLER ITEM FOR UTILIZING DEAD SPACE, BUT...
AH, YES...
I DID CARRY SUCH A THING.

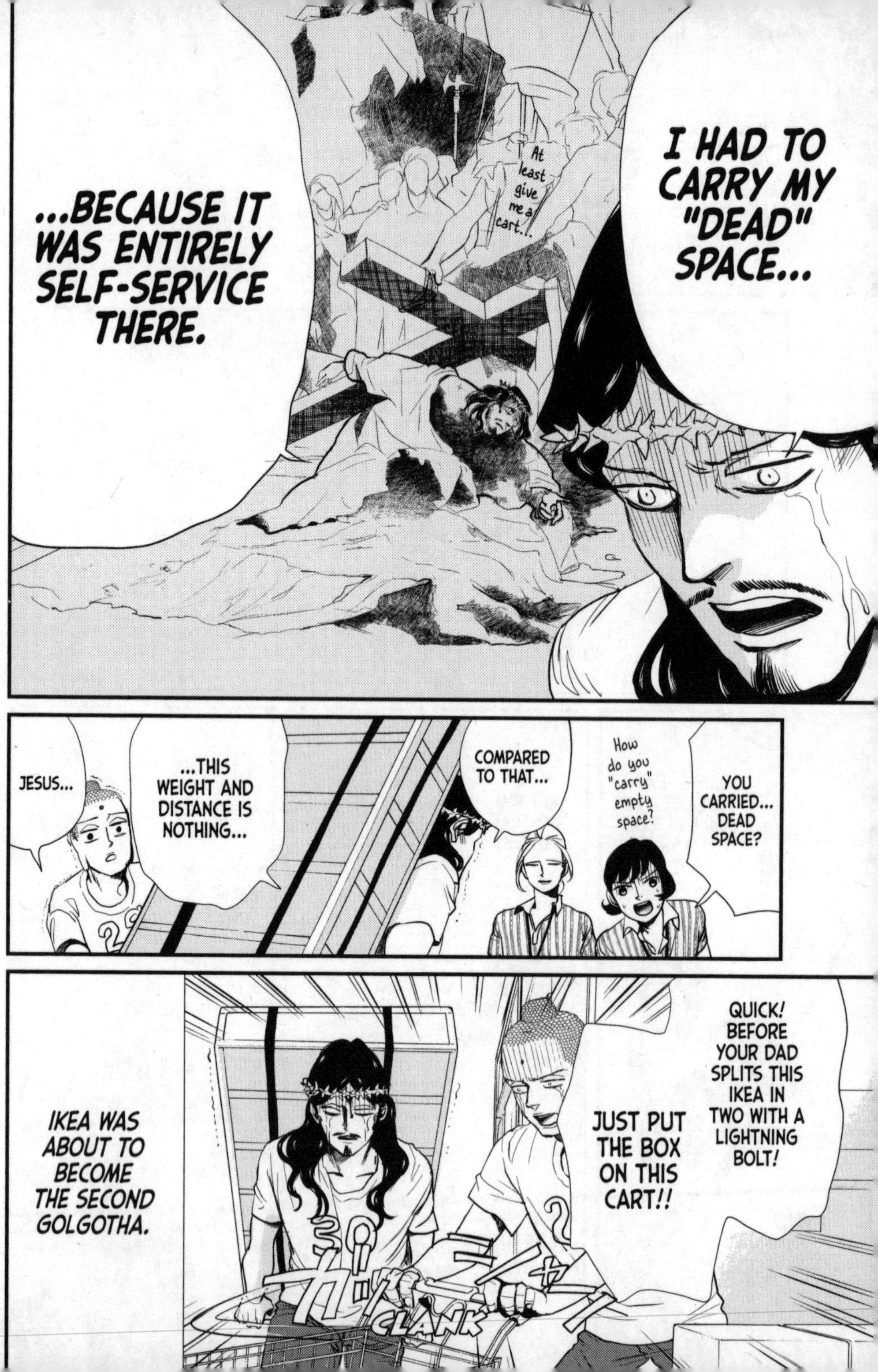
I HAD TO CARRY MY "DEAD" SPACE...
At least give me a cart...
...BECAUSE IT WAS ENTIRELY SELF-SERVICE THERE.
YOU CARRIED... DEAD SPACE?
How do you "carry" empty space?
COMPARED TO THAT...
...THIS WEIGHT AND DISTANCE IS NOTHING...
JESUS...
QUICK! BEFORE YOUR DAD SPLITS THIS IKEA IN TWO WITH A LIGHTNING BOLT!
JUST PUT THE BOX ON THIS CART!!
CLANK
IKEA WAS ABOUT TO BECOME THE SECOND GOLGOTHA.

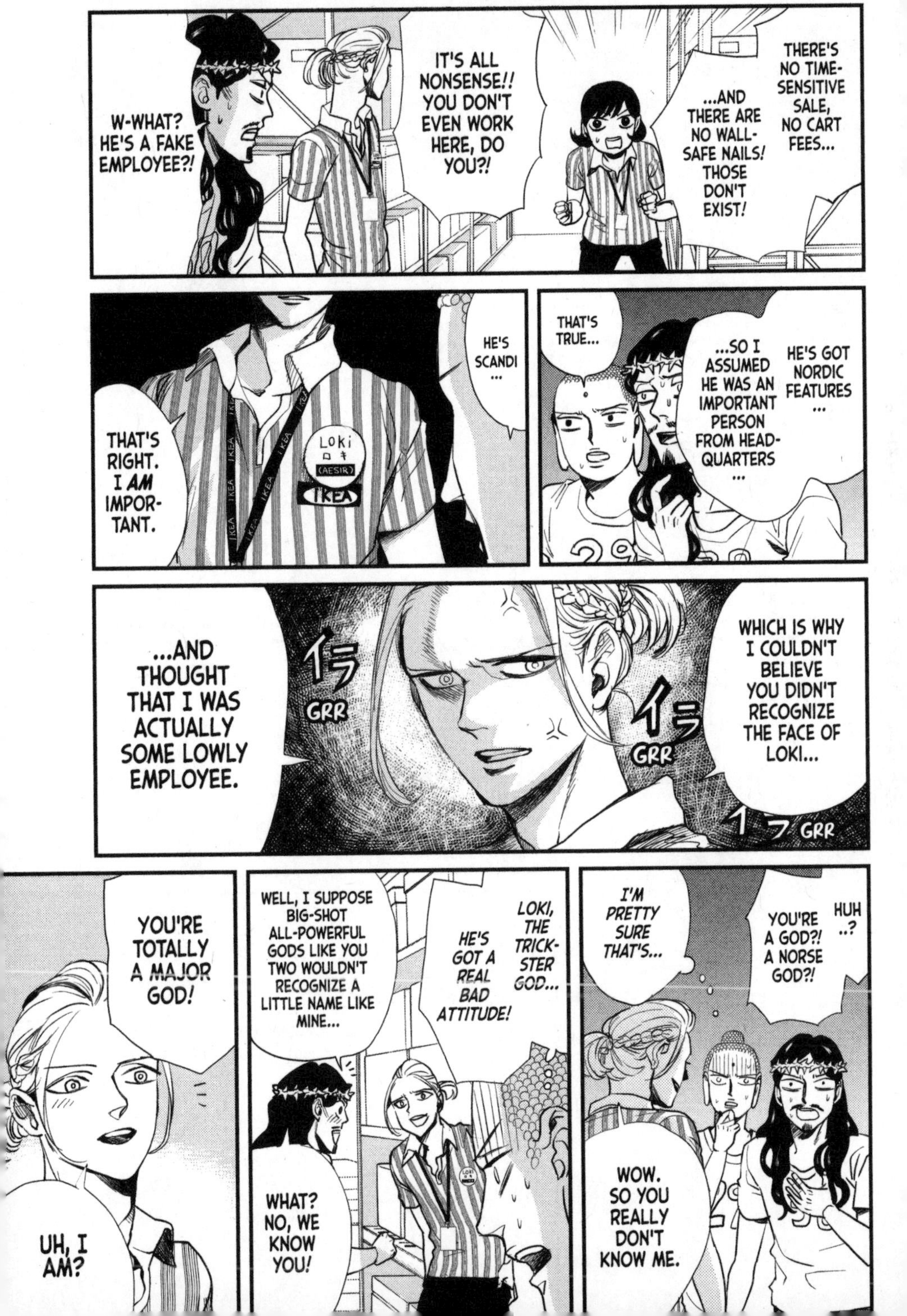
THERE'S NO TIME-SENSITIVE SALE, NO CART FEES...
...AND THERE ARE NO WALL-SAFE NAILS! THOSE DON'T EXIST!
IT'S ALL NONSENSE!! YOU DON'T EVEN WORK HERE, DO YOU?!
W-WHAT? HE'S A FAKE EMPLOYEE?!
HE'S GOT NORDIC FEATURES...
...SO I ASSUMED HE WAS AN IMPORTANT PERSON FROM HEAD-QUARTERS...
THAT'S TRUE...
HE'S SCANDI...
LOKi
ロキ
(AESIR)
IKEA
THAT'S RIGHT. I *AM* IMPOR-TANT.
WHICH IS WHY I COULDN'T BELIEVE YOU DIDN'T RECOGNIZE THE FACE OF LOKI...
イラ GRR
イラ GRR
イラ GRR
...AND THOUGHT THAT I WAS ACTUALLY SOME LOWLY EMPLOYEE.
HUH ..?
YOU'RE A GOD?! A NORSE GOD?!
I'M PRETTY SURE THAT'S...
WOW. SO YOU REALLY DON'T KNOW ME.
LOKI, THE TRICK-STER GOD...
HE'S GOT A REAL BAD ATTITUDE!
WELL, I SUPPOSE BIG-SHOT ALL-POWERFUL GODS LIKE YOU TWO WOULDN'T RECOGNIZE A LITTLE NAME LIKE MINE...
WHAT? NO, WE KNOW YOU!
YOU'RE TOTALLY A MAJOR GOD!
UH, I AM?

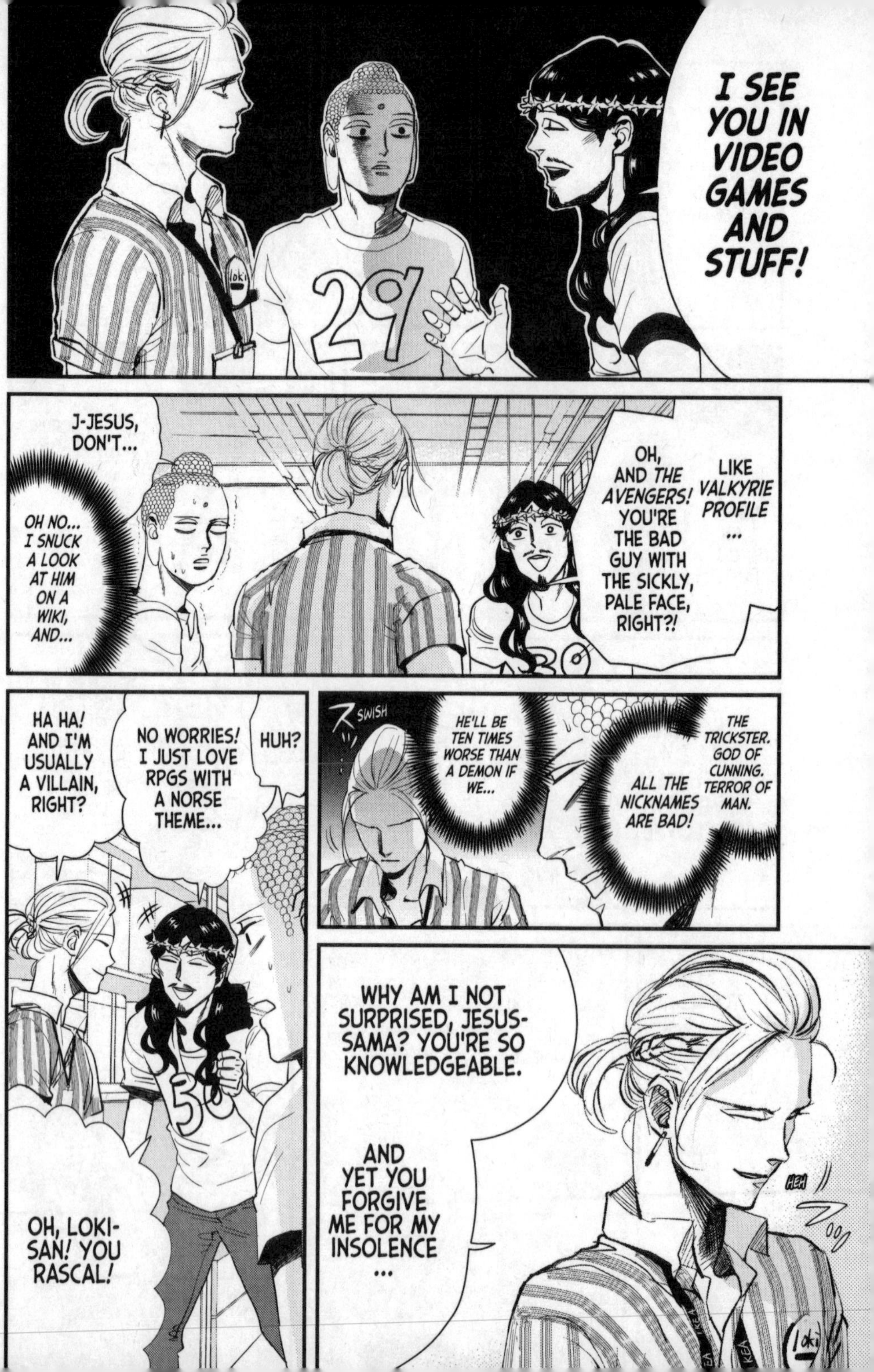
I SEE YOU IN VIDEO GAMES AND STUFF!
LIKE VALKYRIE PROFILE ...
OH, AND THE AVENGERS! YOU'RE THE BAD GUY WITH THE SICKLY, PALE FACE, RIGHT?!
J-JESUS, DON'T...
OH NO... I SNUCK A LOOK AT HIM ON A WIKI, AND...
THE TRICKSTER. GOD OF CUNNING. TERROR OF MAN.
ALL THE NICKNAMES ARE BAD!
HE'LL BE TEN TIMES WORSE THAN A DEMON IF WE...
SWISH
WHY AM I NOT SURPRISED, JESUS-SAMA? YOU'RE SO KNOWLEDGEABLE.
AND YET YOU FORGIVE ME FOR MY INSOLENCE ...
HEH
HUH?
NO WORRIES! I JUST LOVE RPGS WITH A NORSE THEME...
HA HA! AND I'M USUALLY A VILLAIN, RIGHT?
OH, LOKI-SAN! YOU RASCAL!

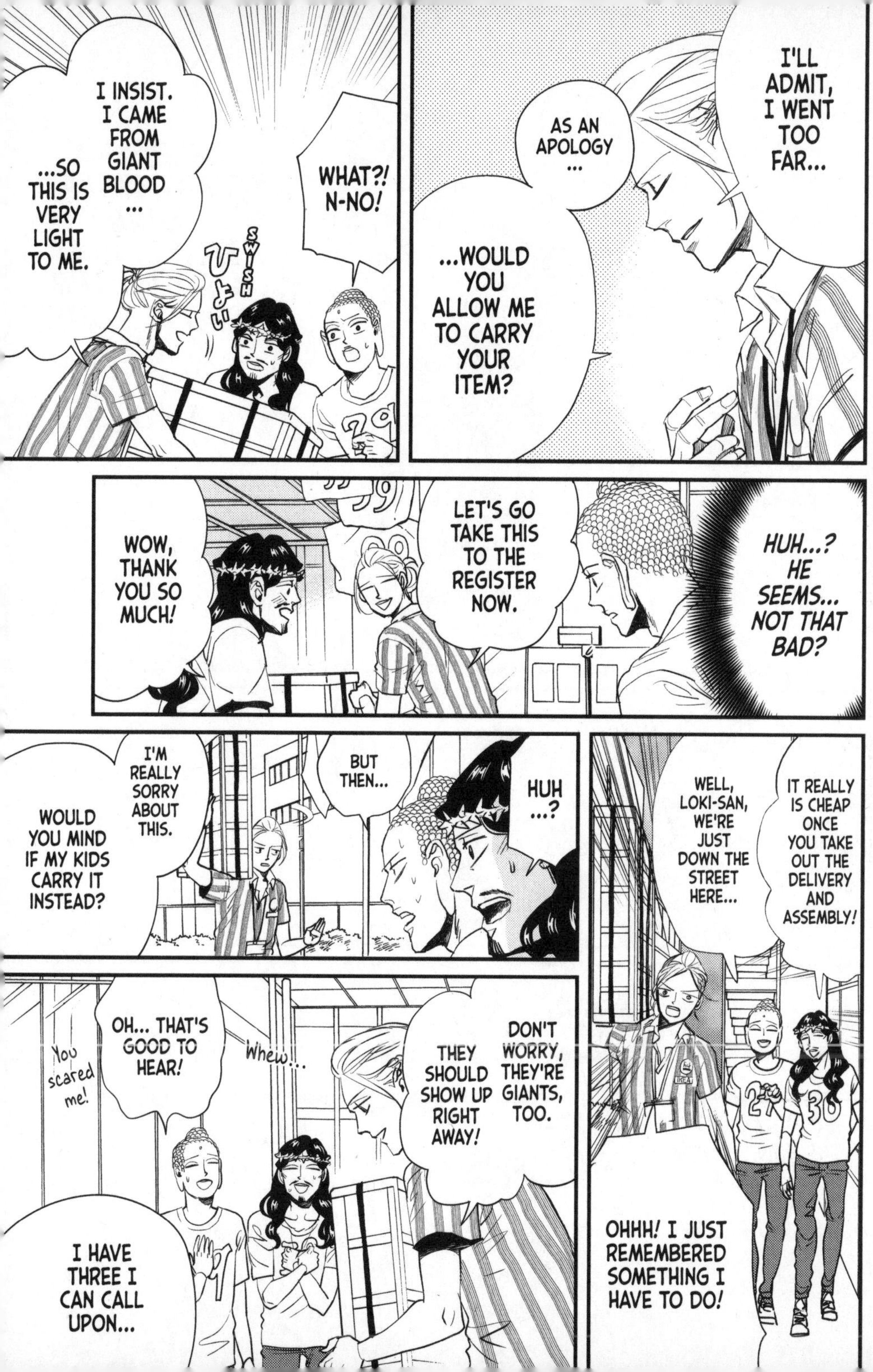
I'LL ADMIT, I WENT TOO FAR...
AS AN APOLOGY...
...WOULD YOU ALLOW ME TO CARRY YOUR ITEM?
WHAT?! N-NO!
I INSIST. I CAME FROM GIANT BLOOD...
...SO THIS IS VERY LIGHT TO ME.
SWISH
HUH...? HE SEEMS... NOT THAT BAD?
LET'S GO TAKE THIS TO THE REGISTER NOW.
WOW, THANK YOU SO MUCH!
IT REALLY IS CHEAP ONCE YOU TAKE OUT THE DELIVERY AND ASSEMBLY!
WELL, LOKI-SAN, WE'RE JUST DOWN THE STREET HERE...
OHHH! I JUST REMEMBERED SOMETHING I HAVE TO DO!
HUH...?
BUT THEN...
I'M REALLY SORRY ABOUT THIS.
WOULD YOU MIND IF MY KIDS CARRY IT INSTEAD?
DON'T WORRY, THEY'RE GIANTS, TOO.
THEY SHOULD SHOW UP RIGHT AWAY!
Whew...
OH... THAT'S GOOD TO HEAR!
You scared me!
I HAVE THREE I CAN CALL UPON...

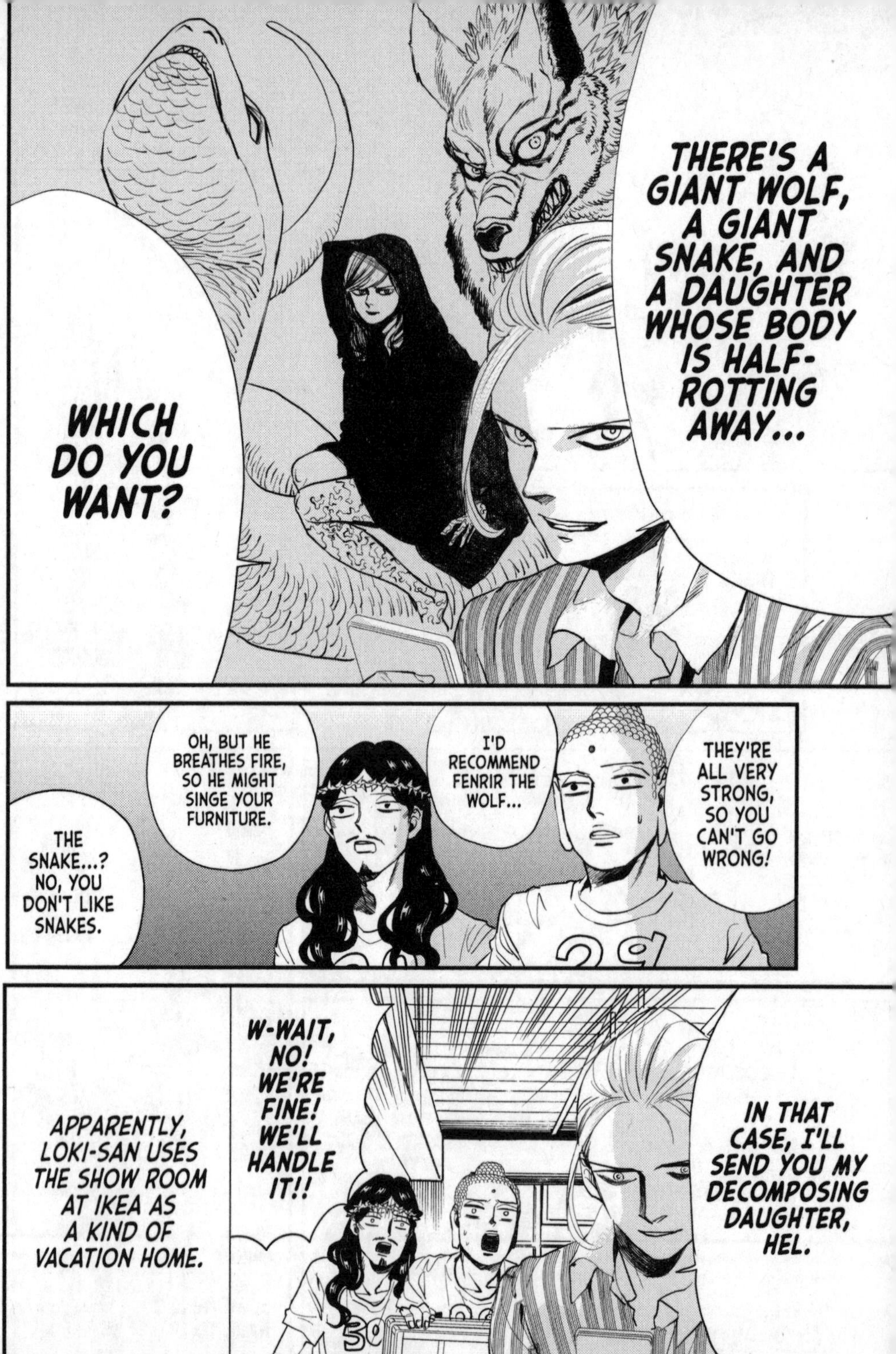
THERE'S A GIANT WOLF, A GIANT SNAKE, AND A DAUGHTER WHOSE BODY IS HALF-ROTTING AWAY...
WHICH DO YOU WANT?
THEY'RE ALL VERY STRONG, SO YOU CAN'T GO WRONG!
I'D RECOMMEND FENRIR THE WOLF...
OH, BUT HE BREATHES FIRE, SO HE MIGHT SINGE YOUR FURNITURE.
THE SNAKE...? NO, YOU DON'T LIKE SNAKES.
IN THAT CASE, I'LL SEND YOU MY DECOMPOSING DAUGHTER, HEL.
W-WAIT, NO! WE'RE FINE! WE'LL HANDLE IT!!
APPARENTLY, LOKI-SAN USES THE SHOW ROOM AT IKEA AS A KIND OF VACATION HOME.

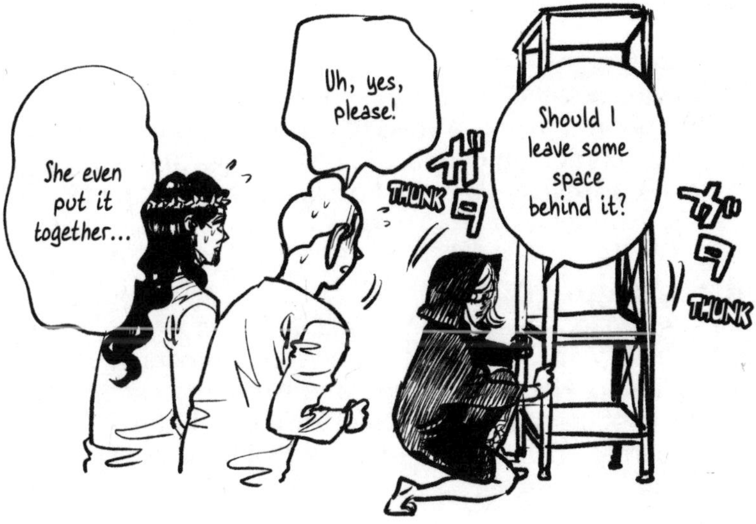
ガタ
THUNK
Should I leave some space behind it?
ガタ
THUNK
Uh, yes, please!
She even put it together...

SAINT☆YOUNG MEN

CHAPTER 86 TRANSLATION NOTES

Ikea, page 96

In this panel, Buddha is imagining that the name Ikea was actually derived from *Ike-ya,* meaning "pond store" in Japanese.

Baldr, page 100

A son of Odin and brother to Thor. Baldr is known mostly for his tragic death, caused by Loki. Baldr was impervious to all weapons but mistletoe; when Loki learned this secret, he fashioned a weapon out of mistletoe that he gave to the blind god Hod, who accidentally killed Baldr with it.

Golgotha, page 102

The site at which Jesus was crucified. According to the Gospels, it was located just outside of Jerusalem's walls, although the exact location is unclear and disputed.

Valkyrie Profile, page 104

A series of Norse-mythology-themed RPGs, starting with 1999's *Valkyrie Profile.* The player controls a valkyrie named Lenneth who recruits various mortal warriors after death to be einherjar, those heroes who spend the afterlife in Valhalla. Loki is the final villain of the game.

Loki's children, page 105

According to the sagas used as source material, Loki has three children: Fenrir the giant wolf; Jormungand the World Serpent; and Hel, the ruler of the land of Hel (or Helheim), a realm where some gods go after death, especially after old age or sickness. Hel is described as being partially blue of skin. After his death, Baldr spends his time trapped under Hel's watch.

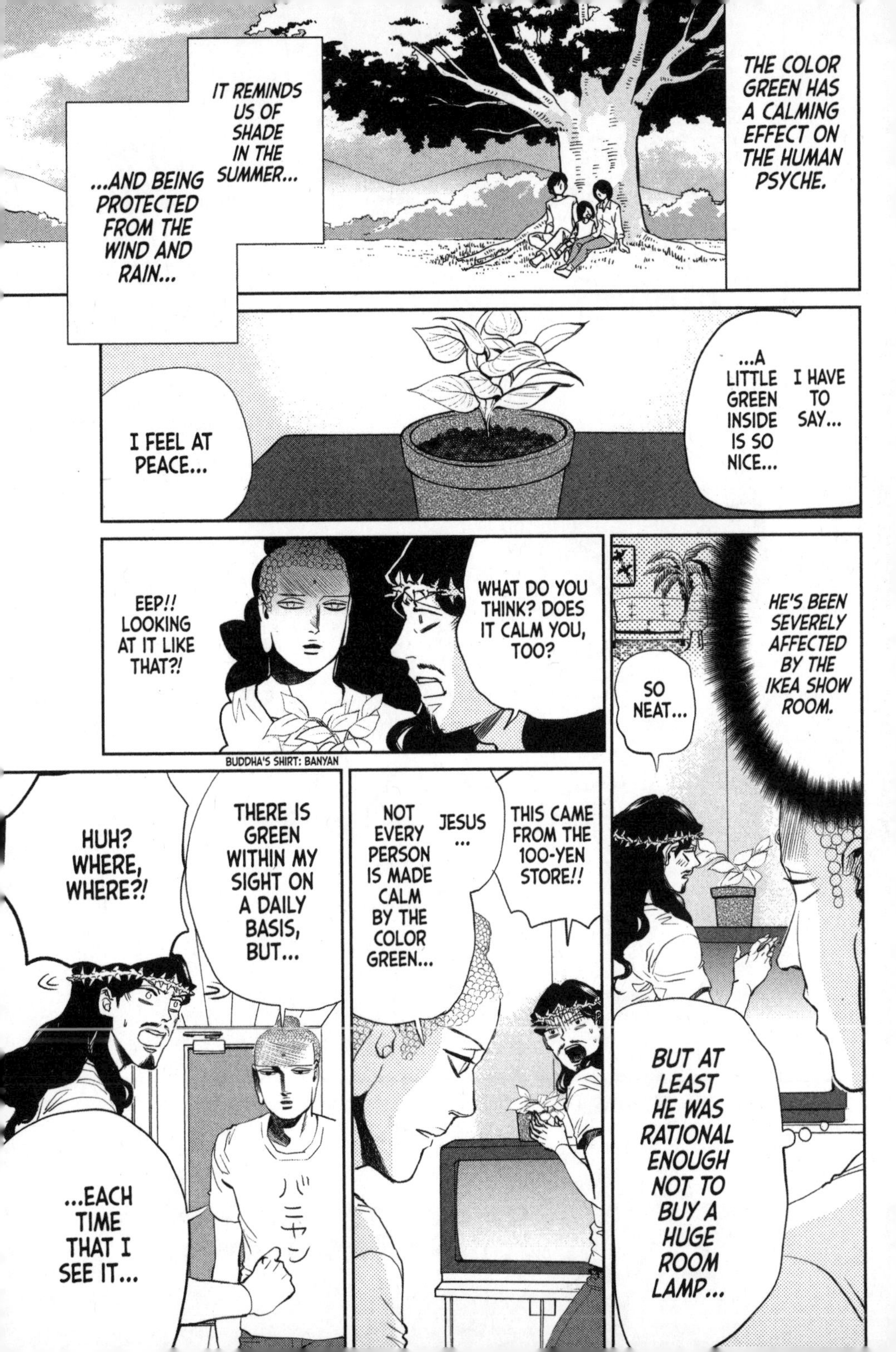

THE COLOR GREEN HAS A CALMING EFFECT ON THE HUMAN PSYCHE.
IT REMINDS US OF SHADE IN THE SUMMER...
...AND BEING PROTECTED FROM THE WIND AND RAIN...
I HAVE TO SAY...
...A LITTLE GREEN INSIDE IS SO NICE...
I FEEL AT PEACE...
HE'S BEEN SEVERELY AFFECTED BY THE IKEA SHOW ROOM.
SO NEAT...
BUT AT LEAST HE WAS RATIONAL ENOUGH NOT TO BUY A HUGE ROOM LAMP...
WHAT DO YOU THINK? DOES IT CALM YOU, TOO?
EEP!! LOOKING AT IT LIKE THAT?!
BUDDHA'S SHIRT: BANYAN
THIS CAME FROM THE 100-YEN STORE!!
JESUS...
NOT EVERY PERSON IS MADE CALM BY THE COLOR GREEN...
THERE IS GREEN WITHIN MY SIGHT ON A DAILY BASIS, BUT...
HUH? WHERE, WHERE?!
...EACH TIME THAT I SEE IT...

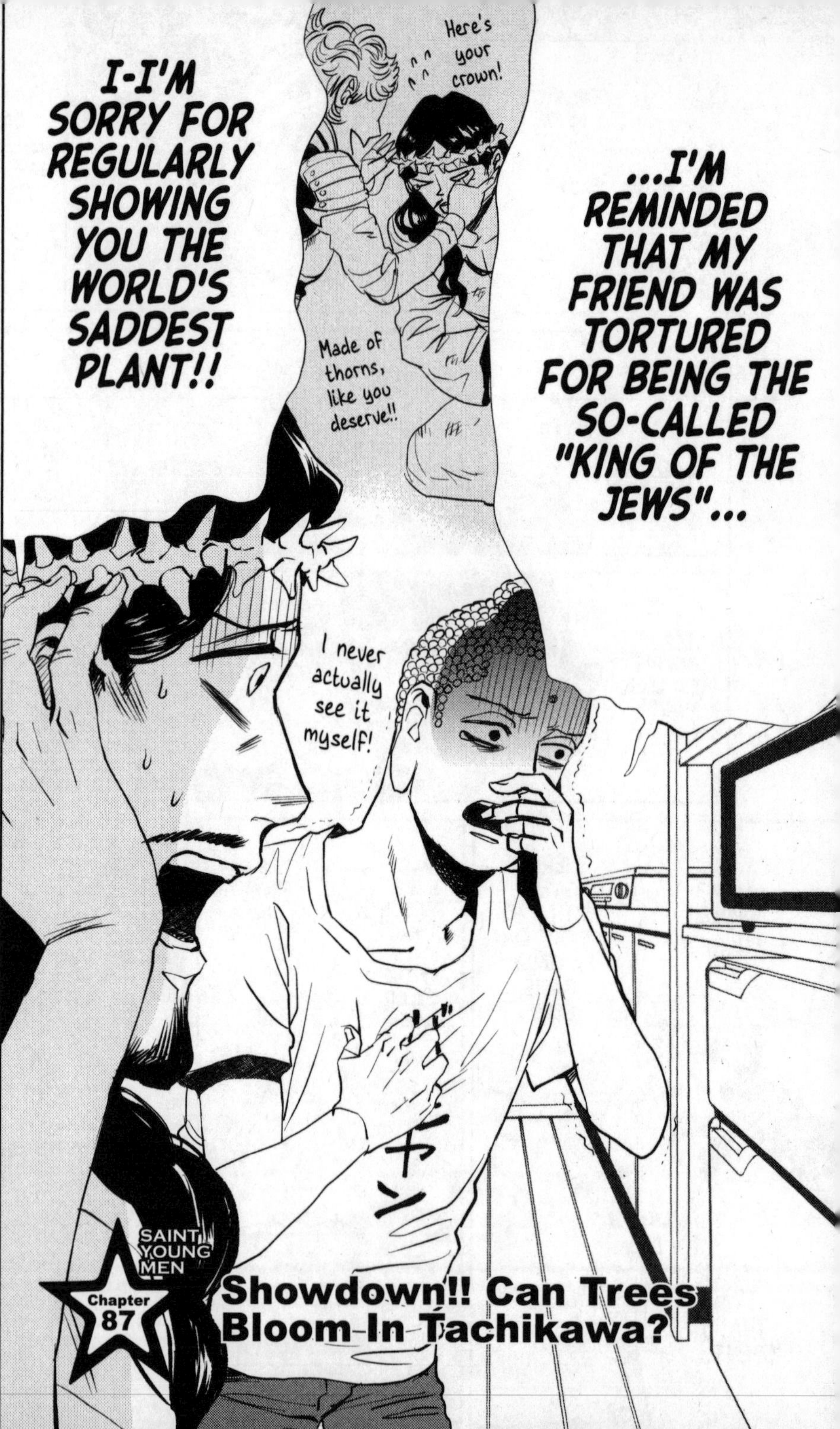
...I'M REMINDED THAT MY FRIEND WAS TORTURED FOR BEING THE SO-CALLED "KING OF THE JEWS"...
Here's your crown!
Made of thorns, like you deserve!!
I-I'M SORRY FOR REGULARLY SHOWING YOU THE WORLD'S SADDEST PLANT!!
I never actually see it myself!
ギャン
OR MAYBE IT'S JUST IN FASHION.
SAINT YOUNG MEN
Chapter 87
Showdown!! Can Trees Bloom In Tachikawa?

BUDDHA
HE'S FROM INDIA, BUT THE COOLER PART CLOSE TO THE HIMALAYAS. HIS ASCETIC TRAINING HASN'T KICKED IN THIS YEAR, PERHAPS BECAUSE IT'S SO HOT THAT IT MELTED HIS SENSORS.

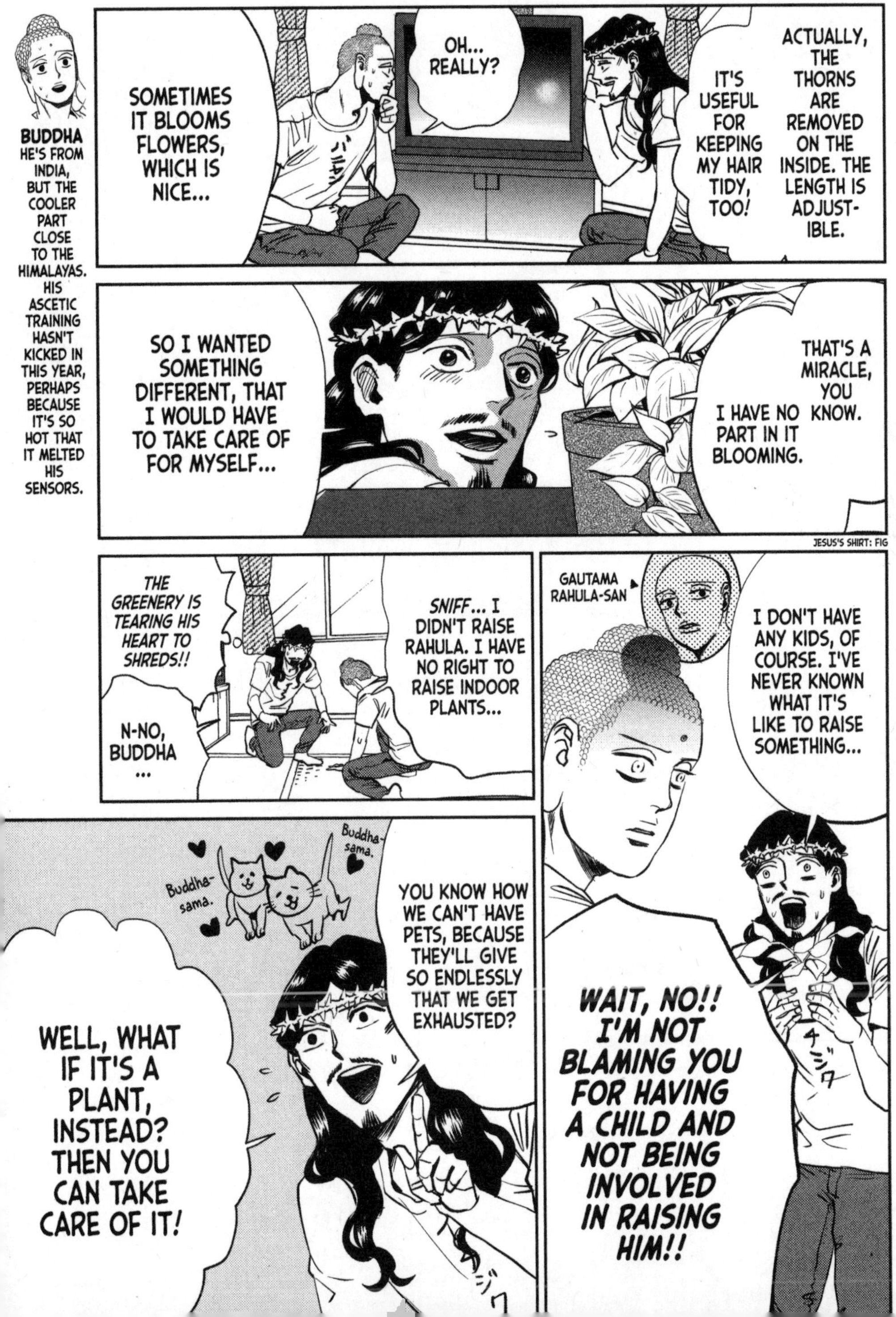

ACTUALLY, THE THORNS ARE REMOVED ON THE INSIDE. THE LENGTH IS ADJUSTIBLE.
IT'S USEFUL FOR KEEPING MY HAIR TIDY, TOO!
OH... REALLY?
SOMETIMES IT BLOOMS FLOWERS, WHICH IS NICE...
THAT'S A MIRACLE, YOU KNOW.
I HAVE NO PART IN IT BLOOMING.
SO I WANTED SOMETHING DIFFERENT, THAT I WOULD HAVE TO TAKE CARE OF FOR MYSELF...
JESUS'S SHIRT: FIG
GAUTAMA RAHULA-SAN
I DON'T HAVE ANY KIDS, OF COURSE. I'VE NEVER KNOWN WHAT IT'S LIKE TO RAISE SOMETHING...
WAIT, NO!! I'M NOT BLAMING YOU FOR HAVING A CHILD AND NOT BEING INVOLVED IN RAISING HIM!!
SNIFF... I DIDN'T RAISE RAHULA. I HAVE NO RIGHT TO RAISE INDOOR PLANTS...
THE GREENERY IS TEARING HIS HEART TO SHREDS!!
N-NO, BUDDHA...
Buddha-sama.
Buddha-sama.
YOU KNOW HOW WE CAN'T HAVE PETS, BECAUSE THEY'LL GIVE SO ENDLESSLY THAT WE GET EXHAUSTED?
WELL, WHAT IF IT'S A PLANT, INSTEAD? THEN YOU CAN TAKE CARE OF IT!

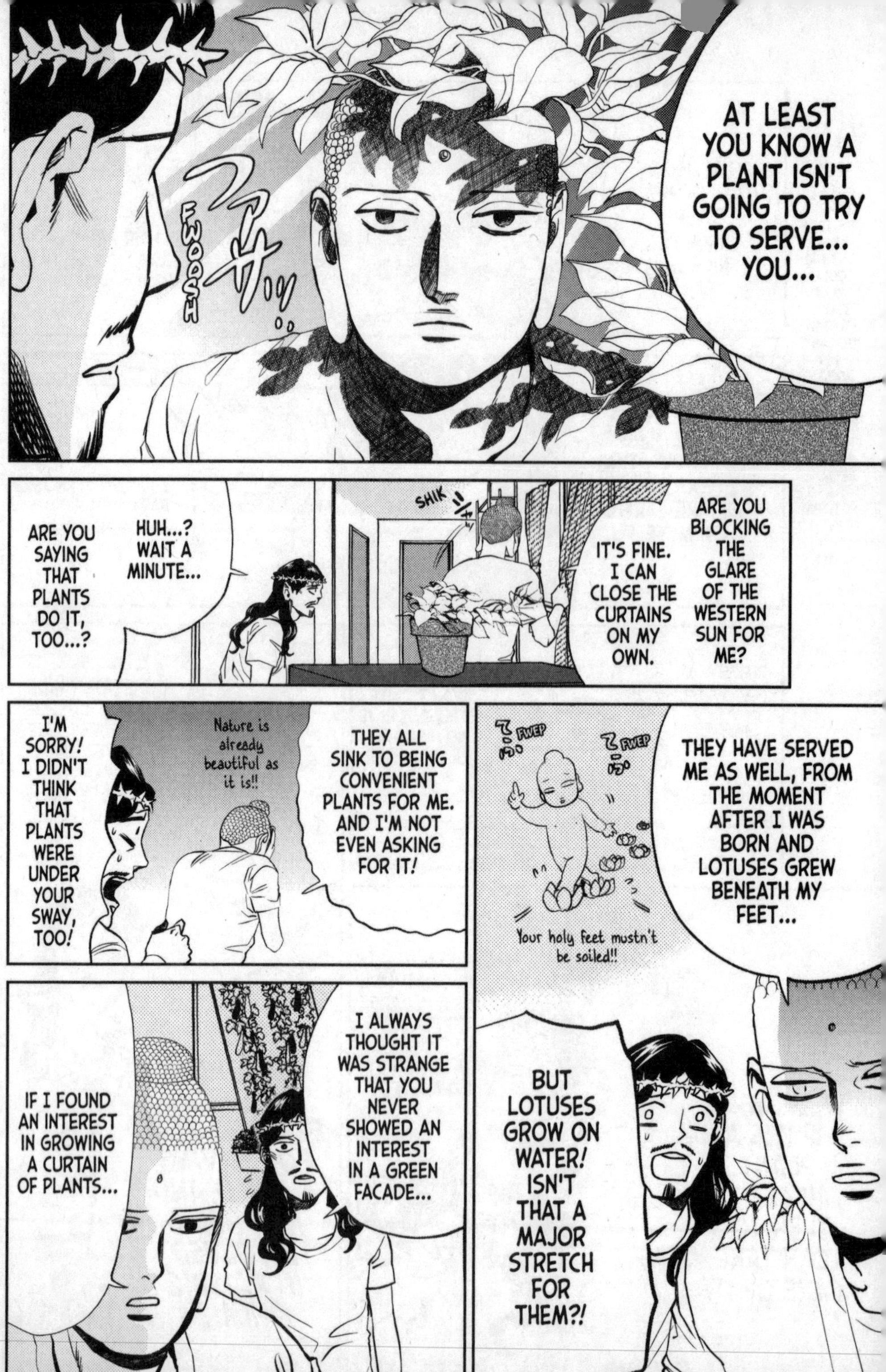
AT LEAST YOU KNOW A PLANT ISN'T GOING TO TRY TO SERVE... YOU...
FWOOSH
ARE YOU BLOCKING THE GLARE OF THE WESTERN SUN FOR ME?
SHIK
IT'S FINE. I CAN CLOSE THE CURTAINS ON MY OWN.
HUH...? WAIT A MINUTE...
ARE YOU SAYING THAT PLANTS DO IT, TOO...?
THEY HAVE SERVED ME AS WELL, FROM THE MOMENT AFTER I WAS BORN AND LOTUSES GREW BENEATH MY FEET...
FWEP
FWEP
Your holy feet mustn't be soiled!!
THEY ALL SINK TO BEING CONVENIENT PLANTS FOR ME. AND I'M NOT EVEN ASKING FOR IT!
Nature is already beautiful as it is!!
I'M SORRY! I DIDN'T THINK THAT PLANTS WERE UNDER YOUR SWAY, TOO!
BUT LOTUSES GROW ON WATER! ISN'T THAT A MAJOR STRETCH FOR THEM?!
I ALWAYS THOUGHT IT WAS STRANGE THAT YOU NEVER SHOWED AN INTEREST IN A GREEN FACADE...
IF I FOUND AN INTEREST IN GROWING A CURTAIN OF PLANTS...

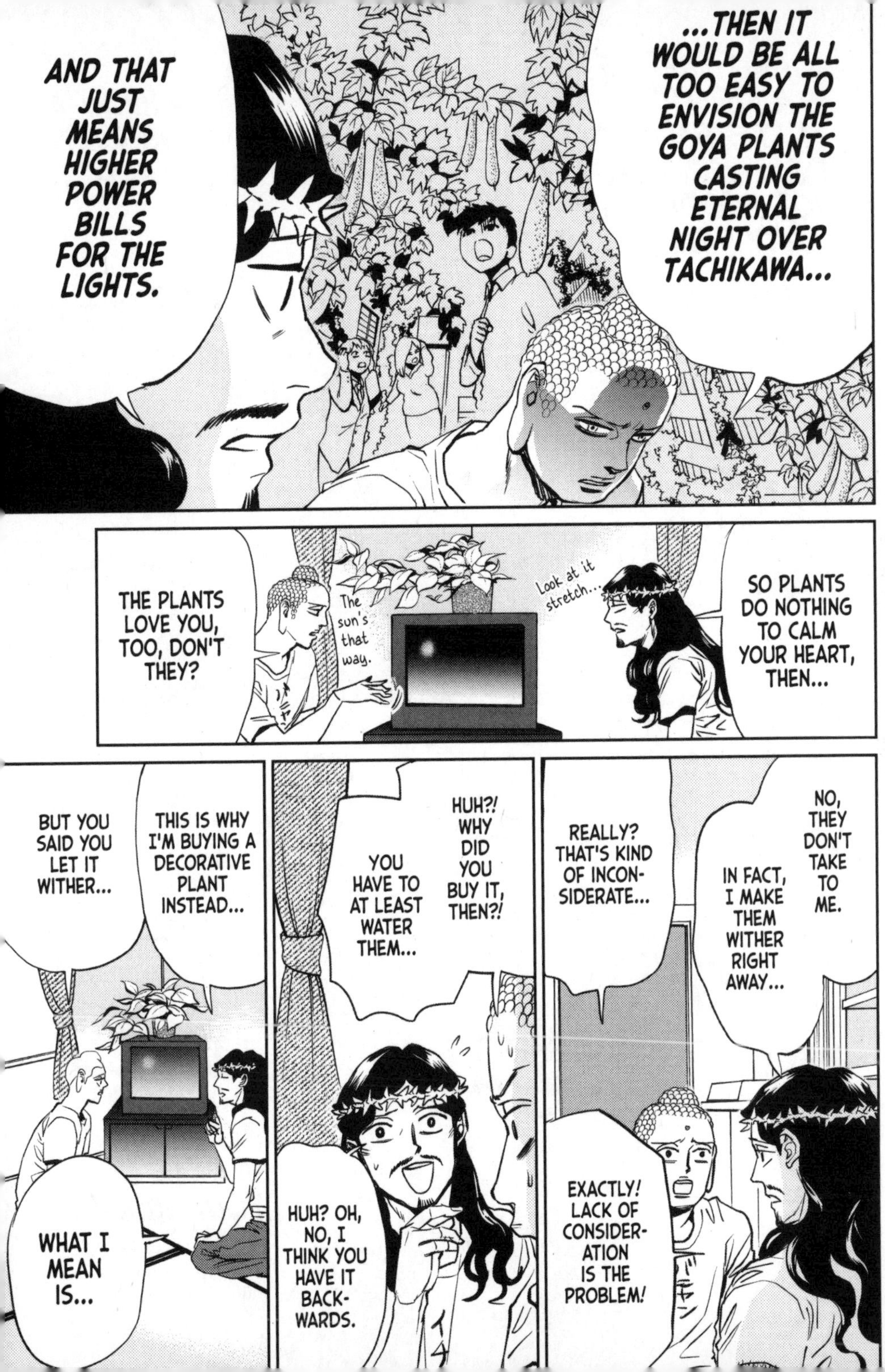
...THEN IT WOULD BE ALL TOO EASY TO ENVISION THE GOYA PLANTS CASTING ETERNAL NIGHT OVER TACHIKAWA...
AND THAT JUST MEANS HIGHER POWER BILLS FOR THE LIGHTS.
SO PLANTS DO NOTHING TO CALM YOUR HEART, THEN...
Look at it stretch...
The sun's that way.
THE PLANTS LOVE YOU, TOO, DON'T THEY?
NO, THEY DON'T TAKE TO ME.
IN FACT, I MAKE THEM WITHER RIGHT AWAY...
REALLY? THAT'S KIND OF INCON-SIDERATE...
EXACTLY! LACK OF CONSIDER-ATION IS THE PROBLEM!
HUH?! WHY DID YOU BUY IT, THEN?!
YOU HAVE TO AT LEAST WATER THEM...
HUH? OH, NO, I THINK YOU HAVE IT BACK-WARDS.
THIS IS WHY I'M BUYING A DECORATIVE PLANT INSTEAD...
BUT YOU SAID YOU LET IT WITHER...
WHAT I MEAN IS...

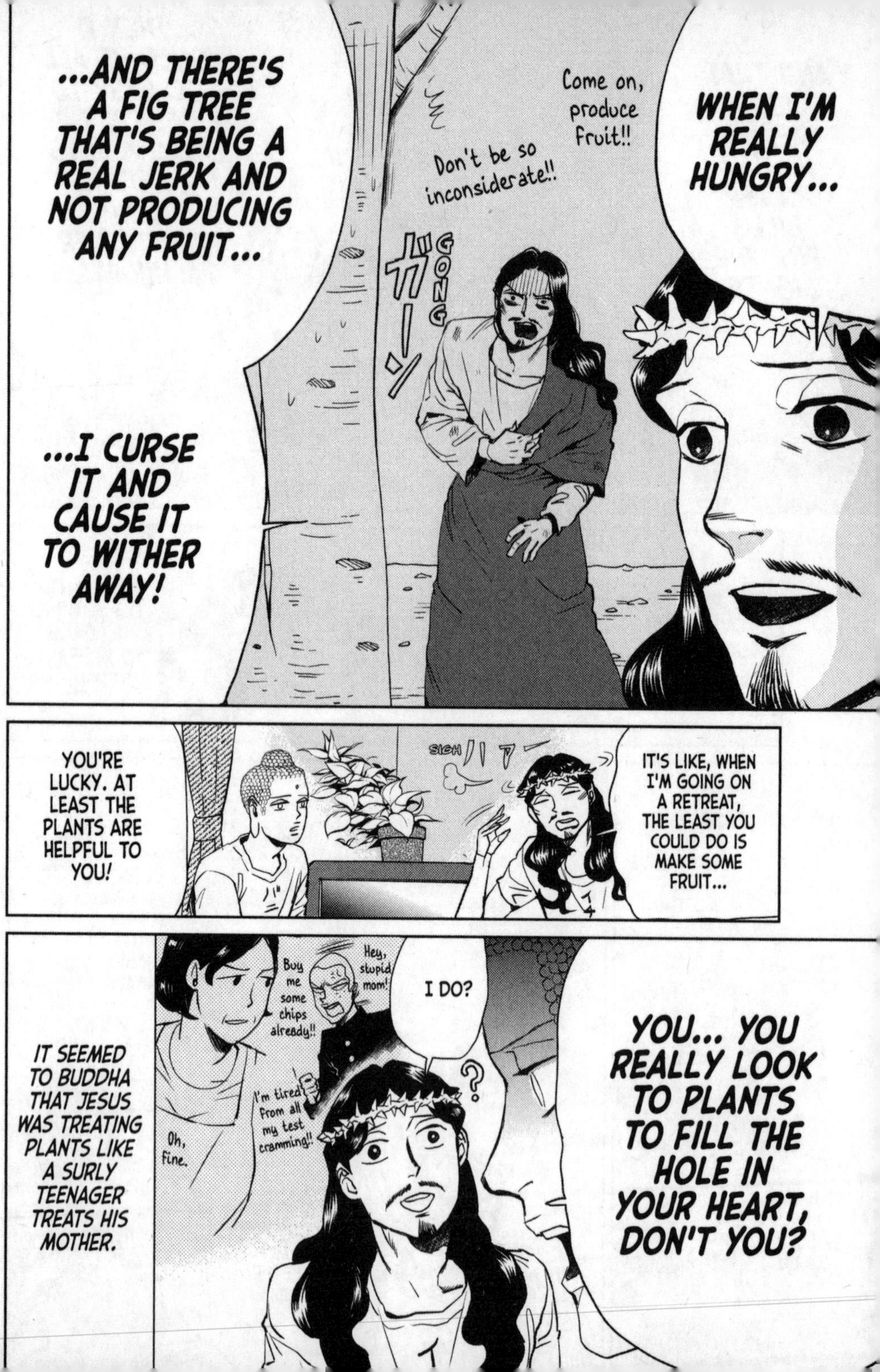
WHEN I'M REALLY HUNGRY...
...AND THERE'S A FIG TREE THAT'S BEING A REAL JERK AND NOT PRODUCING ANY FRUIT...
Come on, produce fruit!!
Don't be so inconsiderate!!
GONG
...I CURSE IT AND CAUSE IT TO WITHER AWAY!
IT'S LIKE, WHEN I'M GOING ON A RETREAT, THE LEAST YOU COULD DO IS MAKE SOME FRUIT...
SIGH
YOU'RE LUCKY. AT LEAST THE PLANTS ARE HELPFUL TO YOU!
YOU... YOU REALLY LOOK TO PLANTS TO FILL THE HOLE IN YOUR HEART, DON'T YOU?
I DO?
Hey, stupid mom!
Buy me some chips already!!
I'm tired from all my test cramming!!
Oh, Fine.
IT SEEMED TO BUDDHA THAT JESUS WAS TREATING PLANTS LIKE A SURLY TEENAGER TREATS HIS MOTHER.

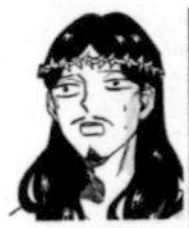

JESUS
"SUMMER HEAT, BEGONE!" I WANT TO SAY, BUT I CAN'T, BECAUSE IF DAD HEARS IT, HE'LL START A NEW ICE AGE. AT LEAST BUDDHA WON'T MIND IF I BUY EXTRA ICE CREAM.

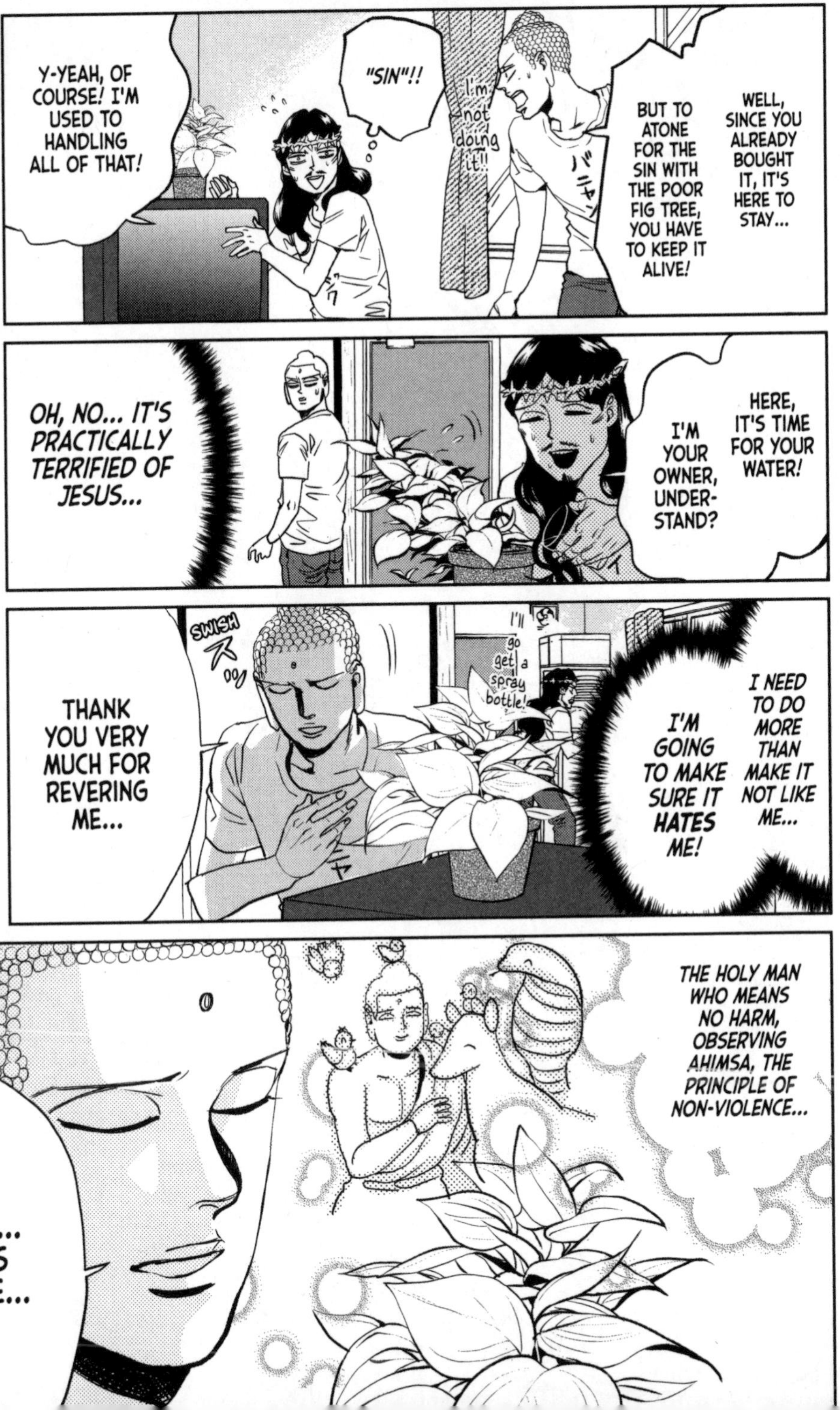
WELL, SINCE YOU ALREADY BOUGHT IT, IT'S HERE TO STAY...
BUT TO ATONE FOR THE SIN WITH THE POOR FIG TREE, YOU HAVE TO KEEP IT ALIVE!
I'm not doing it!!
"SIN"!!
Y-YEAH, OF COURSE! I'M USED TO HANDLING ALL OF THAT!
HERE, IT'S TIME FOR YOUR WATER!
I'M YOUR OWNER, UNDER-STAND?
OH, NO... IT'S PRACTICALLY TERRIFIED OF JESUS...
I NEED TO DO MORE THAN MAKE IT NOT LIKE ME...
I'M GOING TO MAKE SURE IT HATES ME!
I'll go get a spray bottle!
SWISH
THANK YOU VERY MUCH FOR REVERING ME...
THE HOLY MAN WHO MEANS NO HARM, OBSERVING AHIMSA, THE PRINCIPLE OF NON-VIOLENCE...
YES... IT'S TRUE...

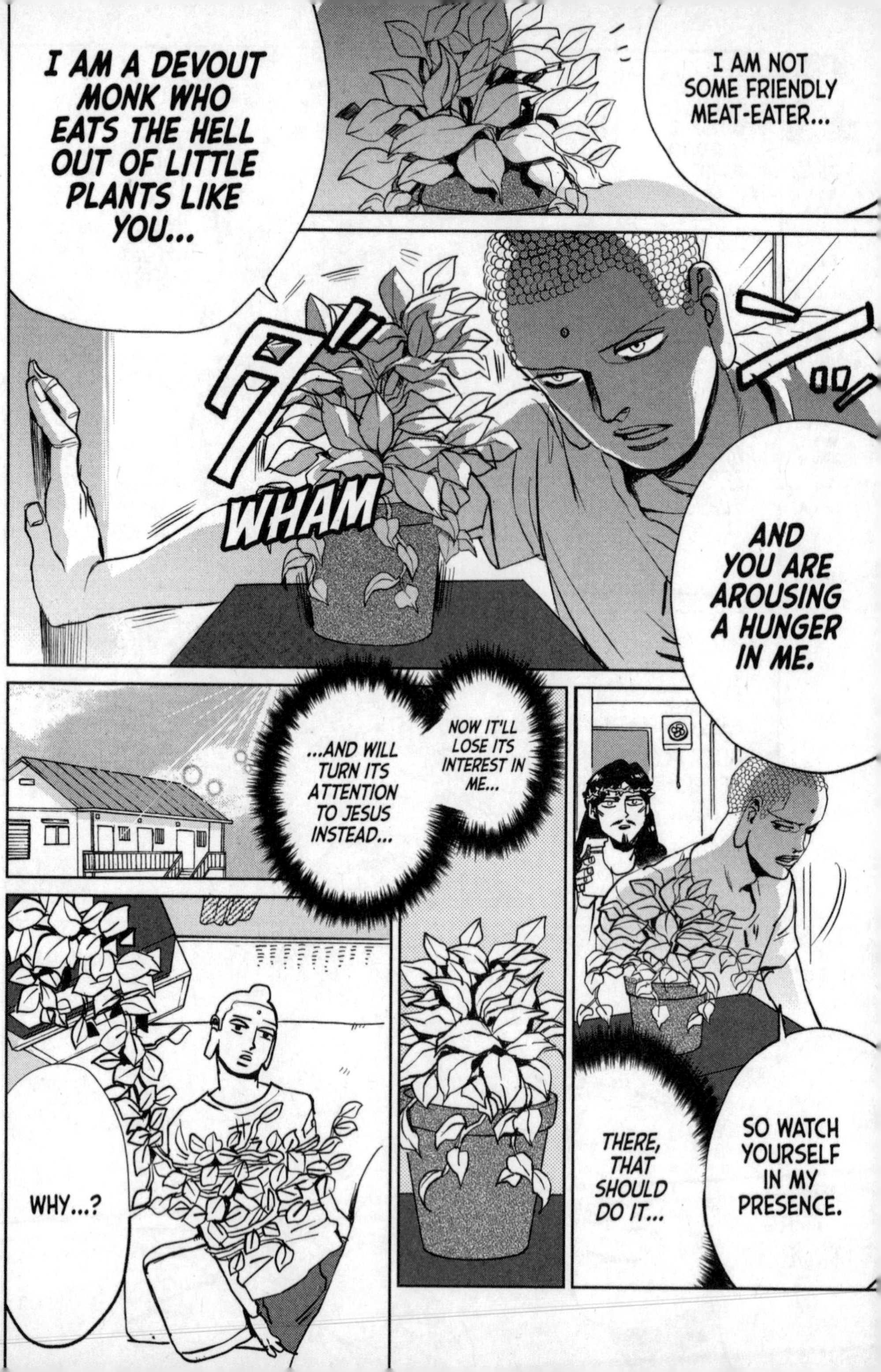
I AM NOT SOME FRIENDLY MEAT-EATER...
I AM A DEVOUT MONK WHO EATS THE HELL OUT OF LITTLE PLANTS LIKE YOU...
WHAM
AND YOU ARE AROUSING A HUNGER IN ME.
SO WATCH YOURSELF IN MY PRESENCE.
THERE, THAT SHOULD DO IT...
NOW IT'LL LOSE ITS INTEREST IN ME...
...AND WILL TURN ITS ATTENTION TO JESUS INSTEAD...
WHY...?

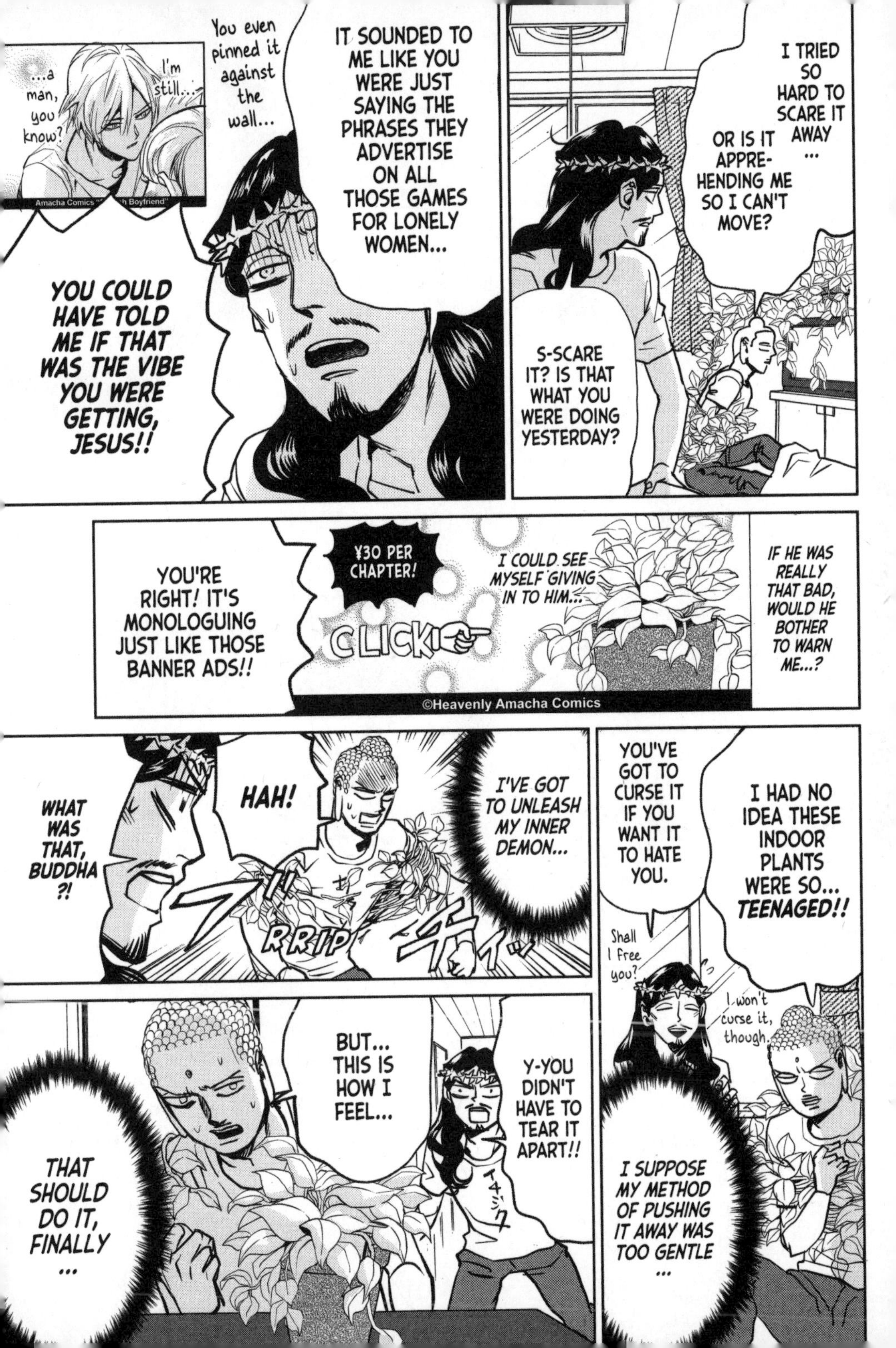
I TRIED SO HARD TO SCARE IT AWAY...
OR IS IT APPREHENDING ME SO I CAN'T MOVE?
S-SCARE IT? IS THAT WHAT YOU WERE DOING YESTERDAY?
IT SOUNDED TO ME LIKE YOU WERE JUST SAYING THE PHRASES THEY ADVERTISE ON ALL THOSE GAMES FOR LONELY WOMEN...
You even pinned it against the wall...
I'm still...
...a man, you know?
YOU COULD HAVE TOLD ME IF THAT WAS THE VIBE YOU WERE GETTING, JESUS!!
IF HE WAS REALLY THAT BAD, WOULD HE BOTHER TO WARN ME...?
I COULD SEE MYSELF GIVING IN TO HIM...
¥30 PER CHAPTER!
CLICK
YOU'RE RIGHT! IT'S MONOLOGUING JUST LIKE THOSE BANNER ADS!!
©Heavenly Amacha Comics
I HAD NO IDEA THESE INDOOR PLANTS WERE SO... TEENAGED!!
YOU'VE GOT TO CURSE IT IF YOU WANT IT TO HATE YOU.
Shall I free you?
I won't curse it, though.
I SUPPOSE MY METHOD OF PUSHING IT AWAY WAS TOO GENTLE...
I'VE GOT TO UNLEASH MY INNER DEMON...
HAH!
RRIP
WHAT WAS THAT, BUDDHA?!
Y-YOU DIDN'T HAVE TO TEAR IT APART!!
BUT... THIS IS HOW I FEEL...
THAT SHOULD DO IT, FINALLY...

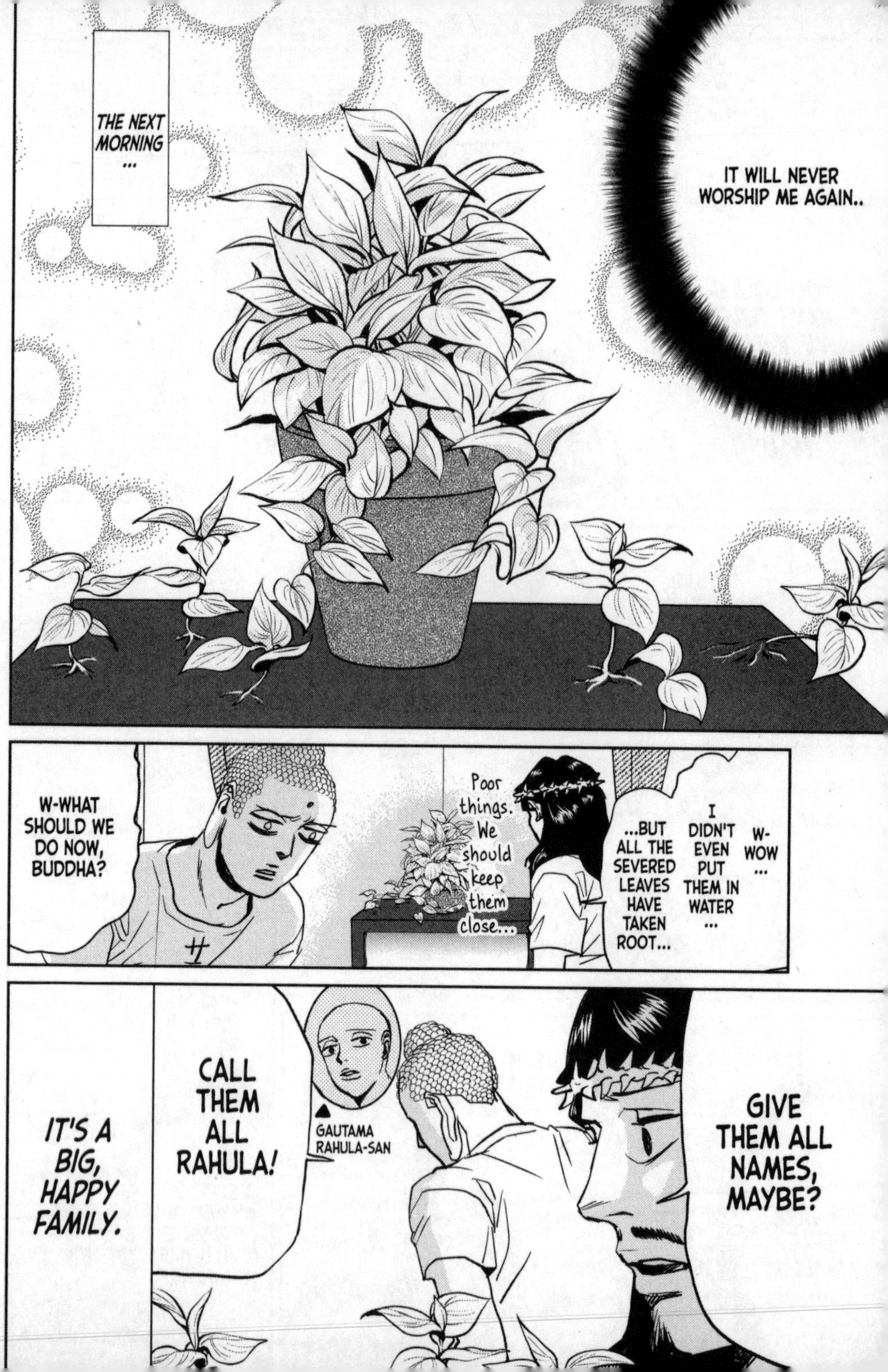
IT WILL NEVER WORSHIP ME AGAIN..
THE NEXT MORNING ...
W-WOW ...
I DIDN'T EVEN PUT THEM IN WATER ...
...BUT ALL THE SEVERED LEAVES HAVE TAKEN ROOT...
Poor things. We should keep them close...
W-WHAT SHOULD WE DO NOW, BUDDHA?
GIVE THEM ALL NAMES, MAYBE?
CALL THEM ALL RAHULA!
GAUTAMA RAHULA-SAN
IT'S A BIG, HAPPY FAMILY.

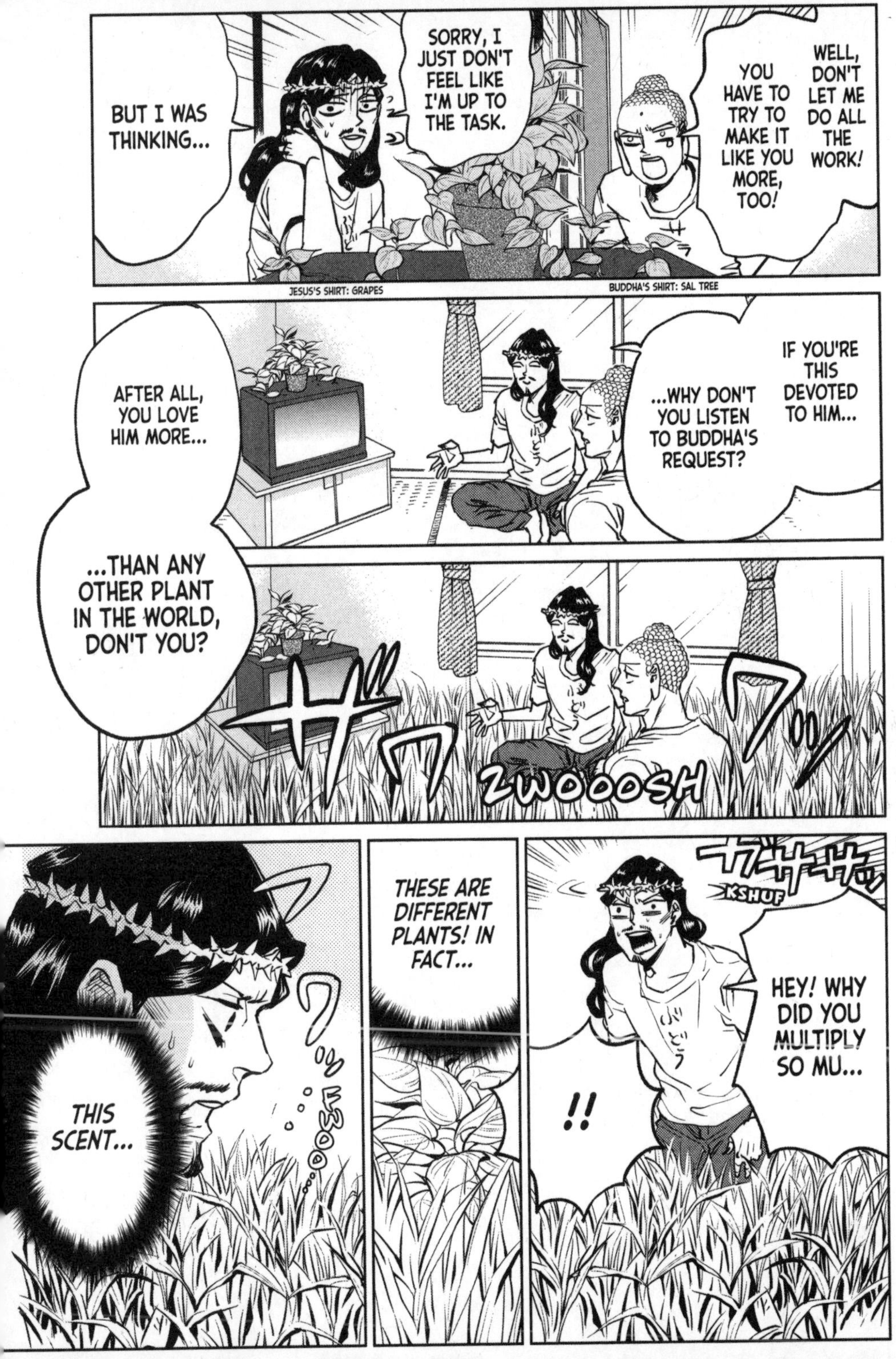

WELL, DON'T LET ME DO ALL THE WORK!
YOU HAVE TO TRY TO MAKE IT LIKE YOU MORE, TOO!
SORRY, I JUST DON'T FEEL LIKE I'M UP TO THE TASK.
BUT I WAS THINKING...
BUDDHA'S SHIRT: SAL TREE
JESUS'S SHIRT: GRAPES
IF YOU'RE THIS DEVOTED TO HIM...
...WHY DON'T YOU LISTEN TO BUDDHA'S REQUEST?
AFTER ALL, YOU LOVE HIM MORE...
...THAN ANY OTHER PLANT IN THE WORLD, DON'T YOU?
ZWOOOSH
KSHUF
HEY! WHY DID YOU MULTIPLY SO MU...
!!
THESE ARE DIFFERENT PLANTS! IN FACT...
FWOO
THIS SCENT...

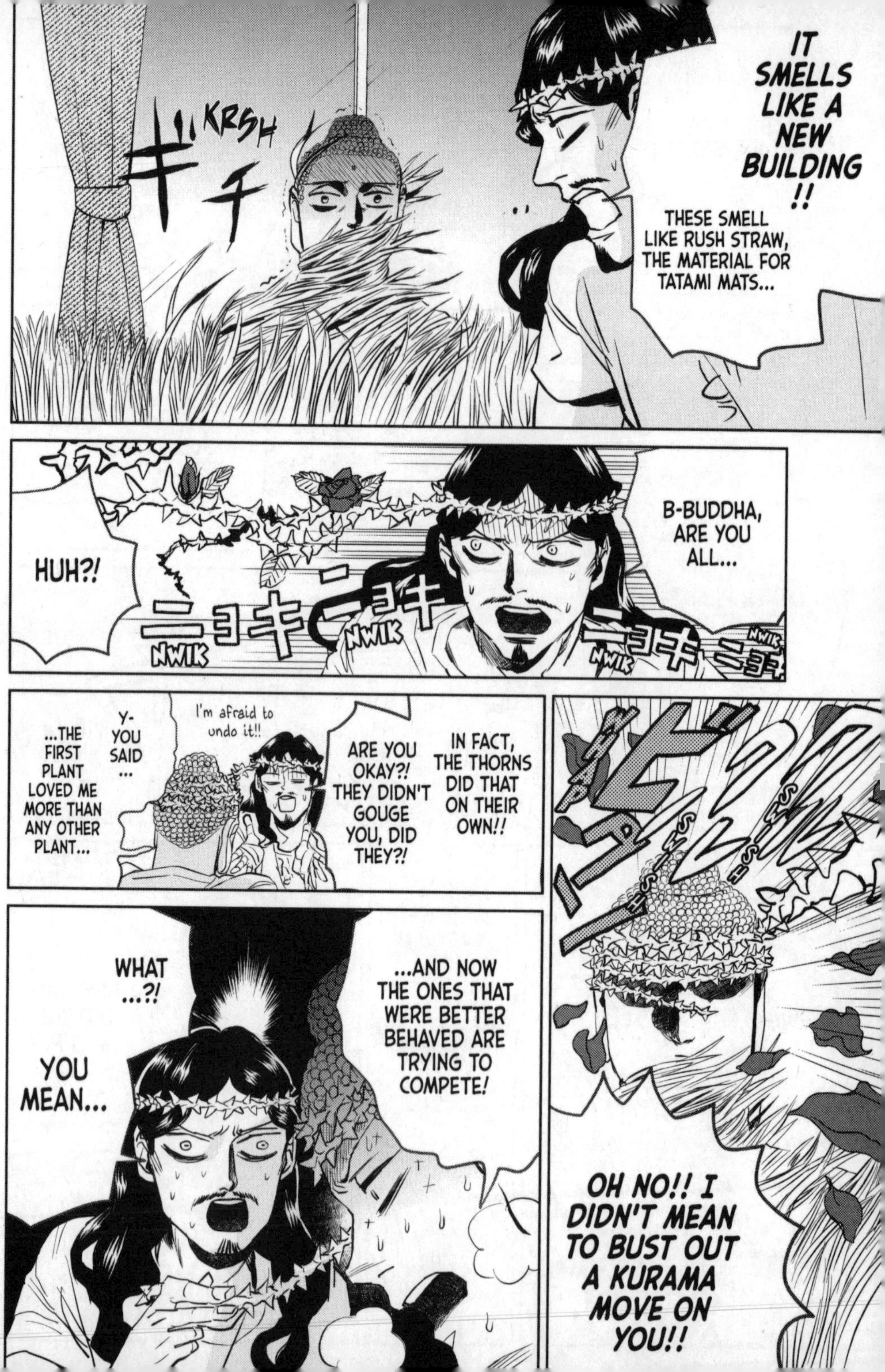
IT SMELLS LIKE A NEW BUILDING!!
THESE SMELL LIKE RUSH STRAW, THE MATERIAL FOR TATAMI MATS...
KRSH
B-BUDDHA, ARE YOU ALL...
NWIK
NWIK
NWIK
NWIK
HUH?!
OH NO!! I DIDN'T MEAN TO BUST OUT A KURAMA MOVE ON YOU!!
IN FACT, THE THORNS DID THAT ON THEIR OWN!!
ARE YOU OKAY?! THEY DIDN'T GOUGE YOU, DID THEY?!
I'm afraid to undo it!!
Y- YOU SAID...
...THE FIRST PLANT LOVED ME MORE THAN ANY OTHER PLANT...
...AND NOW THE ONES THAT WERE BETTER BEHAVED ARE TRYING TO COMPETE!
WHAT...?!
YOU MEAN...

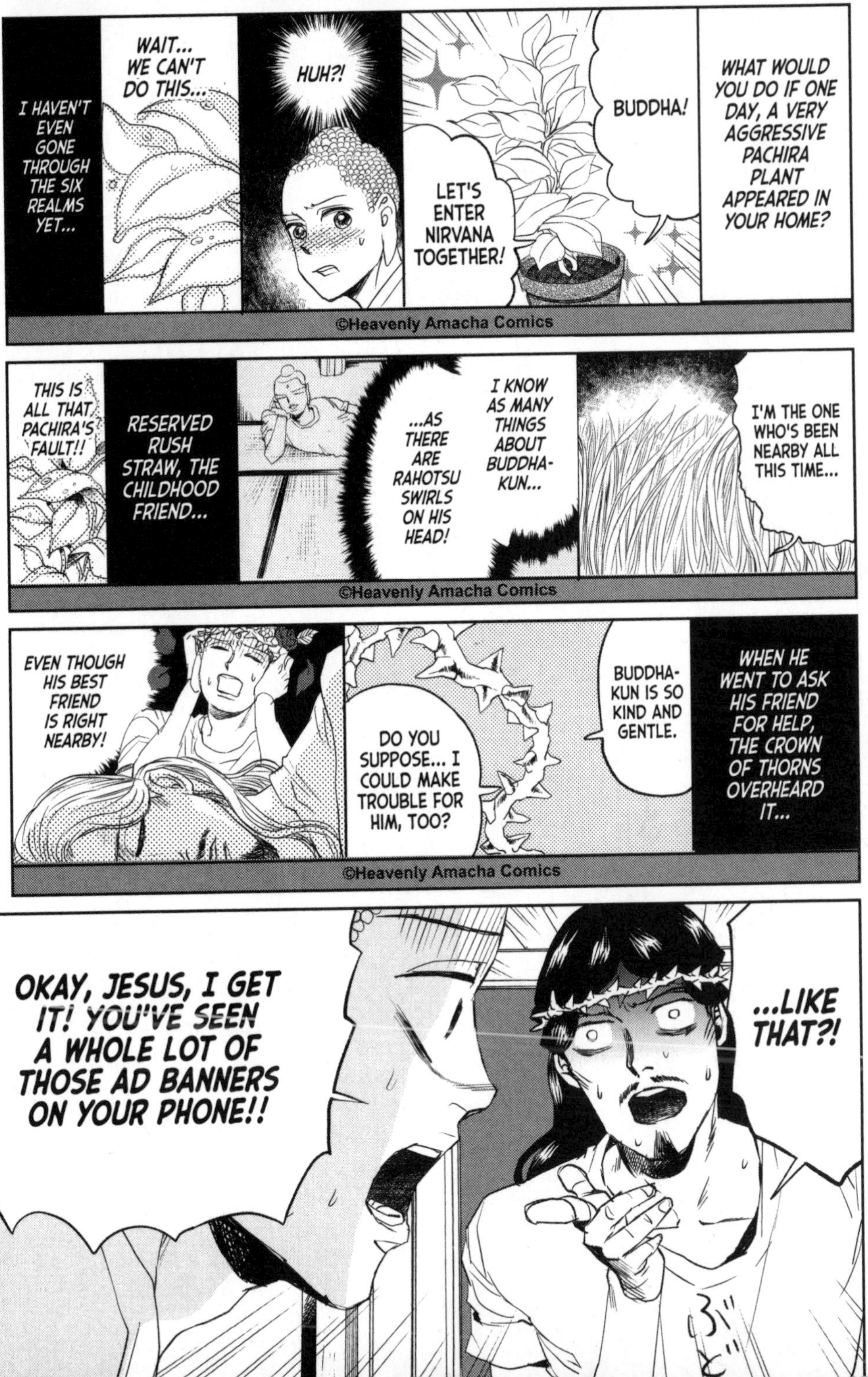
WHAT WOULD YOU DO IF ONE DAY, A VERY AGGRESSIVE PACHIRA PLANT APPEARED IN YOUR HOME?
BUDDHA!
LET'S ENTER NIRVANA TOGETHER!
HUH?!
WAIT... WE CAN'T DO THIS...
I HAVEN'T EVEN GONE THROUGH THE SIX REALMS YET...
©Heavenly Amacha Comics
I'M THE ONE WHO'S BEEN NEARBY ALL THIS TIME...
I KNOW AS MANY THINGS ABOUT BUDDHA-KUN...
...AS THERE ARE RAHOTSU SWIRLS ON HIS HEAD!
RESERVED RUSH STRAW, THE CHILDHOOD FRIEND...
THIS IS ALL THAT PACHIRA'S FAULT!!
©Heavenly Amacha Comics
WHEN HE WENT TO ASK HIS FRIEND FOR HELP, THE CROWN OF THORNS OVERHEARD IT...
BUDDHA-KUN IS SO KIND AND GENTLE.
DO YOU SUPPOSE... I COULD MAKE TROUBLE FOR HIM, TOO?
EVEN THOUGH HIS BEST FRIEND IS RIGHT NEARBY!
©Heavenly Amacha Comics
...LIKE THAT?!
OKAY, JESUS, I GET IT! YOU'VE SEEN A WHOLE LOT OF THOSE AD BANNERS ON YOUR PHONE!!

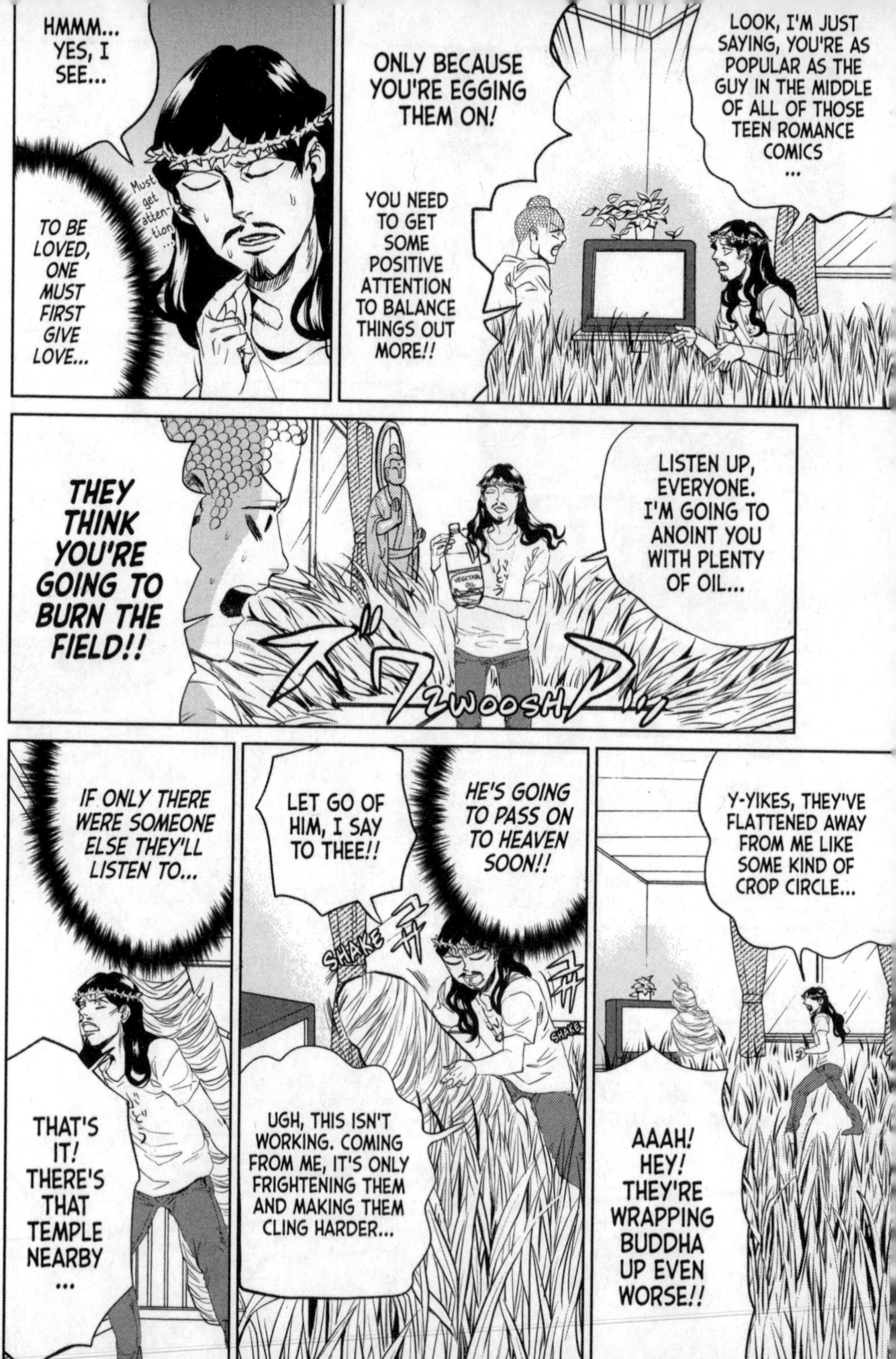
LOOK, I'M JUST SAYING, YOU'RE AS POPULAR AS THE GUY IN THE MIDDLE OF ALL OF THOSE TEEN ROMANCE COMICS ...
ONLY BECAUSE YOU'RE EGGING THEM ON!
YOU NEED TO GET SOME POSITIVE ATTENTION TO BALANCE THINGS OUT MORE!!
HMMM... YES, I SEE...
Must get atten- tion ...
TO BE LOVED, ONE MUST FIRST GIVE LOVE...
LISTEN UP, EVERYONE. I'M GOING TO ANOINT YOU WITH PLENTY OF OIL...
VEGETABLE OIL
THEY THINK YOU'RE GOING TO BURN THE FIELD!!
ZWOOSH
Y-YIKES, THEY'VE FLATTENED AWAY FROM ME LIKE SOME KIND OF CROP CIRCLE...
AAAH! HEY! THEY'RE WRAPPING BUDDHA UP EVEN WORSE!!
HE'S GOING TO PASS ON TO HEAVEN SOON!!
LET GO OF HIM, I SAY TO THEE!!
SHAKE
SHAKE
UGH, THIS ISN'T WORKING. COMING FROM ME, IT'S ONLY FRIGHTENING THEM AND MAKING THEM CLING HARDER...
IF ONLY THERE WERE SOMEONE ELSE THEY'LL LISTEN TO...
THAT'S IT! THERE'S THAT TEMPLE NEARBY ...

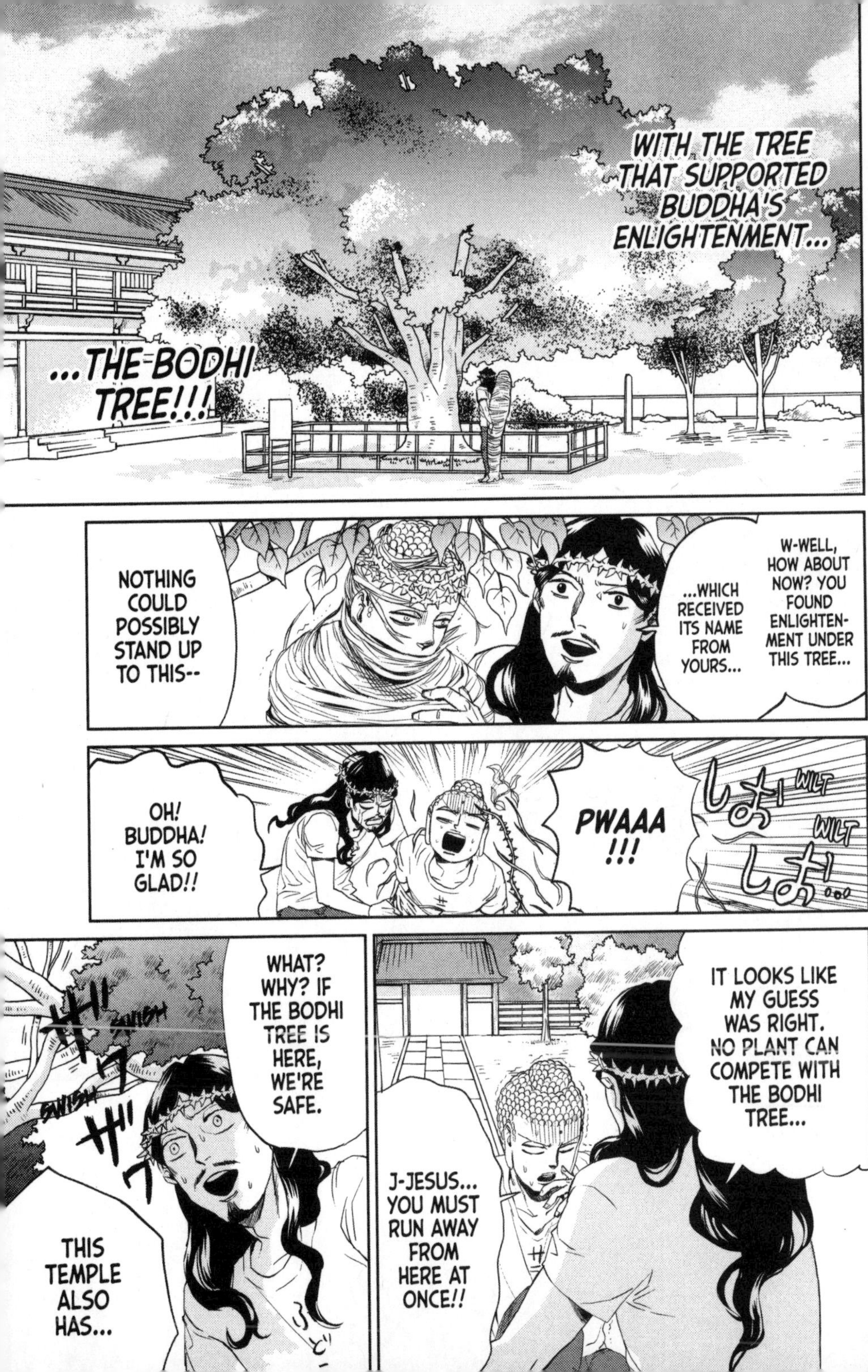
WITH THE TREE THAT SUPPORTED BUDDHA'S ENLIGHTENMENT...
...THE BODHI TREE!!!
W-WELL, HOW ABOUT NOW? YOU FOUND ENLIGHTEN-MENT UNDER THIS TREE...
...WHICH RECEIVED ITS NAME FROM YOURS...
NOTHING COULD POSSIBLY STAND UP TO THIS--
WILT WILT
PWAAA !!!
OH! BUDDHA! I'M SO GLAD!!
IT LOOKS LIKE MY GUESS WAS RIGHT. NO PLANT CAN COMPETE WITH THE BODHI TREE...
J-JESUS... YOU MUST RUN AWAY FROM HERE AT ONCE!!
WHAT? WHY? IF THE BODHI TREE IS HERE, WE'RE SAFE.
SWISH SWISH
THIS TEMPLE ALSO HAS...

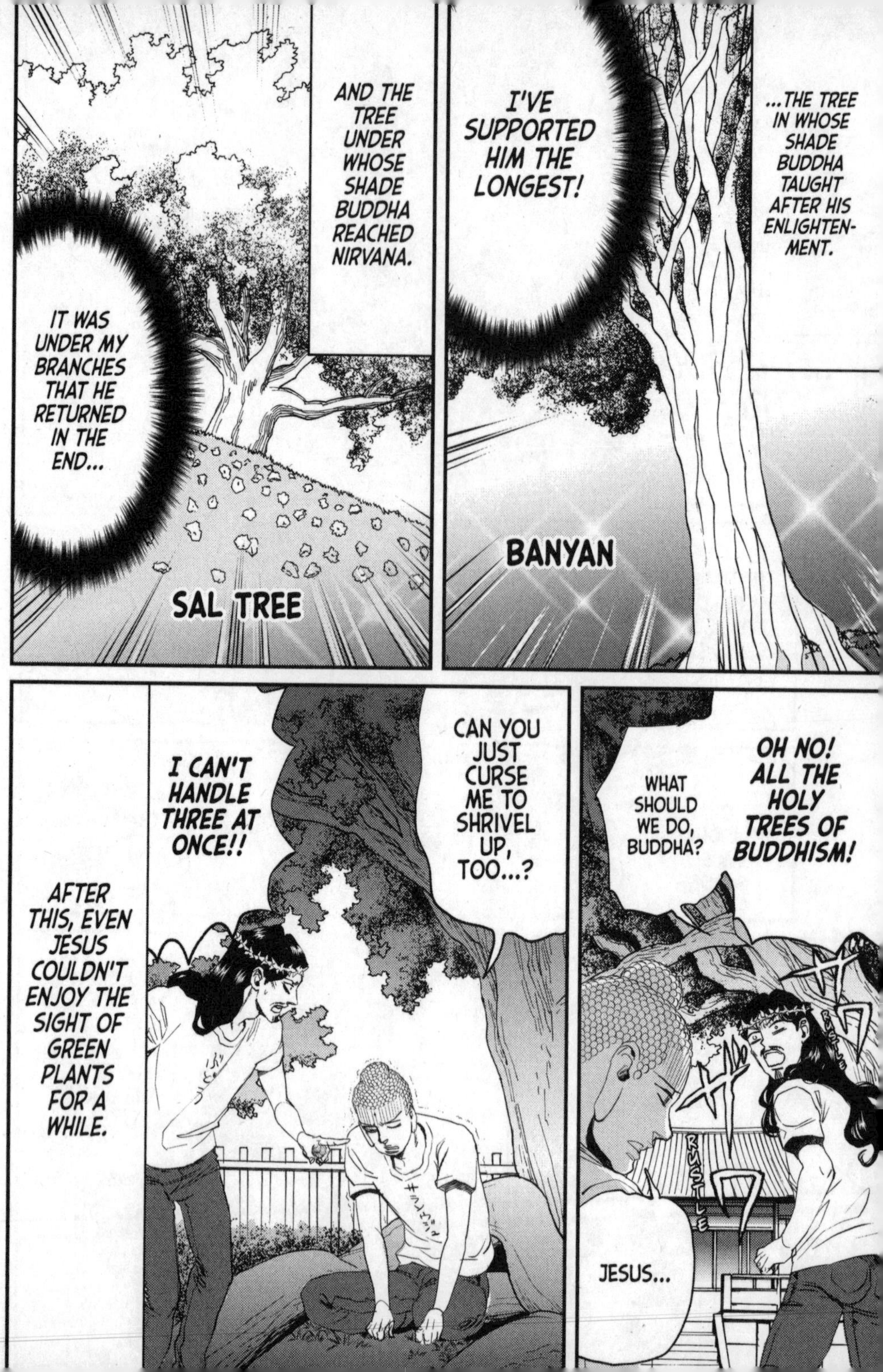
...THE TREE IN WHOSE SHADE BUDDHA TAUGHT AFTER HIS ENLIGHTENMENT.
I'VE SUPPORTED HIM THE LONGEST!
BANYAN
AND THE TREE UNDER WHOSE SHADE BUDDHA REACHED NIRVANA.
IT WAS UNDER MY BRANCHES THAT HE RETURNED IN THE END...
SAL TREE
OH NO! ALL THE HOLY TREES OF BUDDHISM!
WHAT SHOULD WE DO, BUDDHA?
RUSTLE
RUSTLE
JESUS...
CAN YOU JUST CURSE ME TO SHRIVEL UP, TOO...?
I CAN'T HANDLE THREE AT ONCE!!
AFTER THIS, EVEN JESUS COULDN'T ENJOY THE SIGHT OF GREEN PLANTS FOR A WHILE.

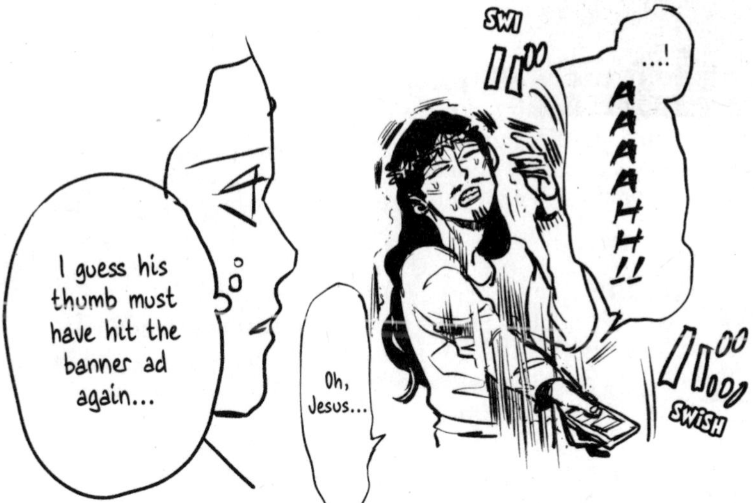
SWI
...!
AAAAHH!!
SWISH
Oh, Jesus...
I guess his thumb must have hit the banner ad again...

SAINT☆YOUNG MEN

CHAPTER 87 TRANSLATION NOTES

Banyan, page 109

A relative of the bodhi tree, which is the tree under which the Buddha was said to have reached enlightenment. The banyan tree, by contrast, has some of the widest canopy coverage on earth, because it grows down roots that, when they find soil, grow into full-sized trunks of their own. Thus, the banyan is often compared to the cycle of Samsara: without beginning or end.

Fig tree, page 111

There are a number of stories in the Gospels about fig trees. In one parable, Jesus compares the budding of a fig tree, signaling the coming of the season, to the coming of the kingdom of God. In another parable, a man with a barren fig tree wants to cut it down, but his gardener pleads with him to wait one more year, in case it will bear fruit.

Goya, page 113

A type of vegetable found in Asia and Africa, commonly called "bitter melon." In Okinawa, where it is a regular part of cuisine, it is called goya. The vines can grow up to 16 feet in length.

Pinning against the wall, page 117

A romantic scenario that became a recent trend in Japan called *kabe-don*, meaning "wall-thump." It refers to one person approaching a submissive romantic target who is standing against or near a wall, and aggressively pushing their arm against the wall (the "*don*") over the target's shoulder, to trap them there.

Sal tree, page 119

A type of tree found in India. It is known as the tree that the Buddha died beneath, and is one of the Three Holy Trees of Buddhism, along with the ashoka tree (where the Buddha was born) and bodhi or banyan tree (where the Buddha reached enlightenment).

Kurama, page 120

One of the principal characters from the classic '90s series *Yu Yu Hakusho* by Yoshihiro Togashi. Kurama is a fox demon who carries a rose that turns into a whip of thorns.

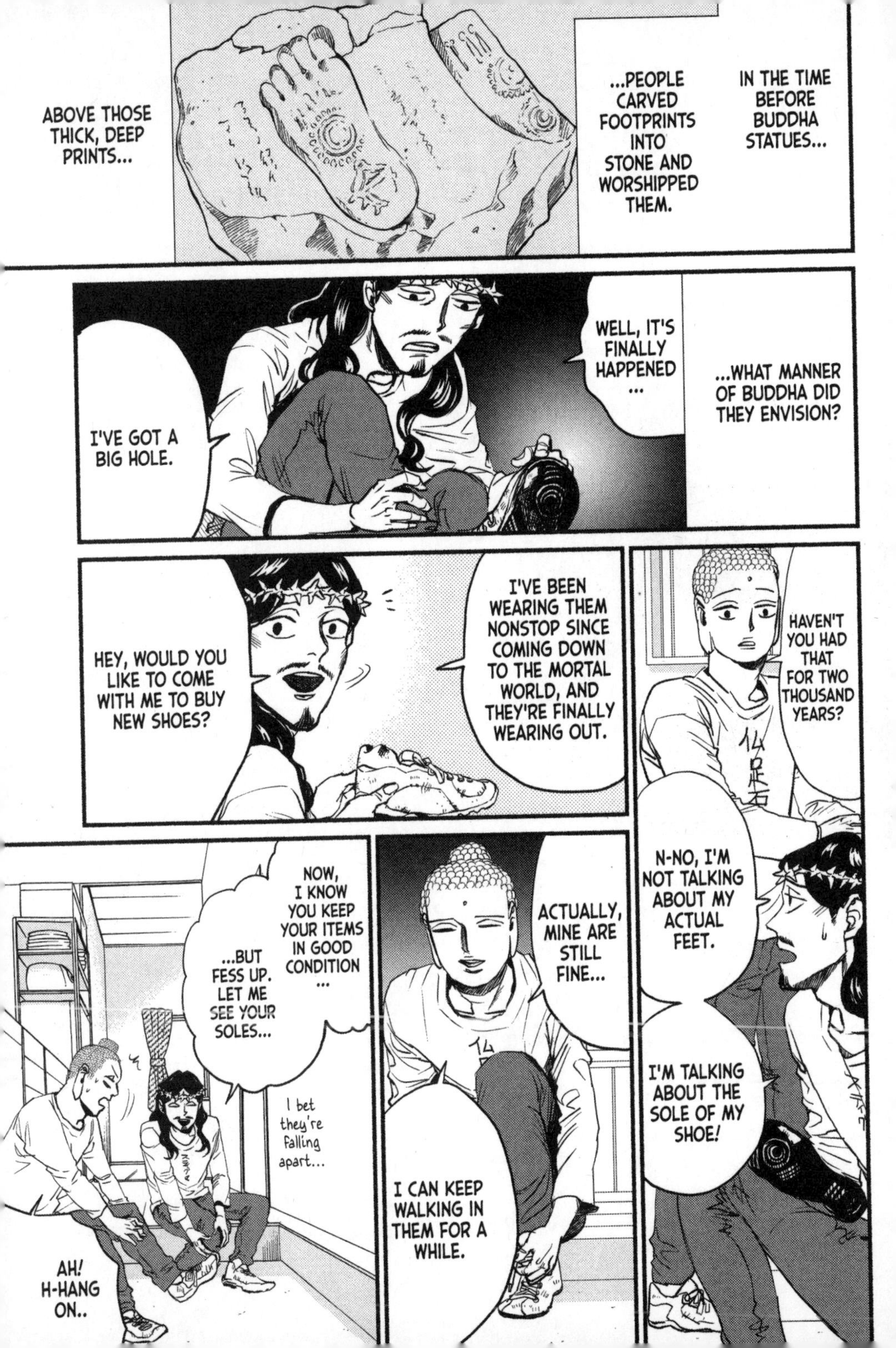
IN THE TIME BEFORE BUDDHA STATUES...
...PEOPLE CARVED FOOTPRINTS INTO STONE AND WORSHIPPED THEM.
ABOVE THOSE THICK, DEEP PRINTS...
...WHAT MANNER OF BUDDHA DID THEY ENVISION?
WELL, IT'S FINALLY HAPPENED...
I'VE GOT A BIG HOLE.
HAVEN'T YOU HAD THAT FOR TWO THOUSAND YEARS?
N-NO, I'M NOT TALKING ABOUT MY ACTUAL FEET.
I'M TALKING ABOUT THE SOLE OF MY SHOE!
I'VE BEEN WEARING THEM NONSTOP SINCE COMING DOWN TO THE MORTAL WORLD, AND THEY'RE FINALLY WEARING OUT.
HEY, WOULD YOU LIKE TO COME WITH ME TO BUY NEW SHOES?
ACTUALLY, MINE ARE STILL FINE...
I CAN KEEP WALKING IN THEM FOR A WHILE.
NOW, I KNOW YOU KEEP YOUR ITEMS IN GOOD CONDITION...
...BUT FESS UP. LET ME SEE YOUR SOLES...
I bet they're falling apart...
AH! H-HANG ON..

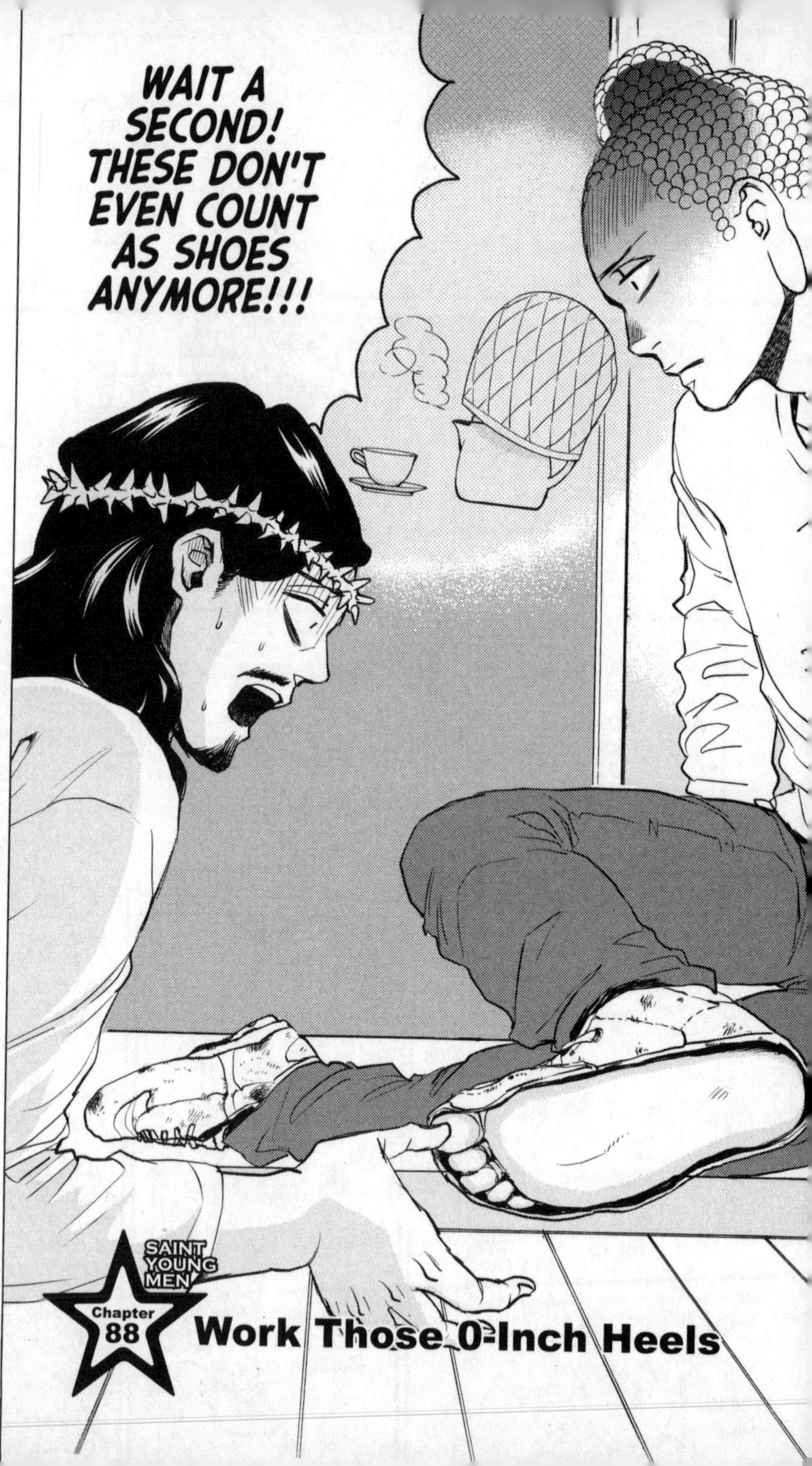
WAIT A SECOND! THESE DON'T EVEN COUNT AS SHOES ANYMORE!!!
SAINT YOUNG MEN
Chapter 88
Work Those 0-Inch Heels

THE BUDDHIST VERSION OF THE DE-CLUTTERING CRAZE EXTENDS TO SHOE SOLES.

BUDDHA
AUTUMN IS THE SEASON OF NEW RICE! WITH MATSUDA-SAN'S HOMEMADE UMEBOSHI AND NUKAZUKE, OUR MEALS ARE AMAZING NOW.

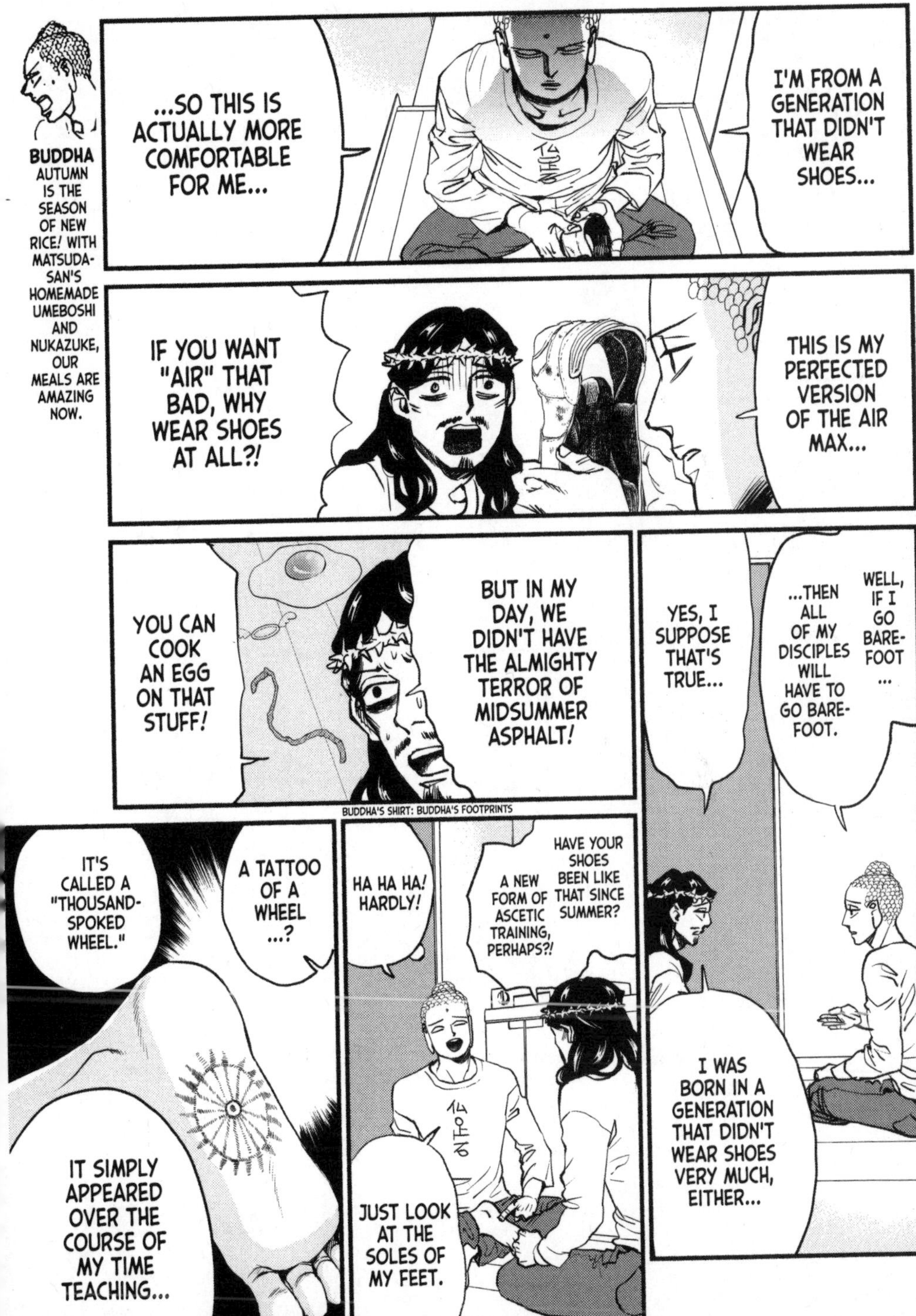
I'M FROM A GENERATION THAT DIDN'T WEAR SHOES...
...SO THIS IS ACTUALLY MORE COMFORTABLE FOR ME...
THIS IS MY PERFECTED VERSION OF THE AIR MAX...
IF YOU WANT "AIR" THAT BAD, WHY WEAR SHOES AT ALL?!
WELL, IF I GO BAREFOOT...
...THEN ALL OF MY DISCIPLES WILL HAVE TO GO BAREFOOT.
YES, I SUPPOSE THAT'S TRUE...
I WAS BORN IN A GENERATION THAT DIDN'T WEAR SHOES VERY MUCH, EITHER...
BUT IN MY DAY, WE DIDN'T HAVE THE ALMIGHTY TERROR OF MIDSUMMER ASPHALT!
YOU CAN COOK AN EGG ON THAT STUFF!
BUDDHA'S SHIRT: BUDDHA'S FOOTPRINTS
HAVE YOUR SHOES BEEN LIKE THAT SINCE SUMMER?
A NEW FORM OF ASCETIC TRAINING, PERHAPS?!
HA HA HA! HARDLY!
JUST LOOK AT THE SOLES OF MY FEET.
A TATTOO OF A WHEEL...?
IT'S CALLED A "THOUSAND-SPOKED WHEEL."
IT SIMPLY APPEARED OVER THE COURSE OF MY TIME TEACHING...

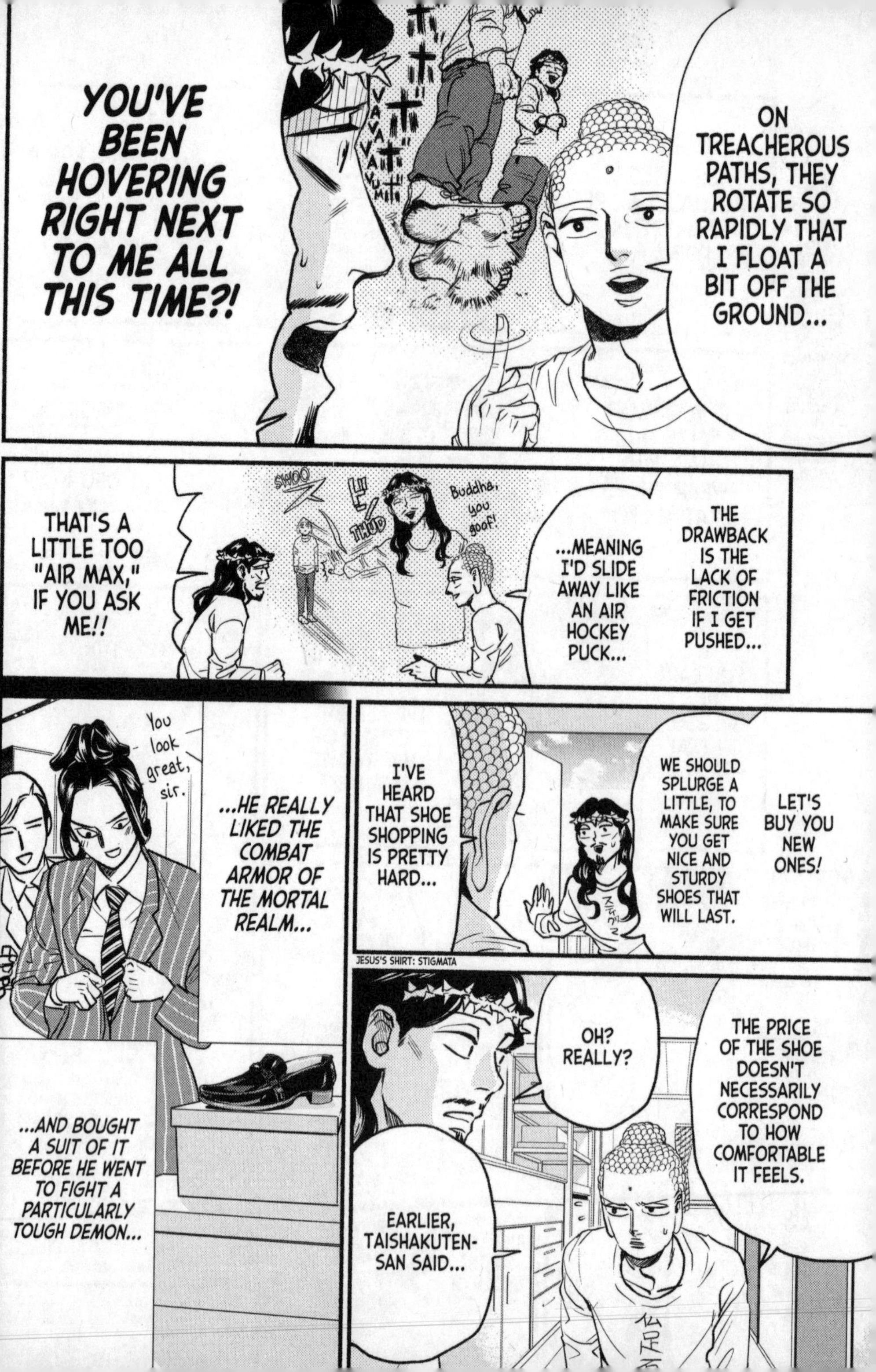
ON TREACHEROUS PATHS, THEY ROTATE SO RAPIDLY THAT I FLOAT A BIT OFF THE GROUND...
YOU'VE BEEN HOVERING RIGHT NEXT TO ME ALL THIS TIME?!
THE DRAWBACK IS THE LACK OF FRICTION IF I GET PUSHED...
...MEANING I'D SLIDE AWAY LIKE AN AIR HOCKEY PUCK...
Buddha, you goof!
SHOO
THUD
THAT'S A LITTLE TOO "AIR MAX," IF YOU ASK ME!!
LET'S BUY YOU NEW ONES!
WE SHOULD SPLURGE A LITTLE, TO MAKE SURE YOU GET NICE AND STURDY SHOES THAT WILL LAST.
I'VE HEARD THAT SHOE SHOPPING IS PRETTY HARD...
JESUS'S SHIRT: STIGMATA
THE PRICE OF THE SHOE DOESN'T NECESSARILY CORRESPOND TO HOW COMFORTABLE IT FEELS.
OH? REALLY?
EARLIER, TAISHAKUTEN-SAN SAID...
...HE REALLY LIKED THE COMBAT ARMOR OF THE MORTAL REALM...
You look great, sir.
...AND BOUGHT A SUIT OF IT BEFORE HE WENT TO FIGHT A PARTICULARLY TOUGH DEMON...

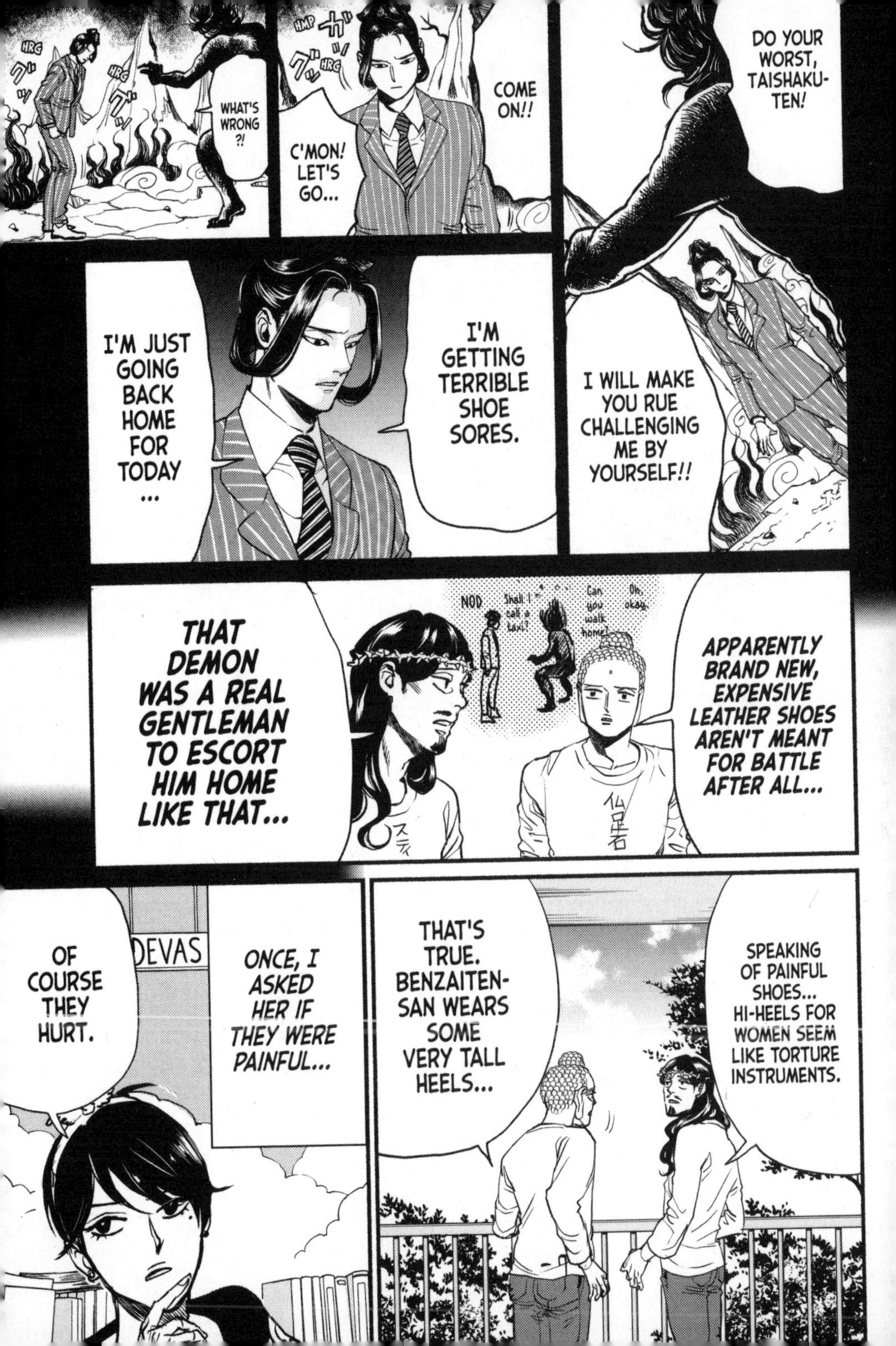
DO YOUR WORST, TAISHAKU-TEN!
I WILL MAKE YOU RUE CHALLENGING ME BY YOURSELF!!
HMP
HRG
COME ON!!
C'MON! LET'S GO...
HRG
HRG
WHAT'S WRONG?!
I'M GETTING TERRIBLE SHOE SORES.
I'M JUST GOING BACK HOME FOR TODAY...
APPARENTLY BRAND NEW, EXPENSIVE LEATHER SHOES AREN'T MEANT FOR BATTLE AFTER ALL...
Oh, okay.
Can you walk home?
Shall I call a taxi?
NOD
THAT DEMON WAS A REAL GENTLEMAN TO ESCORT HIM HOME LIKE THAT...
SPEAKING OF PAINFUL SHOES... HI-HEELS FOR WOMEN SEEM LIKE TORTURE INSTRUMENTS.
THAT'S TRUE. BENZAITEN-SAN WEARS SOME VERY TALL HEELS...
ONCE, I ASKED HER IF THEY WERE PAINFUL...
DEVAS
OF COURSE THEY HURT.

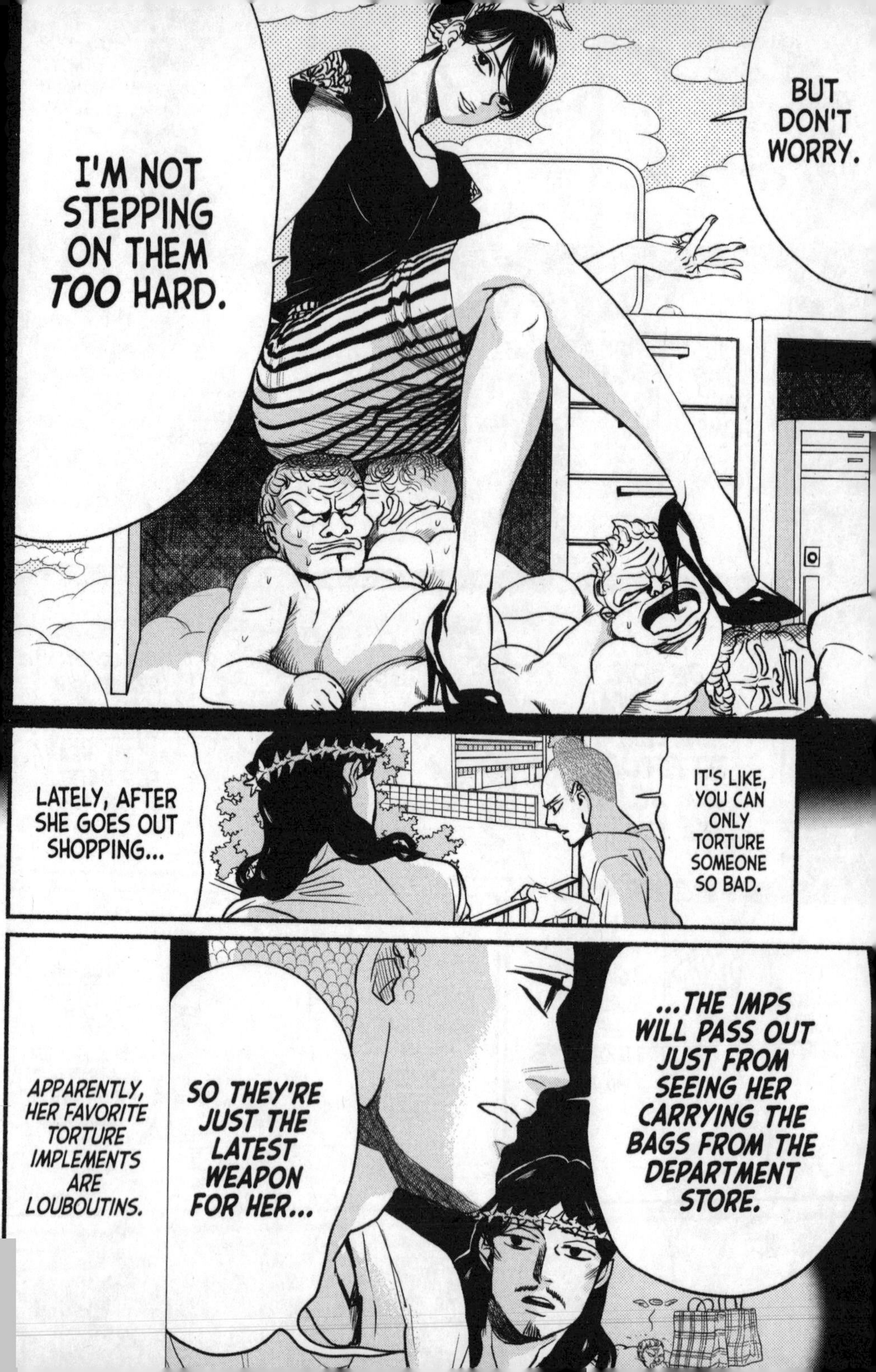
BUT DON'T WORRY.
I'M NOT STEPPING ON THEM *TOO* HARD.
IT'S LIKE, YOU CAN ONLY TORTURE SOMEONE SO BAD.
LATELY, AFTER SHE GOES OUT SHOPPING...
...THE IMPS WILL PASS OUT JUST FROM SEEING HER CARRYING THE BAGS FROM THE DEPARTMENT STORE.
SO THEY'RE JUST THE LATEST WEAPON FOR HER...
APPARENTLY, HER FAVORITE TORTURE IMPLEMENTS ARE LOUBOUTINS.

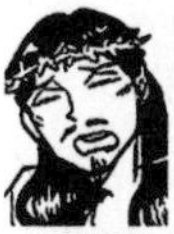

JESUS
WHAT I LOVE ABOUT THE AUTUMN IS THE FULL MOON FESTIVAL! LATELY, I'VE STARTED TO SEE THE RABBIT IN THE PATTERN ON THE MOON.

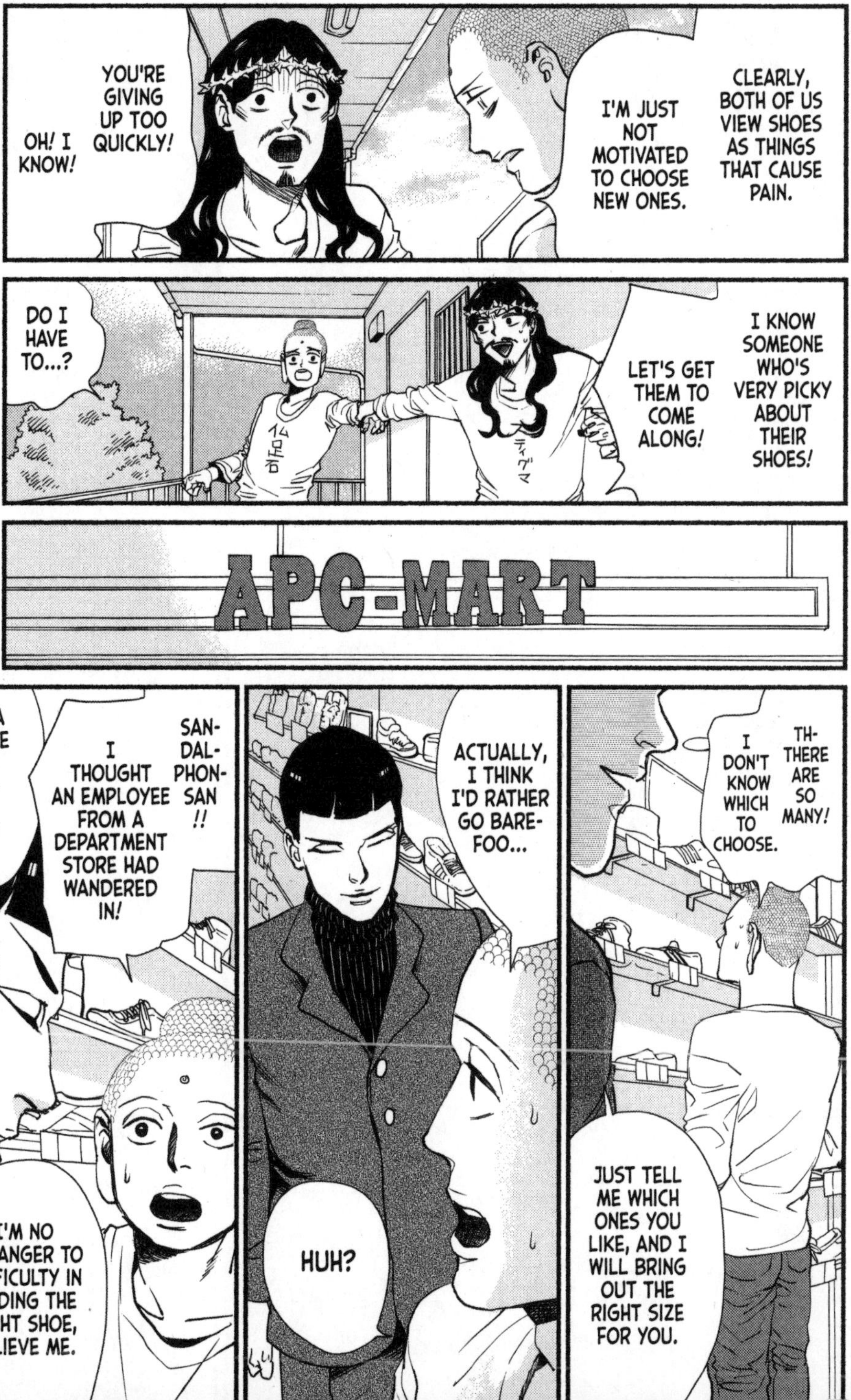

CLEARLY, BOTH OF US VIEW SHOES AS THINGS THAT CAUSE PAIN.
I'M JUST NOT MOTIVATED TO CHOOSE NEW ONES.
YOU'RE GIVING UP TOO QUICKLY!
OH! I KNOW!
I KNOW SOMEONE WHO'S VERY PICKY ABOUT THEIR SHOES!
LET'S GET THEM TO COME ALONG!
DO I HAVE TO...?
APC-MART
TH-THERE ARE SO MANY!
I DON'T KNOW WHICH TO CHOOSE.
JUST TELL ME WHICH ONES YOU LIKE, AND I WILL BRING OUT THE RIGHT SIZE FOR YOU.
ACTUALLY, I THINK I'D RATHER GO BARE-FOO...
HUH?
SAN-DAL-PHON-SAN!!
I THOUGHT AN EMPLOYEE FROM A DEPARTMENT STORE HAD WANDERED IN!
I GOT A MESSAGE FROM JESUS-SAMA ABOUT YOU.
I'M NO STRANGER TO DIFFICULTY IN FINDING THE RIGHT SHOE, BELIEVE ME.

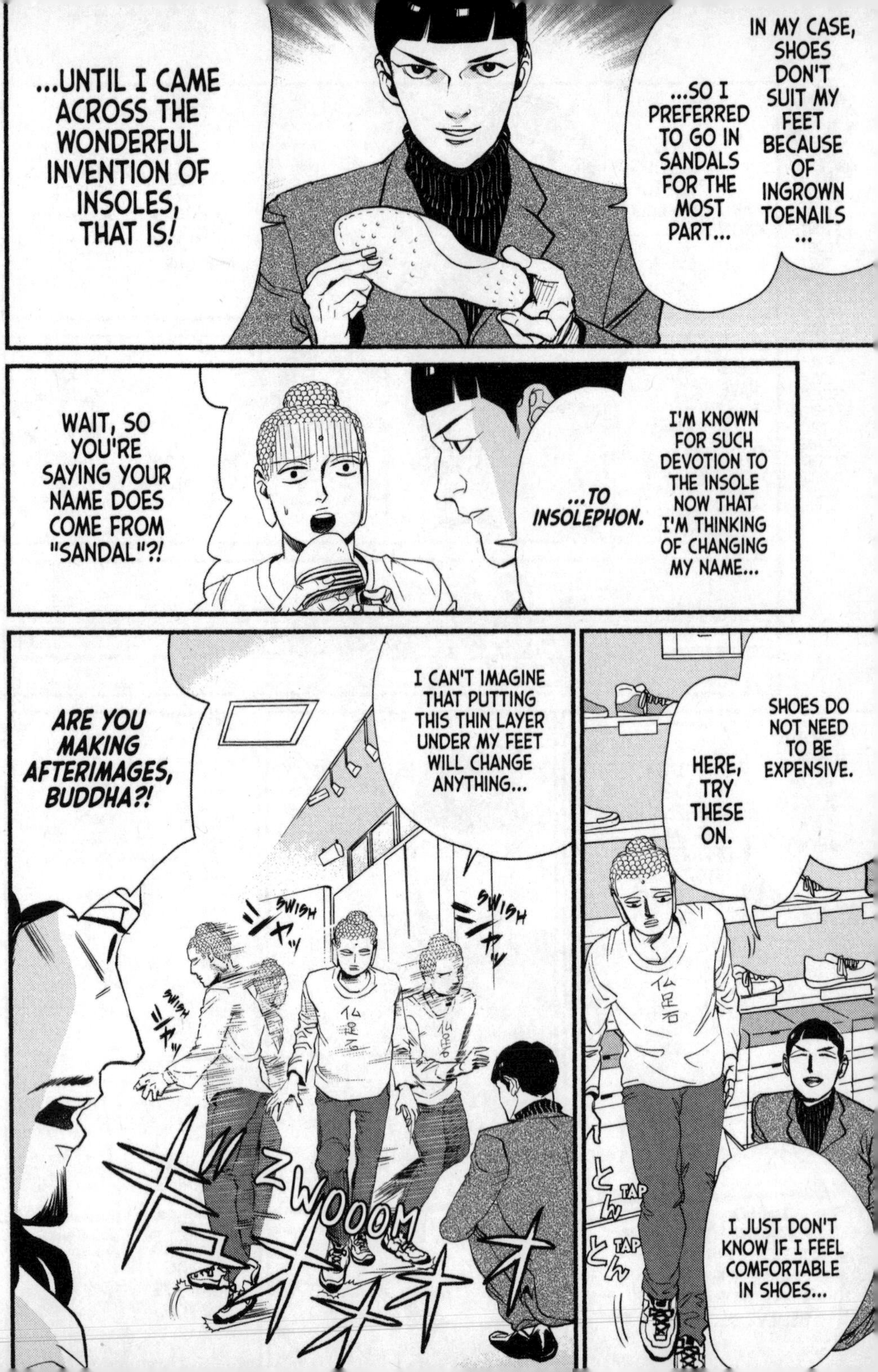
IN MY CASE, SHOES DON'T SUIT MY FEET BECAUSE OF INGROWN TOENAILS...
...SO I PREFERRED TO GO IN SANDALS FOR THE MOST PART...
...UNTIL I CAME ACROSS THE WONDERFUL INVENTION OF INSOLES, THAT IS!
I'M KNOWN FOR SUCH DEVOTION TO THE INSOLE NOW THAT I'M THINKING OF CHANGING MY NAME...
...TO INSOLEPHON.
WAIT, SO YOU'RE SAYING YOUR NAME DOES COME FROM "SANDAL"?!
SHOES DO NOT NEED TO BE EXPENSIVE.
HERE, TRY THESE ON.
TAP
TAP
I JUST DON'T KNOW IF I FEEL COMFORTABLE IN SHOES...
I CAN'T IMAGINE THAT PUTTING THIS THIN LAYER UNDER MY FEET WILL CHANGE ANYTHING...
SWISH
SWISH
SWISH
ZWOOOM
ARE YOU MAKING AFTERIMAGES, BUDDHA?!

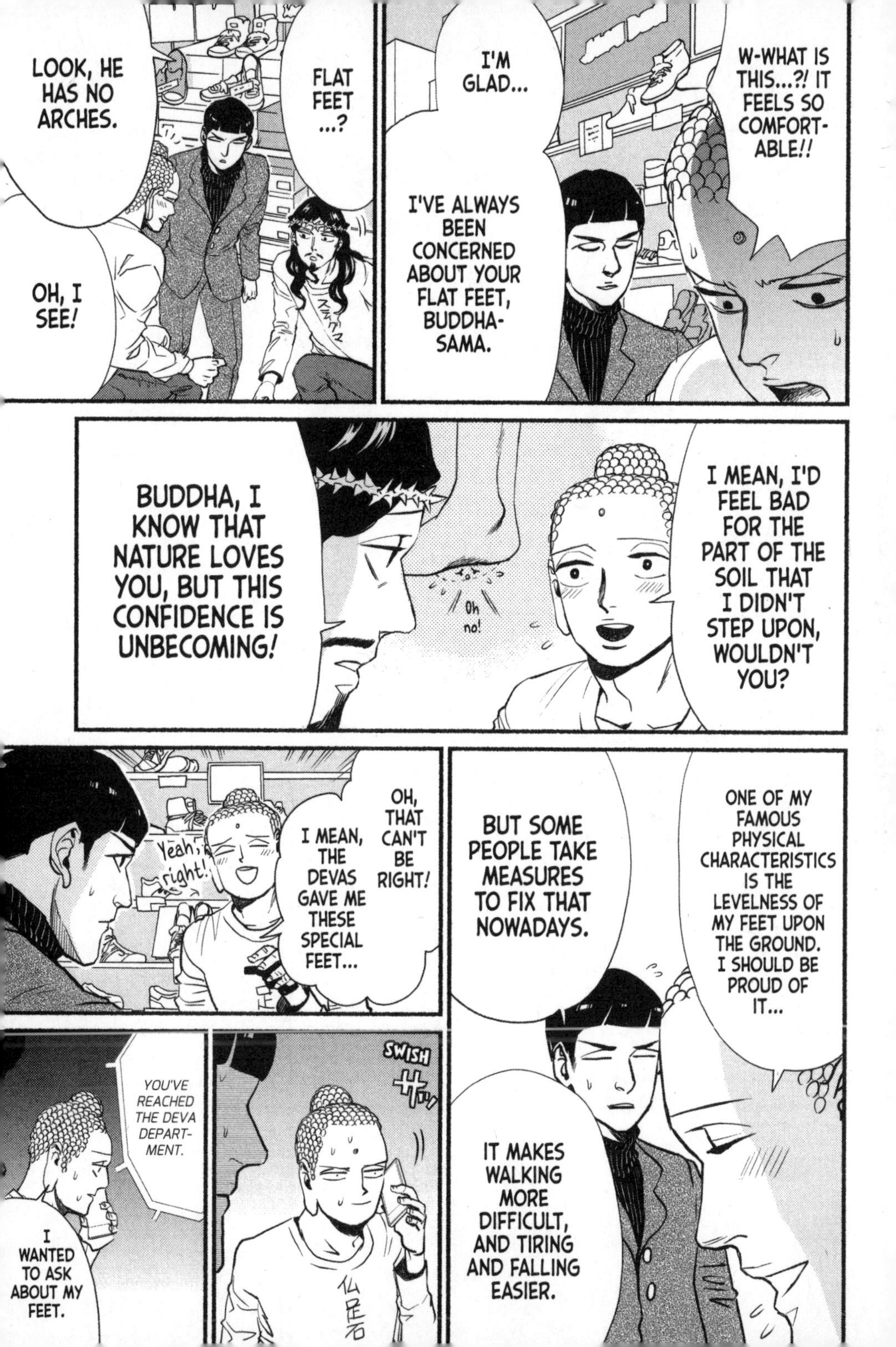
W-WHAT IS THIS...?! IT FEELS SO COMFORTABLE!!
I'M GLAD...
I'VE ALWAYS BEEN CONCERNED ABOUT YOUR FLAT FEET, BUDDHA-SAMA.
FLAT FEET ...?
LOOK, HE HAS NO ARCHES.
OH, I SEE!
I MEAN, I'D FEEL BAD FOR THE PART OF THE SOIL THAT I DIDN'T STEP UPON, WOULDN'T YOU?
Oh no!
BUDDHA, I KNOW THAT NATURE LOVES YOU, BUT THIS CONFIDENCE IS UNBECOMING!
ONE OF MY FAMOUS PHYSICAL CHARACTERISTICS IS THE LEVELNESS OF MY FEET UPON THE GROUND. I SHOULD BE PROUD OF IT...
BUT SOME PEOPLE TAKE MEASURES TO FIX THAT NOWADAYS.
IT MAKES WALKING MORE DIFFICULT, AND TIRING AND FALLING EASIER.
OH, THAT CAN'T BE RIGHT!
I MEAN, THE DEVAS GAVE ME THESE SPECIAL FEET...
Yeah, right!
SWISH
YOU'VE REACHED THE DEVA DEPARTMENT.
I WANTED TO ASK ABOUT MY FEET.

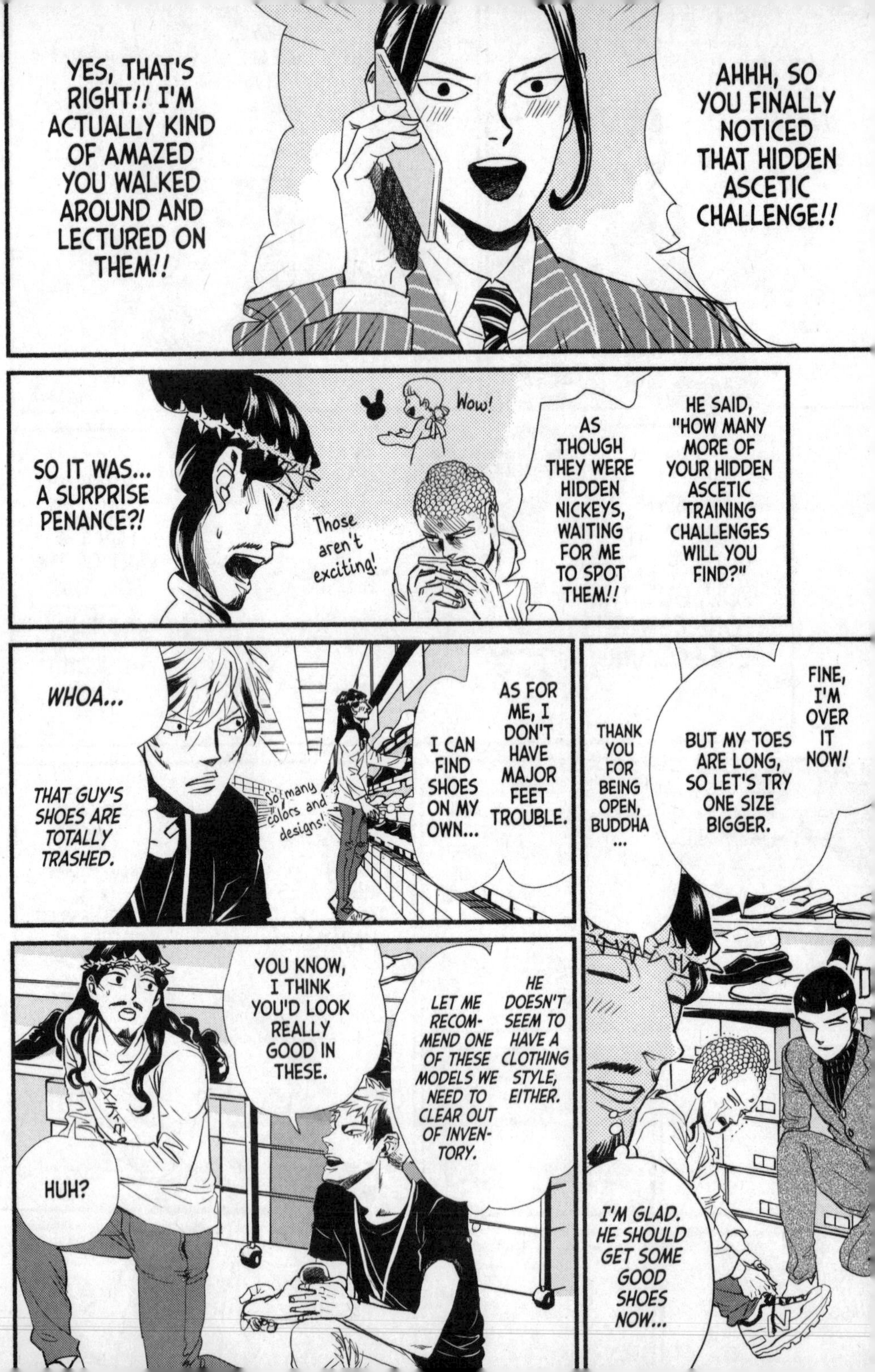
AHHH, SO YOU FINALLY NOTICED THAT HIDDEN ASCETIC CHALLENGE!!
YES, THAT'S RIGHT!! I'M ACTUALLY KIND OF AMAZED YOU WALKED AROUND AND LECTURED ON THEM!!
HE SAID, "HOW MANY MORE OF YOUR HIDDEN ASCETIC TRAINING CHALLENGES WILL YOU FIND?"
AS THOUGH THEY WERE HIDDEN NICKEYS, WAITING FOR ME TO SPOT THEM!!
Wow!
Those aren't exciting!
SO IT WAS... A SURPRISE PENANCE?!
FINE, I'M OVER IT NOW!
BUT MY TOES ARE LONG, SO LET'S TRY ONE SIZE BIGGER.
THANK YOU FOR BEING OPEN, BUDDHA ...
I'M GLAD. HE SHOULD GET SOME GOOD SHOES NOW...
AS FOR ME, I DON'T HAVE MAJOR FEET TROUBLE.
I CAN FIND SHOES ON MY OWN...
So many colors and designs!
WHOA...
THAT GUY'S SHOES ARE TOTALLY TRASHED.
HE DOESN'T SEEM TO HAVE A CLOTHING STYLE, EITHER.
LET ME RECOMMEND ONE OF THESE MODELS WE NEED TO CLEAR OUT OF INVENTORY.
YOU KNOW, I THINK YOU'D LOOK REALLY GOOD IN THESE.
HUH?

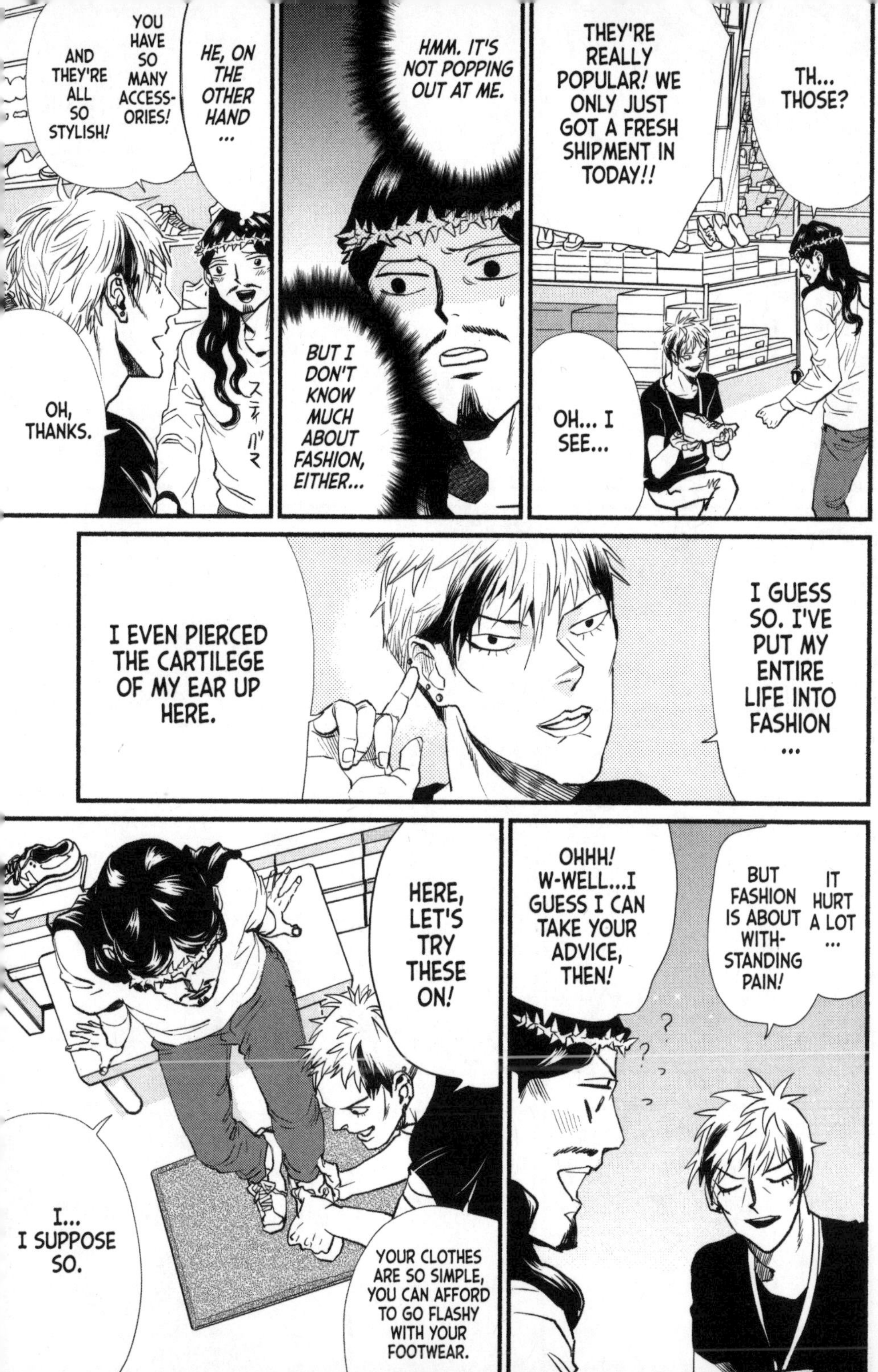
TH... THOSE?
THEY'RE REALLY POPULAR! WE ONLY JUST GOT A FRESH SHIPMENT IN TODAY!!
OH... I SEE...
HMM. IT'S NOT POPPING OUT AT ME.
BUT I DON'T KNOW MUCH ABOUT FASHION, EITHER...
HE, ON THE OTHER HAND ...
YOU HAVE SO MANY ACCESSORIES!
AND THEY'RE ALL SO STYLISH!
OH, THANKS.
スティグマ
I GUESS SO. I'VE PUT MY ENTIRE LIFE INTO FASHION ...
I EVEN PIERCED THE CARTILEGE OF MY EAR UP HERE.
IT HURT A LOT ...
BUT FASHION IS ABOUT WITH-STANDING PAIN!
OHHH! W-WELL...I GUESS I CAN TAKE YOUR ADVICE, THEN!
HERE, LET'S TRY THESE ON!
YOUR CLOTHES ARE SO SIMPLE, YOU CAN AFFORD TO GO FLASHY WITH YOUR FOOTWEAR.
I... I SUPPOSE SO.

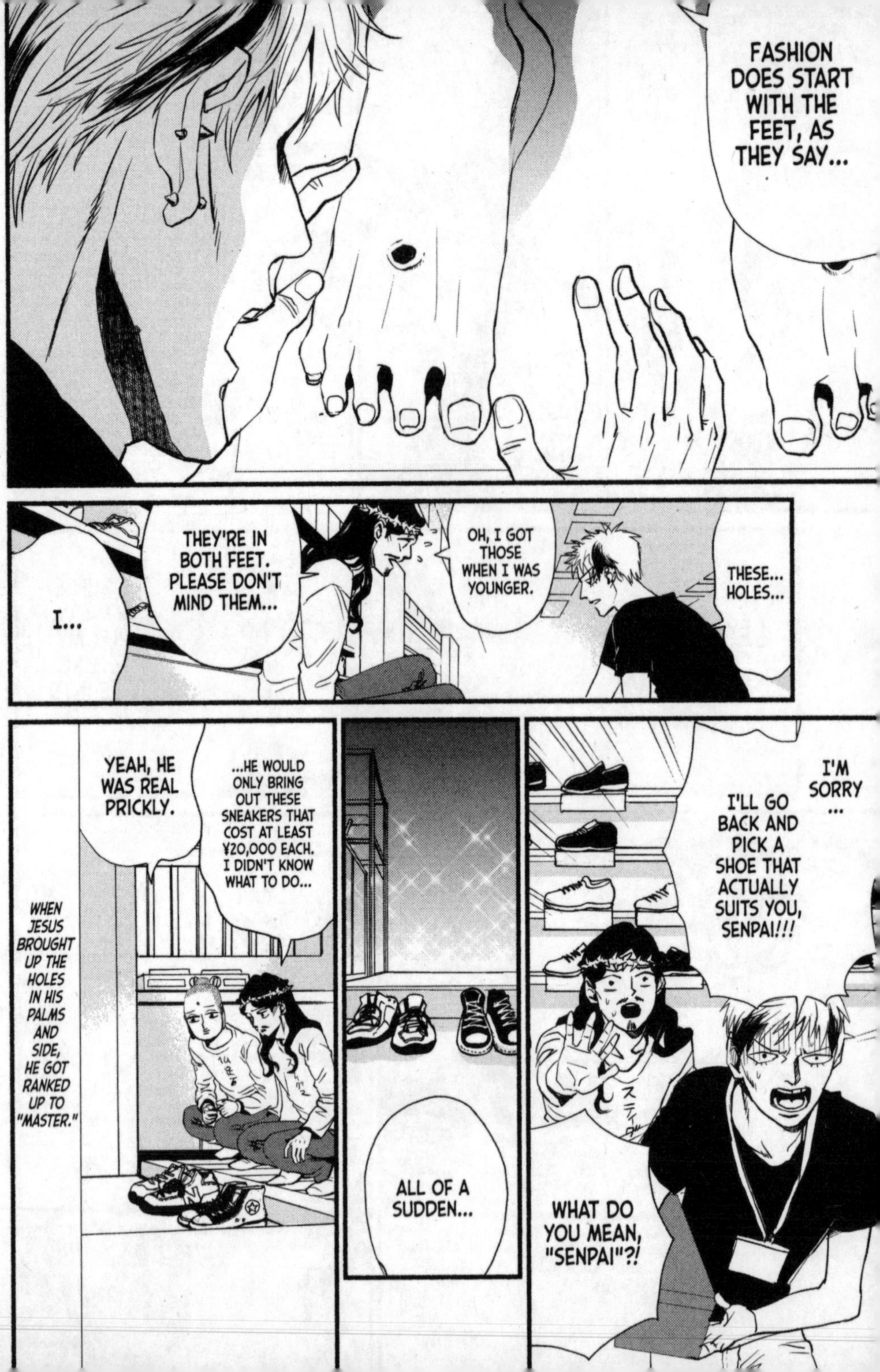
FASHION DOES START WITH THE FEET, AS THEY SAY...
THESE... HOLES...
OH, I GOT THOSE WHEN I WAS YOUNGER.
THEY'RE IN BOTH FEET. PLEASE DON'T MIND THEM...
I...
I'M SORRY ...
I'LL GO BACK AND PICK A SHOE THAT ACTUALLY SUITS YOU, SENPAI!!!
WHAT DO YOU MEAN, "SENPAI"?!
ALL OF A SUDDEN...
...HE WOULD ONLY BRING OUT THESE SNEAKERS THAT COST AT LEAST ¥20,000 EACH. I DIDN'T KNOW WHAT TO DO...
YEAH, HE WAS REAL PRICKLY.
WHEN JESUS BROUGHT UP THE HOLES IN HIS PALMS AND SIDE, HE GOT RANKED UP TO "MASTER."

"A shoe that actually suits you"

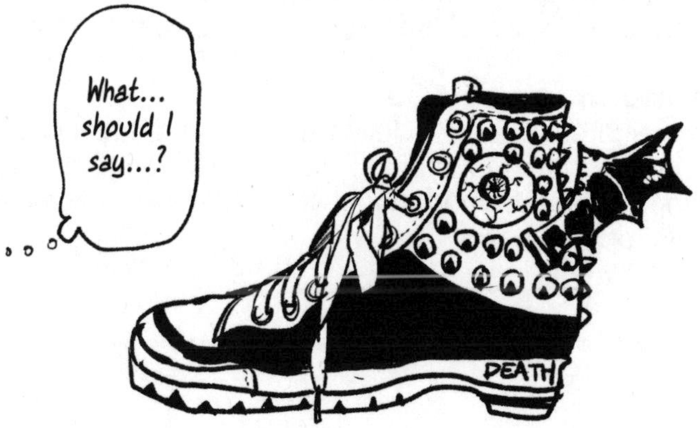
What... should I say...?
DEATH

SAINT ☆ YOUNG MEN

CHAPTER 88 TRANSLATION NOTES

Buddha's footprint, page 127
A piece of Buddhist iconography and art. In ancient India, it was common to worship the feet of gurus and gods, with placing one's head at feet level representing the hierarchical difference. Footprints purported to belong to the Buddha (in stone or other materials) were a representation of the Buddha's physical presence upon the earth. They are often decorated with dharma wheels and similar symbols.

Umeboshi, page 128
A salted and pickled Japanese plum. Umeboshi are very sour and salty, which makes them a popular side dish to eat in small amounts with rice or in rice balls. The salt and citric acid make them healthy as well.

Nukazuke, page 128
A pickled vegetable found in Japanese cuisine. The pickling source, *nuka*, is a sand-like mixture based on rice bran that is left in a "nuka bed" for long periods, and the food meant for pickling is buried inside the mixture for the desired length of time. It has a rich, yeasty flavor.

Rabbit on the moon, page 133
In many East Asian cultures, there is a folklore tradition of seeing a rabbit in the markings on the surface of the moon. In Japan, the rabbit is using a mortar and pestle to pound mochi, the glutinous rice cakes eaten around the end of the year.

PERFECT WORLD

Rie Aruga

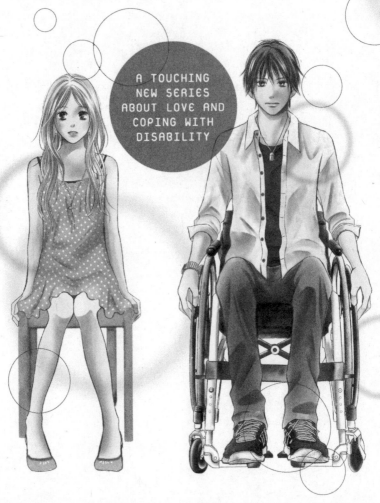

A TOUCHING
NEW SERIES
ABOUT LOVE AND
COPING WITH
DISABILITY

An office party reunites Tsugumi with her high school crush Itsuki. He's realized his dream of becoming an architect, but along the way, he experienced a spinal injury that put him in a wheelchair. Now Tsugumi's rekindled feelings will butt up against prejudices she never considered — and Itsuki will have to decide if he's ready to let someone into his heart...

"Depicts with great delicacy and courage the difficulties some with disabilities experience getting involved in romantic relationships... Rie Aruga refuses to romanticize, pushing her heroine to face the reality of disability. She invites her readers to the same tasks of empathy, knowledge and recognition."
—Slate.fr

"An important entry [in manga romance]... The emotional core of both plot and characters indicates thoughtfulness... [Aruga's] research is readily apparent in the text and artwork, making this feel like a real story."
—Anime News Network

KC
KODANSHA
COMICS

MAGIC KNIGHT RAYEARTH

25TH ANNIVERSARY EDITION

CLAMP

A BELOVED CLASSIC MAKES ITS STUNNING RETURN IN THIS GORGEOUS, LIMITED EDITION BOX SET!

This tale of three Tokyo teenagers who cross through a magical portal and become the champions of another world is a modern manga classic. The box set includes three volumes of manga covering the entire first series of *Magic Knight Rayearth*, plus the series's super-rare full-color art book companion, all printed at a larger size than ever before on premium paper, featuring a newly-revised translation and lettering, and exquisite foil-stamped covers. A strictly limited edition, this will be gone in a flash!

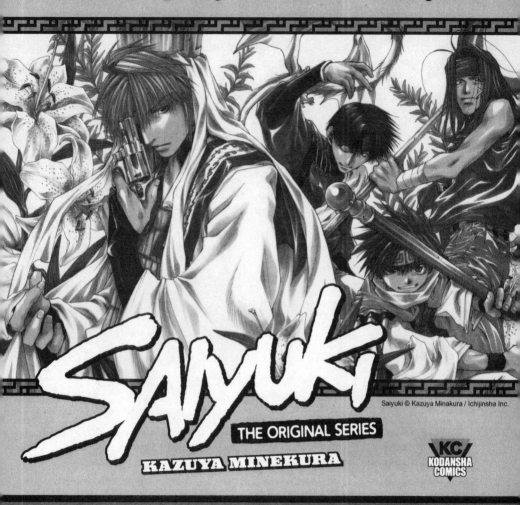

The adorable new odd-couple cat comedy manga from the creator of the beloved *Chi's Sweet Home*, in full color!

Sue & Tai-chan

Konami Kanata

Sue is an aging housecat who's looking forward to living out her life in peace... but her plans change when the mischievous black tomcat Tai-chan enters the picture! Hey! Sue never signed up to be a catsitter! *Sue & Tai-chan* is the latest from the reigning meow-narch of cute kitty comics, Konami Kanata.

KC
KODANSHA COMICS

Saint Young Men 6 copyright © 2015 Hikaru Nakamura
English translation copyright © 2021 Hikaru Nakamura

Published in the United States by Kodansha Comics, an imprint of Kodansha USA Publishing, LLC, New York.

Publication rights for this English edition arranged through Kodansha Ltd., Tokyo.

First published in Japan in 2015 by Kodansha Ltd., Tokyo as *Seinto oniisan*, volumes 11 & 12.

ISBN 978-1-64651-164-8

Original cover design by Hiroshi Niigami (NARTI;S)

Printed in the United States of America.

www.kodanshacomics.com

9 8 7 6 5 4 3 2 1
Translation: Stephen Paul
Lettering: E.K. Weaver
Editing: Nathaniel Gallant
Kodansha Comics edition cover design by Phil Balsman

Publisher: Kiichiro Sugawara

Director of publishing services: Ben Applegate
Associate director of operations: Stephen Pakula
Publishing services managing editors: Alanna Ruse, Madison Salters
Assistant production managers: Emi Lotto, Angela Zurlo